Constitutional Law
and the Criminal Justice System:
A Case Book

Lore Rutz-Burri, J.D.

Professor Emeritus, Southern Oregon University

Acknowledgement:

This book is dedicated to my longtime friend, Cherie Hull, in appreciation for her expertise in the finer details of copy editing and project management. She is a talented, generous, and adventuresome person, and I am so thankful to have her assistance on this last book endeavor.

Chapter One: Foundational Principles

The United States Constitution[1] plays a significant role in the American criminal justice system: it establishes federalism, requires the separation of powers between the three branches of government, and limits Congress's ability to pass laws not directly related to either its enumerated or implied powers. The Constitution says other things about criminal law and procedure as well. For example,

> ➢ Article I of the Constitution restricts Congress from passing any laws that are retroactively applied (the Ex Post Facto Clause), or that are directed at named individuals (Bills of Attainder);

> ➢ the First Amendment limits Congress's ability to pass laws that limit free speech, freedom of religion, freedom of assembly and association;

> ➢ the Second Amendment limits Congress's ability to regulate the possession of firearms;

> ➢ the Fourth, Fifth, Sixth and Eighth Amendments have provisions that govern criminal procedure during the investigative, pretrial, and trial phases of the criminal justice process;

> ➢ the Eighth Amendment sets limits on the government's ability to impose certain punishments;

> ➢ the Due Process Clause of the Fifth and Fourteenth Amendment require that criminal justice procedures be fundamentally fair.

> ➢ the Fourteenth Amendment's Equal Protection Clause requires that, at a minimum, there be some rational reason for treating people differently.

To understand the laws that govern substantive criminal law and criminal procedures in the United States, it is helpful to understand our sources of law. This text primarily focuses on case law developed by the United States Supreme Court[2,] but other important sources of criminal procedural include: federal and state constitutions; case law developed by the state courts; state and federal codes, statutes, ordinances, or any law enacted by a legislative body[3]; administrative laws enacted by

---

[1] This text will use the term "Constitution" to mean the federal, United States Constitution. State constitutions will be distinguished and specifically identified. Instead of referring to the Amendments to the United States Constitution by number and full title "First Amendment to the Constitution of the United State" in sentences, they will simply be referred to as "the First Amendment." In citing to specific article and section numbers of provisions of the United States Constitution, they will similarly be abbreviated (for example, Const. Art I, Sec. 9 or Art I, § 9, or U.S. Const. amend. XIV, §2).

[2] The Supreme Court of the United States will be referred to as the "Court" (with a capital C) but will sometimes, for clarity, refer to the U.S. Supreme Court as "the Supreme Court." All other state and federal courts will be distinguished and specifically identified.

[3] Most substantive criminal law is legislatively created by statutes. State legislatures and U.S. Congress enact laws which take the form of statutes or congressional acts. Statutes are written statements, enacted into law by an affirmative vote of both chambers of the legislature and accepted (or not vetoed) by the governor or President. State legislatures may also

administrative agencies[4]; and the common law[5] that derived from custom. In some states, initiatives and referendum also are a source of criminal substantive and procedural law.[6]

THE CONSTITUTION

The Constitution is a result of a compromise between federalists (those who wanted a strong federal/national government) and the anti-federalist (those who wanted stronger state governments).[7]

---

establish legal standards through interstate compacts (for example, the Uniform Extradition Act, or the Uniform Fresh Pursuit Act). Congress makes federal law through passing acts and approving treaties between the United States and other nation states. Local legislators, city and town councilors, and county commissioners also make laws through the enactment of local ordinances.

[4] State and federal legislatures cannot keep up with the task of enacting legislation on all the myriad subjects that must be regulated by law. In each branch of government, various administrative agencies exist with authority to create administrative law. At the federal level, for example, the Environmental Protection Agency enacts regulations against environmental crimes. At the state level, the Department of Motor Vehicles enacts crimes and violations concerning drivers' license suspension. Administrative regulations are enforceable by the courts provided that the agency has acted within the scope of its delegated authority from the legislature.

[5] Although some refer to the law decided in judicial case decisions as "common law", this text refers to common law as the laws brought over from England to the United States. LaFave describes the process by which common law was derived in England.

> . . . Although there were some early criminal statutes [in England], in the main the criminal law was originally common law. Thus, by the 1600s the judges, not the legislature, had created and defined the felonies of murder, suicide, manslaughter, burglary, arson, robbery, larceny rape, sodomy and mayhem; and such misdemeanors as assault, battery, false imprisonment, libel, perjury, and intimidation of jurors. During the period from 1660 . . . to 1860 the process continued with the judges creating new crimes when the need arose and punishing those who committed them: blasphemy (1676), conspiracy (1664), sedition (18th century), forgery (1727), attempt (1784), solicitation (1801). From time to time the judges, when creating new misdemeanors, spoke of the court's power to declare criminal any conduct tending to "outrage decency" or "corrupt public morals" . . . thus, they found running naked in the streets, publishing an obscene book, and grave-snatching to be common law crimes.

> Of course, sometimes the courts refused to denote as criminal some forms of anti-social conduct. At times their refusal seemed irrational, causing the legislature to step in and enact a statute: thus, false pretenses, embezzlement, incest and other matters became statutory crimes in England. ... Some immoral conduct, mostly of a sexual nature (such as private acts of adultery or fornication, and seduction without conspiracy) was punished by ecclesiastical courts in England. The common law courts never punished these activities as criminal, and thus, they never became English common law crimes.

> At the same time that judges were developing new crimes, they were also developing new common law defenses to crime, such as self-defense, insanity, infancy, and coercion. ...

> About the middle of the nineteenth century, the process of creating new crimes almost came to a standstill in England. ...

> The original colonists in American who emigrated from England brought with them the common law with its then existing statutory modifications . . . so far as applicable to the conditions in America."

[6] In several states, citizens have the power to enact laws through direct democracy by putting "ballot measures" or "propositions" up for a vote. This type of lawmaking by the people started primarily in the Western states around the turn of the 20th century. Initiatives, referendums, and referrals have some slight differences, but generally, these ballot measures ultimately find their way into either statutes or the constitution, and so they are included in this section on legislative law. For example, Oregon Ballot Measure 11, establishing minimum mandatory sentences for 17 person felonies, was voted on in November 1994 and took effect April 1, 1995. It is now found in the Oregon Revised Statutes as ORS 137.700. Proposition 36, overwhelmingly approved by Californians in 2012, significantly amended the "three strikes" sentencing laws, they approved in 1994. Initiatives, referendums and referrals can be effective in quickly changing the criminal law (for example, mandatory sentencing in the 1980s) and is a way to circumvent what could have been a contentious legislative process (for example, the decriminalization of marijuana).

[7] There is a rich history about the political squabbles and compromises that existed when the federal constitution took effect, but it is beyond the scope of this text. Essentially, the statesmen had opposing viewpoints concerning how strong the

The Constitution declares itself to be the "supreme Law of the Land," but this does not mean that the Constitution always controls the outcome of a case. Although the Supreme Court frequently and generally has the final say on what is and what is not constitutional, occasionally state courts interpret their own constitutions and find that they guarantee more rights to their citizens than does the U.S. Constitution. When this occurs, state constitutions control the outcomes for that state.

The Bill of Rights (the first ten amendments to the Constitution) originally applied to the federal government only. However, in 1868 the Fourteenth Amendment became an important tool for making states also follow the provisions of the Bill of the Rights. It was drafted to enforce the Civil Rights Act passed in 1866 in the post-Civil War states. Section 1 of the Fourteenth Amendment enjoins (stops) the states from depriving any person of life, liberty, or property, without due process of law. It prohibits states from adopting any laws that abridge the privileges and immunities of the citizens of the United States and requires that states not deny any person equal protection under the law. U.S. Const. amend. XIV, § 2. Thus, since 1868 state and federal courts began reviewing the action of state actors to ensure they also complied with the U.S. Constitution.

Making these rights articulated in the federal constitution applicable to citizens of each state is referred to as "incorporating the Bill of Rights" or the "incorporation debate." Over decades, the Court debated whether the Bill of Rights should be incorporated all together in one-fell swoop (called total incorporation) or piece-by-piece (called selective incorporation). The case-by-case, bit-by-bit approach won out. In a series of decisions—many of which you will read in this text-- the Court has held that the Due Process Clause of the Fourteenth Amendment makes enforceable against the states those provisions of the Bill of Rights that are "implicit in the concept of ordered liberty." *Palko v. Connecticut*, 302 U.S. 319 (1937). For example, in 1925 the Court recognized that the First Amendment protections of free speech and free press apply to states as well as to the federal government. *Gitlow v. New York*, 268 U.S. 652 (1925). In the 1960s, the Court selectively incorporated many of the procedural guarantees[8] of the Bill of Rights. The Court also used the Fourteenth Amendment to extend substantive guarantees[9] of the Bill of Rights to the states. For example, the Court, in *McDonald v. City of Chicago*, 561 U.S. 742 (2010), held that the Second Amendment's right to bear arms also applied to the states, and in *Timbs v. Indiana*, 586 U.S. ___ (2018), the Court incorporated the no excess fines clause of the Eighth Amendment. Since 2018, the Court has taken the approach that when a right is incorporated to the states through the Fourteenth Amendment, then "there will be no light between" (meaning there is no difference) how it is applied (and its remedies) in federal cases and in state cases. See, e.g., *Timbs* (above) and *Ramos v. Louisiana*, 590 U.S. ___ (2020),

The following excerpt from *McDonald v. City of Chicago*, 561 U.S. 3025 (2010), discusses the incorporation debate. As you read, be aware that the cases of *Betts* and *Wolf* noted in one of the final paragraphs (highlighting how the remedies for rights now incorporated to the states may not, themselves, have been incorporated) were both overturned by subsequent cases in the 1960s. Also, as mentioned above, the approach of allowing a right to look and feel differently when applied to the federal government than when it applies to the states has, since 2018, been disavowed.

---

national government should be and how strong state governments should be. Even as the original federal constitution was being circulated and ratified, the framers were thinking about the provisions that became known as the Bill of Rights.

[8] Procedural guarantees include, for example, freedom from unreasonable search and seizure, the right to a fair trial, the right to a jury trial, or due process.

[9] Substantive guarantees include, for example, equal protection of law, the right to be free from cruel and unusual punishment.

We have previously held that most of the provisions of the Bill of Rights apply with full force to both the Federal Government and the States.

…

The Bill of Rights … originally applied only to the Federal Government. In *Barron ex rel. Tiernan v. Mayor of Baltimore*, 7 Pet. 243 (1833), the Court, in an opinion by Chief Justice Marshall, explained that this question was "of great importance" but "not of much difficulty." Id., at 247. In less than four pages, the Court firmly rejected the proposition that the first eight Amendments operate as limitations on the States, holding that they apply only to the Federal Government. …

The constitutional Amendments adopted in the aftermath of the Civil War fundamentally altered our country's federal system. The provision at issue in this case, §1 of the Fourteenth Amendment, provides, among other things, that a State may not abridge "the privileges or immunities of citizens of the United States" or deprive "any person of life, liberty, or property, without due process of law."

…

In the late 19th century, the Court began to consider whether the Due Process Clause prohibits the States from infringing rights set out in the Bill of Rights. … . Five features of the approach taken during the ensuing era should be noted.

First, the Court viewed the due process question as entirely separate from the question whether a right was a privilege or immunity of national citizenship.

Second, the Court explained that the only rights protected against state infringement by the Due Process Clause were those rights "of such a nature that they are included in the conception of due process of law." … While it was "possible that some of the personal rights safeguarded by the first eight Amendments against National action [might] also be safeguarded against state action," the Court stated, this was "not because those rights are enumerated in the first eight Amendments." *Twining*, at 99.

The Court used different formulations in describing the boundaries of due process. For example, in T*wining*, the Court referred to "immutable principles of justice which inhere in the very idea of free government which no member of the Union may disregard." 211 U. S., at 102 (internal quotation marks omitted). In *Snyder v. Massachusetts*, 291 U. S. 97, 105 (1934), the Court spoke of rights that are "so rooted in the traditions and conscience of our people as to be ranked as fundamental." And in *Palko*, the Court famously said that due process protects those rights that are "the very essence of a scheme of ordered liberty" and essential to "a fair and enlightened system of justice." 302 U. S., at 325.

Third, in some cases decided during this era the Court "can be seen as having asked, when inquiring into whether some particular procedural safeguard was required of a State, if a civilized system could be imagined that would not accord the particular protection." *Duncan v. Louisiana*, 391 U. S. 145, 149, n. 14 (1968). …Similarly, the Court found that due process did not provide a right against compelled incrimination in part because this right "has no place in the jurisprudence of civilized and free countries outside the domain of the common law." *Twining*, supra, at 113.

Fourth, the Court during this era was not hesitant to hold that a right set out in the Bill of Rights failed to meet the test for inclusion within the protection of the Due Process Clause. The Court found that some such rights qualified. See, e.g., *Gitlow v. New York*, 268 U. S. 652, 666 (1925) (freedom of speech and press); *Near v. Minnesota ex rel. Olson*, 283 U. S. 697 (1931) (same); *Powell*, supra (assistance of counsel in capital cases); *De*

Jonge, supra (freedom of assembly); *Cantwell v. Connecticut*, 310 U. S. 296 (1940) (free exercise of religion). But others did not. See, e.g., *Hurtado*, supra (grand jury indictment requirement); *Twining*, supra (privilege against self-incrimination).

Finally, even when a right set out in the Bill of Rights was held to fall within the conception of due process, the protection or remedies afforded against state infringement sometimes differed from the protection or remedies provided against abridgment by the Federal Government. To give one example, in *Betts* the Court held that, although the Sixth Amendment required the appointment of counsel in all federal criminal cases in which the defendant was unable to retain an attorney, the Due Process Clause required appointment of counsel in state criminal proceedings only where "want of counsel in [the] particular case . . . result[ed] in a conviction lacking in . . . fundamental fairness." 316 U. S., at 473 (1942). Similarly, in *Wolf v. Colorado*, 338 U. S. 25 (1949), the Court held that the "core

of the Fourth Amendment" was implicit in the concept of ordered liberty and thus "enforceable against the States through the Due Process Clause" but that the exclusionary rule, which applied in federal cases, did not apply to the States. Id., at 27-28, 33.

2

An alternative theory regarding the relationship between the Bill of Rights and §1 of the Fourteenth Amendment was championed by Justice Black. This theory held that §1 of the Fourteenth Amendment totally incorporated all of the provisions of the Bill of Rights. . . . [T]he Court never has embraced Justice Black's "total incorporation" theory.

3

[T]he Court eventually moved in that direction by initiating what has been called a process of "selective incorporation," i.e., the Court began to hold that the Due Process Clause fully incorporates particular rights contained in the first eight Amendments.

JUDICIAL REVIEW AND THE RULE OF LAW

The term "rule of law" has recently become widely used. It means that no person or government entity is above the law. According to Professor Philip Reichel, there is a three-step process that leads to a justice system based on rule of law.[10] The first step in that process involves recognizing fundamental rights. Fundamental rights, for example, could include the presumption of innocence, the right to have a trial, or the right to associate with whomever we want. The second step involves writing down these fundamental rights in a place where people can find them. In the United States, we have identified our fundamental rights in our Constitution, but not every country with rule of law has a constitution. For example, England has no constitution — instead, the Magna Carta and its Bill of Rights identify and articulate in writing England's fundamental values. The third and final step involves implementing a procedure or mechanism in which the government or individuals are held accountable to these fundamental principles. In the United States, the mechanism we use is judicial review. Judicial review, one of the hallmarks of our judicial system, arose out of the Court's decision in *Marbury v. Madison,* 5 U.S. 237 (1803). In *Marbury*, Chief Justice John Marshall held that the Court has the power to decide what the Constitution means and the ability to review acts of Congress and strike them down if they conflict with the Constitution. Courts also engage in judicial review when they strike down police action (an executive branch action) finding such actions (such as a search or a seizure) conflict with the Constitution. Most of the cases you will read in the following pages are the written manifestations of the Court engaging in judicial review.

---

[10]See, Phillip Reichel, Comparative Criminal Justice Systems: Topical Approach (2000).

States courts also engage in judicial review and interpret their own state constitutions, state laws, and state administrative rules. Each state is autonomous, and under the "adequate and state grounds doctrine" the Court must allow states to interpret their own constitutions. Sometimes, however, the Court finds it difficult to determine whether the state is interpreting its own constitution (in which case the Court adopts a "hands off" approach and will not review the action) or whether the state is interpreting the federal constitution (in which case the Court may review the action). *Michigan v. Long,* 463 U.S. 1032 (1983), explains when the Court will weigh in on a state court matter. It held,

> [W]hen . . . a state court decision fairly appears to rest primarily on federal law, or to be interwoven with the federal law, and when the adequacy and independence of any possible state law ground is not clear from the face of the opinion, we will accept as the most reasonable explanation that the state court decided the case the way it did because it believed that federal law required it to do so. If a state court chooses merely to rely on federal precedents as it would on the precedents of all other jurisdictions, then it need only make clear by a plain statement in its judgment or opinion that the federal cases are being used only for the purpose of guidance, and do not themselves compel the result that the court has reached. In this way, both justice and judicial administration will be greatly improved. If the state court decision indicates clearly and expressly that it is alternatively based on bona fide separate, adequate, and independent grounds, we, of course, will not undertake to review the decision.

> . . . It is fundamental that state courts be left free and unfettered by us in interpreting their state constitutions. But it is equally important that ambiguous or obscure adjudications by state courts do not stand as barriers to a determination by this Court of the validity under the federal constitution of state action.

COURT JURISDICTION

To understand the role of courts in developing law known as case law it is essential to understand the concept of jurisdiction. Jurisdiction covers a variety of settings under which a court has legal authority to resolve the matter before it. Jurisdiction is tied to federalism. Federalism results in a "dual court system" -- state courts have jurisdiction over state matters and federal courts have jurisdiction over federal matters. Both federal courts and state courts have a hierarchy that divides trial courts and appellate courts.[11] Trial courts have jurisdiction over pretrial matters, trials,

---

[11] Article III, Section I of the U.S. Constitution provides that

> "[t]he judicial Power of the United States shall be vested in one Supreme Court, and in such inferior Courts as the Congress may from time to time ordain and establish. The Judges, both of the supreme and inferior Courts, shall hold their Offices during good Behavior, and shall, at stated Times, receive for their Services a Compensation, which shall not be diminished during their continuation in office."

The highest court in the federal court system is the U.S. Supreme Court (Court). The Court is comprised of a chief justice and eight associate justices. All justices are nominated and appointed by the President of the United States with the advice and consent of the Senate and have lifetime tenure (but may be removed by impeachment). A federal act fixed the number of justices at nine, but Congress could alter the number of justices on the Court. The justices always meet as one panel (*en banc*) unlike most appellate courts in which judges sit in panels of three. The Court begins its term of service the first Monday in October and continues its session through the end of June the following year. Court cases are argued and decided during this period, and decisions are "handed down" or announced throughout the court session. Although the Court can act as a trial court, it does so rarely. Mostly, the Court acts as an appellate court and decides cases brought before it either through a petition for a writ of certiorari or a petition for a writ of habeas corpus. The Court has discretion whether to hear these writs, and at least four justices must agree to accept review before the Court will consider a case. If four justices can't agree to hear the case, then the last decision made in the case remains.

sentencing, and probation and parole violations. Trial courts deal with facts. Did the defendant stab the victim? Was the eyewitness able to clearly see the stabbing? Did the probationer willfully violate terms of probation? Trial courts determine legal guilt and impose punishments. Appellate courts, on the other hand, review the decisions of the trial courts. Appellate courts are primarily concerned with matters of law. Did the trial judge properly instruct the jury about the controlling law? Did the trial court properly suppress evidence in a pretrial hearing? Does the statute allow the defendant to raise a particular defense? Appellate courts review the trial record for legal error and then correct legal errors made by trial courts and develop law when new legal questions arise. In some instances, appellate courts determine if there is legally sufficient evidence to uphold a conviction (that is, do the facts shown at trial support the verdict.)

To understand how appellate courts review lower court decisions, one must understand the concept of "standards of review." A standard of review refers to a level of scrutiny the appellate court employs in deciding questions of law, questions of fact, and mixed questions of fact and law. Perhaps the best way to think about standard of review is to relate it to the deference an appellate court must give to the findings of the lower courts. In some instances, the appellate court gives great deference to the conclusions and findings made by the trial judge and jury; in other instances, the appellate court may substitute its own opinion and need not defer to the trial judge at all. From time to time, the appellate courts may recognize and correct "plain error" (error obvious on its face) that it sees when reviewing the record even though the parties have failed to mention it in their appellate briefs.

The intermediate courts of appeals for the federal system are the United States Courts of Appeals. These are also called the U.S. Circuit Courts. There are thirteen federal judicial circuits — twelve are based on regional jurisdiction, and the thirteenth is based on subject matter jurisdiction from around the nation (called the Court of Appeals for the Federal Circuit). Except for the D.C. Circuit, all of the regional jurisdiction circuits are comprised of at least three states. Each Circuit has at least six judges and the largest circuit, the Ninth Circuit, has twenty-eight judges. The number of federal court of appeals judges varies constantly. Judges are nominated and appointed for life terms by the President of the United States with advice and consent of the Senate, and can be removed only by impeachment. Judges sit either *en banc* or in panels of three or five judges.

The primary trial courts for the federal system are the U.S. District Courts. Each state has between one and four judicial districts, and there are ninety-four judicial districts in the states, Guam, Puerto Rico, and the Virgin Islands. U.S. District Court judges are appointed for life terms by the President of the United States with advice and consent of Senate, and can be removed only by impeachment. In practice the senior U.S. Senator from the state makes recommendations for appointment to the U.S. District Court.

U.S. magistrate courts were established to relieve the district court judges of heavy caseloads. Magistrate judges have limited authority such as trying minor offenses, holding bail hearings, issuing warrants, reviewing habeas corpus petitions, and holding pretrial conferences. In contrast to the other judges in the federal system, magistrate judges are Article I judges and not Article III judges because their positions were not created by Article III of the U.S. Constitution. Instead, their positions were created by Congress under its authority in Article I Section 8 to "constitute Tribunals inferior to the supreme Court." Magistrate judges are appointed by federal district court judges to either eight-year (full time) or four-year (part time) terms.

The structure of the states' court systems varies, but each state has trial courts ("courts of original jurisdiction") and appellate courts. All states have supreme courts. (Texas and Oklahoma have two supreme courts). Thirty-five states have intermediate appellate courts, and in fifteen states, cases are appealed directly to the state supreme court. Each state has trial courts of general jurisdiction (for serious cases) and trial courts of limited jurisdiction (for petty offenses). The names of the general jurisdiction courts vary and include: circuit courts, district courts, superior courts, commonwealth courts, and supreme court. Likewise, the limited jurisdiction courts have various names including: district court, county court, municipal court, justice-of-the-peace court. Some states divide their trial courts by subject matter jurisdiction such as probate, juvenile, domestic relation.

CASE LAW

The term "case law" refers to legal rules announced in opinions written by appellate judges when deciding cases before them. Case law (judicial opinions) is what results from the appellate courts doing their job reviewing what happened in the lower courts. Judicial decisions written by these appellate judges reflect that court's interpretation of constitutions, statutes, common law, or administrative regulations (recall, these are the sources of criminal law). When courts interpret a statute, the statute and its interpretation control how the law will be enforced and applied in the future. The same is true when courts interpret federal and state constitutions. When deciding cases and interpreting the law, judges are bound by precedent, a doctrine known as "stare decisis."[12]

Stare Decisis

The doctrine of *stare decisis* comes from a Latin phrase that states, "to stand by the decisions and not disturb settled points." If case decisions in the past have held that a particular rule governs a certain fact situation, that rule should govern all later cases presenting the same fact situation. Thus, trial courts (and appellate courts) follow the controlling case law that has already been announced in appellate court decisions from their own jurisdiction. Trial courts rely upon precedent when they decide questions of law.[13] Under the doctrine of *stare decisis,* past appellate court decisions form precedent that judge "must" follow in similar subsequent cases. The Court in *Vasquez v. Hillery*, 474 U.S. 254 (1986), held that stare decisis "permits society to presume that bedrock principles are founded in the law rather than in the proclivities of individuals, and thereby contribute to the integrity of our constitutional system of government, both in appearance and fact."

The advantages of *stare decisis* include: efficiency, equality, predictability, the wisdom of past experience, and the image of limited authority.[14] Efficiency occurs because each trial judge and appellate judge does not have to work out a solution to every legal question.[15] Equality results when one rule of law is applied to all persons in the same setting. "Identical cases brought before different judges should, to the extent humanly possible, produce identical results. ... *Stare decisis* assists in providing uniform standards of law for similar cases decided in the same state. It provides a common grounding used by all judges throughout the jurisdiction."[16] *Stare decisis* provides stability in allowing individuals to count on the rules of law that have been applied in the past. Stare decisis also ensures proper recognition of the wisdom and experience of the past. Justice Cardozo observed that "no single judge is likely to have 'a vision at once so keen and so broad' as to ensure that his new ideas of wise policy are indeed the most beneficial for society."[17] Since stare decisis is not absolute, courts can still reject past precedent, but it requires a judge to "think long and hard before he departs from the findings of his predecessors over the years."[18] Finally, stare decisis enhances the image of the courts as the impartial interpreter of the law.

Stare decisis decreases the leeway granted to the individual judge to settle controversies in accordance with his own personal desires. ... Indeed, the doctrine of *stare decisis* indirectly serves to

---

[12] Although stare decisis is a foundational principle in American jurisprudence (our theory of law), recently it has taken a beating in the Court. Legal podcasts such as Strict Scrutiny and Amicus have alleged that many current justices embrace a new "vibe" way of deciding cases and feel that "stare decisis is for suckers." See, e.g., https://crooked.com/podcast-series/strict-scrutiny/

[13] Questions of law include what a statute means, what the law states, how the constitution should be interpreted, whether a particular law even applies under the facts in the case before them. Questions of fact, on the other hand, are decided by jurors (or judges in bench trials) and include, for example: how fast was the defendant driving, what color hat the defendant was wearing, whether the gun went off accidentally?

[14] See, H. Kerper, Introduction to the Criminal Justice System, (2d. ed., 1979), supra at 47-49.

[15] Id. at 49.

[16] Id.

[17] Benjamin Cardozo, The Growth of Law, 141 (1924).

[18] Kerper, *supra* at 49

restrict the law-making role of the judge even in those cases presenting "open issues" not resolved by past precedent. ... A sudden change in the composition of the judiciary, even at the highest level, should not present an equally sudden change in the substance of the law.[19]

In the federal system all federal courts must follow the decisions of the Supreme Court -- it is the final interpreter of the federal constitution and federal statutes. If, however, the Supreme Court has not ruled on an issue, then the federal trial courts (U.S. District Courts and U.S. Magistrate Courts) and federal appellate courts (Circuit Courts of Appeals) must follow decisions from their own circuit. Each circuit is treated, in effect, as its own jurisdiction, and the court of appeals for the various circuits are free to disagree with each other.

Because *stare decisis* is not an absolute rule, courts may reject precedent by overruling earlier decisions. One factor that courts will consider before overruling earlier case law is the strength of the precedent. Another factor is the field of law involved. Courts are more reluctant to override precedents governing property or trade where commercial enterprises are more likely to have relied quite heavily on the precedent.[20] Courts also consider the initial source of precedent--for example statutory interpretation. For example, if the courts decided in 1950 that the statute meant that individuals could graze their cattle on federal lands without being in violation of any trespass laws, and then the federal government did not subsequently change the law, the legislature's inaction indicates the interpretation was probably right. The most compelling basis upon which a court will overturn precedent is if it perceives the presence or absence of changed circumstances. For example, scientific or technological developments may warrant the application of new rules.[21] One final ground for overruling a prior decision is general changes in the spirit of the times. For example, in *Trop v. Dulles,* 356 U.S. 86 (1958), the Court looked to "evolving standards of decency."

If there are no binding precedents in its own state[22], a state court may find persuasive case law from other states. In those cases, the court is not bound by stare decisis to follow those decisions. When there is no precedent or controlling case, the case or issue is referred to as "a matter of first impression." In cases of first impression, courts must decide what the relevant rule should be. Courts will look to relevant statutes, legislative history, and cases involving similar situations.[23]

The situation may be a new one. ... Yet the judges do not throw up their hands and say the case may not be decided; they decide it. Maybe they can use some settled law in an analogous situation. ... Even if there is no available analogy, or if there are competing analogies, the judge will make (some prefer to say discover) the law to apply to the new situation. The new law will be decided according to the judges' ideas (ideas they acquire as members of society) of what is moral, right, just; of what will further sound public policy, in light of customs and traditions of the people of which the judges are members.[24]

---

[19] *Id.* at 50-51.

[20] *See*, Kerper, *supra* at 52.

[21] Technological changes result in new rules. For example, at common law, in order to prove the crime of murder, the state had to prove that the victim died within one year and a day of the attack (in order to prove that it was the defendant's act that caused the victim's death). Medical science now makes it possible to trace the source of fatal blow, so many murder statutes no longer include the "year and a day rule."

[22] Trial judges are not required to follow the decisions of other trial judges within the state.

[23] For example, if a court had to decide whether a *private* citizen could lawfully use deadly force to apprehend a fleeing thief, it could point to an earlier case holding that police officers could not lawfully use deadly force to apprehend a fleeing thief. The court would observe that police officers have greater authority to apprehend criminals than do private citizens and would hold that the private citizen may not use deadly force to apprehend a fleeing thief.

[24] LaFave, *supra* at 69.

Judicial Law-Making Versus Law-Applying

At times, people criticize judges for being "judicial activists." At the heart of this criticism is the sentiment that judges have exceeded their authority to interpret and apply the law and have ventured into the realm of making law—a legislative function. It is not necessarily easy, however, to apply the law to the facts of a case. Facts can be messy, the law can be less than clear, and not everyone will agree on the appropriate meaning of the law's mandate. LaFave notes,

> There is something of a dispute among those who like to speculate on the workings of the judicial mind as to whether courts first decide how a defective statute ought to be interpreted and then display whatever canons of statutory construction will make this interpretation look inevitable, or whether the courts actually first use the applicable canons and second reach the result. Doubtless the truth lies somewhere in between--some judges are apt to do it one way, some the others; some cases lend themselves to one technique, some to the other. ... [M]ost of the rules are stated in a way which ends with the exception that the rule does not apply if the meaning of the statute is clear, but a good deal of discretion remains in the courts as to when a statute is clear and when it is ambiguous. (Footnotes omitted.) [25]

> Judges rely on several tools or approaches when interpreting the language of a statute.[26] First, judges may take a "strict constructionist approach" and look at the plain meaning of the statute. This approach suggests that the wording of a statute is central to the meaning to the law. The strict constructionist approach often relies on dictionary-like tools to discover the meaning of words. "Where the language is plain and admits of no more than one meaning, the duty of interpretation does not arise."[27] Judges can, and do, still disagree whether the language of the statute is plain.

> Second, judges may look at the intent of the framers or the legislators who wrote the law. Generally, this approach would require an examination of legislative history, including the record of legislative hearings and floor debates. More legislative history exists at the federal level (see, for example, the Congressional Record) than at the state level. Sometimes figuring out the framers' intent is easy, but sometimes their purpose is not readily apparent. Moreover, different lawmakers may have had different intentions when they voted to pass the law.

> When interpreting an ambiguous statute, the court will seek to find the intention of the legislature. At times it is clear that the legislature never thought of the particular fact situation now in question, in which case "intention of the legislature" may mean simply "intention the legislature would have had if it had thought of this problem," to be determined from a consideration of the general purpose the legislature had in mind in enacting the statute. In order to help solve the often-difficult problem of the legislature's intention, the courts have a large assortment of rules and maxims at their disposal. (Footnotes omitted.)

> . . .

> The use of legislative history as an aid to statutory interpretation has its limits. While a good deal of legislative history can be mined for a federal statute, most state legislatures, although they may go through much the same motions a Congress, do not keep as good a written record of their work. Elaborate committee reports are seldom made, and it is rare for a record to be kept of legislative debates. ... (Footnotes omitted.)

> It should be noted also that not all judges are enamored of the use of legislative history in interpreting ambiguous statutes. And in any event, legislative history is less likely to be

---

[25] *Id.* at 80.
[26] See, https://www.acslaw.org/expertforum/in-pursuit-of-progressive-jurisprudence/
[27] *Caminetti v. United States*, 242 U.S. 470 (1917).

controlling in construing criminal statutes than civil statutes. If one purpose of a criminal statute is to warn the public of what conduct will get them into criminal trouble, that is, if prospective criminals are entitled to fair warning--then the public should be able to ascertain the line between permitted and prohibited conduct from the statute itself. (Footnotes omitted.)[28]

Third, judges may look at the original understanding or original meaning of the law.[29] The court focuses on how the law would have been understood by the common person in the period during which the law was first implemented. This approach might yield different interpretations because different people could have had different understandings of what the law meant.

Fourth, judges may interpret the law based on precedent. One drawback to this approach is that facts of the earlier cases will always differ somewhat from the facts in the new case the court is trying to interpret. Another difficulty occurs when the court is faced with a new situation or a new law and there is no precedent to guide the court. LaFave identified the difficulty in adhering too closely to precedent:

Sometimes a court, having earlier construed a criminal statute strictly in favor of the defendant, later decides that its earlier construction was wrong. ... Obviously, other things being equal, courts should interpret statutes correctly, regardless of past mistakes. On the other hand, it may not be fair to . . . change the rule now. The difficulty lies in the Anglo-American theory of precedents that case law operates retroactively, and in particular that case law which overrules earlier precedents operates retroactively. When faced with this problem-- that of overruling or following an earlier erroneous interpretation . . . [one] court felt obliged to follow case precedent with an invitation to the legislature to change the rule of for the future; but [another court overruled the precedent.]

The choice, however, is not necessarily between following the precedent (thus letting a defendant off but perpetuating a bad decision) and retroactively overruling it (thus eliminating a bad precedent but putting the defendant behind bars). There are two techniques by which the defendant may go free even if the precedent is overruled. It is not impossible for the court to overrule for the future only, letting the defendant go but stating in the opinion that anyone who from now on conducts himself the way this defendant did will be guilty of the crime. The second method is to overrule the erroneous precedent but to give the defendant the defense of mistake of law induced by an appellate court. ... Some courts have gone so far as to say that the adoption of a new interpretation of an old statute is forbidden by ex post facto constitutional provision if the new interpretation is harder on the defendant than the old. (Footnotes omitted.)[30]

Finally, in deciding what a statute means, courts utilize common law doctrines, such as the "rule of lenity," which directs the court to interpret ambiguous terms in a light that is favorable to the defendant. One Latin maxim *"expressio unius est exclusion alterius"* (the inclusion of one is the exclusion of all others), holds that when a legislative body includes specific items within a statute, the assumption is that it intends to exclude all other terms. Another maxim, *"in pari materia"* (on the same matter or subject) instructs the court to determine an ambiguous statute in light of other statutes on the same subject. Sometimes a statute's title throws some light on the meaning of an ambiguous statute.[31] Yet another

---

[28] LaFave, *supra* at 86-89.
[29] For a discussion of the differences between originalism and textualism see, https://pacificlegal.org/originalism-vs-textualism-vs-living-constitutionalism/
[30] LaFave, supra at 96-97.
[31] See, LaFave, supra at 89.

maxim, *ejusdem genaris,* holds that where criminal statutes list specific items followed by a general catchall phrase, usually introduced by the words "or other", the general phrase may be construed to be limited to things of the same kinds as the specific items.[32] Courts also look for a "striking change of expression" (meaning the use of different language) because when the legislature uses different language in two parts of the same statute, this can be an indication of different legislative intent. Finally, general rules of interpretation hold that specific language controls over general language and latter statutes control over earlier statutes. So, as you can see, there is a lot of guidance for judges to follow when determining how to best interpret other sources of law.

Reading Appellate Decisions

Many court opinions begin by explaining the procedural history of a case — tracing the case's progress from the state or federal trial court to the initial court of appeals and up to the U.S. Supreme Court. The procedural history includes the decisions of each court and may indicate the standard of review — the criteria, level of scrutiny, and deference the court must give to the lower courts. Frequently, the issue the appellate court must decide is not whether the jury reached the right or wrong decision, but whether the trial court failed to apply the law correctly (for example, by telling the jury to apply an incorrect statement of law (called a jury instruction). As you read these cases, pay attention to how the trial court verdict was challenged in the appellate courts. Challenges take many forms and are not necessarily referred to as "appeals." They include: motions for directed verdicts, motions for judgment notwithstanding the verdict, motions for a new trial, a direct appeal (called either a petition for a writ of certiorari or a petition for review), a petition for writ of habeas corpus, and finally a petition for post-conviction relief.

Motions for Directed Verdict and Judgment Notwithstanding the Verdict

Defendants can raise motions for directed verdict at the close of the prosecution's case. Basically, through this motion the defendant asks the judge to direct (or impose) a verdict of not guilty. The standard of review for the trial judge to follow in this motion is whether, in viewing all the evidence in the state's favor, there is any evidence upon which the jury could find beyond a reasonable doubt the elements that the state needs to prove. If this motion is unsuccessful, the defendant can again raise this motion at the close of the defendant's case in chief. Finally, the defendant can raise a similar motion, called a motion for a judgment notwithstanding the verdict (of guilty), after the jury returns a guilty verdict.

Motion for a New Trial

Prior to sentencing, the defendant can also make a motion for a new trial. These motions are rare, but if the defendant can point to some prejudicial error that would be clear on its face, the judge may grant this motion -- for example, if the defendant can point to some impropriety in the jury deliberations that was discovered after the verdict was returned but before sentence was imposed.

Direct Challenges to Convictions—Appeals

An appeal is a direct attack on the defendant's conviction. There is no constitutional right to an appeal, but the federal government and every state provides an "appeal of right" to all defendants convicted at trial. If the defendant has pled guilty to the charges, then the right to appeal is very limited. The defendant who waived trial and entered a guilty plea can only appeal whether the sentence given is one that is allowed by law. Some states allow defendants sentenced to death to appeal directly to the state supreme court rather than to the state's intermediate court of appeals.

---

[32] *Id.* at 90.

Generally, after the defendant is convicted, there is a very narrow window in which he or she can file an appeal. Most defendants wishing to file an appeal must seek out a different attorney than their trial attorney. Trial attorneys generally represent the defendant through imposition of sentence, but most defense attorneys do not handle the defendant's appeal (nor do the prosecutors handle cases which have been appealed.) Instead, there is a cadre of attorneys who specialize in appellate work. For the state, these attorneys are generally found in the state's department of justice, criminal appeals division. For indigent defendants there may be a state public defenders' office (as opposed to local contract or public defenders or privately-obtained defense attorneys). As you will read in later pages, defendants are entitled to counsel for their representation on appeals of right, but they are not entitled to representation on their discretionary appeals.

The defendant's appellate attorney will prepare an appellate brief alleging mistakes (called errors) which were made during the course of the trial. No trial is free from error, and courts will only reverse a conviction if there is "prejudicial error." Prejudicial error is error that affected the outcome of the case. Prejudicial error is also called harmful error, and certain types of errors (plain error or structural error) are automatically considered harmful to the defendant because they affect basic rights.

Appeals involve reviewing what took place at trial, and to do that review, the appellate court will need a copy of the trial transcript. Until 1956 the State did not have to provide a transcript for an indigent defendant who wished to appeal a conviction but in *Griffin v. Illinois,* 351 U.S. 12 (1956), the court held that the due process and equal protection clauses of the Fourteenth Amendment require that all indigent defendants be furnished a transcript. Justice Black wrote,

> "…In criminal trials a state can no more discriminate on account of poverty than on account of religion, race or color… . It is true that a state is not required by the federal constitution to provide appellate review at all. … But this is not to say that a State that does grant appellate review can do so in a way that discriminates against some convicted defendant on account of their poverty. … There can be no equal justice where the kind of trial a man gets depends on the amount of money he has."

Professional ethical rules dictate that attorneys cannot forward claims they know to be meritless, and this puts attorneys in a bind when their clients insist on filing an appeal that the attorney believes has no merit. *Anders v. California* , 386 U.S. 768 (1967) examined the issue of attorney's filing "frivolous" appellate briefs on behalf of their indigent clients. In that case, the Court that there was no due process violation when an attorney indicated in the brief (now known as "Anders briefs") that the appeal would be frivolous.

> "A state court is free to adopt a procedure for appellate counsel to follow when, after careful review of the record, he or she determines that there is no merit to review and to file for an appeal would only be frivolous. In order to comport with the demands of the Fourteenth Amendment, the procedure must reasonably ensure that an indigent's appeal will be resolved in a way that is related to the appeal's merit."

Most appeals result in a review by the appellate court, followed by the court affirming the holding of the trial court without writing an opinion — an "awop" (affirm without opinion). Other options for the appellate courts include an affirmation with a written opinion, a reversal of the lower court, a reversal of the lower court's holding with a remand decision (sending it back to be done again).

The final step in a direct attack on a conviction (appeal) is through a *petition for writ of certiorari* to the U.S. Supreme Court. Approximately 8500 cases are filed with the U.S. Supreme Court each year, and, in most, the Court denies the petition.[33]

Collateral Challenges To Conviction

Sometimes trial errors are not obvious from the transcript, and most of the times the defendant does not get relief from his or her direct challenge to the conviction. But the defendant has two more attacks that can be made upon the conviction. The first is called a petition for a writ of habeas corpus, and the second is called post-conviction relief.

Collateral Challenge: Petition for Writ of Habeas Corpus

A *writ of habeas corpus* (a Latin term which means "you have the body"), also known as "the Great Writ" is found in the U.S. Constitution. It is available to individuals who are confined and who have "exhausted their appellate remedies" (meaning they have lost on their appeal of right and their discretionary appeals have either been denied or they lost there too). A habeas corpus writ is a civil suit by the detained person against the person or entity detaining him. It could be a warden or the

---

[33] In the past decades the Court has annually reviewed, and issued opinions on, between 80 and 90 petitions for writs of certiorari or petitions for writ of habeas corpus from both state and federal courts. In the 2022-2023 term, the Court accepted only 52 cases for review. That said. the Court has been reviewing (and criticized for reviewing) and more and more cases on its "shadow docket." Cases on the shadow docket are not fully briefed by the parties nor have there been oral arguments presented. In the April 14, 2021 publication of the American Bar Association O'Connell stated,

> "First coined in 2015 by law professor William Baude, the term "shadow docket" refers to the thousands of decisions the Supreme Court hands down each term that "defy its normal procedural regularity." Unlike the 60-70 cases the Justices hear on the "merits" docket, where the Court receives full briefings, hears oral arguments, and delivers lengthy, signed opinions, cases decided by way of the "shadow docket" lack such public deliberation and transparency. According to Court watchers and analysts, increasingly often in recent years, the Justices are handing down one- or two-sentence summary decisions late at night in controversial cases like those involving the recent federal executions. These shadow docket orders often do not include information about how each Justice voted or why the majority came to a certain conclusion, potentially leaving lower courts in the dark about how to apply Supreme Court precedent moving forward. In the case of the federal death penalty cases, the government often relied on these unsigned emergency orders from SCOTUS, typically handed down the night of the scheduled execution, to clear away any remaining legal barriers preventing the execution from moving forward. Recognizing this recent shift in Supreme Court practice, on February 18th, 2021, the House Judiciary Committee held a hearing on the shadow docket, listening to legal experts explain the history of the practice, why Congress should be concerned when SCOTUS doesn't "show its work," and suggestions for reform. . . .

> The shadow docket . . . has existed since the very formation of the U.S. Supreme Court. As Stephen Vladeck, professor at University of Texas Law School, explained in his testimony at the hearing, this legal approach to resolving cases was typically reserved for denials of uncontroversial petitions for certiorari, denying emergency relief applications for cases that clearly didn't meet the "emergency" criteria, granting parties more time to file briefs, and other typically unremarkable scenarios. To seek emergency relief from the Court on the shadow docket and thus side-step the formal appeals process, an applicant must prove that they will suffer "irreparable harm" if their request is not immediately granted. While only eight such applications for emergency relief were filed by the Department of Justice between 2001 and 2017, the Trump administration filed 41 such applications in just four years. Not only has the size of the shadow docket grown considerably as a result, but the types of cases the Supreme Court has been deciding via this emergency relief method have changed as well. The Court has begun resolving politically-charged disputes over the border wall, COVID-19 safety restrictions, and federal executions using the once "anodyne" shadow docket.

> . . . [O]f the eight emergency relief applications filed by the Bush and Obama administrations between 2001 and 2017, only one resulted in a public dissent; but of the 36 heard under the Trump administration, 27 applications resulted in such dissenting opinions, demonstrating the more polarizing nature of recent shadow docket decisions even amongst the Justices themselves."

director of the state's department of corrections.[34] This text contains several cases which were reviewed by the court not as direct appeals, but rather as writs of habeas corpus.

Writs of habeas corpus are often brought because information comes to light that shows that defendant's rights were violated after the permissible time for filing an appeal. Another reason may be because there is a violation not apparent from the trial record. One of the most frequent allegations on a habeas corpus writ is that a person's received ineffective assistance of counsel.

Collateral Challenge: Federal Writ of Habeas Corpus by State Prisoners

A person held in a state prison or jail after being convicted of a state crime may file a writ of habeas corpus in state court — generally the trial court of general jurisdiction. Many of the Court decisions in this text involved state court prisoners who have challenged their convictions all the way up the federal system as well. The federal courts do not have to provide a federal writ of habeas corpus to state prisoners, but historically they have. As the workload has increased in the federal courts, the types of habeas corpus claims have been restricted, and the limits on habeas corpus writs have increased. Federal writs of habeas corpus from state court prisoners start through the state system and then are filed in the Federal District Court (after the defendant has "exhausted state remedies".) *Stone v. Powell,* 428 U.S. 465 (1976) imposed a major limitation on state prisoner's ability to seek habeas corpus in federal courts by holding that federal courts would no longer review petitions from petitioner's whose sole complaint involved an illegal search and seizure under the Fourth Amendment. The second major impediment to filing writs of habeas corpus in federal court is the Congressional Antiterrorism and Effective Death Penalty Act of 1997. This Act requires that prisoners combine all their allegations into one habeas petition that must be filed within one year after the state remedies have been exhausted. This Act has effectively curbed the practice of repeated writ writing by prisoners.

Habeas corpus "work" is technical, and decisions surrounding writs of habeas corpus are fairly intricate. Most attorneys, with the exception of federal public defenders and state public defenders (as opposed to local public defenders), are generally unfamiliar with the process and the mechanics of filing these writs. Many prisoners file their own writs of habeas corpus, relying on prison library resources and "jailhouse" lawyers for assistance.

Del Carmen compares direct appeals with the writ of habeas corpus[35]:

Appeal	Writ of Habeas Corpus
A direct attack upon the conviction	A collateral attack, meaning separate case from the criminal conviction
Part of the criminal proceeding	A civil proceeding
Purpose is to reverse the conviction	Purpose is to secure release from prison
Filed only after conviction	May be filed anytime a person is deprived of freedom illegally by a public officer, before or after conviction — with some exceptions
Accused has been convicted and may be either free or incarcerated.	Person is serving time or is detained illegally, cannot be filed by a person who is free

---

[34] See, e.g., *Humphry v. Wilson* in Chapter 11.
[35] See, Del Carmen, R., Criminal Procedure: Law and Practice (7th ed., 2007), at 66. (Table includes this author's inserts).

Appeal	Writ of Habeas Corpus
Based on any type of error made during the trial	Based on a violation of a constitutional right, usually, but not necessarily, during trial.
Must be undertaken within a certain period of time after conviction, otherwise the right of action lapses	Right of action does not lapse, may be filed while the person is serving time in prison (must be) [Under AEDPA, there are time limits based on time since state remedies were exhausted]
All issues must be raised from the trial record (i.e., evidence must be demonstrated in trial transcript)	New testimony may be presented

Collateral Challenge: Post-Conviction Relief (PCR)

The second type of collateral attack on a conviction is called "post-conviction relief." Post-conviction relief is a remedy provided by a state statute that allows individuals who are not being held in custody to challenge their conviction under certain circumstances. If, for example, Joe was convicted of assault, but was given a no-jail sentence, he would be able to challenge his conviction by taking an appeal. But, assume that after the time allowed for an appeal, Joe found out that the prosecutor and his defense attorney had conspired to make sure he was convicted. Joe would not be able to file a writ of habeas corpus because he is not in custody. Here is where post-conviction relief statutes may provide an avenue for Joe to challenge his conviction. State PCR statutes vary widely, but generally a PCR suit is more similar to a habeas corpus action (except for the in-custody requirement) than a direct appeal.

Issues Raised in Collateral Attacks

To the extent possible, defendants should challenge any claims of error on direct appeal. But because appellate courts must review a record of what took place during pre-trial hearings or at trial, some injustices (errors) may have occurred that are not or cannot be captured "on the record" (i.e., in the trial transcript). In those cases, those issues are raised in habeas corpus petitions or a post-conviction relief suit. For example, the fact that defense counsel or the judge slept through major portions of the trial would likely not be reflected in the trial transcript. The defendant would perhaps have a habeas corpus claim of ineffective assistance of counsel or a general due process/fair trial challenge. Similarly, if it came to light after trial that the prosecutor's office knowingly failed to disclose the existence of a lab report that tended to exonerate the defendant, the discovery of this failure would likely happen long after the time for direct appeal had passed, so a petition for habeas corpus or a post-conviction relief action would be appropriate. Defendant would raise a claim of discovery violation under *Brady v. Maryland* (discussed in Chapter Eight). Newly discovered evidence, recanted eyewitness testimony, and DNA tests are other reasons defendants raise their claims in collateral rather than direct appeals.

Occasionally, the Court must decide whether a holding in one case should be applied retroactively to another case. In *Teague v. Lane,* 489 U.S. 288 (1989), the Court held that "new constitutional rules of criminal procedure generally should not be applied retroactively to cases on collateral review" (habeas and pcr) and "such new rules will not be applicable to those cases that have become final before the new rules were announced." However, a new rule *should* be applied retroactively "if it requires the observance of 'those procedures that . . . are implicit in the concept of ordered liberty.'" What this suggests is that the Court will have to decide this on a case-by-case, issue-by-issue basis.

A CASE BOOK

A case book is a text book comprised primarily of the excerpts of written opinions of court cases rather than a summary of each case. Although it may be simpler just to read a compilation of case summaries, reading a case book helps students see how the law develops in light of the set of facts presented in each case. All but a few of the cases in this book are U.S. Supreme Court cases. The Court decides a handful of substantive criminal law and criminal procedure cases each year, and after so many years there are hundreds of cases that one could be expected to know. This book does not include every such case, but it does include most of the really important ones. These "seminal" or "pivotal" cases contribute to a change in the way things are viewed or done in the criminal justice system. Although this book also contains summaries (not excerpts) of many cases, the full decisions of these summarized cases are easy to access once you understand about case citations.

Case Citations

Case citations indicate the location of the written court opinions within books that compile judicial opinions. The case citation provides a very specific location for that particular case in the same way an "APA citation" provides the location for a journal article. For example, the official citation of *Mapp v. Ohio* is 367 US 643 (1961). "367" indicates volume 367. "US" means the United States Reports. United States Reports is the official series of books published by the U.S. government containing U.S. Supreme Court Cases. "643" means the case starts on page 643. (1961) is the year the case was published. Thus, before the internet, lawyers would go to the library (or pay for a subscription to have the books in their law offices), find the United States Reports (a series of books on the shelves), take down the book with 367 embossed on its spine, flip it open to page 643, and there he or she would find the written decision of *Mapp v. Ohio*. A quotation from *Mapp v. Ohio* may be cited as 367 US 643, 650. This citation indicates that the quoted material is found on page 650.

Mapp v. Ohio is also cited as 367 U.S. 643; 81 S.Ct. 1684; 6 L.Ed.2d 1081 (1961). The 81 S.Ct. 1684 indicates volume 81 of the Supreme Court Reporter, page 1684. Supreme Court Reporters are books published by West Publishing Company, a private publisher; likewise, 6 L.Ed.2d 1081 indicates Law Edition Second. Law Edition Second are books published by LexisNexis, a private publisher. The volume and page numbers are indicated in the same way as in the official publications

In this book you will occasionally see case citations with "F.2d" which stands for the Federal Reports, Second Series and "F.3d" which stands for Federal Reports, Third Series. These are reported decisions of the federal courts of appeal and are published by West Publishing Company. "F.Supp" stands for the Federal Supplement and cases with these citations are the reported decisions of federal district courts—the trial courts.[36]

State courts generally publish appellate decisions in an official reporter and through a private publisher. Official citations for state cases follow the individual rules of citation adopted by the state, and these citations vary tremendously. West Publishing Company publishes seven regional reporters comprised of state court decisions within that region. The regional reporters are Pacific Reporters (P), the Atlantic Reporter (A), the North Eastern Reporter (N.E.), the North Western Reporter (N.W.), the South Eastern Reporter (S.E.), the Southern Reporter (S) and South Western Reporter (S.W.). These regional reporters may have multiple series, so a citation showing P.3d or N.W.3d means the third series of the Pacific Reporters or North Western Reporters. Each of the regional reporters covers several states cases.

---

[36]"F.Supp." cases are the exception to the general rule that trial court decisions are not published.

Locating A Case — Doing Legal Research

Since most people have access to the Internet, going to the library to look up cases in the reporters is primarily a thing of the past. Although law schools teach a variety of legal research strategies that are not discussed in this book, internet sources, such as Findlaw and Academic Universe, allow for easy retrieval of case law. The easiest way to access a full case decision of the U.S. Supreme Court is to type the case title into the search engine (for example, google). This works well when the case name is known, but not so well when trying to research an area of law.

Case Briefs

Case briefs are tools to help readers focus on the key facts, principles, holdings and legal reasoning of the case. Briefing a case requires readers to summarize the most important information in a judicial opinion. Case briefs differ from appellate briefs which are prepared by the party who is appealing a legal decision. An appellate brief has consequences in real life, but a case brief does not. An appellant will challenge the decision from the lower court and will write an appellant's brief setting forth all the errors that the appellant alleges occurred at or before trial. The format, page length, and appropriate citation format used in appellate briefs are dictated by court rules. The trend is to require digital submission of these briefs, but some jurisdictions still require paper filing, and when they do so, even the weight and color of the paper used is regulated by rules. Failure to follow these rules may result in the appeal being dismissed. Fortunately, case briefs are fairly flexible. In fact, there is no agreement among scholars on how a case should be briefed, so it's a good idea to follow whatever format your professor provides. The guiding principle is that briefs should be brief — concise and precise. Basic elements of a simple case brief include:

> ➢ Case title
>
> ➢ Citation
>
> ➢ Year Decided
>
> ➢ Facts
>
> ➢ Main Issue or Question Presented
>
> ➢ "Court's Decision" or "Answer" or "Holding"
>
> ➢ Holding, Ruling, or Legal Reasoning, Rationale

Some professors want students to include the rationale of any dissenting or concurring opinions as well (dissents and concurring opinions are discussed below).

Some General Tips When "Briefing A Case"

Fact Section

Ask yourself, "What minimum facts must be included so that somebody who has not read the whole case will nonetheless understand it." The amount of detail required is up to you — you must determine what facts are important or unimportant. Keep the important and weed out the unimportant. Generally, when cases involve substantive criminal law, you will want to include some description of what the defendant did and some statement of what the controlling or disputed law was. In cases involving criminal procedure, you will want to include some statement of what the defendant did and probably a statement of what the police, prosecutor, or courts did.

Procedural History

Some professors want students to include a statement of the procedural history of the case in their brief. The procedural history section identifies where the case came from, what happened with the case at the trial court, the appellate court, etc. Some professors believe the "holding" refers to whether the court reversed, affirmed, or reversed and remanded the case, others believe it includes the answer/ruling. You will just need to defer to your professor on this.

Main Issue/Question Presented Section

The issue or question presented should be in the form of a question. The issue should not be so broad as to apply to every case even remotely similar in facts nor so narrow as to be applicable only to the peculiar facts of this case. The ultimate procedural question "should the court grant or deny the appeal?" is found in every case and the answer would not be helpful in a brief. Similarly, the question "Are police seizures without probable cause valid?" is too broad. "Was the police seizure of something that feels like a lump in a suspect's pocket valid?" is probably too narrow. "Was the seizure of crack cocaine from defendant's pocket valid under a stop and frisk?" is about right. Generally, there will only be one question presented, but there may be two or even more issues presented. If the issues cannot be merged, the must be stated as separate issues.

Decision/Holding/Answer

Your response should answer directly the question asked in the main issue or question presented section of the brief. It may be as simple as, "yes" or "no." Some professors want the holding to be spelled out. For instance, "No. When searching a suspect incident to arrest, the police may also search within arm's reach of the suspect."

Rationale/Legal Reasoning/Ruling

Ask why the court decided the case as it did. State in brief, exact and clear language what the court said. In some cases, the rationale should be taken verbatim from the case itself. The rationale, or legal reasoning, is the most important element of the case brief because it states not only the rule announced by the court but also the majority of the judges' reasoning why they decided as they did. It is what becomes precedent and thus applicable to similar cases decided by the court in the future.

Judgment/Disposition

The judgment of the case states what is going to happen to the judgment of the court immediately below and, ultimately, to the defendant or convicted offender. Common judgments include "affirmed," "reversed" or "reversed and remanded." Affirmed means that the appellate court upheld the judgment of the court immediately below it. "Reversed" means the appellate court set aside or nullified the lower court's judgment, and "remanded" means that the appellate court sent the case back to the lower court for further action. The most common disposition of a case is to "affirm the case without a written opinion" (AWOP) because the appellate courts are not required to write or publish an opinion. The cases in this text are extraordinary in that the U.S. Supreme Court accepted review and published an opinion.

Types of Judicial Opinions

Majority opinions: Each of the nine U.S. Supreme Court justices[37] has a vote, so generally it will take five justices to have a majority. Sometimes, however, not all nine justices will participate in a case, and in those cases a majority can be made of less than five justices. When the chief justice is in the majority, he or she determines who will write the majority opinion. When the chief justice is not in the majority, then the most senior judge in the majority determines who will write the opinion. In most intermediate appellate court settings, members sit together in panels of three, but occasionally

---

[37] By now, you may have noticed that the term "justice" is reserved for members of the federal and state supreme courts, while all other trial and appellate judges are referred to as "judge."

the intermediate appellate court will sit "*en banc*"(all together), in both scenarios, the majority opinion will be written by a judge who is in the numerical majority.

Dissenting Opinions (also called "dissents"): If justices don't agree with the court's majority decision, they can write their own dissenting opinions explaining why they don't agree with the result reached by the majority. Sometimes, other justices will "join" on a dissenting opinion; other times, they will write their own dissenting opinions.

Concurring Opinions: Sometimes, justices agree with the result of the majority opinion (to affirm or reverse, for example) but for a different reason. In this case, they will write a separate opinion, called a concurring opinion, giving their own reasons for reaching the decision. Like dissenting opinions, concurring opinions are sometimes joined by other justices. Sometimes justices will write a concurring opinion even if they agree with the holding and rationale, but have some additional point they wish to make.

Plurality Opinions: If not enough justices agree with a result for the same reason, a decision called a plurality opinion will be written by a justice who agrees with the sentiment of the largest number of justices. For example, suppose seven justices agree with the result (to affirm) and four of these justices agree that the reason to affirm rests with the Fourth Amendment, but three of the justices think that the reason to affirm rests with the Fifth Amendment, then one of the four justices will write the plurality opinion. Plurality opinions control only the result in the present case and technically have no precedential value. Nevertheless, several plurality decisions in this book have been repeatedly referred to in subsequent court cases (for example, *United States v. Mendenhall*,446 U.S. 544 (1980)).

Per Curiam: A per curiam opinion is an unsigned opinion, written anonymously — the individual judge authoring the opinion is not listed. Per curiam decisions are frequently, but not necessarily, unanimous decisions

Professor Samaha noted the effect of reading not only the majority opinion but also accompanying dissenting and concurring opinions. He stated,

> "[t]he conflicting arguments and reasoning in the majority, plurality, concurring and dissenting opinions challenge you to think about the issues in the cases, because, most of the time, all the justices argue their views of the case convincingly. First, the majority opinion, then the concurring opinion(s), and finally the dissenting opinions present arguments that will sway your opinion one way and then another. This is good. It teaches you that here's more than one reasonable position on all the important issues in the law of criminal procedure. Reasonable people do disagree."[38]

---

[38]Joel Samaha, Criminal Procedure, 14 (7th ed., 2007)

Chapter Two: Constitutional Limits On Substantive Criminal Law

Recall from our discussion of the rule of law in Chapter One that judicial review is the mechanism by which all individuals and governments in general are held accountable to those fundamental values in our society that have been reduced to writing--primarily in our constitutions. State and federal constitutions will, from time-to-time, limit the ability of the legislative and executive branch to pass certain types of criminal laws and engage in certain behaviors against individuals in the United States (both citizens and non-citizens alike). In other words, when Congress, state legislators, local county and municipal councils create laws that run up against some constitutional protections, courts may (and should) strike down those Acts, statutes, and ordinances. We then can refer to these protections or fundamental values as constitutional limits on the government's ability to regulate certain types of behavior. Although many of the fundamental values articulated in the Constitution do not involve the criminal justice system, this chapter focuses on those limits that do. (Appendix A sets out several cases which involve important fundamental rights that do not necessarily involve the criminal justice system in case you are interested.)

The drafters of the federal Constitution were so concerned about two historic abuses by English Parliament--ex post facto laws and bills of attainder--that they prohibited Congress from passing these types of laws in original body of the Constitution. See, Const. Art. I, § 9. Most of the other limitations on substantive criminal law, however, were not part of the original Constitution but were adopted by the states in 1791 in the "Bill of Rights" (the first ten amendments). These amendments added several constraints on Congress that had not yet been resolved by the time of the Constitutional Convention. The impact of the Bill of Rights was to place substantial checks on the federal government's ability to define crimes.

EX POST FACTO LAWS

Ex post facto laws are ones that are applied retroactively. For example, assume that Cheryl catches and squashes a centipede on January 1st. In response the city council, on January 2nd, passes a law that makes centipede-squashing a misdemeanor. The prohibition against ex post facto laws protects Cheryl from being prosecuted under this new law. Any attempt by the state to prosecute Cheryl using the new law applied retroactively would violate the provision against ex post facto laws. One of the reasons that ex post facto laws are problematic is because they violate the principle of legality which holds that individuals are entitled to know, in advance, what the law prohibits. Without the protection against ex post facto laws, Cheryl would only be able to guess at what types of laws could ensnare her at any time in the future.

Modern legislatures are generally careful not to draft statutes that violate ex post facto prohibitions. However, courts occasionally find a law to be retroactive in ways that the legislature failed to consider. When that happens, the court will strike down the law. For example, the Court struck down Florida sentencing guidelines in 1987 to the extent they reduced time off for an inmate's good behavior because it had the effect of increasing the punishment for those who committed crimes before the enactment of the guidelines. *Miller v. Florida*, 482 U.S. 423 (1987). Conversely, in *Smith v. Doe*, 538 U.S. 84 (2003), defendants who had committed crimes before Alaska Sex Offender Registration Law (Megan's Law) was passed were nevertheless required to register under the act. The Court held that the act was not punitive in nature, and therefore the ex post facto limitation did not apply.

The following cases involve the Court deciding whether a state law violated the Constitution's ex post facto prohibition.

STOGNER v. CALIFORNIA, 539 U.S. 607 (2003)

JUSTICE BREYER delivered the opinion of the Court.

I

In 1993, California enacted a new criminal statute of limitations governing sex-related child abuse crimes. The new statute permits prosecution for those crimes where "[t]he limitation period specified in [prior statutes of limitations] has expired"--provided that (1) a victim has reported an allegation of abuse to the police, (2) "there is independent evidence that clearly and convincingly corroborates the victim's allegation," and (3) the prosecution is begun within one year of the victim's report. A related provision, added to the statute in 1996, makes clear that a prosecution satisfying these three conditions "shall revive any cause of action barred by [prior statutes of limitations]." The statute thus authorizes prosecution for criminal acts committed many years beforehand--and where the original limitations period has expired--as long as prosecution begins within a year of a victim's first complaint to the police.

In 1998, a California grand jury indicted Marion Stogner, the petitioner, charging him with sex-related child abuse committed decades earlier--between 1955 and 1973. Without the new statute allowing revival of the State's cause of action, California could not have prosecuted Stogner. The statute of limitations governing prosecutions at the time the crimes were allegedly committed had set forth a 3-year limitations period. And that period had run 22 years or more before the present prosecution was brought.

Stogner moved for the complaint's dismissal. He argued that the Federal Constitution's *Ex Post Facto* Clause, Art. I, §10, cl. 1, forbids revival of a previously time-barred prosecution. The trial court agreed that such a revival is unconstitutional. But the California Court of Appeal reversed, citing a recent, contrary decision by the California Supreme Court. Stogner then moved to dismiss his indictment, arguing that his prosecution is unconstitutional under both the *Ex Post Facto* Clause and the Due Process Clause, Amdt. 14, §1. The trial court denied Stogner's motion, and the Court of Appeal upheld that denial. . . . We granted certiorari to consider Stogner's constitutional claims.

II

The law at issue here created a new criminal limitations period that extends the time in which prosecution is allowed. It authorized criminal prosecutions that the passage of time had previously barred. Moreover, it was enacted after prior limitations periods for Stogner's alleged offenses had expired. Do these features of the law, taken together, produce the kind of retroactivity that the Constitution forbids? We conclude that they do.

First, the new statute threatens the kinds of harm that, in this Court's view, the *Ex Post Facto* Clause seeks to avoid. Long ago the Court pointed out that the Clause protects liberty by preventing governments from enacting statutes with "manifestly *unjust and oppressive*" retroactive effects. *Calder* v. *Bull,* 3 Dall. 386, 391

(1798). Judge Learned Hand later wrote that extending a limitations period after the State has assured "a man that he has become safe from its pursuit ... seems to most of us unfair and dishonest." *Falter* v. *United States.* In such a case, the government has refused "to play by its own rules," *Carmell* v. *Texas.* It has deprived the defendant of the "fair warning," that might have led him to preserve exculpatory evidence. ... And a Constitution that permits such an extension, by allowing legislatures to pick and choose when to act retroactively, risks both "arbitrary and potentially vindictive legislation," and erosion of the separation of powers. ...

Second, the kind of statute at issue falls literally within the categorical descriptions of *ex post facto* laws set forth by Justice Chase more than 200 years ago in *Calder* v. *Bull* --a categorization that this Court has recognized as providing an authoritative account of the scope of the *Ex Post Facto* Clause. ...

In his alternative description, Chase traced these four categories back to Parliament's earlier abusive acts, as follows:

Category 1: "Sometimes they respected the crime, by declaring acts to be treason, which were not treason, when committed."

Category 2: "[A]t other times they inflicted punishments, where the party was not, by law, liable to any punishment."

Category 3: "[I]n other cases, they inflicted greater punishment, than the law annexed to the offence."

Category 4: "[A]t other times, they violated the rules of evidence (to supply a deficiency of legal proof) by admitting one witness, when the existing law required two; by receiving evidence without oath; or the oath of the wife against the husband; or other testimony, which the courts of justice would not admit." 3 Dall., at 389.

The second category--including any "law that *aggravates a crime,* or makes it *greater* than it was, when committed," -- describes California's statute as long as those

words are understood as Justice Chase understood them--*i.e.,* as referring to a statute that "inflict[s] *punishments,* where the party was not, by *law,* liable to *any punishment,*" ... After (but not before) the original statute of limitations had expired, a party such as Stogner was not "liable to any punishment." California's new statute therefore "aggravated" Stogner's alleged crime, or made it "greater than it was, when committed," in the sense that, and to the extent that, it "inflicted punishment" for past criminal conduct that (when the new law was enacted) did not trigger any such liability. ...

So to understand the second category (as applying where a new law inflicts a punishment upon a person not then subject to that punishment, to any degree) explains why and how that category differs from both the first category (making criminal noncriminal behavior) and the third category (aggravating the punishment). And this understanding is consistent, in relevant part, with Chase's second category examples--examples specifically provided to illustrate Chase's *alternative* description of laws " 'inflict[ing] *punishments,* where the party was not, by *law,* liable to *any punishment.*' " ...

In finding that California's law falls within the literal terms of Justice Chase's second category, we do not deny that it may fall within another category as well. Justice Chase's fourth category, for example, includes any "law that alters the *legal* rules of *evidence,* and receives less, or different, testimony, than the law required at the time of the commission of the offence, *in order to convict the offender.*" This Court has described that category as including laws that diminish "the quantum of evidence required to convict."...

Significantly, a statute of limitations reflects a legislative judgment that, after a certain time, no quantum of evidence is sufficient to convict. And that judgment typically rests, in large part, upon evidentiary concerns--for example, concern that the passage of time has eroded memories or made witnesses or other evidence unavailable. ...

Consequently, to resurrect a prosecution after the relevant statute of limitations has expired is to eliminate a currently existing conclusive presumption forbidding prosecution, and thereby to permit conviction on a quantum of evidence where that quantum, at the time the new law is enacted, would have been legally insufficient. And, in that sense, the new law would "violate" previous evidence-related legal rules by authorizing the courts to " 'receiv[e] evidence . . . which the courts of justice would not [previously have] admit[ted]' " as sufficient proof of a crime. ... Nonetheless, given Justice Chase's description of the second category, we need not explore the fourth category, or other categories, further.

In sum, California's law subjects an individual such as Stogner to prosecution long after the State has, in effect, granted an amnesty, telling him that he is "at liberty to return to his country ... and that from henceforth he may cease to preserve the proofs of his innocence," It retroactively withdraws a complete defense to prosecution after it has already attached, and it does so in a manner that allows the State to withdraw this defense at will and with respect to individuals already identified. "Unfair" seems to us a fair characterization.

IV

The statute before us is unfairly retroactive as applied to Stogner. A long line of judicial authority supports characterization of this law as *ex post facto*. For the reasons stated, we believe the law falls within Justice Chase's second category of *ex post facto* laws. We conclude that a law enacted after expiration of a previously applicable limitations period violates the *Ex Post Facto* Clause when it is applied to revive a previously time-barred prosecution.

THE FIRST AMENDMENT

The First Amendment lists several restrictions on Congress's power to create legislation. Through the Fourteenth Amendment's Due Process Clause, these restrictions also apply to state legislation. The First Amendment provides,

Congress shall make no law respecting an establishment of religion, or prohibiting the free exercise thereof; or abridging the freedom of speech, or of the press; or the right of the people peaceably to assemble, and to petition the Government for a redress of grievances.

Freedom Of Religion

Religious freedom was particularly important to the new colonists, and it is the first right set forth in the Bill of Rights. The First Amendment prohibits Congress from making laws that restrict the freedom of religion. It comprises two separate clauses: The Establishment Clause and the Exercise Clause.

The Establishment Clause

The First Amendment states, "Congress shall make no law respecting an establishment of religion." The "Establishment Clause" has little to do with criminal law or procedure and basically provides that Congress cannot create a national church or prescribe a religion; government cannot set up a religion and require people to be part of that religion.

It is, however, impossible to completely separate the church and the state. For example, even church buildings have to conform to building codes. Nevertheless, the First Amendment tries to ensure that government neither favors, nor is hostile toward, one religion over another. Questions raised by cases interpreting the Establishment Clause is how much governmental interaction is necessary for one to conclude it is establishing a religion? Is providing federal financial aid to students who want to go to a private religious based school sufficient connection? (Generally, no). Is it okay for a school to have a Christmas tree? A minute of prayer?

Generally, when studying criminal law, we get to dodge the bullet on Establishment Clause questions because they are beyond the scope of the criminal law. But essentially, in order to survive an Establishment Clause challenge, the state law must: (1) have a primary secular (non-religious) purpose; (2) have a principal effect that neither advances nor inhibits religion; and (3) not generate excessive entanglement between government and religion. The cases in the Establishment Clause area show the struggle between changing norms and constitutional interpretations.

The Exercise Clause

The second aspect of religious freedom has a much clearer connection to the criminal law. The First Amendment states, "Congress shall make no law . . . prohibiting the free exercise [of religion]." The free exercise of religion involves the freedom to believe and the freedom to act.

The First Amendment was intended to allow every one under the jurisdiction of the United States to entertain such notions respecting his relations to his Maker and the duties they impose as may be approved by his judgment and conscience, and to exhibit his sentiments in such form of worship, as he may think proper, not injurious to the rights of others. *Davis v. Beason*, 133 U.S. 33 (1890).

A few examples highlight how the substantive criminal law can impact a person's exercise of his or her religion. Is Edie entitled to smoke peyote as part of her religious practice while incarcerated or does the correctional staff have a right to deny her that right even assuming it is a legitimate exercise of her religion? Can the court force parents who are practicing Jehovah's Witnesses to allow a life-saving blood transfusion for their minor child? If they refuse, and their child dies will they successfully be prosecuted for criminally negligent homicide? Note that courts generally recognize the right of adults to refuse medical treatment for themselves based on their personal religious beliefs, but when adults make similar decisions for their children, they may violate the criminal law. "Parents may be free to become martyrs themselves. But it does not follow that they are free in identical circumstances to make martyrs of their children before they have reached the age of full legal discretion when they can make that choice for themselves." *Prince v. Massachusetts*, 321 U.S. 158 (1944).

When Free Exercise Of Religion Conflicts With Criminal Law

When religion and criminal law conflict, the courts will generally look at whether the criminal statute is one of general applicability (for example, criminally negligent homicide) or whether it is more inclined to target religious practices. The Constitution permits the former but not the latter. The courts have distinguished between laws which incidentally prohibit some exercise of religious practice and laws which are written specifically to stop a religious practice.

One free exercise case, *People v. Woody*, 394 P.2d 813 (Cal. 1964), involved the convictions of several members of the Native American Church for possession of peyote. The California Supreme Court reversed their convictions, finding that the defendants' sacramental use of peyote was central for the members of that church and thus was protected by the First Amendment. In 1990, however, the Court decided *Employment Division v. Smith*, 492 U.S. 872 (1990) in which two American Indian drug counselors in Oregon lost their jobs because they used peyote as part of a religious ritual in their church. They sought unemployment benefits, but Oregon refused to pay. The Court upheld the Employment Division's refusal. It reasoned that because respondents' ingestion of peyote was constitutionally prohibited under Oregon law, Oregon could deny respondents unemployment compensation when they were dismissed from their jobs because of their drug use. The Court tried to make clear in *Smith* that the Free Exercise Clause does not allow individuals to avoid the responsibilities and consequences of a generally applicable criminal statute.

Three years after the *Smith* case, the Court in *Church of the Lukimi Babalu Aye, Inc. v. City of Hialeah*, 508 U.S. 520 (1993) unanimously struck down a statute that made it an offense to "unnecessarily kill, torment, torture, or mutilate an animal in a public or private ritual or ceremony not for the primary purpose of food consumption." The Court found that the "laws in question were enacted by officials who did not understand, failed to perceive or chose to ignore the fact that their official actions violated the Nation's essential commitment to religious freedom." The Court specifically noted that the City of Hialeah had criminalized and targeted activity practiced by a religious group and was not enacting a general criminal prohibition against the slaughter of animals.

In response to *Smith*, Congress passed, and President Clinton signed, the Religious Freedom Restoration Act of 1993; Pub. L. No. 103-141, 107 Stat. 1488 (November 16, 1993) the explicit purpose of which was to overturn the *Smith* holding. Congress intended to limit government's interference with religious practices. The Court, however, struck down this act holding that it was a legislative encroachment on the judicial right of the courts to interpret the U.S. Constitution. See, *City of Boerne, Texas v. Flores*, 521 U.S. 507 (1997).

In 2000 Congress again attempted to limit government's ability to impede the exercise of religion by passing the Religious Land Use and Institutionalized Persons Act of 2000 (RLUIPA). It provides that no government shall impose a substantial burden on the religious exercise of an institutionalized person unless the government demonstrates that the burden is the least restrictive means of furthering a compelling governmental interest. The Court had to determine the constitutionality the government's actions under this Act in *Holt v. Hobbs* (below).

In *Fulton v. City of Philadelphia*, 593 U.S. ____ (2021), one question presented was whether the Smith decision should be overturned. The City of Philadelphia had barred the Catholic Social Services (CSS) from placing children in foster homes because CSS had adopted a policy that prohibited licensing same-sex couples as foster parents. CSS sued Philadelphia asking the court to renew its contract arguing that its right to free exercise of religion and free speech allowed it to reject qualified same-sex couples simply because they were same-sex couples (rather than any reason related to their qualifications for child care). The Court, in a surprisingly unanimous opinion, held in favor of CSS.

Chief Justice Roberts wrote the opinion finding that Philadelphia violated CSS's free exercise of religion by requiring it to "curtail its mission" or to certify same-sex couples as foster parents, in violation of its stated religious beliefs." He noted that according to *Smith*, a neutral, generally applicable law may incidentally burden religion, but the Philadelphia law was not neutral and generally applicable because it allowed for exceptions to the anti-discrimination requirement at the sole discretion of the Commissioner.

Although unanimous in the holding, there were several concurring opinions written: Justice Barrett acknowledged several arguments for overruling *Smith*, but agreed with the majority that the facts of the case did not trigger *Smith*; Justice Alito noted he would overrule Smith, and replace it with a rule that any law that burdens religious exercise must be subject to strict scrutiny; and Justice Gorsuch's opinion criticized the majority's circumvention of *Smith*.

The following cases examine whether the government went too far in restricting the defendant's actions in a way that violated their free exercise of religion.

CANTWELL v. CONNECTICUT, 10 U.S. 296 (1949)

MR. JUSTICE ROBERTS, delivered the opinion of the Court.

Newton Cantwell and his two sons, Jesse and Russell, members of a group known as Jehovah's witnesses, and claiming to be ordained ministers, were arrested in New Haven, Connecticut, and each was charged by information in five counts, with statutory and common law offenses. After trial in the Court of Common Pleas of New Haven County each of them was convicted on the third count, (the statutory count), and on the fifth count, which charged commission of the common law offense of inciting a breach of the peace. On appeal to the Supreme Court the conviction of all three on the third count was affirmed. The conviction of Jesse Cantwell, on the fifth count, was also affirmed, but the conviction of Newton and Russell on that count was reversed and a new trial ordered as to them.

[They argued] . . . the statute under which the third count was drawn was offensive to the due process clause of the Fourteenth Amendment because, on its face and as construed and applied, it denied them freedom of speech and prohibited their free exercise of religion. In like manner they made the point that they could not be found guilty on the fifth count, without violation of the Amendment.

. . .

. . . On the day of their arrest the appellants were engaged in going singly from house to house on Cassius Street in New Haven. They were individually equipped with a bag containing books and pamphlets on religious subjects, a portable phonograph and a set of records, each of which, when played, introduced, and was a description of, one of the books. Each appellant asked the person who responded to his call for permission to play one of the records. If permission was granted he asked the person to buy the book described and, upon refusal, he solicited such contribution towards the publication of the pamphlets as the listener was willing to make.

If a contribution was received a pamphlet was delivered upon condition that it would be read.

Cassius Street is in a thickly populated neighborhood, where about ninety per cent of the residents are Roman Catholics. A phonograph record, describing a book entitled 'Enemies', included an attack on the Catholic religion. None of the persons interviewed were members of Jehovah's witnesses.

The statute under which the appellants were charged [in count three] provides:

> 'No person shall solicit money, services, subscriptions or any valuable thing for any alleged religious, charitable or philanthropic cause, from other than a member of the organization for whose benefit such person is soliciting or within the county in which such person or organization is located unless such cause shall have been approved by the secretary of the public welfare council. Upon application of any person in behalf of such cause, the secretary shall determine whether such cause is a religious one or is a bona fide object of charity or philanthropy and conforms to reasonable standards of efficiency and integrity, and, if he shall so find, shall approve the same and issue to the authority in charge a certificate to that effect. Such certificate may be revoked at any time. Any person violating any provision of this section shall be fined not more than one hundred dollars or imprisoned not more than thirty days or both.'

The appellants claimed that their activities were not within the statute but consisted only of distribution of books, pamphlets, and periodicals. The State Supreme Court construed the finding of the trial court to be that 'in addition to the sale of the books and the distribution of the pamphlets the defendants were also soliciting contributions or donations of money for an alleged religious cause, and thereby came within the purview of the statute. It overruled the contention that the Act, as applied to the appellants, offends the due process clause of the Fourteenth Amendment, because it abridges or denies religious freedom and liberty of speech and press. The court stated that it was the solicitation that brought the appellants within the sweep of the Act and not their other activities in the dissemination of literature. It declared the legislation constitutional as an effort by the State to protect the public against fraud and imposition in the solicitation of funds for what purported to be religious, charitable, or philanthropic causes.

…

First. We hold that the statute, as construed and applied to the appellants, deprives them of their liberty without due process of law in contravention of the Fourteenth Amendment. The fundamental concept of liberty embodied in that Amendment embraces the liberties guaranteed by the First Amendment. The First Amendment declares that Congress shall make no law respecting an establishment of religion or prohibiting the free exercise thereof. The Fourteenth Amendment has rendered the legislatures of the states as incompetent as Congress to enact such laws. The constitutional inhibition of legislation on the subject of religion has a double aspect. On the one hand, it forestalls compulsion by law of the acceptance of any creed or the practice of any form of worship. Freedom of conscience and freedom to adhere to such religious organization or form of worship as the individual may choose cannot be restricted by law. On the other hand, it safeguards the free exercise of the chosen form of religion. Thus the Amendment embraces two concepts, - freedom to believe and freedom to act. The first is absolute but, in the nature of things, the second cannot be. Conduct remains subject to regulation for the protection of society. The freedom to act must have appropriate definition to preserve the enforcement of that protection. In every case the power to regulate must be so exercised as not, in attaining a permissible end, unduly to infringe the protected freedom. No one would contest the proposition that a state may not, by statute, wholly deny the right to preach or to disseminate religious views. Plainly such a previous and absolute restraint would violate the terms of the guarantee. It is equally clear that a state may by general and non-discriminatory legislation regulate the times, the places, and the manner of soliciting upon its streets, and of holding meetings thereon; and may in other respects safeguard the peace, good order and comfort of the community, without unconstitutionally invading the liberties protected by the Fourteenth Amendment. The appellants are right in their insistence that the Act in question is not such a regulation. If a certificate is procured, solicitation is permitted without restraint but, in the absence of a certificate, solicitation is altogether prohibited.

The appellants urge that to require them to obtain a certificate as a condition of soliciting support for their views amounts to a prior restraint on the exercise of their religion within the meaning of the Constitution. The State insists that the Act, as construed by the Supreme Court of Connecticut, imposes no previous restraint upon the dissemination of religious views or teaching but merely safeguards against the perpetration of frauds under the cloak of religion. Conceding that this is so, the question remains whether the method adopted by Connecticut to that end transgresses the liberty safeguarded by the Constitution.

The general regulation, in the public interest, of solicitation, which does not involve any religious test and does not unreasonably obstruct or delay the collection of funds, is not open to any constitutional objection, even though the collection be for a religious purpose. Such regulation would not constitute a prohibited previous restraint on the free exercise of religion or interpose an inadmissible obstacle to its exercise.

It will be noted, however, that the Act requires an application to the secretary of the public welfare council of the State; that he is empowered to determine whether the cause is a religious one, and that the issue of a certificate depends upon his affirmative action. If he finds that the cause is not that of religion, to solicit for it becomes a crime. He is not to issue a certificate as a matter of course. His decision to issue or refuse it involves appraisal of facts, the exercise of judgment, and the formation of an opinion. He is authorized to withhold his approval if he determines that the cause is not a religious one. Such a censorship of religion as the means of determining its right to survive is a denial of liberty protected by the First Amendment and included in the liberty which is within the protection of the Fourteenth.

The State asserts that if the licensing officer acts arbitrarily, capriciously, or corruptly, his action is subject to judicial correction. ...

. . . The line between a discretionary and a ministerial act is not always easy to mark and the statute has not been construed by the State court to impose a mere ministerial duty on the secretary of the welfare council. Upon his decision as to the nature of the cause, the right to solicit depends. Moreover, the availability of a judicial remedy for abuses in the system of licensing still leaves that system one of

previous restraint which, in the field of free speech and press, we have held inadmissible. A statute authorizing previous restraint upon the exercise of the guaranteed freedom by judicial decision after trial is as obnoxious to the Constitution as one providing for like restraint by administrative action.

. . . Even the exercise of religion may be at some slight inconvenience in order that the state may protect its citizens from injury. Without doubt a state may protect its citizens from fraudulent solicitation by requiring a stranger in the community, before permitting him publicly to solicit funds for any purpose, to establish his identity and his authority to act for the cause which he purports to represent. The state is likewise free to regulate the time and manner of solicitation generally, in the interest of public safety, peace, comfort or convenience. But to condition the solicitation of aid for the perpetuation of religious views or systems upon a license, the grant of which rests in the exercise of a determination by state authority as to what is a religious cause, is to lay a forbidden burden upon the exercise of liberty protected by the Constitution.

HOLT v. HOBBS,
574 U.S. 352 (2015)

FACTS (Official Summary)

Section 3 of the Religious Land Use and Institutionalized Persons Act of 2000 (RLUIPA) provides that "[n]o government shall impose a substantial burden on the religious exercise" of an institutionalized person unless the government demonstrates that the burden "is the least restrictive means of furthering [a] compelling governmental interest."

Petitioner is an Arkansas inmate and devout Muslim who wishes to grow a ½-inch beard in accordance with his religious beliefs. Respondent Arkansas Department of Correction (Department) prohibits its prisoners from growing beards, with the single exception that inmates with diagnosed skin

conditions may grow ¼-inch beards. Petitioner sought an exemption on religious grounds and, although he believes that his faith requires him not to trim his beard at all, he proposed a compromise under which he would be allowed to maintain a ½-inch beard. Prison officials denied his request, and petitioner sued in Federal District Court. At an evidentiary hearing before a Magistrate Judge, Department witnesses testified that beards compromised prison safety because they could be used to hide contraband and because an inmate could quickly shave his beard to disguise his identity. The Magistrate Judge recommended dismissing petitioner's complaint, emphasizing that prison officials are entitled to deference on security matters and that the prison permitted petitioner to exercise his religion in other ways. The

District Court adopted the recommendation in full, and the Eighth Circuit affirmed, holding that the Department had satisfied its burden of showing that the grooming policy was the least restrictive means of furthering its compelling security interests, and reiterating that courts should defer to prison officials on matters of security.

JUSTICE ALITO, J., delivered the opinion for a unanimous Court.

(a) Under RLUIPA, the challenging party bears the initial burden of proving that his religious exercise is grounded in a sincerely held religious belief and that the government's action substantially burdens his religious exercise. Here, petitioner's sincerity is not in dispute, and he easily satisfies the second obligation. The Department's policy forces him to choose between "engag[ing] in conduct that seriously violates [his] religious belie[f]," or contravening the grooming policy and risking disciplinary action. In reaching the opposite conclusion, the District Court misunderstood the analysis that RLUIPA demands. First, the District Court erred by concluding that the grooming policy did not substantially burden petitioner's religious exercise because he could practice his religion in other ways. Second, the District Court erroneously suggested that the burden on petitioner's religious exercise was slight because petitioner testified that his religion would "credit" him for attempting to follow his religious beliefs, even if that attempt proved unsuccessful. RLUIPA, however, applies to religious exercise regardless of whether it is "compelled." Finally, the District Court improperly relied on petitioner's testimony that not all Muslims believe that men must grow beards. Even if petitioner's belief were idiosyncratic, RLUIPA's guarantees are "not limited to beliefs which are shared by all of the members of a religious sect."

(b) Once the challenging party satisfies his burden, the burden shifts to the government to show that substantially burdening the religious exercise of the "particular claimant" is "the least restrictive means of furthering [a]

compelling governmental interest." The Department fails to show that enforcing its beard prohibition against petitioner furthers its compelling interests in preventing prisoners from hiding contraband and disguising their identities.

(i) While the Department has a compelling interest in regulating contraband, its argument that this interest is compromised by allowing an inmate to grow a ½-inch beard is unavailing, especially given the difficulty of hiding contraband in such a short beard and the lack of a corresponding policy regulating the length of hair on the head. RLUIPA does not permit the unquestioning deference required to accept the Department's assessment. Even if the Department could show that denying petitioner a ½-inch beard furthers its interest in rooting out contraband, it would still have to show that its policy is the least restrictive means of furthering that interest, a standard that is "exceptionally demanding" and requires the government to "sho[w] that it lacks other means of achieving its desired goal without imposing a substantial burden on the exercise of religion by the objecting part[y]." Here, the Department fails to establish that its security concerns cannot be satisfied by simply searching a ½-inch beard.

(ii) Even if the Department's grooming policy furthers its compelling interest in prisoner identification, its policy still violates RLUIPA as applied in the present circumstances. As petitioner argues, requiring inmates to be photographed both with and without beards and then periodically thereafter is a less restrictive means of solving the Department's identification concerns. The Department fails to show why its prison system is so different from the many institutions that allow facial hair that the dual-photo method cannot be employed at its institutions. It also fails to show why the security risk presented by a prisoner shaving a ½-inch beard is so different from the risk of a prisoner shaving a mustache, head hair, or ¼-inch beard.

(c) In addition to the Department's failure to prove that petitioner's proposed alternatives would not sufficiently serve its security interests, the Department also fails to adequately explain the substantial under-inclusiveness of its policy, since it permits ¼-inch beards for prisoners with medical conditions and more than ½ inch of hair on the head. Its failure to pursue its proffered objectives with regard to such "analogous nonreligious conduct" suggests that its interests "could be achieved by narrower ordinances that burdened religion to a far lesser degree." Nor does the Department explain why the vast majority of States and the Federal Government can permit inmates to grow ½-inch beards, either for any reason or for religious reasons, but it cannot. Such evidence requires a prison, at a minimum, to offer persuasive reasons why it believes it must take a different course.

The Department's grooming policy violates RLUIPA insofar as it prevents petitioner from growing a ½-inch beard in accordance with his religious beliefs.

Other Cases: Establishment Clause

Stone v. Graham, 449 U.S. 39 (1980)

SUMMARY: The Court struck down a Kentucky law requiring the posting of the Ten Commandments in all classrooms.

The American Legion v. American Humanist Association, 588 U.S. ___ (2019)

SUMMARY: The Court held that when a local government displays and maintains a large memorial cross, it does not violate the Establishment Clause. This case reiterated the three-prong analysis courts employ when evaluating whether a law establishes a religion in violation of the First Amendment.

Kennedy v. Bremerton School District, 597 U.S. ___ (2022)

SUMMARY: The Court majority held that the Bremerton School District had violated football coach Kennedy's constitutional rights to free speech and exercise of religion by "firing him" (there is a factual dispute whether he was fired or not) for repeatedly engaging in prayer at the 50-yard line after football games.

The majority decided this case based on free exercise and free speech, and gave short shrift to the Establishment Clause. Justice Sotomayor, however, wrote a dissenting opinion refuting the Court's characterization of the facts before the Court, but more important for our purposes here, she had the following to say about the Establishment Clause.

"Official-led prayer strikes at the core of our constitutional protections for the religious liberty of students and their parents, as embodied in both the Establishment Clause and the Free Exercise Clause of the First Amendment. The Court now charts a different path, yet again paying almost exclusive attention to the Free Exercise Clause's protection for individual religious exercise while giving short shrift to the Establishment Clause's prohibition on state establishment of religion. ...

The Establishment Clause prohibits States from adopting laws "respecting an establishment of religion." Amdt. 1; see Wallace v. Jaffree, 472 U. S. 38, 49 (1985) (recognizing the Clause's incorporation against the States). ... The Establishment Clause protects ... freedom by "command[ing] a separation of church and state." At its core, this means forbidding "sponsorship, financial support, and active involvement of the sovereign in religious activity." In the context of public schools, it means that a State cannot use "its public school system to aid any or all religious faiths or sects in the dissemination of their doctrines and ideals. Indeed, "[t]he Court has been particularly vigilant in monitoring compliance with the Establishment Clause in elementary and secondary schools." The reasons motivating this vigilance inhere in the nature of schools themselves and the young people they serve. Two are relevant here.

First, government neutrality toward religion is particularly important in the public school context given the role public schools play in our society. "'The public school is at once the symbol of our democracy and the most pervasive means for promoting our common destiny,'" meaning that "'[i]n no activity of the State is it more vital to keep out divisive forces than in its schools.'" Families "entrust public schools with the education of their children . . . on the understanding that the classroom will not purposely be used to advance religious views that may conflict with the private beliefs of the student and his or her family." Accordingly, the Establishment Clause "proscribes public schools from 'conveying or attempting to convey a message that religion or a particular religious belief is favored or preferred'" or otherwise endorsing religious beliefs.

Second, schools face a higher risk of unconstitutionally "coerc[ing] . . . support or participat[ion] in religion or its exercise" than other government entities. The State "exerts great authority and coercive power" in schools as a general matter "through mandatory attendance requirements." Moreover, the State exercises that great authority over children, who are uniquely susceptible to "subtle coercive pressure." Children are particularly vulnerable to coercion because of their "emulation of teachers as role models" and "susceptibility to peer pressure." Accordingly, this Court has emphasized that "the State may not, consistent with the Establishment Clause, place primary and secondary school children" in the dilemma of choosing between "participating, with all that implies, or protesting" a religious exercise in a public school.

Given the twin Establishment Clause concerns of endorsement and coercion, it is unsurprising that the Court has consistently held integrating prayer into public school activities to be unconstitutional, including when student participation is not a formal requirement or prayer is silent. See Wallace, (mandatory moment of silence for prayer); School Dist. of Abington Township v. Schempp, (nonmandatory recitation of Bible verses and prayer); Engel, (nonmandatory recitation of one-sentence prayer). The Court also has held that incorporating a nondenominational general benediction into a graduation ceremony is unconstitutional. Finally, this Court has held that including prayers in student football games is unconstitutional, even when delivered by students rather than staff and even when students themselves initiated the prayer.

Under these precedents, the Establishment Clause violation at hand is clear.

Freedom Of Speech

In general, the government may neither require, nor substantially interfere with, individual expression. Most First Amendment cases do not involve the government compelling expression—for example a student may not be compelled to pledge allegiance to the American Flag. Justice Jackson observed,

> If there is any fixed star in our constitutional constellation, it is that no official, high or petty, can prescribe what shall be orthodox in politics, nationalism, religion, or other matters of opinion or force citizens to confess by word or act their faith therein. If there are any circumstances which permit an exception, they do not now occur to us.

> We think the action of the local authorities in compelling the flag salute and pledge transcends constitutional limitations on their power, and invades the sphere of intellect and spirit which it is the purpose of the First Amendment to our Constitution to reserve from all official control. *West Virginia State Board of Education v. Barnette*, 319 U.S. 624, 642 (1943).

Instead, most cases involve a statute that limits an individual's expression. Although the First Amendment's protection of free speech is broad, it is not absolute. In the case below, the Court indicated certain types of speech that are not considered worthy of protection.

CHAPLINSKY v. NEW HAMPSHIRE, 315 U.S. 568 (1942)

MR. JUSTICE MURPHY delivered the opinion of the Court.

Appellant, a member of the sect known as Jehovah's Witnesses, was convicted in the municipal court of Rochester, New Hampshire, for violation of Chapter 378, Section 2, of the Public Laws of New Hampshire: 'No person shall address any offensive, derisive or annoying word to any other person who is lawfully in any street or other public place, nor call him by any offensive or derisive name, nor make any noise or exclamation in his presence and hearing with intent to deride, offend or annoy him, or to prevent him from pursuing his lawful business or occupation.'

The complaint charged that appellant 'with force and arms, in a certain public place in said city of Rochester, to wit, on the public sidewalk on the easterly side of Wakefield Street, near unto the entrance of the City Hall, did unlawfully repeat, the words following, addressed to the complainant, that is to say, 'You are a God damned racketeer' and 'a damned Fascist and the whole government of Rochester are Fascists or agents of Fascists' the same being offensive, derisive and annoying words and names'.

Upon appeal there was a trial de novo of appellant before a jury in the Superior Court. He was found guilty and the judgment of conviction was affirmed by the Supreme Court of the State.

By motions and exceptions, appellant raised the questions that the statute was invalid under the Fourteenth Amendment of the Constitution of the United States in that it placed an unreasonable restraint on freedom of speech, freedom of the press, and freedom of worship, and because it was vague and indefinite. These contentions were overruled and the case comes here on appeal.

There is no substantial dispute over the facts. Chaplinsky was distributing the literature of his sect on the streets of Rochester on a busy Saturday afternoon. Members of the local citizenry complained to the City Marshal, Bowering, that Chaplinsky was denouncing all religion as a 'racket'. Bowering told them that Chaplinsky was lawfully engaged, and then warned Chaplinsky that the crowd was getting restless. Some time later a disturbance occurred and the traffic officer on duty at the busy intersection started with Chaplinsky for the police station, but did not inform him that he was under arrest or that he was going to be arrested. On the way they encountered Marshal Bowering who had been advised that a riot was under way and was therefore hurrying to the scene. Bowering repeated his earlier warning to Chaplinsky who then addressed to Bowering the words set forth in the complaint.

Chaplinsky's version of the affair was slightly different. He testified that when he met Bowering, he asked him to arrest the ones responsible for the disturbance. In reply Bowering cursed him and told him to come along. Appellant admitted that he said the words charged in the complaint with the exception of the name of the Deity.

Over appellant's objection the trial court excluded as immaterial testimony relating to appellant's mission 'to preach the true facts of the Bible', his treatment at the hands of the crowd, and the alleged neglect of duty on the part of the police. This action was approved by the court below which held that neither provocation nor the truth of the utterance would constitute a defense to the charge.

It is now clear that 'Freedom of speech and freedom of the press, which are protected by the First Amendment from infringement by Congress, are among the fundamental personal rights and liberties which are protected by the Fourteenth Amendment from invasion by state action'. Freedom of worship is similarly sheltered.

Appellant assails the statute as a violation of all three freedoms, speech, press and worship, but only an attack on the basis of free speech is warranted. The spoken, not the written, word is involved. And we cannot conceive that cursing a public officer is the exercise of religion in any sense of the term. But even if the activities of the appellant which preceded the incident could be viewed as religious in character, and therefore entitled to the protection of the Fourteenth Amendment, they would not cloak him with immunity from the legal consequences for concomitant acts committed in violation of a valid criminal statute. We turn, therefore, to an examination of the statute itself.

Allowing the broadest scope to the language and purpose of the Fourteenth Amendment, it is well understood that the right of free speech is not absolute at all times and under all circumstances. There are certain well-defined and narrowly limited classes of speech, the prevention and punishment of which has never been thought to raise any Constitutional problem. These include the lewd and obscene, the profane, the libelous, and the insulting or 'fighting' words-those which by their very utterance inflict injury or tend to incite an immediate breach of the peace. It has been well observed that such utterances are no essential part of any exposition of ideas, and are of such slight social value as a step to truth that any benefit that may be derived from them is clearly outweighed by the social interest in order and morality. Resort to epithets or personal abuse is not in any proper sense communication of information or opinion safeguarded by the Constitution. …

The state statute here challenged comes to us authoritatively construed by the highest court of New Hampshire. It has two provisions-the first relates to words or names addressed to another in a public place; the second refers to noises and exclamations. The court said: 'The two provisions are distinct. One may stand separately from the other. Assuming, without holding, that the second were unconstitutional, the first could stand if constitutional.' We accept that construction of severability and limit our consideration to the first provision of the statute. On the authority of its earlier decisions, the state court declared that the statute's purpose was to preserve the public peace, no words being 'forbidden except such as have a direct tendency to cause acts of violence by the person to whom, individually, the remark is addressed'. It was further said: 'The word 'offensive' is not to be defined in terms of what a particular addressee thinks. ... The test is what men of common intelligence would understand would be words likely to cause an average addressee to fight. . . . Derisive and annoying words can be taken as coming within the purview of the statute as heretofore interpreted only when they have this characteristic of plainly tending to excite the addressee to a breach of the peace. ... The statute, as construed, does no more than prohibit the face-to-face words plainly likely to cause a breach of the peace by the addressee, words whose speaking constitute a breach of the peace by the speaker-including 'classical fighting words', words in current use less 'classical' but equally likely to cause violence, and other disorderly words, including profanity, obscenity and threats.'

We are unable to say that the limited scope of the statute as thus construed contravenes the constitutional right of free expression. It is a statute narrowly drawn and limited to define and punish specific conduct lying within the domain of state power, the use in a public place of words likely to cause a breach of the peace. This conclusion necessarily disposes of appellant's contention that the statute is so vague and indefinite as to render a conviction thereunder a violation of due process. A statute punishing verbal acts, carefully drawn so as not unduly to impair liberty of expression, is not too vague for a criminal law.

Nor can we say that the application of the statute to the facts disclosed by the record substantially or unreasonably impinges upon the privilege of free speech. Argument is unnecessary to demonstrate that the appellations 'damn racketeer' and 'damn Fascist' are epithets likely to provoke the average person to retaliation, and thereby cause a breach of the peace.

The refusal of the state court to admit evidence of provocation and evidence bearing on the truth or falsity of the utterances is open to no Constitutional objection. Whether the facts sought to be proved by such evidence constitute a defense to the charge or may be shown in mitigation are questions for the state court to determine. Our function is fulfilled by a determination that the challenged statute, on its face and as applied, does not contravene the Fourteenth Amendment.

Other Cases: Free Speech

Cantwell v. Connecticut, 10 U.S. 296 (1949)

Facts: See case excerpt above

…

The facts which were held to support the conviction of Jesse Cantwell on the fifth count were that he stopped two men in the street, asked, and received, permission to play a phonograph record, and played the record 'Enemies', which attacked the religion and church of the two men, who were Catholics. Both were incensed by the contents of the record and were tempted to strike Cantwell unless he went away. On being told to be on his way he left their presence. There was no evidence that he was personally offensive or entered into any argument with those he interviewed.

The court held that the charge was not assault or breach of the peace or threats on Cantwell's part, but invoking or inciting others to breach of the peace, and that the facts supported the conviction of that offense.

…

Second. We hold that, in the circumstances disclosed, the conviction of Jesse Cantwell on the fifth count must be set aside. Decision as to the lawfulness of the conviction demands the weighing of two conflicting interests. The fundamental law declares the interest of the United States that the free exercise of religion be not prohibited and that freedom to communicate information and opinion be not abridged. The state of Connecticut has an obvious interest in the preservation and protection of peace and good order within her borders. We must determine whether the alleged protection of the State's interest, means to which end would, in the absence of limitation by the federal Constitution, lie wholly within the State's discretion, has been pressed, in this instance, to a point where it has come into fatal collision with the overriding interest protected by the federal compact.

Conviction on the fifth count was not pursuant to a statute . . . [rather] . . . the judgment is based on a common law concept of the most general and undefined nature. The court below has held that the petitioner's conduct constituted the commission of an offense under the State law, and we accept its decision as binding upon us to that extent.

The offense known as breach of the peace embraces a great variety of conduct destroying or menacing public order and tranquility. It includes not only violent acts but acts and words likely to produce violence in others. No one would have the hardihood to suggest that the principle of freedom of speech sanctions incitement to riot or that religious liberty connotes the privilege to exhort others to physical attack upon those belonging to another sect. When clear and present danger of riot, disorder, interference with traffic upon the public streets, or other immediate threat to public safety, peace, or order, appears, the power of the state to prevent or punish is obvious. Equally obvious is it that a state may not unduly suppress free communication of views, religious or other, under the guise of conserving desirable conditions. Here we have a situation analogous to a conviction under a statute sweeping in a great variety of conduct under a general and indefinite characterization, and leaving to the executive and judicial branches too wide a discretion in its application.

Having these considerations in mind, we note that Jesse Cantwell, on April 26, 1938, was upon a public street, where he had a right to be, and where he had a right peacefully to impart his views to others. There is no showing that his deportment was noisy, truculent, overbearing or offensive. He requested of two pedestrians permission to play to them a phonograph record.

The permission was granted. It is not claimed that he intended to insult or affront the hearers by playing the record. It is plain that he wished only to interest them in his propaganda. The sound of the phonograph is not shown to have disturbed residents of the street, to have drawn a crowd, or to have impeded traffic. Thus far he had invaded no right or interest of the public or of the men accosted.

The record played by Cantwell embodies a general attack on all organized religious systems as instruments of Satan and injurious to man; it then singles out the Roman Catholic Church for strictures couched in terms which naturally would offend not only persons of that persuasion, but all others who respect the honestly held religious faith of their fellows. The hearers were in fact highly offended. One of them said he felt like hitting Cantwell and the other that he was tempted to throw Cantwell off the street. The one who testified he felt like hitting Cantwell said, in answer to the question 'Did you do anything else or have any other reaction?' 'No, sir, because he said he would take the victrola and he went.' The other witness testified that he told Cantwell he had better get off the street before something happened to him and that was the end of the matter as Cantwell picked up his books and walked up the street.

Cantwell's conduct, in the view of the court below, considered apart from the effect of his communication upon his hearers, did not amount to a breach of the peace. One may, however, be guilty of the offense if he commits acts or make statements likely to provoke violence and disturbance of good order, even though no such eventuality be intended. Decisions to this effect are many, but examination discloses that, in practically all, the provocative language which was held to amount to a breach of the peace consisted of profane, indecent, or abusive remarks directed to the person of the hearer.

Resort to epithets or personal abuse is not in any proper sense communication of information or opinion safeguarded by the Constitution, and its punishment as a criminal act would raise no question under that instrument.

We find in the instant case no assault or threatening of bodily harm, no truculent bearing, no intentional discourtesy, no personal abuse. On the contrary, we find only an effort to persuade a willing listener to buy a book or to contribute money in the interest of what Cantwell, however misguided others may think him, conceived to be true religion.

…

The essential characteristic of these liberties… [of religious and political belief] …is, that under their shield many types of life, character, opinion and belief can develop unmolested and unobstructed. Nowhere is this shield more necessary than in our own country for a people composed of many races and of many creeds. There are limits to the exercise of these liberties. The danger in these times from the coercive activities of those who in the delusion of racial or religious conceit would incite violence and breaches of the peace in order to deprive others of their equal right to the exercise of their liberties, is emphasized by events familiar to all. These and other transgressions of those limits the states appropriately may punish. Although the contents of the record not unnaturally aroused animosity, we think that, in the absence of a statute narrowly drawn to define and punish specific conduct as constituting a clear and present danger to a substantial interest of the State, the petitioner's communication, considered in the light of the constitutional guarantees, raised no such clear and present menace to public peace and order as to render him liable to conviction of the common law offense in question.

Words Lacking In Value (Not Protected Speech)

As you just read, the Court in *Chaplinsky v. New Hampshire* said that certain types of speech are so inherently lacking in value as not to merit any First Amendment protection.

Libel and Slander

One major limitation to the freedom of speech guaranteed by the First Amendment is the civil causes of action known as libel (a written defamatory statement), and slander (a spoken defamatory statement). Libel and slander involve defamatory speech (oral or written) that harms another person's reputation. People can sue others who say something that injures their reputation. Public officials must have a thicker skin, however. In order for public officials to recover damages for slander or liable, the statement made against them must have been made with actual malice (with knowledge that it was false or with reckless disregard whether it was false or not). *New York Times v. Sullivan* , 376 U.S. 254 (1964).

Profanity

Although *Chaplinsky* identified profanity as speech not worthy of protection, today courts generally hold that profanity is protected speech. Many states' laws and local ordinances still prohibit public profanity, but these provisions are largely unenforced and are likely to be struck down if challenged.

COHEN v. CALIFORNIA,
403 U.S. 15 (1971)

MR. JUSTICE HARLAN delivered the opinion of the Court.

Appellant Paul Robert Cohen was convicted in the Los Angeles Municipal Court of violating that part of California Penal Code 415 which prohibits "maliciously and willfully disturb[ing] the peace or quiet of any neighborhood or person . . . by . . . offensive conduct . . . ." He was given 30 days' imprisonment. The facts [are] as follows:

"On April 26, 1968, the defendant was observed in the Los Angeles County Courthouse in the corridor outside of division 20 of the municipal court wearing a jacket bearing the words `Fuck the Draft' which were plainly visible. There were women and children present in the corridor. The defendant was arrested. The defendant testified that he wore the jacket knowing that the words were on the jacket as a means of informing the public of the depth of his feelings against the Vietnam War and the draft."

"The defendant did not engage in, nor threaten to engage in, nor did anyone as the result of his conduct in fact commit or threaten to commit any act of violence. The defendant did not make any loud or unusual noise, nor was there any evidence that he uttered any sound prior to his arrest."

In affirming the conviction the Court of Appeal held that "offensive conduct" means "behavior which has a tendency to provoke others to acts of violence or to in turn disturb

the peace," and that the State had proved this element because, on the facts of this case, "[i]t was certainly reasonably foreseeable that such conduct might cause others to rise up to commit a violent act against the person of the defendant or attempt to forcibly remove his jacket.". . . We now reverse.

. . .

I

...

The conviction quite clearly rests upon the asserted offensiveness of the words Cohen used to convey his message to the public. The only "conduct" which the State sought to punish is the fact of communication. Thus, we deal here with a conviction resting solely upon "speech," not upon any separately identifiable conduct... . [T]he State certainly lacks power to punish Cohen for the underlying content of the message the inscription conveyed. At least so long as there is no showing of an intent to incite disobedience to or disruption of the draft, Cohen could not, consistently with the First and Fourteenth Amendments, be punished for asserting the evident position on the inutility or immorality of the draft his jacket reflected.

Appellant's conviction, then, rests squarely upon his exercise of the "freedom of speech" protected from arbitrary governmental interference by the Constitution and can be justified, if at all, only as a valid regulation of the manner in which he exercised that freedom, not as a permissible prohibition on the substantive message it conveys. This does not end the inquiry, of course, for the First and Fourteenth Amendments have never been thought to give absolute protection to every individual to speak whenever or wherever he pleases, or to use any form of address in any circumstances that he chooses.

. . .

In this regard, persons confronted with Cohen's jacket were in a quite different posture than, say, those subjected to the raucous emissions of sound trucks blaring outside their residences. Those in the Los Angeles courthouse could effectively avoid further bombardment of their sensibilities simply by averting their eyes. . . . Given the subtlety and complexity of the factors involved, if Cohen's "speech" was otherwise entitled to constitutional protection, we do not think the fact that some unwilling "listeners" in a public building may have been briefly exposed to it can serve to justify this breach of the peace conviction. . . .

II

. . . [The issue in this case] . . . is whether California can excise, as "offensive conduct," one particular scurrilous epithet from the public discourse, either upon the theory of the court below that its use is inherently likely to cause violent reaction or upon a more general assertion that the States, acting as guardians of public morality, may properly remove this offensive word from the public vocabulary.

The rationale of the California court is plainly untenable. . . . We have been shown no evidence that substantial numbers of citizens are standing ready to strike out physically at whoever may assault their sensibilities with execrations like that uttered by Cohen. There may be some persons about with such lawless and violent proclivities, but that is an insufficient base upon which to erect, consistently with constitutional values, a governmental power to force persons who

wish to ventilate their dissident views into avoiding particular forms of expression. . . .

. . .

At the outset, we cannot overemphasize that, in our judgment, most situations where the State has a justifiable interest in regulating speech will fall within one or more of the various established exceptions . . . to the usual rule that governmental bodies may not prescribe the form or content of individual expression. . . . The constitutional right of free expression is powerful medicine in a society as diverse and populous as ours. It is designed and intended to remove governmental restraints from the arena of public discussion, putting the decision as to what views shall be voiced largely into the hands of each of us, in the hope that use of such freedom will ultimately produce a more capable citizenry and more perfect polity and in the belief that no other approach would comport with the premise of individual dignity and choice upon which our political system rests.

To many, the immediate consequence of this freedom may often appear to be only verbal tumult, discord, and even offensive utterance. These are, however, within established limits, in truth necessary side effects of the broader enduring values which the process of open debate permits us to achieve. That the air may at times seem filled with verbal cacophony is, in this sense not a sign of weakness but of strength. We cannot lose sight of the fact that, in what otherwise might seem a trifling and annoying instance of individual distasteful abuse of a privilege, these fundamental societal values are truly implicated. . . .

Against this perception of the constitutional policies involved, we discern certain more particularized considerations that peculiarly call for reversal of this conviction. First, the principle contended for by the State seems inherently boundless. How is one to distinguish this from any other offensive word? Surely the State has no right to cleanse public debate to the point where it is grammatically palatable to the most squeamish among us. Yet no readily ascertainable general principle exists for stopping short of that result were we to affirm the judgment below. For, while the particular four-letter word being litigated here is perhaps more distasteful than most others of its genre, it is nevertheless often true that one man's vulgarity is another's lyric. Indeed, we think it is largely because governmental officials cannot make principled distinctions in this area that the Constitution leaves matters of taste and style so largely to the individual.

Additionally, we cannot overlook the fact, because it is well illustrated by the episode involved here, that much linguistic expression serves a dual communicative function: it conveys not only ideas capable of relatively precise, detached explication, but otherwise inexpressible emotions as well. In fact, words are often chosen as much for their emotive as their cognitive force. We cannot sanction the view that the Constitution, while solicitous of the cognitive content of individual speech, has little or no regard for that emotive function

which, practically speaking, may often be the more important element of the overall message sought to be communicated. …

Finally, and in the same vein, we cannot indulge the facile assumption that one can forbid particular words without also running a substantial risk of suppressing ideas in the process. Indeed, governments might soon seize upon the censorship of particular words as a convenient guise for banning the expression of unpopular views. We have been able, as noted above, to discern little social benefit that might result from running the risk of opening the door to such grave results.

It is, in sum, our judgment that, absent a more particularized and compelling reason for its actions, the State may not, consistently with the First and Fourteenth Amendments, make the simple public display here involved of this single four-letter expletive a criminal offense. …

Other Cases: Profanity

Iancu v. Brunetti, 588 U.S. ___ (2019)

SUMMARY: The Court held that the trademark office's refusal to register Brunetti's trademark "fuct" under Section 2 of the Lantham Act, which prohibits the federal registration of "immoral" or "scandalous" marks, violated the Free Speech Clause of the First Amendment.

Mahanoy Area School District, Petitioner v. B. L., , 594 U.S. ___ (2021)

JUSTICE BREYER delivered the opinion of the Court.

A public high school student used, and transmitted to her Snapchat friends, vulgar language and gestures criticizing both the school and the school's cheerleading team. The student's speech took place outside of school hours and away from the school's campus. In response, the school suspended the student for a year from the cheerleading team. We must decide whether the Court of Appeals for the Third Circuit correctly held that the school's decision violated the First Amendment. [W]e do

agree . . . that the school's disciplinary action violated the First Amendment.

I A

. . . [Details of snaps, context . . .omitted]

After discussing the matter with the school principal, the coaches decided that because the posts used profanity in connection with a school extracurricular activity, they violated team and school rules. As a result, the coaches suspended B. L. from the junior varsity cheerleading squad for the upcoming year. B. L.'s subsequent apologies did not move school officials. The school's athletic director, principal, superintendent, and school board, all affirmed B. L.'s suspension from the team. In response, B. L., together with her parents, filed this lawsuit in Federal District Court.

B

The District Court found in B. L.'s favor. …

On appeal, a panel of the Third Circuit affirmed the District Court's conclusion. In so doing, the majority noted that this Court [the U.S. Supreme Court] had previously held in *Tinker* that a public high school could not constitutionally prohibit a peaceful student political demonstration consisting of "'pure speech'" on school property during the school day. In reaching its conclusion in *Tinker*, this Court emphasized that there was no evidence the student protest would "substantially interfere with the work of the school or impinge upon the rights of other students." But the Court also said that: "[C]onduct by [a] student, in class or out of it, which for any reason—whether it stems from time, place, or type of behavior—materially disrupts classwork or involves substantial disorder or invasion of the rights of others is . . . not immunized by the constitutional guarantee of freedom of speech."

Many courts have taken this statement as setting a standard—a standard that allows schools considerable freedom on campus to discipline students for conduct that the First Amendment might otherwise protect. But here, the panel majority held that this additional freedom did "not apply to off-campus speech," which it defined as "speech that is outside school-owned, -operated, or -supervised channels and that is not reasonably interpreted as bearing the school's imprimatur.". Because B. L.'s speech took place off campus, the panel concluded that the *Tinker* standard did not apply and the school consequently could not discipline B. L. for engaging in a form of pure speech.

A concurring member of the panel agreed with the majority's result but wrote that the school had not sufficiently justified disciplining B. L. because, whether the *Tinker* standard did or did not apply, B. L.'s speech was not substantially disruptive.

C

The school district filed a petition for certiorari in this Court, asking us to decide "[w]hether [*Tinker*], which holds that public school officials may regulate speech that would materially and substantially disrupt the work and discipline of the school, applies to student speech that occurs off campus." We granted the petition.

II

We have made clear that students do not "shed their constitutional rights to freedom of speech or expression," even "at the school house gate." ... But we have also made clear that courts must apply the First Amendment "in light of the special characteristics of the school environment ... One such characteristic, which we have stressed, is the fact that schools at times stand in loco parentis, i.e., in the place of parents. ... This Court has previously outlined three specific categories of student speech that schools may regulate in certain circumstances: (1) "indecent," "lewd," or "vulgar" speech uttered during a school assembly on school grounds; (2) speech, uttered during a class trip, that promotes "illegal drug use," and (3) speech that others may reasonably perceive as "bear[ing] the imprimatur of the school," such as that appearing in a school-sponsored newspaper.

Finally, in *Tinker,* we said schools have a special interest in regulating speech that "materially disrupts classwork or involves substantial disorder or invasion of the rights of others." These special characteristics call for special leeway when schools regulate speech that occurs under its supervision.

Unlike the Third Circuit, we do not believe the special characteristics that give schools additional license to regulate student speech always disappear when a school regulates speech that takes place off campus. The school's regulatory interests remain significant in some off-campus circumstances. The parties' briefs, and those of amici, list several types of off-campus behavior that may call for school regulation. These include serious or severe bullying or harassment targeting particular individuals; threats aimed at teachers or other students; the failure to follow rules concerning lessons, the writing of papers, the use of computers, or participation in other online school activities; and breaches of school security devices, including material maintained within school computers.

. . .

. . . Thus, we do not now set forth a broad, highly general First Amendment rule stating just what counts as "off campus" speech and whether or how ordinary First Amendment standards must give way off campus to a school's special need to prevent, e.g., substantial disruption of learning-related activities or the protection of those who make up a school community.

We can, however, mention three features of off-campus speech that often, even if not always, distinguish schools' efforts to regulate that speech from their efforts to regulate on-campus speech. Those features diminish the strength of the unique educational characteristics that might call for special First Amendment leeway.

First, a school, in relation to off-campus speech, will rarely stand in loco parentis. The doctrine of in loco parentis treats school administrators as standing in the place of students' parents under circumstances where the children's actual parents cannot protect, guide, and discipline them. Geographically speaking, off-campus speech will normally fall within the zone of parental, rather than school-related, responsibility.

Second, from the student speaker's perspective, regulations of off-campus speech, when coupled with regulations of on-campus speech, include all the speech a student utters during the full 24-hour day. That means courts must be more skeptical of a school's efforts to regulate off-campus speech, for doing so may mean the student cannot engage in that kind of speech at all. When it comes to political or religious speech that occurs outside school or a school program or activity, the school will have a heavy burden to justify intervention.

Third, the school itself has an interest in protecting a student's unpopular expression, especially when the expression takes place off campus. America's public schools are the nurseries of democracy. Our representative democracy only works if we protect the "marketplace of ideas." This free exchange facilitates an informed public opinion, which, when transmitted to lawmakers, helps produce laws that reflect the People's will. That protection must include the protection of unpopular ideas, for popular ideas have less need for protection. Thus, schools have a strong interest in ensuring that future generations understand the workings in practice of the well-known aphorism, "I disapprove of what you say, but I will defend to the death your right to say it." …

… Taken together, these three features of much off-campus speech mean that the leeway the First Amendment grants to schools in light of their special characteristics is diminished. We leave for future cases to decide where, when, and how these features mean the speaker's off-campus location will make the critical

difference. This case can, however, provide one example.

III

Consider B. L.'s speech. Putting aside the vulgar language, the listener would hear criticism, of the team, the team's coaches, and the school—in a word or two, criticism of the rules of a community of which B. L. forms a part. This criticism did not involve features that would place it outside the First Amendment's ordinary protection. B. L.'s posts, while crude, did not amount to fighting words. [*Chaplinsky*] And while B. L. used vulgarity, her speech was not obscene as this Court has understood that term. [*Cohen*] To the contrary, B. L. uttered the kind of pure speech to which, were she an adult, the First Amendment would provide strong protection. …

Consider too when, where, and how B. L. spoke. Her posts appeared outside of school hours from a location outside the school. She did not identify the school in her posts or target any member of the school community with vulgar or abusive language. B. L. also transmitted her speech through a personal cellphone, to an audience consisting of her private circle of Snapchat friends. These features of her speech, while risking transmission to the school itself, nonetheless (for reasons we have just explained) diminish the school's interest in punishing B. L.'s utterance.

But what about the school's interest, here primarily an interest in prohibiting students from using vulgar language to criticize a school team or its coaches—at least when that criticism might well be transmitted to other students, team members, coaches, and faculty? We can break that general interest into three parts.

First, we consider the school's interest in teaching good manners and consequently in punishing the use of vulgar language aimed at part of the school community. (indicating that coaches removed B. L. from the cheer team because "there was profanity in [her] Snap and it was directed towards cheerleading"). The strength of this anti-vulgarity interest is weakened considerably by the fact that B. L. spoke outside the school on her own time. See *Morse*, (clarifying that although a school can regulate a student's use of sexual innuendo in a speech given within the school, if the student "delivered the same speech in a public forum outside the school context, it would have been protected"); see also *Fraser,* (noting that if the student in *Fraser* "had given the same speech outside of the school environment, he could not have been penalized simply because government officials considered his language to be inappropriate").

B. L. spoke under circumstances where the school did not stand in loco parentis. . . . Together, these facts convince us that the school's interest in teaching good manners is not sufficient, in this case, to overcome B. L.'s interest in free expression.

Second, the school argues that it was trying to prevent disruption, if not within the classroom, then within the bounds of a school-sponsored extracurricular activity. But we can find no evidence in the record of the sort of "substantial disruption" of a school activity or a threatened harm to the rights of others that might justify the school's action. ...

Third, the school presented some evidence that expresses (at least indirectly) a concern for team morale. One of the coaches testified that the school decided to suspend B. L., not because of any specific negative impact upon a particular member of the school community, but "based on the fact that there was negativity put out there that could impact students in the school." There is little else, however, that suggests any serious decline in team morale—to the point where it could create a substantial interference in, or disruption of, the school's efforts to maintain team cohesion. ...

It might be tempting to dismiss B. L.'s words as unworthy of the robust First Amendment protections discussed herein. But sometimes it is necessary to protect the superfluous in order to preserve the necessary. ...

...

Obscenity

Obscene materials are considered to lack "redeeming social importance" and are not constitutionally protected. Distinguishing between obscenity and protected speech is not easy, and the Court has conceded that obscenity cannot be defined with "God-like precision." Justice Stewart pronounced that the only viable test seemed to be that he "knew obscenity when...[he]...saw it." *Jacobellis v. Ohio*, 378 U.S. 184 (1964). In *Miller v. California,* 413 U.S. 15 (1973) the Court finally defined obscenity, holding that it was limited to works that, when "taken as a whole, in light of contemporary community standards, appeal to the prurient interest in sex; are patently offensive; and lack serious literary, artistic, political, or scientific value." Still, the concept remains somewhat vague. Under this definition, for example, a medical textbook portraying individuals engaged in sexual intercourse would probably not constitute obscenity because the book could have scientific value. The Court has found that obscenity refers only to "hard-core" pornography.

The growth of Internet pornography has led to serious national and international child pornography rings, and police and prosecutors no longer target violators of traditional obscenity laws, instead they have directed their resources to aggressively fighting child pornography. Legislators have tried, but found it difficult, to draft child pornography statutes that survive First Amendment challenges. (These laws have been successfully challenged on grounds of overbreadth, a doctrine you will read about later in this chapter. See, e.g., *Ashcroft v. American Civil Liberties Union et al.,* 542 U.S. 656 (2004).)

Words That Cause Civil Unrest (Not Protected Speech)

Clear And Present Danger

Being able to speak against the government has always been recognized as an important right; however, it is not an absolute right. Early on, the Court had to grapple with speech that caused unrest. One of the first tests, enunciated in *Gitlow v. New York*, 268 U.S. 652 (1925), was the "clear and present danger test." This test asks whether words are so potentially dangerous as to not be protected by the First Amendment. In *Gitlow* the Court held that "a state in the exercise of its police power may punish those who abuse this freedom by utterances inimical to the public welfare, tending to corrupt public morals, and incite to crime, or disturbing the public peace" at 667. Gitlow had been indicted under a New York law that prohibited the advocacy of the overthrow of the government by force or violence. In 1940 Congress enacted the Alien Registration Act of 1940 (known as "the Smith Act), that made advocating overthrow of the government by force or violence unlawful.[39] The Court ultimately struck down the Smith Act in 1957.

Incitement To Violent Action

The Court continued to modify the test after *Chaplinsky*; in the 1950s the Court began to talk in terms of whether the speech "provoked others to imminent violent action." When it did so, it was no longer protected speech. In *Feiner v. New York*, 340 U S 315, 320 (1951), the Court ruled, "when clear and present danger of riot, disorder, interference with traffic upon the public streets, or other immediate threat to public safety, peace, or order, appears, the power of the State to prevent or punish is obvious." On the other hand, in *Terminiello v. Chicago*, 337 U.S. 1, 4 (1947), the Supreme Court had stressed that a speaker could not be punished for speech that merely "stirs to anger, invites dispute, brings about a condition of unrest, or creates a disturbance."

Imminent Lawless Action

In *Brandenburg v. Ohio*, 395 U.S. 444 (1969), (see below) the Court reviewed an Ohio statute prohibiting criminal syndicalism which Ohio courts interpreted as advocating violence to achieve political change and announced an "imminent lawless action test." Under this test, if the government demonstrates that (1) the speaker subjectively intended incitement, (2) in context, the words used were likely to produce imminent, lawless action, and (3) the words used by the speaker objectively encouraged and urged incitement, then the words are not protected speech. The Court reversed the conviction of a Ku Klux Klan leader saying that the constitutional guarantees of free speech and free press do not permit a state to forbid advocacy. "People cannot be prosecuted merely for advocating violence; there must be "imminent lawless action" to justify a criminal penalty on public expression." The *Brandenburg* approach was frequently cited in the second impeachment trial of former president Donald Trump, and it has been termed the "balancing test," a position taken by the appellate courts to balance society's need for law and order and for effective law enforcement against the rights of individuals. Although modified slightly through subsequent case interpretations, the imminent lawless action test enunciated in *Brandenburg* is still the test used by the Court today.

Other Cases: Words that Cause Civil Unrest

Feiner v. New York, 340 U.S. 315 (1951)	box on the sidewalk, was addressing the crowd through a loud-speaker system attached to an automobile. Although the purpose of his speech was to urge his listeners to attend a meeting to be held that night in the Syracuse Hotel, in its course he was making derogatory remarks concerning President Truman, the American Legion, the Mayor of Syracuse, and other local political officials.
…	
On the evening of March 8, 1949, petitioner Irving Feiner was addressing an open-air meeting at the corner of South McBride and Harrison Streets in the City of Syracuse. At approximately 6:30 p. m., the police received a telephone complaint concerning the meeting, and two officers were detailed to investigate. One of these officers went to the scene immediately, the other arriving some twelve minutes later. They found a crowd of about seventy-five or eighty people, both Negro and white, filling the sidewalk and spreading out into the street. Petitioner, standing on a large wooden	The police officers made no effort to interfere with petitioner's speech, but were first concerned with the effect of the crowd on both pedestrian and vehicular traffic. They observed the situation from the opposite side of the street, noting that some pedestrians were forced to walk in the street to

---

[39] Pub.Law 54 Stat. 670, 18 U.S.C. Section 2385.

avoid the crowd. Since traffic was passing at the time, the officers attempted to get the people listening to petitioner back on the sidewalk. The crowd was restless and there was some pushing, shoving and milling around. One of the officers telephoned the police station from a nearby store, and then both policemen crossed the street and mingled with the crowd without any intention of arresting the speaker.

At this time, petitioner was speaking in a "loud, high-pitched voice." He gave the impression that he was endeavoring to arouse the Negro people against the whites, urging that they rise up in arms and fight for equal rights. The statements before such a mixed audience "stirred up a little excitement." Some of the onlookers made remarks to the police about their inability to handle the crowd and at least one threatened violence if the police did not act. There were others who appeared to be favoring petitioner's arguments. Because of the feeling that existed in the crowd both for and against the speaker, the officers finally "stepped in to prevent it from resulting in a fight." One of the officers approached the petitioner, not for the purpose of arresting him, but to get him to break up the crowd. He asked petitioner to get down off the box, but the latter refused to accede to his request and continued talking. The officer waited for a minute and then demanded that he cease talking. Although the officer had thus twice requested petitioner to stop over the course of several minutes, petitioner not only ignored him but continued talking. During all this time, the crowd was pressing closer around petitioner and the officer. Finally, the officer told petitioner he was under arrest and ordered him to get down from the box, reaching up to grab him. Petitioner stepped down, announcing over the microphone that "the law has arrived, and I suppose they will take over now." In all, the officer had asked petitioner to get down off the box three times over a space of four or five minutes. Petitioner had been speaking for over a half hour.

. . .

 . . . The trial judge heard testimony supporting and contradicting the judgment of the police officers that a clear danger of disorder was threatened. After weighing this contradictory evidence, the trial judge reached the conclusion that the police officers were justified in taking action to prevent a breach of the peace. The

exercise of the police officers' proper discretionary power to prevent a breach of the peace was thus approved by the trial court and later by two courts on review. The courts below recognized petitioner's right to hold a street meeting at this locality, to make use of loud-speaking equipment in giving his speech, and to make derogatory remarks concerning public officials and the American Legion. They found that the officers in making the arrest were motivated solely by a proper concern for the preservation of order and protection of the general welfare, and that there was no evidence which could lend color to a claim that the acts of the police were a cover for suppression of petitioner's views and opinions. Petitioner was thus neither arrested nor convicted for the making or the content of his speech. Rather, it was the reaction which it actually engendered.

… No one would have the hardihood to suggest that the principle of freedom of speech sanctions incitement to riot or that religious liberty connotes the privilege to exhort others to physical attack upon those belonging to another sect. When clear and present danger of riot, disorder, interference with traffic upon the public streets, or other immediate threat to public safety, peace, or order, appears, the power of the State to prevent or punish is obvious." *Cantwell v. Connecticut*, 310 U.S. at 308. The findings of the New York courts as to the condition of the crowd and the refusal of petitioner to obey the police requests, supported as they are by the record of this case, are persuasive that the conviction of petitioner for violation of public peace, order and authority does not exceed the bounds of proper state police action. This Court respects, as it must, the interest of the community in maintaining peace and order on its streets. We cannot say that the preservation of that interest here encroaches on the constitutional rights of this petitioner.

We are well aware that the ordinary murmurings and objections of a hostile audience cannot be allowed to silence a speaker, and are also mindful of the possible danger of giving overzealous police officials complete discretion to break up otherwise lawful public meetings. "A State may not unduly suppress free communication of views, religious or other, under the guise of conserving desirable conditions." But we are not faced here with such a situation. It is one thing to say that the police cannot be used as an instrument for the suppression of unpopular views, and another to say that, when as here the speaker passes the bounds of argument or persuasion and undertakes incitement to riot, they are powerless to prevent a breach of the peace. Nor in this case can we condemn the considered judgment of three New York courts approving the means which the police, faced with a crisis, used in the exercise of their power and duty to preserve peace and order. The findings of the state courts as to the existing situation and the imminence of greater disorder coupled with petitioner's deliberate defiance of the police officers convince us that we should not reverse this conviction in the name of free speech.

MR. JUSTICE BLACK, dissenting.

The record before us convinces me that petitioner, a young college student, has been sentenced to the penitentiary for the unpopular views he expressed on matters of public interest while lawfully making a street-corner speech in Syracuse, New York. Today's decision, however, indicates that we must blind ourselves to this fact because the trial judge fully accepted the testimony of the prosecution witnesses on all important points. Many times in the past this Court has said that despite findings below, we will examine the evidence for ourselves to ascertain whether federally protected rights have been denied; otherwise review here would fail of its purpose in safeguarding constitutional guarantees. Even a partial abandonment of this rule marks a dark day for civil liberties in our Nation.

But still more has been lost today. Even accepting every "finding of fact" below, I think this conviction makes a mockery of the free speech guarantees of the First and Fourteenth Amendments. The end result of the affirmance here is to approve a simple and readily available technique by which cities and states can with impunity subject all speeches, political or otherwise, on streets or elsewhere, to the supervision and censorship of the local police. I will have no part or parcel in this holding which I view as a long step toward totalitarian authority.

…

The Court's opinion apparently rests on this reasoning: The policeman, under the circumstances detailed, could reasonably conclude that serious fighting or even riot was imminent; therefore, he could stop petitioner's speech to prevent a breach of peace; accordingly, it was "disorderly conduct" for petitioner to continue speaking in disobedience of the officer's request. As to the existence of a dangerous situation on the street corner, it seems far-fetched to suggest that the "facts" show any imminent threat of riot or uncontrollable disorder. It is neither unusual nor unexpected that some people at public street meetings mutter, mill about, push, shove, or disagree, even violently, with the speaker. Indeed, it is rare where controversial topics are discussed that an outdoor crowd does not do some or all of these things. Nor does one isolated threat to assault the speaker forebode disorder. Especially should the danger be discounted where, as here, the person threatening was a man whose wife and two small children accompanied him and who, so far as the record shows, was never close enough to petitioner to carry out the threat.

Moreover, assuming that the "facts" did indicate a critical situation, I reject the implication of the Court's opinion that the police had no obligation to protect petitioner's constitutional right to talk. The police of course have power to prevent breaches of the peace. But if, in the name of preserving order, they ever can interfere with a lawful public speaker, they first must make all reasonable efforts to protect him. Here the policemen did not even pretend to try to protect petitioner. … Their duty was to protect petitioner's right to talk, even to the extent of arresting the man who threatened to interfere. Instead, they shirked that duty and acted only to suppress the right to speak.

…

MR. JUSTICE DOUGLAS, with whom MR. JUSTICE MINTON concurs, dissenting.

…

Public assemblies and public speech occupy an important role in American life. One high function of the police is to protect these lawful gatherings so that the speakers may exercise their constitutional rights. When unpopular causes are sponsored from the public platform, there will commonly be mutterings and unrest and heckling from the crowd. When a speaker mounts a platform it is not unusual to find him resorting to exaggeration, to vilification of ideas and men, to the making of false charges. But those extravagances, as we emphasized in Cantwell v. Connecticut, 310 U.S. 296, do not justify penalizing the speaker by depriving him of the platform or by punishing him for his conduct.

A speaker may not, of course, incite a riot any more than he may incite a breach of the peace by the use of "fighting words." But this record shows no such extremes. It shows an unsympathetic audience and the threat of one man to haul the speaker from the stage. It is against that kind of threat that speakers need police protection. If they do not receive it and instead the police throw their weight on the side of those who would break up the meetings, the police become the new censors of speech. Police censorship has all the vices of the censorship from city halls which we have repeatedly struck down.

Brandenburg v. Ohio, 395 U.S. 444 (1969)

The appellant, a leader of a Ku Klux Klan group, was convicted under the Ohio Criminal Syndicalism statute for "advocat[ing] . . . the duty, necessity, or propriety of crime, sabotage, violence, or unlawful methods of terrorism as a means of accomplishing industrial or political reform" and for "voluntarily assembl[ing] with any society, group, or assemblage of persons formed to teach or advocate the doctrines of criminal syndicalism." Ohio Rev. Code Ann. § 2923.13. He was fined $1,000 and sentenced to one to 10 years' imprisonment. The appellant challenged the constitutionality of the criminal syndicalism statute under the First and Fourteenth Amendments to the United States Constitution. …

The record shows that a man, identified at trial as the appellant, telephoned an announcer-reporter on the staff of a Cincinnati television station and invited him to come to a Ku Klux Klan "rally" to be held at a farm in Hamilton County. With the cooperation of the organizers, the reporter and a cameraman attended the meeting and filmed the events. Portions of the films were later broadcast on the local station and on a national network. The prosecution's case rested on the films and on testimony identifying the appellant as the person who communicated with the reporter and who spoke at the rally. The State also introduced into evidence several articles appearing in the film, including a pistol, a rifle, a shotgun, ammunition, a Bible, and a red hood worn by the speaker in the films. One film showed 12 hooded figures, some of whom carried firearms. They were gathered around a large wooden cross, which they burned. No one was present other than the participants and the newsmen who made the film. Most of the words uttered during the scene were

incomprehensible when the film was projected, but scattered phrases could be understood that were derogatory of Negroes and, in one instance, of Jews. Another scene on the same film showed the appellant, in Klan regalia, making a speech. The speech, in full, was as follows:

"This is an organizers' meeting. We have had quite a few members here today which are—we have hundreds, hundreds of members throughout the State of Ohio. I can quote from a newspaper clipping from the Columbus, Ohio Dispatch, five weeks ago Sunday morning. The Klan has more members in the State of Ohio than does any other organization. We're not a revengent organization, but if our President, our Congress, our Supreme Court, continues to suppress the white, Caucasian race, it's possible that there might have to be some revengeance taken.

"We are marching on Congress July the Fourth, four hundred thousand strong. From there we are dividing into two groups, one group to march on St. Augustine, Florida, the other group to march into Mississippi. Thank you."

The second film showed six hooded figures one of whom, later identified as the appellant, repeated a speech very similar to that recorded on the first film. The reference to the possibility of "revengeance" was omitted, and one sentence was added: "Personally, I believe the nigger should be returned to Africa, the Jew returned to Israel." Though some of the figures in the films carried weapons, the speaker did not.

… [T]he constitutional guarantees of free speech and free press do not permit a State to forbid or proscribe advocacy of the use of force or of law violation except where such advocacy is directed to inciting or producing imminent lawless action and is likely to incite or produce such action. As we said in *Noto v. United States*, 367 U. S. 290, 297-298 (1961), "the mere abstract teaching . . . of the moral propriety or even moral necessity for a resort to force and violence, is not the same as preparing a group for violent action and steeling it to such action." A statute which fails to draw this distinction impermissibly intrudes upon the freedoms guaranteed by the First and Fourteenth Amendments. It sweeps within its condemnation speech which our Constitution has immunized from governmental control.

Measured by this test, Ohio's Criminal Syndicalism Act cannot be sustained. The Act punishes persons who "advocate or teach the duty, necessity, or propriety" of violence "as a means of accomplishing industrial or political reform"; or who publish or circulate or display any book or paper containing such advocacy; or who "justify" the commission of violent acts "with intent to exemplify, spread or advocate the propriety of the doctrines of criminal syndicalism"; or who "voluntarily assemble" with a group formed "to teach or advocate the doctrines of criminal syndicalism." Neither the indictment nor the trial judge's instructions to the jury in any way refined the statute's bald definition of the crime in terms of mere advocacy not distinguished from incitement to imminent lawless action.

Accordingly, we are here confronted with a statute which, by its own words and as applied, purports to punish mere advocacy and to forbid, on pain of criminal punishment, assembly with others merely to advocate the described type of action. Such a statute falls within the condemnation of the First and Fourteenth Amendments.

MR. JUSTICE BLACK, concurring.

... [T]he "clear and present danger" doctrine should have no place in the interpretation of the First Amendment.

MR. JUSTICE DOUGLAS, concurring.

While I join the opinion of the Court, I desire to enter a caveat.

The "clear and present danger" test was adumbrated by Mr. Justice Holmes in a case arising during World War I. ... [The opinion then discusses the various cases in 1918 and 1919 in which the court applied "clear and present danger" as a test of whether the anti-war speech should be protected or not].

Those, then, were the World War I cases that put the gloss of "clear and present danger" on the First Amendment. Whether the war power ... is adequate to sustain that doctrine is debatable. The dissents in [the prior cases discussed] show how easily "clear and present danger" is manipulated to crush what Brandeis called "[t]he fundamental right of free men to strive for better conditions through new legislation and new institutions" by argument and discourse even in time of war. Though I doubt if the "clear and present danger" test is congenial to the First Amendment in time of a declared war, I am certain it is not reconcilable with the First Amendment in days of peace.

True Threats

One type of problematic speech is speech involving direct threats. What if the threat is not directly aimed or sent to the victim, but is instead posted on a Facebook page or other social media? Consider the case of Roger Stone who, while awaiting trial for lying to Congress, posted a picture of U.S. District Court Judge Amy Berman Jackson (the judge handling his case) with a gun crosshair/scope superimposed on her image.[40] Is this a real threat? What about posting the names and addresses of doctors who perform abortions on a site dedicated to anti-abortion protesting?[41]

Many states have stalking laws that prohibit repeated and unwanted contact and some of the prohibited contact involves speech. In an important Oregon case, *State v. Rangel*, 328 Or. 224 (1999) the defendant claimed that Oregon's stalking law violated his rights to free speech under the Oregon and federal constitutions and was overbroad. The Oregon Supreme Court's opinion states,

> The gist of the crime of stalking is knowingly alarming or coercing another through repeated and unwanted "contacts." Where the state relies on one or more "contacts" that constitute speech or writing rather than physical force or other behaviors ... the definition of "coerce" in [the statute] ... expressly requires proof of a threat. ... We conclude that ... the legislature contemplated ... that a speech-based contact would be punishable as an element of stalking only if it constitutes a threat."

---

[40] See, https://www.bbc.com/news/world-us-canada-47326451
[41] See, e.g, https://nypost.com/2022/07/16/dr-caitlin-bernard-who-gave-10-year-old-an-abortion-faced-kidnapping-threat/

Hate Speech versus Hate Crimes

Hate speech raises interesting First Amendment concerns. Hate speech is defined as speech that denigrates, humiliates, and attacks individuals on account of some race, religion, ethnicity, nationality, gender, sexual orientation, or other personal characteristics and preferences (hate crimes target categories of people named specifically in the statute). Hate speech can be verbal (screaming derogatory names at someone), written (writing derogatory comments or posting written comments on social media platforms) or symbolic (burning crosses on someone's yard, for example). Because it constitutes expression, it is generally protected by the Constitution unless it falls within one of the recognized exceptions to the First Amendment.

Hate speech must be distinguished from hate crimes or criminal offenses directed against a member of a specific groups. Hate crime statutes have been upheld because they target conduct rather than expression. The most important two rulings from the Court that highlight the distinction between hate speech and hate crimes are *R.A.V. v. St. Paul*, 505 U.S. 377 (1992), and *Wisconsin v. Mitchell*, 508 U.S. 475 (1993). They are discussed in the following case of *People v. Rokicki*, 718 N.E. 2d 333 (Ill. App. 1999).

PEOPLE v. ROKICKI, 718 N.E.2d 333 (Ill. App. 1999)

JUSTICE HUTCHINSON delivered the opinion of the court

Defendant, Kenneth Rokicki was charged in a single-count indictment with hate crime . . . based on the predicate offense of disorderly conduct. Following a bench trial, defendant was convicted, sentenced to 2 years' probation and ordered . . . to perform 100 hours of community service and attend anger management counseling. [Defendant appealed] contending that the hate crime statute is unconstitutionally overly broad and chills expression protected by the first amendment to the United States Constitution. We affirm.

FACTS

. . .

Donald Delaney testified that he is a store manager of a Pizza Hut in South Elgin. On October 20, 1995 at approximately 1:30 p.m., defendant entered the restaurant. The victim was a server there and took defendant's order. The victim requested payment, and the defendant refused to tender payment to him. Delaney who was nearby, stepped in and completed the sale. Defendant told Delaney not to let "that faggot" touch his food. When defendant's pizza came out of the oven, Delaney was on the telephone, and the victim began to slice the pizza. Delaney saw defendant approaching the counter with an irritated expression and hung up the telephone. Before Delaney could intervene, defendant leaned over the counter and began yelling at the victim and pounding his fist on the counter. Defendant directed a series of epithets at the victim including "Mary," "faggot," and "Molly Homemaker." Defendant continued yelling for 10 minutes and, when not pounding his fist shook his finger at the victim. Delaney asked defendant to leave several times and threatened to call the police. However, Delaney did not call the police because he was standing between the victim and the defendant and feared that the defendant would physically attack the victim if Delaney moved. Eventually Delaney returned defendant's money and defendant left the establishment.

The victim testified that he was working at the South Elgin Pizza Hut on October 20, 1995. Defendant entered the restaurant and ordered a pizza. When defendant's pizza came out of the oven, the victim began to slice it. Defendant then began yelling at the victim and pounding his fist on the counter. Defendant appeared very angry and seemed very serious. The victim, who is much smaller than defendant, testified that he was terrified by defendant's outburst and remained frightened for several days thereafter. Eventually, the manager gave defendant a refund and defendant left the restaurant. The victim followed defendant into the parking lot, recorded the license number of his car, and called the police.

Christopher Merritt, a sergeant with the South Elgin police department, testified that, at 2:20 P.M. on October 20, 1995, defendant entered the police station and said he wished to report an incident at the Pizza Hut. Defendant told Merritt that he was upset because a homosexual was working at the restaurant and he wanted someone "normal" to touch his food. Defendant stated that he became angry when the victim touched his food. He called the victim a "Mary," pounded on the counter, and was subsequently kicked out of the restaurant. Merritt asked defendant what he meant by a "Mary," and defendant responded that a "Mary" was a homosexual. Merritt conducted only a brief interview of defendant because shortly after defendant arrived at the police station Merritt was dispatched to the Pizza Hut.

Deborah Hagedorn, an employee at the Pizza Hut in St. Charles, testified that in 1995 defendant came into the restaurant and asked for the address of the district manager for Pizza Hut. When asked why he wanted the address, defendant complained that he had been arrested at the South Elgin restaurant because he did not want a "f___g faggot" touching his food.

Defendant testified that he was upset because the victim had placed his fingers in his mouth and had not washed his hands before cutting the pizza. Defendant admitted calling the victim "Mary" but denied that he intended to suggest the victim was a homosexual. Defendant stated that he used the term "Mary" because the victim would not stop talking and "it was like arguing with a woman." Defendant denied yelling and denied directing other derogatory terms toward the victim. Defendant admitted giving a statement to Merritt but denied telling him that he pounded his fist on the counter or used homosexual slurs. Defendant testified that he went to the St. Charles Pizza Hut but that Hagedorn was not present during his conversation with the manager. Defendant testified that he complained about the victim's hygiene but did not use any homosexual slurs.

The trial court found defendant guilty of a hate crime. In a posttrial motion, defendant argued that the hate crime statute was unconstitutional. The trial court denied defendant's motion and sentenced him to two years' probation. As part of the probation, the trial court ordered Defendant not to enter Pizza Hut restaurants, not to contact the victim, to perform 100 hours' community service, and attend anger management counseling. Defendant timely appeals.

ISSUE

On appeal, Defendant does not challenge the sufficiency of the evidence against him. Defendant contends only that the hate crime statute is unconstitutional when the predicate offense is disturbing the peace. Defendant argues that the statute is overly broad and impermissibly chills free speech.

ANALYSIS

… The Illinois hate crime statute … reads in part as follows:

> A person commits a hate crime when, by reason of the actual or perceived race, color, creed, religion, ancestry, gender, sexual orientation, physical or mental disability, or national origin of another individual or group of individuals, [she or] he commits assault, battery, aggravated assault, misdemeanor theft, criminal trespass to residence, misdemeanor criminal damage to property, criminal trespass to vehicle, criminal trespass to real property, mob action or disorderly conduct. . . .

. . .

1. Infringement on Free Speech Rights

The issue presented in this case highlights the limits imposed by the first amendment on a state's power to regulate its citizens' speech and thought. In a pair of cases decided in 1992 and 1993, the Supreme Court staked out the boundary between a state's unconstitutional regulation of unpopular beliefs in the market place of ideas and the permissible regulation of conduct motivated by those beliefs. See *R.A.V. v. City of St. Paul*, 505 U.S. 377. . . (1992); Wisconsin v. Mitchell, 508 U.S. 476 . . . (1993). Our analysis of defendant's claims is controlled by these two cases, and we will begin by examining them.

In *R.A.V.*, the petitioner was alleged to have burned a crudely constructed wooden cross on the lawn of the residence of an African-American family and was charged with violating St. Paul's Bias-Motivated Crime Ordinance. The ordinance declared that anyone who places a burning cross, Nazi swastika, or other symbol on private or public property knowing that the symbol would arouse " 'anger, alarm or resentment in others on the basis of race, color, creed, religion, or gender commits disorderly conduct and shall be guilty of a misdemeanor.' " The Minnesota Supreme Court found that the ordinance was constitutional because it could be construed to reach only "fighting words," which are outside the protection of the first amendment. The United States Supreme Court held that, even when a statute addresses speech that is otherwise prescribable, the state may not discriminate on the basis of the content. The *R.A.V.* Court then found that the St. Paul ordinance violated the first amendment because it would allow the proponents of racial tolerance and equality to use fighting words to argue in favor of tolerance and equality but would prohibit similar use by those opposed to racial tolerance and equality.

One year later, the United States Supreme Court revisited the issue in *Mitchell* The defendant in *Mitchell* was convicted of aggravated battery, which carried a maximum term of two years' incarceration. However, the defendant was sentenced to a term of four years' incarceration under a Wisconsin statute that enhanced the penalty for an offense when the defendant intentionally selected a victim because of his or her " 'race, religion, color, disability, sexual orientation, national origin or ancestry.' " The Wisconsin Supreme Court reversed the conviction and held that the statute was unconstitutional under *R.A.V.*, holding that the legislature cannot "criminalize bigoted thought with which it disagrees."

The *Mitchell* Court held that, unlike the ordinance in *R.A.V.*, the Wisconsin statute was aimed solely at conduct unprotected by the first amendment. The Court noted that, although a defendant may not be punished for his or her abstract beliefs, motive has traditionally been used as a factor in sentencing. The Court also observed that, although the statute punished the defendant for his discriminatory motive, motive played the same role in federal and state antidiscrimination statutes that had withstood first amendment challenges. The Court further held that a state legislature could reasonably conclude that bias-motivated crimes cause greater societal harm warranting stiffer penalties because such offenses are more likely to provoke retaliatory crimes, inflict distinct emotional harms on their victims, and incite community unrest. Consequently, the Court found that the Wisconsin statute did not infringe upon free speech rights.

…

The overbreadth doctrine protects the freedom of speech guaranteed by the first amendment by invalidating laws so broadly written that the fear of prosecution would discourage people from exercising that freedom. A law regulating conduct is facially overly broad if it (1) criminalizes a substantial amount of protected behavior, relative to the law's plainly legitimate sweep, and (2) is not susceptible to a limiting construction that avoids constitutional problems. A statute should not be invalidated for being overly broad unless its overbreadth is both real and substantial.

. . .

In this case, defendant is not being punished merely because he holds an unpopular view on homosexuality or because he expressed those views loudly or in a passionate manner. Defendant was charged with hate crime because he allowed those beliefs to motivate unreasonable conduct. Defendant remains free to believe what he will regarding people who are homosexual, but he may not force his opinions on others by shouting, pounding on a counter, and disrupting a lawful business. Defendant's conduct exceeded the bounds of spirited debate, and the first amendment does not give him the right to harass or terrorize anyone. Therefore, because the hate crime statute requires conduct beyond mere expression, . . . we . . . conclude that…the Illinois hate crime statute constitutionally regulates conduct without infringing upon free speech.

2. Content Discrimination

Defendant cites *R.A.V.* and argues that the hate crime statute is constitutionally impermissible because it discriminates based on the content of an offender's beliefs. Defendant argues that the statute enhances disorderly conduct to hate crime when the conduct is motivated by, e.g., an offender's views on race or sexual orientation but that it treats identical conduct differently if motivated, e.g., by an offender's beliefs regarding abortion or animal rights. The *R.A.V.* Court invalidated the St. Paul ordinance because it favored some political views over others. The Court stated as follows:

"[T]he ordinance applies only to 'fighting words' that insult, or provoke violence, 'on the basis of race, color, creed, religion or gender.' Displays containing abusive invective, no matter how vicious or severe, are permissible unless they are addressed to one of the specified disfavored topics. Those who wish to use 'fighting words' in connection with other ideas to express hostility, for example, on the basis of political affiliation, union membership, or homosexuality are not covered." *R.A.V.* 505 U.S. at 291. …

In *R.A.V.*, the Court recognized several limitations to its content discrimination analysis, including statutes directed at conduct rather than speech, which sweep up a particular subset of prescribable speech. … We too decide that the legislature was free to determine as a matter of sound public policy that bias-motivated crimes create greater harm than identical conduct not motivated by bias and should be punished more harshly. Consequently, we reject defendant's content discrimination argument.

3. Chilling Effect

Defendant also argues that the hate crime statute chills free expression because individuals will be deterred from expressing unpopular views out of fear that such expression will later be used to justify a hate crime charge. We disagree. The overbreadth doctrine should be used sparingly and only when the constitutional infirmity is both real and substantial…. The *Mitchell* Court rejected identical arguments and held that any possible chilling effects were too speculative to support an overbreadth claim. … [W]e find defendant's argument speculative, and we cannot conclude that individuals will refrain from expressing controversial beliefs simply because they fear that their statements might be used as evidence of motive if they later commit an offense identified in the hate crime statute.

CONCLUSION

We hold that the hate crime statute is not facially unconstitutional when the predicate offense is disorderly conduct because (1) the statute reaches only conduct and does not punish speech itself; (2) the statute does not impermissibly discriminate based on content; and (3) the statute does not chill the exercise of first amendment rights. Defendant contends only that the statute is unconstitutional and does not challenge the sufficiency of the evidence against him or assert any other basis for reversal. Accordingly, we affirm defendant's conviction.

Virginia v. Black,
538 U.S. 343 (2003)

SUMMARY: The Court upheld a law banning cross burning with "an intent to intimidate a person or group of persons." Justice O'Connor wrote the plurality decision concluding that "the First Amendment permits Virginia to outlaw cross burnings done with intent to intimidate because burning a cross is a particularly virulent form of intimidation."

R.A.V. v. City of St. Paul, 505 U.S. 377 (1992)

SUMMARY: Several Caucasian juveniles burned a cross inside the fenced-in yard of an African-American family. They were charged under a statute that provided,

> "whoever places on public or private property a symbol, object, including and not limited to, a burning cross or Nazi swastika, which one knows or has reasonable grounds to know arouses anger, alarm or resentment ... on the basis of race, color, creed, religion or gender commits disorderly conduct ... shall be guilty of a misdemeanor."

The Court held that the ordinance was unconstitutional noting,

> "Let there be no mistake about our belief that burning a cross in someone's front yard is reprehensible. But St. Paul

has sufficient means at its disposal to prevent such behavior without adding the First Amendment to the fire."

The Court gave the example that St. Paul could have prosecuted the juveniles for trespass, menacing, reckless burning or arson, or criminal mischief.

Wisconsin v. Mitchell, 508 U.S. 475 (1993)

SUMMARY: Todd Mitchell challenged a group of other young African-American males by asking whether they were hyped up to move on white people?" As a young Caucasian male approached the group, Mitchell exclaimed, "There goes a white boy, go and get him." He then led a group assault on the victim. The trial court increased his sentence after conviction because of his "intentional selection of the person against whom the crime is committed because of the race ... of that person." Mitchell claimed he was being punished more severely for harboring and acting on racially discriminatory views in violation of the First Amendment. The Court held that the Wisconsin statute that enhanced the punishment of individuals convicted of hate crimes did not violate the defendant's First Amendment rights because Mitchell was being punished for a harmful act rather than for the fact that his act was motivated by racist views. It noted that acts based on discriminatory motives are likely to provoke retaliatory crimes, inflict distinct emotional harms on their victims and incite community unrest.

Symbolic Speech And Expressive Conduct

The Constitution protects symbolic speech and expressive conduct. "Freedom of expression is a broad concept embracing speech, publication, performances, and demonstrations. Even wearing symbols is considered to be constitutionally protected symbolic speech." See, *Tinker v. Des Moines Independent Community School District,* 393 U.S. 503 (1969). Expressive conduct includes: "sit-ins" to protest racial segregation, civilians wearing American military uniforms to protest the Vietnam War, and "picketing" over a variety of issues.

One form of expressive conduct the Court has frequently considered is flag burning. Scheb noted,

> Without question, the most controversial application of the concept of expressive conduct have been the Supreme Court's decisions holding that public burning of the American flag is protected by the First Amendment. In *Texas v. Johnson,* . . . the Court invalidated a Texas statute banning flag desecration. ... In *United States v. Eichman* ... the Supreme Court invalidated ... [the Flag Protection Act of 1989] ... as well, saying that "punishing

desecration of the flag dilutes the very freedom that makes this emblem so revered, and worth revering." … On several occasions, Congress has attempted to pass a constitutional amendment to overturn the Supreme Court's flag burning decisions, but in every instance the measure has failed to receive the necessary two thirds vote in the Senate. Scheb, supra at 68-69.

TEXAS v. JOHNSON, 491 U.S. 397 (1989)

JUSTICE BRENNAN delivered the opinion of the Court.

After publicly burning an American flag as a means of political protest, Gregory Lee Johnson was convicted of desecrating a flag in violation of Texas law. This case presents the question whether his conviction is consistent with the First Amendment. We hold that it is not.

I

While the Republican National Convention was taking place in Dallas in 1984, respondent Johnson participated in a political demonstration dubbed the "Republican War Chest Tour." As explained in literature distributed by the demonstrators and in speeches made by them, the purpose of this event was to protest the policies of the Reagan administration and of certain Dallas-based corporations. The demonstrators marched through the Dallas streets, chanting political slogans and stopping at several corporate locations to stage "die-ins" intended to dramatize the consequences of nuclear war. On several occasions they spray-painted the walls of buildings and overturned potted plants, but Johnson himself took no part in such activities. He did, however, accept an American flag handed to him by a fellow protestor who had taken it from a flagpole outside one of the targeted buildings.

The demonstration ended in front of Dallas City Hall, where Johnson unfurled the American flag, doused it with kerosene, and set it on fire. While the flag burned, the protestors chanted: "America, the red, white, and blue, we spit on you." After the demonstrators dispersed, a witness to the flag burning collected the flag's remains and buried them in his backyard. No one was physically injured or threatened with injury, though several witnesses testified that they had been seriously offended by the flag burning.

Of the approximately 100 demonstrators, Johnson alone was charged with a crime. The only criminal offense with which he was charged was the desecration of a venerated object. … After a trial, he was convicted, sentenced to one year in prison, and fined $2,000. The Court of Appeals for the Fifth District of Texas at Dallas affirmed Johnson's conviction, but the Texas Court of Criminal Appeals reversed, holding that the State could not, consistent with the First Amendment, punish Johnson for burning the flag in these circumstances.

The Court of Criminal Appeals began by recognizing that Johnson's conduct was symbolic speech protected by the First Amendment: "Given the context of an organized demonstration, speeches, slogans, and the distribution of literature, anyone who observed appellant's act would have understood the message that appellant intended to convey. The act for which appellant was convicted was clearly `speech' contemplated by the First Amendment." To justify Johnson's conviction for engaging in symbolic speech, the State asserted two interests: preserving the flag as a symbol of national unity and preventing breaches of the peace. The Court of Criminal Appeals held that neither interest supported his conviction.

Acknowledging that this Court had not yet decided whether the Government may criminally sanction flag desecration in order to preserve the flag's symbolic value, the Texas court nevertheless concluded that our decision in *West Virginia State Board of Education v. Barnette* suggested that furthering this interest by curtailing speech was impermissible. "Recognizing that the right to differ is the centerpiece of our First Amendment freedoms," the court explained, "a government cannot mandate by fiat a feeling of unity in its citizens. Therefore, that very same government cannot carve out a symbol of unity and prescribe a set of approved messages to be associated with that symbol when it cannot mandate the status or feeling the symbol purports to represent." Noting that the State had not shown that the flag was in "grave and immediate danger," of being stripped of its symbolic value, the Texas court also decided that the flag's special status was not endangered by Johnson's conduct.

As to the State's goal of preventing breaches of the peace, the court concluded that the flag-desecration statute was not drawn narrowly enough to encompass only those flag burnings that were likely to result in a serious disturbance of the peace. And in fact, the court emphasized, the flag burning in this particular case did not threaten such a reaction. "`Serious offense' occurred," the court admitted, "but there was no breach of peace nor does the record reflect that the situation was potentially explosive. One cannot equate `serious offense' with incitement to breach the peace." The court also stressed that another Texas statute, prohibited breaches of the peace. ... [T]he court decided that [this statute] demonstrated Texas' ability to prevent disturbances of the peace without punishing this flag desecration. ...

Because it reversed Johnson's conviction on the ground that 42.09 was unconstitutional as applied to him, the state court did not address Johnson's argument that the statute was, on its face, unconstitutionally vague and overbroad. We granted certiorari ... and now affirm.

II

Johnson was convicted of flag desecration for burning the flag rather than for uttering insulting words. This fact somewhat complicates our consideration of his conviction under the First Amendment. We must first determine whether Johnson's burning of the flag constituted expressive conduct, permitting him to invoke the First Amendment in challenging his conviction. If his conduct was expressive, we next decide whether the State's regulation is related to the suppression of free expression. If the State's regulation is not related to expression, then the less stringent standard we announced in *United States v. O'Brien* for regulations of noncommunicative conduct controls. If it is, then we are outside of *O'Brien's* test, and we must ask whether this interest justifies Johnson's conviction under a more demanding standard. A third possibility is that the State's asserted interest is simply not implicated on these facts, and in that event the interest drops out of the picture.

The First Amendment literally forbids the abridgment only of "speech," but we have long recognized that its protection does not end at the spoken or written word. While we have rejected "the view that an apparently limitless variety of conduct can be labeled `speech' whenever the person engaging in the conduct intends thereby to express an idea," we have acknowledged that conduct may be "sufficiently imbued with elements of communication to fall within the scope of the First and Fourteenth Amendments,"

In deciding whether particular conduct possesses sufficient communicative elements to bring the First Amendment into play, we have asked whether "[a]n intent to convey a particularized message was present, and [whether] the likelihood was great that the message would be understood by those who viewed it." Hence, we have recognized the expressive nature of students' wearing of black armbands to protest American military involvement in Vietnam, *Tinker v. Des Moines Independent Community School District*. ; of a sit-in by blacks in a "whites only" area to protest segregation, *Brown v. Louisiana*; of the wearing of American military uniforms in a dramatic presentation criticizing American involvement in Vietnam,

Schacht v. United States; and of picketing about a wide variety of causes, see, e.g., *Food Employees v. Logan Valley Plaza, Inc.*, [and] *United States v. Grace*.

Especially pertinent to this case are our decisions recognizing the communicative nature of conduct relating to flags. Attaching a peace sign to the flag, refusing to salute the flag, and displaying a red flag, we have held, all may find shelter under the First Amendment. ... That we have had little difficulty identifying an expressive element in conduct relating to flags should not be surprising. The very purpose of a national flag is to serve as a symbol of our country; it is, one might say, "the one visible manifestation of two hundred years of nationhood." Thus, we have observed:

> "[T]he flag salute is a form of utterance. Symbolism is a primitive but effective way of communicating ideas. The use of an emblem or flag to symbolize some system, idea, institution, or personality, is a short cut from mind to mind. Causes and nations, political parties, lodges and ecclesiastical groups seek to knit the loyalty of their followings to a flag or banner, a color or design."

...

The State of Texas conceded for purposes of its oral argument in this case that Johnson's conduct was expressive conduct, and this concession seems to us as prudent. Johnson burned an American flag as part - indeed, as the culmination - of a political demonstration that coincided with the convening of the Republican Party and its renomination of Ronald Reagan for President. The expressive, overtly political nature of this conduct was both intentional and overwhelmingly apparent. At his trial, Johnson explained his reasons for burning the flag as follows: "The American Flag was burned as Ronald Reagan was being renominated as President. And a more powerful statement of symbolic speech, whether you agree with it or not, couldn't have been made at that time. It's quite a [juxtaposition]. We had new patriotism and no

patriotism." In these circumstances, Johnson's burning of the flag was conduct "sufficiently imbued with elements of communication" . . . to implicate the First Amendment.

III

The government generally has a freer hand in restricting expressive conduct than it has in restricting the written or spoken word. ... A law directed at the communicative nature of conduct must, like a law directed at speech itself, be justified by the substantial showing of need that the First Amendment requires." It is, in short, not simply the verbal or nonverbal nature of the expression, but the governmental interest at stake, that helps to determine whether a restriction on that expression is valid.

...

The State offers two separate interests to justify this conviction: preventing breaches of the peace and preserving the flag as a symbol of nationhood and national unity. We hold that the first interest is not implicated on this record and that the second is related to the suppression of expression.

A

Texas claims that its interest in preventing breaches of the peace justifies Johnson's conviction for flag desecration. However, no disturbance of the peace actually occurred or threatened to occur because of Johnson's burning of the flag. Although the State stresses the disruptive behavior of the protestors during their march toward City Hall, it admits that "no actual breach of the peace occurred at the time of the flagburning or in response to the flagburning." The State's emphasis on the protestors' disorderly actions prior to arriving at City Hall is not only somewhat surprising given that no charges were brought on the basis of this conduct, but it also fails to show that a disturbance of the peace was a likely reaction to Johnson's conduct. The only evidence offered by the State at trial to show the reaction to Johnson's actions was the testimony of several persons who had been seriously offended by the flag burning. Id., at 6-7.

The State's position, therefore, amounts to a claim that an audience that takes serious offense at particular expression is necessarily likely to disturb the peace and that the expression may be prohibited on this basis. Our precedents do not countenance such a presumption. On the contrary, they recognize that a principal "function of free speech under our system of government is to invite dispute. It may indeed best serve its high purpose when it induces a condition of unrest, creates dissatisfaction with conditions as they are, or even stirs people to anger." *Terminiello v. Chicago.* … It would be odd indeed to conclude both that "if it is the speaker's opinion that gives offense, that consequence is a reason for according it constitutional protection," and that the government may ban the expression of certain disagreeable ideas on the unsupported presumption that their very disagreeableness will provoke violence.

Thus, we have not permitted the government to assume that every expression of a provocative idea will incite a riot, but have instead required careful consideration of the actual circumstances surrounding such expression, asking whether the expression "is directed to inciting or producing imminent lawless action and is likely to incite or produce such action." *Brandenburg v. Ohio*, (reviewing circumstances surrounding rally and speeches by Ku Klux Klan). To accept Texas' arguments that it need only demonstrate "the potential for a breach of the peace," and that every flag burning necessarily possesses that potential, would be to eviscerate our holding in Brandenburg. This we decline to do.

Nor does Johnson's expressive conduct fall within that small class of "fighting words" that are "likely to provoke the average person to retaliation, and thereby cause a breach of the peace." *Chaplinsky v. New Hampshire.* … No reasonable onlooker would have regarded Johnson's generalized expression of dissatisfaction with the policies of the Federal Government as a direct personal insult or an invitation to exchange fisticuffs.

We thus conclude that the State's interest in maintaining order is not implicated on these facts. The State need not worry that our holding will disable it from preserving the peace. We do not suggest that the First Amendment forbids a State to prevent "imminent lawless action." And, in fact, Texas already has a statute specifically prohibiting breaches of the peace . . . which tends to confirm that Texas need not punish this flag desecration in order to keep the peace.

B

The State also asserts an interest in preserving the flag as a symbol of nationhood and national unity. In *Spence*, we acknowledged that the government's interest in preserving the flag's special symbolic value "is directly related to expression in the context of activity" such as affixing a peace symbol to a flag. We are equally persuaded that this interest is related to expression in the case of Johnson's burning of the flag. …

IV

It remains to consider whether the State's interest in preserving the flag as a symbol of nationhood and national unity justifies Johnson's conviction.

As in Spence, "[w]e are confronted with a case of prosecution for the expression of an idea through activity," and "[a]ccordingly, we must examine with particular care the interests advanced by [petitioner] to support its prosecution." Johnson was not, we add, prosecuted for the expression of just any idea; he was prosecuted for his expression of dissatisfaction with the policies of this country, expression situated at the core of our First Amendment values.

Moreover, Johnson was prosecuted because he knew that his politically charged expression would cause "serious offense." If he had burned the flag as a means of disposing of it because it was dirty or torn, he would not have been convicted of flag desecration under this

Texas law: federal law designates burning as the preferred means of disposing of a flag "when it is in such condition that it is no longer a fitting emblem for display," and Texas has no quarrel with this means of disposal. The Texas law is thus not aimed at protecting the physical integrity of the flag in all circumstances, but is designed instead to protect it only against impairments that would cause serious offense to others. Texas concedes as much: "Section 42.09(b) reaches only those severe acts of physical abuse of the flag carried out in a way likely to be offensive. The statute mandates intentional or knowing abuse, that is, the kind of mistreatment that is not innocent, but rather is intentionally designed to seriously offend other individuals."

Whether Johnson's treatment of the flag violated Texas law thus depended on the likely communicative impact of his expressive conduct. Our decision in *Boos v. Barry* ... tells us that this restriction on Johnson's expression is content based. In *Boos*, we considered the constitutionality of a law prohibiting "the display of any sign within 500 feet of a foreign embassy if that sign tends to bring that foreign government into 'public odium' or 'public disrepute.'" Rejecting the argument that the law was content neutral because it was justified by "our international law obligation to shield diplomats from speech that offends their dignity," we held that "[t]he emotive impact of speech on its audience is not a 'secondary effect'" unrelated to the content of the expression itself.

According to the principles announced in *Boos*, Johnson's political expression was restricted because of the content of the message he conveyed. We must therefore subject the State's asserted interest in preserving the special symbolic character of the flag to "the most exacting scrutiny."

Texas argues that its interest in preserving the flag as a symbol of nationhood and national unity survives this close analysis. ... The State's argument is not that it has an interest simply in maintaining the flag as a symbol of something, no matter what it symbolizes;

indeed, if that were the State's position, it would be difficult to see how that interest is endangered by highly symbolic conduct such as Johnson's. Rather, the State's claim is that it has an interest in preserving the flag as a symbol of nationhood and national unity, a symbol with a determinate range of meanings. According to Texas, if one physically treats the flag in a way that would tend to cast doubt on either the idea that nationhood and national unity are the flag's referents or that national unity actually exists, the message conveyed thereby is a harmful one and therefore may be prohibited. ...

If there is a bedrock principle underlying the First Amendment, it is that the government may not prohibit the expression of an idea simply because society finds the idea itself offensive or disagreeable. ...

In short, nothing in our precedents suggests that a State may foster its own view of the flag by prohibiting expressive conduct relating to it. To bring its argument outside our precedents, Texas attempts to convince us that even if its interest in preserving the flag's symbolic role does not allow it to prohibit words or some expressive conduct critical of the flag, it does permit it to forbid the outright destruction of the flag. The State's argument cannot depend here on the distinction between written or spoken words and nonverbal conduct. That distinction, we have shown, is of no moment where the nonverbal conduct is expressive, as it is here, and where the regulation of that conduct is related to expression, as it is here. ...

Texas' focus on the precise nature of Johnson's expression, moreover, misses the point of our prior decisions: their enduring lesson, that the government may not prohibit expression simply because it disagrees with its message, is not dependent on the particular mode in which one chooses to express an idea. If we were to hold that a State may forbid flag burning wherever it is likely to endanger the flag's symbolic role, but allow it wherever burning a flag promotes that role - as where, for example, a person ceremoniously burns a dirty flag - we would be saying that when it comes to impairing the flag's physical integrity, the flag itself may be used as a symbol - as a substitute for the written or spoken word or a "short cut from mind to mind" - only in one direction. We would be permitting a State to "prescribe what shall be orthodox" by saying that one may burn the flag to convey one's attitude toward it and its referents only if one does not endanger the flag's representation of nationhood and national unity.

We never before have held that the Government may ensure that a symbol be used to express only one view of that symbol or its referents. ...

. . .

There is . . . no indication ... that a separate juridical category exists for the American flag alone. ... The First Amendment does not guarantee that other concepts virtually sacred to our Nation as a whole - such as the principle that discrimination on the basis of race is odious and destructive - will go unquestioned in the marketplace of ideas. We decline, therefore, to create for the flag an exception to the joust of principles protected by the First Amendment.

It is not the State's ends, but its means, to which we object. It cannot be gainsaid that there is a special place reserved for the flag in this Nation, and thus we do not doubt that the government has a legitimate interest in making efforts to "preserv[e] the national flag as an unalloyed symbol of our country." We reject the suggestion, urged at oral argument by counsel for Johnson, that the government lacks "any state interest whatsoever" in regulating the manner in which the flag may be displayed. Congress has, for example, enacted precatory regulations describing the proper treatment of the flag, and we cast no doubt on the legitimacy of its interest in making such recommendations. To say that the government has an interest in encouraging proper treatment of the flag, however, is not to say that it may criminally punish a person for burning a flag as a means of political protest. "National unity as an end which officials may

foster by persuasion and example is not in question. The problem is whether under our Constitution compulsion as here employed is a permissible means for its achievement."

. . .

We are tempted to say, in fact, that the flag's deservedly cherished place in our community will be strengthened, not weakened, by our holding today. Our decision is a reaffirmation of the principles of freedom and inclusiveness that the flag best reflects, and of the conviction that our toleration of criticism such as Johnson's is a sign and source of our strength.

…

The way to preserve the flag's special role is not to punish those who feel differently about these matters. It is to persuade them that they are "wrong." To courageous, self-reliant men, with confidence in the power of free and fearless reasoning applied through the processes of popular government, no danger flowing from speech can be deemed clear and present, unless the incidence of the evil apprehended is so imminent that it may befall before there is opportunity for full discussion. If there be time to expose through discussion the falsehood and fallacies, to avert the evil by the processes of education, the remedy to be applied is more speech, not enforced silence." *Whitney v. California*, 274 U.S. 357, 377 (1927) (Brandeis, J., concurring). And, precisely because it is our flag that is involved, one's response to the flag burner may exploit the uniquely persuasive power of the flag itself. We can imagine no more appropriate response to burning a flag than waving one's own, no better way to counter a flag burner's message than by saluting the flag that burns, no surer means of preserving the dignity even of the flag that burned than by - as one witness here did - according its remains a respectful burial. We do not consecrate the flag by punishing its desecration, for in doing so we dilute the freedom that this cherished emblem represents.

V

Johnson was convicted for engaging in expressive conduct. The State's interest in preventing breaches of the peace does not support his conviction because Johnson's conduct did not threaten to disturb the peace. Nor does the State's interest in preserving the flag as a symbol of nationhood and national unity justify his criminal conviction for engaging in political expression. …

JUSTICE KENNEDY, concurring.

I write not to qualify the words JUSTICE BRENNAN chooses so well, for he says with power all that is necessary to explain our ruling. I join his opinion without reservation, but with a keen sense that this case, like others before us from time to time, exacts its personal toll. This prompts me to add to our pages these few remarks.

The case before us illustrates better than most that the judicial power is often difficult in its exercise. We cannot here ask another Branch to share responsibility, as when the argument is made that a statute is flawed or incomplete. For we are presented with a clear and simple statute to be judged against a pure command of the Constitution. The outcome can be laid at no door but ours.

The hard fact is that sometimes we must make decisions we do not like. We make them because they are right, right in the sense that the law and the Constitution, as we see them, compel the result. And so great is our commitment to the process that, except in the rare case, we do not pause to express distaste for the result, perhaps for fear of undermining a valued principle that dictates the decision. This is one of those rare cases.

. . .

With all respect to those views, I do not believe the Constitution gives us the right to rule as the dissenting Members of the Court urge, however painful this judgment is to announce. Though symbols often are what we ourselves make of them, the flag is constant in expressing beliefs Americans share, beliefs in law and peace and that freedom which sustains the human spirit. The case here today forces recognition of the costs to which those beliefs commit us. It is poignant but fundamental that the flag protects those who hold it in contempt.

For all the record shows, this respondent was not a philosopher and perhaps did not even possess the ability to comprehend how repellent his statements must be to the Republic itself. But whether or not he could appreciate the enormity of the offense he gave, the fact remains that his acts were speech, in both the technical and the fundamental meaning of the Constitution. So I agree with the Court that he must go free.

CHIEF JUSTICE REHNQUIST, with whom JUSTICE WHITE and JUSTICE O'CONNOR join, dissenting.

… For more than 200 years, the American flag has occupied a unique position as the symbol of our Nation, a uniqueness that justifies a governmental prohibition against flag burning in the way respondent Johnson did here.

. . .

The American flag … has come to be the visible symbol embodying our Nation. It does not represent the views of any particular political party, and it does not represent any particular political philosophy. The flag is not simply another "idea" or "point of view" competing for recognition in the marketplace of ideas. Millions and millions of Americans regard it with an almost mystical reverence regardless of what sort of social, political, or philosophical beliefs they may have. I cannot agree that the First Amendment invalidates the Act of Congress, and the laws of 48 of the 50 States, which make criminal the public burning of the flag.

. . .

…[T]he Court insists that the Texas statute prohibiting the public burning of the American flag infringes on respondent Johnson's freedom of expression. Such freedom, of course, is not absolute.

. . .

. . . Here it may equally well be said that the public burning of the American flag by Johnson was no essential part of any exposition of ideas, and at the same time it had a tendency to incite a breach of the peace. Johnson was free to make any verbal denunciation of the flag that he wished; indeed, he was free to burn the flag in private. He could publicly burn other symbols of the Government or effigies of political leaders. He did lead a march through the streets of Dallas, and conducted a rally in front of the Dallas City Hall. He engaged in a "die-in" to protest nuclear weapons. He shouted out various slogans during the march, including: "Reagan, Mondale which will it be? Either one means World War III"; "Ronald Reagan, killer of the hour, Perfect example of U.S. power"; and "red, white and blue, we spit on you, you stand for plunder, you will go under." For none of these acts was he arrested or prosecuted; it was only when he proceeded to burn publicly an American flag stolen from its rightful owner that he violated the Texas statute.

[Johnson's acts] . . . like *Chaplinsky's* provocative words, conveyed nothing that could not have been conveyed and was not conveyed just as forcefully in a dozen different ways. As with "fighting words," so with flag burning, for purposes of the First Amendment: It is "no essential part of any exposition of ideas, and [is] of such slight social value as a step to truth that any benefit that may be derived from [it] is clearly outweighed" by the public interest in avoiding a probable breach of the peace. The highest courts of several States have upheld state statutes prohibiting the public burning of the flag on the grounds that it is so inherently inflammatory that it may cause a breach of public order. ...

. . . [F]ive years ago we said ... that "the First Amendment does not guarantee the right to employ every conceivable method of communication at all times and in all places." The Texas statute deprived Johnson of only one rather inarticulate symbolic form of protest - a form of protest that was profoundly offensive to many - and left him with a full panoply of other symbols and every conceivable form of verbal expression to express his deep disapproval of national policy. Thus, in no way can it be said that Texas is punishing him because his hearers - or any other group of people - were profoundly opposed to the message that he sought to convey. Such opposition is no proper basis for restricting speech or expression under the First Amendment. It was Johnson's use of this particular symbol, and not the idea that he sought to convey by it or by his many other expressions, for which he was punished.

. . .

. . . Surely one of the high purposes of a democratic society is to legislate against conduct that is regarded as evil and profoundly offensive to the majority of people - whether it be murder, embezzlement, pollution, or flag burning.

. . .

JUSTICE STEVENS, dissenting.

As the Court analyzes this case, it presents the question whether the State of Texas, or indeed the Federal Government, has the power to prohibit the public desecration of the American flag. The question is unique. In my judgment rules that apply to a host of other symbols, such as state flags, armbands, or various privately promoted emblems of political or commercial identity, are not necessarily controlling. Even if flag burning could be considered just another species of symbolic speech under the logical application of the rules that the Court has developed in its interpretation of the First Amendment in other contexts, this case has an intangible dimension that makes those rules inapplicable.

A country's flag is a symbol of more than "nationhood and national unity." It also signifies the ideas that characterize the society that has chosen that emblem as well as the special history that has animated the growth and power of those ideas. The fleurs-de-lis and the tricolor both symbolized "nationhood and national unity," but they had vastly different meanings. The message conveyed by some flags - the swastika, for example - may survive long after it has outlived its usefulness as a symbol of regimented unity in a particular nation.

So it is with the American flag. It is more than a proud symbol of the courage, the determination, and the gifts of nature that transformed 13 fledgling Colonies into a world power. It is a symbol of freedom, of equal opportunity, of religious tolerance, and of good will for other peoples who share our aspirations. The symbol carries its message to dissidents both at home and abroad who may have no interest at all in our national unity or survival.

The value of the flag as a symbol cannot be measured. Even so, I have no doubt that the interest in preserving that value for the future is both significant and legitimate. Conceivably that value will be enhanced by the Court's conclusion that our national commitment to free expression is so strong that even the United States as ultimate guarantor of that freedom is without power to prohibit the desecration of its unique symbol. But I am unpersuaded. The creation of a federal right to post bulletin boards and graffiti on the Washington Monument might enlarge the market for free expression, but at a cost I would not pay. Similarly, in my considered judgment, sanctioning the public desecration of the flag will tarnish its value - both for those who cherish the ideas for which it waves and for those who desire to don the robes of martyrdom by burning it. That tarnish is not justified by the trivial burden on free expression occasioned by requiring that an available, alternative mode of expression - including uttering words critical of the flag. . . .

Other Cases: Expressive Conduct

Barnes v. Glen Theatre, Inc, 501 U.S. 560 (1991)

SUMMARY: Indiana had a public indecency law which required exotic dancers to wear pasties and G-strings. Two establishments wanted to provide totally nude dancing entertainment and did not want the law to be enforced against them. They sued to enjoin the inforcement of that law asserting that the law's prohibition against total nudity in public places violates the First Amendment. The U.S. District Court (trial court) held that nude dancing was not expressive conduct, but the Court of Appeals (intermediate court of appeals) reversed, finding that nonobscene nude dancing performed for entertainment was protected expression and that the statute infringed the constitution because its purpose was to prevent the message of eroticism. The case was then appealed to the U.S. Supreme Court which held that the enforcement of Indiana's public indecency law to prevent totally nude dancing did not violate the First Amendment's guarantee of freedom of expression.]

CHIEF JUSTICE RHENQUIST'S (Official Summary)

(a) Nude dancing of the kind sought to be performed here is expressive conduct within the outer perimeters of the First Amendment, although only marginally so.

b) Applying the four-part test of *United States v. O'Brien*, 391 U.S. 367, 376 -377 - which rejected the contention that symbolic speech is entitled to full First Amendment protection - the statute is justified despite its incidental limitations on some expressive activity. The law is clearly within the State's constitutional power. And it furthers a substantial governmental interest in protecting societal order and morality. Public indecency statutes reflect moral disapproval of people appearing in the nude among strangers in public places, and this particular law follows a line of state laws, dating back to 1831, banning public nudity. The States' traditional police power is defined as the authority to provide for the public health, safety, and morals, and such a basis for legislation has been upheld. This governmental interest is unrelated to the suppression of free expression, since public nudity is the evil the State seeks to prevent, whether or not it is combined with expressive activity. The law does not proscribe nudity in these establishments because the dancers are conveying an erotic message. To the contrary, an erotic performance may be presented without any state interference, so long as the performers wear a scant amount of clothing. Finally, the incidental restriction on First Amendment freedom is no greater than is essential to the furtherance of the governmental interest. Since the statutory prohibition is not a means to some greater end, but an end itself, it is without cavil that the statute is narrowly tailored.

JUSTICE SCALIA concurring opinion, omitted.

JUSTICE SOUTER concurring opinion, omitted (cited and applied the O'Brien test (below)).

United States v. O'Brien, 391 U.S. 367 (1968)

SUMMARY: This case established the test the Court uses when deciding whether the government impermissibly limited symbolic speech/expressive conduct. It was discussed in *Texas v. Johnson* and adhered to in *Barnes v. Glen Theatre*.

David O'Brien burned his draft card at a Boston courthouse and claimed he was expressing his opposition to war when he was charged with violating a federal law making it a crime to mutilate a draft card. The 7-1 opinion in favor of the government and authored by Chief Justice Earl Warren stated,

> "[W]e think it clear, that a government regulation is sufficiently justified if it is within the constitutional power of the Government; if it furthers an important or substantial governmental interest; if the governmental interest is unrelated to the suppression of free expression; and if the incidental restriction on alleged First Amendment freedoms is not greater than is essential to the furtherance of that interest."

Frederick v. Morse, 551 U.S. 393 (2007)

SUMMARY: At a school-supervised event, Frederick held up a banner with the message "Bong Hits 4 Jesus." His school principal, Deborah Morse took away the banner and suspended Frederick for ten day -- citing the school's policy against the display of material that promotes the use of illegal drugs. Frederick sued under 42 U.S.C. 1983, the federal civil rights statute, alleging a violation of his First Amendment right to freedom of speech. The District Court found no constitutional violation, and even if there were, Morse had qualified immunity. The Ninth Circuit Court of Appeals, citing the Tinker case, found that Frederick was punished for his message rather than for any disturbance and ruled the punishment was unconstitutional. Furthermore, the principal had no qualified immunity, because any reasonable principal would have known that Morse's actions were unlawful.

The Court reversed by a 5-4 vote, holding that school officials can prohibit students from displaying messages that promote illegal drug use. Chief Justice John Roberts's majority opinion held that although students do have some right to political speech even while in school, this right does not extend to pro-drug messages that may undermine the school's important mission to discourage drug use. The majority held that Frederick's message, though "cryptic," was reasonably interpreted as promoting marijuana use - equivalent to "[Take] bong hits" or "bong hits [are a good thing]."

In ruling for Morse, the Court affirmed that the speech rights of public-school students are not as extensive as those adults normally enjoy, and that the highly protective standard set by Tinker would not always be applied.

In concurring opinions, Justice Thomas expressed his view that the right to free speech does not apply to students and his wish to see Tinker overturned altogether, while Justice Alito stressed that the decision applied only to pro-drug messages and not to broader political speech.

The dissent conceded that the principal should have had immunity from the lawsuit, but argued that the majority opinion was "[...] deaf to the constitutional imperative to permit unfettered debate, even among high-school students [...]." See, https://www.oyez.org/cases/2006/06-278)

Freedom Of Association And Assembly

The First Amendment protects the right of people to peacefully assemble. *DeJonge v. Oregon,* 299 U.S. 353 (1937), held that freedom of peaceful meeting is as fundamental as freedom of speech and the press to democracy. The right of association is not specifically mentioned in the Constitution; but it is considered a natural right and thus protected by the Constitution.

> Notwithstanding the appropriate caution against reading into the Constitution rights not explicitly defined, this Court has acknowledged that certain unarticulated rights are implicit in enumerated guarantees. For example, the rights of association and of privacy, the right to be presumed innocent, and the right to be judged by a standard of proof beyond a reasonable doubt in a criminal trial, as well as the right to travel, appear nowhere in the Constitution or Bill of Rights. Yet these important but unarticulated rights have nonetheless been found to share constitutional protection in common with explicit guarantees. ... Fundamental rights, even though not expressly guaranteed, have been recognized by the Court as indispensable to the enjoyment of rights explicitly defined. Richmond Newspapers, Inc. v. Virginia, 488 U.S. 555, 579 (1980).

Although the First Amendment limits the legislature's ability to pass any laws infringing on a person's freedom of assembly, the Court has approved the right of government officials to put limits on the ability to congregate when necessary to maintain public order.

Forums

The amount of protection afforded to speech depends, in large part, on where the person is speaking and where people are assembling. The Court refers to specific speaking locations as "forums" and has identified different types of forums: traditional public forum, designated public forums, and non-public forums. Some refer to these as public forums, quasi-public forums, and private forums.

Public forums are property generally used for purposes of public assembly, communicating thoughts between citizens and discussing public questions.

> Traditional public forums include public parks, sidewalks, and areas that have been traditionally open to political speech and debate. Speakers in these areas enjoy the strongest First Amendment protections. In traditional public forums, the government may not discriminate against speakers based on their views." This is called "viewpoint discrimination." The government may, however, subject speech to reasonable, content-neutral restrictions on its time, place, and manner. When considering government restrictions of speech in traditional public forums, courts use "strict scrutiny." Under strict scrutiny, restrictions are allowed only if they serve a compelling state interest and are narrowly tailored to meet the needs of that interest.[42]

Quasi-public forums (places where people frequently congregate) include areas such as shopping stores and other privately owned building or property to which the public has general access; and

> Sometimes, the government opens public property for public expression even though the public property is not a traditional public forum. These [types of properties] are designated public forums. After opening a designated public forum, the government is not obligated to keep it open. However, so long as the government does keep the forum open, speech in the forum receives the same First Amendment protections as speech in traditional public forums.

---

[42] See, http://www.law.cornell.edu/wex/forums.

Examples of designated public forums include municipal theatres and meeting rooms at state universities. [43]

The government may limit access to a designated public forum to certain classes or types of speech. In these "limited forums," although the government may discriminate against classes of speakers or types of speech, it may not exercise viewpoint discrimination. For example, the government may limit access to public school meeting rooms by only allowing speakers conducting school-related activities. It may not, however, exclude speakers from a religious group simply because they intend to express religious views.[44]

Non-public forums (like an airport) are privately owned property

Nonpublic forums are forums for public speech that are neither traditional public forums nor designated public forums. Government restrictions on speech in nonpublic forums must be reasonable, and may not discriminate based on speakers' viewpoints. Examples of nonpublic forums include airport terminals and a public school's internal mail system. [45] ...

Private property (like an individual's home) are not forums.

Finally, some public property is not a forum at all, and thus is not subject to this forum analysis. For example, public television broadcasters are not subject to forum analysis when they decide what shows to air.

Courts will be more likely to strike down ordinances and laws that limit the right to assemble in public forums and less likely to strike down regulations of assemblies in quasi-public and non-public forums. The more public the forum, the less the government will be allowed to restrict people's freedom of assembly.

Time, Manner, And Place Restrictions

The right of assembly is not absolute. Even at the most public of forums, the government can impose reasonable time, reasonable place, and reasonable manner restrictions on assemblies. Governments may not ban assemblies in the public forum so long as they are peaceful and do not impede the operations of government or the activities of other citizens.

The following case addresses many First Amendment rights to free speech (free expression) and to assembly.

COX v. LOUISIANA,
379 U.S. 536 (1965)

...

[Cox, the appellant] was convicted of violating a Louisiana "disturbing the peace" statute, which provides:

Whoever with intent to provoke a breach of the peace, or under circumstances such that a breach of the peace may be occasioned thereby crowds or congregates with others . . .

in or upon . . . a public street or public highway, or upon a public sidewalk, or any other public place or building . . . and who fails or refuses to disperse and move on . . . when ordered so to do by any law enforcement officer of any municipality, or parish, in which such act or acts are committed, or by any law enforcement officer of the state of Louisiana, or any other authorized

---

[43] Id.
[44] Id.
[45] Id.

person . . . shall be guilty of disturbing the peace.

…It is clear to us that, on the facts of this case, which are strikingly similar to those present in *Edwards v. South Carolina,* and *Fields v. South Carolina,* Louisiana infringed appellant's rights of free speech and free assembly by convicting him under this statute.

… We hold that Louisiana may not constitutionally punish appellant under this statute for engaging in the type of conduct which this record reveals, and also that the statute as authoritatively interpreted by the Louisiana Supreme Court is unconstitutionally broad in scope.

The Louisiana courts have held that appellant's conduct constituted a breach of the peace under state law, . . . but our independent examination of the record, which we are required to make, shows no conduct which the State had a right to prohibit as a breach of the peace.

Appellant led a group of young college students who wished "to protest segregation" and discrimination against Negroes and the arrest of 23 fellow students. They assembled peaceably at the State Capitol building and marched to the courthouse where they sang, prayed and listened to a speech. A reading of the record reveals agreement on the part of the State's witnesses that Cox had the demonstration "very well controlled," and, until the end of Cox's speech, the group was perfectly "orderly." Sheriff Clemmons testified that the crowd's activities were not "objectionable" before that time. They became objectionable, according to the Sheriff himself, when Cox, concluding his speech, urged the students to go uptown and sit in at lunch counters. The Sheriff testified that the sole aspect of the program to which he objected was

> [t]he inflammatory manner in which he [Cox] addressed that crowd and told them to go on up town, go to four places on the protest list, sit down and if

they don't feed you, sit there for one hour.

Yet this part of Cox's speech obviously did not deprive the demonstration of its protected character under the Constitution as free speech and assembly. … The State argues, however, that, while the demonstrators started out to be orderly, the loud cheering and clapping by the students in response to the singing from the jail converted the peaceful assembly into a riotous one. The record, however, does not support this assertion. It is true that the students, in response to the singing of their fellows who were in custody, cheered and applauded. However, the meeting was an outdoor meeting, and a key state witness testified that, while the singing was loud, it was not disorderly. There is, moreover, no indication that the mood of the students was ever hostile, aggressive, or unfriendly. Our conclusion that the entire meeting, from the beginning until its dispersal by tear gas was, orderly and not riotous is confirmed by a film of the events taken by a television news photographer, which was offered in evidence as a state exhibit. We have viewed the film, and it reveals that the students, though they undoubtedly cheered and clapped, were well behaved throughout. … The singing and cheering do not seem to us to differ significantly from the constitutionally protected activity of the demonstrators in *Edwards,* who loudly sang "while stamping their feet and clapping their hands."

Our conclusion that the record does not support the contention that the students' cheering, clapping and singing constituted a breach of the peace is confirmed by the fact that these were not relied on as a basis for conviction by the trial judge, who, rather, stated as his reason for convicting Cox of disturbing the peace that

> [i]t must be recognized to be inherently dangerous and a breach of the peace to bring 1,500 people, colored people, down in the predominantly white business district in the City of Baton Rouge and congregate across the street from the courthouse and sing songs as

described to me by the defendant as the CORE national anthem carrying lines such as "black and white together" and to urge those 1,500 people to descend upon our lunch counters and sit there until they are served. That has to be an inherent breach of the peace, and our statute 14:103.1 has made it so.

Finally, the State contends that the conviction should be sustained because of fear expressed by some of the state witnesses that "violence was about to erupt" because of the demonstration. It is virtually undisputed, however, that the students themselves were not violent, and threatened no violence. The fear of violence seems to have been based upon the reaction of the group of white citizens looking on from across the street. One state witness testified that "he felt the situation was getting out of hand" as, on the courthouse side of St. Louis Street, "were small knots or groups of white citizens who were muttering words, who seemed a little bit agitated." A police officer stated that the reaction of the white crowd was not violent, but "was rumblings." Others felt the atmosphere became "tense" because of "mutterings," "grumbling," and "jeering" from the white group. There is no indication, however, that any member of the white group threatened violence. And this small crowd, estimated at between 100 and 300, was separated from the students by "seventy-five to eighty" armed policemen, including "every available shift of the City Police," the "Sheriff's Office in full complement," and "additional help from the State Police," along with a "fire truck and the Fire Department." As Inspector Trigg testified, they could have handled the crowd

. . .

III

THE OBSTRUCTING PUBLIC PASSAGES CONVICTION

...

[Cox was also convicted of a Louisiana statute against obstructing public passages. The Louisiana Supreme Court upheld his conviction on that charge. We conclude] ... There is no doubt from the record in this case that this far sidewalk was obstructed, and thus, as so construed, appellant violated the statute.

Appellant, however, contends that, as so construed and applied in this case, the statute is an unconstitutional infringement on freedom of speech and assembly. This contention, on the facts here presented, raises an issue with which this Court has dealt in many decisions, that is, the right of a State or municipality to regulate the use of city streets and other facilities to assure the safety and convenience of the people in their use and the concomitant right of the people of free speech and assembly.

... The rights of free speech and assembly, while fundamental in our democratic society, still do not mean that everyone with opinions or beliefs to express may address a group at any public place and at any time. The constitutional guarantee of liberty implies the existence of an organized society maintaining public order, without which liberty itself would be lost in the excesses of anarchy. The control of travel on the streets is a clear example of governmental responsibility to insure this necessary order. A restriction in that relation, designed to promote the public convenience in the interest of all, and not susceptible to abuses of discriminatory application, cannot be disregarded by the attempted exercise of some civil right which, in other circumstances, would be entitled to protection. One would not be justified in ignoring the familiar red light because this was thought to be a means of social protest. Nor could one, contrary to traffic regulations, insist upon a street meeting in the middle of Times Square at the rush hour as a form of freedom of speech or assembly. Governmental authorities have the duty and responsibility to keep their streets open and available for movement. A group of demonstrators could not insist upon the right to cordon off street, or entrance to a public or private building, and allow no one to pass who did not agree to listen to their exhortations.

We emphatically reject the notion urged by appellant that the First and Fourteenth Amendments afford the same kind of freedom to those who would communicate ideas by conduct such as patrolling, marching, and picketing on streets and highways, as these amendments afford to those who communicate ideas by pure speech. …

We have no occasion in this case to consider the constitutionality of the uniform, consistent, and nondiscriminatory application of a statute forbidding all access to streets and other public facilities for parades and meetings. Although the statute here involved on its face precludes all street assemblies and parades, it has not been so applied and enforced by the Baton Rouge authorities. . . . From all the evidence before us, it appears that the authorities in Baton Rouge permit or prohibit parades or street meetings in their completely uncontrolled discretion.

…

This Court has recognized that the lodging of such broad discretion in a public official allows him to determine which expressions of view will be permitted and which will not. This thus sanctions a device for the suppression of the communication of ideas and permits the official to act as a censor. Also inherent in such a system allowing parades or meetings only with the prior permission of an official is the obvious danger to the right of a person or group not to be denied equal protection of the laws. … It is clearly unconstitutional to enable a public official to determine which expressions of view will be permitted and which will not or to engage in invidious discrimination among persons or groups either by use of a statute providing a system of broad discretionary licensing power or, as in this case, the equivalent of such a system by selective enforcement of an extremely broad prohibitory statute.

It is, of course, undisputed that appropriate, limited discretion, under properly drawn statutes or ordinances, concerning the time, place, duration, or manner of use of the streets for public assemblies may be vested in administrative officials, provided that such limited discretion is exercised with "uniformity of method of treatment upon the facts of each application, free from improper or inappropriate considerations and from unfair discrimination" . . . [and with] a "systematic, consistent and just order of treatment, with reference to the convenience of public use of the highways. . . ."

But here it is clear that the practice in Baton Rouge allowing unfettered discretion in local officials in the regulation of the use of the streets for peaceful parades and meetings is an unwarranted abridgment of appellant's freedom of speech and assembly secured to him by the First Amendment, as applied to the States by the Fourteenth Amendment. It follows, therefore, that appellant's conviction for violating the statute as so applied and enforced must be reversed.

Other Cases: Freedom of Assembly/Speech

Wood v. Moss, et al. 572 U.S. ___ (2014).

SUMMARY: While on the campaign trail for re-election, George W. Bush stopped over in Jacksonville, Oregon. Law enforcement officers permitted a group of Bush supporters and protestors to assemble on opposite sides of the street along the motorcade route. President Bush made a last-minute change of plans to have dinner at the Jacksonville Inn, which prompted the Secret Service agents to move the protestors to an area two blocks away

The protesters sued the agents, alleging that the agents engaged in viewpoint discrimination in violation of the First Amendment when they moved the protesters away from the Inn but allowed the supporters to remain in their original location. The agents moved to dismiss the suit which the District Court denied. The agents filed an interlocutory appeal to the Ninth Circuit Court of Appeals which reversed. holding that protesters had failed to state a First Amendment claim.

The Court held that the government officials were entitled to qualified immunity.

OPINION (official):

Government officials may not exclude from public places persons engaged in peaceful expressive activity solely because the government actor fears, dislikes, or disagrees with the views expressed. ... The fundamental right to speak, however, does not leave people at liberty to publicize their views " 'whenever and however and wherever they please.' "

The doctrine of qualified immunity protects government officials from liability for civil damages "unless a plaintiff pleads facts showing (1) that the official violated a statutory or constitutional right, and (2) that the right was 'clearly established' at the time of the challenged conduct." ... The "dispositive inquiry . . . is whether it would [have been] clear to a reasonable officer" in the agents' position "that [their] conduct was unlawful in the situation [they] confronted." ... This Court has recognized the overwhelming importance of safeguarding the President. ...Mindful that officers may be faced with unanticipated security situations, the key question addressed is whether it should have been clear to the agents that the security perimeter they established violated the First Amendment.

(b) The protesters assert, and the Ninth Circuit agreed, that the agents violated clearly established federal law by denying them "equal access to the President." No decision of which the Court is aware, however, would alert Secret Service agents engaged in crowd control that they bear a First Amendment obligation to make sure that groups with conflicting views are at all times in equivalent positions. Nor would the maintenance of equal access make sense in the situation the agents here confronted, where only the protesters, not the supporters, had a direct line of sight to the patio where the President was dining. The protesters suggest that the agents could have moved the supporters out of the motorcade's range as well, but there would have been no security rationale for such a move.

(c) . . . A White House manual directs the President's advance team to "work with the Secret Service ... to designate a protest area ... preferably not in view of the event site or motorcade route." The manual guides the conduct of the political advance team, not the Secret Service, whose own written guides explicitly prohibit "agents from discriminating between anti-government and pro-government demonstrators." Even assuming, as the protesters maintain, that other agents, at other times and places, have assisted in shielding the President from political speech, this case is scarcely one in which the agents lacked a valid security reason for their actions.

THE OVERBREADTH (DUE PROCESS) DOCTRINE[46]

One court-created doctrine that defendants raise that is closely related to, and often involves, the First Amendment is the doctrine of "overbreadth." The Court first discussed the overbreadth doctrine in *Thornhill v. Alabama*, 310 U.S. 88 (1940) determining that courts should strike down criminal laws that are written so broadly that they infringe on a person's constitutionally protected right. A law is overbroad when it prohibits what the constitution protects.

Frequently speech is impermissibly prohibited by an overly broad statute. "The overbreadth doctrine encourages legislatures consider free speech issues when drafting legislation because these statutes will be especially vulnerable to constitutional challenges. The threat of a court invalidating a statute as overbroad incentivizes the legislatures to narrowly tailor their statutes." *Thornhill, at 90.* In *Coates (see, below)* in addition to finding the statute too vague--the Court found that the ordinance was overly broad because it criminalized speech and assembly that are protected by the First Amendment. The cases of *R. A.V.* and *Mitchell (*above, and discussed in *People v. Rokicki)* also

---

[46] You have already read a bit about overbreadth challenges in the cases of *Cox v. Louisiana* (above) and *People v. Rokicki* (above).

addressed the primary concern of the overbreadth doctrine and the chilling effect that their relevant statutes had on people's behavior. If a statute seems to prohibit what is protected (speech), then individuals will refrain from engaging in that type of speech, even though the Constitution considers it a fundamental right.

Because statutes that are overbroad have a "chilling effect" on people's behavior, they may be challenged even by persons not charged with violating the law. Generally, the law requires a person have "standing" -- that is, a specific personal interest in the outcome of the case -- before he or she can challenge a statute. However, "[t]he overbreadth doctrine creates a distinct exception to the standing requirement, and, in effect, allows any litigant willing to challenge an allegedly overbroad statute to bring suit."[47],

When applying the overbreadth doctrine, a court considers the constitutionality of a statute on its face rather than how it is applied under the facts of the case before it. However, even if the Court finds a statute to be overbroad, it will not necessarily declare the statute "void for overbreadth." For example, the Court refused to strike down a child pornography statute that defendant argued was overbroad in *New York v. Ferber,* 458 U.S. 747 (1982), finding that although the statute might possibly be applied to punish constitutionally protected artistic expression, a statute should not be invalidated for overbreadth if its legitimate reach "dwarfs its arguably impermissible applications." Fifteen years later, however, the Court struck down the Communications Decency Act of 1996 in *Reno v. American Civil Liberties Union,* 521 U.S. 844 (1997), finding that Congress had attempted to ban "indecent" as well as "obscene" speech from the Internet and thus swept within its ambit constitutionally protected speech as well as obscenity.[48]

Courts will analyze a statute to see which phrases or clauses make it potentially overbroad and then, to the extent possible, will narrow that statute without necessarily declaring it void. The following case involves the defendant challenging an ordinance as overbroad.

HOUSTON v. HILL,
482 U.S. 451 (1987)

SUMMARY:

Hill shouted at police in an attempt to divert their attention from his friend during a confrontation. Hill was arrested for "willfully . . . interrupt[ing] a city policeman . . . by verbal challenge during an investigation" in violation of a municipal ordinance making it unlawful for any person "to assault, strike or in any manner oppose, molest, abuse or interrupt any policeman in the execution of his duty." He was acquittal in Municipal Court, but still brought suit in Federal District Court challenging the ordinance's constitutionality. The District Court held that the ordinance was not unconstitutionally vague or overbroad on

---

[47] Christopher Pierce, The "Strong Medicine" of the Overbreadth Doctrine: When Statutory Exceptions Are No More than a Placebo, 64 (1) Fed. Comm. L.J. at 182.

[48] In response to this decision, Congress passed the Child Online Protection Act in 1998, but it never took effect due to a series of permanent injunctions granted by the Third Circuit Court of Appeals. In Ashcroft v. Free Speech Coalition, 535 U.S. 234 (2002), the U.S. Supreme Court struck down the federal child pornography law because it intruded on free speech rights. In 2004, the Supreme Court once again faced this issue (see, *Ashcroft v. American Civil Liberties Union,* 542 U.S. 656 (2004)). The Court upheld the injunction granted by the lower court stopping the implementation of COPA. The Court stated,

> "Content-based prohibitions, enforced by severe criminal penalties, have the constant potential to be a repressive force in the lives and thoughts of a free people. To guard against that threat the Constitution demands that content-based restrictions on speech be presumed invalid, *R.A.V. v. St. Paul* and that the Government bear the burden of showing their constitutionality. *United States v. Playboy Entertainment Group, Inc..* This is true even when Congress twice has attempted to find a constitutional means to restrict, and punish, the speech in question."

its face, but the Court of Appeals reversed, finding that the ordinance was substantially overbroad, since its literal wording punished and might deter a significant range of protected speech.

SYLLABUS OF THE OPINION (official)[49]

A municipal ordinance that makes it unlawful to interrupt a police officer in the performance of his duty is substantially overbroad, and therefore invalid on its face under the First Amendment. The ordinance in question criminalizes a substantial amount of, and is susceptible of regular application to, constitutionally protected speech, and accords the police unconstitutional enforcement discretion, as is demonstrated by evidence indicating that, although the ordinance's plain language is violated scores of times daily, only those individuals chosen by police in their unguided discretion are arrested. Appellant's [the city of Houston's] argument that the ordinance is not substantially overbroad because it does not inhibit the exposition of ideas, but simply bans unprotected "core criminal conduct," is not persuasive. Since the ordinance's language making it unlawful to "assault" or "strike" a police officer is expressly preempted by the State Penal Code, its enforceable portion prohibits verbal interruptions of police, and thereby deals with speech, rather than with core criminal conduct. Moreover, although speech might be prohibited if it consists of "fighting words" that by their very utterance inflict injury or tend to incite an immediate breach of the peace, the ordinance in question is not limited to such expressions, but broadly applies to speech that "in any manner . . . interrupt[s] any policeman," and thereby impermissibly infringes the constitutionally protected freedom of individuals verbally to oppose or challenge police action. Appellant's contention that the ordinance's sweeping nature is both inevitable and essential to maintain public order is also without merit, since the ordinance is not narrowly tailored to prohibit only disorderly conduct or fighting words, but impermissibly provides police with unfettered discretion to arrest individuals for words or conduct that are simply annoying or offensive.

2. [The Court struck down the statute, declaring it void rather than limiting or narrowing the statute or sending it back to the state for it to limit/narrow the statute stating,]

. . .Even if this case did not involve a First Amendment facial challenge, . . . the ordinance in question is plain and unambiguous, and thus is not susceptible to a limiting construction. Moreover, it cannot be limited by severing discrete unconstitutional subsections, since its enforceable portion is unconstitutional in its entirety.

3. Although the preservation of liberty depends in part upon the maintenance of social order, the First Amendment requires that officers and municipalities respond with restraint in the face of verbal challenges to police action, since a certain amount of expressive disorder is inevitable in a society committed to individual freedom, and must be protected if that freedom would survive.

. . .

Other Cases: Void for Overbreadth

Cox v. Louisiana

FACTS: see above

There is an additional reason why this [Cox's] conviction cannot be sustained. The statute at issue in this case, as authoritatively interpreted by the Louisiana Supreme Court, is unconstitutionally vague in its overly broad scope. The statutory crime consists of two elements: (1) congregating with others "with intent to provoke a breach of the peace, or under circumstances such that a breach of the peace may be occasioned," and (2) a refusal to move on after having been ordered to do so by a

---

[49] (See, www.oyez.org/cases/1986/86-243).

law enforcement officer. While the second part of this offense is narrow and specific, the first element is not. The Louisiana Supreme Court in this case defined the term "breach of the peace" as "to agitate, to arouse from a state of repose, to molest, to interrupt, to hinder, to disquiet."

…

[T]he conviction under this statute must be reversed, as the statute is unconstitutional in that it sweeps within its broad scope activities that are constitutionally protected free speech and assembly. Maintenance of the opportunity for free political discussion is a basic tenet of our constitutional democracy. As Chief Justice Hughes stated in Stromberg v. California, 283 U.S. 359, 369:

> A statute which, upon its face and as authoritatively construed, is so vague and indefinite as to permit the punishment of the fair use of this opportunity is repugnant to the guaranty of liberty contained in the Fourteenth Amendment.

THE VOID-FOR-VAGUENESS DOCTRINE

No specific constitutional provision bans overly vague laws. Instead, the Due Process Clauses of the Fifth and Fourteenth Amendments require clarity in criminal statutes. Due process requires that individuals receive notice of criminal conduct, and vaguely written laws don't provide that notice. If the government writes a law that is vague, then individuals may have to guess at whether their behavior is allowed or prohibited. The Court has repeatedly struck down laws that are so vague that a person of ordinary intelligence could not reasonably understand them or determine when they applied. The Court has also struck down laws that give excessive discretion to law enforcement officials to decide who can be arrested or prosecuted. When dealing with statutes that may be too vague, the Court will sometimes throw the statute a lifeline by upholding them if, through judicial interpretation, they can be construed with sufficient specificity. Police, prosecutors, judges, and jurors must also have a reasonably clear statement of what is prohibited behavior. Requiring laws not be vague ensures the uniform and nondiscriminatory enforcement of law.

Generally, the court presumes laws are constitutional (they are not vague, or overbroad, or retroactive, etc.), and the burden of proving otherwise falls on the defendant. In the context of claiming void-for-vagueness, the defendant,

> "[M]ust show that upon examining the statute, an individual of ordinary intelligence would not understand what he is required to do under the law. Thus, to escape responsibility . . . [the defendant] must prove that he could not reasonably understand that . . . [the law in question] prohibited the acts in which he is engaged. … The party alleging that a statute is unconstitutional must prove this assertion beyond a reasonable doubt. "State v. Anderson, 566 N.E. 2d 1224 (Ohio, 1991).

The following cases involve the courts determining whether a substantive law violates the requirement that laws not be too vague. As you read these cases note whether the court was primarily focused on the due process concern of giving citizens notice or the concern of discriminatory enforcement of the law.

STATE v. METZGER,
319 N.W. 2d 459 (Neb. 1982)

KRIVOSHA delivered the opinion of the court.

Metzger lived in a garden-level apartment located in Lincoln, Nebraska. A large window in the apartment faces a parking lot which is situated on the north side of the apartment building. At about 7:45 a. m. on April 30, 1981, another resident of the apartment, while parking his automobile in a space directly in front of Metzger's apartment window, observed Metzger standing naked with his arms at his sides in his apartment window for a period of 5 seconds. The resident testified that he saw Metzger's body from his thighs on up.

The resident called the police department and two officers arrived at the apartment at about 8 a. m. The officers testified that they observed Metzger standing in front of the window eating a bowl of cereal. They testified that Metzger was standing within a foot of the window and his nude body, from the mid-thigh on up, was visible.

The pertinent portion of § 9.52.100 of the Lincoln Municipal Code, under which Metzger was charged, provides as follows:

> It shall be unlawful for any person within the City of Lincoln ... to commit any indecent, immodest or filthy act in the presence of any person, or in such a situation that persons passing might ordinarily see the same.

…The…issue presented to us by this appeal is whether the ordinance, as drafted, is so vague as to be unconstitutional. We believe that it is. There is no argument that a violation of the municipal ordinance in question is a criminal act. Since the ordinance in question is criminal in nature, it is a fundamental requirement of due process of law that such criminal ordinance be reasonably clear and definite….

A criminal statute cannot rest upon an uncertain foundation. The crime and the elements constituting it must be so clearly expressed that the ordinary person can intelligently choose in advance what course it is lawful for him to pursue. Penal statutes prohibiting the doing of certain things and providing a punishment for their violation should not admit of such a double meaning that the citizen may act upon one conception of its requirements and the courts upon another. A statute which forbids the doing of an act in terms so vague that men of common intelligence must necessarily guess as to its meaning and differ as to its application violates the first essential elements of due process of law. It is not permissible to enact a law which in effect spreads an all-inclusive net for the feet of everybody upon the chance that, while the innocent will surely be entangled in its meshes, some wrongdoers may also be caught….

Several other jurisdictions which have viewed ordinances with the same general intent in mind have reached similar conclusions. In the case of *State v. Sanders*, 245 S.E.2d 397 (1978), the South Carolina Court of Appeals was presented with a statute making it a misdemeanor for members of the opposite sex to occupy the same bedroom at a hotel for "any immoral purpose." In finding the ordinance too vague and indefinite to comply with constitutional due process standards, the court said:

> A criminal statute or ordinance must be sufficiently definite to inform citizens of common intelligence of the particular acts which are forbidden. [The statute] fails to define with sufficient precision exactly what the term "any immoral purpose" may encompass. The word *immoral* is not equivalent to the word *illegal*; hence, enforcement of [the statute] may involve legal acts which, nevertheless, are immoral in the view of many citizens. One must necessarily speculate, therefore, as to what acts are immoral. If the legislative intent of [the statute] is to proscribe illicit sexual intercourse the statute could have specifically so provided.

…The ordinance . . . makes it unlawful for anyone to commit any 'indecent, immodest or filthy act.' We know of no way in which the standards required of a criminal act can be met in those broad, general terms. . . . The dividing line between what is lawful and what is unlawful in terms of 'indecent,' 'immodest,' or 'filthy' is simply too broad to satisfy the constitutional requirements of due process. Both lawful and unlawful acts can be embraced within such broad definitions. That cannot be permitted. One is not able to determine in advance what is lawful and what is unlawful.

We do not attempt . . . to determine whether Metzger's actions in a particular case might not be made unlawful, nor do we intend to encourage such behavior. Indeed, it may be possible that a governmental subdivision using sufficiently definite language could make such an act as committed by Metzger unlawful. We simply do not decide that question at this time

because of our determination that the ordinance in question is so vague as to be unconstitutional.

We therefore believe. . . [that the ordinance] . . . must be declared invalid. Because the ordinance is therefore declared invalid, the conviction cannot stand.

CITY OF CHICAGO v. MORALES et al., 527 U.S. 41(1999)

In 1992, the Chicago City Council enacted the Gang Congregation Ordinance, which prohibits "criminal street gang members" from "loitering" with one another or with other persons in any public place. The question presented is whether the Supreme Court of Illinois correctly held that the ordinance violates the Due Process Clause of the Fourteenth Amendment to the Federal Constitution.

I

Before the ordinance was adopted, the city council's Committee on Police and Fire conducted hearings to explore the problems created by the city's street gangs, and more particularly, the consequences of public loitering by gang members. Witnesses included residents of the neighborhoods where gang members are most active, as well as some of the aldermen who represent those areas. Based on that evidence, the council made a series of findings that are included in the text of the ordinance and explain the reasons for its enactment.

The council found that a continuing increase in criminal street gang activity was largely responsible for the city's rising murder rate, as well as an escalation of violent and drug related crimes. It noted that in many neighborhoods throughout the city, "the burgeoning presence of street gang members in public places has intimidated many law abiding citizens." Furthermore, the council stated that gang members "establish control over identifiable areas ... by loitering in those areas and intimidating others from entering

those areas; and . . . [m]embers of criminal street gangs avoid arrest by committing no offense punishable under existing laws when they know the police are present . . . ." It further found that "loitering in public places by criminal street gang members creates a justifiable fear for the safety of persons and property in the area" and that "[a]ggressive action is necessary to preserve the city's streets and other public places so that the public may use such places without fear." Moreover, the council concluded that the city "has an interest in discouraging all persons from loitering in public places with criminal gang members."

The ordinance creates a criminal offense punishable by a fine of up to $500, imprisonment for not more than six months, and a requirement to perform up to 120 hours of community service. Commission of the offense involves four predicates. First, the police officer must reasonably believe that at least one of the two or more persons present in a "public place" is a "criminal street gang membe[r]." Second, the persons must be "loitering," which the ordinance defines as "remain[ing] in any one place with no apparent purpose." Third, the officer must then order "all" of the persons to disperse and remove themselves "from the area." Fourth, a person must disobey the officer's order. If any person, whether a gang member or not, disobeys the officer's order, that person is guilty of violating the ordinance.

Two months after the ordinance was adopted, the Chicago Police Department promulgated General Order 92-4 to provide guidelines to govern its enforcement. That order purported to establish limitations on the enforcement discretion of police officers "to ensure that the anti-gang loitering ordinance is not enforced in an arbitrary or discriminatory way." The limitations confine the authority to arrest gang members who violate the ordinance to sworn "members of the Gang Crime Section" and certain other designated officers, and establish detailed criteria for defining street gangs and membership in such gangs. In addition, the order directs district commanders to "designate areas in which the presence of gang members has a demonstrable effect on the activities of law abiding persons in the surrounding community," and provides that the ordinance "will be enforced only within the designated areas. The city, however, does not release the locations of these "designated areas" to the public.

II

During the three years of its enforcement, the police issued over 89,000 dispersal orders and arrested over 42,000 people for violating the ordinance. In the ensuing enforcement proceedings, two trial judges upheld the constitutionality of the ordinance, but eleven others ruled that it was invalid. In respondent Youkhana's case, the trial judge held that the "ordinance fails to notify individuals what conduct is prohibited, and it encourages arbitrary and capricious enforcement by police."

The Illinois Appellate Court affirmed the trial court's ruling . . . persuaded that the ordinance impaired the freedom of assembly of non-gang members in violation of the First Amendment to the Federal Constitution and Article I of the Illinois Constitution, that it was unconstitutionally vague, that it improperly criminalized status rather than conduct, and that it jeopardized rights guaranteed under the Fourth Amendment.

The Illinois Supreme Court affirmed. It held "that the gang loitering ordinance violates due process of law in that it is impermissibly vague on its face and an arbitrary restriction on personal liberties." The court did not reach

the contentions that the ordinance "creates a status offense, permits arrests without probable cause or is overbroad."

In support of its vagueness holding, the court pointed out that the definition of "loitering" in the ordinance drew no distinction between innocent conduct and conduct calculated to cause harm. "Moreover, the definition of 'loiter' provided by the ordinance does not assist in clearly articulating the proscriptions of the ordinance." Furthermore, it concluded that the ordinance was "not reasonably susceptible to a limiting construction which would affirm its validity."

We granted certiorari and now affirm. Like the Illinois Supreme Court, we conclude that the ordinance enacted by the city of Chicago is unconstitutionally vague.

(Official summaries)

JUSTICE STEVENS concluded that the ordinance's broad sweep violates the requirement that a legislature establish minimal guidelines to govern law enforcement. *Kolender v. Lawson.*

The ordinance encompasses a great deal of harmless behavior: In any public place in Chicago, persons in the company of a gang member "shall" be ordered to disperse if their purpose is not apparent to an officer. Moreover, the Illinois Supreme Court interprets the ordinance's loitering definition-- "to remain in any one place with no apparent purpose"--as giving officers absolute discretion to determine what activities constitute loitering. This Court has no authority to construe the language of a state statute more narrowly than the State's highest court. The three features of the ordinance that, the city argues, limit the officer's discretion-- (1) it does not permit issuance of a dispersal order to anyone who is moving along or who has an apparent purpose; (2) it does not permit an arrest if individuals obey a dispersal order; and (3) no order can issue unless the officer reasonably believes that one of the loiterers is a gang member--are insufficient. Finally, the Illinois Supreme Court is correct that General

Order 92-4 is not a sufficient limitation on police discretion.

JUSTICE STEVENS, joined by JUSTICE SOUTER and JUSTICE GINSBURG, concluded:

1. It was not improper for the state courts to conclude that the ordinance, which covers a significant amount of activity in addition to the intimidating conduct that is its factual predicate, is invalid on its face. An enactment may be attacked on its face as impermissibly vague if, inter alia, it fails to establish standards for the police and public that are sufficient to guard against the arbitrary deprivation of liberty. The freedom to loiter for innocent purposes is part of such "liberty." The ordinance's vagueness makes a facial challenge appropriate. This is not an enactment that simply regulates business behavior and contains a scienter requirement. It is a criminal law that contains no mens rea requirement, and infringes on constitutionally protected rights.

2. Because the ordinance fails to give the ordinary citizen adequate notice of what is forbidden and what is permitted, it is impermissibly vague. See, e.g., *Coates v. Cincinnati*. The term "loiter" may have a common and accepted meaning, but the ordinance's definition of that term--"to remain in any one place with no apparent purpose"-- does not. It is difficult to imagine how any Chicagoan standing in a public place with a group of people would know if he or she had an "apparent purpose." This vagueness about what loitering is covered and what is not dooms the ordinance. The city's principal response to the adequate notice concern--that loiterers are not subject to criminal sanction until after they have disobeyed a dispersal order--is unpersuasive for at least two reasons. First, the fair notice requirement's purpose is to enable the ordinary citizen to conform his or her conduct to the law. See *Lanzetta v. New Jersey*. A dispersal order, which is issued only after prohibited conduct has occurred, cannot retroactively provide adequate notice of the boundary between the permissible and the impermissible applications of the ordinance.

Second, the dispersal order's terms compound the inadequacy of the notice afforded by the ordinance, which vaguely requires that the officer "order all such persons to disperse and remove themselves from the area," and thereby raises a host of questions as to the duration and distinguishing features of the loiterers' separation.

JUSTICE O'CONNOR, joined by JUSTICE BREYER, concluded that, as construed by the Illinois Supreme Court, the Chicago ordinance is unconstitutionally vague because it lacks sufficient minimal standards to guide law enforcement officers; in particular, it fails to provide any standard by which police can judge whether an individual has an "apparent purpose." This vagueness alone provides a sufficient ground for affirming the judgment below, and there is no need to consider the other issues briefed by the parties and addressed by the plurality. It is important to courts and legislatures alike to characterize more clearly the narrow scope of the Court's holding. Chicago still has reasonable alternatives to combat the very real threat posed by gang intimidation and violence, including, e.g., adoption of laws that directly prohibit the congregation of gang members to intimidate residents, or the enforcement of existing laws with that effect. Moreover, the ordinance could have been construed more narrowly to avoid the vagueness problem, by, e.g., adopting limitations that restrict the ordinance's criminal penalties to gang members or interpreting the term "apparent purpose" narrowly and in light of the Chicago City Council's findings. This Court, however, cannot impose a limiting construction that a state supreme court has declined to adopt. See, e.g., *Kolender v. Lawson*. The Illinois Supreme Court misapplied this Court's precedents, particularly *Papachristou v. City of Jacksonville*, to the extent it read them as requiring it to hold the ordinance vague in all of its applications.

JUSTICE KENNEDY concluded that, as interpreted by the Illinois Supreme Court, the Chicago ordinance unconstitutionally reaches a broad range of innocent conduct, and, therefore, is not necessarily saved by the requirement that the citizen disobey a dispersal order before there is a violation. Although it can be assumed that disobeying some police commands will subject a citizen to prosecution whether or not the citizen knows why the order is given, it does not follow that any unexplained police order must be obeyed without notice of its lawfulness. The predicate of a dispersal order is not sufficient to eliminate doubts regarding the adequacy of notice under this ordinance. A citizen, while engaging in a wide array of innocent conduct, is not likely to know when he may be subject to such an order based on the officer's own knowledge of the identity or affiliations of other persons with whom the citizen is congregating; nor may the citizen be able to assess what an officer might conceive to be the citizen's lack of an apparent purpose.

JUSTICE BREYER concluded that the ordinance violates the Constitution because it delegates too much discretion to the police, and it is not saved by its limitations requiring that the police reasonably believe that the person ordered to disperse (or someone accompanying him) is a gang member, and that he remain in the public place "with no apparent purpose." Nor does it violate this Court's usual rules governing facial challenges to forbid the city to apply the unconstitutional ordinance in this case. There is no way to distinguish in the ordinance's terms between one application of unlimited police discretion and another. It is unconstitutional, not because a policeman applied his discretion wisely or poorly in a particular case, but rather because the policeman enjoys too much discretion in every case. And if every application of the ordinance represents an exercise of unlimited discretion, then the ordinance is invalid in all its applications. See *Lanzetta v. New Jersey*. Contrary to Justice Scalia 's suggestion, the ordinance does not escape facial invalidation simply because it may provide fair warning to some individual defendants that it prohibits the conduct in which they are engaged. This ordinance is unconstitutional, not because it provides insufficient notice, but because it

does not provide sufficient minimal standards to guide the police. See Coates v. Cincinnati.

JUSTICE SCALIA, dissenting.

The citizens of Chicago were once free to drive about the city at whatever speed they wished. At some point Chicagoans (or perhaps Illinoisans) decided this would not do, and imposed prophylactic speed limits designed to assure safe operation by the average (or perhaps even subaverage) driver with the average (or perhaps even subaverage) vehicle. This infringed upon the "freedom" of all citizens, but was not unconstitutional.

Similarly, the citizens of Chicago were once free to stand around and gawk at the scene of an accident. At some point Chicagoans discovered that this obstructed traffic and caused more accidents. They did not make the practice unlawful, but they did authorize police officers to order the crowd to disperse, and imposed penalties for refusal to obey such an order. Again, this prophylactic measure infringed upon the "freedom" of all citizens, but was not unconstitutional.

Until the ordinance that is before us today was adopted, the citizens of Chicago were free to stand about in public places with no apparent purpose--to engage, that is, in conduct that appeared to be loitering. In recent years, however, the city has been afflicted with criminal street gangs. As reflected in the record before us, these gangs congregated in public places to deal in drugs, and to terrorize the neighborhoods by demonstrating control over their "turf." Many residents of the inner city felt that they were prisoners in their own homes. Once again, Chicagoans decided that to eliminate the problem it was worth restricting some of the freedom that they once enjoyed. The means they took was similar to the second, and more mild, example given above rather than the first: Loitering was not made unlawful, but when a group of people occupied a public place without an apparent purpose and in the company of a known gang member, police officers were authorized to order them to disperse, and the failure to obey such an order was made unlawful. See

Chicago Municipal Code §8-4-015 (1992). The minor limitation upon the free state of nature that this prophylactic arrangement imposed upon all Chicagoans seemed to them (and it seems to me) a small price to pay for liberation of their streets.

The majority today invalidates this perfectly reasonable measure by ignoring our rules governing facial challenges, by elevating loitering to a constitutionally guaranteed right, and by discerning vagueness where, according to our usual standards, none exists.

. . .

The fact is that the present ordinance is entirely clear in its application, cannot be violated except with full knowledge and intent, and vests no more discretion in the police than innumerable other measures authorizing police orders to preserve the public peace and safety. As suggested by their tortured analyses, and by their suggested solutions that bear no relation to the identified constitutional problem, the majority's real quarrel with the Chicago Ordinance is simply that it permits (or indeed requires) too much harmless conduct by innocent citizens to be proscribed. . . .

But in our democratic system, how much harmless conduct to proscribe is not a judgment to be made by the courts. So long as constitutionally guaranteed rights are not affected, and so long as the proscription has a rational basis, all sorts of perfectly harmless activity by millions of perfectly innocent people can be forbidden--riding a motorcycle without a safety helmet, for example, starting a campfire in a national forest, or selling a safe and effective drug not yet approved by the FDA. All of these acts are entirely innocent and harmless in themselves, but because of the risk of harm that they entail, the freedom to engage in them has been abridged. The citizens of Chicago have decided that depriving themselves of the freedom to "hang out" with a gang member is necessary to eliminate pervasive gang crime and intimidation--and that the elimination of the one is worth the deprivation of the other. This Court has no business second-guessing either the degree of necessity or the fairness of the trade.

Other Cases: Void for Vagueness

Johnson v. United States, 135 S.Ct. 2551 (2015)

SUMMARY: Defendant was convicted of being a felon in possession of a firearm. Prosecution sought to increase his sentence under the act based on prior firearm possession convictions. Court concluded that the residual clause of the Career Armed Criminal Act, 18 U.S.C. 924 was so unclear and uncertain that it was unconstitutionally vague. Court found that the clause failed to give any guidance on what degree of potential risk was enough to make the act applicable in a given case.

Coates v. Cincinnati, 402 U.S. 611 (1971)

SUMMARY: Defendant was convicted of violating an ordinance that made it illegal for three or more people gathered on a sidewalk to "annoy" passersby. Court held that because what annoys one person may not annoy the other, "the ordinance was vague . . . in the sense that no conduct is specified at all. "

Papachristou v. City of Jacksonville, 405 U.S. 156 (1972)

SUMMARY: Defendant was convicted of violating an ordinance that made being a "vagrant" a crime and defining vagrants as "rogues and vagabonds" "dissolute persons," or "common night walkers." In this landmark decision, the Court struck down a Jacksonville, Florida ordinance that prohibited various forms of vagrancy, including loitering and "prowling by auto." Court held the ordinance was unconstitutional because it did not give fair notice of prohibited conduct. Justice Douglas objected to the unfettered discretion the ordinance placed in the hands of the police, saying it allowed for "arbitrary and discriminatory enforcement of the law."

SUMMARY: The Court struck down a statute criminalizing any person who "loiters or wanders upon the streets or from place to place without apparent reason or business and who refuses to identify himself and to account for his presence when requested to do so."

"As presently drafted and as construed by the state courts, [the statute] contains no standard for determining what a suspect has to do in order to satisfy the requirement to provide a "credible and reliable" identification. As such, the statute vests virtually complete discretion in the hands of police to determine whether the suspect has satisfied the statute and must be permitted to go on his way in the absence of probable cause to arrest. An individual, whom police may think is suspicious, but do not have probable cause to believe has committed a crime, is entitled to walk the public streets 'only at the whim of any police officer' who happens to stop that individual under [the statute]."

See also, ***Warren v. State***, 572 So.2d 1376 (Fl. S. Ct., 1991)(Statute making it a crime to keep a "house of ill fame" was unconstitutionally vague); ***State v. Lara***, 853 P.2d 1168 (Kan. Ct. App., 1993) (Statute making criminal "excessive and unusual" motor vehicle noises held not void for vagueness); ***State v. Bohannon***, 814 P.2d 694 (Wash. Ct. App, 1991)(Statute making it a crime for causing a minor to engage in "sexually explicit conduct" held not void for vagueness); ***United States v. White***, 882 F.2d. 250, 252 (7th Circuit, 1989)(The "vagueness doctrine" is "designed more to limit the discretion of police and prosecutors than to ensure that statutes are intelligible to persons pondering criminal activity.")

RIGHT TO BEAR ARMS

The poorly-drafted Second Amendment to the U.S. Constitution states, "A well regulated Militia, being necessary to the security of a free state, the right of the people to keep and bear arms shall not be infringed." There are thousands of local, state, and federal prohibitions against the sale, possession, and use of certain firearms and ammunition. Arguably, these laws seem to conflict with the Second Amendment's "right to keep and bear arms." Thus, Courts and commentators have been left debating its reach and application to modern circumstances.

In *United States v. Miller,* 307 U.S. 174 (1939), the Court upheld a federal law criminalizing the interstate shipment of sawed-off shotguns. The Court held the phrase "to keep and bear arms shall not be infringed" needed to be interpreted in context with the phrase "a well-regulated militia." Since possession of sawed-off shotguns had no reasonable relationship to serving the militia, the statute (regulating shotguns) was not unconstitutional. In 1980 the Court reaffirmed this reasoning in *Lewis v. United States*, 445 U.S. 55, 58 (1980) stating, "The Second Amendment guarantees no right to keep and bear a firearm that does not have some reasonable relationship to the preservation of efficiency of a well-regulated militia."

In *District of Columbia v. Heller*, 554 U.S. 570 (2008), however, the Court declared the right to keep and bear arms was a personal right tied to a natural right of self-defense that had nothing to do with being part of a militia. Washington, D.C. had enacted an ordinance that created a complete ban on handguns and required that any weapons kept at home must be unloaded and non-functional. Heller, a special police officer in D.C., was authorized to carry a handgun at his job at the Federal Judicial Center. He applied to register his personal gun, but the government refused. He sued to enjoin the District of Columbia from enforcing the ordinance, arguing that he (and others) had a constitutional right to possess a weapon in his home for his personal safety. The Court did not define the scope of the right to keep and bear arms, nor did it indicate whether the Second Amendment was applicable to the states through the Fourteenth Amendment, but it did hold that the D.C. ordinance was too restrictive, nevertheless noting that the right to bear arms was subject to reasonable government regulations.

In Chicago, gun owners challenged Chicago ordinances which were virtually identical to the ordinance in *Heller*. They asked the Court to hold that the Second Amendment applied to the states through the Fourteenth Amendment. In a five-four decision, the U.S. Supreme Court held that an individual's right to keep and bear arms is was applicable to the states and incorporated through the 14th Amendment's Due Process Clause. Writing for the majority in *McDonald v. City of Chicago*, Justice Alito observed: "It is clear that the Framers and ratifiers of the Fourteenth Amendment counted the right to keep and bear arms among those fundamental rights necessary to our system of ordered liberty. ... The Fourteenth Amendment makes the Second Amendment right to keep and bear arms fully applicable to the States." Although not ruling on the constitutionality of this gun ban, the Court made it clear that such restrictive bans are unconstitutional. The *McDonald* Court reaffirmed what it said in Heller -- the Second Amendment only protects a right to possess a firearm in the home for lawful uses such as self-defense and stressed that some firearm regulation is constitutionally permissible and the Second Amendment right to possess firearms is not unlimited. The Second Amendment does not guarantee a right to possess any firearm, anywhere, and for any purpose. The dissent argued that the right to own guns was not "fundamental" and therefore states and localities should be free to regulate, or even ban, them. Dissenting justices maintained that *Heller* was incorrectly decided, and--even if correct--they would not have extended its applicability to states.

As of June 23, 2022, the Court has changed its mind. In *New York State Rifle & Pistol Association, Inc. v. Bruen*, ___ U.S. ___ (2022) the court held that individuals have a right to possess a handgun outside their home for personal protection and the 1913 New York law prohibiting this was inconsistent with the Second Amendment.[50] This decision prompted the Court to instruct lower courts to reconsider their holdings and throw out several other gun restrictions in light of this opinion. One commentator indicated that the *Bruen* decision "created confusion about which firearms restrictions were constitutional."[51] New York (and other states) passed legislation in response to *Bruen* restricting possession of concealed firearms. New York's new law was immediately challenged, and on January 11, 2023 the U.S. Supreme Court (without ruling on the merits of the challenges or law) in an unsigned emergency order allowed those restrictions to remain in effect while the legal challenges are pending.[52]

Other Cases: Right to Bear Arms

Moore v. Madigan, 708 F.3d 901 (2013) (7th Cir),	*Young v. State, 896 F.3d 1044 (9th Cir.2018)*
SUMMARY: The Court of Appeals found unconstitutional a flat ban by Illinois statute on carrying a loaded firearm within accessible reach outside the home. The law allowed exceptions by police officers, security personnel, hunters and members of target shooting clubs. The Court, found that although the need for self-defense noted in *Heller* and *McDonald* was most acute inside a home, this did not mean that it was not acute outside the home.	SUMMARY: The Ninth Circuit Court of Appeals struck down Hawaii's "place to keep" statutes which required that gun owners keep their firearms at the place of business, residence, or sojourn. Individuals could petition chief of police for license for concealed carry based on reason to fear injury to person or property and could obtain open license carry permit based on urgency or need to protect. 2-1 majority found that under the statute, law-abiding citizens in Hawaii were foreclosed from exercising the core Second Amendment right to bear arms in self-defense.

---

[50] https://www.reuters.com/world/us/us-supreme-court-orders-lower-courts-reconsider-gun-law-challenges-2022-06-30/
[51] https://abcnews.go.com/US/supreme-court-decision-creates-confusion-firearm-restrictions-constitutional/story?id=96364133
[52] https://www.cnn.com/2023/01/11/politics/supreme-court-new-york-gun-law/index.html; https://www.nytimes.com/2023/01/11/us/new-york-gun-law-supreme-court.html;

THE RIGHT TO PRIVACY

The Constitution also limits government's ability to pass laws that violate a person's right to privacy. If you were to scour the Constitution you would not find the words "right to privacy," but the Court has held that the right to privacy is inherent in several of the Amendments and thus falls in the "penumbra" of the Constitution. Having the right to privacy has been equated to being free from governmental intrusion over certain areas of one's life.

The right to privacy is a fundamental right. As such, courts employ strict scrutiny over statutes that would limit a person's right to be free from governmental intrusion in a private matter. Even employing strict scrutiny, sometimes the government can enact laws (such as laws that criminalize the possession of child pornography) which pass constitutional muster. The test of whether a statute passes a strict scrutiny exam is whether the state can show a compelling state interest in regulating the behavior, and show there is no more suitable means of control. The state obviously has a compelling interest in protecting children from being victimized by the pornography industry. And yet, as you just read, Congress has had difficulty crafting statutes that address child pornography that are not too broad and do not violate the First Amendment.

The dust as not settled on the Court's decision in *Dobbs v. Jackson Women's Health Organization, No. 19-1392,*[53] 597 U.S. ___, so in February 2023 (as of this latest editing), it is unclear what remains of the right to privacy and the viability of earlier Court cases decided on the basis of privacy rights. Abortion, same sex marriage, and other rights that were well-established (or were becoming well-established) may be in jeopardy. In the past, this author has been able to "dodge the bullet" and say that those really were merely tangential to the criminal justice system so we need not delve in too deep. However, many states are posed to criminalize the seeking of an abortion, obtaining an abortion, counseling in favor of abortion, and so it is no longer feasible to avoid grappling with the intersection between personal privacy interests and criminal prosecutions. In fact, historically, these cases came to the Court as a result of some criminal prosecution (consider, e.g., Griswold where the defendant was prosecuted and fined for counseling married couples about birth control). Moreover, it appears that much fallout from the *Dobbs* holding will involve criminal prosecutions of individuals who aid and assist others in procuring abortions contrary to state laws.

The following case involves the right to privacy. Note the earlier privacy cases the Court discussed in *Lawrence* and consider how the *Dobbs* rationale and holding may upend those prior decisions.

LAWRENCE v. TEXAS,
539 U.S. 558 (2003)

Justice Kennedy delivered the opinion of the Court.

Liberty protects the person from unwarranted government intrusions into a dwelling or other private places. In our tradition the State is not omnipresent in the home. And there are other spheres of our lives and existence, outside the home, where the State should not be a dominant presence. Freedom extends beyond spatial bounds. Liberty presumes an autonomy of self that includes freedom of thought, belief, expression, and certain intimate conduct. The instant case involves liberty of the person both in its spatial and more transcendent dimensions.

I

The question before the Court is the validity of a Texas statute making it a crime for two persons of the same sex to engage in certain intimate sexual conduct.

In Houston, Texas, officers of the Harris County Police Department were dispatched to a private residence in response to a reported weapons disturbance. They entered an apartment where one of the petitioners, John Geddes Lawrence, resided. The right of the police to enter does not seem to have been questioned. The officers observed Lawrence and another man, Tyron Garner, engaging in a sexual act. The two petitioners were arrested, held in custody overnight, and charged and convicted before a Justice of the Peace.

[They were charged with "deviate sexual intercourse, namely anal sex with a member of the same sex (man)"]

The petitioners exercised their right to a trial *de novo* in Harris County Criminal Court. They challenged the statute as a violation of the Equal Protection Clause of the Fourteenth Amendment and of a like provision of the Texas Constitution. Those contentions were rejected. The petitioners, having entered a plea of *nolo contendere*, were each fined $200 and assessed court costs of $141.25.

[Appeals were taken through the Texas appellate courts which rejected Lawrence's constitutional claims.]

We granted certiorari to consider three questions:

"1. Whether Petitioners' criminal convictions under the Texas "Homosexual Conduct" law–which criminalizes sexual intimacy by same-sex couples, but not identical behavior by different-sex couples–violate the Fourteenth Amendment guarantee of equal protection of laws?

"2. Whether Petitioners' criminal convictions for adult consensual sexual intimacy in the home violate their vital interests in liberty and privacy protected by the Due Process Clause of the Fourteenth Amendment?

"3. Whether *Bowers* v. *Hardwick* … should be overruled?"

The petitioners were adults at the time of the alleged offense. Their conduct was in private and consensual.

II

We conclude the case should be resolved by determining whether the petitioners were free as adults to engage in the private conduct in the exercise of their liberty under the Due Process Clause of Fourteenth Amendment to the Constitution. For this inquiry we deem it necessary to reconsider the Court's holding in *Bowers*.

There are broad statements of the substantive reach of liberty under the Due Process Clause, . . . but the most pertinent beginning point is our decision in *Griswold* v. *Connecticut,* 381 U.S. 479 (1965).

In *Griswold* the Court invalidated a state law prohibiting the use of drugs or devices of contraception and counseling or aiding and abetting the use of contraceptives. The Court described the protected interest as a right to privacy and placed emphasis on the marriage relation and the protected space of the marital bedroom. *Id.,* at 485.

After *Griswold* it was established that the right to make certain decisions regarding sexual conduct extends beyond the marital relationship. In *Eisenstadt* v. *Baird,* 405 U.S. 438 (1972), the Court invalidated a law prohibiting the distribution of contraceptives to unmarried persons. The case was decided under the Equal Protection Clause, but with respect to unmarried persons, the Court went on to state the fundamental proposition that the law impaired the exercise of their personal rights. It … [stated]:

"It is true that in *Griswold* the right of privacy in question inhered in the marital relationship.… . If the right of privacy means anything, it is the right of the *individual*, married or single, to be free from unwarranted governmental intrusion into matters so fundamentally affecting a person as the decision whether to bear or beget a child." *Id.,* at 453.

Roe v. Wade . . . recognized the right of a woman to make certain fundamental decisions affecting her destiny and confirmed once more that the protection of liberty under the Due Process Clause has a substantive dimension of fundamental significance in defining the rights of the person.

In *Carey* v. *Population Services Int'l.* (1977), the Court confronted a New York law forbidding sale or distribution of contraceptive devices to persons under 16 years of age. Although there was no single opinion for the Court, the law was invalidated.
Both *Eisenstadt* and *Carey*, as well as the holding and rationale in *Roe*, confirmed that the reasoning of *Griswold* could not be confined to the protection of rights of married adults. This was the state of the law with respect to some of the most relevant cases when the Court
considered *Bowers* v. *Hardwick.*

The facts in *Bowers* had some similarities to the instant case. A police officer, whose right to enter seems not to have been in question, observed Hardwick, in his own bedroom, engaging in intimate sexual conduct with another adult male. The conduct was in violation of a Georgia statute making it a criminal offense to engage in sodomy. One difference between the two cases is that the Georgia statute prohibited the conduct whether or not the participants were of the same sex, while the Texas statute, as we have seen, applies only to participants of the same sex. Hardwick was not prosecuted, but he brought an action in federal court to declare the state statute invalid. He alleged he was a practicing homosexual and that the criminal prohibition violated rights guaranteed to him by the Constitution. The Court . . . sustained the Georgia law.

The Court began its substantive discussion in *Bowers* as follows: "The issue presented is whether the Federal Constitution confers a fundamental right upon homosexuals to engage in sodomy and hence invalidates the laws of the many States that still make such conduct illegal and have done so for a very long time." *Id.,* at 190. That statement, we now conclude, discloses the Court's own failure to appreciate the extent of the liberty at stake. To say that the issue in *Bowers* was simply the right to engage in certain sexual conduct demeans the claim the individual put forward, just as it would demean a married couple were it to be said marriage is simply about the right to have sexual intercourse. The laws involved in *Bowers* and here are, to be sure, statutes that purport to do no more than prohibit a particular sexual act. Their penalties and purposes, though, have more far-reaching consequences, touching upon the most private human conduct, sexual behavior, and in the most private of places, the home. The statutes do seek to control a personal relationship that, whether or not entitled to formal recognition in the law, is within the liberty of persons to choose without being punished as criminals.

This, as a general rule, should counsel against attempts by the State, or a court, to define the meaning of the relationship or to set its boundaries absent injury to a person or abuse of an institution the law protects. It suffices for us to acknowledge that adults may choose to enter upon this relationship in the confines of their homes and their own private lives and still retain their dignity as free persons. When sexuality finds overt expression in intimate conduct with another person, the conduct can be but one element in a personal bond that is more enduring. The liberty protected by the Constitution allows homosexual persons the right to make this choice.

[The Court discusses the history of sodomy laws as set forth in *Bowers*]

Laws prohibiting sodomy do not seem to have been enforced against consenting adults acting in private. A substantial number of sodomy prosecutions and convictions for which there are surviving records were for predatory acts against those who could not or did not consent, as in the case of a minor or the victim of an assault. As to these, one purpose for the prohibitions was to ensure there would be no lack of coverage if a predator committed a sexual assault that did not constitute rape as defined by the criminal law.

The policy of punishing consenting adults for private acts was not much discussed in the early legal literature. We can infer that one reason for this was the very private nature of the conduct. Despite the absence of prosecutions, there may have been periods in which there was public criticism of homosexuals as such and an insistence that the criminal laws be enforced to discourage their practices. But far from possessing "ancient roots," *Bowers*, 478 U.S., at 192, American laws targeting same-sex couples did not develop until the last third of the 20th century.

In summary, the historical grounds relied upon in *Bowers* are more complex than the majority opinion and the concurring opinion by Chief Justice Burger indicate. Their historical premises are not without doubt and, at the very least, are overstated.

It must be acknowledged, of course, that the Court in *Bowers* was making the broader point that for centuries there have been powerful voices to condemn homosexual conduct as immoral. The condemnation has been shaped by religious beliefs, conceptions of right and acceptable behavior, and respect for the traditional family. For many persons these are not trivial concerns but profound and deep convictions accepted as ethical and moral principles to which they aspire and which thus determine the course of their lives. These considerations do not answer the question before us, however. The issue is whether the majority may use the power of the State to enforce these views on the whole society through operation of the criminal law. "Our obligation is to define the liberty of all, not to mandate our own moral code." *Planned Parenthood of Southeastern Pa. v. Casey,* 505 U.S. 833, 850 (1992).

… In all events we think that our laws and traditions in the past half century are of most relevance here. These references show an emerging awareness that liberty gives substantial protection to adult persons in deciding how to conduct their private lives in matters pertaining to sex.

This emerging recognition should have been apparent when *Bowers* was decided. In 1955 the American Law Institute promulgated the Model Penal Code and made clear that it did not recommend or provide for "criminal penalties for consensual sexual relations conducted in private." … It justified its decision on three grounds: (1) The prohibitions undermined respect for the law by penalizing conduct many people engaged in; (2) the statutes regulated private conduct not harmful to others; and (3) the laws were arbitrarily enforced and thus invited the danger of blackmail. …

…

The doctrine of *stare decisis* is essential to the respect accorded to the judgments of the Court and to the stability of the law. It is not, however, an inexorable command. *Payne* v. *Tennessee*, 501 U.S. 808, 828 (1991) ("*Stare decisis* is not an inexorable command; rather, it 'is a principle of policy and not a mechanical formula of adherence to the latest decision' ") (quoting *Helvering* v. *Hallock*, 309 U.S. 106, 119 (1940))). …

The rationale of *Bowers* does not withstand careful analysis. In his dissenting opinion in *Bowers* Justice Stevens came to these conclusions:

> "Our prior cases make two propositions abundantly clear. First, the fact that the governing majority in a State has traditionally viewed a particular practice as immoral is not a sufficient reason for upholding a law prohibiting the practice; neither history nor tradition could save a law prohibiting miscegenation from constitutional attack. Second, individual decisions by married persons, concerning the intimacies of their physical relationship, even when not intended to produce offspring, are a form of "liberty" protected by the Due Process Clause of

the Fourteenth Amendment. Moreover, this protection extends to intimate choices by unmarried as well as married persons." 478 U.S., at 216.

Justice Stevens' analysis, in our view, should have been controlling in *Bowers* and should control here.

Bowers was not correct when it was decided, and it is not correct today. It ought not to remain binding precedent.
Bowers v. *Hardwick* should be and now is overruled.

The present case does not involve minors. It does not involve persons who might be injured or coerced or who are situated in relationships where consent might not easily be refused. It does not involve public conduct or prostitution. It does not involve whether the government must give formal recognition to any relationship that homosexual persons seek to enter. The case does involve two adults who, with full and mutual consent from each other, engaged in sexual practices common to a homosexual lifestyle. The petitioners are entitled to respect for their private lives. The State cannot demean their existence or control their destiny by making their private sexual conduct a crime. Their right to liberty under the Due Process Clause gives them the full right to engage in their conduct without intervention of the government. "It is a promise of the Constitution that there is a realm of personal liberty which the government may not enter." *Casey*, *supra*, at 847. The Texas statute furthers no legitimate state interest which can justify its intrusion into the personal and private life of the individual.

. . .

Other Cases: Right to Privacy

Stanley v. Georgia, 384 U.S. 557 (1969) SUMMARY: The court found that individuals have the right to privacy in possessing pornography depicting adult subjects.	***Richmond Newspapers, Inc. v. Virginia, 448 U.S. 555 (1980)*** SUMMARY: The Court held that "certain unarticulated rights . . . [including the right to privacy] . . . are implicit in the enumerated guarantees."
Griswold v. Connecticut, 381 U.S. 479 (1965) SUMMARY: This was the first case to recognize a constitutional right to privacy. The Court, in that case, struck down a statute that punished using or assisting someone to use birth control. Physicians had been found guilty and ordered to pay a $100.00 fine for providing counseling and contraceptives to married people. Court noted that the Ninth Amendment means that rights not spelled out in the in the Constitution (enumerated rights), nevertheless exist. The Court held that a married couple's use of contraceptives was protected by the constitutional right to privacy.	***Satz v. Perlmutter, 379 So.2d 359 (Fla.1980)*** SUMMARY: The Court found that an adult with a terminal illness had a protected right of privacy in the decision to refuse medical treatment that would unnaturally prolong life.
	Gilbert v. State, 487 So. 2d 1185 (Fla. App. 1986). SUMMARY: The Court refused to extend the right to privacy as a justification for euthanasia or doctor-assisted suicide.
In re Quinlan, 355 A.2d 647 (N.J. 1976) Family members have the constitutionally protected right to privacy in their decision to remove a comatose woman from extraordinary means of life support.	***Gonzalez v. Oregon, 546 U.S. 243 (2006)*** SUMMARY: The Court held that Oregon's Death with Dignity Act survived challenges by the U.S. Attorney General who had attempted to invalidate the law arguing that physicians were

violating the Federal Controlled Substance Act when they prescribed drugs that would be used to commit suicide. The Court held that the U.S. Attorney General was encroaching on the practice of medicine--traditionally a state regulated profession. Although not necessarily a right to privacy case, this decision limits the federal government's ability to regulate in this area which most would hold to be a private decision.

EQUAL PROTECTION UNDER THE LAW

The Fourteenth Amendment tells state governments that they should not deprive their citizens of equal protections of law. The federal constitution contains no Equal Protection Clause, but in 1954, the Court employed a "reverse incorporation" theory and found that the protection was implied within the Due Process Clause of the Fifth Amendment. Justice Warren wrote, "The concepts of equal protection and due process, both stemming from our American ideal of fairness, are not mutually exclusive." Equal protection is more explicit safeguard against discrimination but "discrimination may be so unjustifiable as to be violative of due process." He opined that it would be unthinkable that the Equal Protection Clause applied to the states, but did not apply to the federal government. *Bolling v. Sharpe, 347 U.S. 497 (1954)*.

Basically, equal protection of laws means legislators cannot write laws that treat people differently. But obviously, in some circumstances, they do. It is one thing to treat people differently based on age or employment or educational level, and the government may do so if it has a good reason (a rational basis), but it is quite another to treat people differently because of their sex or race. As you will read, the Court now employs three levels of scrutiny in deciding whether a law violates equal protections: rational basis scrutiny, heightened scrutiny, or strict scrutiny. The level of scrutiny courts employ is contingent upon the nature of the classification. (Who is being treated differently than whom.)

Most classifications will be governed by rational basis scrutiny. The classifications are presumed valid so long as they are rationally related to a constitutionally permissible state interest. For example, in *Westbrook v. Alaska*, Westbrook was convicted of underaged drinking. The issue was whether the state could permissibly restrict underage drinking and impose a minimum age of 21. The Court held that the state had shown a reasonable interest in regulating and ensuring responsible drinking and that the age requirement was rationally related to that interest. Accordingly, it upheld the statute.

Classifications based on sex or other "quasi-suspect classifications" are subjected to heightened, intermediate scrutiny. These laws will only survive challenge when they bear a fair and substantial relationship to a legitimate state end or "important government interest." Finally, classifications based on race are subject to strict scrutiny. To survive strict scrutiny, the court must find that the government had a compelling state interest and that there is no way to promote that interest other than through the differential treatment. As Justice Stewart noted in his concurring opinion in *Michael M. v. Sonoma County Superior Court* (see below), "The Constitution is violated when government, state or federal, invidiously classifies similarly situated people on the basis of the immutable characteristics with which they were born. Thus, detrimental racial classifications by government always violate the Constitution, for the simple reason that, so far as the Constitution is concerned, people of different races are always similarly situated. "

The cases below explore whether a statute can survive an equal protections challenge.

WEBSTER v. PEOPLE OF THE VIRGIN ISLANDS,
S.Ct. Crim No. 2012-0012 (VI Supreme Ct. 2014)

CABRET, ASSOCIATE JUSTICE delivered the opinion of the court:

Patrick Webster, Jr., was convicted in the Superior Court of aggravated assault and battery and disturbing the peace, both as acts of domestic violence, and unauthorized use of a vehicle. Webster appeals, arguing that the aggravated assault statute contains unconstitutional sex-based classifications and that the evidence was insufficient to establish the other charges. For the reasons that follow, we reverse Webster's assault conviction and affirm his convictions for disturbing the peace and unauthorized use of a vehicle.

FACTS

On May 4, 2011, at approximately 1 a.m., Webster went into the bedroom of his mother Vernice Webster while she was sleeping to ask for the keys to her car. When she refused, Webster searched the room for the keys while his mother went to the kitchen. When he could not find the keys, Webster grabbed Vernice by the throat and the wrap she was wearing, pulling her back into the bedroom and then repeatedly pushing her down onto her bed, demanding the keys. Still refusing to give Webster the keys, Vernice returned to the kitchen, ending up on the floor with Webster standing over her holding a wine bottle. Webster once again dragged his mother into the bedroom and threw her onto her mattress several more times. Vernice finally retrieved the keys from a bathroom cabinet and gave them to Webster, who disabled the house phone and took Vernice's cell phone before leaving with the car.

After he left, Vernice went to a neighbor to call 911. Once police arrived, they noticed bruises and minor scratches on her collarbone and forearm, and observed that the bedroom was "ransacked." The responding officers took Vernice to her sister's house for the night because she was afraid that Webster would return to the house. She returned home in the morning with Officer Vernon Williams, where they found the car outside and Webster asleep in his bedroom. Williams then arrested Webster. The following day, Vernice went to the hospital complaining of back pain caused by the altercation.

. . .

. . . [T]he trial concluded . . . there was not enough evidence to support a conviction for third-degree assault with a deadly weapon or the use of a dangerous weapon during a crime of violence, but entered convictions against Webster for aggravated assault and battery, disturbing the peace, and unauthorized use of a vehicle. The court also found that aggravated assault and disturbing the peace were acts of domestic violence as defined by 16 V.I.C. § 91(b). . . . [T]he Superior Court sentenced Webster to a suspended ten-month prison sentence and a $1,000 fine for aggravated assault and battery, a concurrent sixty-day sentence for disturbing the peace, a concurrent one-year suspended sentence for unauthorized use of a vehicle, and placed him on supervised probation for one year. Webster filed a timely notice of appeal on February 8, 2012

DISCUSSION

Webster argues that his conviction for aggravated assault must be reversed because the statute under which he was convicted, 14 V.I.C. § 298(5), violates constitutional principles assuring equal protection of the laws. He further asserts that the evidence was insufficient to support his convictions for disturbing the peace and unauthorized use of a vehicle. We address each argument in turn.

14 V.I.C. § 298(5)

For the first time on appeal, Webster argues that because 14 V.I.C. § 298(5) enhances simple assault to aggravated assault based only on the respective sexes of the attacker and the victim, it violates the Equal Protection Clause of the Fourteenth Amendment to the

United States Constitution. Because he did not raise this argument before the Superior Court, we review it only for plain error. "Under plain error review, there must be an error, that was plain, that affected the defendant's substantial rights." "Even then, this Court will only reverse where the error seriously affects the fairness, integrity, or public reputation of judicial proceedings." ... In conducting this review, we must first determine whether the Superior Court erred by entering a conviction against Webster under an unconstitutional statute.

The Superior Court entered the conviction under section 298, which enumerates nine aggravating circumstances that enhance a simple assault to an aggravated assault. ... Webster argues that by making his sex an aggravating factor, section 298(5) denies him equal protection of the law.

"The Equal Protection Clause of the Fourteenth Amendment 'is essentially a direction that all persons similarly situated should be treated alike.'" *Lawrence v. Texas.* Here, it is evident that section 298(5) creates a sex-based classification on its face, upgrading an assault from simple to aggravated in all instances in which the defendant is male and the victim is female. While most statutory classifications—such as those contained in tax policy and economic regulations—must meet only rational basis review, *see Heller v. Doe* (rational basis review is satisfied by "any reasonably conceivable state of facts that could provide a rational basis for the classification"), an explicitly sex-based statutory classification—like those based on race, national origin, or alienage—must satisfy heightened constitutional scrutiny.

In the case of a sex-based classification, this heightened level of scrutiny is intermediate. Unlike rational basis review—where it is the defendant's burden to "negat[e] every conceivable basis that might support the government's statutory classification,"— intermediate scrutiny requires the People to carry the burden of establishing that there is an "exceedingly persuasive justification" for the classification by showing that it "serves important governmental objectives and that the discriminatory means employed are substantially related to the achievement of those objectives." We must closely examine the People's justifications "free of fixed notions concerning the roles and abilities of males and females," as generalizations and stereotypes about the respective characteristics of men and women cannot satisfy intermediate scrutiny.

The People concedes that it bears the burden of demonstrating the constitutionality of section 298(5) and asserts that "the statute identifies men because of the demonstrable fact that they are physically different from women." The People also contends that "[t]he Government's objective in having a gender based statute is to protect women from physically aggressive and overpowering men as was the situation in this case." The People further insists that the "[L]egislature could easily have determined that assaults and batteries by physically larger and stronger men are more likely to cause greater physical injuries to women than similar assaults by females." While the People may be correct that the Legislature *could* have enacted section 298(5) with the aim of protecting women from assaults by physically larger and stronger men, a justification "hypothesized or invented *post hoc* in response to litigation" cannot meet intermediate scrutiny. Instead, "a tenable justification must describe actual state purposes, not rationalizations for actions in fact differently grounded."

. . .

... While it is undoubtedly true that the Legislature "can take into account . . . physical differences when classifying crimes relating to physical violence," section 298(5) does not do this. Instead, this provision makes any assault committed by a man upon a woman an aggravated assault regardless of the physical differences between the attacker and the victim, providing no additional protections to a man assaulted by a physically stronger woman, or a woman assaulted by a physically stronger woman. By using sex as a proxy for the relative physical characteristics of the attacker and the victim, section 298(5) rests entirely on "archaic and stereotypic notions" that have been specifically rejected by the United States Supreme Court. As the Supreme Court explained, "if the statutory objective is to . . . 'protect' members of one gender because they are presumed to suffer from an inherent handicap or to be innately inferior, the objective itself is illegitimate." Legislative classifications such as this "carry the inherent risk of reinforcing stereotypes about the 'proper place' of women and their need for special protection." Finally, it would seem apparent that if the Legislature's objective was to take into account "physical differences when classifying crimes relating to physical violence," this purpose would have been better served by enacting a statute that actually takes into account physical differences in classifying violent crimes. And when governmental objectives are as well-served by a sex-neutral law that does not "carr[y] with it the baggage of sexual stereotypes," the government "cannot be permitted to classify on the basis of sex." Therefore, even if the Legislature enacted 14 V.I.C. § 298(5) with the objective of providing greater protections to women who are attacked by physically stronger men, because the statute fails to take into account the relative physical prowess of the attacker and the victim, we cannot say that the "discriminatory means employed are substantially related to the achievement of those objectives." In arguing that section 298(5) does not violate equal protection, the People relies heavily on *Gov't of the V.I. v. Prescott*. But *Prescott* . . . applied rational basis review long after the United States Supreme Court held that sex-based statutory classifications must satisfy intermediate scrutiny. ... The only recent case cited is *State v. Wright*, 563 S.E.2d 311 (S.C. 2002), in which the South Carolina Supreme Court upheld a sex-based sentencing enhancement. But despite appropriately identifying intermediate scrutiny, the *Wright* court relied

almost entirely on cases utilizing rational basis review in upholding that statute. ...

Accordingly, by providing that any assault committed by a male upon a female is automatically aggravated in nature, 14 V.I.C. § 298(5) violates the Equal Protection Clause of the Fourteenth Amendment, and the Superior Court committed error in entering a conviction against Webster under this section.

Despite this error, because Webster failed to raise the constitutionality of section 298(5) before the Superior Court, we will only exercise our discretion to reverse his conviction if the Superior Court's error was plain and affected Webster's substantial rights, and affirming Webster's conviction would "seriously affect[] the fairness, integrity, or public reputation of judicial proceedings."

... In the case of sex-based statutory classifications, the United States Supreme Court has repeatedly instructed that courts must apply heightened constitutional scrutiny, requiring a careful examination of whether an "exceedingly persuasive justification" motivated the Legislature's use of this otherwise impermissible classification. ... Given this longstanding precedent from the United States Supreme Court, the Superior Court's error in entering a conviction under section 298(5)—a statute containing an explicit sex-based classification—is plain under current law.

Furthermore, there is no doubt that this error affected Webster's substantial rights . . . and that affirming Webster's conviction under a facially unconstitutional statute would clearly affect the integrity and public reputation of judicial proceedings. . . . Accordingly, because the Superior Court committed plain error in entering a conviction against Webster under a statute that violates the Equal Protection Clause of the Fourteenth Amendment, we reverse Webster's conviction for aggravated assault under 14 V.I.C. § 298(5).

LOVING v. VIRGINIA,
388 U.S. 1 (1967)

MR. CHIEF JUSTICE WARREN delivered the opinion of the Court.

This case presents a constitutional question never addressed by this Court: whether a statutory scheme adopted by the State of Virginia to prevent marriages between persons solely on the basis of racial classifications violates the Equal Protection and Due Process Clauses of the Fourteenth Amendment. For reasons which seem to us to reflect the central meaning of those constitutional commands, we conclude that these statutes cannot stand consistently with the Fourteenth Amendment.

In June 1958, two residents of Virginia, Mildred Jeter, a Negro woman, and Richard Loving, a white man, were married in the District of Columbia pursuant to its laws. Shortly after their marriage, the Lovings returned to Virginia and established their marital abode in Caroline County. At the October Term, 1958, of the Circuit Court of Caroline County, a grand jury issued an indictment charging the Lovings with violating Virginia's ban on interracial marriages. On January 6, 1959, the Lovings pleaded guilty to the charge and were sentenced to one year in jail; however, the trial judge suspended the sentence for a period of 25 years on the condition that the Lovings leave the State and not return to Virginia together for 25 years. ...

After their convictions, the Lovings took up residence in the District of Columbia. On November 6, 1963, they filed a motion in the state trial court to vacate the judgment and set aside the sentence on the ground that the statutes which they had violated were repugnant to the Fourteenth Amendment. . . . On January 22, 1965, the state trial judge denied the motion to vacate the sentences, and the Lovings perfected an appeal to the Supreme Court of Appeals of Virginia. On February 11, 1965, the three-judge District Court continued the case to allow the Lovings to present their constitutional claims to the highest state court.

The [Virginia] Supreme Court of Appeals upheld the constitutionality of the antimiscegenation statutes and, after modifying the sentence, affirmed the convictions. The Lovings appealed this decision. ...

[The statutes under which appellants were convicted and sentenced were part of a comprehensive statutory scheme aimed at prohibiting and punishing interracial marriages and punishing individuals violating the statute by incarceration in a penitentiary for a minimum of one year and a maximum of five years. The laws also voided without judicial proceedings all interracial marriages.]

The Lovings have never disputed in the course of this litigation that Mrs. Loving is a "colored person" or that Mr. Loving is a "white person" within the meanings given those terms by the Virginia statutes.

I

In upholding the constitutionality of these provisions in the decision below, the Supreme Court of Appeals of Virginia referred to its 1955 decision in *Naim v. Naim* as stating the reasons supporting the validity of these laws. In Naim, the state court concluded that the State's legitimate purposes were "to preserve the racial integrity of its citizens," and to prevent "the corruption of blood," "a mongrel breed of citizens," and "the obliteration of racial pride," obviously an endorsement of the doctrine of White Supremacy. The court also reasoned that marriage has traditionally been subject to state regulation without federal intervention, and, consequently, the regulation of marriage should be left to exclusive state control by the Tenth Amendment.

While the state court is no doubt correct in asserting that marriage is a social relation subject to the State's police power, the State does not contend in its argument before this Court that its powers to regulate marriage are unlimited notwithstanding the commands of the Fourteenth Amendment. ... Instead, the State argues that the meaning of the Equal Protection Clause, is only that state penal laws containing an interracial element as part of the definition of the offense must apply equally to whites and Negroes in the sense that members of each race are punished to the same degree. Thus, the State contends that, because its miscegenation statutes punish equally both the white and the Negro participants in an interracial marriage, these statutes, despite their reliance on racial classifications, do not constitute an invidious discrimination based upon race. The second argument advanced by the State assumes the validity of its equal application theory. The argument is that, if the Equal Protection Clause does not outlaw miscegenation statutes because of their reliance on racial classifications, the question of constitutionality would thus become whether there was any rational basis for a State to treat interracial marriages differently from other marriages. On this question, the State argues, the scientific evidence is substantially in doubt and, consequently, this Court should defer to the wisdom of the state legislature in adopting its policy of discouraging interracial marriages.

Because we reject the notion that the mere "equal application" of a statute containing racial classifications is enough to remove the classifications from the Fourteenth Amendment's proscription of all invidious racial discriminations, we do not accept the State's contention that these statutes should be upheld if there is any possible basis for concluding that they serve a rational purpose. The mere fact of equal application does not mean that our analysis of these statutes should follow the approach we have taken in cases involving no racial discrimination. ... In these cases, involving distinctions not drawn according to race, the Court has merely asked whether there is any rational foundation for the discriminations, and has deferred to the wisdom of the state legislatures. In the case at bar, however, we deal with statutes containing racial classifications, and the fact of equal application does not immunize the statute from the very heavy burden of justification which the Fourteenth Amendment has traditionally required of state statutes drawn according to race.

... We have rejected the proposition that . . . the requirement of equal protection of the laws is satisfied by penal laws defining offenses based on racial classifications so long as white and Negro participants in the offense were similarly punished.

. . . [T]he Equal Protection Clause requires the consideration of whether the classifications drawn by any statute constitute an arbitrary and invidious discrimination. The clear and central purpose of the Fourteenth Amendment was to eliminate all official state sources of invidious racial discrimination in the States.

There can be no question but that Virginia's miscegenation statutes rest solely upon distinctions drawn according to race. The statutes proscribe generally accepted conduct if engaged in by members of different races. Over the years, this Court has consistently repudiated "[d]istinctions between citizens solely because of their ancestry" as being "odious to a free people whose institutions are founded upon the doctrine of equality." At the very least, the Equal Protection Clause demands that racial classifications, especially suspect in criminal statutes, be subjected to the "most rigid scrutiny," *Korematsu v. United States*, and, if they are ever to be upheld, they must be shown to be necessary to the accomplishment of some permissible state objective, independent of the racial discrimination which it was the object of the Fourteenth Amendment to eliminate. Indeed, two members of this Court have already stated that they "cannot conceive of a valid legislative purpose . . . which makes the color of a person's skin the test of whether his conduct is a criminal offense."

There is patently no legitimate overriding purpose independent of invidious racial discrimination which justifies this classification. The fact that Virginia prohibits only interracial marriages involving white persons demonstrates that the racial classifications must stand on their own justification, as measures designed to maintain White Supremacy. We have consistently denied the constitutionality of measures which restrict the rights of citizens on account of race. There can be no doubt that restricting the freedom to marry solely because of racial classifications violates the central meaning of the Equal Protection Clause.

II

These statutes also deprive the Lovings of liberty without due process of law in violation of the Due Process Clause of the Fourteenth Amendment. The freedom to marry has long been recognized as one of the vital personal rights essential to the orderly pursuit of happiness by free men.

Marriage is one of the "basic civil rights of man," fundamental to our very existence and survival. To deny this fundamental freedom on so unsupportable a basis as the racial classifications embodied in these statutes, classifications so directly subversive of the principle of equality at the heart of the Fourteenth Amendment, is surely to deprive all the State's citizens of liberty without due process of law. The Fourteenth Amendment requires that the freedom of choice to marry not be restricted by invidious racial discriminations. Under our Constitution, the freedom to marry, or not marry, a person of another race resides with the individual and cannot be infringed by the State.

...

MR. JUSTICE STEWART, concurring.

I have previously expressed the belief that "it is simply not possible for a state law to be valid under our Constitution which makes the criminality of an act depend upon the race of the actor." Because I adhere to that belief, I concur in the judgment of the Court.

Other Cases: Equal Protections

Michael M. v. Sonoma County Superior Court, 450 U.S. 464 (1981)

SUMMARY: At approximately midnight on June 3, 1978, Michael M. and two friends approached Sharon, a 16 1/2-year-old female, and her sister as they waited at a bus stop. Michael M and Sharon, who had already been drinking, moved away from the others and began to kiss. After being struck in the face for rebuffing petitioner's initial advances, Sharon submitted to sexual intercourse with petitioner. Michael M., a 17-and-1/2-year-old male, was found guilty of violating California's "statutory rape" law. The law defined unlawful sexual intercourse as "an act of sexual intercourse accomplished with a female not the wife of the perpetrator, where the female is under the age of 18 years." The statute made men alone criminally liable for such conduct. Michael M. challenged the constitutionality of the law. The Court had to decide whether California's statutory rape law violated the Fourteenth Amendment's Equal Protection Clause and unconstitutionally discriminated on the basis of gender?

In a plurality [split] decision, the Court held that the law did not violate the Equal Protection Clause of the Fourteenth Amendment, noting that "young men and young women are not similarly situated with respect to the problems and the risks of sexual intercourse." The Court found that the state had a strong interest in preventing "illegitimate pregnancy." The Court also noted that "[i]t is hardly unreasonable for a legislature acting to protect minor females to exclude them from punishment. Moreover, the risk of pregnancy itself constitutes a substantial deterrence to young females. No similar natural sanctions deter males."]

JUSTICE REHNQUIST announced the judgment of the Court and delivered an opinion, in which THE CHIEF JUSTICE, JUSTICE STEWART, and JUSTICE POWELL joined.

. . .

As is evident from our opinions, the Court has had some difficulty in agreeing upon the proper approach and analysis in cases involving challenges to gender-based classifications. . . . Our cases have held, however, that the traditional minimum rationality test takes on a somewhat "sharper focus" when gender-based classifications are challenged. In *Reed v. Reed*, for example, the Court stated that a gender-based classification will be upheld if it bears a "fair and substantial relationship" to legitimate state ends, while in *Craig v. Boren* the Court restated the test to require the classification to bear a "substantial relationship" to "important governmental objectives."

Underlying these decisions is the principle that a legislature may not "make overbroad generalizations based on sex which are entirely unrelated to any differences between men and women or which demean the ability or social status of the affected class." But because the Equal Protection Clause does not "demand that a statute necessarily apply equally to all persons" or require "`things which are different in fact . . . to be treated in law as though they were the same,'" this Court has consistently upheld statutes where the gender classification is not invidious, but rather realistically reflects the fact that the sexes are not similarly situated in certain circumstances. As the Court has stated, a legislature may "provide for the special problems of women."

. . .

The justification for the statute offered by the State, and accepted by the Supreme Court of California, is that the legislature sought to prevent illegitimate teenage pregnancies. That finding, of course, is entitled to great deference. And although our cases establish that the State's asserted reason for the enactment of a statute may be rejected, if it "could not have been a goal of the legislation," this is not such a case.

We are satisfied not only that the prevention of illegitimate pregnancy is at least one of the "purposes" of the statute, but also that the State has a strong interest in preventing such pregnancy. . . .

We need not be medical doctors to discern that young men and young women are not similarly situated with respect to the problems and the risks of sexual intercourse. Only women may become pregnant, and they suffer disproportionately the profound physical, emotional, and psychological consequences of sexual activity. The statute at issue here protects women from sexual intercourse at an age when those consequences are particularly severe.

The question thus boils down to whether a State may attack the problem of sexual intercourse and teenage pregnancy directly by prohibiting a male from having sexual intercourse with a minor female. We hold that such a statute is sufficiently related to the State's objectives to pass constitutional muster.

Because virtually all of the significant harmful and inescapably identifiable consequences of teenage pregnancy fall on the young female, a legislature acts well within its authority when it elects to punish only the participant who, by nature, suffers few of the consequences of his conduct. It is hardly unreasonable for a legislature acting to protect minor females to exclude them from punishment. Moreover, the risk of pregnancy itself constitutes a substantial deterrence to young females. No similar natural sanctions deter males. A criminal sanction imposed solely on males thus serves to roughly "equalize" the deterrents on the sexes.

. . .

JUSTICE STEWART, concurring:

. . .

The Constitution is violated when government, state or federal, invidiously classifies similarly situated people on the basis of the immutable characteristics with which they were born. Thus, detrimental racial classifications by government always violate the Constitution, for the simple reason that, so far as the Constitution is concerned, people of different races are always similarly situated. By contrast, while detrimental gender classifications by government often violate the Constitution, they do not always do so, for the reason that there are differences between males and females that the Constitution necessarily recognizes. In this case we deal with the most basic of these differences: females can become pregnant as the result of sexual intercourse; males cannot.

. . . Gender-based classifications may not be based upon administrative convenience, or upon archaic assumptions about the proper roles of the sexes. But we have recognized that in certain narrow circumstances men and women are not similarly situated; in these circumstances a gender classification based on clear differences between the sexes is not invidious, and a legislative classification realistically based upon those differences is not unconstitutional. "[G]ender-based classifications are not invariably invalid. When men and women are not in fact similarly situated in the area covered by the legislation in question, the Equal Protection Clause is not violated."

. . .

E

In short, the Equal Protection Clause does not mean that the physiological differences between men and women must be disregarded. While those differences must never be permitted to become a pretext for invidious discrimination, no such discrimination is presented by this case. The Constitution surely does not require a State to pretend that demonstrable differences between men and women do not really exist.

JUSTICE BRENNAN, with whom JUSTICES WHITE and MARSHALL join, dissenting. Omitted.

JUSTICE STEVENS, dissenting. Omitted.

Craig v. Boren, 429 U.S. 190 (1976)

SUMMARY: An Oklahoma law prohibited the sale of "nonintoxicating" 3.2 percent beer to males under the age of 21 and to females under the age of 18. Curtis Craig, a male then between the ages of 18 and 21, and Carolyn Whitener, a licensed vendor challenged the law as discriminatory. The Court was faced with the question of whether the statute violated the Fourteenth Amendment's Equal Protection Clause by establishing different drinking ages for men and women.

JUSTICE BRENNAN (MAJORITY OPINION):

… *Reed* emphasized that statutory classifications that distinguish between males and females are "subject to scrutiny under the Equal Protection Clause." To withstand constitutional challenge, previous cases establish that classifications by gender must serve important governmental objectives and must be substantially related to achievement of those objectives. Thus, in *Reed*, the objectives of "reducing the workload on probate courts," and "avoiding intrafamily controversy were deemed of insufficient

importance to sustain use of an overt gender criterion in the appointment of administrators of intestate decedents' estates. Decisions following *Reed* similarly have rejected administrative ease and convenience as sufficiently important objectives to justify gender-based classifications.

Reed v. Reed has also provided the underpinning for decisions that have invalidated statutes employing gender as an inaccurate proxy for other, more germane bases of classification. Hence, "archaic and overbroad" generalizations, concerning the financial position of servicewomen and working women could not justify use of a gender line in determining eligibility for certain governmental entitlements. Similarly, increasingly outdated misconceptions concerning the role of females in the home rather than in the "marketplace and world of ideas" were rejected as loose-fitting characterizations incapable of supporting state statutory schemes that were premised upon their accuracy. In light of the weak congruence between gender and the characteristic or trait that gender purported to represent, it was necessary that the legislatures choose either to realign their substantive laws in a gender-neutral fashion, or to adopt procedures for identifying those instances where the sex-centered generalization actually comported with fact.

In this case, too, "Reed, we feel, is controlling . . .." We turn then to the question whether, under Reed, the difference between males and females with respect to the purchase of 3.2% beer warrants the differential in age drawn by the Oklahoma statute. We conclude that it does not.

JUSTICE POWELL, concurring opinion omitted.

JUSTICE STEVENS, concurring opinion omitted.

JUSTICE REHNQUIST, dissenting:

The Court's disposition of this case is objectionable on two grounds. First is its conclusion that men challenging a gender-based statute which treats them less favorably than women may invoke a more stringent standard of judicial review than pertains to most other types of classifications. Second is the Court's enunciation of this standard, without citation to any source, as being that "classifications by gender must serve important governmental objectives and must be substantially related to achievement of those objectives." The only redeeming feature of the Court's opinion, to my mind, is that it apparently signals a retreat . . . from [the] view that sex is a "suspect" classification for purposes of equal protection analysis. I think the Oklahoma statute challenged here need pass only the "rational basis" equal protection analysis . . . , and I believe that it is constitutional under that analysis.

. . .

The Court's conclusion that a law which treats males less favorably than females "must serve important governmental objectives and must be substantially related to achievement of those objectives" apparently comes out of thin air. The Equal Protection Clause contains no such language, and none of our previous cases adopt that standard. I would think we have had enough difficulty with the two standards of review which our cases have recognized - the norm of "rational basis," and the "compelling state interest" required where a "suspect classification" is involved - so as to counsel weightily against the insertion of still another "standard" between those two. How is this Court to divine what objectives are important? How is it to determine whether a particular law is "substantially" related to the achievement of such objective, rather than related in some other way to its achievement? …

I would have thought that if this Court were to leave anything to decision by the popularly elected branches of the Government, where no constitutional claim other than that of equal protection is invoked, it would be the decision as to what governmental objectives to be achieved by law are "important," and which are not. As for the second part of the Court's new test, the Judicial Branch is probably in no worse position than the Legislative or Executive Branches to determine if there is any rational relationship between a classification and the purpose which it might be thought to serve.

The applicable rational-basis test is one which

> "permits the States a wide scope of discretion in enacting laws which

affect some groups of citizens differently than others. The constitutional safeguard is offended only if the classification rests on grounds wholly irrelevant to the achievement of the State's objective. State legislatures are presumed to have acted within their constitutional power despite the fact that, in practice, their laws result in some inequality. A statutory discrimination will not be set aside if any state of facts reasonably may be conceived to justify it."
McGowan v. Maryland.

Our decisions indicate that application of the Equal Protection Clause in a context not justifying an elevated level of scrutiny does not demand "mathematical nicety" or the elimination of all inequality. Those cases recognize that the practical problems of government may require rough accommodations of interests, and hold that such accommodations should be respected unless no reasonable basis can be found to support them. Whether the same ends might have been better or more precisely served by a different approach is no part of the judicial inquiry under the traditional minimum rationality approach.

United States v. Windsor, 570 U.S. 744 (2013)

SUMMMARY: The Court struck down part of the Defense of Marriage Act (DOMA), a federal law which defined marriage as "only a legal union between one man and one woman." The law had in effect denied federal benefits to same-sex couples whose marriages were recognized under state law. The Court found no legitimate purpose of the law overcomes the purpose and effect of the law which was to injure demean and deny equal statutes to same sex marriages.

Obergefell v. Hodges, 576 U.S. ___ (2015)

The Fourteenth Amendment's Equal Protection Clause (and the Due Process Clause) guarantees same-sex couples the same fundamental right to marry as is afforded to opposite sex couples and ruled that the state prohibitions on same-sex marriage were unconstitutional.

SECTION THREE: CONSTITUTIONAL RIGHTS IN THE INVESTIGATORY PHASE, PART I

Chapter 3: Applicability of the Fourth Amendment

The Fourth Amendment to the United States Constitution states,

The right of the people to be secure in their persons, houses, papers and effects, against unreasonable searches and seizures, shall not be violated, and no warrants shall issue but upon probable cause, supported by oath or affirmation, and particularly describing the place to be searched and the person or things to be seized.

As stated in hundreds of cases, the Fourth Amendment prohibits unreasonable searches and seizures. Thus, the Constitution limits government's ability to detain people (affect their liberty interest), take their stuff (affect their proprietary interest), and look at or into their homes, things, or person (affect their privacy interest). Let's be clear, the Fourth Amendment and its surrounding case law is complex, voluminous, and ever-changing. So, brace yourself. It is easy to get lost in the weeds on this,[54] but if you were to consider the following questions (and their "sub-questions") in the following order, you will have a flow-chart on how to approach the Fourth Amendment and a "search and seizure" analysis.

Chapter Three discusses the questions about applicability or scope of the Fourth Amendment—who it restrains, who it protects, where (location) it is applicable, and what it constrains (searches and seizures).

1. Was there a *governmental* action? (Who was the actor, was it a governmental entity?) Who does the Fourth Amendment restrain? For example, does the amendment only apply to police, or does it extend to any governmental agent? Note that if there is not a government action, then the Fourth Amendment's protection is not available (although there may be some private complaint against a private citizen that can be brought.)

---

[54] One tricky thing about all the search and seizure cases is that they all inter-relate. You will read a case in one section defining searches or seizures (the topics in this chapter), but then you will see there is also a question about whether the search was reasonable, consent was given, or the exclusionary rule should apply. Rarely, will the facts involved in a "search and seizure case" decided by the Court take on only one Fourth Amendment issue. For example, the *Mendenhall* Court addressed whether the government action was a seizure and whether Mendenhall consented to the searches; *in Hodari D*, the Court examined whether the government action was a seizure, and whether drugs were properly considered abandoned property; the *Place* Court addressed whether a dog sniff is a search and also whether Place's luggage was appropriately seized. So, how do you, the reader, approach these cases and keep them straight? First, one approach is to consider their chronology. When was the case decided? If some case is inconsistent with another, ask which case came first. Was there precedent that had to be followed? Overruled? The following chapters attempt to follow a "flow chart" search and seizure analysis, but you may nevertheless find that a case "fits" better and illustrates one aspect of search and seizure law more than the area where the author has chosen to discuss it. When fitting it all together and attempting to analyze a new scenario (as the Court might), consider all these cases as "tools in your toolbelt." Some of the cases clearly are used more appropriately in deciding a specific issue, but then there are some cases that are "multi-purpose tools" and have a lot to say about search and seizure jurisprudence in general.

2. Who was the person whose rights were "violated." Another way of asking this is "who does the Fourth Amendment protect --Does the Fourth Amendment only protect citizens or does it protect any person?

3. Where did the government action occur? Do Fourth Amendment protections reach other countries or just American soil?

4. Is the government action that took place even covered by the Fourth Amendment? Specifically, is the government action a "search" (as defined by cases)? Is the government action in question a "seizure" (as defined by cases)? Note that if the government action is not a "search" or a "seizure" then the Fourth Amendment "is not implicated" (meaning the Amendment does not limit the government from doing that action.

Chapter Four covers the questions about the warrant requirement specifically mentioned in the Fourth Amendment. In addition to exploring the necessary components of a valid warrant, you will read what a proper execution of the warrant looks like. Chapter Four answers the following questions in the flow chart of search and seizure.

5. Assuming there is a governmental action, against a protected person, in a protected place that is either a search or seizure as defined by case law, was there a warrant?

6. If there was a warrant, was it valid?

> Was there an affidavit sworn to by an oath or affirmation that supported the warrant application?

> Did the warrant and affidavit spell out in particular (in enough detail) the place or person to be searched or seized?

> Was there probable cause to support the warrant? What is probable cause anyway --how does it differ from hunches, reasonable suspicion, absolute certainty, for example. What facts can be considered to develop probable cause?

> Did a neutral and detached magistrate review and issue the warrant?

7. If the warrant was valid, was it executed properly?

> Did the government violate anyone's rights while executing the warrant by using too much force?

> Did the government violate anyone's rights by going outside the scope of the warrant?

> By the time the government executed the warrant, was it stale?

> Did the government agents knock and announce their presence when searching a home?

> Did the government improperly restrain someone while executing the warrant

> Can the government seize property seen in plain view during the execution of a search warrant which is not listed on the warrant?

Finally, Chapter Five covers questions surrounding the reasonableness of searches or seizures that were done without a warrant. The government must overcome the presumption that such warrantless searches are unconstitutional, but it can do so by pointing to the Court's case law which established that some warrantless searches and seizures are in fact reasonable and therefore fall under some "well-delineated exceptions to the warrant requirement."

8. If there was no warrant, was the search or seizure nevertheless reasonable?

> Were the actions reasonable because the action was arguably within a group of well-delineated exceptions to the warrant requirement?

> What are the conditions of those well-delineated exceptions to the warrant requirement and were they met in this circumstance?

9. If there was no warrant, nor was it reasonable to act without a warrant, what remedies are there available?

> Should the evidence be excluded from defendant's trial

> Does the exclusionary rule apply or is there an exception to the exclusionary rule that applies in these circumstances?

So, let's get started with our search and seizure analysis by examining the applicability of the Fourth Amendment.

WAS THERE A GOVERNMENTAL ACTION?

The Fourth Amendment applies only to searches and seizures that are the product of government action. Who qualifies as a government actor has been broadly construed and encompasses any governmental actor or an agent of the government actor — not just the police. See e.g., *Dow Chemical Co v. United States,* 476 U.S. 227 (1986) (employee of the Environmental Protection Agency) *and New Jersey v. T.L.O.,* 469 U.S. 325 (1985) (school employees). A private-party search becomes a government search if "the government coerces, dominates or directs the actions" of the person conducting the search. *United States v. Smythe*, 84 F.3d 1240, 1242 (10th Cir 1996).

WHOM DOES THE FOURTH AMENDMENT PROTECT?

Implicit from the case of *United States v. Montoya De Hernandez,* 473 U.S 531 (1985) (see below), is that the citizenship of the person being searched and or seized is irrelevant. Rosa Montoya De Hernandez was a Colombian woman flying from Colombia who was seized and searched at the airport in the United States because she was suspected to be smuggling drugs through swallowing balloons. The issue in the case was whether her warrantless searches at the international border was reasonable. The case never mentioned her citizenship, and seemed to assume that generally, the government's conduct was governed by the Fourth Amendment

WHERE DID THE GOVERNMENTAL ACTION OCCUR?

In *United States v. Verdugo-Urquidez*, 494 U.S. 259 (1990), a joint operation between Mexican police and U.S. Marshals resulted in the defendant, a resident and citizen of Mexico believed to be one of the leaders of a large and violent drug smuggling operation in Mexico and the United States, being arrested and transported to the United States. His property in Mexico was searched and the evidence found in that search was used in his trial in the United States. The question before the Court was whether the Fourth Amendment applied to the search and seizure by United States agents of the property which was owned by a non-resident and located in a foreign country. The Court held that it does not.

"The available historical data show … that the purpose of the Fourth Amendment was to protect the people of the United States against arbitrary action by their own Government; it was never suggested that the provision was intended to restrain the actions of the Federal Government against aliens *outside* of the United States territory. . . ."

Similarly, in 1990 the United States invaded Panama and forcibly abducted former Panamanian leader Manuel Noriega who had been indicted in Miami in 1989. Noriega was brought to the United States, tried and convicted in 1992. The Court found no Fourth Amendment violation for the actions occurring in Panama. After the events of September 11, 2001, the United States began (or increased) the practice of government renditions. Renditions (also known extraordinary or forceful renditions) involve government-sponsored abduction and transporting an individual to a country with more lax laws governing interrogation techniques and detention. These practices probably draw their authority from the Court's interpretation that the Fourth Amendment does not applying to action outside of the U.S., regardless of citizenship status.

IS THE GOVERNMENTAL ACTION A SEARCH?

The Fourth Amendment protects against unreasonable searches and seizures. If the government action is not considered a search or seizure, is it not protected by the Fourth Amendment. So, in deciding whether the Constitution limited the government's action, we must consider whether the action meets the Court's definition of what constitutes a "search" or a "seizure." In this section, we examine how the Court has defined what is a search.

What Is A Search?

In *Olmstead v. United States, 277 U.S. 438 (1928),* the Court analyzed whether a search had occurred by focusing on whether the government had trespassed onto an individual's property. The facts in *Olmstead* involve a liquor distribution ring throughout the Pacific Northwest. The opinion reflects the government's grave concern with fighting the illegal distribution of liquor at that time (during prohibition). At issue in the case was whether the government wiretap of the defendant's home was an impermissible search and thus a violation of the Fourth Amendment. Justice Brandeis, dissented, arguing against the "trespass doctrine" embraced by the majority, opining that the Fourth Amendment is about the "right to be left alone." This sentiment became the cornerstone of modern Fourth Amendment jurisprudence on searches and privacy interests.

From 1967 (*Katz v. United States, 389 U.S. 347*) until 2012 (*United States v. Jones,* 565 U.S. 400 (2012)), the Court focused on an individual's right to be left alone under the circumstances and whether the government had interfered with a person's reasonable expectation of privacy in deciding whether a governmental action constituted a search. Most cases in the next three chapters were decided under the privacy doctrine enunciated in *Katz.*

In 2012, the Court revisited the *Olmstead* trespass doctrine that was long considered dead. In two cases, *Jones* and *Jardines v. Florida,* the court majority decided the case by pointing to the trespass doctrine, stating that the privacy doctrine added to, but did not supplant, the trespass doctrine.

Olmstead: A Search Is A Governmental Intrusion/Trespass On A Protected Space.

OLMSTEAD v. UNITED STATES
277 U.S. 438 (1928)

CHIEF JUSTICE TAFT delivered the opinion of the Court.

The single question. . . [for the court is] whether the use of evidence of private telephone conversations between the defendants and others, intercepted by means of

wire tapping, amounted to a violation of the 4th and 5th Amendments.

The evidence in the records discloses a conspiracy of amazing magnitude to import, possess and sell liquor unlawfully. It involved the employment of not less than fifty persons, of two seagoing vessels for the transportation of liquor to British Columbia, of smaller vessels for coastwise transportation to the state of Washington, the purchase and use of a ranch beyond the suburban limits of Seattle, with a large underground cache for storage and a number of smaller caches in that city, the maintenance of a central office manned with operators, the employment of executives, salesmen, deliverymen, dispatchers, scouts, bookkeepers, collectors and an attorney. In a bad month sales amounted to $176,000; the aggregate for a year must have exceeded two million of dollars.

Olmstead was the leading conspirator and the general manager of the business. He made a contribution of $10,000 to the capital; eleven others contributed $1,000 each. The profits were divided one-half to Olmstead and the remainder to the other eleven. Of the several offices in Seattle the chief one was in a large office building. In this there were three telephones on three different lines. There were telephones in an office of the manager in his own home, at the homes of his associates, and at other places in the city. Communication was had frequently with Vancouver, British Columbia. Times were fixed for the deliveries of the "stuff," to places along Puget Sound near Seattle, and from there the liquor was removed and deposited in the caches already referred to. One of the chief men was always on duty at the main office to receive orders by the telephones and to direct their filing by a corps of men stationed in another room — the "bull pen." The call numbers of the telephones were given to those known to be likely customers. At times the sales amounted to 200 cases of liquor per day.

The information which led to the discovery of the conspiracy and its nature and extent was largely obtained by intercepting messages on the telephones of the conspirators by four Federal prohibition officers. Small wires were inserted along the ordinary telephone wires from the residences of four of the petitioners and those leading from the chief office. The insertions were made without trespass upon any property of the defendants. They were made in the basement of the large office building. The taps from house lines were made in the streets near the houses.

The gathering of evidence continued for many months. . . . Many of the intercepted conversations were not merely reports but parts of the criminal acts. The evidence also disclosed the difficulties to which the conspirators were subjected, the reported news of the capture of vessels, the arrest of their men and the seizure of cases of liquor in garages and other places. It showed the dealing by Olmstead, the chief conspirator, with members of the Seattle police, the messages to them which secured the release of arrested members of the conspiracy, and also direct promises to officers of payments as soon as opportunity offered. . . .

The [Fourth] Amendment itself shows that the search is to be of material things — the person, the house, his papers or his effects. The description of the warrant necessary to make the proceeding lawful is that it must specify the place to be searched and the person or things to be seized. . . .

The Amendment does not forbid what was done here. There was no searching. There was no seizure. The evidence was secured by the use of the sense of hearing and that only. There was no entry of the house or offices of the defendants.

The language of the Amendment can not be extended and expanded to include telephone wires reaching to the whole world from the defendant's house or office. The intervening wires are not part of his house or office, any more than are the highways along which they are stretched. . . .

…[O]ne who installs in his house a telephone instrument with connecting wires intends to project his voice to those quite outside, and that the wires beyond his house and messages while passing over them are not within the protection of the 4th Amendment. Here those who intercepted the projected voices were not in the house of either party to the conversation. …

We think, therefore, that the wire tapping here disclosed did not amount to a search or seizure within the meaning of the 4th Amendment. ...

JUSTICE BRANDEIS, dissenting:

[The founders of the Constitution] conferred, as against the government, the right to be let alone — the most comprehensive of rights and the right most valued by civilized men. To protect that right, every unjustifiable intrusion by the government upon the privacy of the individual, whatever the means employed, must be deemed a violation of the 4th Amendment. ...

...It is, of course, immaterial where the physical connection with the telephone wires leading into the defendants' premises was made. And it is also immaterial that the intrusion was in aid of law enforcement. Experience should teach us to be most on our guard to protect liberty when the government's purposes are beneficent. Men born to freedom are naturally alert to repel invasion of their liberty by evil-minded rulers.

The greatest dangers to liberty lurk in insidious encroachment by men of zeal, well-meaning, but without understanding. ...

Decency, security, and liberty alike demand that government officials shall be subjected to the same rules of conduct that are commands to the citizen. In a government of laws, existence of the government will be imperiled if it fails to observe the law scrupulously. Our government is the potent, the omnipresent, teacher. For good or for ill, it teaches the whole people by its example. Crime is contagious. If the government becomes a law-breaker, it breeds contempt for law; it invites every man to become a law unto himself; it invites anarchy. To declare that in the administration of the criminal law the end justifies the means — to declare that the government may commit crimes in order to secure the conviction of a private criminal — would bring terrible retribution. Against that pernicious doctrine this court should resolutely set its face.

Katz: A Search Is A Governmental Intrusion On A Person's Privacy Interest

The Court considers the degree of intrusion into a zone of privacy in determining whether a search has occurred. "Under the Fourth Amendment, a search occurs when government officials invade a defendant's legitimate expectation of privacy." *Oliver v. United States* (1984); *Katz v. United States* (1967). "Official conduct that does not compromise any legitimate interest in privacy is not a search subject to the Fourth Amendment." *Illinois v. Caballes* (2005). "A defendant is not entitled to suppression unless the defendant demonstrates that the defendant has standing -- that the search violated his or her own personal Fourth Amendment right to a legitimate expectation of privacy." *Minnesota v. Carter*, 525 U.S 83 (1978). Although, a government agent's minimal intrusion into an area in which the defendant has a reasonable expectation of privacy may not violate the Fourth Amendment (see, e.g., *Maryland v. Wilson*, 519 U.S. 408 (1997), when "the Government uses a device that is not in general public use [e.g., a thermal imaging device], to explore details of the home that would previously have been unknowable without physical intrusion, the surveillance is a "search" and is presumptively unreasonable without a warrant." *Kyllo v. United States*, 533 U.S., at 40.

As we will explore in greater detail later in this chapter, the Court has concluded that individuals do not have an expectation of privacy in an open field (see, *Oliver v. United States, below);* outside the curtilage of a home (see, *Dunn v. United States*, below); in property they abandon or garbage they leave at the curb (see, *California v. Greenwood*, 486 U.S. 35 (1988); in a telephone number dialed on a phone (see, *Smith v. Maryland*, below); in the odor of controlled substances that may be detected by trained dogs from outside a vehicle (see, *Illinois v. Caballes*, below). The Court also has concluded that a person has a diminished expectation of privacy in an area outside a business (see, e.g., *Dow Chemical Co. v. United States*, 476 U.S. 227 (1986) or inside a car (see, e.g., *United*

States v. Knotts, 460 U.S. 276 (1983) (but see, *Byrd v. United States*, 584 U.S. ____ (2018) where Court held that a person may have a privacy interest in a rental car even when they are not the registered renter). But generally, activities conducted privately within a home are protected by the Fourth Amendment. "In the home . . . all details are intimate details, because the entire area is held safe from prying eyes." *Kyllo v. United States,* 533 U.S. 27 (2001).

KATZ v. UNITED STATES
389 U.S. 347 (1967)

JUSTICE STEWART delivered the opinion of the Court.

The petitioner was convicted … [for]… transmitting wagering information by telephone from Los Angeles to Miami and Boston in violation of a federal statute. At trial the Government was permitted, over the petitioner's objection, to introduce evidence of the petitioner's end of telephone conversations, overheard by FBI agents who had attached an electronic listening and recording device to the outside of the public telephone booth from which he had placed his calls. . . .

… [T]he parties have attached great significance to the characterization of the telephone booth from which the petitioner placed his calls. The petitioner has strenuously argued that the booth was a "constitutionally protected area." The Government has maintained with equal vigor that it was not. But this effort to decide whether or not a given "area," viewed in the abstract, is "constitutionally protected" deflects attention from the problem presented by this case. For the Fourth Amendment protects people, not places. What a person knowingly exposes to the public, even in his own home or office, is not a subject of Fourth Amendment protection. But what he seeks to preserve as private, even in an area accessible to the public, may be constitutionally protected.

The Government stresses the fact that the telephone booth from which the petitioner made his calls was constructed partly of glass, so that he was as visible after he entered it as he would have been if he had remained outside. But what he sought to exclude when he entered the booth was not the intruding eye — it was the uninvited ear. He did not shed his right to do so simply because he made his calls from a place where he might be seen. No less than an individual in a business office, in a friend's apartment, or in a taxicab, a person in a telephone booth may rely upon the protection of the Fourth Amendment. One who occupies it, shuts the door behind him, and pays the toll that permits him to place a call is surely entitled to assume that the words he utters into the mouthpiece will not be broadcast to the world. To read the Constitution more narrowly is to ignore the vital role that the public telephone has come to play in private communication.

The Government contends, however, that the activities of its agents in this case should not be tested by Fourth Amendment requirements, for the surveillance technique they employed involved no physical penetration of the telephone booth from which the petitioner placed his calls. It is true that the absence of such penetration was at one time thought to foreclose further Fourth Amendment inquiry, . . .for that Amendment was thought to limit only searches and seizures of tangible property. But "[t]he premise that property interests control the right of the Government to search and seize has been discredited." Thus, although a closely divided Court supposed in *Olmstead* that surveillance without any trespass and without the seizure of any material object fell outside the ambit of the Constitution, we have since departed from the narrow view on which that decision rested. Indeed, we have expressly held that the Fourth Amendment governs not only the seizure of tangible items, but extends as well to the recording of oral statements overheard without any "technical trespass under . . .local property law." Once this much is acknowledged, and once it is recognized that the Fourth Amendment protects people — and not simply "areas" — against unreasonable searches and seizures it becomes clear that the reach of the Amendment cannot turn upon the presence or absence of a physical intrusion into any given enclosure.

We conclude that the underpinnings of . . .[*Olmstead v. United States*] . . .have been so eroded by our subsequent decisions that the "trespass" doctrine there enunciated can no longer be regarded as controlling. The Government's activities in electronically listening to and recording the petitioner's words violated the privacy upon which he justifiably relied while using the telephone booth and thus constituted a "search and seizure" within the meaning of the Fourth Amendment. The fact that the electronic device employed to achieve that end did not happen to penetrate the wall of the booth can have no constitutional significance.

The question remaining for decision, then, is whether the search and seizure conducted in this case complied with constitutional standards. In that regard, the Government's position is that its agents acted in an entirely defensible manner. They did not begin their electronic surveillance until investigation of the petitioner's activities had established a strong probability that he was using the telephone in question to transmit gambling information to persons in other States, in violation of federal law. Moreover, the surveillance was limited, both in scope and in duration, to the specific purpose of establishing the contents of the petitioner's unlawful telephone communications. The agents confined their surveillance to the brief periods during which he used the telephone booth, and they took great care to overhear only the conversations of the petitioner himself.

Accepting this account of the Government's actions as accurate, it is clear that this surveillance was so narrowly circumscribed that a duly authorized magistrate, properly notified of the need for such investigation, specifically informed of the basis on which it was to proceed, and clearly apprised of the precise intrusion it would entail, could constitutionally have authorized, with appropriate safeguards, the very limited search and seizure that the Government asserts in fact took place. ...

JUSTICE HARLAN, concurring.

As the Court's opinion states, "the Fourth Amendment protects people, not places." The question, however, is what protection it affords to those people. Generally, as here, the answer to that question requires reference to a "place." My understanding of the rule that has emerged from prior decisions is that there is a twofold requirement, first that a person have exhibited an actual (subjective) expectation of privacy and, second, that the expectation be one that society is prepared to recognize as "reasonable." Thus a man's home is, for most purposes, a place where he expects privacy, but objects, activities, or statements that he exposes to the "plain view" of outsiders are not "protected" because no intention to keep them to himself has been exhibited. On the other hand, conversations in the open would not be protected against being overheard, for the expectation of privacy under the circumstances would be unreasonable.

The critical fact in this case is that "[o]ne who occupies it [a telephone booth], shuts the door behind him, and pays the toll that permits him to place a call is surely entitled to assume" that his conversation is not being intercepted. The point is not that the booth is "accessible to the public" at other times, but that it is a temporarily private place whose momentary occupants' expectations of freedom from intrusion are recognized as reasonable. . . .

JUSTICE BLACK, dissenting.

[F]or me the language of the Amendment is the crucial place to look in construing a written document such as our Constitution. . . .

The first clause [of the Fourth Amendment] protects "persons, houses, papers, and effects, against unreasonable searches and seizures. ..." These words connote the idea of tangible things with size, form, and weight, things capable of being searched, seized, or both. The second clause of the Amendment still further established its Framers' purpose to limit its protection to tangible things by providing that no warrants shall issue but those "particularly describing the place to be searched, and the persons or things to be seized." A

conversation overheard by eavesdropping, whether by plain snooping or wire-tapping, is not tangible and, under the normally accepted meanings of the words, can neither be searched nor seized. …I must conclude that the Fourth Amendment simply does not apply to eavesdropping. …

Jones -- A Search Is A Governmental Intrusion On A Person's Privacy Interest Or A Trespass Into A Protected Space.

UNITED STATES v. JONES
565 U.S. 400 (2012)

JUSTICE SCALIA delivered the opinion of the Court.

We decide whether the attachment of a Global-Positioning-System (GPS) tracking device to an individual's vehicle, and subsequent use of that device to monitor the vehicle's movements on public streets, constitutes a search or seizure within the meaning of the Fourth Amendment.

I

In 2004 respondent Antoine Jones, owner and operator of a nightclub in the District of Columbia, came under suspicion of trafficking in narcotics and was made the target of an investigation by a joint FBI and Metropolitan Police Department task force. Officers employed various investigative techniques, including visual surveillance of the nightclub, installation of a camera focused on the front door of the club, and a pen register and wiretap covering Jones's cellular phone.

Based in part on information gathered from these sources, in 2005 the Government applied to the United States District Court for the District of Columbia for a warrant authorizing the use of an electronic tracking device on the Jeep Grand Cherokee registered to Jones's wife. A warrant issued, authorizing installation of the device in the District of Columbia and within 10 days.

On the 11th day, and not in the District of Columbia but in Maryland, agents installed a GPS tracking device on the undercarriage of the Jeep while it was parked in a public parking lot. Over the next 28 days, the Government used the device to track the vehicle's movements, and once had to replace the device's battery when the vehicle was parked in a different public lot in Maryland. By means of signals from multiple satellites, the device established the vehicle's location within 50 to 100 feet, and communicated that location by cellular phone to a Government computer. It relayed more than 2,000 pages of data over the 4-week period.

The Government ultimately obtained a multiple-count indictment charging Jones and several alleged co-conspirators with … conspiracy to distribute and possess with intent to distribute five kilograms or more of cocaine and 50 grams or more of cocaine base … . Before trial, Jones filed a motion to suppress evidence obtained through the GPS device. The District Court … [suppressed] … the data obtained while the vehicle was parked in the garage adjoining Jones's residence. It held the remaining data admissible, because " '[a] person traveling in an automobile on public thoroughfares has no reasonable expectation of privacy in his movements from one place to another.' " …

[There was a hung jury, and then a retrial; the government again introduced GPS locational data admitted in the first trial which had connected Jones to the stash house, the drugs, and the cash. Jury convicted Jones and court sentenced him to life in prison. Jones appealed and the D.C. Circuit appeals court reversed his conviction, finding that the use of evidence obtained without a warrant violated his Fourth Amendment rights.]

II
A

We hold that the Government's installation of a GPS device on a target's vehicle, and its use of that device to monitor the vehicle's movements, constitutes a "search."

It is important to be clear about what occurred in this case: The Government physically occupied private property for the purpose of obtaining information. We have no doubt that such a physical intrusion would have been considered a "search" within the meaning of the Fourth Amendment when it was adopted. . . .

The text of the Fourth Amendment reflects its close connection to property, since otherwise it would have referred simply to "the right of the people to be secure against unreasonable searches and seizures"; the phrase "in their persons, houses, papers, and effects" would have been superfluous.

Consistent with this understanding, our Fourth Amendment jurisprudence was tied to common-law trespass, at least until the latter half of the 20th century. Thus, in *Olmstead v. United States* we held that wiretaps attached to telephone wires on the public streets did not constitute a Fourth Amendment search because "[t]here was no entry of the houses or offices of the defendants,". . .

Our later cases, of course, have deviated from that exclusively property-based approach. In *Katz v. United States*, we said that "the Fourth Amendment protects people, not places," and found a violation in attachment of an eavesdropping device to a public telephone booth. Our later cases have applied the analysis of Justice Harlan's concurrence in that case, which said that a violation occurs when government officers violate a person's "reasonable expectation of privacy," . . .

The Government contends that the Harlan standard shows that no search occurred here, since Jones had no "reasonable expectation of privacy" in the area of the Jeep accessed by Government agents (its underbody) and in the locations of the Jeep on the public roads, which were visible to all. But we need not address the Government's contentions, because Jones's Fourth Amendment rights do not rise or fall with the *Katz* formulation. At bottom, we must "assur[e] preservation of that degree of privacy against government that existed when the Fourth Amendment was adopted." *Kyllo*. As explained, for most of our history the Fourth Amendment was understood to embody a particular concern for government trespass upon the areas ("persons, houses, papers, and effects") it enumerates. *Katz* did not repudiate that understanding. . . ."[W]e [do not] believe that *Katz*, by holding that the Fourth Amendment protects persons and their private conversations, was intended to withdraw any of the protection which the Amendment extends to the home . . . ."

Katz did not erode the principle "that, when the Government does engage in physical intrusion of a constitutionally protected area in order to obtain information, that intrusion may constitute a violation of the Fourth Amendment." . . .

The Government contends that several of our post-*Katz* cases foreclose the conclusion that what occurred here constituted a search. It relies principally on two cases in which we rejected Fourth Amendment challenges to "beepers," electronic tracking devices that represent another form of electronic monitoring. The first case, United States v. *Knotts*, 460 US 276 (1983), upheld against Fourth Amendment challenge the use of a "beeper" that had been placed in a container of chloroform, allowing law enforcement to monitor the location of the container. We said that there had been no infringement of Knotts' reasonable expectation of privacy since the information obtained — the location of the automobile carrying the container on public roads, and the location of the off-loaded container in open fields near Knotts' cabin — had been voluntarily conveyed to the public. But as we have discussed, the *Katz* reasonable-expectation-of-privacy test has been added to, not substituted for, the common-law trespassory test. The holding in *Knotts* addressed only the former, since the latter was not at issue. The beeper had been placed in the container before it came into *Knotts'* possession, with the consent of the then-owner. Knotts did not challenge that installation, and we specifically declined to consider its effect on the Fourth Amendment analysis. . . .

[In *Karo* we said the government] . . . came into physical contact with the container only before it belonged to the defendant Karo; and the transfer of the container with the unmonitored beeper inside did not convey any information and thus did not invade Karo's privacy. That conclusion is perfectly consistent with the one we reach here. Karo accepted the container as it came to him, beeper and all, and was therefore not entitled to object to the beeper's presence, even though it was used to monitor the container's location.

. . .

B

This Court has to date not deviated from the understanding that mere visual observation does not constitute a search. We accordingly held in *Knotts* that "[a] person traveling in an automobile on public thoroughfares has no reasonable expectation of privacy in his movements from one place to another." Thus, even assuming that the concurrence is correct to say that "[t]raditional surveillance" of Jones for a 4-week period "would have required a large team of agents, multiple vehicles, and perhaps aerial assistance," our cases suggest that such visual observation is constitutionally permissible. It may be that achieving the same result through electronic means, without an accompanying trespass, is an unconstitutional invasion of privacy, but the present case does not require us to answer that question.

. . .

JUSTICE SOTOMAYOR, concurring.

I join the Court's opinion because I agree that a search within the meaning of the Fourth Amendment occurs, at a minimum, "[w]here, as here, the Government obtains information by physically intruding on a constitutionally protected area." In this case, the Government installed a Global Positioning System (GPS) tracking device on respondent Antoine Jones' Jeep without a valid warrant and without Jones' consent, then used that device to monitor the Jeep's movements over the course of four weeks. The Government usurped Jones' property for the purpose of conducting surveillance on him, thereby invading privacy interests long afforded, and undoubtedly entitled to, Fourth Amendment protection.

Of course, the Fourth Amendment is not concerned only with trespassory intrusions on property. Rather, even in the absence of a trespass, "a Fourth Amendment search occurs when the government violates a subjective expectation of privacy that society recognizes as reasonable." In *Katz*, this Court enlarged its then-prevailing focus on property rights by announcing that the reach of the Fourth Amendment does not "turn upon the presence or absence of a physical intrusion." As the majority's opinion makes clear, however, *Katz's* reasonable-expectation-of-privacy test augmented, but did not displace or diminish, the common-law trespassory test that preceded it. Thus, "when the Government does engage in physical intrusion of a constitutionally protected area in order to obtain information, that intrusion may constitute a violation of the Fourth Amendment." *United States v. Knotts*....[T]he trespassory test applied in the majority's opinion reflects an irreducible constitutional minimum: When the Government physically invades personal property to gather information, a search occurs. The reaffirmation of that principle suffices to decide this case.

Nonetheless . . . physical intrusion is now unnecessary to many forms of surveillance. With increasing regularity, the Government will be capable of duplicating the monitoring undertaken in this case by enlisting factory- or owner-installed vehicle tracking devices or GPS-enabled smartphones. In cases of electronic or other novel modes of surveillance that do not depend upon a physical invasion on property, the majority opinion's trespassory test may provide little guidance. But "[s]ituations involving merely the transmission of electronic signals without trespass would remain subject to *Katz* analysis." ... [T]he same technological advances that have made possible nontrespassory surveillance techniques will also affect the *Katz* test by shaping the evolution of societal privacy expectations. Under that rubric, I agree with Justice Alito that, at the very least, "longer term GPS monitoring in investigations of most offenses impinges on expectations of privacy."

In cases involving even short-term monitoring, some unique attributes of GPS surveillance relevant to the *Katz* analysis will require particular attention. GPS monitoring generates a precise, comprehensive record of a person's public movements that reflects a wealth of detail about her familial, political, professional, religious, and sexual associations. ... The Government can store such records and efficiently mine them for information years into the future. And because GPS monitoring is cheap in comparison to conventional surveillance techniques and, by design, proceeds surreptitiously, it evades the ordinary checks that constrain abusive law enforcement practices: "limited police resources and community hostility."

Awareness that the Government may be watching chills associational and expressive freedoms. And the Government's unrestrained power to assemble data that reveal private aspects of identity is susceptible to abuse. The net result is that GPS monitoring — by making available at a relatively low cost such a substantial quantum of intimate information about any person whom the Government, in its unfettered discretion, chooses to track — may "alter the relationship between citizen and government in a way that is inimical to

democratic society." *United States v. Cuevas-Perez.*

I would take these attributes of GPS monitoring into account when considering the existence of a reasonable societal expectation of privacy in the sum of one's public movements. I would ask whether people reasonably expect that their movements will be recorded and aggregated in a manner that enables the Government to ascertain, more or less at will, their political and religious beliefs, sexual habits, and so on. I do not regard as dispositive the fact that the Government might obtain the fruits of GPS monitoring through lawful conventional surveillance techniques. ... I would also consider the appropriateness of entrusting to the Executive, in the absence of any oversight from a coordinate branch, a tool so amenable to misuse, especially in light of the Fourth Amendment's goal to curb arbitrary exercises of police power to and prevent "a too permeating police surveillance." ...

More fundamentally, it may be necessary to reconsider the premise that an individual has no reasonable expectation of privacy in information voluntarily disclosed to third parties. This approach is ill suited to the digital age, in which people reveal a great deal of information about themselves to third parties in the course of carrying out mundane tasks. People disclose the phone numbers that they dial or text to their cellular providers; the URLs that they visit and the e-mail addresses with which they correspond to their Internet service providers; and the books, groceries, and medications they purchase to online retailers. Perhaps, as Justice Alito notes, some people may find the "tradeoff" of privacy for convenience "worthwhile," or come to accept this "diminution of privacy" as "inevitable," and perhaps not. I for one doubt that people would accept without complaint the warrantless disclosure to the Government of a list of every Web site they had visited in the last week, or month, or year. But whatever the societal expectations, they can attain constitutionally protected status only if our Fourth Amendment jurisprudence ceases to treat secrecy as a prerequisite for privacy. I would not assume that all information voluntarily disclosed to some member of the public for a limited purpose is, for that reason alone, disentitled to Fourth Amendment protection. ...

Resolution of these difficult questions in this case is unnecessary, however, because the Government's physical intrusion on Jones' Jeep supplies a narrower basis for decision. I therefore join the majority's opinion.

JUSTICE ALITO, with whom JUSTICE GINSBURG, JUSTICE BREYER, and JUSTICE KAGAN join, concurring in the judgment.

...

I would analyze the question presented in this case by asking whether respondent's reasonable expectations of privacy were violated by the long-term monitoring of the movements of the vehicle he drove.

The Fourth Amendment prohibits "unreasonable searches and seizures," and the Court makes very little effort to explain how the attachment or use of the GPS device fits within these terms. The Court does not contend that there was a seizure. A seizure of property occurs when there is "some meaningful interference with an individual's possessory interests in that property," *United States v. Jacobsen*, and here there was none. Indeed, the success of the surveillance technique that the officers employed was dependent on the fact that the GPS did not interfere in any way with the operation of the vehicle, for if any such interference had been detected, the device might have been discovered.

The Court's reasoning in this case is very similar to that in the Court's early decisions involving wiretapping and electronic eavesdropping, namely, that a technical trespass followed by the gathering of evidence constitutes a search. In the early electronic surveillance cases, the Court concluded that a Fourth Amendment search occurred when private conversations were monitored as a result of an "unauthorized physical penetration into the premises occupied" by the defendant. *Silverman v. United States.* In Silverman, police officers listened to conversations in an attached home by inserting a "spike mike" through the wall that this house shared with the vacant house next door. This procedure was held to be a search because the mike made contact with a heating duct on the other side of the wall and thus "usurp[ed] ... an integral part of the premises."

...

This trespass-based rule was repeatedly criticized. ...

Katz v. United States finally did away with the old approach, holding that a trespass was not required for a Fourth Amendment violation. ... What mattered, the Court now held, was whether the conduct at issue "violated the privacy upon which [the defendant] justifiably relied while using the telephone booth."

Under this approach, as the Court later put it when addressing the relevance of a technical trespass, "an actual trespass is neither necessary nor sufficient to establish a constitutional violation." ...

II

. . . .

In sum, the majority is hard pressed to find support in post-*Katz* cases for its trespass-based theory.

...

IV

A

The *Katz* expectation-of-privacy test ... is not without its own difficulties. It involves a degree of circularity, and judges are apt to confuse their own expectations of privacy with those of the hypothetical reasonable person to which the *Katz* test looks. In addition, the *Katz* test rests on the assumption that this hypothetical reasonable person has a well-developed and stable set of privacy expectations. But technology can change those expectations. Dramatic technological change may lead to periods in which popular expectations are in flux and may ultimately produce significant changes in popular attitudes. New technology may provide increased convenience or security at the expense of privacy, and many people may find the tradeoff worthwhile. And even if the public does not welcome the diminution of privacy that new technology entails, they may eventually reconcile themselves to this development as inevitable.

On the other hand, concern about new intrusions on privacy may spur the enactment of legislation to protect against these intrusions. This is what ultimately happened with respect to wiretapping. After *Katz*, Congress did not leave it to the courts to develop a body of Fourth Amendment case law governing that complex subject. Instead, Congress promptly enacted a comprehensive statute. . . .

B

Recent years have seen the emergence of many new devices that permit the monitoring of a person's movements. In some locales, closed-circuit television video monitoring is becoming ubiquitous. On toll roads, automatic toll collection systems create a precise record of the movements of motorists who choose to make use of that convenience. Many motorists purchase cars that are equipped with devices that permit a central station to ascertain the car's location at any time so that roadside assistance may be provided if needed and the car may be found if it is stolen.

Perhaps most significant, cell phones and other wireless devices now permit wireless carriers to track and record the location of users — and as of June 2011, it has been reported, there were more than 322 million wireless devices in use in the United States. For older phones, the accuracy of the location information depends on the density of the tower network, but new "smart phones," which are equipped with a GPS device, permit more precise tracking. For example, when a user

activates the GPS on such a phone, a provider is able to monitor the phone's location and speed of movement and can then report back real-time traffic conditions after combining ("crowdsourcing") the speed of all such phones on any particular road. Similarly, phone-location-tracking services are offered as "social" tools, allowing consumers to find (or to avoid) others who enroll in these services. The availability and use of these and other new devices will continue to shape the average person's expectations about the privacy of his or her daily movements.

V

In the pre-computer age, the greatest protections of privacy were neither constitutional nor statutory, but practical. Traditional surveillance for any extended period of time was difficult and costly and therefore rarely undertaken. The surveillance at issue in this case — constant monitoring of the location of a vehicle for four weeks — would have required a large team of agents, multiple vehicles, and perhaps aerial assistance. Only an investigation of unusual importance could have justified such an expenditure of law enforcement resources. Devices like the one used in the present case, however, make long-term monitoring relatively easy and cheap. In circumstances involving dramatic technological change, the best solution to privacy concerns may be legislative. A legislative body is well situated to gauge changing public attitudes, to draw detailed lines, and to balance privacy and public safety in a comprehensive way.

To date, however, Congress and most States have not enacted statutes regulating the use of GPS tracking technology for law enforcement purposes. The best that we can do in this case is to apply existing Fourth Amendment doctrine and to ask whether the use of GPS tracking in a particular case involved a degree of intrusion that a reasonable person would not have anticipated.

Under this approach, relatively short-term monitoring of a person's movements on public streets accords with expectations of privacy that our society has recognized as reasonable. But the use of longer term GPS monitoring in investigations of most offenses impinges on expectations of privacy. For such offenses, society's expectation has been that law enforcement agents and others would not — and indeed, in the main, simply could not — secretly monitor and catalogue every single movement of an individual's car for a very long period. In this case, for four weeks, law enforcement agents tracked every movement that respondent made in the vehicle he was driving. We need not identify with precision the point at which the tracking of this vehicle became a search, for the line was surely crossed before the 4-week mark. Other cases may present more difficult questions. But where uncertainty exists with respect to whether a certain period of GPS surveillance is long enough to constitute a Fourth Amendment search, the police may always seek a warrant. …

For these reasons, I conclude that the lengthy monitoring that occurred in this case constituted a search under the Fourth Amendment. I therefore agree with the majority that the decision of the Court of Appeals must be affirmed.

Scenarios That Are Not Searches Under Katz.

Katz announced the standard which the Court has followed (at least primarily) for nearly six decades. If the majority of a court, after considering the circumstances of the case, decided that a person would not have a reasonable expectation of privacy, then what the government did was not a "search" and the action was not protected by the Fourth Amendment. The following cases demonstrate the various scenarios where the Court has found that no search took place using the Katz definition of search.

Plain Or Open View

If the government agent sees something which is in plain view (open view) then it is not a search because people who expose things to public view do not have a reasonable expectation of privacy Neither plain view nor open view rules are needed when a lawful observation is made by an officer from an area that is not protected by a privacy interest. In those circumstances, under the *Katz* definition, a search is not occurring.

The "plain view doctrine" is an exception to the warrant requirement specifically dealing with seizures of items without the benefit of a warrant. The doctrine and cases are discussed in far greater detail in Chapter Four. But simply, the doctrine holds that when police see evidence of a crime with their unaided senses from a place where they have a lawful right to be, they may seize it without stopping and getting a warrant.

Expectations Of Privacy In An Era Of Technology And Aerial Surveillance.

One of the requirements of the plain view doctrine is that the observation is made with unaided senses. The court has reviewed the use of emerging technology and aerial surveillance in deciding whether an individual had an expectation of privacy.

DOW CHEMICAL CO. V. UNITED STATES
476 U.S. 227 (1986)

[Facts Summarized:

Instead of getting an administrative search warrant to inspect Dow Chemical's industrial plant, the government employed an aerial photographer who used a standard precision aerial mapping camera to take photographs of the facility from various altitudes, all which were within lawful navigable airspace. Dow Chemical claimed the government violated its Fourth Amendment rights and sued the EPA alleging it acted beyond its statutory investigative authority. The District Court agreed, but the Circuit Court of Appeals reversed saying that what the EPA did was not a search.]

Court Opinion:

[The] EPA's taking, without a warrant, of aerial photographs of petitioner's plant complex from an aircraft lawfully in public navigable airspace was not a search prohibited by the Fourth Amendment. The open areas of an industrial plant complex such as petitioner's are not analogous to the "curtilage" of a dwelling, which is entitled to protection as a place where the occupants have a reasonable and legitimate expectation of privacy that society is prepared to accept. The intimate activities associated with family privacy and the home and its curtilage simply do not reach the outdoor areas or spaces between structures and buildings of a manufacturing plant. For purposes of aerial surveillance, the open areas of an industrial complex are more comparable to an "open field" in which an individual may not legitimately demand privacy. Here, EPA was not employing some unique sensory device not available to the public, but rather was employing a conventional, albeit precise, commercial camera commonly used in mapmaking. The photographs were not so revealing of intimate details as to raise constitutional concerns. The mere fact that human vision is enhanced somewhat, at least to the degree here, does not give rise to constitutional problems.

[The Court suggested, however, that "surveillance of private property using highly sophisticated surveillance equipment not generally available to the public, such as satellite technology, might be constitutionally proscribed absent a warrant."]

CALIFORNIA v. CIRAOLO
476 U.S. 207 (1986)

CHIEF JUSTICE BURGER delivered the opinion of the court.

(Official Summary)

The Santa Clara, Cal., police received an anonymous telephone tip that marijuana was growing in respondent's backyard, which was enclosed by two fences and shielded from view at ground level. Officers who were trained in marijuana identification secured a private airplane, flew over respondent's house at an altitude of 1,000 feet, and readily identified marijuana plants growing in the yard. A search warrant was later obtained on the basis of one of the officer's naked-eye observations; a photograph of the surrounding area taken from the airplane was attached as an exhibit. The warrant was executed, and marijuana plants were seized. After the California trial court denied respondent's motion to suppress the evidence of the search, he pleaded guilty to a charge of cultivation of marijuana. The California Court of Appeal reversed on the ground that the warrantless aerial observation of respondent's yard violated the Fourth Amendment.

Held: The Fourth Amendment was not violated by the naked-eye aerial observation of respondent's backyard.

The touchstone of Fourth Amendment analysis is whether a person has a constitutionally protected reasonable expectation of privacy, which involves the two inquiries of whether the individual manifested a subjective expectation of privacy in the object of the challenged search, and whether society is willing to recognize that expectation as reasonable. In pursuing the second inquiry, the test of legitimacy is not whether the individual chooses to conceal assertedly "private activity," but whether the government's intrusion infringes upon the personal and societal values protected by the Fourth Amendment.

On the record here, respondent's expectation of privacy from all observations of his backyard was unreasonable. That the backyard and its crop were within the "curtilage" of respondent's home did not itself bar all police observation. The mere fact that an individual has taken measures to restrict some views of his activities does not preclude an officer's observation from a public vantage point where he has a right to be and which renders the activities clearly visible. The police observations here took place within public navigable airspace, in a physically nonintrusive manner. The police were able to observe the plants readily discernible to the naked eye as marijuana, and it was irrelevant that the observation from the airplane was directed at identifying the plants and that the officers were trained to recognize marijuana. Any member of the public flying in this airspace who cared to glance down could have seen everything that the officers observed. The Fourth Amendment simply does not require police traveling in the public airways at 1,000 feet to obtain a warrant in order to observe what is visible to the naked eye.

JUSTICE POWELL, with whom JUSTICE BRENNAN, JUSTICE MARSHALL, and JUSTICE BLACKMUN join, dissenting.

…

Respondent contends that the police intruded on his constitutionally protected expectation of privacy when they conducted aerial surveillance of his home and photographed his backyard without first obtaining a warrant. The Court rejects that contention, holding that respondent's expectation of privacy in the curtilage of his home, although reasonable as to intrusions on the ground, was unreasonable as to surveillance from the navigable airspace. In my view, the Court's holding rests on only one obvious fact, namely, that the airspace generally is open to all persons for travel in airplanes. The Court does not explain why this single fact deprives citizens of their privacy interest in outdoor activities in an enclosed curtilage.

II

A

…

As the decision in *Katz* held, and dissenting opinions written by Justices of this Court prior to *Katz* recognized, a standard that defines a Fourth Amendment "search" by reference to whether police have physically invaded a "constitutionally protected area" provides no real protection against surveillance techniques made possible through technology. Technological advances have enabled police to see people's activities and associations, and to hear their conversations, without being in physical proximity. Moreover, the capability now exists for police to conduct intrusive surveillance without any physical penetration of the walls of homes or other structures that citizens may believe shelters their privacy. Looking to the Fourth Amendment for protection against such "broad and unsuspected governmental incursions" into the "cherished privacy of law-abiding citizens," the Court in *Katz* abandoned its inquiry into whether police had committed a physical trespass. *Katz* announced a standard under which the occurrence of a search turned not on the physical position of the police conducting the surveillance, but on whether the surveillance in question had invaded a constitutionally protected reasonable expectation of privacy.

Our decisions following the teaching of *Katz* illustrate that this inquiry "normally embraces two discrete questions." "The first is whether the individual, by his conduct, has exhibited an actual (subjective) expectation of privacy.' The second is whether that subjective expectation "is `one that society is prepared to recognize as "reasonable."'" While the Court today purports to reaffirm this analytical framework, its conclusory rejection of respondent's expectation of privacy in the yard of his residence as one that "is unreasonable," represents a turning away from the principles that have guided our Fourth Amendment inquiry. The Court's rejection of respondent's Fourth Amendment claim is curiously at odds with its purported reaffirmation of the curtilage doctrine, both in this decision and its companion case, *Dow Chemical Co. v. United States*, and particularly with its conclusion in *Dow* that society is prepared to recognize as reasonable expectations of privacy in the curtilage.

...

In deciding whether an area is within the curtilage, courts "have defined the curtilage, as did the common law, by reference to the factors that determine whether an individual reasonably may expect that an area immediately adjacent to the home will remain private. The lower federal courts have agreed that the curtilage is "an area of domestic use immediately surrounding a dwelling and usually, but not always, fenced in with the dwelling. Those courts also have held that whether an area is within the curtilage must be decided by looking at all of the facts. Relevant facts include the proximity between the area claimed to be curtilage and the home, the nature of the uses to which the area is put, and the steps taken by the resident to protect the area from observation by people passing by.

III

A

The Court begins its analysis of the Fourth Amendment issue posed here by deciding that respondent had an expectation of privacy in his backyard. I agree with that conclusion because of the close proximity of the yard to the house, the nature of some of the activities respondent conducted there, and because he had taken steps to shield those activities from the view of passersby. The Court then implicitly acknowledges that society is prepared to recognize his expectation as reasonable with respect to ground-level surveillance, holding that the yard was within the curtilage, an area in which privacy interests have been afforded the "most heightened" protection. As the foregoing discussion of the curtilage doctrine demonstrates, respondent's yard

unquestionably was within the curtilage. Since Officer Shutz could not see into this private family area from the street, the Court certainly would agree that he would have conducted an unreasonable search had he climbed over the fence, or used a ladder to peer into the yard without first securing a warrant.

The Court concludes, nevertheless, that Shutz could use an airplane -- a product of modern technology -- to intrude visually into respondent's yard. The Court argues that respondent had no reasonable expectation of privacy from aerial observation. It notes that Shutz was "within public navigable airspace," when he looked into and photographed respondent's yard. It then relies on the fact that the surveillance was not accompanied by a physical invasion of the curtilage. Reliance on the *manner* of surveillance is directly contrary to the standard of *Katz,* which identifies a constitutionally protected privacy right by focusing on the interests of the individual and of a free society. Since *Katz,* we have consistently held that the presence or absence of physical trespass by police is constitutionally irrelevant to the question whether society is prepared to recognize an asserted privacy interest as reasonable.

The Court's holding, therefore, must rest solely on the fact that members of the public fly in planes and may look down at homes as they fly over them. The Court does not explain why it finds this fact to be significant. One may assume that the Court believes that citizens bear the risk that air travelers will observe activities occurring within backyards that are open to the sun and air. This risk, the Court appears to hold, nullifies expectations of privacy in those yards even as to purposeful police surveillance from the air. The Court finds support for this conclusion in *United States v. Knotts,* 460 U. S. 276 (1983).

This line of reasoning is flawed. First, the actual risk to privacy from commercial or pleasure aircraft is virtually nonexistent. Travelers on commercial flights, as well as private planes used for business or personal reasons, normally obtain at most a fleeting, anonymous, and nondiscriminating glimpse of the landscape and buildings over which they pass. The risk that a passenger on such a plane might observe private activities, and might connect those activities with particular people, is simply too trivial to protect against. It is no accident that, as a matter of common experience, many people build fences around their residential areas, but few build roofs over their backyards. Therefore, contrary to the Court's suggestion, people do not "*knowingly expos[e]*" their residential yards "*`to the public'*" merely by failing to build barriers that prevent aerial surveillance.

…[T]he Court fails to acknowledge the qualitative difference between police surveillance and other uses made of the airspace. Members of the public use the airspace for travel, business, or pleasure, not for the purpose of observing activities taking place within residential yards. Here, police conducted an overflight at low altitude solely for the purpose of discovering evidence of crime within a private enclave into which they were constitutionally forbidden to intrude at ground level without a warrant. It is not easy to believe that our society is prepared to force individuals to bear the risk of this type of warrantless police intrusion into their residential areas.

B

Since respondent had a reasonable expectation of privacy in his yard, aerial surveillance undertaken by the police for the purpose of discovering evidence of crime constituted a "search" within the meaning of the Fourth Amendment. "Warrantless searches are presumptively unreasonable, though the Court has recognized a few limited exceptions to this general rule." This case presents no such exception. …

IV

Some may believe that this case, involving no physical intrusion on private property, presents "the obnoxious thing in its mildest and least repulsive form." But this Court recognized long ago that the essence of a Fourth Amendment violation is "not the breaking of [a person's] doors, and the rummaging of his drawers," but rather is "the invasion of his indefeasible right of personal security, personal liberty and private property." Rapidly advancing technology now permits police to conduct surveillance in the home itself, an area where privacy interests are most cherished in our society, without any physical trespass. While the rule in *Katz* was designed to prevent silent and unseen invasions of Fourth Amendment privacy rights in a variety of settings, we have consistently afforded heightened protection to a person's right to be left alone in the privacy of his house. The Court fails to enforce that right or to give any weight to the longstanding presumption that warrantless intrusions into the home are unreasonable. I dissent.

KYLLO v. UNITED STATES
533 U.S. 27 (2001)

JUSTICE SCALIA delivered the opinion of the Court.

[In 1991 agents of the U.S. Department of Interior were investigating the defendant. They used a thermos imaging device which detected infrared radiation not visible to the naked eye. They scanned Kylo's home from a parked car parked across the street from the front of the house and a street from the back of the house.] . . . The scan showed that the roof over the garage and a side wall of petitioners' home were relatively hot compared to the rest of the home and substantially warmer than neighboring homes in the triplex. Agent Elliott concluded that petitioner was using halide lights to grow marijuana in his house, which indeed he was. Based on tips from informants, utility bills, and the thermal imaging, a Federal Magistrate Judge issued a warrant authorizing a search of petitioners' home, and the agents found an indoor growing operation involving more than 100 plants.

The present case involves officers on a public street engaged in more than naked-eye surveillance of a home. We have previously reserved judgment as to how much technological enhancement of ordinary perception from such a vantage point, if any, is too much. . . .

We think that obtaining by sense-enhancing technology any information regarding the interior of the home that could not otherwise have been obtained without physical intrusion into a constitutionally protected area, . . . constitutes a search at least where (as here) the technology in question is not in general public use. This assures preservation of that degree of privacy against government that existed when the Fourth Amendment was adopted. On the basis of this criterion, the information obtained by the thermal imager in this case was the product of a search.

The Government maintains, however, that the thermal imaging must be upheld because it detected only heat radiating from the external surface of the house. . ... The dissent makes this its leading point, . . . contending that there is a fundamental difference between what it calls off-the-wall observations and through-the-wall surveillance. But just as a thermal imager captures only heat emanating from a house, so also a powerful directional microphone picks up only sound emanating from a house and a satellite capable of scanning from many miles away would pick up only visible light emanating from a house. We rejected such a mechanical interpretation of the Fourth Amendment in *Katz*, where the eavesdropping device picked up only sound waves that reached the exterior of the phone booth. Reversing that approach would leave the homeowner at the mercy of advancing technology including imaging technology that could discern all human activity in the home. While the technology used in the present case was relatively crude, the rule we adopt must take account of more sophisticated systems that are already in use or in development. . . .

The Government also contends that the thermal imaging was constitutional because it did not detect private activities occurring in private areas. . . . The Fourth Amendment's protection of the home has never been tied to measurement of the quality or quantity of information obtained. . . . In the home, our cases show, *all* details are intimate details, because the entire area is held safe from prying government eyes. . . .

. . .

We have said that the Fourth Amendment draws a firm line at the entrance to the house. . . . That line, we think, must be not only firm but also bright, which requires clear specification of those methods of surveillance that require a warrant. While it is certainly possible to conclude from the videotape of the thermal imaging that occurred in this case that no significant compromise of the homeowner's privacy has occurred, we must take the long view, from the original meaning of the Fourth Amendment forward. . . .

Where, as here, the Government uses a device that is not in general public use, to explore details of the home that would previously have been unknowable without physical intrusion, the surveillance is a search and is presumptively unreasonable without a warrant. . . .

JUSTICE STEVENS, with whom THE CHIEF JUSTICE, JUSTICE O'CONNOR, and JUSTICE KENNEDY join, dissenting.

All that the infrared camera did in this case was passively measure heat emitted from the exterior surfaces of petitioner's home; all that those measurements showed were relative differences in emission levels, vaguely indicating that some areas of the roof and outside walls were warmer than others. As still images from the infrared scans show, . . . no details regarding the interior of petitioner's home were revealed. Unlike an x-ray scan, or other possible through-the-wall techniques, the detection of infrared radiation emanating from the home did not accomplish an unauthorized physical penetration into the premises . . . nor did it obtain information that it could not have obtained by observation from outside the curtilage of the house. . . .

Indeed, the ordinary use of the senses might enable a neighbor or passerby to notice the heat emanating from a building, particularly if it is vented, as was the case here. ... Nor, in my view, does such observation become an unreasonable search if made from a distance with the aid of a device that merely discloses that the exterior of one house, or one area of the house, is much warmer than another. Nothing more occurred in this case.

Thus, the notion that heat emissions from the outside of a dwelling is a private matter implicating the protections of the Fourth Amendment (the text of which guarantees the right of people to be secure *in* their houses against unreasonable searches and seizures (emphasis added)) is not only unprecedented but also quite difficult to take seriously. Heat waves, like aromas that are generated in a kitchen, or in a laboratory or opium den, enter the public domain if and when they leave a building. A subjective expectation that they would remain private is not only implausible but also surely not one that society is prepared to recognize as reasonable. ...

To be sure, the homeowner has a reasonable expectation of privacy concerning what takes place within the home, and the Fourth Amendment's protection against physical invasions of the home should apply to their functional equivalent. But the equipment in this case did not penetrate the walls of petitioners home, and while it did pick up details of the home that were exposed to the public . . . it did not obtain any information regarding the *interior* of the home. . . .

Since what was involved in this case was nothing more than drawing inferences from off-the-wall surveillance, rather than any through-the-wall surveillance, the officers conduct did not amount to a search and was perfectly reasonable. . . .

Other Cases: Technological Enhancements

Texas v. Brown, 460 US 730 (1983).

The "use of artificial means to illuminate a darkened area does not constitute a search, and thus triggers no Fourth Amendment protection. "

United States v. Knotts, 460 U.S. 276 (1973).

Monitoring an electronic beeper on a public highway and in the 'open fields' of private property does not constitute a search or seizure under the Fourth Amendment.

United States v. Karo, 468 U.S. 705 (1984).

The Fourth Amendment is violated when officers, without a warrant, monitor a beeper in a private residence. *United States v. Karo*, 468 U.S. 705 (1984).

United States v. Dubrofsky, 581 F.2d 208 (1978)

SUMMARY: A package was mailed from Thailand to California and was intercepted by customs officials in San Francisco. A lawful customs search revealed ten plastic bags of heroin in the hollowed-out walls of the package. Customs turned the package over to the DEA, which removed the heroin and replaced it with six bags of white powder and two gags of heroin and electric beepers that allowed agents to follow the package and tell when the it had been opened.

The package was resealed and sent to the post office for a controlled delivery. On May 17 Dubrofsky picked up the parcel and drove to the residence of Ms. Cheryl Lovejoy in Santa Cruz. He was followed by federal agents and local police.

Soon after Dubrofsky entered Lovejoy's house the beeper changed tones, indicating that the package had been opened. Six or seven officers approached the residence and requested entry. Ms. Lovejoy admitted them, was informed of their purpose, and indicated that Dubrofsky was in the basement. The agents went there and discovered that the basement was locked from the outside. They obtained the combination from Ms. Lovejoy, opened the door, and ordered Dubrofsky to come out. Dubrofsky obeyed and was arrested.

After the arrest, Ms. Lovejoy was informed that she was a suspect in the investigation. She was given a Miranda warning, and her consent was requested to search the basement. Although a written consent was apparently given after the search, evidence at the suppression hearing indicates that Ms. Lovejoy gave a valid oral consent prior to the search. The package, heroin, heroin substitute, and the beepers were found in the basement.

Later that day a warrant was obtained to search Dubrofsky's home in Boulder Creek. The warrant was issued in San Francisco and telephonically relayed to an agent waiting at Dubrofsky's home. The agent performing the search never saw the warrant nor was informed of the specific items authorized to be seized. A passport, an alien registration card, a small amount of heroin, narcotics paraphernalia, a phone bill, a plane ticket, and a loan document were discovered in the search.

II. Installation and Use of the Electronic Surveillance Devices.

Dubrofsky contends that the installation and subsequent use of the electronic surveillance devices was a search falling within the Fourth Amendment's protections. We disagree.

A two-step analysis is required for problems presented by the use of electronic surveillance devices in law enforcement activities. First, it must be determined if the Fourth Amendment was violated when the device was installed. If installation of the device was proper, the court must then determine if the continued surveillance by the device violates a reasonable expectation of privacy.

There is no question that the initial opening of the package by customs agents was lawful. Customs officials are authorized to inspect incoming international mail when they have a "reasonable cause to suspect" that the mail contains contraband. *United States v. Ramsey* "Reasonable cause to suspect" is a considerably milder standard than probable cause." Substantial quantities of narcotics are imported into the United States from Thailand, and it is reasonable to suspect that a crated package like the one in controversy contains

contraband. Therefore, the package was lawfully opened, and the mere insertion of the devices did not violate any Fourth Amendment right. Such rights, we recognize, easily can be violated by the installation of beepers, but this is not such a case.

The actual use of the devices, providing continued surveillance of the package and indicating when it was opened, presents a different problem. Electronic tracking devices continually broadcast "here I am" and when appropriate "the package has been opened." This intrusion, though, is slight and is not an impermissible search. Transmitting the package's location is merely an aid to what can be accomplished by visual surveillance. Permissible techniques of surveillance include more than the five senses of officers and their unaided physical abilities. Binoculars, dogs that track and sniff out contraband, searchlights, fluorescent powders, automobiles and airplanes, burglar alarms, radar devices, and bait money contribute to surveillance without violation of the Fourth Amendment in the usual case. On the other hand, wiretaps, breaking and entering, and many other searches and seizures fall on the other side of the line. The issue before us is whether the mere presence of the beeper, it having been attached without violating the Fourth Amendment, sufficiently resembles a wiretap to require the "antecedent justification" that a warrant would provide. We hold that it does not. We acknowledge that a beeper which said "the package is being opened" and related much more might well be considered equivalent to a wiretap. However, a beeper which says no more than "the package is being opened" does not constitute an intrusion entitled to the protection of *Katz*. It is but another surveillance aid previously affixed to the package without violating the Fourth Amendment. It no more violates the Fourth Amendment than would the use of binoculars designed for night by an officer located on the roof of a building whose owner had given him permission to enter, ascend, and survey.

…

Consent And Expectations Of Privacy

A person who allows another to look at something or someplace no longer has a reasonable expectation of privacy in that thing or place. Accordingly, consent "searches" aren't really searches at all. In order to be valid, consent must be voluntary. (See, *Schneckloth v. Bustamonte*, 412 U.S. 218 (1973)). Consent may justify a "search" of a person or the person's property. Police do not need probable cause to "search" when an individual with proper authority gives consent to "search", but they must examine only those areas properly covered within the scope of consent given.

Voluntariness Of Consent

The key case examining the voluntariness of consent is *Schneckloth v. Bustamonte*, 412 U.S. 218 (1973). In it, the Court focused on whether, under the totality of the circumstances, the suspect voluntarily consented to the search. It specifically noted that valid, voluntary, consent does not require the person to know that he or she has the right to refuse consent. It is a question of fact (meaning something the jury has to decide) whether voluntary consent has been given, see, *Mendenhall,* and even a person who has been arrested may give valid, voluntary, consent to search. *United States v. Watson*, 423 U.S. 411 (1976). The test for voluntariness is an objective test --consent is involuntary when it is the product of coercion or threat, express or implied.

SCHNECKLOTH v. BUSTAMONTE
412 U.S. 218 (1973)

JUSTICE STEWART delivered the opinion of the court.

. . . .

While on routine patrol in Sunnyvale, California, at approximately 2:40 in the morning, Police Officer James Rand stopped an automobile when he observed that one headlight and its license plate light were burned out. Six men were in the vehicle. Joe Alcala and the respondent, Robert Bustamonte, were in the front seat with Joe Gonzales, the driver. Three older men were seated in the rear. When, in response to the policeman's question, Gonzales could not produce a driver's license, Officer Rand asked if any of the other five had any evidence of identification. Only Alcala produced a license, and he explained that the car was his brother's. After the six occupants had stepped out of the car at the officer's request and after two additional policemen had arrived, Officer Rand asked Alcala if he could search the car. Alcala replied, "Sure, go ahead." Prior to the search no one was threatened with arrest and, according to Officer Rand's uncontradicted testimony, it "was all very congenial at this time." Gonzales testified that Alcala actually helped in the search of the car, by opening the trunk and glove compartment. In Gonzales' words: "[T]he police officer asked Joe [Alcala], he goes, `Does the trunk open?' And Joe said, `Yes.' He went to the car and got the keys and opened up the trunk." Wadded up under the left rear seat, the police officers found three checks that had previously been stolen from a car wash.

Not only officer Rand, but Gonzales, the driver of the automobile, testified that Alcala's assent to the search of his brother's automobile was freely, even casually given. At the time of the request to search the automobile the atmosphere, according to Rand, was `congenial' and there had been no discussion of any crime. As noted, Gonzales said Alcala even attempted to aid in the search

. . . .

The precise question in this case . . . is what must the prosecution prove to demonstrate that a consent was "voluntarily" given. And upon that question there is a square conflict of views between the state and federal courts that have reviewed the search involved in the case before us. The Court of Appeals for the Ninth

Circuit concluded that it is an essential part of the State's initial burden to prove that a person knows he has a right to refuse consent. The California courts have followed the rule that voluntariness is a question of fact to be determined from the totality of all the circumstances, and that the state of a defendant's knowledge is only one factor to be taken into account in assessing the voluntariness of a consent.

[The Court analyzed the voluntariness-due process cases decided in the context of confessions and interrogations and pointed to 30 different cases where the Court had to decide whether the confession had been voluntarily given.]

...

The significant fact about all of these decisions is that none of them turned on the presence or absence of a single controlling criterion; each reflected a careful scrutiny of all the surrounding circumstances. In none of them did the Court rule that the Due Process Clause required the prosecution to prove as part of its initial burden that the defendant knew he had a right to refuse to answer the questions that were put. While the state of the accused's mind, and the failure of the police to advise the accused of his rights, were certainly factors to be evaluated in assessing the "voluntariness" of an accused's responses, they were not in and of themselves determinative.

While knowledge of the right to refuse consent is one factor to be taken into account, the government need not establish such knowledge as the sine qua non of an effective consent. As with police questioning, two competing concerns must be accommodated in determining the meaning of a "voluntary" consent - the legitimate need for such searches and the equally important requirement of assuring the absence of coercion.

[Bustamonte argues] . . . that the Court's decision in the *Miranda* case requires the conclusion that knowledge of a right to refuse is an indispensable element of a valid consent. [But the] . . . considerations that informed the

Court's holding in *Miranda* are simply inapplicable in the present case.

In this case, there is no evidence of any inherently coercive tactics - either from the nature of the police questioning or the environment in which it took place.

It is also argued that the failure to require the Government to establish knowledge as a prerequisite to a valid consent, will relegate the Fourth Amendment to the special province of "the sophisticated, the knowledgeable and the privileged." We cannot agree. The traditional definition of voluntariness we accept today has always taken into account evidence of minimal schooling, low intelligence, and the lack of any effective warnings to a person of his rights; and the voluntariness of any statement taken under those conditions has been carefully scrutinized to determine whether it was in fact voluntarily given.

Our decision today is a narrow one. We hold only that when the subject of a search is not in custody and the State attempts to justify a search on the basis of his consent, the Fourth and Fourteenth Amendments require that it demonstrate that the consent was in fact voluntarily given, and not the result of duress or coercion, express or implied. Voluntariness is a question of fact to be determined from all the circumstances, and while the subject's knowledge of a right to refuse is a factor to be taken into account, the prosecution is not required to demonstrate such knowledge as a prerequisite to establishing a voluntary consent.

JUSTICE MARSHALL, dissenting.

. . . .

[T]his case deals not with "coercion," but with "consent," a subtly different concept to which different standards have been applied in the past. Freedom from coercion is a substantive right, guaranteed by the Fifth and Fourteenth Amendments. Consent, however, is a mechanism by which substantive requirements, otherwise applicable, are avoided. In the context of the Fourth

Amendment, the relevant substantive requirements are that searches be conducted only after evidence justifying them has been submitted to an impartial magistrate for a determination of probable cause. There are, of course, exceptions to these requirements based on a variety of exigent circumstances that make it impractical to invalidate a search simply because the police failed to get a warrant. But none of the exceptions relating to the overriding needs of law enforcement are applicable when a search is justified solely by consent. On the contrary, the needs of law enforcement are significantly more attenuated, for probable cause to search may be lacking but a search permitted if the subject's consent has been obtained. Thus, consent searches are permitted, not because such an exception to the requirements of probable cause and warrant is essential to proper law enforcement, but because we permit our citizens to choose whether or not they wish to exercise their constitutional rights. Our prior decisions simply do not support the view that a meaningful choice has been made solely because no coercion was brought to bear on the subject.

. . . .

I am at a loss to understand why consent "cannot be taken literally to mean a `knowing' choice." In fact, I have difficulty in comprehending how a decision made without knowledge of available alternatives can be treated as a choice at all.

If consent to search means that a person has chosen to forgo his right to exclude the police from the place they seek to search, it follows that his consent cannot be considered a meaningful choice unless he knew that he could in fact exclude the police. . . . I can think of no other situation in which we would say that a person agreed to some course of action if he convinced us that he did not know that there was some other course he might have pursued. I would therefore hold, at a minimum, that the prosecution may not rely on a purported consent to search if the subject of the search did not know that he could refuse to give consent.

Other Cases: Consent

Florida v. Bostick, 501 U.S. 429 (1991)

SUMMARY: Two officers, with badges and insignia, boarded a bus. They explained their presence on the bus as "being on the lookout for illegal drugs." Without any suspicion, they approached Bostick and asked him for consent to search his bag and told him that he had the right to refuse consent. Bostick, instead, gave consent.

The Court found Bostick's consent to be voluntary. In addition, the Court held that the officer's conduct in boarding buses, questioning passengers, and requesting consent to search luggage "was not a "seizure" that vitiated consent; under these circumstances, which included notice of the right to refuse consent, a reasonable person would have felt free to decline the request for consent or otherwise terminate the encounter."

Ohio v. Robinette, 519 U.S. 33 (1996)

SUMMARY: Police officer stopped a motorist for speeding, issued a warning, and returned his driver's license. The officer then asked the driver if he was carrying any contraband. Robinette answered that he was not. The officer then asked if he could search the car, and Robinette gave consent. The officer did not inform him that he was "free to go." Police searched and contraband was found. The Court found that the search was constitutional and that the officer was not required to tell Robinette that he was free to go.

HOLDING: A person who is lawfully stopped for a traffic infraction need not be advised that he or she is free to leave before the officer can lawfully request consent to search for evidence of an unrelated offense.

Note: State law varies on this and may hold that failure to tell the person that they are free to go may extend the length of the permissible seizure and make it an unlawful stop.

Scope Of Consent

The scope of a consent search (where the police may look) is limited by the scope of the consent given (where the suspect says the police may look). In deciding whether a search exceeded the scope of consent, the court asks how a reasonable person would have understood the conversation between the officer and the suspect or third party when consent was given. For example, a retail store does not consent to a general search of the entire store nor all of its customers just because it has invited the public to enter. *Lo-Ji Sales, Inc. v. New York*, 442 U.S. 319 (1979).

FLORIDA v. JIMENO
500 U.S. 248 (1991)

CHIEF JUSTICE REHNQUIST delivered the opinion of the Court.

...

This case began when a Dade County police officer, Frank Trujillo, overheard respondent, Enio Jimeno, arranging what appeared to be a drug transaction over a public telephone. Believing that respondent might be involved in illegal drug trafficking, Officer Trujillo followed his car. The officer observed respondent make a right turn at a red light without stopping. He then pulled respondent over to the side of the road in order to issue him a traffic citation. Officer Trujillo told respondent that he had been stopped for committing a traffic infraction. The officer went on to say that he had reason to believe that respondent was carrying narcotics in his car, and asked permission to search the car. He explained that respondent did not have to consent to a search of the car. Respondent stated that he had nothing to hide and gave Trujillo permission to search the automobile. After two passengers stepped out of respondent's car, Officer Trujillo went to the passenger side, opened the door, and saw a folded, brown paper bag on the floorboard. The officer picked up the bag, opened it, and found a kilogram of cocaine inside.

We granted certiorari to determine whether consent to search a vehicle may extend to closed containers found inside the vehicle.... .

We have long approved consensual searches because it is no doubt reasonable for the police to conduct a search once they have been permitted to do so. The standard for measuring the scope of a suspect's consent under the Fourth Amendment is that of "objective" reasonableness - what would the typical reasonable person have understood by the exchange between the officer and the suspect? The question before us, then, is whether it is reasonable for an officer to consider a suspect's general consent to a search of his car to include consent to examine a paper bag lying on the floor of the car. We think that it is.

The scope of a search is generally defined by its expressed object. In this case, the terms of the search's authorization were simple. Respondent granted Officer Trujillo permission to search his car, and did not place any explicit limitation on the scope of the search. Trujillo had informed respondent that he believed respondent was carrying narcotics, and that he would be looking for narcotics in the car. We think that it was objectively reasonable for the police to conclude that the general consent to search respondent's car included consent to search containers within that car which might bear drugs. A reasonable person may be expected to know that narcotics are generally carried in some form of a container. "Contraband goods rarely are strewn across the trunk or floor of a car." The authorization to search in this case, therefore, extended beyond the surfaces of the car's interior to the paper bag lying on the car's floor.

...A suspect may, of course, delimit as he chooses the scope of the search to which he consents. But if his consent would reasonably be understood to extend to a particular container, the Fourth Amendment provides no grounds for requiring a more explicit authorization.

UNITED STATES v. RODNEY
956 F. 2d 295 (CA. D.C. 1992)

THOMAS, Circuit Justice:

The principal question presented is whether a consent to a body search for drugs, without more, authorizes the sort of careful frisk described in *Terry v. Ohio*. We hold that it does.

On February 17, 1990, Dylan Rodney stepped off a bus that had arrived in Washington, D.C., from New York City. As Rodney left the bus station, Detective Vance Beard, dressed in plain clothes and carrying a concealed weapon, approached him from behind. A second officer waited nearby. Beard displayed identification and asked if Rodney would talk to him. Rodney agreed. Beard asked Rodney whether he lived in either Washington or New York. Rodney replied that he lived in Florida, but had come to Washington to try to find his wife. She lived on Georgia Avenue, Rodney said, although he was unable to identify any more precise location. Beard asked Rodney whether he was carrying drugs in his travel bag. After Rodney said no, Beard obtained permission to search the bag. As he did so, the other officer advanced to within about five feet of Rodney. The search failed to turn up any contraband.

Beard then asked Rodney whether he was carrying drugs on his person. After Rodney again said no, Beard requested permission to conduct a body search. Rodney said "sure" and raised his arms above his head. Beard placed his hands on Rodney's ankles and, in one sweeping motion, ran them up the inside of Rodney's legs. As he passed over the crotch area, Beard felt small, rock-like objects. Rodney exclaimed: "That's me!" Detecting otherwise, Beard placed Rodney under arrest.

At the police station, Beard unzipped Rodney's pants and retrieved a plastic bag containing a rock-like substance that was identified as cocaine base. Rodney was charged with possession and intent to distribute. On April 10, 1990, Rodney moved to suppress the crack. Rodney argued (1) that he had not consented voluntarily to the body search; (2) that even if he had done so, the consent did not include a search of his crotch area; and (3) that his arrest was unsupported by probable cause.

The district court found that Rodney had "[given] his consent voluntarily to [the] search [of] his person and belongings." Rodney entered a conditional guilty plea, reserving the right to withdraw it if this court reversed the denial of his suppression motion.

Rodney first contends that the district court erred in finding that his consent to the body search was voluntary, and therefore not prohibited by the Fourth Amendment.

On this record, we find no clear error. On the one hand, some evidence suggests an involuntary consent. Rodney testified that he thought three, rather than two, officers were covering him; that the officers were much bigger than he; and that he was young (twenty-four) and relatively uneducated (to the tenth grade) at the time. He also testified that before the events leading to his arrest, he had had four unpleasant encounters with the police: each time he had refused their request to search him, but each time they had searched him anyway. On the other hand, Beard's testimony indicates that the police conduct here bore no resemblance to the sort of "aggressive questioning, intimidating actions, or prolonged police presence," that might invalidate a consent. During the encounter, according to Beard, his gun was concealed; he wore plain clothes and spoke in a conversational tone; and no other officer came within five feet of Rodney. The district court could have weighed Beard's evidence more heavily than Rodney's. Thus, even assuming that the court credited Rodney's testimony in addition to Beard's, the court committed no clear error in finding the consent voluntary.

Rodney next argues that even if he consented voluntarily to the body search, he did not consent to the search of his crotch area. A consensual search cannot exceed the scope of the consent. The scope of the consent is measured by a test of " 'objective' reasonableness": it depends on how broadly a reasonable observer would have interpreted the consent under the circumstances. Here, Rodney clearly consented to a search of his body for drugs. We conclude that a reasonable person would have understood that consent to encompass the search undertaken here.

Under *Jimeno*, "[t]he scope of a search is generally defined by its expressed object." In this case, Rodney authorized a search for drugs. Dealers frequently hide drugs near their genitals. Indeed, Beard testified that his colleagues make up to 75 percent of their drug recoveries from around the crotch area. For these reasons, we conclude that a request to conduct a body search for drugs reasonably includes a request to conduct some search of that area.

Although *Jimeno* states the test "generally" used to determine the scope of a consent to search, we doubt that the Supreme Court would have us apply that test unflinchingly in the context of body searches. At some point, we suspect, a body search would become so intrusive that we would not infer consent to it from a generalized consent, regardless of the stated object of the search. For example, although drugs can be hidden virtually anywhere on or in one's person, a generalized consent to a body search for drugs surely does not validate everything up to and including a search of body cavities.

The search undertaken here, however, was not unusually intrusive, at least relative to body searches generally. It involved a continuous sweeping motion over Rodney's outer garments, including the trousers covering his crotch area. In this respect, the search was no more invasive than the typical pat-down frisk for weapons … .

…

We conclude that the frisk of Rodney's fully-clothed body involved nothing so intrusive, relative to body searches generally, as to require a separate consent above and beyond the consent to a body search that Rodney had given voluntarily.

Withdrawing Consent

Federal circuit courts and state courts that have unanimously held that people can withdraw their consent. In *United States v. Sanders*, 424 F.3d 768, at 774 (8th Circuit, Iowa, 2005) the court held that "any such withdrawal must be supported by unambiguous acts or unequivocal statements." Similarly, in *United States v. Gray*,   369 F.3d 1024 (2004) (8th Cir., Ark.), the defendant's motion to suppress evidence obtained during a traffic stop was denied. He agreed that he voluntarily consented to the search but argued that he later withdrew that permission.

"After obtaining consent at approximately 11:09 a.m., Drown searched the vehicle and its contents for some 20 minutes without incident. Shortly after 11:30 a.m., Gray and Lawrence began expressing concern about the length of the search. Gray testified that he stated "[t]his is ridiculous" and asked how long the search was going to take. He admitted, however, that he did not ask to leave during this initial conversation, and it is undisputed that Drown [the officer] continued looking through the vehicle.

A few minutes later, at approximately 11:33 a.m., Drown received a phone call, following which Gray and Drown had a second conversation, the content of which they recall differently.

Drown testified that Gray merely asked that the search be speeded up and did not withdraw consent, whereas Gray testified that he attempted to withdraw consent by again indicating that the length of the search was "ridiculous" and twice saying that he and Lawrence were "ready to go now." Depending on whose testimony is credited, Drown responded to this second conversation by either asking or telling Gray about using the canine. In any event, Drown moved the luggage that was outside the vehicle away from the vehicle's exterior and then conducted the canine search.

Withdrawal of consent need not be effectuated through particular "magic words," but an intent to withdraw consent must be made by unequivocal act or statement. *United States v. Ross,* 263 F.3d 844, 846 (8th Cir.2001). The district court found that Gray and Lawrence made "protests to leave," but concluded that "there was no specific request to leave, and under the circumstances, ... Trooper Drown was reasonable in continuing the search beyond the initial contact at 11:30." The district court further found that when the defendants became "more strident about their desire to leave," Trooper Drown decided to use Rudy, and only about nine or ten minutes elapsed between the time Gray first began objecting and the time Rudy alerted."[55]

Third Party Consent

Can police can get consent to search from a third party — someone who is not the owner of the property or premise? Conversely stated, may a third person authorize the police to search something or someplace that is not necessarily theirs? The pivotal issue is whether the person had the authority to give the consent. Authority arises from shared access, use, and control, and is not based necessarily on ownership or relationship. For example, a homeowner cannot consent to a police search of a home they have rented to a tenant merely because they are the home owner. In fact, landlord-tenant law limits the landlord's authority to enter the property themselves. Likewise, parents don't have authority to consent to the police searching their child's room, simply because it is their home (or the child is their child). More facts need to be known (Did the parents frequently go into the child's room? was there a separate lock to the child's room and did the child have a key when the parent's did not?)

Sometimes police may reasonably believe that a person has authority to consent when, in fact, they do not. In *Illinois v. Rodriguez,* 497 U.S. 177 (1990) (below) the Court distinguished between actual authority (one who, in fact, has the legal authority to consent for someone else) and apparent authority (one who the officers reasonably believed had authority, but in fact did not). In *Georgia v. Randolph,* 547 U.S. 104 (2006) (discussed in *Fernandez* below), the Court examined the situation where a husband and wife were both present when the police asked for consent to search. He objected, she did not. *Fernandez v. California,* 571 U.S. ___ (2014), revisited *Randolph* in the context of a co-habitant who was arrested and thus removed from the property — but when he was there, he had emphatically refused consent.

ILLINOIS v. RODRIGUEZ
497 U.S. 177 (1990)

JUSTICE SCALIA delivered the opinion of the Court.

[Facts Summarized: Police contacted Gail Fischer at her mom's home. Gail had been severely beaten and told police that Rodriguez had done the beating in an apartment that she

had just fled from. She said Rodriguez was asleep at the apartment. Fischer repeatedly referred to the apartment as "our apartment" and had mentioned that she had clothes and furniture there. It was unclear to the Court whether she indicated specifically that she

---

[55] Note that this case was decided prior to the *Rodriguez v. United States,* 575 U.S. ___ (2015) discussed in Chapter Three, and it is likely that the nine-to-ten-minute delay would render this an illegal seizure.

currently lived at the apartment or only that she used to live there.]

The police officers drove to the apartment on South California, accompanied by Fischer. They did not obtain an arrest warrant for Rodriguez, nor did they seek a search warrant for the apartment. At the apartment, Fischer unlocked the door with her key and gave the officers permission to enter. They moved through the door into the living room, where they observed in plain view drug paraphernalia and containers filled with white powder that they believed (correctly, as later analysis showed) to be cocaine. They proceeded to the bedroom, where they found Rodriguez asleep and discovered additional containers of white powder in two open attache cases. The officers arrested Rodriguez and seized the drugs and related paraphernalia.

Rodriguez was charged with possession of a controlled substance with intent to deliver. He moved to suppress all evidence seized at the time of his arrest, claiming that Fischer had vacated the apartment several weeks earlier and had no authority to consent to the entry. . . .

The Fourth Amendment generally prohibits the warrantless entry of a person's home, whether to make an arrest or to search for specific objects. The prohibition does not apply, however, to situations in which voluntary consent has been obtained, either from the individual whose property is searched, or from a third party who possesses common authority over the premises, The State of Illinois contends that that exception applies in the present case.

[The state courts held] . . . "Common authority" rests "on mutual use of the property by persons generally having joint access or control for most purposes . . . ." The burden of establishing that common authority rests upon the State. On the basis of this record, it is clear that burden was not sustained. The evidence showed that, although Fischer, with her two small children, had lived with Rodriguez beginning in December, 1984, she had moved out on July 1, 1985, almost a month before the search at issue here, and had gone to live with her mother. She took her and her children's clothing with her, though leaving behind some furniture and household effects. During the period after July 1, she sometimes spent the night at Rodriguez's apartment, but never invited her friends there and never went there herself when he was not home. Her name was not on the lease, nor did she contribute to the rent. She had a key to the apartment, which she said at trial she had taken without Rodriguez's knowledge (though she testified at the preliminary hearing that Rodriguez had given her the key). On these facts, the State has not established that, with respect to the South California apartment, Fischer had "joint access or control for most purposes." To the contrary, the Appellate Court's determination of no common authority over the apartment was obviously correct.

The State contends that, even if Fischer did not in fact have authority to give consent, it suffices to validate the entry that the law enforcement officers reasonably believed she did.

Respondent asserts that permitting a reasonable belief of common authority to validate an entry would cause a defendant's Fourth Amendment rights to be "vicariously waived." . . . We disagree.

. . . .

What [Rodriguez] is assured by the Fourth Amendment is not that no government search of his house will occur unless he consents, but that no such search will occur that is "unreasonable." There are various elements, of course, that can make a search of a person's house "reasonable" - one of which is the consent of the person or his cotenant. The essence of respondent's argument is that we should impose upon this element a requirement that we have not imposed upon other elements that regularly compel government officers to exercise judgment regarding the facts: namely, the requirement that their judgment be not only responsible, but correct.

"Reasonableness," with respect to this necessary element, does not demand that the government be factually correct in its assessment that that is what a search will produce. Warrants need only be supported by "probable cause," which demands no more than a proper "assessment of probabilities in particular factual contexts. ... "

... We see no reason to depart from this general rule [that searches be reasonable] with respect to facts bearing upon the authority to consent to a search. Whether the basis for such authority exists is the sort of recurring factual question to which law enforcement officials must be expected to apply their judgment, and all the Fourth Amendment requires is that they answer it reasonably. The Constitution is no more violated when officers enter without a warrant because they reasonably (though erroneously) believe that the person who has consented to their entry is a resident of the premises than it is violated when they enter without a warrant because they reasonably (though erroneously) believe they are in pursuit of a violent felon who is about to escape.

[W]hat we hold today does not suggest that law enforcement officers may always accept a person's invitation to enter premises. Even when the invitation is accompanied by an explicit assertion that the person lives there, the surrounding circumstances could conceivably be such that a reasonable person would doubt its truth and not act upon it without further inquiry. As with other factual determinations bearing upon search and seizure, determination of consent to enter must "be judged against an objective standard: would the facts available to the officer at the moment . . . `warrant a man of reasonable caution in the belief'" that the consenting party had authority over the premises? If not, then warrantless entry without further inquiry is unlawful unless authority actually exists. But if so, the search is valid.

JUSTICE MARSHALL, with whom JUSTICE BRENNAN and JUSTICE STEVENS join, dissenting.

...

Because the sole law enforcement purpose underlying third-party consent searches is avoiding the inconvenience of securing a warrant, a departure from the warrant requirement is not justified simply because an officer reasonably believes a third party has consented to a search of the defendant's home. In holding otherwise, the majority ignores our longstanding view that "the informed and deliberate determinations of magistrates . . . as to what searches and seizures are permissible under the Constitution are to be preferred over the hurried action of officers and others who may happen to make arrests.

A search conducted pursuant to an officer's reasonable but mistaken belief that a third party had authority to consent is thus on an entirely different constitutional footing from one based on the consent of a third party who in fact has such authority. Even if the officers reasonably believed that Fischer had authority to consent, she did not, and Rodriguez's expectation of privacy was therefore undiminished. Rodriguez accordingly can challenge the warrantless intrusion into his home as a violation of the Fourth Amendment.

. . .

Unlike searches conducted pursuant to the recognized exceptions to the warrant requirement, third-party consent searches are not based on an exigency, and therefore serve no compelling social goal. Police officers, when faced with the choice of relying on consent by a third party or securing a warrant, should secure a warrant, and must therefore accept the risk of error should they instead choose to rely on consent

Our cases demonstrate that third-party consent searches are free from constitutional challenge only to the extent that they rest on consent by a party empowered to do so. . . .That a person who allows another joint access over his property thereby limits his expectation of privacy does not justify trampling the rights of a person who has not similarly relinquished any of his privacy expectation.

FERNANDEZ v. CALIFORNIA
571 U.S. 292 (2014)

JUSTICE ALITO delivered the opinion of the Court.

Our cases firmly establish that police officers may search jointly occupied premises if one of the occupants consents. In *Georgia v. Randolph* we recognized a narrow exception to this rule, holding that the consent of one occupant is insufficient when another occupant is present and objects to the search. In this case, we consider whether *Randolph* applies if the objecting occupant is absent when another occupant consents. Our opinion in *Randolph* took great pains to emphasize that its holding was limited to situations in which the objecting occupant is physically present. We therefore refuse to extend *Randolph* to the very different situation in this case, where consent was provided by an abused woman well after her male partner had been removed from the apartment they shared.

…

The Fourth Amendment prohibits unreasonable searches and seizures and provides that a warrant may not be issued without probable cause, but "the text of the Fourth Amendment does not specify when a search warrant must be obtained." Our cases establish that a warrant is generally required for a search of a home, but "the ultimate touchstone of the Fourth Amendment is `reasonableness,'" And certain categories of permissible warrantless searches have long been recognized.

Consent searches occupy one of these categories. "Consent searches are part of the standard investigatory techniques of law enforcement agencies" and are "a constitutionally permissible and wholly legitimate aspect of effective police activity." It would be unreasonable — indeed, absurd — to require police officers to obtain a warrant when the sole owner or occupant of a house or apartment voluntarily consents to a search.

The owner of a home has a right to allow others to enter and examine the premises, and there is no reason why the owner should not be permitted to extend this same privilege to police officers if that is the owner's choice. Where the owner believes that he or she is under suspicion, the owner may want the police to search the premises so that their suspicions are dispelled. This may be particularly important where the owner has a strong interest in the apprehension of the perpetrator of a crime and believes that the suspicions of the police are deflecting the course of their investigation. An owner may want the police to search even where they lack probable cause, and if a warrant were always required, this could not be done. And even where the police could establish probable cause, requiring a warrant despite the owner's consent would needlessly inconvenience everyone involved — not only the officers and the magistrate but also the occupant of the premises, who would generally either be compelled or would feel a need to stay until the search was completed.

While it is clear that a warrantless search is reasonable when the sole occupant of a house or apartment consents, what happens when there are two or more occupants? Must they all consent? Must they all be asked? Is consent by one occupant enough? The Court faced that problem 40 years ago in *United States v. Matlock* (1974). In that case, Matlock and a woman named Graff were living together in a house that was also occupied by several of Graff's siblings and by her mother, who had rented the house. While in the front yard of the house, Matlock was arrested for bank robbery and was placed in a squad car. Although the police could have easily asked him for consent to search the room that he and Graff shared, they did not do so. Instead, they knocked on the door and obtained Graff's permission to search. The search yielded incriminating evidence, which the defendant sought to suppress, but this Court held that Graff's consent justified the warrantless search. As the Court put it, "the consent of one who possesses common authority over premises or effects is valid as against the absent, nonconsenting person with whom that authority is shared."

. . . .

B

While consent by one resident of jointly occupied premises is generally sufficient to justify a warrantless search, we recognized a narrow exception to this rule in *Georgia v. Randolph* (2006). In that case, police officers responded to the Randolphs' home after receiving a report of a domestic dispute. When the officers arrived, Janet Randolph informed the officers that her estranged husband, Scott Randolph, was a cocaine user and that there were "items of drug evidence" in the house. The officers first asked Scott for consent to search, but he "unequivocally refused." The officers then turned to Janet, and she consented to the search, which produced evidence that was later used to convict Scott for possession of cocaine.

…

III

In this case, petitioner was not present when Rojas consented, but petitioner still contends that *Randolph* is controlling. He advances two main arguments. First, he claims that his absence should not matter since he was absent only because the police had taken him away. Second, he maintains that it was sufficient that he objected to the search while he was still present. Such an objection, he says, should remain in effect until the objecting party "no longer wishes to keep the police out of his home." Neither of these arguments is sound.

A

…

We … hold that an occupant who is absent due to a lawful detention or arrest stands in the same shoes as an occupant who is absent for any other reason.

This conclusion does not "make a mockery of *Randolph*," as petitioner protests. It simply accepts *Randolph* on its own terms. The *Randolph* holding unequivocally requires the presence of the objecting occupant in every situation other than the one mentioned in the dictum discussed above.

B

This brings us to petitioner's second argument, viz., that his objection, made at the threshold of the premises that the police wanted to search, remained effective until he changed his mind and withdrew his objection. This argument is inconsistent with *Randolph*'s reasoning…

…

Petitioner's rule would . . .require the police and ultimately the courts to determine whether, after the passage of time, an objector still had "common authority" over the premises, and this would often be a tricky question. …

Another problem concerns the procedure needed to register a continuing objection. Would it be necessary for an occupant to object while police officers are at the door? If presence at the time of consent is not needed, would an occupant have to be present at the premises when the objection was made? Could an objection be made pre-emptively? Could a person like Scott Randolph, suspecting that his estranged wife might invite the police to view his drug stash and paraphernalia, register an objection in advance? Could this be done by posting a sign in front of the house? Could a standing objection be registered by serving notice on the chief of police?

Finally, there is the question of the particular law enforcement officers who would be bound by an objection. Would this set include just the officers who were present when the objection was made? Would it also apply to other officers working on the same investigation? Would it extend to officers who were unaware of the objection? How about officers assigned to different but arguably related cases? Would it be limited by law enforcement agency?

If *Randolph* is taken at its word — that it applies only when the objector is standing in the door saying "stay out" when officers propose to make a consent search — all of these problems disappear.

. . . .

C

Petitioner argues strenuously that his expansive interpretation of *Randolph* would not hamper law enforcement because in most cases where officers have probable cause to arrest a physically present objector they also have probable cause to search the premises that the objector does not want them to enter, but this argument misunderstands the constitutional status of consent searches. A warrantless consent search is reasonable and thus consistent with the Fourth Amendment irrespective of the availability of a warrant. Even with modern technological advances, the warrant procedure imposes burdens on the officers who wish to search, the magistrate who must review the warrant application, and the party willing to give consent. When a warrantless search is justified, requiring the police to obtain a warrant may "unjustifiably interfer[e] with legitimate law enforcement strategies." Such a requirement may also impose an unmerited burden on the person who consents to an immediate search, since the warrant application procedure entails delay. Putting the exception the Court adopted in *Randolph* to one side, the lawful occupant of a house or apartment should have the right to invite the police to enter the dwelling and conduct a search. Any other rule would trample on the rights of the occupant who is willing to consent. Such an occupant may want the police to search in order to dispel "suspicion raised by sharing quarters with a criminal." And an occupant may want the police to conduct a thorough search so that any dangerous contraband can be found and removed. In this case, for example, the search resulted in the discovery and removal of a sawed-off shotgun to which Rojas' 4-year-old son had access.

Denying someone in Rojas' position the right to allow the police to enter *her* home would also show disrespect for her independence. Having beaten Rojas, petitioner would bar her from controlling access to her own home until such time as he chose to relent. The Fourth Amendment does not give him that power.

JUSTICE SCALIA, concurring. Omitted.

JUSTICE THOMAS, concurring.

… I write separately to make clear the extent of my disagreement with *Randolph*.

JUSTICE GINSBURG, with whom JUSTICE SOTOMAYOR and JUSTICE KAGAN join, dissenting.

The warrant requirement . . .ranks among the "fundamental distinctions between our form of government, where officers are under the law, and the police-state where they are the law." The Court has accordingly declared warrantless searches, in the main, "*per se* unreasonable." If this main rule is to remain hardy, the Court has explained, exceptions to the warrant requirement must be "few in number and carefully delineated."

Instead of adhering to the warrant requirement, today's decision tells the police they may dodge it, nevermind ample time to secure the approval of a neutral magistrate. Suppressing the warrant requirement, the Court shrinks to petite size our holding in *Georgia v. Randolph,* that "a physically present inhabitant's express refusal of consent to a police search [of his home] is dispositive as to him, regardless of the consent of a fellow occupant," …

United States v. Dubrofsky, 581 F.2d 208 (1978)

SUMMARY (see above for summary of facts):

After the arrest, Ms. Lovejoy was informed that she was a suspect in the investigation. She was given a Miranda warning, and her consent was requested to search the basement. Although a written consent was apparently given after the search, evidence at the suppression hearing indicates that Ms. Lovejoy gave a valid oral consent prior to the search. The package, heroin, heroin substitute, and the beepers were found in the basement.

…

III. Lovejoy's Consent to Search the Basement.

Dubrofsky contends that Ms. Lovejoy did not voluntarily consent to the search of her basement and that she had no authority to consent to that search. We disagree with both these arguments.

It was found at the suppression hearing that Ms. Lovejoy gave a knowing and voluntary consent to search the basement. Findings of fact made at a suppression hearing will be overturned on appeal only if clearly erroneous. We find nothing in the record to indicate that the findings of the magistrate at the suppression hearing are clearly erroneous, and therefore hold that Ms. Lovejoy's consent was voluntary.

Dubrofsky's argument that Ms. Lovejoy had no authority to consent to the search also fails. Authority justifying consent to search need only rest on mutual use of the property. A party who has a key to the premises and access throughout the residence can also give a valid consent to search. As the permanent resident of the house, Ms. Lovejoy more than meets these minimum requirements for authority to consent to a search.

Dubrofsky urges that *Chapman v. United States, and Stoner v. California (*1964) are controlling. These cases involved hotel and apartment searches authorized by clerks and landlords and have no effect here. There the focus was on an owner relinquishing control over a section of the premises to a business tenant. The facts here are very different. Ms. Lovejoy never relinquished control over the basement. She had valid authority to consent to the search.

United States v. Matlock, 415 U.S. 164 (1974)

SUMMARY: A roommate gave the police consent to search a common area. The Court stated,

> "Consent of one who possesses common authority over premises or effects is valid as against the absent, nonconsenting person with whom that authority is shared. … Common authority is, of course, not to be implied from the mere property interest a third party has in the property. The authority which justifies the third party consent does not rest upon the law of property, with its attendant historical and legal refinements, but rests rather on the mutual use of the property by persons generally having joint access or control for most purposes, so that it is reasonable to recognize that any of the cohabitants has the right to permit the inspection in his own right and that the others have assumed the risk that one of their number might permit the common area to be searched."

Stoner v. California, 376 U.S. 483 (1964).

SUMMARY: A hotel clerk did not have authority to consent to a police search of a guest's room. The Court said,

> "It is important to bear in mind that it was the petitioner's constitutional right which was at stake here, and not the night clerk's or the hotel's."

Chapman v. California, 386 US 18 (1967)

HOLDING: A landlord may not give consent to a police search into a tenant's apartment or house, even though the landlord has a general right of entry for normal inspection purposes.

Open Fields And Curtilage

The following cases, decided under the Katz search definition (privacy), demonstrate how the court distinguishes between open fields and area called "curtilage." One question to consider is whether the outcome of these cases would have been different if the Court's current definition of a search as seen in *Jones* had been controlling (privacy or a trespass)

OLIVER v. UNITED STATES
466 U.S. 170 (1984)

JUSTICE POWELL delivered the opinion of the Court.

The "open fields" doctrine, first enunciated by this Court in *Hester v. United States* permits police officers to enter and search a field without a warrant. We granted certiorari in these cases to clarify confusion that has arisen as to the continued vitality of the doctrine.

Acting on reports that marihuana was being raised on the farm of petitioner Oliver, two narcotics agents of the Kentucky State Police went to the farm to investigate. Arriving at the farm, they drove past petitioner's house to a locked gate with a "No Trespassing" sign. A footpath led around one side of the gate. The agents walked around the gate and along the road for several hundred yards, passing a barn and a parked camper. At that point, someone standing in front of the camper shouted: "No hunting is allowed, come back up here." The officers shouted back that they were Kentucky State Police officers, but found no one when they returned to the camper. The officers resumed their investigation of the farm and found a field of marihuana over a mile from petitioner's home.

Petitioner was arrested and indicted for "manufactur[ing]" a "controlled substance." After a pretrial hearing, the District Court suppressed evidence of the discovery of the marihuana field. Applying *Katz v. United States*, the court found that petitioner had a reasonable expectation that the field would remain private because petitioner "had done all that could be expected of him to assert his privacy in the area of farm that was searched." He had posted "No Trespassing" signs at regular intervals and had locked the gate at the entrance to the center of the farm. Further, the court noted that the field itself is highly secluded: it is bounded on all sides by woods, fences, and embankments and cannot be seen from any point of public access. The court concluded that this was not an "open" field that invited casual intrusion.

The . . . [Court of Appeals] . . . concluded that *Katz*. . .had not impaired the vitality of the open fields doctrine of *Hester*. Rather, the open fields doctrine was entirely compatible with *Katz'* emphasis on privacy. The court reasoned that the "human relations that create the need for privacy do not ordinarily take place" in open fields, and that the property owner's common-law right to exclude trespassers is insufficiently linked to privacy to warrant the Fourth Amendment's protection. We granted certiorari.

...

The rule announced in *Hester v. United States* was founded upon the explicit language of the Fourth Amendment. . . . As Justice Holmes explained for the Court in his characteristically laconic style: "[T]he special protection accorded by the Fourth Amendment to the people in their 'persons, houses, papers, and effects,' is not extended to the open fields. The distinction between the latter and the house is as old as the common law."

We conclude . . . that the government's intrusion upon the open fields is not one of those "unreasonable searches" proscribed by the text of the Fourth Amendment.

. . . .

No single factor determines whether an individual legitimately may claim under the Fourth Amendment that a place should be free of government intrusion not authorized by warrant. In assessing the degree to which a search infringes upon individual privacy, the Court has given weight to such factors as the intention of the Framers of the Fourth Amendment, the uses to which the individual has put a location, and our societal understanding that certain areas deserve the most scrupulous protection from government invasion. . . These factors are equally relevant to determining whether the government's intrusion upon open fields without a warrant or probable cause violates reasonable expectations of privacy and is therefore a search proscribed by the Amendment.

[A]n individual may not legitimately demand privacy for activities conducted out of doors in fields, except in the area immediately surrounding the home. This rule is true to the conception of the right to privacy embodied in the Fourth Amendment.

[O]pen fields do not provide the setting for those intimate activities that the Amendment is intended to shelter from government interference or surveillance. There is no societal interest in protecting the privacy of those activities, such as the cultivation of crops, that occur in open fields. Moreover, as a practical matter these lands usually are accessible to the public and the police in ways that a home, an office, or commercial structure would not be. It is not generally true that fences or "No Trespassing" signs effectively bar the public from viewing open fields in rural areas. And both petitioner Oliver and respondent Thornton concede that the public and police lawfully may survey lands from the air. For these reasons, the asserted expectation of privacy in open fields is not an expectation that "society recognizes as reasonable."

[T]he common law distinguished "open fields" from the "curtilage," the land immediately surrounding and associated with the home. The distinction implies that only the curtilage, not the neighboring open fields, warrants the Fourth Amendment protections that attach to the home. At common law, the curtilage is the area to which extends the intimate activity associated with the "sanctity of a man's home and the privacies of life," and therefore has been considered part of the home itself for Fourth Amendment purposes. . . .

. . . .

[W]e reject the suggestion that steps taken to protect privacy establish that expectations of privacy in an open field are legitimate. It is true, of course, that petitioner Oliver and respondent Thornton, in order to conceal their criminal activities, planted the marihuana upon secluded land and erected fences and "No Trespassing" signs around the property. And it may be that because of such precautions, few members of the public stumbled upon the marihuana crops seized by the police. Neither of these suppositions demonstrates, however, that the expectation of privacy was legitimate in the sense required by the Fourth Amendment. The test of legitimacy is not whether the individual chooses to conceal assertedly "private" activity. Rather, the correct inquiry is whether the government's intrusion infringes upon the personal and societal values protected by the Fourth Amendment. As we have explained, we find no basis for concluding that a police inspection of open fields accomplishes such an infringement.

Nor is the government's intrusion upon an open field a "search" in the constitutional sense because that intrusion is a trespass at common law. The existence of a property right is but one element in determining whether expectations of privacy are legitimate. "`The premise that property interests control the right of the Government to search and seize has been discredited.'"

...

JUSTICE WHITE, concurring in part and concurring in the judgment.

... However reasonable a landowner's expectations of privacy may be, those expectations cannot convert a field into a "house" or an "effect."

JUSTICE MARSHALL, with whom JUSTICE BRENNAN and JUSTICE STEVENS join, dissenting.

In each of these consolidated cases, police officers, ignoring clearly visible "No Trespassing" signs, entered upon private land in search of evidence of a crime. At a spot that could not be seen from any vantage point accessible to the public, the police discovered contraband, which was subsequently used to incriminate the owner of the land. In neither case did the police have a warrant authorizing their activities.

The Court holds that police conduct of this sort does not constitute an "unreasonable search" within the meaning of the Fourth Amendment. The Court reaches that startling conclusion by two independent analytical routes. First, the Court argues that, because the Fourth Amendment by its terms renders people secure in their "persons, houses, papers, and effects," it is inapplicable to trespasses upon land not lying within the curtilage of a dwelling. Second, the Court contends that "an individual may not legitimately demand privacy for activities conducted out of doors in fields, except in the area immediately surrounding the home." Because I cannot agree with either of these propositions, I dissent.

. . . .

The liberty shielded by the Fourth Amendment, as we have often acknowledged, is freedom "from unreasonable government intrusions into . . . legitimate expectations of privacy." That freedom would be incompletely protected if only government conduct that impinged upon a person, house, paper, or effect were subject to constitutional scrutiny. Accordingly, we have repudiated the proposition that the Fourth Amendment applies only to a limited set of locales or kinds of property. In *Katz v. United States*, we expressly rejected a proffered locational theory of the coverage of the Amendment, holding that it "protects people, not places." Since that time we have consistently adhered to the view that the applicability of the provision depends solely upon "whether the person invoking its protection can claim a `justifiable,' a `reasonable,' or a `legitimate expectation of privacy' that has been invaded by government action." The Court's contention that, because a field is not a house or effect, it is not covered by the Fourth Amendment is inconsistent with this line of cases and with the understanding of the nature of constitutional adjudication from which it derives.

The second ground for the Court's decision is its contention that any interest a landowner might have in the privacy of his woods and fields is not one that "society is prepared to recognize as `reasonable.'"

We have frequently acknowledged that privacy interests are not coterminous with property rights. However, because "property rights reflect society's explicit recognition of a person's authority to act as he wishes in certain areas, [they] should be considered in determining whether an individual's expectations of privacy are reasonable." Indeed, the Court has suggested that, insofar as "[o]ne of the main rights attaching to property is the right to exclude others, . . . one who owns or lawfully possesses or controls property will in all likelihood have a legitimate expectation of privacy by virtue of this right to exclude."

It is undisputed that Oliver and Thornton each owned the land into which the police intruded. That fact alone provides considerable support for their assertion of legitimate privacy interests in their woods and fields. But even more telling is the nature of the sanctions that Oliver and Thornton could invoke, under local law, for violation of their property rights. . . .An intrusion into "any place from which [the intruder] may lawfully be excluded and which is posted in a manner prescribed by law or in a manner reasonably likely to come to the attention of intruders or which is fenced or otherwise enclosed" is a crime. Thus, positive law not only recognizes the legitimacy of Oliver's and Thornton's insistence that strangers keep off their land, but subjects those who refuse to respect their wishes to the most severe of penalties - criminal liability. Under these circumstances, it is hard to credit the Court's assertion that Oliver's and Thornton's expectations of privacy were not of a sort that society is prepared to recognize as reasonable.

The uses to which a place is put are highly relevant to the assessment of a privacy interest asserted therein. If, in light of our shared sensibilities, those activities are of a kind in which people should be able to engage without fear of intrusion by private persons or government officials, we extend the protection of the Fourth Amendment to the space in question, even in the absence of any entitlement derived from positive law.

Privately owned woods and fields that are not exposed to public view regularly are employed in a variety of ways that society acknowledges deserve privacy. Many landowners like to take solitary walks on their property, confident that they will not be confronted in their rambles by strangers or policemen. Others conduct agricultural businesses on their property. Some landowners use their secluded spaces to meet lovers, others to gather together with fellow worshippers, still others to engage in sustained creative endeavor. Private land is sometimes used as a refuge for wildlife, where flora and fauna are protected from human intervention of any kind. Our respect for the freedom of landowners to use their posted "open fields" in ways such as these partially explains the seriousness with which the positive law regards deliberate invasions of such spaces, and substantially reinforces the landowners' contention that their expectations of privacy are "reasonable."

Whether a person "took normal precautions to maintain his privacy" in a given space affects whether his interest is one protected by the Fourth Amendment. The reason why such precautions are relevant is that we do not insist that a person who has a right to exclude others exercise that right. A claim to privacy is therefore strengthened by the fact that the claimant somehow manifested to other people his desire that they keep their distance.

Certain spaces are so presumptively private that signals of this sort are unnecessary; a homeowner need not post a "Do Not Enter" sign on his door in order to deny entrance to uninvited guests. Privacy interests in other spaces are more ambiguous, and the taking of precautions is consequently more important; placing a lock on one's footlocker strengthens one's claim that an examination of its contents is impermissible. Still other spaces are, by positive law and social convention, presumed accessible to members of the public unless the owner manifests his intention to exclude them.

Undeveloped land falls into the last-mentioned category. If a person has not marked the boundaries of his fields or woods in a way that informs passersby that they are not welcome, he cannot object if members of the public enter onto the property. There is no reason why he should have any greater rights as against government officials. Accordingly, we have held that an official may, without a warrant, enter private land from which the public is not excluded and make observations from that vantage point. Fairly read, the case on which the majority so heavily relies, *Hester v. United States*, (1924), affirms little more than the foregoing unremarkable proposition. . . .

A very different case is presented when the owner of undeveloped land has taken precautions to exclude the public. As indicated above, a deliberate entry by a private citizen onto private property marked with "No Trespassing" signs will expose him to criminal liability. I see no reason why a government official should not be obliged to respect such unequivocal and universally understood manifestations of a landowner's desire for privacy.

In sum, examination of the three principal criteria we have traditionally used for assessing the reasonableness of a person's expectation that a given space would remain private indicates that interests of the sort asserted by Oliver and Thornton are entitled to constitutional protection. An owner's right to insist that others stay off his posted land is firmly grounded in positive law. Many of the uses to which such land may be put deserve privacy. And, by marking the boundaries of the land with warnings that the public should not intrude, the owner has dispelled any ambiguity as to his desires.

The police in these cases proffered no justification for their invasions of Oliver's and Thornton's privacy interests; in neither case was the entry legitimated by a warrant or by one of the established exceptions to the warrant requirement. I conclude, therefore, that the searches of their land violated the Fourth Amendment, and the evidence obtained in the course of those searches should have been suppressed.

A clear, easily administrable rule emerges from the analysis set forth above: Private land marked in a fashion sufficient to render entry thereon a criminal trespass under the law of the State in which the land lies is protected by the Fourth Amendment's proscription of unreasonable searches and seizures. One of the advantages of the foregoing rule is that it draws upon a doctrine already familiar to both citizens and government officials. In each jurisdiction, a substantial body of statutory and case law defines the precautions a landowner must take in order to avail himself of the sanctions of the criminal law. The police know

that body of law, because they are entrusted with responsibility for enforcing it against the public; it therefore would not be difficult for the police to abide by it themselves.

By contrast, the doctrine announced by the Court today is incapable of determinate application. Police officers, making warrantless entries upon private land, will be obliged in the future to make on-the-spot judgments as to how far the curtilage extends, and to stay outside that zone. In addition, we may expect to see a spate of litigation over the question of how much improvement is necessary to remove private land from the category of "unoccupied or undeveloped area" to which the "open fields exception" is now deemed applicable.

The Court's holding not only ill serves the need to make constitutional doctrine "workable for application by rank-and-file, trained police officers," it withdraws the shield of the Fourth Amendment from privacy interests that clearly deserve protection. By exempting from the coverage of the Amendment large areas of private land, the Court opens the way to investigative activities we would all find repugnant.

. . . .

UNITED STATES v. DUNN
480 U.S. 294 (1987)

[Official Syllabus}

In 1980, Drug Enforcement Administration agents, having discovered that one Carpenter had bought large quantities of chemicals and equipment used to make controlled substances, placed tracking "beepers" in some of the equipment and one of the chemical containers, which, when transported in Carpenter's truck, led the agents to respondent's ranch. Aerial photographs of the ranch showed the truck backed up to a barn behind the ranch house. The ranch was completely encircled by a perimeter fence, and contained several interior barbed wire fences, including one around the house approximately

50 yards from the barn, and a wooden fence enclosing the front of the barn, which had an open overhang and locked, waist-high gates. Without a warrant, officers crossed the perimeter fence, several of the barbed wire fences, and the wooden fence in front of the barn. They were led there by the smell of chemicals, and, while there, could hear a motor running inside. They did not enter the barn but stopped at the locked gate and shined a flashlight inside, observing what they took to be a drug laboratory. They then left the ranch, but entered it twice the next day to confirm the laboratory's presence. They obtained a search warrant and executed it, arresting respondent

and seizing chemicals and equipment, as well as bags of amphetamines they discovered in the house. . . . Respondent and Carpenter were convicted of conspiracy to manufacture controlled substances and related offenses. However, the Court of Appeals reversed, holding that the barn was within the residence's curtilage and therefore within the Fourth Amendment's protective ambit.]

JUSTICE WHITE delivered the opinion of the Court.

We granted the Government's petition for certiorari to decide whether the area near a barn, located approximately 50 yards from a fence surrounding a ranch house, is, for Fourth Amendment purposes, within the curtilage of the house.

… [T]he Fourth Amendment protects the curtilage of a house and that the extent of the curtilage is determined by factors that bear upon whether an individual reasonably may expect that the area in question should be treated as the home itself. We identified the central component of this inquiry as whether the area harbors the "intimate activity associated with the `sanctity of a man's home and the privacies of life.'" … [W]we believe that curtilage questions should be resolved with particular reference to four factors: the proximity of the area claimed to be curtilage to the home, whether the area is included within an enclosure surrounding the home, the nature of the uses to which the area is put, and the steps taken by the resident to protect the area from observation by people passing by. . . . We do not suggest that combining these factors produces a finely tuned formula that, when mechanically applied, yields a "correct" answer to all extent-of-curtilage questions. Rather, these factors are useful analytical tools only to the degree that, in any given case, they bear upon the centrally relevant consideration - whether the area in question is so intimately tied to the home itself that it should be placed under the home's "umbrella" of Fourth Amendment protection. Applying these factors to respondent's barn and to the area immediately surrounding it, we have little difficulty in concluding that this

area lay outside the curtilage of the ranch house.

First. The record discloses that the barn was located 50 yards from the fence surrounding the house and 60 yards from the house itself. Standing in isolation, this substantial distance supports no inference that the barn should be treated as an adjunct of the house.

Second. It is also significant that respondent's barn did not lie within the area surrounding the house that was enclosed by a fence. We noted in Oliver, supra, that "for most homes, the boundaries of the curtilage will be clearly marked; and the conception defining the curtilage - as the area around the home to which the activity of home life extends - is a familiar one easily understood from our daily experience." Viewing the physical layout of respondent's ranch in its entirety, it is plain that the fence surrounding the residence serves to demark a specific area of land immediately adjacent to the house that is readily identifiable as part and parcel of the house. Conversely, the barn - the front portion itself enclosed by a fence - and the area immediately surrounding it, stands out as a distinct portion of respondent's ranch, quite separate from the residence.

Third. It is especially significant that the law enforcement officials possessed objective data indicating that the barn was not being used for intimate activities of the home. …

Fourth. Respondent did little to protect the barn area from observation by those standing in the open fields. Nothing in the record suggests that the various interior fences on respondent's property had any function other than that of the typical ranch fence; the fences were designed and constructed to corral livestock, not to prevent persons from observing what lay inside the enclosed areas.

The officers lawfully viewed the interior of respondent's barn, and their observations were properly considered by the Magistrate in issuing a search warrant for respondent's premises.

JUSTICE BRENNAN, with whom JUSTICE MARSHALL joins, dissenting.

The Government agents' intrusions upon Ronald Dunn's privacy and property violated the Fourth Amendment for two reasons. First, the barnyard invaded by the agents lay within the protected curtilage of Dunn's farmhouse. Second, the agents infringed upon Dunn's reasonable expectation of privacy in the barn and its contents. Our society is not so exclusively urban that it is unable to perceive or unwilling to preserve the expectation of farmers and ranchers that barns and their contents are protected from (literally) unwarranted government intrusion.

…

A barn, like a factory, a plant, or a warehouse, is a business place not open to the general public. Like these other business establishments, the barn, and any area immediately surrounding or adjacent to it from which the public is excluded, should receive protection. A business operator is undisputably entitled to constitutional protection within the premises when steps have been taken to ensure privacy.

For the police habitually to engage in such surveillance - without a warrant - is constitutionally intolerable. Because I believe that farmers' and ranchers' expectations of privacy in their barns and other outbuildings are expectations society would regard as reasonable, and because I believe that sanctioning the police behavior at issue here does violence to the purpose and promise of the Fourth Amendment, I dissent.

Abandoned Property

People have no privacy interest in items they throw out or discard. Accordingly, the Court has consistently held that warrantless searches of abandoned property do not violate the Fourth Amendment. The seminal case on abandoned property is *California v. Greenwood.*

CALIFORNIA v. GREENWOOD
486 U.S. 35 (1988)

JUSTICE WHITE delivered the opinion of the Court.

The issue here is whether the Fourth Amendment prohibits the warrantless search and seizure of garbage left for collection outside the curtilage of a home. We conclude, in accordance with the vast majority of lower courts that have addressed the issue, that it does not.

[Facts Summarized: Laguna Beach Police Officer, Jenny Stracner, got information that Greenwood was involved in the illegal drug trade; she further investigated and surveilled his home. She asked the trash collector to set aside Greenwood's garbage. He did, and she searched it and found items indicating drugs. She then got a warrant, executed the warrant and found lots of drugs. Greenwood was arrested. He posted bail and moved back home. There were further reports of drug trafficking. This lead to another garbage investigation and more drugs were found. Then there was another warrantmore drugs and evidence of drug trafficking. Greenwood was again arrested.]

The warrantless search and seizure of the garbage bags left at the curb outside the Greenwood house would violate the Fourth Amendment only if respondents manifested a subjective expectation of privacy in their garbage that society accepts as objectively reasonable. . . . Respondents do not disagree with this standard.

They assert, however, that they had, and exhibited, an expectation of privacy with respect to the trash that was searched by the police: The trash, which was placed on the street for collection at a fixed time, was contained in opaque plastic bags, which the garbage collector was expected to pick up, mingle with the trash of others, and deposit at the garbage dump. The trash was only temporarily on the street, and there was little likelihood that it would be inspected by anyone.

It may well be that respondents did not expect that the contents of their garbage bags would become known to the police or other members of the public. An expectation of privacy does not give rise to Fourth Amendment protection, however, unless society is prepared to accept that expectation as objectively reasonable.

Here, we conclude that respondents exposed their garbage to the public sufficiently to defeat their claim to Fourth Amendment protection. It is common knowledge that plastic garbage bags left on or at the side of a public street are readily accessible to animals, children, scavengers, snoops, and other members of the public. Moreover, respondents placed their refuse at the curb for the express purpose of conveying it to a third party, the trash collector, who might himself have sorted through respondents' trash or permitted others, such as the police, to do so. Accordingly, having deposited their garbage "in an area particularly suited for public inspection and, in a manner of speaking, public consumption, for

the express purpose of having strangers take it," respondents could have had no reasonable expectation of privacy in the inculpatory items that they discarded.

Furthermore, as we have held, the police cannot reasonably be expected to avert their eyes from evidence of criminal activity that could have been observed by any member of the public. Hence, "[w]hat a person knowingly exposes to the public, even in his own home or office, is not a subject of Fourth Amendment protection."

[Court noted that] . . . individual States may surely construe their own constitutions as imposing more stringent constraints on police conduct than does the Federal Constitution.

JUSTICE BRENNAN, with whom JUSTICE MARSHALL joins, dissenting.

. . .

Scrutiny of another's trash is contrary to commonly accepted notions of civilized behavior. I suspect, therefore, that members of our society will be shocked to learn that the Court, the ultimate guarantor of liberty, deems unreasonable our expectation that the aspects of our private lives that are concealed safely in a trash bag will not become public.

Other Cases: Abandoned Property

Smith v. Ohio, 494 U.S. 541 (1990)	abandoned, and not merely set aside or concealed.)
SUMMARY: Suspect threw a sack onto the hood of a car when approached by the police. Court found that he did not abandon the sack, but instead attempted to protect it. Note: this shows that to lose Fourth Amendment protections, the property must actually be	***Abel v. United States, 362 U.S. 217 (1960)***
	HOLDING: The warrantless seizure of items abandoned in a hotel wastepaper basket did not violate the Fourth Amendment.

Dog Sniffs

The Court has examined "dog sniffs" in several cases: The first dealt with the use of a dog to detect contraband. (*United States v. Place* (1983).) The *Place* Court held that a dog sniff of a passenger's luggage in an airport was not a search, the Court ultimately decided it on seizure grounds -- so the case excerpt is found later in the chapter. Since *Place* the Court has examined drug detection dog sniffs in *Illinois v. Caballes* (2005), *Florida v. Jardines (2013)* and *Florida v. Harris (2013)*, and then in *Rodriguez v. United States* (2015)

Illinois v. Caballes, 543 U.S. 405 (2005)

SUMMARY: State Trooper Gillette stopped Caballes for speeding on an interstate highway. A second trooper, Graham, part of the drug interdiction team, overheard the transmission and headed to the scene with his drug-detection dog. When Graham got to where Gillette and Caballes were, he walked the dog around Caballes car while Gillette was writing the warning ticket. The dog alerted to the presence of drugs. Based on the alert, troopers searched the trunk, found marijuana and arrested Caballes. The entire incident lasted no longer than 10 minutes.

OPINION:

Official conduct that does not "compromise any legitimate interest in privacy" is not a search subject to the Fourth Amendment. . . Any interest in possessing contraband cannot be deemed "legitimate," and thus, governmental conduct that only reveals the possession of contraband compromises no legitimate privacy interest. This is because the expectation that certain facts will not come to the attention of the authorities" is not the same as an interest in "privacy that society is prepared to consider reasonable."

Although Caballes argues that the error rates, particularly the existence of false positives, call into question the premise that drug-detection dogs alert only to contraband, the record contains no evidence or findings that support his argument. Moreover, Caballes does not suggest that an erroneous alert, in and of itself, reveals any legitimate private information, and, in this case the trial judge found that the dog sniff was sufficiently reliable to establish probable cause.

[T]he use of a well-trained narcotics-detection dog — one that does not expose noncontraband items that otherwise would remain hidden from public view during a lawful traffic stop, generally does not implicate legitimate privacy interests. In this case the dog sniff was performed on the exterior of Caballes' car while he was lawfully seized for a traffic violation. Any intrusion on Caballes's privacy expectation does not rise to the level of a constitutionally cognizable infringement.

A dog sniff conducted during a concededly lawful traffic stop that reveals no information other than the location of a substance that no individual has any right to possess does not violate the Fourth Amendment.

Florida v. Jardines, 569 U.S. 1 (2013)

SUMMARY: Drug detection dog and its handler went up to the front door but never went into the home. The State, relying on *Caballes*, argued that there was no reasonable expectation of privacy in narcotics or contraband. The defendant argued that this was not the type of dog sniff in *Caballes,* but rather this was a search of something in his home — an area that the Court has afforded the highest level of privacy. The Court's majority analyzed the case under the reinvigorated trespass analysis it had just announced in *U.S. v. Jones* (see above), rather than under a *Katz* privacy analysis.

Court agreed with the defendant and found the dog sniff at the door was a violation of the Fourth Amendment.

Justice Kagen's concurring opinion indicated that she would have been content to analyze the case under the privacy doctrine, and likened the dog's sniff, to enhanced technology and would have found a violation of the Fourth Amendment based on the Kyllo decision.

Florida v. Harris, 568 U.S. 237 (2013)

SUMMARY: The issue before the court was whether a particular dog was sufficiently trained and reliable. Police had stopped a car and found that the driver seemed nervous. A drug detection dog was brought to sniff around the car. The dog alerted. The police searched that area and pseudoephedrine was found.

The defendant filed a motion to suppress arguing that the dog was not properly trained. The motion was denied and defendant was convicted. He appealed, and the Florida Supreme Court opined that to adequately show a dog's accuracy the State needed to show training certification records. The Florida Supreme Court found several problems with the state's argument that the alert, by itself, was sufficient to constitute probable cause. It noted that there could be handler error, false alerts, and misleading residual odors.

The Court refused to enunciate a per se test that a dog alert constituted probable cause, but instead held that the totality of the circumstance test should be employed. The dog's training is one factor to be considered in the probable cause determination.

Bank Records, Pen Registers, E-Mails, And Cell Phone Records—

In 1976 the Court held that people do not have a legitimate expectation of privacy in their bank account data. In *United States v. Miller*, 425 U.S. 435 (1976), federal treasury agents served subpoenas on the presidents of Miller's banks demanding that bank records be produced at the grand jury. The banks didn't tell Miller about the subpoenas but ordered their employees to make the records available and to provide copies of any documents the agents desired.

> Miller urges that he has a Fourth Amendment interest in the records kept by banks because. . . he has a reasonable expectation of privacy [in the records]. ... We ... perceive no legitimate expectation of privacy in their contents. The checks are not confidential communications but negotiable instruments to be used in commercial transactions. All of the documents obtained, including financial statements and deposit slips, contain only information voluntarily conveyed to the banks and exposed to their employees in the ordinary course of business. . .

> The depositor takes the risk, in revealing his affairs to another, that the information will be conveyed by that person to the Government. This Court has held repeatedly that the Fourth Amendment does not prohibit the obtaining of information revealed to a third party and conveyed by him to Government authorities, even if the information is revealed on the assumption that it will be used only for a limited purpose and the confidence placed in the third party will not be betrayed.

Similarly, In *Smith v. Maryland*, 442 U.S. 735 (1979) the Court held that using a pen register is not a search under the meaning of the Fourth Amendment. A pen register is a device that records the phone numbers that are dialed from a particular phone number. (This common feature on every cell phone today used to be something that only the telephone company had access to.) Justice Blackman stated,

> Telephone users . . . typically know that they must convey numerical information to the phone company; that the phone company has facilities for recording this information; and that the phone company does in fact record this information for a variety of legitimate business purposes. Although subjective expectations cannot be scientifically gauged, it is too much to believe that telephone subscribers, under these circumstances, harbor any general expectation that the numbers they dial will remain secret.

> Second, even if petitioner did harbor some subjective expectation that the phone numbers he dialed would remain private, this expectation is not "one that society is prepared to recognize as 'reasonable.'" . . . This Court consistently has held that a person has no legitimate expectation of privacy in information he voluntarily turns over to third parties. . . .

> [P]etitioner can claim no legitimate expectation of privacy here. When he used his phone, petitioner voluntarily conveyed numerical information to the telephone company and "exposed" that information to its equipment in the ordinary course of business. In so doing, petitioner assumed the risk that the company would reveal to police the numbers he dialed.

> . . . The installation and use of a pen register, consequently, was not a "search," and no warrant was required.

Federal courts have extended the Court's reasoning in *Smith* and *Miller* to utility records and cell phone records. In response, Congress, in 1994, provided legislation to protect individual privacy for cordless phones following up on legislation to protect against eavesdropping on cellular phones. The Communications Assistance for Law Enforcement Act of 1994 did, however, require telecommunications carriers ensure that their equipment and services were complying with electronic surveillance by law enforcement. More recently courts have been faced with the question of whether people have a right to privacy from government access to cell phone records which reveal location and movement phone use over several months. In *Carpenter v. United States*, 585 U.S. at ____ (2018) the Court was presented with the question of whether a Fourth Amendment search occurs when the government access historical cell phone records that provide a comprehensive chronicle of the user's past movements.

CARPENTER V. UNITED STATES
585 U.S. ___ (2018)

Facts: In April 2011, police arrested four men in connection with a series of armed robberies. One of the men confessed to the crimes and gave the FBI his cell phone number and the numbers of the other participants. The FBI used this information to apply for three orders from magistrate judges to obtain "transactional records" for each of the phone numbers, which the judges granted under the Stored Communications Act, 18 U.S.C. 2703(d). That Act provides that the government may require the disclosure of certain telecommunications records when "specific and articulable facts show[] that there are reasonable grounds to believe that the contents of a wire or electronic communication, or the records or other information sought, are relevant and material to an ongoing criminal investigation." The transactional records obtained by the government include the date and time of calls, and the approximate location where calls began and ended based on their connections to cell towers—"cell site" location information (CSLI).

Based on the cell-site evidence, the government charged Timothy Carpenter with, among other offenses, aiding and abetting robbery that affected interstate commerce, in violation of the Hobbs Act, 18 U.S.C. 1951. Carpenter moved to suppress the government's cell-site evidence on Fourth Amendment grounds, arguing that the FBI needed a warrant based on probable cause to obtain the records. The

district court denied the motion to suppress, and the Sixth Circuit affirmed.

Official Summary

1. The Government's acquisition of Carpenter's cell-site records was a Fourth Amendment search.

…

(b) The digital data at issue—personal location information maintained by a third party—does not fit neatly under existing precedents but lies at the intersection of two lines of cases. One set addresses a person's expectation of privacy in his physical location and movements. See, *e.g., United States* v. *Jones,* 565 U. S. 400 (five Justices concluding that privacy concerns would be raised by GPS tracking). The other addresses a person's expectation of privacy in information voluntarily turned over to third parties. See *United States* v. *Miller,* 425 U. S. 435 (no expectation of privacy in financial records held by a bank), and *Smith,* 442 U. S. 735 (no expectation of privacy in records of dialed telephone numbers conveyed to telephone company).

(c) Tracking a person's past movements through CSLI partakes of many of the qualities of GPS monitoring considered in *Jones*—it is detailed, encyclopedic, and effortlessly compiled. At the same time, however, the fact that the individual continuously reveals his location to his wireless carrier implicates the third-party principle of *Smith* and *Miller*. Given the unique nature of cell-site records, this Court declines to extend *Smith* and *Miller* to cover them.

(1) A majority of the Court has already recognized that individuals have a reasonable expectation of privacy in the whole of their physical movements. Allowing government access to cell-site records—which "hold for many Americans the 'privacies of life,' " *Riley v. California*, 573 U. S. ___, ___ (contravenes that expectation. In fact, historical cell-site records present even greater privacy concerns than the GPS monitoring considered in *Jones*: They give the Government near perfect surveillance and allow it to travel back in time to retrace a person's whereabouts, subject only to the five-year retention policies of most wireless carriers. The Government contends that CSLI data is less precise than GPS information, but it thought the data accurate enough here to highlight it during closing argument in Carpenter's trial. At any rate, the rule the Court adopts "must take account of more sophisticated systems that are already in use or in development,"... and the accuracy of CSLI is rapidly approaching GPS-level precision.

(2) The Government contends that the third-party doctrine governs this case, because cell-site records, like the records in *Smith* and *Miller*, are "business records," created and maintained by wireless carriers. But there is a world of difference between the limited types of personal information addressed in *Smith* and *Miller* and the exhaustive chronicle of location information casually collected by wireless carriers.

The third-party doctrine partly stems from the notion that an individual has a reduced expectation of privacy in information knowingly shared with another. *Smith* and *Miller*, however, did not rely solely on the act of sharing. They also considered "the nature of the particular documents sought" and limitations on any "legitimate 'expectation of privacy' concerning their contents." ... In mechanically applying the third-party doctrine to this case

the Government fails to appreciate the lack of comparable limitations on the revealing nature of CSLI.

Nor does the second rationale for the third-party doctrine—voluntary exposure—hold up when it comes to CSLI. Cell phone location information is not truly "shared" as the term is normally understood. First, cell phones and the services they provide are "such a pervasive and insistent part of daily life" that carrying one is indispensable to participation in modern society. ... Second, a cell phone logs a cell-site record by dint of its operation, without any affirmative act on the user's part beyond powering up.

(d) This decision is narrow. It does not express a view on matters not before the Court; does not disturb the application of *Smith* and *Miller* or call into question conventional surveillance techniques and tools, such as security cameras; does not address other business records that might incidentally reveal location information; and does not consider other collection techniques involving foreign affairs or national security.

2. The Government did not obtain a warrant supported by probable cause before acquiring Carpenter's cell-site records. It acquired those records pursuant to a court order under the Stored Communications Act, which required the Government to show "reasonable grounds" for believing that the records were "relevant and material to an ongoing investigation." 18 U. S. C. §2703(d). That showing falls well short of the probable cause required for a warrant. Consequently, an order issued under §2703(d) is not a permissible mechanism for accessing historical cell-site records. Not all orders compelling the production of documents will require a showing of probable cause. A warrant is required only in the rare case where the suspect has a legitimate privacy interest in records held by a third party. And even though the Government will generally need a warrant to access CSLI, case-specific exceptions—*e.g.*, exigent circumstances—may support a warrantless search.

SUMMARY OF DISSENTING OPINIONS:[56]

Justice Anthony Kennedy: Cell-site records are no different from the many other kinds of business records the government has a lawful right to obtain by compulsory process. He would limit the Fourth Amendment to its property-based origins.

Justice Thomas dissent: Emphasized the property-based approach to Fourth Amendment questions. Case should not turn on whether a search occurred, but whose property was searched. By focusing on this latter question, Justice Thomas reasoned, the only logical conclusion would be that the information did not belong to Carpenter.

Justice Alito dissent: Distinguish between an actual search and an order "merely requiring a party to look through its own records and produce specified documents"—with the former being far more intrusive than the latter. Criticized majority for "allow[ing] a defendant to object to the search of a third party's property," a departure from long-standing Fourth Amendment doctrine.

Justice Gorsuch dissent: Emphasized the "original understanding" of the Fourth Amendment and laments the Court's departure from it.

IS THE GOVERNMENTAL ACTION A SEIZURE?

Seizing People

The Court distinguishes between non-seizures ("mere encounters") of individuals, and seizures of individuals, including limited seizures (stops), full-blown seizures (arrests). The Court has also examined seizures of individuals in the context of traffic stops, random patrol stops, checkpoint stops, and roadblocks. (The reasonableness of the latter, warrantless traffic stops is dealt with in Chapter Five.)

According to the Court, police officers need "no particularized suspicion" to approach individuals and question them. In *Florida v. Royer*, 460 U.S. 491 (1983) the Court stated,

"Law enforcement officials do not violate the Fourth Amendment by merely approaching an individual on the street or in another public place, by asking him if he is willing to answer some questions, by putting questions to him if the person is willing to listen, or by offering in evidence in a criminal prosecution his voluntary answers to such questions."

The Court reiterated the differences between mere encounters and seizures in *Florida v. Bostick*, 401 U.S. 429 (1991). In that case two uniformed officers boarded a bus in Fort Lauderdale, Florida that was en route from Miami to Atlanta. The officers approached Bostick and asked him for identification and his bus ticket. The officers then asked him for consent to search his bag and told Bostick he could refuse consent. Bostick nevertheless consented to the search of his luggage that uncovered cocaine. Bostick moved to suppress the cocaine in court, arguing that it was illegally seized. The Court overruled the Florida Supreme Court's finding that "working the busses" was per se unconstitutional:

"The appropriate test is whether, taking into account all of the circumstances surrounding the encounter, a reasonable person would feel free to decline the officers' request to otherwise terminate the encounter. . . . [A] seizure does not occur simply because a police officer approaches an individual and asks a few questions. So long as a reasonable person would feel free 'to disregard the police and go about his business,' the encounter is consensual and

---

56

See,https://supreme.justia.com/cases/federal/us/585/16-402/#tab-opinion-3919271

no reasonable suspicion is required. The encounter will not trigger Fourth Amendment scrutiny unless it loses its consensual nature.

There is no doubt that if this same encounter had taken place before Bostick boarded the bus or in the lobby or the bus terminal, it would not rise to the level of a seizure. The Court has dealt with similar encounters in airports and has found them to be 'the sort of consensual encounters that implicate no Fourth Amendment interest.' We have stated that even when officers have no basis for suspecting a particular individual, they may generally ask questions of that individual and request consent to search his or her luggage — as long as the police do not convey a message that compliance with their requests is required."

Temporary Seizures: Stops

Terry v. Ohio, 392 U.S. 1 (1968), created an entirely "new" level of Fourth Amendment analysis. (Although stops and frisks were not really new because officers had been doing these investigative stops that some states called "stops and frisk" for some time, the Court in *Terry* officially affirmed these practices.) The Fourth Amendment governs searches and seizures, and seems to require that probable cause is needed for a seizure to be reasonable. In *Terry* though, the Court held that some seizures and searches were reasonable even with facts that didn't meet the probable cause standard of sufficiency of evidence.

TERRY v. OHIO
392 U.S. 1 (1968)

CHIEF JUSTICE WARREN delivered the opinion of the Court.

. . . Officer McFadden testified . . . [at a motion to suppress hearing] that while he was patrolling in plain clothes in downtown Cleveland at approximately 2:30 in the afternoon his attention was attracted by two men, Chilton and Terry, standing on the corner of Huron Road and Euclid Avenue. He had never seen the two men before, and he was unable to say precisely what first drew his eye to them. However, he testified that he had been a policeman for 39 years and a detective for 35 and that he had been assigned to patrol this vicinity of downtown Cleveland for shoplifters and pickpockets for 30 years. He explained that he had developed routine habits of observation over the years and that he would "stand and watch people or walk and watch people at many intervals of the day." He added: "Now, in this case when I looked over they didn't look right to me at the time."

His interest aroused, Officer McFadden took up a post of observation in the entrance to a store 300 to 400 feet away from the two men. "I get more purpose to watch them when I

seen their movements," he testified. He saw one of the men leave the other one and walk southwest on Huron Road, past some stores. The man paused for a moment and looked in a store window, then walked on a short distance, turned around and walked back toward the corner, pausing once again to look in the same store window. He rejoined his companion at the corner, and the two conferred briefly. Then the second man went through the same series of motions, strolling down Huron Road, looking in the same window, walking on a short distance, turning back, peering in the store window again, and returning to confer with the first man at the corner. The two men repeated this ritual alternately between five and six times apiece — in all roughly a dozen trips. At one point, while the two were standing together on the corner, a third man approached them and engaged them briefly in conversation. This man then left the two other and walked west on Euclid Avenue. Chilton and Terry resumed their measured pacing, peering, and conferring. After this had gone on for 10 to 12 minutes, the two men walked off together, heading west on Euclid Avenue, following the path taken earlier by the third man.

By this time Officer McFadden had become thoroughly suspicious. He testified that after observing this elaborately casual and oft-repeated reconnaissance of the store window on Huron Road, he suspected the two men of "casing a job, a stick-up," and that he considered it his duty as a police officer to investigate further. He added that he feared "they may have a gun." Thus, Officer McFadden followed Chilton and Terry and saw them stop in front of Zucker's store to talk to the same man who had conferred with them earlier on the street corner. Deciding that the situation was ripe for direct action, Officer McFadden approached the three men, identified himself as a police officer and asked for their names. At this point his knowledge was confined to what he had observed. He was not acquainted with any of the three men by name or by sight, and he had received no information concerning them from any other source. When the men "mumbled something" in response to his inquiries, Officer McFadden grabbed petitioner Terry, spun him around so that they were facing the other two, with Terry between McFadden and the other, and patted down the outside of his clothing. In the left breast pocket of Terry's overcoat Officer McFadden felt a pistol. He reached inside the overcoat pocket, but was unable to remove the gun. At this point, keeping Terry between himself and the other, the officer ordered all three men to enter Zucker's store. As they went in, he removed Terry's overcoat completely, removed a .38-caliber revolver from the pocket and ordered all three men to face the wall with their hands raised. Officer McFadden proceeded to pat down the outer clothing of Chilton and the third man, Katz. He discovered another revolver in the outer pocket of Chilton's overcoat, but no weapons were found on Katz. The officer testified that he only patted the men down to see whether they had weapons, and that he did not put his hands beneath the outer garments of either Terry or Chilton until he felt their guns. So far as appears from the record, he never placed his hands beneath Katz' outer garments. Officer McFadden seized Chilton's gun, asked the proprietor of the store to call a police wagon, and took all three men to the station, where Chilton and Terry were formally charged with carrying concealed weapons.

On the motion to suppress the guns the prosecution took the position that they had been seized following a search incident to a lawful arrest. The trial court rejected this theory, stating that it "would be stretching the facts beyond reasonable comprehension" to find that Officer McFadden had probable cause to arrest the men before he patted them down for weapons. However, the court denied the defendants' motion on the ground that Officer McFadden, on the basis of his experience, "had reasonable cause to believe . . .that the defendants were conducting themselves suspiciously, and some interrogation should be made of their action." Purely for his own protection, the court held, the officer had the right to pat down the outer clothing of these men, who he had reasonable cause to believe might be armed. The court distinguished between a investigatory "stop" and an arrest, and between a "frisk" of the outer clothing for weapons and a full-blown search for evidence of crime. The frisk, it held, was essential to the proper performance of the officer's investigatory duties, for without it, "the answer to the police officer may be a bullet, and a loaded pistol discovered during the frisk is admissible."

We granted certiorari … to determine whether the admission of the revolvers in evidence violated petitioner's rights under the Fourth Amendment, made applicable to the States by the Fourteenth. … We affirm the conviction.

Unquestionably petitioner was entitled to the protection of the Fourth Amendment as he walked down the street in Cleveland. … The question is whether in all the circumstances of this on-the-street encounter, his right to personal security was violated by an unreasonable search and seizure. …

In this case there can be no question … that Officer McFadden "seized" petitioner and subjected him to a "search" when he took hold of him and patted down the outer surfaces of his clothing. We must decide whether at that point it was reasonable for Officer McFadden to have interfered with petitioner's personal security as he did. And in determining whether the seizure and search were "unreasonable" our inquiry is a dual one — whether the officer's action was justified at its inception, and whether it was reasonably related in scope to the circumstances which justified the interference in the first place.

[W]e deal here with an entire rubric of police conduct — necessarily swift action predicated upon the on-the-spot observations of the officer on the beat — which historically has not been, and as a practical matter could not be, subjected to the warrant procedure. Instead, the conduct involved in this case must be tested by the Fourth Amendment's general proscription against unreasonable searches and seizures.

Nonetheless, the notions which underlie both the warrant procedure and the requirement of probable cause remain fully relevant in this context. In order to assess the reasonableness of Officer McFadden's conduct as a general proposition, it is necessary "first to focus upon the governmental interest which allegedly justifies official intrusion upon the constitutionally protected interests of the private citizen," for there is "no ready test for determining reasonableness other than by balancing the need to search [or seize] against the invasion which the search [or seizure] entails." . . .And in justifying the particular intrusions the police officer must be able to point to specific and articulable facts which, taken together with rational inferences from those facts, reasonably warrant that intrusion. …

Applying these principles to this case, we consider first the nature and extent of the governmental interests involved. One general interest is of course that of effective crime prevention and detection; it is this interest which underlies the recognition that a police officer may in appropriate circumstances and in an appropriate manner approach a person for purposes of investigating possible criminal behavior even though there is no probable cause to make an arrest. …

The crux of this case, however, is not the propriety of Officer McFadden's taking steps to investigate petitioner's suspicious behavior, but rather, whether there was justification for McFadden's invasion of Terry's personal security by searching him for weapons in the course of that investigation. We are now concerned with more than the governmental interest in investigating crime; in addition, there is the more immediate interest of the police officer in taking steps to assure himself that the person with whom he is dealing is not armed with a weapon that could unexpectedly and fatally be used against him. Certainly it would be unreasonable to require that police officers take unnecessary risks in the performance of their duties. …

In view of these facts, we cannot blind ourselves to the need for law enforcement officers to protect themselves and other prospective victims of violence in situations where they may lack probable cause for an arrest. When an officer is justified in believing that the individual whose suspicious behavior he is investigating at close range is armed and presently dangerous to the officer or to others, it would appear to be clearly unreasonable to deny the officer the power to take necessary measures to determine whether the person is in fact carrying a weapon and to neutralize the threat of physical harm.

We must consider, however, the nature and quality of the intrusion on individual rights which must be accepted if police officers are to be conceded the right to search for weapons in situations where probable cause to arrest for crime is lacking. Even a limited search of the outer clothing for weapons constitutes a severe, though brief, intrusion upon cherished personal security, and it must surely be an annoying, frightening, and perhaps humiliating experience. …

We conclude that the revolver seized from Terry was properly admitted in evidence against him. At the time he seized petitioner and searched him for weapons, Officer McFadden had reasonable grounds to believe that petitioner was armed and dangerous, and it was necessary for the protection of himself and others to take swift measures to discover the true facts and neutralize the threat of harm if it materialized. The policeman carefully restricted his search to what was appropriate to the discovery of the particular items which he sought. Each case of this sort will, of course, have to be decided on its own facts. We merely hold today that where a police officer observes unusual conduct which leads him reasonably to conclude in light of his experience that criminal activity may be afoot and that the persons with whom he is dealing may be armed and presently dangerous, where in the course of investigating this behavior he identifies himself as a policeman and makes reasonable inquiries, and where nothing in the initial stages of the encounter serves to dispel his reasonable fear for his own or others' safety, he is entitled for the protection of himself and others in the area to conduct a carefully limited search of the outer clothing of such persons in an attempt to discover weapons which might be used to assault him. Such a search is a reasonable search under the Fourth Amendment, and any weapons seized may properly be introduced in evidence against the person from whom they were taken.

JUSTICE DOUGLAS, dissenting.

I agree that petitioner was "seized" within the meaning of the Fourth Amendment. I also agree that frisking petitioner and his companions for guns was a "search." But it is a mystery how that "search" and that "seizure" can be constitutional by Fourth Amendment standards, unless there was "probable cause" to believe that (1) a crime had been committed or (2) a crime was in the process of being committed or (3) a crime was about to be committed.

…

[P]olice officers up to today have been permitted to effect arrests or searches without warrants only when the facts within their personal knowledge would satisfy the constitutional standard of probable cause. At the time of their "seizure" without a warrant they must possess facts concerning the person arrested that would have satisfied a magistrate that "probable cause" was indeed present. The term "probable cause" rings a bell of certainty that is not sounded by phrases such as "reasonable suspicion. …"

The infringement on personal liberty of any "seizure" of a person can only be "reasonable" under the Fourth Amendment if we require the police to possess "probable cause" before they seize him. Only that line draws a meaningful distinction between an officer's mere inkling and the presence of facts within the officer's personal knowledge which would convince a reasonable man that the person seized has committed, is committing, or is about to commit a particular crime.

What Constitutes A Stop?

The Court has examined what constitutes a seizure of a person in several cases. In Terry, as you just read, the Court defined a seizure (a "stop") stating, "Only when the officer, by means of physical force or show of authority, has in some way restrained the liberty of a citizen may we conclude that a 'seizure' has occurred." *Terry v. Ohio*, 392 U.S. 1 (1968). In *Torres v. Madrid*, 592 U.S. ___ (2021) the Court examined what constitutes a seizure in the context of a police shooting. The Court simply held that, "The application of physical force to the body of a person with intent to restrain is a seizure even if the person does not submit and is not subdued." This definition somewhat modifies the holding in *California v. Hodari D..*, 499 U.S. 621 (1991), (no stop occurs, even when police officers attempt to exert authority over suspect, if he had not actually submitted to the officer's show of authority). Prior to *Hodari D.,* a plurality of the Court stated, a person is "seized within the meaning of the Fourth Amendment only if, in view of all the circumstances surrounding the incident, a reasonable person would have believed that he was not free to leave." *United States v. Mendenhall*, 446 U.S. 544 (1980).

TORRES V. MADRID,
592 U.S. ___ (2021)

OFFICIAL SUMMARY (CASE SYLLABUS): Respondents Janice Madrid and Richard Williamson, officers with the New Mexico State Police, arrived at an Albuquerque apartment complex to execute an arrest warrant and approached petitioner Roxanne Torres, then standing near a Toyota FJ Cruiser. The officers attempted to speak with her as she got into the driver's seat. Believing the officers to be carjackers, Torres hit the gas to escape. The officers fired their service pistols 13 times to stop Torres, striking her twice. Torres managed to escape and drove to a hospital 75 miles away, only to be airlifted back to a hospital in Albuquerque, where the police arrested her the next day. Torres later sought damages from the officers under 42 U. S. C. §1983. She claimed that the officers used excessive force against her and that the shooting constituted an unreasonable seizure under the Fourth Amendment. [The Tenth Circuit (the appellate court) affirmed the trial U.S. District Court (the trial court)'s ruling in favor of the police holding hat "a suspect's continued flight after being shot by police negates a Fourth Amendment excessive-force claim."]

HOLDING: The application of physical force to the body of a person with intent to restrain is a seizure even if the person does not submit and is not subdued.

(a) … This Court's precedents have interpreted the term "seizure" by consulting the common law of arrest, the "quintessential" seizure of the person. … In *Hodari D.*, this

Court explained that the common law considered the application of physical force to the body of a person with the intent to restrain to be an arrest—not an attempted arrest—even if the person does not yield. …

The analysis does not change because the officers used force from a distance to restrain Torres. The required "corporal seising or touching the defendant's body," … can be as readily accomplished by a bullet as by the end of a finger. The focus of the Fourth Amendment is "the privacy and security of individuals," not the particular form of governmental intrusion.

The application of force, standing alone, does not satisfy the rule recognized in this decision. A seizure requires the use of force with intent to restrain, as opposed to force applied by accident or for some other purpose. ... The appropriate inquiry is whether the challenged conduct objectively manifests an intent to restrain. *Michigan* v. *Chesternut*, … This test does not depend on either the subjective motivation of the officer or the subjective perception of the suspect. Finally, a seizure by force lasts only as long as the application of force unless the suspect submits. *Hodari D.*,

…

(c) The officers seized Torres by shooting her with the intent to restrain her movement. This Court does not address the reasonableness of the seizure, the damages caused by the seizure, or the officers' entitlement to qualified immunity.

BRENDLIN v. CALIFORNIA
551 U.S. 249 (2007)

JUSTICE SOUTER delivered the opinion of the Court.

When a police officer makes a traffic stop, the driver of the car is seized within the meaning of the Fourth Amendment. The question in

this case is whether the same is true of a passenger. We hold that a passenger is seized as well and so may challenge the constitutionality of the stop.

Early in the morning of November 27, 2001, Deputy Sheriff Robert Brokenbrough and his partner saw a parked Buick with expired registration tags. In his ensuing conversation with the police dispatcher, Brokenbrough learned that an application for renewal of registration was being processed. The officers saw the car again on the road, and this time Brokenbrough noticed its display of a temporary operating permit with the number "11," indicating it was legal to drive the car through November. The officers decided to pull the Buick over to verify that the permit matched the vehicle, even though, as Brokenbrough admitted later, there was nothing unusual about the permit or the way it was affixed. Brokenbrough asked the driver, Karen Simeroth, for her license and saw a passenger in the front seat, petitioner Bruce Brendlin, whom he recognized as "one of the Brendlin brothers." He recalled that either Scott or Bruce Brendlin had dropped out of parole supervision and asked Brendlin to identify himself. Brokenbrough returned to his cruiser, called for backup, and verified that Brendlin was a parole violator with an outstanding no-bail warrant for his arrest. While he was in the patrol car, Brokenbrough saw Brendlin briefly open and then close the passenger door of the Buick. Once reinforcements arrived, Brokenbrough went to the passenger side of the Buick, ordered him out of the car at gunpoint, and declared him under arrest. When the police searched Brendlin incident to arrest, they found an orange syringe cap on his person. A patdown search of Simeroth revealed syringes and a plastic bag of a green leafy substance, and she was also formally arrested. Officers then searched the car and found tubing, a scale, and other things used to produce methamphetamine.

Brendlin ... did not assert that his Fourth Amendment rights were violated by the search of Simeroth's vehicle, . . . but claimed only that the traffic stop was an unlawful seizure of his person. The trial court denied the suppression motion after finding that the stop was lawful and Brendlin was not seized until Brokenbrough ordered him out of the car and formally arrested him. Brendlin pleaded guilty, subject to appeal on the suppression issue, and was sentenced to four years in prison

. . . .

We granted certiorari to decide whether a traffic stop subjects a passenger, as well as the driver, to Fourth Amendment seizure. . . .

A person is seized by the police and thus entitled to challenge the government's action under the Fourth Amendment when the officer, " 'by means of physical force or show of authority,' " terminates or restrains his freedom of movement, *Florida v. Bostick*. . . . Thus, an "unintended person . . . [may be] the object of the detention," so long as the detention is "willful" and not merely the consequence of "an unknowing act." . . . A police officer may make a seizure by a show of authority and without the use of physical force, but there is no seizure without actual submission; otherwise, there is at most an attempted seizure, so far as the Fourth Amendment is concerned. . . .

When the actions of the police do not show an unambiguous intent to restrain or when an individual's submission to a show of governmental authority takes the form of passive acquiescence, there needs to be some test for telling when a seizure occurs in response to authority, and when it does not. The test was devised by Justice Stewart in *United States v. Mendenhall*, (1980), who wrote that a seizure occurs if "in view of all of the circumstances surrounding the incident, a reasonable person would have believed that he was not free to leave," ... Later on, the Court adopted Justice Stewart's touchstone, but added that when a person "has no desire to leave" for reasons unrelated to the police presence, the "coercive effect of the encounter" can be measured better by asking whether "a reasonable person would feel free to decline the officers' requests or otherwise terminate the encounter," *Florida v. Bostick*. ...

The law is settled that in Fourth Amendment terms a traffic stop entails a seizure of the driver "even though the purpose of the stop is limited and the resulting detention quite brief." And although we have not, until today, squarely answered the question whether a passenger is also seized, we have said over and over in dicta that during a traffic stop an officer seizes everyone in the vehicle, not just the driver.

We have come closest to the question here in two cases dealing with unlawful seizure of a passenger, and neither time did we indicate any distinction between driver and passenger that would affect the Fourth Amendment analysis. *Delaware v. Prouse* considered grounds for stopping a car on the road and held that Prouse's suppression motion was properly granted. We spoke of the arresting officer's testimony that Prouse was in the back seat when the car was pulled over, described Prouse as an occupant, not as the driver, and referred to the car's "occupants" as being seized, . . . Justification for stopping a car was the issue again in *Whren v. United States*, where we passed upon a Fourth Amendment challenge by two petitioners who moved to suppress drug evidence found during the course of a traffic stop. . . . Both driver and passenger claimed to have been seized illegally when the police stopped the car; we agreed and held suppression unwarranted only because the stop rested on probable cause.

The State concedes that the police had no adequate justification to pull the car over . . . , but argues that the passenger was not seized and thus cannot claim that the evidence was tainted by an unconstitutional stop. We resolve this question by asking whether a reasonable person in Brendlin's position when the car stopped would have believed himself free to "terminate the encounter" between the police and himself. We think that in these circumstances any reasonable passenger would have understood the police officers to be exercising control to the point that no one in the car was free to depart without police permission.

A traffic stop necessarily curtails the travel a passenger has chosen just as much as it halts the driver, diverting both from the stream of traffic to the side of the road, and the police

activity that normally amounts to intrusion on "privacy and personal security" does not normally (and did not here) distinguish between passenger and driver. . . . An officer who orders one particular car to pull over acts with an implicit claim of right based on fault of some sort, and a sensible person would not expect a police officer to allow people to come and go freely from the physical focal point of an investigation into faulty behavior or wrongdoing. If the likely wrongdoing is not the driving, the passenger will reasonably feel subject to suspicion owing to close association; but even when the wrongdoing is only bad driving, the passenger will expect to be subject to some scrutiny, and his attempt to leave the scene would be so obviously likely to prompt an objection from the officer that no passenger would feel free to leave in the first place. . . .

It is also reasonable for passengers to expect that a police officer at the scene of a crime, arrest, or investigation will not let people move around in ways that could jeopardize his safety. In *Maryland v. Wilson* . . . we held that during a lawful traffic stop an officer may order a passenger out of the car as a precautionary measure, without reasonable suspicion that the passenger poses a safety risk. . . . In fashioning this rule, we invoked our earlier statement that " '[t]he risk of harm to both the police and the occupants is minimized if the officers routinely exercise unquestioned command of the situation.' " . . . What we have said in these opinions probably reflects a societal expectation of " 'unquestioned [police] command' " at odds with any notion that a passenger would feel free to leave, or to terminate the personal encounter any other way, without advance permission. . . .

. . . .

Brendlin was seized from the moment Simeroth's car came to a halt on the side of the road, and it was error to deny his suppression motion on the ground that seizure occurred only at the formal arrest. It will be for the state courts to consider in the first instance whether suppression turns on any other issue. The judgment of the Supreme Court of California is vacated, and the case is remanded for further proceedings not inconsistent with this opinion.

Other Cases: What is a Seizure

United States v. Mendenhall, 446 U.S. 544 (1980)

SUMMARY: DEA agents contacted Mendenhall at the airport. She consented to go with them upstairs, and upstairs she allowed them to search her purse and later her person (a strip search resulted in finding two heroin packages hidden on her person. The question was whether she was seized either downstairs initially or when she went upstairs at the request of the agents.

…

PLURALITY OPINION: It was on the basis of this evidence that the District Court denied the respondent's motion to suppress. The court concluded that the agents' conduct in initially approaching the respondent and asking to see her ticket and identification was a permissible investigative stop under the standards of *Terry v. Ohio*, and *United States v. Brignoni-Ponce*, finding that this conduct was based on specific and articulable facts that justified a suspicion of criminal activity. The court also found that the respondent had not been placed under arrest or otherwise detained when she was asked to accompany the agents to the DEA office, but had accompanied the agents "`voluntarily in a spirit of apparent cooperation.'" It was the court's view that no arrest occurred until after the heroin had been found. Finally, the trial court found that the respondent "gave her consent to the search [in the DEA office] and . . . such consent was freely and voluntarily given."

[T]he Government concedes that its agents had neither a warrant nor probable cause to believe that the respondent was carrying narcotics when the agents conducted a search of the respondent's person. It is the Government's position, however, that the search was conducted pursuant to the respondent's consent, and thus was excepted from the requirements of both a warrant and probable cause. …

Evidently, the Court of Appeals concluded that the respondent's apparent consent to the search was in fact not voluntarily given and was in any event the product of earlier official conduct violative of the Fourth Amendment. We must first consider, therefore, whether such conduct occurred, either on the concourse or in the DEA office at the airport.

The Fourth Amendment's requirement that searches and seizures be founded upon an objective justification, governs all seizures of the person, "including seizures that involve only a brief detention short of traditional arrest. Accordingly, if the respondent was "seized" when the DEA agents approached her on the concourse and asked questions of her, the agents' conduct in doing so was constitutional only if they reasonably suspected the respondent of wrongdoing. But "[o]bviously, not all personal intercourse between policemen and citizens involves `seizures' of persons. Only when the officer, by means of physical force or show of authority, has in some way restrained the liberty of a citizen may we conclude that a `seizure' has occurred."

The Court in *Sibron v. New York*, . . . indicated that not every encounter between a police officer and a citizen is an intrusion requiring an objective justification. In that case, a police officer, before conducting what was later found to have been an unlawful search, approached Sibron in a restaurant and told him to come outside, which Sibron did. . . . The record was "barren of any indication whether Sibron accompanied [the officer] outside in submission to a show of force or authority which left him no choice, or whether he went voluntarily in a spirit of apparent cooperation with the officer's investigation." Plainly, in the latter event, there was no seizure until the police officer in some way demonstrably curtailed Sibron's liberty.

We adhere to the view that a person is "seized" only when, by means of physical force or a show of authority, his freedom of movement is restrained. Only when such restraint is imposed is there any foundation whatever for invoking constitutional safeguards. The purpose of the Fourth Amendment is not to eliminate all contact between the police and the citizenry, but "to prevent arbitrary and oppressive interference by enforcement officials with the privacy and personal security of individuals." *United States v. Martinez-Fuerte.* As long as the person to whom questions are put remains free to disregard the questions and walk away, there has been no intrusion upon that person's liberty or privacy as would under the Constitution require some particularized and objective justification.

Moreover, characterizing every street encounter between a citizen and the police as a "seizure," while not enhancing any interest secured by the Fourth Amendment, would impose wholly unrealistic restrictions upon a wide variety of legitimate law enforcement practices. The Court has on other occasions referred to the acknowledged need for police questioning as a tool in the effective enforcement of the criminal laws. ..

We conclude that a person has been "seized" within the meaning of the Fourth Amendment only if, in view of all of the circumstances surrounding the incident, a reasonable person would have believed that he was not free to leave. Examples of circumstances that might indicate a seizure, even where the person did not attempt to leave, would be the threatening presence of several officers, the display of a weapon by an officer, some physical touching of the person of the citizen, or the use of language or tone of voice indicating that compliance with the officer's request might be compelled. In the absence of some such evidence, otherwise inoffensive contact between a member of the public and the police cannot, as a matter of law, amount to a seizure of that person.

On the facts of this case, no "seizure" of the respondent occurred. The events took place in the public concourse. The agents wore no uniforms and displayed no weapons. They did not summon the respondent to their presence, but instead approached her and identified themselves as federal agents. They requested, but did not demand to see the respondent's identification and ticket. Such conduct, without more, did not amount to an intrusion upon any constitutionally protected interest. The respondent was not seized simply by reason of the fact that the agents approached her, asked her if she would show them her ticket and identification, and posed to her a few questions. Nor was it enough to establish a seizure that the person asking the questions was a law enforcement official. In short, nothing in the record suggests that the respondent had any objective reason to believe that she was not free to end the conversation in the concourse and proceed on her way, and for that reason we conclude that the agents' initial approach to her was not a seizure.

Our conclusion that no seizure occurred is not affected by the fact that the respondent was not expressly told by the agents that she was free to decline to cooperate with their inquiry, for the voluntariness of her responses does not depend upon her having been so informed. ...

Although we have concluded that the initial encounter between the DEA agents and the respondent on the concourse at the Detroit Airport did not constitute an unlawful seizure, it is still arguable that the respondent's Fourth Amendment protections were violated when she went from the concourse to the DEA office. Such a violation might in turn infect the subsequent search of the respondent's person.

The question whether the respondent's consent to accompany the agents was in fact voluntary or was the product of duress or coercion, express or implied, is to be determined by the totality of all the circumstances, and is a matter which the Government has the burden of proving. The respondent herself did not testify at the hearing. The Government's evidence showed that the respondent was not told that she had to go to the office, but was simply asked if she would accompany the officers. There were neither threats nor any show of force. The respondent had been questioned only briefly, and her ticket and identification were returned to her before she was asked to accompany the officers.

On the other hand, it is argued that the incident would reasonably have appeared coercive to the respondent, who was 22 years old and had not been graduated from high school. It is additionally suggested that the respondent, a female and a Negro, may have felt unusually threatened by the officers, who were white males. While these factors were not irrelevant, neither were they decisive, and the totality of the evidence in this case was plainly adequate to support the District Court's finding that the respondent voluntarily consented to accompany the officers to the DEA office.

We conclude that the District Court's determination that the respondent consented to the search of her person "freely and voluntarily" was sustained by the evidence and that the Court of Appeals was, therefore, in error in setting it aside. Accordingly, the judgment of the Court of Appeals is reversed, and the case is remanded to that court for further proceedings.

CHIEF JUSTICE BLACKMUN, and JUSTICE POWELL also join all but Part II-A of this opinion. Omitted.

JUSTICE WHITE, with whom JUSTICE BRENNAN, JUSTICE MARSHALL, and JUSTICE STEVENS join, dissenting. Omitted.

Florida v. Royer, (1983),

SUMMARY: The Court adopted *Mendenhall* as the appropriate standard for determining when police questioning crosses the threshold from a consensual encounter to a forcible stop. ...

The citizen "may not be detained even momentarily without reasonable, objective grounds for doing so; and his refusal to listen or answer does not, without more, furnish those grounds. The rule looks, not to the subjective perceptions of the person questioned, but rather, to the objective characteristics of the encounter that may suggest whether a reasonable person would have felt free to leave."

Michigan v. Chesternut, 486 U.S. 567 (1988),

SUMMARY: Chesternut began running when he saw a police officer's car approaching. Officers followed him to "see where he was going." As the officers drove alongside Chesternut, they observed him pull a number of packets from his pocket and throw them away. The officers stopped and seized the packets. After examining the packets, they concluded that they might be contraband and then arrested Chesternut. A subsequent search (incident to arrest) revealed more drugs. Chesternut was charged with felony narcotics possession. The Court found that the officer's investigatory pursuit of Chesternut to "see where he was going" was not a seizure under the Fourth amendment. The court noted that a seizure occurs when a reasonable person, viewing the police conduct and surrounding circumstances, would conclude that he or she is not free to leave.

"No bright-line rule applicable to all investigatory pursuits can be fashioned. Rather, the appropriate test is whether a reasonable man, viewing the particular police conduct as a whole and within the setting of all the surrounding circumstances, would have concluded that the police had in some manner restrained his liberty so that he was not free to leave . . . . Under this test, respondent [Chesternut] was not 'seized' before he discarded the drug packets. ... The record does not reflect that the police activated a siren or flashers; commanded respondent to halt or displayed any weapons; or operated the car aggressively to block his course or to control his direction or speed. Thus, respondent could not reasonably have believed that he was not free to disregard the police presence and go about his business. The police, therefore, were not required to have a particularized and objective basis for suspecting him of criminal activity in order to pursue him."

Brower v. County of Inyo, 489 U.S. 593 (1989)

SUMMARY: Brower had stolen a car and eluded the police in a chase of more than 20 miles. The police placed an 18-wheeled truck across both lanes of a highway, behind a curve, and in a manner in which the police car's headlights would blind Brower. Brower was killed in the crash as a result of the roadblock. Bower's heirs sued for damages against the police alleging a violation of Brower's constitutional right against unreasonable search and seizure. In addition to looking at the reasonableness of the seizure, the Court specifically noted that a police roadblock to stop a fleeing suspect was a form of seizure under the Fourth Amendment. It stated, "Consistent with the language, history, and judicial construction of the Fourth Amendment, a seizure occurs when governmental termination of a person's movement is effected through means intentionally applied. Because the complaint alleges the Brower was stopped by the instrumentality set in motion or put in place to stop him, it states of a claim of Fourth Amendment seizure." (The Court allowed the suit to continue).

California v. Hodari D., 499 U.S. 621 (1991)

Late one evening in April, 1988, Officers Brian McColgin and Jerry Pertoso were on patrol in a high-crime area of Oakland, California. They were dressed in street clothes but wearing jackets with "Police" embossed on both front and back. Their unmarked car proceeded west on Foothill Boulevard, and turned south onto 63rd Avenue. As they rounded the corner, they saw four or five youths huddled around a small red car parked at the curb. When the youths saw the officers' car approaching, they apparently panicked, and took flight. The respondent here, Hodari D., and one companion ran west through an alley; the others fled south. The red car also headed south, at a high rate of speed.

The officers were suspicious, and gave chase. McColgin remained in the car and continued south on 63rd Avenue; Pertoso left the car, ran back north along 63rd, then west on Foothill Boulevard, and turned south on 62nd Avenue. Hodari, meanwhile, emerged from the alley onto 62nd and ran north. Looking behind as he ran, he did not turn and see Pertoso until the officer was almost upon him, whereupon he tossed away what appeared to be a small rock. A moment later, Pertoso tackled Hodari, handcuffed him, and radioed for assistance. Hodari was found to be carrying $130 in cash and a pager; and the rock he had discarded was found to be crack cocaine.

In the juvenile proceeding brought against him, Hodari moved to suppress the evidence relating to the cocaine. The court denied the motion without opinion. The California Court of Appeal reversed, holding that Hodari had been "seized" when he saw Officer Pertoso running towards him, that this seizure was unreasonable under the Fourth Amendment, and that the evidence of cocaine had to be suppressed as the fruit of that illegal seizure. . . .

As this case comes to us, the only issue presented is whether, at the time he dropped the drugs, Hodari had been "seized" within the meaning of the Fourth Amendment. If so, respondent argues, the drugs were the fruit of that seizure and the evidence concerning them was properly excluded. If not, the drugs were abandoned by Hodari and lawfully recovered by the police, and the evidence should have been admitted. . . .

. . . .

To say that an arrest is effected by the slightest application of physical force, despite the arrestee's escape, is not to say that, for Fourth Amendment purposes, there is a continuing arrest during the period of fugitivity. If, for example, Pertoso had laid his hands upon Hodari to arrest him, but Hodari had broken away and had then cast away the cocaine, it would hardly be realistic to say that that disclosure had been made during the course of an arrest. The present case, however, is even one step further removed. It does not involve the application of any physical force; Hodari was untouched by Officer Pertoso at the time he discarded the cocaine. His defense relies instead upon the proposition that a seizure occurs "when the officer, by means of physical force or show of authority, has in some way restrained the liberty of a citizen." Hodari contends (and we accept as true for purposes of this decision) that Pertoso's pursuit qualified as a "show of authority" calling upon Hodari to halt. The narrow question before us is whether, with respect to a show of authority as with respect to application of physical force, a seizure occurs even though the subject does not yield. We hold that it does not.

The word "seizure" readily bears the meaning of a laying on of hands or application of physical force to restrain movement, even when it is ultimately unsuccessful. . . . It does not remotely apply, however, to the prospect of a policeman yelling "Stop, in the name of the law!" at a fleeing form that continues to flee. That is no seizure. . . . An arrest requires either physical force (as described above) or, where that is absent, submission to the assertion of authority.

Respondent contends that his position is sustained by the so-called Mendenhall test, formulated by Justice Stewart's opinion in United States v. Mendenhall (1980), and adopted by the Court in later cases "[A] person has been `seized' within the meaning of the Fourth Amendment only if, in view of all the circumstances surrounding the incident, a reasonable person would have believed that he was not free to leave." In seeking to rely upon that test here, respondent fails to read it carefully. It says that a person has been seized "only if," not that he has been seized "whenever"; it states a necessary, but not a sufficient, condition for seizure - or, more precisely, for seizure effected through a "show of authority." Mendenhall establishes that the

test for existence of a "show of authority" is an objective one: not whether the citizen perceived that he was being ordered to restrict his movement, but whether the officer's words and actions would have conveyed that to a reasonable person.

…

In sum, assuming that Pertoso's pursuit in the present case constituted a "show of authority" enjoining Hodari to halt, since Hodari did not comply with that injunction, he was not seized until he was tackled. The cocaine abandoned while he was running was, in this case, not the fruit of a seizure, and his motion to exclude evidence of it was properly denied.

JUSTICE STEVENS, with whom JUSTICE MARSHALL joins, dissenting. Omitted

How Long Can A Stop Last?

Under the Fourth Amendment any investigatory detention must be temporary and last no longer than is necessary to effectuate the purpose of the stop. *Terry* noted that detentions must be brief. *United States v. Sharpe*, 470 U.S. 675 (1985) examined what "brief" means with the Court deciding that whether a stop is too long depends, not only on the length of time of the stop, but also on the surrounding circumstances—finding that the appropriate test is whether the length of time employed was reasonable. The dissent in *Sharpe* noted that the time should not be extended simply because of how unprepared the police were. In assessing reasonableness, courts take into account whether the police diligently pursued their investigation, and no rigid time limitation has ever been imposed. More recently, however, in *Rodriguez v. United States 575 U.S. 348 (2015)* the Court examined whether a dog sniff conducted at a traffic stop impermissibly extended the duration of the stop.

RODRIGUEZ v. UNITED STATES
575 U.S. 348 (2015)

JUSTICE GINSBURG delivered the opinion of the Court.

In *Illinois v. Caballes* this Court held that a dog sniff conducted during a lawful traffic stop does not violate the Fourth Amendment's proscription of unreasonable seizures. This case presents the question whether the Fourth Amendment tolerates a dog sniff conducted after completion of a traffic stop. We hold that a police stop exceeding the time needed to handle the matter for which the stop was made violates

the Constitution's shield against unreasonable seizures. A seizure justified only by a police-observed traffic violation, therefore, "become[s] unlawful if it is prolonged beyond the time reasonably required to complete th[e] mission" of issuing a ticket for the violation. The Court so recognized in *Caballes*, and we adhere to the line drawn in that decision.

I

[Facts Summarized: K-9 deputy Struble was on patrol with his dog Floyd when he pulled Rodriguez over for driving on the highway shoulder against Nebraska law. Struble did the paperwork and questioning of Rodriguez and Pollman, the passenger in the car. Struble did the necessary records check and got all the documents back to Rodriguez and gave him a written warning. Struble did not consider Rodriguez free to leave, but "although the justification for the traffic stop was out of the way," he asked for permission to walk his dog around the car. Rodriguez said no. Struble told Rodriguez to get out of the car and stand in front of the patrol car which Rodriguez did.

A second deputy arrived, and Struble walked Floyd twice around the car. The dog alerted to the presence of drugs halfway through Struble's second pass. All told, seven or eight minutes had elapsed from the time Struble issued the written warning until the dog indicated the presence of drugs. A search of the vehicle revealed a large bag of methamphetamine.

Rodriguez was indicted, and unsuccessfully moved to suppress the evidence seized from his car on the ground, among others, that Struble had prolonged the traffic stop without reasonable suspicion in order to conduct the dog sniff. Although the Magistrate Judge [*pretrial motions judge*] found no probable cause nor reasonable suspicion, he nevertheless followed the Eighth Circuit's precedent which allowed de minimus intrusions on the Fourth Amendment right and was therefore permissible.]

The District Court [*trial court*] adopted the Magistrate Judge's factual findings and legal conclusions and denied Rodriguez's motion to suppress. The court noted that, in the Eighth Circuit, "dog sniffs that occur within a short time following the completion of a traffic stop are not constitutionally prohibited if they constitute only de minimis intrusions." The court thus agreed with the Magistrate Judge that the "7 to 10 minutes" added to the stop by the dog sniff "was not of constitutional significance." Impelled by that decision, Rodriguez entered a conditional guilty plea and was sentenced to five years in prison.

The Eighth Circuit [*appellate court*] affirmed. The "seven- or eight-minute delay" in this case, the opinion noted, resembled delays that the court had previously ranked as permissible. The Court of Appeals thus ruled that the delay here constituted an acceptable "*de minimis* intrusion on Rodriguez's personal liberty." Given that ruling, the court declined to reach the question whether Struble had reasonable suspicion to continue Rodriguez's detention after issuing the written warning.

We granted certiorari to resolve a division among lower courts on the question whether police routinely may extend an otherwise-completed traffic stop, absent reasonable suspicion, in order to conduct a dog sniff. ...

II

A seizure for a traffic violation justifies a police investigation of that violation. "[A] relatively brief encounter," a routine traffic stop is "more analogous to a so-called '*Terry* stop' ... than to a formal arrest." Like a *Terry* stop, the tolerable duration of police inquiries in the traffic-stop context is determined by the seizure's "mission" — to address the traffic violation that warranted the stop ...and attend to related safety concerns. Because addressing the infraction is the purpose of the stop, it may "last no longer than is necessary to effectuate th[at] purpose." Authority for the seizure thus ends when tasks tied to the traffic infraction are — or reasonably should have been — completed. ...

Our decisions in *Caballes* and *Johnson* heed these constraints. In both cases, we concluded that the Fourth Amendment tolerated certain unrelated investigations that did not lengthen the roadside detention. In *Caballes*, however, we cautioned that a traffic stop "can become unlawful if it is prolonged beyond the time reasonably required to complete th[e] mission" of issuing a warning ticket. And we repeated that admonition in *Johnson*: The seizure remains lawful only "so long as [unrelated] inquiries do not measurably extend the duration of the stop." . . . An officer, in other words, may conduct certain unrelated checks during an otherwise lawful traffic stop. But . . . he may not do so in a way that prolongs the stop, absent the reasonable suspicion ordinarily demanded to justify detaining an individual.

Beyond determining whether to issue a traffic ticket, an officer's mission includes "ordinary inquiries incident to [the traffic] stop." Typically such inquiries involve checking the driver's license, determining whether there are outstanding warrants against the driver, and inspecting the automobile's registration and proof of insurance. These checks serve the same objective as enforcement of the traffic code: ensuring that vehicles on the road are operated safely and responsibly.

A dog sniff, by contrast, is a measure aimed at "detect[ing] evidence of ordinary criminal wrongdoing." Candidly, the Government acknowledged at oral argument that a dog sniff, unlike the routine measures just mentioned, is not an ordinary incident of a traffic stop. Lacking the same close connection to roadway safety as the ordinary inquiries, a dog sniff is not fairly characterized as part of the officer's traffic mission.

…

…Traffic stops are "especially fraught with danger to police officers," so an officer may need to take certain negligibly burdensome precautions in order to complete his mission safely. On-scene investigation into other crimes, however, detours from that mission. So too do safety precautions taken in order to facilitate such detours. Thus, even assuming that the imposition here was no more intrusive than the exit order in *Mimms*, the dog sniff could not be justified on the same basis. Highway and officer safety are interests different in kind from the Government's endeavor to detect crime in general or drug trafficking in particular.

The Government argues that an officer may "incremental[ly]" prolong a stop to conduct a dog sniff so long as the officer is reasonably diligent in pursuing the traffic-related purpose of the stop, and the overall duration of the stop remains reasonable in relation to the duration of other traffic stops involving similar circumstances. The Government's argument, in effect, is that by completing all traffic-related tasks expeditiously, an officer can earn bonus time to pursue an unrelated criminal investigation. The reasonableness of a seizure, however, depends on what the police in fact do. In this regard, the Government acknowledges that "an officer always has to be reasonably diligent." How could diligence be gauged other than by noting what the officer actually did and how he did it? If an officer can complete traffic-based inquiries expeditiously, then that is the amount of "time reasonably required to complete [the stop's] mission." As we said in *Caballes* and reiterate today, a traffic stop "prolonged beyond" that point is "unlawful." The critical question, then, is not whether the dog sniff occurs before or after the officer issues a ticket, . . . but whether conducting the sniff "prolongs" — *i.e.,* adds time to — "the stop."

Seizing Property

Under the Fourth Amendment a seizure of property occurs when the government meaningfully interferes with an individual's possessory interest. The general principles set forth in *Terry* regarding stops of individuals are applicable to the temporary detention of property. Investigatory detention of property, like that of a "stop" of an individual, must be temporary and last no longer than is necessary to effectuate the purpose of the stop. When officers seek to seize and detain the property for a prolonged period, the best course of action is to seek a warrant. In *Chambers v. Maroney* 399 U.S. 42, 51 (1970) for example, the court found it reasonable to seize and impound an automobile on the basis of probable cause, for whatever period is necessary to obtain a warrant for the search. The court has also held that "freezing a scene" (not allowing anyone to enter a house or move a car) until the officers can get a warrant is valid under the Fourth Amendment. Thus, it is sometimes lawful to temporarily detain a person's property to investigate its connection to a crime. The temporary detention of property often arises in the context of detaining a car for the purpose of allowing a drug-sniffing dog to arrive. (See, *United States v. Place,* 462 U.S. 696 (1983) and *Illinois v. Caballes*, 543 U.S. 405 (2005), below). Under certain circumstances, investigative detentions of personal property have been found to be constitutionally valid under the Fourth Amendment.

UNITED STATES v. PLACE
462 U.S. 696 (1983)

Justice O'Connor delivered the opinion of the Court.

This case presents the issue whether the Fourth Amendment prohibits law enforcement authorities from temporarily detaining personal luggage for exposure to a trained narcotics detection dog on the basis of reasonable suspicion that the luggage contains narcotics. Given the enforcement problems associated with the detection of narcotics trafficking and the minimal intrusion that a properly limited detention would entail, we conclude that the Fourth Amendment does not prohibit such a detention. On the facts of this case, however, we hold that the police conduct exceeded the bounds of a permissible investigative detention of the luggage.

[Facts Summarized: Place's behavior made law enforcement at Miami airport suspicious. They approached Place and requested his tickets and identification. Place consented to a search of his suitcases by a dog, but his flight was about to depart so they did not do so. Place had made comments to them that made them even more suspicious, so they checked out the information he had given and it didn't check out. They contacted New York DEA agents, who then waited for Place to arrive at La Guardia Airport. Place's behavior also made them suspicious so they approached him after he had claimed his two bags and called for a limo service. They approached Place and he said he knew they were cops and that he had spotted them as soon as he deplaned. He told them what had happened in Miami but stated that the Miami police had searched his baggage. DEA agents got his identification on which they ran a warrants check. Place refused to consent to search of his luggage, and they told him they were going to keep his bags and go apply for a warrant. They told Place he could accompany him. He declined.]

…

The agents then took the bags to Kennedy Airport, where they subjected the bags to a "sniff test" by a trained narcotics detection dog. The dog reacted positively to the smaller of the two bags but ambiguously to the larger bag. Approximately 90 minutes had elapsed since the seizure of respondent's luggage. Because it was late on a Friday afternoon, the agents retained the luggage until Monday morning, when they secured a search warrant from a Magistrate for the smaller bag. Upon opening that bag, the agents discovered 1,125 grams of cocaine.

Where law enforcement authorities have probable cause to believe that a container holds contraband or evidence of a crime, but have not secured a warrant, the Court has interpreted the Amendment to permit seizure of the property, pending issuance of a warrant to examine its contents, if the exigencies of the circumstances demand it or some other recognized exception to the warrant requirement is present. . . .

In this case, the Government asks us to recognize the reasonableness under the

Fourth Amendment of warrantless seizures of personal luggage from the custody of the owner on the basis of less than probable cause, for the purpose of pursuing a limited course of investigation, short of opening the luggage, that would quickly confirm or dispel the authorities' suspicion. Specifically, we are asked to apply the principles of *Terry v. Ohio*, supra, to permit such seizures on the basis of reasonable, articulable suspicion, premised on objective facts, that the luggage contains contraband or evidence of a crime. In our view, such application is appropriate.

We must balance the nature and quality of the intrusion on the individual's Fourth Amendment interests against the importance of the governmental interests alleged to justify the intrusion. When the nature and extent of the detention are minimally intrusive of the individual's Fourth Amendment interests, the opposing law enforcement interests can support a seizure based on less than probable cause.

We examine first the governmental interest offered as a justification for a brief seizure of luggage from the suspect's custody for the purpose of pursuing a limited course of investigation. The Government contends that, where the authorities possess specific and articulable facts warranting a reasonable belief that a traveler's luggage contains narcotics, the governmental interest in seizing the luggage briefly to pursue further investigation is substantial. We agree.

The context of a particular law enforcement practice, of course, may affect the determination whether a brief intrusion on Fourth Amendment interests on less than probable cause is essential to effective criminal investigation. Because of the inherently transient nature of drug courier activity at airports, allowing police to make brief investigative stops of persons at airports on reasonable suspicion of drug-trafficking substantially enhances the likelihood that police will be able to prevent the flow of narcotics into distribution channels.

. . . .

In sum, we conclude that when an officer's observations lead him reasonably to believe that a traveler is carrying luggage that contains narcotics, the principles of *Terry* and its progeny would permit the officer to detain the luggage briefly to investigate the circumstances that aroused his suspicion, provided that the investigative detention is properly limited in scope.

The purpose for which respondent's luggage was seized, of course, was to arrange its exposure to a narcotics detection dog. Obviously, if this investigative procedure is itself a search requiring probable cause, the initial seizure of respondent's luggage for the purpose of subjecting it to the sniff test - no matter how brief - could not be justified on less than probable cause.

The Fourth Amendment "protects people from unreasonable government intrusions into their legitimate expectations of privacy." We have affirmed that a person possesses a privacy interest in the contents of personal luggage that is protected by the Fourth Amendment. A "canine sniff" by a well-trained narcotics detection dog, however, does not require opening the luggage. It does not expose noncontraband items that otherwise would remain hidden from public view, as does, for example, an officer's rummaging through the contents of the luggage. Thus, the manner in which information is obtained through this investigative technique is much less intrusive than a typical search. Moreover, the sniff discloses only the presence or absence of narcotics, a contraband item. Thus, despite the fact that the sniff tells the authorities something about the contents of the luggage, the information obtained is limited. This limited disclosure also ensures that the owner of the property is not subjected to the embarrassment and inconvenience entailed in less discriminate and more intrusive investigative methods.

In these respects, the canine sniff is sui generis. We are aware of no other investigative procedure that is so limited both in the manner in which the information is obtained and in the content of the information revealed by the procedure. Therefore, we conclude that the particular course of investigation that the agents intended to pursue here - exposure of respondent's luggage, which was located in a public place, to a trained canine - did not constitute a "search" within the meaning of the Fourth Amendment.

There is no doubt that the agents made a "seizure" of Place's luggage for purposes of the Fourth Amendment when, following his refusal to consent to a search, the agent told Place that he was going to take the luggage to a federal judge to secure issuance of a warrant. …

At the outset, we must reject the Government's suggestion that the point at which probable cause for seizure of luggage from the person's presence becomes necessary is more distant than in the case of a *Terry* stop of the person himself. The premise of the Government's argument is that seizures of property are generally less intrusive than seizures of the person. While true in some circumstances, that premise is faulty on the facts we address in this case. The precise type of detention we confront here is seizure of personal luggage from the immediate possession of the suspect for the purpose of arranging exposure to a narcotics detection dog. Particularly in the case of detention of luggage within the traveler's immediate possession, the police conduct intrudes on both the suspect's possessory interest in his luggage as well as his liberty interest in proceeding with his itinerary. The person whose luggage is detained is technically still free to continue his travels or carry out other personal activities pending release of the luggage. Moreover, he is not subjected to the coercive atmosphere of a custodial confinement or to the public indignity of being personally detained. Nevertheless, such a seizure can effectively restrain the person since he is subjected to the possible disruption of his travel plans in

order to remain with his luggage or to arrange for its return. Therefore, when the police seize luggage from the suspect's custody, we think the limitations applicable to investigative detentions of the person should define the permissible scope of an investigative detention of the person's luggage on less than probable cause. Under this standard, it is clear that the police conduct here exceeded the permissible limits of a *Terry*-type investigative stop.

The length of the detention of respondent's luggage alone precludes the conclusion that the seizure was reasonable in the absence of probable cause … [T]he brevity of the invasion of the individual's Fourth Amendment interests is an important factor in determining whether the seizure is so minimally intrusive as to be justifiable on reasonable suspicion. Moreover, in assessing the effect of the length of the detention, we take into account whether the police diligently pursue their investigation. We note that here the New York agents knew the time of Place's scheduled arrival at La Guardia, had ample time to arrange for their additional investigation at that location, and thereby could have minimized the intrusion on respondent's Fourth Amendment interests. Thus, although we decline to adopt any outside time limitation for a permissible *Terry* stop, we have never approved a seizure of the person for the prolonged 90-minute period involved here and cannot do so on the facts presented by this case.

Although the 90-minute detention of respondent's luggage is sufficient to render the seizure unreasonable, the violation was exacerbated by the failure of the agents to accurately inform respondent of the place to which they were transporting his luggage, of the length of time he might be dispossessed, and of what arrangements would be made for return of the luggage if the investigation dispelled the suspicion. In short, we hold that the detention of respondent's luggage in this case went beyond the narrow authority possessed by police to detain briefly luggage reasonably suspected to contain narcotics.

We conclude that, under all of the circumstances of this case, the seizure of respondent's luggage was unreasonable under the Fourth Amendment. Consequently, the evidence obtained from the subsequent search of his luggage was inadmissible, and Place's conviction must be reversed. The judgment of the Court of Appeals, accordingly, is affirmed.

Chapter Four: Warrants

WAS THERE A VALID WARRANT?

Searches and seizures conducted by the government without a warrant are *per se* unreasonable unless they fall within one of the few specifically established and carefully delineated exceptions to the warrant requirement. In addition to requiring a warrant, the Fourth Amendment specifies what is needed to make a warrant valid. It states: ". . . no Warrants shall issue, but upon probable cause, supported by Oath or affirmation, and particularly describing the place to be searched, and the persons or things to be seized." In addition to requiring a valid warrant, the police must execute the warrant in a lawful manner. This chapter examines the warrant requirement, what makes a warrant valid, what limits there are in the execution of a warrant. This chapter also examines a court-created remedy known as the "exclusionary rule" which is not actually part of the Fourth Amendment, but has been deemed necessary to encourage compliance with the Fourth Amendment's requirements.[57]

WHAT ARE THE COMPONENTS OF A VALID WARRANT?

Probable Cause

The Fourth Amendment states that warrants must be issued on probable cause. The probable cause standard of evidence has been used as the touchstone of Fourth Amendment action. Judges may issue warrants only if they find the evidence is sufficient to establish probable cause to arrest an individual, search an individual, or search or seize property. For an arrest warrant to be issued the judge must find there is probable cause to believe that a crime was committed and that the person to be arrested is the one who committed the crime. For a search warrant the judge must find that there is probable cause to believe that the search will discover things specified in the application. Probable cause must be determined from the "four corners" of the affidavit. This means that every fact that the judge considers must be mentioned on the warrant affidavit.

"Objective Basis" Or "Objective Justification" Continuum

When we talk about law, we talk about proof -- evidence that can prove a certain point. How much proof the government has can range from very little to a whole lot. There is a continuum that starts with no proof, works its way up to a hunch, and then continues until there is enough proof to establish some point to an absolute certainty. The stops on this continuum or the level of proof are sometimes referred to as either "objective basis" or "objective justification." Probable cause is one level of objective basis. Other levels of objective basis used in the justice system are beyond a reasonable doubt, clear and convincing evidence, preponderance of the evidence, reasonable suspicion, and random/suspicionless actions. The government is required to put on evidence and convince a jury beyond a reasonable doubt of defendant's guilt in a criminal trial. Clear and convincing evidence is required with some criminal defenses (such as with the federal insanity defense) and requires more proof than does the preponderance of the evidence standard but less than the "beyond a reasonable doubt" standard. The preponderance of the evidence standard means that the party will need to have facts that show it is more likely than not that something happened. Preponderance of the evidence is a standard required for some criminal defenses and is the standard of proof used in civil trials. Probable cause is less than proof beyond a reasonable doubt, less than

---

[57] Note that the exclusion of evidence has also been tied to violations of other constitutional guarantees such as the Fifth Amendment's protection against self-incrimination.

proof to a clear and convincing degree and less than proof by a preponderance of the evidence; it is more than reasonable suspicion or no suspicion at all.

The Court has said that probable cause to search exists when "there is a fair probability that contraband or evidence of a crime will be found in a particular place." *Illinois v. Gates*, 462 U.S. 213, 238 (1983). Probable cause, for the purpose of arrest, appears to mean the same "fair probability" standard used by the Court in evaluating searches. Arrests require a fair probability that an offense has been or is being committed by the person who is to be arrested. Probable cause under the Fourth Amendment is generally determined by an essentially *objective standard* (what a reasonable person would think) as opposed to a *subjective standard* (what the arresting officer or what the suspect thought).

Probable Cause Is More Than Reasonable Suspicion

The Court sometimes allows interferences with liberty, property, and privacy rights based on less than probable cause. "In a series of decisions, * * * the Supreme Court has held that reasonable articulable suspicion of criminal activity justifies searches and seizures when the intrusion on individual privacy is minimal and outweighed by an important government interest." *Thirty-Fifth Annual Review of Criminal Procedure*, 35 Geo.L.J. Ann. Rev. Crim. Proc. 18 (2006). These decisions allow the police to do a limited seizure, called a "stop," and a limited search, called a "frisk," but do not allow the issuance of an arrest warrant or a search warrant on based reasonable suspicion. The *Terry* Court for the first time held that government officers can constitutionally interfere with a person's Fourth Amendment liberty rights with proof less than probable cause — as long as the interference is "reasonable." Although the phrase "reasonable suspicion" was not used in *Terry*, this phrase has become known as the

> "standard of evidence that police must have to detain a person for a brief field interrogation. The reasonable suspicion standard is also the basis of certain other warrantless searches. ... A definition of reasonable suspicion is the existence of articulable facts that support an officer's reasonable interference with a person's Fourth Amendment liberty, which facts do not rise to the level of probable cause. In contrast to probable cause, in which evidence creates an inference that a crime has been committed, reasonable suspicion is a lower standard of evidence. Reasonable suspicion exists only when evidence creates a suspicion that criminal activity 'may be afoot'." [58]

Prior to *Terry v. Ohio,* 392 U.S. 1 (1968), any interference with property, liberty or privacy interests on less than probable cause violated the Fourth Amendment. *Terry* created a rule that allows police officers to stop individuals and do a field investigation when they have reasonable suspicion to believe the person was either committing a crime or about to commit a crime. The Court did not define "reasonable suspicion" in *Terry* — in fact those words aren't even within the decision — but in later cases, the Court stated that reasonable suspicion involves some minimal level of objective justification for making a stop that is something more than an unparticularized suspicion or hunch, but less than the level of suspicion required for probably cause. *See, e.g., United States v. Sokolow,* 490 U.S. 1 (1989) (below).

The following cases have, at their core, the issue of whether certain facts constitute probable cause or reasonable suspicion. As you read, take note of all the   information known to the police and how they got that information-- did they see it themselves? Was there an informant?

---

58 Zalman, M., *Constitutional Procedure*, p. 86.

DRAPER v. UNITED STATES
358 U.S. 307 (1959)

JUSTICE WHITTAKER delivered the opinion of the Court.

Petitioner was convicted of knowingly concealing and transporting narcotic drugs. . . . His conviction was based in part on the use in evidence against him of two "envelopes containing [865 grains of] heroin" and a hypodermic syringe that had been taken from his person, following his arrest, by the arresting officer. . . .

The evidence offered at the hearing on the motion to suppress was not substantially disputed. It established that one Marsh, a federal narcotic agent with 29 years' experience, was stationed at Denver; that one Hereford had been engaged as a "special employee" of the Bureau of Narcotics at Denver for about six months, and from time to time gave information to Marsh regarding violations of the narcotic laws, for which Hereford was paid small sums of money, and that Marsh had always found the information given by Hereford to be accurate and reliable. On September 3, 1956, Hereford told Marsh that James Draper (petitioner) recently had taken up abode at a stated address in Denver and "was peddling narcotics to several addicts" in that city. Four days later, on September 7, Hereford told Marsh "that Draper had gone to Chicago the day before [September 6] by train [and] that he was going to bring back three ounces of heroin [and] that he would return to Denver either on the morning of the 8th of September or the morning of the 9th of September also by train." Hereford also gave Marsh a detailed physical description of Draper and of the clothing he was wearing, and said that he would be carrying "a tan zipper bag," and that he habitually "walked real fast."

On the morning of September 8, Marsh and a Denver police officer went to the Denver Union Station and kept watch over all incoming trains from Chicago, but they did not see anyone fitting the description that Hereford had given. Repeating the process on the morning of September 9, they saw a person, having the exact physical attributes and wearing the precise clothing described by Hereford, alight from an incoming Chicago train and start walking "fast" toward the exit. He was carrying a tan zipper bag in his right hand and the left was thrust in his raincoat pocket. Marsh, accompanied by the police officer, overtook, stopped and arrested him. They then searched him and found the two "envelopes containing heroin" clutched in his left hand in his raincoat pocket, and found the syringe in the tan zipper bag. Marsh then took him (petitioner) into custody. Hereford died four days after the arrest and therefore did not testify at the hearing on the motion.

. . . .

The crucial question for us then is whether knowledge of the related facts and circumstances gave Marsh "probable cause" within the meaning of the Fourth Amendment, . . . to believe that petitioner had committed or was committing a violation of the narcotic laws. If it did, the arrest, though without a warrant, was lawful and the subsequent search of petitioner's person and the seizure of the found heroin were validly made incident to a lawful arrest, and therefore the motion to suppress was properly overruled and the heroin was competently received in evidence at the trial.

Petitioner does not dispute this analysis of the question for decision. Rather, he contends (1) that the information given by Hereford to Marsh was "hearsay" and, because hearsay is not legally competent evidence in a criminal trial, could not legally have been considered, but should have been put out of mind, by Marsh in assessing whether he had "probable cause" and "reasonable grounds" to arrest petitioner without a warrant, and (2) that, even if hearsay could lawfully have been considered, Marsh's information should be held insufficient to show "probable cause" and "reasonable grounds" to believe that petitioner had violated or was violating the narcotic laws and to justify his arrest without a warrant.

Considering the first contention, we find petitioner entirely in error. . . .

Nor can we agree with petitioner's second contention that Marsh's information was insufficient to show probable cause and reasonable grounds to believe that petitioner had violated or was violating the narcotic laws and to justify his arrest without a warrant. The information given to narcotic agent Marsh by "special employee" Hereford may have been hearsay to Marsh, but coming from one employed for that purpose and whose information had always been found accurate and reliable, it is clear that Marsh would have been derelict in his duties had he not pursued it. And when, in pursuing that information, he saw a man, having the exact physical attributes and wearing the precise clothing and carrying the tan zipper bag that Hereford had described, alight from one of the very trains from the very place stated by Hereford and start to walk at a "fast" pace toward the station exit, Marsh had personally verified every facet of the information given him by Hereford except whether petitioner had accomplished his mission and had the three ounces of heroin on his person or in his bag. And surely, with every other bit of Hereford's information being thus personally verified, Marsh had "reasonable grounds" to believe that the remaining unverified bit of Hereford's information — that Draper would have the heroin with him — was likewise true.

> "In dealing with probable cause, . . . as the very name implies, we deal with probabilities. These are not technical; they are the factual and practical considerations of everyday life on which reasonable and prudent men, not legal technicians, act." *Brinegar v. United States.* . Probable cause exists where "the facts and circumstances within [the arresting officers'] knowledge and of which they had reasonably trustworthy information [are] sufficient in themselves

to warrant a man of reasonable caution in the belief that an offense has been or is being committed."

We believe that, under the facts and circumstances here, Marsh had probable cause and reasonable grounds to believe that petitioner was committing a violation of the laws of the United States relating to narcotic drugs at the time he arrested him. The arrest was therefore lawful, and the subsequent search and seizure, having been made incident to that lawful arrest, were likewise valid. It follows that petitioner's motion to suppress was properly denied and that the seized heroin was competent evidence lawfully received at the trial.

Affirmed.

JUSTICE DOUGLAS, dissenting.

With all due deference, the arrest made here on the mere word of an informer violated the spirit of the Fourth Amendment . . . . If an arrest is made without a warrant, the offense must be committed in the presence of the officer or the officer must have "reasonable grounds to believe that the person to be arrested has committed or is committing" a violation of the narcotics law. The arresting officers did not have a bit of evidence, known to them and as to which they could take an oath had they gone to a magistrate for a warrant, that petitioner had committed any crime. The arresting officers did not know the grounds on which the informer based his conclusion; nor did they seek to find out what they were. They acted solely on the informer's word. In my view that was not enough.

. . . .

So far as I can ascertain the mere word of an informer, not bolstered by some evidence that a crime had been or was being committed, has never been approved by this Court as "reasonable grounds" for making an arrest without a warrant. . . . Evidence required to prove guilt is not necessary. But the attendant circumstances must be sufficient to give rise in the mind of the arresting officer at least to inferences of guilt. . . .

. . . .

Even when officers had information far more suggestive of guilt than the word of the informer used here, we have not sustained arrests without a warrant. . . . In *Johnson v. United States*, the arresting officer not only had an informer's tip but he actually smelled opium coming out of a room; and on breaking in found the accused. That arrest was held unlawful. Yet the smell of opium is far more tangible direct evidence than an unverified report that someone is going to commit a crime. And in *United States v. Di Re*, an arrest without a warrant of a man sitting in a car, where counterfeit coupons had been found passing between two men, was not justified in absence of any shred of evidence implicating the defendant, a third person. . . . Yet the evidence before those officers was more potent than the mere word of the informer involved in the present case.

I think the correct rule . . .[is]. . . "Mere suspicion is not enough; there must be circumstances represented to the officers through the testimony of their senses sufficient to justify them in a good-faith belief that the defendant had violated the law."

Here the officers had no evidence - apart from the mere word of an informer - that petitioner was committing a crime. The fact that petitioner walked fast and carried a tan zipper bag was not evidence of any crime. The officers knew nothing except what they had been told by the informer. If they went to a magistrate to get a warrant of arrest and relied solely on the report of the informer, it is not conceivable to me that one would be granted. For they could not present to the magistrate any of the facts which the informer may have had. They could swear only to the fact that the informer had made the accusation. They could swear to no evidence that lay in their own knowledge. They could present, on information and belief, no facts which the informer disclosed. No magistrate could issue a warrant on the mere word of an officer, without more.

We said in *United States v. Di Re*, ". . . a search is not to be made legal by what it turns up. In law it is good or bad when it starts and does not change character from its success." In this case it was only after the arrest and search were made that there was a shred of evidence known to the officers that a crime was in the process of being committed.

DISTRICT OF COLUMBIA v. WESBY, et al.
____ U.S. ____ (2018)

JUSTICE THOMAS delivered the opinion of the Court.

This case involves a civil suit against the District of Columbia and five of its police officers, brought by 16 individuals who were arrested for holding a raucous, late-night party in a house they did not have permission to enter. The United States Court of Appeals for the District of Columbia Circuit held that there was no probable cause to arrest the partygoers, and that the officers were not entitled to qualified immunity. We reverse on both grounds.

I

Around 1 a.m. on March 16, 2008, the District's Metropolitan Police Department received a complaint about loud music and illegal activities at a house in Northeast D. C. The caller, a former neighborhood commissioner, told police that the house had been vacant for several months. When officers arrived at the scene, several neighbors confirmed that the house should have been empty. The officers approached the house and, consistent with the complaint, heard loud music playing inside.

After the officers knocked on the front door, they saw a man look out the window and then run upstairs. One of the partygoers opened the door, and the officers entered. They immediately observed that the inside of the house " 'was in disarray' " and looked like " 'a vacant property.' " The officers smelled marijuana and saw beer bottles and cups of liquor on the floor. In fact, the floor was so dirty that one of the partygoers refused to sit on it while being questioned. Although the house had working electricity and plumbing, it had no furniture downstairs other than a few padded metal chairs. The only other signs of habitation were blinds on the windows, food in the refrigerator, and toiletries in the bathroom.

In the living room, the officers found a makeshift strip club. Several women were wearing only bras and thongs, with cash tucked into their garter belts. The women were giving lap dances while other partygoers watched. Most of the onlookers were holding cash and cups of alcohol. After seeing the uniformed officers, many partygoers scattered into other parts of the house.

The officers found more debauchery upstairs. A naked woman and several men were in the bedroom. A bare mattress—the only one in the house—was on the floor, along with some lit candles and multiple open condom wrappers. A used condom was on the windowsill. The officers found one partygoer hiding in an upstairs closet, and another who had shut himself in the bathroom and refused to come out.

The officers found a total of 21 people in the house. After interviewing all 21, the officers did not get a clear or consistent story. Many partygoers said they were there for a bachelor party, but no one could identify the bachelor. Each of the partygoers claimed that someone had invited them to the house, but no one could say who. Two of the women working the party said that a woman named "Peaches" or "Tasty" was renting the house and had given them permission to be there. One of the women explained that the previous owner had recently passed away, and Peaches had just started renting the house from the grandson who inherited it. But the house had no boxes or moving supplies. She did not know

Peaches' real name. And Peaches was not there.

An officer asked the woman to call Peaches on her phone so he could talk to her. Peaches answered and explained that she had just left the party to go to the store. When the officer asked her to return, Peaches refused because she was afraid of being arrested. The sergeant supervising the investigation also spoke with Peaches. At first, Peaches claimed to be renting the house from the owner, who was fixing it up for her. She also said that she had given the attendees permission to have the party. When the sergeant again asked her who had given her permission to use the house, Peaches became evasive and hung up. The sergeant called her back, and she began yelling and insisting that she had permission before hanging up a second time. The officers eventually got Peaches on the phone again, and she admitted that she did not have permission to use the house.

The officers then contacted the owner. He told them that he had been trying to negotiate a lease with Peaches, but they had not reached an agreement. He confirmed that he had not given Peaches (or anyone else) permission to be in the house—let alone permission to use it for a bachelor party. At that point, the officers arrested the 21 partygoers for unlawful entry. The police transported the partygoers to the police station, where the lieutenant decided to charge them with disorderly conduct. The partygoers were released, and the charges were eventually dropped. (Footnote omitted).

II

Respondents, 16 of the 21 partygoers, sued the District and five of the arresting officers … for false arrest and negligent supervision under District law. The partygoers' claims were all "predicated upon the allegation that [they] were arrested without probable cause."

…

We granted certiorari to resolve two questions: whether the officers had probable cause to arrest the partygoers, and whether the officers were entitled to qualified immunity. We address each question in turn.

III

The Fourth Amendment protects "[t]he right of the people to be secure in their persons, houses, papers, and effects, against unreasonable searches and seizures." Because arrests are "seizures" of "persons," they must be reasonable under the circumstances. A warrantless arrest is reasonable if the officer has probable cause to believe that the suspect committed a crime in the officer's presence.

To determine whether an officer had probable cause for an arrest, "we examine the events leading up to the arrest, and then decide 'whether these historical facts, viewed from the standpoint of an objectively reasonable police officer, amount to' probable cause." Because probable cause "deals with probabilities and depends on the totality of the circumstances," it is "a fluid concept" that is "not readily, or even usefully, reduced to a neat set of legal rules." It "requires only a probability or substantial chance of criminal activity, not an actual showing of such activity." Probable cause "is not a high bar."

A

There is no dispute that the partygoers entered the house against the will of the owner. Nonetheless, the partygoers contend that the officers lacked probable cause to arrest them because the officers had no reason to believe that they "knew or should have known" their "entry was unwanted." We disagree. Considering the totality of the circumstances, the officers made an "entirely reasonable inference" that the partygoers were knowingly taking advantage of a vacant house as a venue for their late-night party.

Consider first the condition of the house. Multiple neighbors, including a former neighborhood official, informed the officers that the house had been vacant for several months. (Note omitted.) The house had no furniture, except for a few padded metal chairs and a bare mattress. The rest of the house was empty, save for some fixtures and large

appliances. The house had a few signs of inhabitance—working electricity and plumbing, blinds on the windows, toiletries in the bathroom, and food in the refrigerator. But those facts are not necessarily inconsistent with the house being unoccupied. The owner could have paid the utilities and kept the blinds while he looked for a new tenant, and the partygoers could have brought the food and toiletries. Although one woman told the officers that Peaches had recently moved in, the officers had reason to doubt that was true. There were no boxes or other moving supplies in the house; nor were there other possessions, such as clothes in the closet, suggesting someone lived there.

In addition to the condition of the house, consider the partygoers' conduct. The party was still going strong when the officers arrived after 1 a.m., with music so loud that it could be heard from outside. Upon entering the house, multiple officers smelled marijuana.[5] The party-goers left beer bottles and cups of liquor on the floor, and they left the floor so dirty that one of them refused to sit on it. The living room had been converted into a makeshift strip club. Strippers in bras and thongs, with cash stuffed in their garter belts, were giving lap dances. Upstairs, the officers found a group of men with a single, naked woman on a bare mattress—the only bed in the house—along with multiple open condom wrappers and a used condom.

Taken together, the condition of the house and the conduct of the partygoers allowed the officers to make several " 'common-sense conclusions about human behavior.' " Most homeowners do not live in near-barren houses. And most homeowners do not invite people over to use their living room as a strip club, to have sex in their bedroom, to smoke marijuana inside, and to leave their floors filthy. The officers could thus infer that the partygoers knew their party was not authorized.

The partygoers' reaction to the officers gave them further reason to believe that the partygoers knew they lacked permission to be in the house. Many scattered at the sight of the uniformed officers. Two hid themselves, one in a closet and the other in a bathroom. "[U]nprovoked flight upon noticing the police," we have explained, "is certainly suggestive" of wrongdoing and can be treated as "suspicious behavior" that factors into the totality of the circumstances. In fact, "deliberately furtive actions and flight at the approach of . . . law officers are *strong* indicia of *mens rea*." A reasonable officer could infer that the partygoers' scattering and hiding was an indication that they knew they were not supposed to be there.

The partygoers' answers to the officers' questions also suggested their guilty state of mind. When the officers asked who had given them permission to be there, the partygoers gave vague and implausible responses. They could not say who had invited them. Only two people claimed that Peaches had invited them, and they were working the party instead of attending it. If Peaches was the hostess, it was odd that none of the partygoers mentioned her name. Additionally, some of the partygoers claimed the event was a bachelor party, but no one could identify the bachelor. The officers could have disbelieved them, since people normally do not throw a bachelor party without a bachelor. Based on the vagueness and implausibility of the partygoers' stories, the officers could have reasonably inferred that they were lying and that their lies suggested a guilty mind.

The panel majority relied heavily on the fact that Peaches said she had invited the partygoers to the house. But when the officers spoke with Peaches, she was nervous, agitated, and evasive. ... After initially insisting that she had permission to use the house, she ultimately confessed that this was a lie—a fact that the owner confirmed. Peaches' lying and evasive behavior gave the officers reason to discredit everything she had told them. For example, the officers could have inferred that Peaches lied to them when she said she had invited the others to the house, which was consistent with the fact that hardly anyone at the party knew her name. Or the officers could have inferred that Peaches told the partygoers (like she eventually told the police) that she

was not actually renting the house, which was consistent with how the party-goers were treating it.

Viewing these circumstances as a whole, a reasonable officer could conclude that there was probable cause to believe the partygoers knew they did not have permission to be in the house.

B

In concluding otherwise, the panel majority engaged in an "excessively technical dissection" of the factors supporting probable cause. Indeed, the panel majority failed to follow two basic and well-established principles of law.

First, the panel majority viewed each fact "in isolation, rather than as a factor in the totality of the circumstances." . . . The "totality of the circumstances" requires courts to consider "the whole picture." Our precedents recognize that the whole is often greater than the sum of its parts—especially when the parts are viewed in isolation. Instead of considering the facts as a whole, the panel majority took them one by one. For example, it dismissed the fact that the partygoers "scattered or hid when the police entered the house" because that fact was "not sufficient *standing alone* to create probable cause." Similarly, it found "nothing in the record suggesting that the condition of the house, *on its own*, should have alerted the [partygoers] that they were unwelcome." The totality-of-the-circumstances test "precludes this sort of divide-and-conquer analysis."

Second, the panel majority mistakenly believed that it could dismiss outright any circumstances that were "susceptible of innocent explanation." For example, the panel majority brushed aside the drinking and the lap dances as "consistent with" the partygoers' explanation that they were having a bachelor party. And it similarly dismissed the condition of the house as "entirely consistent with" Peaches being a "new tenant." But probable cause does not require officers to rule out a suspect's innocent explanation for suspicious facts. As we have explained, "the relevant inquiry is not whether particular conduct is 'innocent' or 'guilty,' but the degree of suspicion that attaches to particular types of noncriminal acts." Thus, the panel majority should have asked whether a reasonable officer could conclude— considering all of the surrounding circumstances, including the plausibility of the explanation itself—that there was a "substantial chance of criminal activity."

The circumstances here certainly suggested criminal activity. As explained, the officers found a group of people who claimed to be having a bachelor party with no bachelor, in a near-empty house, with strippers in the living room and sexual activity in the bedroom, and who fled at the first sign of police. The panel majority identified innocent explanations for most of these circumstances in isolation, but again, this kind of divide-and-conquer approach is improper. A factor viewed in isolation is often more "readily susceptible to an innocent explanation" than one viewed as part of a totality. And here, the totality of the circumstances gave the officers plenty of reasons to doubt the partygoers' protestations of innocence.

For all of these reasons, we reverse the D. C. Circuit's holding that the officers lacked probable cause to arrest.

[The Court then analyzed the qualified immunity claim and found that the officers did have qualified immunity.]

JUSTICE GINSBURG AND JUSTICE SOTOMAYOR concurring, omitted.

MARYLAND v. PRINGLE
540 U.S. 366 (2003)

CHIEF JUSTICE REHNQUIST delivered the opinion of the Court.

At 3:16 a.m. on August 7, 1999, a Baltimore County Police officer stopped a Nissan Maxima for speeding. There were three occupants in the car: Donte Partlow, the driver and owner, respondent Pringle, the front-seat passenger, and Otis Smith, the back-seat passenger. The officer asked Partlow for his license and registration. When Partlow opened the glove compartment to retrieve the vehicle registration, the officer observed a large amount of rolled-up money in the glove compartment. The officer returned to his patrol car with Partlow's license and registration to check the computer system for outstanding violations. The computer check did not reveal any violations. The officer returned to the stopped car, had Partlow get out, and issued him an oral warning.

After a second patrol car arrived, the officer asked Partlow if he had any weapons or narcotics in the vehicle. Partlow indicated that he did not. Partlow then consented to a search of the vehicle. The search yielded $763 from the glove compartment and five plastic glassine baggies containing cocaine from behind the back-seat armrest. When the officer began the search, the armrest was in the upright position flat against the rear seat. The officer pulled down the armrest and found the drugs, which had been placed between the armrest and the back seat of the car.

The officer questioned all three men about the ownership of the drugs and money, and told them that if no one admitted to ownership of the drugs he was going to arrest them all. The men offered no information regarding the ownership of the drugs or money. All three were placed under arrest and transported to the police station.

Later that morning, Pringle waived his rights under *Miranda v. Arizona*, (1966), and gave an oral and written confession in which he acknowledged that the cocaine belonged to him, that he and his friends were going to a party, and that he intended to sell the cocaine or "[u]se it for sex." Pringle maintained that the other occupants of the car did not know about the drugs, and they were released.

The Court of Appeals of Maryland [held] that, absent specific facts tending to show Pringle's knowledge and dominion or control over the drugs, "the mere finding of cocaine in the back armrest when [Pringle] was a front seat passenger in a car being driven by its owner is insufficient to establish probable cause for an arrest for possession." . . . We granted certiorari, 538 U. S. 921 (2003), and now reverse.

It is uncontested in the present case that the officer, upon recovering the five plastic glassine baggies containing suspected cocaine, had probable cause to believe a felony had been committed. . . . The sole question is whether the officer had probable cause to believe that Pringle committed that crime.

On many occasions, we have reiterated that the probable-cause standard is a "'practical, nontechnical conception'" that deals with "'the factual and practical considerations of everyday life on which reasonable and prudent men, not legal technicians, act.'" . . . "[P]robable cause is a fluid concept — turning on the assessment of probabilities in particular factual contexts — not readily, or even usefully, reduced to a neat set of legal rules." . . .

The probable-cause standard is incapable of precise definition or quantification into percentages because it deals with probabilities and depends on the totality of the circumstances. . . . We have stated, however, that "[t]he substance of all the definitions of probable cause is a reasonable ground for belief of guilt," . . . and that the belief of guilt must be particularized with respect to the person to be searched or seized . . . .

To determine whether an officer had probable cause to arrest an individual, we examine the events leading up to the arrest, and then decide "whether these historical facts, viewed from the standpoint of an objectively reasonable police officer, amount to" probable cause. . . .

In this case, Pringle was one of three men riding in a Nissan Maxima at 3:16 a.m. There was $763 of rolled-up cash in the glove compartment directly in front of Pringle. Five plastic glassine baggies of cocaine were behind the back-seat armrest and accessible to all three men. Upon questioning, the three men failed to offer any information with respect to the ownership of the cocaine or the money.

We think it an entirely reasonable inference from these facts that any or all three of the occupants had knowledge of, and exercised dominion and control over, the cocaine. Thus a reasonable officer could conclude that there was probable cause to believe Pringle committed the crime of possession of cocaine, either solely or jointly.

[In *Ybarra* we stated:]

> "[A] person's mere propinquity to others independently suspected of criminal activity does not, without more, give rise to probable cause to search that person. *Sibron v. New York*, (1968). Where the standard is probable cause, a search or seizure of a person must be supported by probable cause particularized with respect to that person. This requirement cannot be undercut or avoided by simply pointing to the fact that coincidentally there exists probable cause to search or seize another or to search the premises where the person may happen to be."

We held that the search warrant did not permit body searches of all of the tavern's patrons and that the police could not pat down the patrons for weapons, absent individualized suspicion.

This case is quite different from *Ybarra.* Pringle and his two companions were in a relatively small automobile, not a public tavern. In *Wyoming v. Houghton* (1999), we noted that "a car passenger — unlike the unwitting tavern patron in *Ybarra* — will often be engaged in a common enterprise with the driver, and have the same interest in concealing the fruits or the evidence of their wrongdoing." Here we think it was reasonable for the officer to infer a common enterprise among the three men. The quantity of drugs and cash in the car indicated the likelihood of drug dealing, an enterprise to which a dealer would be unlikely to admit an innocent person with the potential to furnish evidence against him.

In *Di Re*, a federal investigator had been told by an informant, Reed, that he was to receive counterfeit gasoline ration coupons from a certain Buttitta at a particular place. The investigator went to the appointed place and saw Reed, the sole occupant of the rear seat of the car, holding gasoline ration coupons. There were two other occupants in the car: Buttitta in the driver's seat and Di Re in the front passenger's seat. Reed informed the investigator that Buttitta had given him counterfeit coupons. Thereupon, all three men were arrested and searched. After noting that the officers had no information implicating Di Re and no information pointing to Di Re's possession of coupons, unless presence in the car warranted that inference, we concluded

that the officer lacked probable cause to believe that Di Re was involved in the crime. We said "[a]ny inference that everyone on the scene of a crime is a party to it must disappear if the Government informer singles out the guilty person." No such singling out occurred in this case; none of the three men provided information with respect to the ownership of the cocaine or money.

We hold that the officer had probable cause to believe that Pringle had committed the crime of possession of a controlled substance. Pringle's arrest therefore did not contravene the Fourth and Fourteenth Amendments. Accordingly, the judgment of the Court of Appeals of Maryland is reversed, and the case is remanded for further proceedings not inconsistent with this opinion.

FLORIDA v. J.L.
529 U.S. 266 (2000)

JUSTICE GINSBURG delivered the opinion of the Court.

On October 13, 1995, an anonymous caller reported to the Miami-Dade Police that a young black male standing at a particular bus stop and wearing a plaid shirt was carrying a gun. …So far as the record reveals, there is no audio recording of the tip, and nothing is known about the informant. Sometime after the police received the tip — the record does not say how long — two officers were instructed to respond. They arrived at the bus stop about six minutes later and saw three black males "just hanging out [there]." …One of the three, respondent J. L., was wearing a plaid shirt. … Apart from the tip, the officers had no reason to suspect any of the three of illegal conduct. The officers did not see a firearm, and J. L. made no threatening or otherwise unusual movements. … One of the officers approached J. L., told him to put his hands up on the bus stop, frisked him, and seized a gun from J. L.'s pocket. The second officer frisked the other two individuals, against whom no allegations had been made, and found nothing.

J. L., who was at the time of the frisk "10 days shy of his 16th birth[day]," … was charged under state law with carrying a concealed firearm without a license and possessing a firearm while under the age of 18. He moved to suppress the gun as the fruit of an unlawful search, and the trial court granted his motion. The intermediate appellate court reversed, but the Supreme Court of Florida quashed that decision and held the search invalid under the Fourth Amendment. …

…

In the instant case, the officers' suspicion that J. L. was carrying a weapon arose not from any observations of their own but solely from a call made from an unknown location by an unknown caller. Unlike a tip from a known informant whose reputation can be assessed and who can be held responsible if her allegations turn out to be fabricated … "an anonymous tip alone seldom demonstrates the informant's basis of knowledge or veracity." As we have recognized, however, there are situations in which an anonymous tip, suitably corroborated, exhibits "sufficient indicia of reliability to provide reasonable suspicion to make the investigatory stop." ... The question we here confront is whether the tip pointing to J. L. had those indicia of reliability.

In *Alabama v. White* [1990], the police received an anonymous tip asserting that a woman was carrying cocaine and predicting that she would leave an apartment building at a specified time, get into a car matching a particular description, and drive to a named motel. ... Standing alone, the tip would not have justified a *Terry* stop. ... Only after police observation showed that the informant had accurately predicted the woman's movements, we explained, did it become reasonable to think the tipster had inside knowledge about the suspect and therefore to credit his assertion about the cocaine. ... Although the Court held that the suspicion in *White* became reasonable after police surveillance, we regarded the case as borderline. Knowledge about a person's future movements indicates some familiarity with that person's affairs, but having such knowledge does not necessarily imply that the informant knows, in particular, whether that person is carrying hidden contraband. We accordingly classified *White* as a "close case." ...

The tip in the instant case lacked the moderate indicia of reliability present in *White* and essential to the Court's decision in that case. The anonymous call concerning J. L. provided no predictive information and therefore left the police without means to test the informant's knowledge or credibility. That the allegation about the gun turned out to be correct does not suggest that the officers, prior to the frisks, had a reasonable basis for suspecting J. L. of engaging in unlawful conduct: The reasonableness of official suspicion must be measured by what the officers knew before they conducted their search. All the police had to go on in this case was the bare report of an unknown, unaccountable informant who neither explained how he knew about the gun nor supplied any basis for believing he had inside information about J. L. If *White* was a close

case on the reliability of anonymous tips, this one surely falls on the other side of the line.

Florida contends that the tip was reliable because its description of the suspect's visible attributes proved accurate: There really was a young black male wearing a plaid shirt at the bus stop. . . . The United States as *amicus curiae* makes a similar argument, proposing that a stop and frisk should be permitted "when (1) an anonymous tip provides a description of a particular person at a particular location illegally carrying a concealed firearm, (2) police promptly verify the pertinent details of the tip except the existence of the firearm, and (3) there are no factors that cast doubt on the reliability of the tip." ... These contentions misapprehend the reliability needed for a tip to justify a *Terry* stop.

An accurate description of a subject's readily observable location and appearance is of course reliable in this limited sense: It will help the police correctly identify the person whom the tipster means to accuse. Such a tip, however, does not show that the tipster has knowledge of concealed criminal activity. The reasonable suspicion here at issue requires that a tip be reliable in its assertion of illegality, not just in its tendency to identify a determinate person. . . .

...

The facts of this case do not require us to speculate about the circumstances under which the danger alleged in an anonymous tip might be so great as to justify a search even without a showing of reliability. We do not say, for example, that a report of a person carrying a bomb need bear the indicia of reliability we demand for a report of a person carrying a firearm before the police can constitutionally conduct a frisk. Nor do we hold that public safety officials in quarters where the reasonable expectation of Fourth Amendment privacy is diminished, such as airports, . . . cannot conduct protective searches on the basis of information insufficient to justify searches elsewhere.

Finally, the requirement that an anonymous tip bear standard indicia of reliability in order to justify a stop in no way diminishes a police officer's prerogative, in accord with *Terry*, to conduct a protective search of a person who has already been legitimately stopped. We speak in today's decision only of cases in which the officer's authority to make the initial stop is at issue.

In that context, we hold that an anonymous tip lacking indicia of reliability . . . does not justify a stop and frisk whenever and however it alleges the illegal possession of a firearm.

ILLINOIS v. WARDLOW
528 U.S. 119 (2000)

CHIEF JUSTICE REHNQUIST delivered the opinion of the Court.

Respondent Wardlow fled upon seeing police officers patrolling an area known for heavy narcotics trafficking. Two of the officers caught up with him, stopped him and conducted a protective pat-down search for weapons. Discovering a .38-caliber handgun, the officers arrested Wardlow. We hold that the officers' stop did not violate the Fourth Amendment to the United States Constitution.

On September 9, 1995, Officers Nolan and Harvey were working as uniformed officers in the special operations section of the Chicago Police Department. The officers were driving the last car of a four-car caravan converging on an area known for heavy narcotics trafficking in order to investigate drug transactions. The officers were traveling together because they expected to find a crowd of people in the area, including lookouts and customers.

As the caravan passed 4035 West Van Buren, Officer Nolan observed respondent Wardlow standing next to the building holding an opaque bag. Respondent looked in the direction of the officers and fled. Nolan and Harvey turned their car southbound, watched him as he ran through the gangway and an alley, and eventually cornered him on the street. Nolan then exited his car and stopped respondent. He immediately conducted a protective pat-down search for weapons because in his experience it was common for there to be weapons in the near vicinity of narcotics transactions. During the frisk, Officer Nolan squeezed the bag respondent was carrying and felt a heavy, hard object similar to the shape of a gun. The officer then opened the bag and discovered a .38-caliber handgun with five live rounds of ammunition. The officers arrested Wardlow.

The Illinois trial court denied respondent's motion to suppress, finding the gun was recovered during a lawful stop and frisk. Following a stipulated bench trial *[a trial in which both parties have agreed to what the crucial or most important facts are and those facts are then just read into the record as proven without having witnesses examined to develop the record]*, Wardlow was convicted of unlawful use of a weapon by a felon.

. . . .

[A]n officer may, consistent with the Fourth Amendment, conduct a brief, investigatory stop when the officer has a reasonable, articulable suspicion that criminal activity is afoot. While "reasonable suspicion" is a less demanding standard than probable cause and requires a showing considerably less than preponderance of the evidence, the Fourth Amendment requires at least a minimal level of objective justification for making the stop. *United States v. Sokolow*, (1989). The officer must be able to articulate more than an "inchoate and unparticularized suspicion or `hunch' " of criminal activity.

Nolan and Harvey were among eight officers in a four car caravan that was converging on an area known for heavy narcotics trafficking, and the officers anticipated encountering a large number of people in the area, including drug customers and individuals serving as lookouts. It was in this context that Officer Nolan decided to investigate Wardlow after observing him flee. An individual's presence in an area of expected criminal activity, standing alone, is not enough to support a reasonable, particularized suspicion that the person is committing a crime. *Brown v. Texas* (1979). But officers are not required to ignore the relevant characteristics of a location in determining whether the circumstances are sufficiently suspicious to warrant further investigation. Accordingly, we have previously noted the fact that the stop occurred in a "high crime area" among the relevant contextual considerations in a Terry analysis.

In this case, moreover, it was not merely respondent's presence in an area of heavy narcotics trafficking that aroused the officers' suspicion but his unprovoked flight upon noticing the police. Our cases have also recognized that nervous, evasive behavior is a pertinent factor in determining reasonable suspicion. Headlong flight — wherever it occurs — is the consummate act of evasion: it is not necessarily indicative of wrongdoing, but it is certainly suggestive of such. In reviewing the propriety of an officer's conduct, courts do not have available empirical studies dealing with inferences drawn from suspicious behavior, and we cannot reasonably demand scientific certainty from judges or law enforcement officers where none exists. Thus, the determination of reasonable suspicion must be based on commonsense judgments and inferences about human behavior. ... We conclude Officer Nolan was justified in suspecting that Wardlow was involved in criminal activity, and, therefore, in investigating further.

Such a holding is entirely consistent with our decision in *Florida v. Royer*, (1983), where we held that when an officer, without reasonable suspicion or probable cause, approaches an individual, the individual has a right to ignore the police and go about his business. And any "refusal to cooperate, without more, does not furnish the minimal level of objective justification needed for a detention or seizure." *Florida v. Bostick*, (1991). But unprovoked flight is simply not a mere refusal to cooperate. Flight, by its very nature, is not "going about one's business"; in fact, it is just the opposite. Allowing officers confronted with such flight to stop the fugitive and investigate further is quite consistent with the individual's right to go about his business or to stay put and remain silent in the face of police questioning.

JUSTICE STEVENS, with whom JUSTICE SOUTER, JUSTICE GINSBURG, and JUSTICE BREYER join, concurring in part and dissenting in part.

The State of Illinois asks this Court to announce a "bright-line rule" authorizing the temporary detention of anyone who flees at the mere sight of a police officer. Respondent counters by asking us to adopt the opposite per se rule — that the fact that a person flees upon seeing the police can never, by itself, be sufficient to justify a temporary investigative stop of the kind authorized by *Terry v. Ohio*, (1968).

The Court today wisely endorses neither per se rule. Instead, it rejects the proposition that "flight is . . .necessarily indicative of ongoing criminal activity," adhering to the view that "[t]he concept of reasonable suspicion . . . is not readily, or even usefully, reduced to a neat set of legal rules," but must be determined by looking to "the totality of the circumstances — the whole picture." Abiding by this framework, the Court concludes that "Officer Nolan was justified in suspecting that Wardlow was involved in criminal activity."

Although I agree with the Court's rejection of the per se rules proffered by the parties, unlike the Court, I am persuaded that in this case the brief testimony of the officer who seized respondent does not justify the conclusion that he had reasonable suspicion to make the stop.

The question in this case concerns "the degree of suspicion that attaches to" a person's flight — or, more precisely, what "commonsense conclusions" can be drawn respecting the motives behind that flight. A pedestrian may break into a run for a variety of reasons — to catch up with a friend a block or two away, to seek shelter from an impending storm, to arrive at a bus stop before the bus leaves, to get home in time for dinner, to resume jogging after a pause for rest, to avoid contact with a bore or a bully, or simply to answer the call of nature — any of which might coincide with the arrival of an officer in the vicinity. A pedestrian might also run because he or she has just sighted one or more police officers. In the latter instance, the State properly points out "that the fleeing person may be, , (1) an escapee from jail; (2) wanted on a warrant, (3) in possession of contraband, (i.e. drugs, weapons, stolen goods, etc.); or (4) someone who has just committed another type of crime." In short, there are unquestionably circumstances in which a person's flight is suspicious, and undeniably instances in which a person runs for entirely innocent reasons.

Given the diversity and frequency of possible motivations for flight, it would be profoundly unwise to endorse either per se rule. The inference we can reasonably draw about the motivation for a person's flight, rather, will depend on a number of different circumstances. Factors such as the time of day, the number of people in the area, the character of the neighborhood, whether the officer was in uniform, the way the runner was dressed, the direction and speed of the flight, and whether the person's behavior was otherwise unusual might be relevant in specific cases. This number of variables is surely sufficient to preclude either a bright-line rule that always justifies, or that never justifies, an investigative stop based on the sole fact that flight began after a police officer.

...

"[I]t is a matter of common knowledge that men who are entirely innocent do sometimes fly from the scene of a crime through fear of being apprehended as the guilty parties, or from an unwillingness to appear as witnesses. Nor is it true as an accepted axiom of criminal law that `the wicked flee when no man pursueth, but the righteous are as bold as a lion.' ...

In addition to these concerns, a reasonable person may conclude that an officer's sudden appearance indicates nearby criminal activity. And where there is criminal activity there is also a substantial element of danger — either from the criminal or from a confrontation between the criminal and the police. These considerations can lead to an innocent and understandable desire to quit the vicinity with all speed.

Among some citizens, particularly minorities and those residing in high crime areas, there is also the possibility that the fleeing person is entirely innocent, but, with or without justification, believes that contact with the police can itself be dangerous, apart from any criminal activity associated with the officer's sudden presence. For such a person, unprovoked flight is neither "aberrant" nor "abnormal." Moreover, these concerns and fears are known to the police officers themselves, and are validated by law enforcement investigations into their own practices. Accordingly, the evidence supporting the reasonableness of these beliefs is too pervasive to be dismissed as random or rare, and too persuasive to be disparaged as inconclusive or insufficient. In any event, just as we do not require "scientific certainty" for our commonsense conclusion that unprovoked flight can sometimes indicate suspicious motives neither do we require scientific certainty to conclude that unprovoked flight can occur for other, innocent reasons.

Guided by that totality-of-the-circumstances test, the Court concludes that Officer Nolan had reasonable suspicion to stop respondent.

In this respect, my view differs from the Court's. The entire justification for the stop is articulated in the brief testimony of Officer Nolan. Some facts are perfectly clear; others are not. This factual insufficiency leads me to conclude that the Court's judgment is mistaken.

…

This terse testimony is most noticeable for what it fails to reveal. Though asked whether he was in a marked or unmarked car, Officer Nolan could not recall the answer. He was not asked whether any of the other three cars in the caravan were marked, or whether any of the other seven officers were in uniform. Though he explained that the size of the caravan was because "[n]ormally in these different areas there's an enormous amount of people, sometimes lookouts, customers," Officer Nolan did not testify as to whether anyone besides Wardlow was nearby 4035 West Van Buren. Nor is it clear that that address was the intended destination of the caravan. As the Appellate Court of Illinois interpreted the record, "it appears that the officers were simply driving by, on their way to some unidentified location, when they noticed defendant standing at 4035 West Van Buren." Officer Nolan's testimony also does not reveal how fast the officers were driving. It does not indicate whether he saw respondent notice the other patrol cars. And it does not say whether the caravan, or any part of it, had already passed Wardlow by before he began to run.

Indeed, the Appellate Court thought the record was even "too vague to support the inference that . . . defendant's flight was related to his expectation of police focus on him." Presumably, respondent did not react to the first three cars, and we cannot even be sure that he recognized the occupants of the fourth as police officers. The adverse inference is based entirely on the officer's statement: "He looked in our direction and began fleeing."

No other factors sufficiently support a finding of reasonable suspicion. Though respondent was carrying a white, opaque bag under his arm, there is nothing at all suspicious about that. Certainly the time of day — shortly after noon — does not support Illinois' argument. Nor were the officers "responding to any call or report of suspicious activity in the area." Officer Nolan did testify that he expected to find "an enormous amount of people," including drug customers or lookout, and the Court points out that "[i]t was in this context that Officer Nolan decided to investigate Wardlow after observing him flee." This observation, in my view, lends insufficient weight to the reasonable suspicion analysis; indeed, in light of the absence of testimony that anyone else was nearby when respondent began to run, this observation points in the opposite direction.

The State, along with the majority of the Court, relies as well on the assumption that this flight occurred in a high crime area. Even if that assumption is accurate, it is insufficient because even in a high crime neighborhood unprovoked flight does not invariably lead to reasonable suspicion. On the contrary, because many factors providing innocent motivations for unprovoked flight are concentrated in high crime areas, the character of the neighborhood arguably makes an inference of guilt less appropriate, rather than more so. Like unprovoked flight itself, presence in a high crime neighborhood is a fact too generic and susceptible to innocent explanation to satisfy the reasonable suspicion inquiry.

It is the State's burden to articulate facts sufficient to support reasonable suspicion. … In my judgment, Illinois has failed to discharge that burden. I am not persuaded that the mere fact that someone standing on a sidewalk looked in the direction of a passing car before starting to run is sufficient to justify a forcible stop and frisk.

Brinegar v. United States, 338 U.S. 160 (1949)

SUMMARY: An officer on patrol recognized a driver from earlier contacts coming from a known illegal liquor source and heading towards a probably illegal market. The officer stopped Brinegar based on that information. In addition to the oft-cited definition of probable cause the Court stated,…

"Guilt in a criminal case must be proved beyond a reasonable doubt, and by evidence confined to that which long experience in the common law tradition, to some extent embodied in the Constitution, has crystallized into rules of evidence consistent with that standard. . . .

However, if those standards were to be made applicable in determining probable cause for an arrest or for search and seizure, more especially in cases such as this involving moving vehicles used in the commission of crime, few indeed would be the situations in which an officer, charged with protecting the public interest by enforcing the law, could take effective action toward that end. Those standards have seldom been so applied.

'The substance of all the definitions' of probable cause 'is a reasonable ground for belief of guilt.' And this 'means less than evidence which would justify condemnation" or conviction. … [I]it has come to mean more than bare suspicion.'

These long-prevailing standards seek to safeguard citizens from rash and unreasonable interferences with privacy and from unfounded charges of crime. They also seek to give fair leeway for enforcing the law in the community's protection. Because many situations which confront officers in the course of executing their duties are more or less ambiguous, room must be allowed for some mistakes on their part. But the mistakes must be those of reasonable men, acting on facts leading sensibly to their conclusions of probability. The rule of probable cause is a practical, nontechnical conception affording the best compromise that has been found for accommodating these often opposing interests. Requiring more would unduly hamper law enforcement. To allow less would be to leave law-abiding citizens at the mercy of the officers' whim or caprice."

Probable Cause Is More Than A Hunch Or "No Particularized Suspicion"

Can police take any action based on no suspicion at all? What about just a hunch? One quantum of evidence on the objective basis continuum is "no particularized suspicion." This standard means that the police don't necessarily have any reason (or good reason) to think that a person is involved in criminal activity. The officer's interest could be peaked by a "hunch" or general curiosity and the inquisitiveness that goes along with being a police officer. Sometimes government action is random and not even based on hunch. (In Chapter Five you will read cases about random, suspicionless roadblocks, or random school drug testing.)

Police may approach a person on the street and ask them questions for no particular reason. Police have not seized an individual simply by approaching him or her and asking a few questions provided that a reasonable person would feel free to disregard the officer and go about his or her business. These encounters with the citizenry (referred to as "mere encounters") are consensual and need not be supported by reasonable suspicion of criminal activity. See, *United States v. Drayton,* 536 U.S. 194 (2002). Based on the information gained from these encounters, police may develop probable cause. For example, if Sally Police Officer nonchalantly contacts Joe — a person she knows to be a cocaine user and asks, "How you doing Joe, when's the last time you used cocaine?" And Joe honestly replies, "a couple hours ago." And Sally asks, "do you have any on you right now?" and Joe replies, "Yes." Sally now has at least reasonable suspicion to do a more significant field interrogation. Is it probable cause? More facts would be needed to determine that. For example, does Sally know Joe to be an honest, (but rather naïve) individual? Has Joe possessed meth on his person in the past?

Not all judges think alike and agree whether the facts surrounding a case rise to reasonable suspicion, probable cause, or are just hunches. When there is a close question, who decides? In *Ornelas v. United States*, 517 U.S. 690 (1996), the Court established a "standard of review"[59] to apply to a magistrate's determination of whether reasonable suspicion or probable cause exists. The Court held that this determination involves "mixed questions of law and facts," and therefore, a "strict standard of review" is warranted. This means that the appellate court judges get to decide for themselves whether probable cause or reasonable suspicion existed, and they do not have to defer to the trial judge's findings. In drawing conclusions, however, the appellate court should evaluate the facts from the perspective of an "objectively reasonable police officer."

So, how do police know what they know and get enough facts that rise to the level of reasonable suspicion or probable cause?

Basis Of Knowledge

Personal Knowledge And Experience, The Collective Knowledge Of Police, And Criminal Profiles

Police officers are entitled to rely on their specialized training and experience in drawing inferences of criminality from circumstances that might appear innocent or unremarkable to the lay observer. Indeed, courts have relied on, and deferred to, the special expertise of trained investigators in evaluating otherwise ambiguous conduct. (See, e.g., *Terry* and *Westby*, above). Additionally, police officers can base their probable cause determination on information gained from other police officers. For example, police officers may make an arrest or stop based upon a bulletin issued by another police agency, even if the bulletin does not specify the facts constituting probable cause or reasonable suspicion. *United States v. Hensley,* 469 U.S. 221 (1985). When it comes to making an arrest simply based on a suspect fitting a criminal profile, the Court has expressed some concerns however. On the one hand, the Court has held that officers may not rely solely upon general statistics regarding profiles of offenders to construct a basis for an investigative stop or for probable cause. On the other hand, conduct that fits a profile which may be innocent in itself may serve as part of the foundation for reasonable suspicion or probable cause. The articulation of factors in support of probable cause or reasonable suspicion in the form of a profile of the general characteristics of a class of offenders does not somehow detract from their evidentiary significance as seen by a trained agent.

In the following cases the Court examined whether the fact that the suspect fit a profile provide the police probable cause.

UNITED STATES v. SOKOLOW
490 U.S. 1 (1989)

CHIEF JUSTICE REHNQUIST delivered the opinion of the Court.

... This case involves a typical attempt to smuggle drugs through one of the Nation's airports. On a Sunday in July 1984, respondent went to the United Airlines ticket counter at Honolulu Airport, where he purchased two round-trip tickets for a flight to Miami leaving later that day. The tickets were purchased in the names of "Andrew Kray" and "Janet Norian," and had open return dates. Respondent paid $2,100 for the tickets from a large roll of $20 bills, which appeared to contain a total of $4,000. He also gave the ticket agent his home telephone number. The ticket agent noticed that respondent seemed nervous; he was about 25 years old; he was dressed in a black jumpsuit and wore gold jewelry; and he was accompanied by a

---

[59] Standard of review is the test that the appellate courts will apply when deciding whether the lower courts were right or wrong in their decisions about laws or facts in a given case.

woman, who turned out to be Janet Norian. Neither respondent nor his companion checked any of their four pieces of luggage.

After the couple left for their flight, the ticket agent informed Officer John McCarthy of the Honolulu Police Department of respondent's cash purchase of tickets to Miami. Officer McCarthy determined that the telephone number respondent gave to the ticket agent was subscribed to a "Karl Herman," who resided at 348-A Royal Hawaiian Avenue in Honolulu. Unbeknownst to McCarthy (and later to the DEA agents), respondent was Herman's roommate. The ticket agent identified respondent's voice on the answering machine at Herman's number. Officer McCarthy was unable to find any listing under the name "Andrew Kray" in Hawaii. McCarthy subsequently learned that return reservations from Miami to Honolulu had been made in the names of Kray and Norian, with their arrival scheduled for July 25, three days after respondent and his companion had left. He also learned that Kray and Norian were scheduled to make stopovers in Denver and Los Angeles.

On July 25, during the stopover in Los Angeles, DEA agents identified respondent. He "appeared to be very nervous and was looking all around the waiting area.".... Later that day, at 6:30 p.m., respondent and Norian arrived in Honolulu. As before, they had not checked their luggage. Respondent was still wearing a black jumpsuit and gold jewelry. The couple proceeded directly to the street and tried to hail a cab, where Agent Richard Kempshall and three other DEA agents approached them. Kempshall displayed his credentials, grabbed respondent by the arm and moved him back onto the sidewalk. Kempshall asked respondent for his airline ticket and identification; respondent said that he had neither. He told the agents that his name was "Sokolow," but that he was traveling under his mother's maiden name, "Kray." Respondent and Norian were escorted to the DEA office at the airport. There, the couple's luggage was examined by "Donker," a narcotics detector dog, which alerted to

respondent's brown shoulder bag. The agents arrested respondent. He was advised of his constitutional rights and declined to make any statements. The agents obtained a warrant to search the shoulder bag. They found no illicit drugs, but the bag did contain several suspicious documents indicating respondent's involvement in drug trafficking. The agents had Donker reexamine the remaining luggage, and this time the dog alerted to a medium-sized Louis Vuitton bag. By now, it was 9:30 p.m., too late for the agents to obtain a second warrant. They allowed respondent to leave for the night, but kept his luggage. The next morning, after a second dog confirmed Donker's alert, the agents obtained a warrant and found 1,063 grams of cocaine inside the bag.

…

The Court of Appeals held that the DEA agents seized respondent when they grabbed by the arm and moved him back onto the sidewalk. …

The Government does not challenge that conclusion, and we assume — without deciding — that a stop occurred here. Our decision, then, turns on whether the agents had a reasonable suspicion that respondent was engaged in wrongdoing when they encountered him on the sidewalk. In *Terry v. Ohio* ... (1968), we held that the police can stop and briefly detain a person for investigative purposes if the officer has a reasonable suspicion supported by articulable facts that criminal activity "may be afoot," even if the officer lacks probable cause.

The officer, of course, must be able to articulate something more than an "inchoate and unparticularized suspicion or `hunch.'" The Fourth Amendment requires "some minimal level of objective justification" for making the stop. ... That level of suspicion is considerably less than proof of wrongdoing by a preponderance of the evidence. We have held that probable cause means "a fair probability that contraband or evidence of a crime will be found," ... and the level of suspicion required for a *Terry*-stop is obviously less demanding than that for probable cause. ...

The concept of reasonable suspicion, like probable cause, is not "readily, or even usefully, reduced to a neat set of legal rules." ... We think the Court of Appeals' effort to refine and elaborate the requirements of "reasonable suspicion" in this case create unnecessary difficulty in dealing with one of the relatively simple concepts embodied in the Fourth Amendment. In evaluating the validity of a stop such as this, we must consider "the totality of the circumstances — the whole picture." ...

The rule enunciated by the Court of Appeals, in which evidence available to an officer is divided into evidence of "ongoing criminal behavior" on the one hand, and "probabilistic" evidence, on the other, is not in keeping with the quoted statements from our decisions. It also seems to us to draw a sharp line between types of evidence, the probative value of which varies only in degree. The Court of Appeals classified evidence of traveling under an alias, or evidence that the suspect took an evasive or erratic path through an airport, as meeting the test for showing "ongoing criminal activity." But certainly instances are conceivable in which traveling under an alias would not reflect ongoing criminal activity: for example, a person who wished to travel to a hospital or clinic for an operation and wished to conceal that fact. One taking an evasive path through an airport might be seeking to avoid a confrontation with an angry acquaintance or with a creditor. This is not to say that each of these types of evidence is not highly probative, but they do not have the sort of ironclad significance attributed to them by the Court of Appeals.

On the other hand, the factors in this case that the Court of Appeals treated as merely "probabilistic" also have probative significance. Paying $2,100 in cash for two airplane tickets is out of the ordinary, and it is even more out of the ordinary to pay that sum from a roll of $20 bills containing nearly twice that amount of cash. Most business travelers, we feel confident, purchase airline tickets by credit card or check so as to have a record for tax or business purposes, and few vacationers carry with them thousands of dollars in $20 bills. We also think the agents had a reasonable ground to believe that respondent was traveling under an alias; the evidence was by no means conclusive, but it was sufficient to warrant consideration. While a trip from Honolulu to Miami, standing alone, is not a cause for any sort of suspicion, here there was more: surely few residents of Honolulu travel from that city for 20 hours to spend 48 hours in Miami during the month of July.

Any one of these factors is not by itself proof of any illegal conduct and is quite consistent with innocent travel. But we think taken together they amount to reasonable suspicion. ...

We do not agree with respondent that our analysis is somehow changed by the agents' belief that his behavior was consistent with one of the DEA's "drug courier profiles." A court sitting to determine the existence of reasonable suspicion must require the agent to articulate the factors leading to that conclusion, but the fact that these factors may be set forth in a "profile" does not somehow detract from their evidentiary significance as seen by a trained agent.

...

" ... We hold that the agents had a reasonable basis to suspect that respondent was transporting illegal drugs on these facts.

JUSTICE MARSHALL, with whom JUSTICE BRENNAN joins, dissenting.

Because the strongest advocates of Fourth Amendment rights are frequently criminals, it is easy to forget that our interpretations of such rights apply to the innocent and the guilty alike.

...

The reasonable-suspicion standard is a derivation of the probable cause command, applicable only to those brief detentions which fall short of being full-scale searches and seizures and which are necessitated by law-enforcement exigencies such as the need to stop ongoing crimes, to prevent imminent crimes, and to protect law-enforcement officers in highly charged situations. ... By requiring reasonable suspicion as a prerequisite to such seizures, the Fourth Amendment protects innocent persons from being subjected to "overbearing or harassing" police conduct carried out solely on the basis of imprecise stereotypes of what criminals look like, or on the basis of irrelevant personal characteristics such as race. ...

To deter such egregious police behavior, we have held that a suspicion is not reasonable unless officers have based it on "specific and articulable facts."... It is not enough to suspect that an individual has committed crimes in the past, harbors unconsummated criminal designs, or has the propensity to commit crimes. On the contrary; before detaining an individual, law enforcement officers must reasonably suspect that he is engaged in, or poised to commit, a criminal act at that moment. ... The rationale for permitting brief, warrantless seizures is, after all, that it is impractical to demand strict compliance with the Fourth Amendment's ordinary probable-cause requirement in the face of ongoing or imminent criminal activity demanding "swift action predicated upon the on-the-spot observations of the officer on the beat." ... Observations raising suspicions of past criminality demand no such immediate action, but instead should appropriately trigger routine police investigation, which may ultimately generate sufficient information to blossom into probable cause.

Evaluated against this standard, the facts about Andrew Sokolow known to the DEA agents at the time they stopped him fall short of reasonably indicating that he was engaged at the time in criminal activity. It is highly significant that the DEA agents stopped Sokolow because he matched one of the DEA's "profiles" of a paradigmatic drug courier. In my view, a law enforcement officer's mechanistic application of a formula of personal and behavioral traits in deciding

whom to detain can only dull the officer's ability and determination to make sensitive and fact-specific inferences "in light of his experience," ... particularly in ambiguous or border-line cases. Reflexive reliance on a profile of a drug courier characteristics runs a far greater risk than does ordinary, case-by-case police work, of subjecting innocent individuals to unwarranted police harassment and detention. This risk is enhanced by the profile's "chameleon-like way of adapting to any particular set of observations."

... In asserting that it is not "somehow" relevant that the agents who stopped Sokolow did so in reliance on a prefabricated profile of criminal characteristics ... the majority thus ducks serious issues relating to a questionable law enforcement practice, to address the validity of which we granted certiorari in this case. ...

The facts known to the DEA agents at the time they detained the traveler in this case are scarcely ... suggestive of ongoing criminal activity. ... Sokolow gave no indications of evasive activity. On the contrary, the sole behavioral detail about Sokolow noted by the DEA agents was that he was nervous. With news accounts proliferating of plane crashes, near-collisions and air terrorism, there are manifold and good reasons for being agitated while awaiting flight, reasons that have nothing to do with one's involvement in a criminal endeavor.

The remaining circumstantial facts known about Sokolow considered either singly or together, are scarcely indicative of criminal activity. ... [T]he fact that Sokolow took a brief trip to a resort city for which he brought only carry-on luggage also "describe[s] a very large category of presumably innocent travelers." That Sokolow embarked from Miami, "a source city for illicit drugs," is no more suggestive of illegality; thousands of innocent persons travel from "source cities" every day and, judging from the DEA's testimony in past cases, nearly every major city in the country may be characterized as a source or distribution city. That Sokolow had his phone listed in another person's name also does not support the majority's assertion that the DEA agents reasonably believed Sokolow was using an alias; it is commonplace to have one's phone registered in the name of a roommate, which, it later turned out, was precisely what Sokolow had done. That Sokolow was dressed in a black jumpsuit and wore gold jewelry also provides no grounds for suspecting wrongdoing, the majority's repeated and unexplained allusions to Sokolow's style of dress notwithstanding. ... For law enforcement officers to base a search, even in part, on a pop guess that persons dressed in a particular fashion are likely to commit crimes not only stretches the concept of reasonable suspicion beyond recognition,

but also is inimical to the self-expression which the choice of wardrobe may provide. Finally, that Sokolow paid for his tickets in cash indicates no imminent or ongoing criminal activity. ... Making major cash purchases, while surely less common today, may simply reflect the traveler's aversion to, or inability to obtain, plastic money. ...

The fact is that, unlike the taking of patently evasive action ... the use of an alias ... the casing of a store ... the provision of a reliable report from an informant that wrongdoing is imminent ... nothing about the characteristics shown by airport traveler Sokolow reasonably suggests that criminal activity is afoot. ...

Other Cases: Using Profiles to Support Probable Cause

Reid v. Georgia, 448 U.S. 438 (1980)

Per Curiam.

Facts: [Reid, the petitioner] arrived at the Atlanta Airport on a commercial airline flight from Fort Lauderdale, Fla., in the early morning hours of August 14, 1978. The passengers left the plane in a single file and proceeded through the concourse. The petitioner was observed by an agent of the DEA, who was in the airport for the purpose of uncovering illicit commerce in narcotics. Separated from the petitioner by several persons was another man, who carried a shoulder bag like the one the petitioner carried. As they proceeded through the concourse past the baggage claim area, the petitioner occasionally looked backward in the direction of the second man. When they reached the main lobby of the terminal, the second man caught up with the petitioner and spoke briefly with him. They then left the terminal building together.

The DEA agent approached them outside of the building, identified himself as a federal narcotics agent, and asked them to show him their airline ticket stubs and identification, which they did. The airline tickets had been purchased with the petitioner's credit card and indicated that the men had stayed in Fort Lauderdale only one day. According to the agent's testimony, the men appeared nervous during the encounter. The agent then asked them if they would agree to return to the terminal and to consent to a search

of their persons and their shoulder bags. The agent testified that the petitioner nodded his head affirmatively, and that the other responded, "Yeah, okay." As the three of them entered the terminal, however, the petitioner began to run and before he was apprehended, abandoned his shoulder bag. The bag, when recovered, was found to contain cocaine.

[Trial court suppressed the cocaine, because it found that Reid was stopped without reasonable suspicion and the drugs were a result of that illegal seizure. The appellate court reversed that, finding that the stop was permissible because the drug profile gave articulable suspicion and Reid consented to return to terminal for search of his person and found that after Reid attempted to flee and discarded his bag there was then probable cause to search the bag].

The Fourth and Fourteenth Amendments' prohibition of searches and seizures that are not supported by some objective justification governs all seizures of the person, "including seizures that involve only a brief detention short of traditional arrest. ...While the Court has recognized that in some circumstances a person may be detained briefly, without probable cause to arrest him, any curtailment of a person's liberty by the police must be supported at least by a reasonable and articulable suspicion that the person seized is engaged in criminal activity. ...

The appellate court's conclusion in this case that the DEA agent reasonably suspected the petitioner of wrongdoing rested on the fact that the petitioner appeared to the agent to fit the so-called "drug courier profile," a somewhat informal compilation of characteristics believed to be typical of persons unlawfully carrying narcotics. Specifically, the court thought it relevant that (1) the petitioner had arrived from Fort Lauderdale, which the agent testified is a principal place of origin of cocaine sold elsewhere in the country, (2) the petitioner arrived in the early morning, when law enforcement activity is diminished, (3) he and his companion appeared to the agent to be trying to conceal the fact that they were traveling together, and (4) they apparently had no luggage other than their shoulder bags.

We conclude that the agent could not, as a matter of law, have reasonably suspected the petitioner of criminal activity on the basis of these observed circumstances. Of the evidence relied on, only the fact that the petitioner preceded another person and occasionally looked backward at him as they proceeded through the concourse relates to their particular conduct. The other circumstances describe a very large category of presumably innocent travelers, who would be subject to virtually random seizures were the Court to conclude that as little foundation as there was in this case could justify a seizure. Nor can we agree, on this record, that the manner in which the petitioner and his companion walked through the airport reasonably could have led the agent to suspect them of wrongdoing. . . . The agent's belief that the petitioner and his companion were attempting to conceal the fact that they were traveling together, a belief that was more an "inchoate and unparticularized suspicion or 'hunch,'" . . . than a fair inference in the light of his experience, is simply too slender a reed to support the seizure in this case.

Informants

Probable cause may be established on the affidavit by referring to information known by the officer based upon personal observations or conveyed to the officer by other officers who have made observations. Additionally, warrant applications frequently spell out the officer's training and experience to show why seemingly meaningless information may be indicative of criminal behavior. (See, e.g., the majority opinion in *Sokolow,* above). Police officers also rely on second hand information from non-police sources. These sources are referred to as "informants" and they are generally categorized as either named or unnamed informants. (See, e.g., the facts in *Draper and J.L., above*)

To establish probable cause on the basis of informant's statements, the court will require an adequate foundation be established. In the past the court relied on the "*Aguilar/Spinelli*" test that required sufficient information articulated in the affidavit to show that the informant was both reliable and had an adequate basis of knowledge.[60] In 1983, however, the court in *Illinois v. Gates* abandoned

---

[60] The veracity prong concerns the informant's reliability. The affidavit must demonstrate that the informant is believable or that the information is reliable. "Fine distinctions may be drawn between establishing reliability by showing that the informant is credible and establishing reliability by showing that the information comes from circumstances assuring that the particular information is indeed trustworthy on a specific occasion." (Oregon Department of Justice, Oregon Search and Seizure Manual, 2008).
Reliability/veracity considerations include:

> whether the magistrate has sufficient information to make a determination of a confidential informant's trustworthiness;

> whether the confidential informant made statements against his or her own interest (in which case these are deemed to be trustworthy);

> whether the informant is known to have been reliable in the past;

> whether the situation involved a controlled buy where the police have searched the informant prior to the buy, and watch the informant to and from the place of purchase;

that two-pronged test (see below). Some states still maintain the dual-pronged approach and earlier case law refers to them, so it is still important to understand those prongs. Moreover, those factors considered in determining veracity will be part of the "totality of the circumstances" courts will now consider.

As you read *Illinois v. Gates*, note why under the two-pronged approach would have resulted in the warrant not being granted.

ILLINOIS v. GATES
462 U.S. 213 (1983)

JUSTICE REHNQUIST delivered the opinion of the Court.

On May 3, 1978, the Bloomingdale Police Department received by mail an anonymous handwritten letter which read as follows:

This letter is to inform you that you have a couple in your town who strictly make their living on selling drugs. They are Sue and Lance Gates, they live on Greenway, off Bloomingdale Rd. in the condominiums. Most of their buys are done in Florida. Sue his wife drives their car to Florida, where she leaves it to be loaded up with drugs, then Lance flys down and drives it back. Sue flys back

after she drops the car off in Florida. May 3 she is driving down there again and Lance will be flying down in a few days to drive it back. At the time Lance drives the car back he has the trunk loaded with over $100,000.00 in drugs. Presently, they have over $100,000.00 worth of drugs in their basement.

They brag about the fact they never have to work, and make their entire living on pushers.

I guarantee if you watch them carefully you will make a big catch. They are friends with some big drug dealers, who visit their house often.

---

whether there has been independent police corroboration supporting the informant's statements;

whether the corroboration of information was limited to easily identifiable and innocent information (that alone may not establish the informant's veracity;

whether there was cross-corroboration with other informants; whether the information was very detailed (which tends to indicate informant reliability);

whether there was a polygraph examiner that established the reliability of the informant's information (cannot be sole factor);

whether there is any indication of bias or a reason to fabricate by the informant;

whether the informant has a criminal history or background; and

whether the information is from a disinterested citizen (even if unnamed, a disinterested citizen informant is considered more reliable than an interested party.)

The second prong, the basis of knowledge prong, requires the affiant to establish how the informant knows what he or she knows or doesn't know. Some statutes and cases require that the affidavit set forth facts justifying the inference that the informant was in a position to perceive the events the informant reported to the police. Some court considerations involving informant's basis of knowledge include:

whether the affiant set forth the informant's basis of knowledge (if not the information must be disregarded);

whether every assertion of fact from the informant is related to how the police officer or informant came to know that the assertion is true; and

whether the informant personally observed or directly observed what is being reported in the affidavit.

The letter was referred by the Chief of Police of the Bloomingdale Police Department to Detective Mader, who decided to pursue the tip. Mader learned, from the office of the Illinois Secretary of State, that an Illinois driver's license had been issued to one Lance Gates, residing at a stated address in Bloomingdale. He contacted a confidential informant, whose examination of certain financial records revealed a more recent address for the Gates, and he also learned from a police officer assigned to O'Hare Airport that "L. Gates" had made a reservation on Eastern Airlines Flight 245 to West Palm Beach, Fla., scheduled to depart from Chicago on May 5 at 4:15 p.m. Mader then made arrangements with an agent of the Drug Enforcement Administration for surveillance of the May 5 Eastern Airlines flight. The agent later reported to Mader that Gates had boarded the flight, and that federal agents in Florida had observed him arrive in West Palm Beach and take a taxi to the nearby Holiday Inn.

They also reported that Gates went to a room registered to one Susan Gates and that, at 7:00 a.m. the next morning, Gates and an unidentified woman left the motel in a Mercury bearing Illinois license plates and drove northbound on an interstate frequently used by travelers to the Chicago area. In addition, the DEA [Drug Enforcement Administration] agent informed Mader that the license plate number on the Mercury was registered to a Hornet station wagon owned by Gates.

Mader signed an affidavit setting forth the foregoing facts, and submitted it to a judge of the Circuit Court of DuPage County, together with a copy of the anonymous letter. The judge of that court thereupon issued a search warrant for the Gateses' residence and for their automobile. The judge, in deciding to issue the warrant, could have determined that the modus operandi of the Gateses had been substantially corroborated.

At 5:15 a.m. on March 7th, only 36 hours after he had flown out of Chicago, Lance Gates, and his wife, returned to their home in Bloomingdale, driving the car in which they had left West Palm Beach some 22 hours earlier. The Bloomingdale police were awaiting them, searched the trunk of the Mercury, and uncovered approximately 350 pounds of marijuana. A search of the Gateses' home revealed marijuana, weapons, and other contraband.

The Illinois Supreme Court concluded — and we are inclined to agree — that, standing alone, the anonymous letter sent to the Bloomingdale Police Department would not provide the basis for a magistrate's determination that there was probable cause to believe contraband would be found in the Gateses' car and home. The letter provides virtually nothing from which one might conclude that its author is either honest or his information reliable; likewise, the letter gives absolutely no indication of the basis for the writer's predictions regarding the Gateses' criminal activities. Something more was required, then, before a magistrate could conclude that there was probable cause to believe that contraband would be found in the Gateses' home and car. . . .

. . . .

The Illinois court, alluding to an elaborate set of legal rules that have developed among various lower courts to enforce the "two-pronged test," found that the test had not been satisfied. First, the "veracity" prong was not satisfied because, "there was simply no basis [for] . . .conclud[ing] that the anonymous person [who wrote the letter to the Bloomingdale Police Department] was credible." The court indicated that corroboration by police of details contained in the letter might never satisfy the "veracity" prong, and in any event, could not do so if, as in the present case, only "innocent" details are corroborated. . . .In addition, the letter gave no indication of the basis of its writer's knowledge of the Gateses' activities. The Illinois court understood *Spinelli* as permitting the detail contained in a tip to be used to infer that the informant had a reliable basis for his statements, but it thought that the anonymous letter failed to provide sufficient detail to permit such an inference. Thus, it concluded that no showing of probable cause had been made.

We agree with the Illinois Supreme Court that an informant's "veracity," "reliability" and "basis of knowledge" are all highly relevant in determining the value of his report. We do not agree, however, that these elements should be understood as entirely separate and independent requirements to be rigidly exacted in every case. . . . Rather, . . . they should be understood simply as closely intertwined issues that may usefully illuminate the commonsense, practical question whether there is "probable cause" to believe that contraband or evidence is located in a particular place.

This totality-of-the-circumstances approach is far more consistent with our prior treatment of probable cause than is any rigid demand that specific "tests" be satisfied by every informant's tip.

[P]robable cause is a fluid concept — turning on the assessment of probabilities in particular factual contexts — not readily, or even usefully, reduced to a neat set of legal rules. Informants' tips doubtless come in many shapes and sizes from many different types of persons. "Informants' tips, like all other clues and evidence coming to a policeman on the scene, may vary greatly in their value and reliability." Rigid legal rules are ill-suited to an area of such diversity. "One simple rule will not cover every situation."

Moreover, the "two-pronged test" directs analysis into two largely independent channels — the informant's "veracity" or "reliability" and his "basis of knowledge." There are persuasive arguments against according these two elements such independent status. Instead, they are better understood as relevant considerations in the totality-of-the-circumstances analysis that traditionally has guided probable cause determinations: a deficiency in one may be compensated for, in determining the overall reliability of a tip, by a strong showing as to the other, or by some other indicia of reliability. . . .

If, for example, a particular informant is known for the unusual reliability of his predictions of certain types of criminal activities in a locality, his failure, in a particular case, to thoroughly set forth the basis of his knowledge surely should not serve as an absolute bar to a finding of probable cause based on his tip. . . .Likewise, if an unquestionably honest citizen comes forward with a report of criminal activity — which if fabricated would subject him to criminal liability — we have found rigorous scrutiny of the basis of his knowledge unnecessary. . . .

Conversely, even if we entertain some doubt as to an informant's motives, his explicit and detailed description of alleged wrongdoing, along with a statement that the event was observed firsthand, entitles his tip to greater weight than might otherwise be the case.

Unlike a totality-of-the-circumstances analysis, which permits a balanced assessment of the relative weights of all the various indicia of reliability (and unreliability) attending an informant's tip, the "two-pronged test" has encouraged an excessively technical dissection of informants' tips, with undue attention being focused on isolated issues that cannot sensibly be divorced from the other facts presented to the magistrate.

... Finely tuned standards such as proof beyond a reasonable doubt or by a preponderance of the evidence, useful in formal trials, have no place in the magistrate's decision. While an effort to fix some general, numerically precise degree of certainty corresponding to "probable cause" may not be helpful, it is clear that "only the probability, and not a prima facie showing, of criminal activity is the standard of probable cause." . . .

We also have recognized that affidavits "are normally drafted by nonlawyers in the midst and haste of a criminal investigation. Technical requirements of elaborate specificity once exacted under common law pleading have no proper place in this area." . . .

... The rigorous inquiry into the *Spinelli* prongs and the complex superstructure of evidentiary and analytical rules that some have seen implicit in our *Spinelli* decision, cannot be reconciled with the fact that many warrants are — quite properly, . . .issued on the basis of nontechnical common-sense judgments of laymen applying a standard less demanding than those used in more formal legal proceedings. . . .

Similarly, we have repeatedly said that after-the-fact scrutiny by courts of the sufficiency of an affidavit should not take the form of de novo review. A magistrate's determination of probable cause should be paid great deference by reviewing courts."...

. . . .

Ordinary citizens, like ordinary witnesses, generally do not provide extensive recitations of the basis of their everyday observations. Likewise, as the Illinois Supreme Court observed in this case, the veracity of persons supplying anonymous tips is by hypothesis largely unknown and unknowable. As a result, anonymous tips seldom could survive a rigorous application of either of the *Spinelli* prongs. Yet, such tips, particularly when supplemented by independent police investigation, frequently contribute to the solution of otherwise "perfect crimes." While a conscientious assessment of the basis for crediting such tips is required by the Fourth Amendment, a standard that leaves virtually no place for anonymous citizen informants is not.

For all these reasons, we conclude that it is wiser to abandon the "two-pronged test" established by our decisions in *Agular* and *Spinelli*. In its place we reaffirm the totality of the circumstances analysis that traditionally has informed probable cause determinations.

We are convinced that this flexible, easily applied standard will better achieve the accommodation of public and private interests that the Fourth Amendment requires than does the approach that has developed from *Agular* and *Spinelli*. . . .

Stale Information

Information used to form the basis of probable cause stated on a warrant must be current and not stale. If, for example, a police officer has information that the suspect murdered someone and stashed the body, the officer should not wait one or two weeks before going to apply for a warrant to search the residence for evidence of a crime. Why? Well, it is highly likely that, in the intervening week or two, the corpse will be moved and is no longer in the residence. Waiting two weeks to apply for the warrant makes the information (and the body) stale. When the location to be searched is the suspect's residence, the affidavit must also establish probable cause to believe that the evidence is *currently* located in the suspect's residence as well as establishing the probable cause to connect the suspect with the crime — the mere fact that the suspect resides there is not necessarily sufficient to establish the nexus.

Oath Or Affirmation

The Fourth Amendment requires that warrants be supported by statements made under oath or affirmation. To obtain a warrant, an officer must 1) present a written affidavit to a magistrate that requests that a warrant be issued, 2) swear under oath or affirmation that the information in the affidavit is truthful, and 3) convince the magistrate that the information sworn to establishes probable cause to believe a search warrant or arrest warrant is justified. In seeking a warrant, the officer will generally appear before the judge alone. The judge will question the officer about the affidavit, and require that the officer take an oath that the information in the affidavit is correct to the officer's knowledge. The Court has held that defendants may challenge the truthfulness of factual statements made in the affidavit supporting the warrant — even after the warrant had been issued. The hearing in which the defendant challenges the facts in the affidavit is called a "Franks hearing" after the case

Franks v. Delaware, 438 U.S. 154 (1978) in which the Court approved of this process. If those false statements were necessary to the Magistrate Judge's probable-cause determination, the warrant would be "voided." (See e.g., *Herring v. United States*, 555 U.S. 1 (2009) (below).) Sometimes, a telephonic warrant is appropriate. In this case, the judge instructs the officer to make an oath or affirmation telephonically, and then has the officer reaffirm this as soon as the officer can be in the physical presence of the judge.

The Particularity Requirement

Under the Fourth Amendment a warrant must "particularly describe the place to be searched, and the persons or things to be seized." *Maron v. United States*, 275 U.S. 192 (1927) indicates that the goal of the particularity requirement is to guarantee that nothing is left to the discretion of the police. With regard to residences, the warrant affidavit must describe the targeted residence with sufficient details that any officer with the warrant can, with reasonable effort, ascertain and identify the place intended. *Steele v. United States*, 267 US 498 (1925). With regard to a warrant authorizing the search or seizure of a person, the person should be or described in the supporting affidavit and the warrant, itself, must contain a similar description to comply with particularity requirements.

GROH v. RAMIREZ
540 U.S. 551 (2004)

JUSTICE STEVENS delivered the opinion of the Court.

. . .

Respondents, Joseph Ramirez and members of his family, live on a large ranch in Butte-Silver Bow County, Montana. Petitioner, Jeff Groh, has been a Special Agent for the Bureau of Alcohol, Tobacco and Firearms (ATF) since 1989. In February 1997, a concerned citizen informed petitioner that on a number of visits to respondents' ranch the visitor had seen a large stock of weaponry, including an automatic rifle, grenades, a grenade launcher, and a rocket launcher. Based on that information, petitioner prepared and signed an application for a warrant to search the ranch. The application stated that the search was for "any automatic firearms or parts to automatic weapons, destructive devices to include but not limited to grenades, grenade launchers, rocket launchers, and any and all receipts pertaining to the purchase or manufacture of automatic weapons or explosive devices or launchers." . . . Petitioner supported the application with a detailed affidavit, which he also prepared and executed, that set forth the basis for his belief that the listed items were concealed on the ranch. Petitioner then

presented these documents to a Magistrate, along with a warrant form that petitioner also had completed. The Magistrate signed the warrant form.

Although the application particularly described the place to be searched and the contraband petitioner expected to find, the warrant itself was less specific; it failed to identify any of the items that petitioner intended to seize. In the portion of the form that called for a description of the "person or property" to be seized, petitioner typed a description of respondents' two-story blue house rather than the alleged stockpile of firearms. The warrant did not incorporate by reference the itemized list contained in the application. It did, however, recite that the Magistrate was satisfied the affidavit established probable cause to believe that contraband was concealed on the premises, and that sufficient grounds existed for the warrant's issuance.

The day after the Magistrate issued the warrant, petitioner led a team of law enforcement officers, including both federal agents and members of the local sheriff's department, in the search of respondents' premises. Although respondent Joseph Ramirez was not home, his wife and children were. Petitioner states that he orally described the objects of the search to Mrs. Ramirez in person and to Mr. Ramirez by telephone. According to Mrs. Ramirez, however, petitioner explained only that he was searching for " 'an explosive device in a box.' " At any rate, the officers' search uncovered no illegal weapons or explosives. When the officers left, petitioner gave Mrs. Ramirez a copy of the search warrant, but not a copy of the application, which had been sealed. The following day, in response to a request from respondents' attorney, petitioner faxed the attorney a copy of the page of the application that listed the items to be seized. No charges were filed against the Ramirezes.

...

The warrant was plainly invalid. The Fourth Amendment states unambiguously that "no Warrants shall issue, but upon probable cause, supported by Oath or affirmation, and particularly describing the place to be searched, and the persons or things to be seized." The warrant in this case complied with the first three of these requirements: It was based on probable cause and supported by a sworn affidavit, and it described particularly the place of the search. On the fourth requirement, however, the warrant failed altogether. Indeed, petitioner concedes that "the warrant . . .was deficient in particularity because it provided no description of the type of evidence sought."

The fact that the application adequately described the "things to be seized" does not save the warrant from its facial invalidity. The Fourth Amendment by its terms requires particularity in the warrant, not in the supporting documents. ...We do not say that the Fourth Amendment forbids a warrant from cross-referencing other documents. . . [b]ut in this case the warrant did not incorporate other documents by reference, nor did either the affidavit or the application (which had been placed under seal) accompany the warrant. ...

Petitioner argues that even though the warrant was invalid, the search nevertheless was

"reasonable" within the meaning of the Fourth Amendment. He notes that a Magistrate authorized the search on the basis of adequate evidence of probable cause, that petitioner orally described to respondents the items to be seized, and that the search did not exceed the limits intended by the Magistrate and described by petitioner. Thus, petitioner maintains, his search of respondents' ranch was functionally equivalent to a search authorized by a valid warrant. We disagree. This warrant did not simply omit a few items from a list of many to be seized, or misdescribe a few of several items. Nor did it make what fairly could be characterized as a mere technical mistake or typographical error. Rather, in the space set aside for a description of the items to be seized, the warrant stated that the items consisted of a "single dwelling residence . . .blue in color." In other words, the warrant did not describe the items to be seized at all. In this respect the warrant was so obviously deficient that we must regard the search as "warrantless" within the meaning of our case law. ...

We have clearly stated that the presumptive rule against warrantless searches applies with equal force to searches whose only defect is a lack of particularity in the warrant.

. . . .

A particular warrant . . . "assures the individual whose property is searched or seized of the lawful authority of the executing officer, his need to search, and the limits of his power to search." ...

It is incumbent on the officer executing a search warrant to ensure the search is lawfully authorized and lawfully conducted. ... Because petitioner did not have in his possession a warrant particularly describing the things he intended to seize, proceeding with the search was clearly "unreasonable" under the Fourth Amendment. The Court of Appeals correctly held that the search was unconstitutional.

MESSERSCHMIDT V. MILLENDER
565 U.S. 535 (2012)

CHIEF JUSTICE ROBERTS delivered the opinion of the court.

Petitioner police officers conducted a search of respondents' home pursuant to a warrant issued by a neutral magistrate. The warrant authorized a search for all guns and gang-related material, in connection with the investigation of a known gang member for shooting at his ex-girlfriend with a pistol-gripped sawed-off shotgun, because she had "call[ed] the cops" on him. Respondents [the Millenders] brought an action seeking to hold the officers personally liable under 42 U. S. C. §1983, alleging that the search violated their Fourth Amendment rights because there was not sufficient probable cause to believe the items sought were evidence of a crime. In particular, respondents argued that there was no basis to search for all guns simply because the suspect owned and had used a sawed-off shotgun, and no reason to search for gang material because the shooting at the ex-girlfriend for "call[ing] the cops" was solely a domestic dispute. The Court of Appeals for the Ninth Circuit held that the warrant was invalid, and that the officers were not entitled to immunity from personal liability because this invalidity was so obvious that any reasonable officer would have recognized it, despite the magistrate's approval.

. . . .

Messerschmidt prepared two warrants: one to authorize Bowen's arrest and one to authorize the search of 2234 East 120th Street. An attachment to the search warrant described the property that would be the object of the search:

> "All handguns, rifles, or shotguns of any caliber, or any firearms capable of firing ammunition, or firearms or devices modified or designed to allow it [sic] to fire ammunition. All caliber of ammunition, miscellaneous gun parts, gun cleaning kits, holsters which could hold or have held any caliber handgun being sought. Any receipts or paperwork, showing the purchase, ownership, or possession of the handguns being sought. Any firearm for which there is no proof of ownership. Any firearm capable of firing or chambered to fire any caliber ammunition.

> "Articles of evidence showing street gang membership or affiliation with any Street Gang to include but not limited to any reference to 'Mona Park Crips', including writings or graffiti depicting gang membership, activity or identity. Articles of personal property tending to establish the identity of person [sic] in control of the premise or premises. Any photographs or photograph albums depicting persons, vehicles, weapons or locations, which may appear relevant to gang membership, or which may depict the item being sought and or believed to be evidence in the case being investigated on this warrant, or which may depict evidence of criminal activity. Additionally to include any gang indicia that would establish the persons being sought in this warrant, affiliation or membership with the 'Mona Park Crips' street gang."

Two affidavits accompanied Messerschmidt's warrant applications. The first affidavit described Messerschmidt's extensive law enforcement experience, including that he had served as a peace officer for 14 years, that he was then assigned to a "specialized unit" "investigating gang related crimes and arresting gang members for various violations of the law," that he had been involved in "hundreds of gang related incidents, contacts, and or arrests" during his time on the force, and that he had "received specialized training in the field of gang related crimes" and training in "gang related shootings."

The second affidavit — expressly incorporated into the search warrant — explained why Messerschmidt believed there was sufficient probable cause to support the warrant. That affidavit described the facts of the incident involving Kelly and Bowen in great detail, including the weapon used in the assault. The affidavit recounted that Kelly had identified Bowen as the assailant and that she thought Bowen might be found at 2234 East 120th Street. It also reported that Messerschmidt had "conducted an extensive background search on the suspect by utilizing departmental records, state computer records, and other police agency records," and that from that information he had concluded that Bowen resided at 2234 East 120th Street.

The affidavit requested that the search warrant be endorsed for night service because "information provided by the victim and the cal-gang data base" indicated that Bowen had "gang ties to the Mona Park Crip gang" and that "night service would provide an added element of safety to the community as well as for the deputy personnel serving the warrant." The affidavit concluded by noting that Messerschmidt "believe[d] that the items sought" would be in Bowen's possession and that "recovery of the weapon could be invaluable in the successful prosecution of the suspect involved in this case, and the curtailment of further crimes being committed."

Messerschmidt submitted the warrants to his supervisors — Sergeant Lawrence and Lieutenant Ornales — for review. Deputy District Attorney Janet Wilson also reviewed the materials and initialed the search warrant, indicating that she agreed with Messerschmidt's assessment of probable cause. Finally, Messerschmidt submitted the warrants to a magistrate. The magistrate approved the warrants and authorized night service.

The search warrant was served two days later by a team of officers that included Messerschmidt and Lawrence. Sheriff's deputies forced open the front door of 2234 East 120th Street and encountered Augusta

Millender — a woman in her seventies — and Millender's daughter and grandson. As instructed by the police, the Millenders went outside while the residence was secured but remained in the living room while the search was conducted. Bowen was not found in the residence. The search did, however, result in the seizure of Augusta Millender's shotgun, a California Social Services letter addressed to Bowen, and a box of .45-caliber ammunition.

…

Where the alleged Fourth Amendment violation involves a search or seizure pursuant to a warrant, the fact that a neutral magistrate has issued a warrant is the clearest indication that the officers acted in an objectively reasonable manner or, as we have sometimes put it, in "objective good faith." Nonetheless, under our precedents, the fact that a neutral magistrate has issued a warrant authorizing the allegedly unconstitutional search or seizure does not end the inquiry into objective reasonableness. Rather, we have recognized an exception allowing suit when "it is obvious that no reasonably competent officer would have concluded that a warrant should issue." The "shield of immunity" otherwise conferred by the warrant, will be lost, for example, where the warrant was "based on an affidavit so lacking in indicia of probable cause as to render official belief in its existence entirely unreasonable."

According to the Millenders, the officers "failed to provide *any* facts or circumstances from which a magistrate could properly conclude that there was probable cause to seize the broad classes of items being sought," and "[n]o reasonable officer would have presumed that such a warrant was valid." We disagree.

Noting that "the affidavit indicated exactly what item was evidence of a crime — the 'black sawed off shotgun with a pistol grip,' " they argue that "[n]o facts established that Bowen possessed any other firearms, let alone that such firearms (if they existed) were 'contraband or evidence of a crime.'"

Even if the scope of the warrant were overbroad in authorizing a search for all guns when there was information only about a specific one, that specific one was a sawed-off shotgun with a pistol grip, owned by a known gang member, who had just fired the weapon five times in public in an attempt to murder another person, on the asserted ground that she had "call[ed] the cops" on him. Under these circumstances — set forth in the warrant — it would not have been unreasonable for an officer to conclude that there was a "fair probability" that the sawed-off shotgun was not the only firearm Bowen owned. And it certainly would have been reasonable for an officer to assume that Bowen's sawed-off shotgun was illegal. Evidence of one crime is not always evidence of several, but given Bowen's possession of one illegal gun, his gang membership, his willingness to use the gun to kill someone, and his concern about the police, a reasonable officer could conclude that there would be additional illegal guns among others that Bowen owned.

A reasonable officer also could believe that seizure of the firearms was necessary to prevent further assaults on Kelly. California law allows a magistrate to issue a search warrant for items "in the possession of any person with the intent to use them as a means of committing a public offense," and the warrant application submitted by the officers specifically referenced this provision as a basis for the search. Bowen had already attempted to murder Kelly once with a firearm, and had yelled "I'll kill you" as she tried to escape from him. A reasonable officer could conclude that Bowen would make another attempt on Kelly's life and that he possessed other firearms "with the intent to use them" to that end.

. . . .

With respect to the warrant's authorization to search for evidence of gang membership, the Millenders contend that "no reasonable officer could have believed that the affidavit presented to the magistrate contained a sufficient basis to conclude that the gang paraphernalia sought was contraband or evidence of a crime." They argue that "the magistrate [could not] have reasonably concluded, based on the affidavit, that Bowen's gang membership had anything to do with the crime under investigation" because "[t]he affidavit described a 'spousal assault' that ensued after Kelly decided to end her 'on going dating relationship' with Bowen" and "[n]othing in that description suggests that the crime was gang-related."

A reasonable officer could certainly view Bowen's attack as motivated not by the souring of his romantic relationship with Kelly but instead by a desire to prevent her from disclosing details of his gang activity to the police. She was, after all, no longer linked with him as a girlfriend; he had assaulted her in the past; and she had indeed called the cops on him. And, as the affidavit supporting the warrant made clear, Kelly had in fact given the police information about Bowen's gang ties

It would therefore not have been unreasonable — based on the facts set out in the affidavit — for an officer to believe that evidence regarding Bowen's gang affiliation would prove helpful in prosecuting him for the attack on Kelly. . . . Not only would such evidence help to establish motive, either apart from or in addition to any domestic dispute, it would also support the bringing of additional, related charges against Bowen for the assault. . . .

In addition, a reasonable officer could believe that evidence demonstrating Bowen's membership in a gang might prove helpful in impeaching Bowen or rebutting various defenses he could raise at trial. . .

. . . .

Whatever the use to which evidence of Bowen's gang involvement might ultimately have been put, it would not have been "entirely unreasonable" for an officer to believe that the facts set out in the affidavit established a fair probability that such evidence would aid the prosecution of Bowen for the criminal acts at issue.

Whether any of these facts, standing alone or taken together, actually establish probable cause is a question we need not decide. Qualified immunity "gives government officials breathing room to make reasonable but mistaken judgments." The officers' judgment that the scope of the warrant was supported by probable cause may have been mistaken, but it was not "plainly incompetent."

On top of all this, the fact that the officers sought and obtained approval of the warrant application from a superior and a deputy district attorney before submitting it to the magistrate provides further support for the conclusion that an officer could reasonably have believed that the scope of the warrant was supported by probable cause. . . .In light of the foregoing, it cannot be said that "no officer of reasonable competence would have requested the warrant." Indeed, a contrary conclusion would mean not only that Messerschmidt and Lawrence were "plainly incompetent," but that their supervisor, the deputy district attorney, and the magistrate were as well.

. . . .

[In *Groh* we] . . . held that officers who carried out a warrant-approved search were not entitled to qualified immunity because the warrant in question failed to describe the items to be seized *at all*. . . . [But] "even a cursory reading of the warrant in [that] case — perhaps just a simple glance — would have revealed a glaring deficiency that any reasonable police officer would have known was constitutionally fatal."

The instant case is not remotely similar. In contrast to *Groh*, any defect here would not have been obvious from the face of the warrant. . . ."

JUSTICE KAGAN, concurring in part and dissenting in part.

[She agreed that the officers should have received qualified immunity for the search of the firearms but disagreed that they should have any immunity for the search for the gang-related evidence.]

The Court, however, goes astray when it holds that a reasonable officer could have thought the warrant valid in approving a search for evidence of "street gang membership," . . . The problem for the Court is that nothing in the application supports a link between Bowen's gang membership and that shooting. Contra the Court's elaborate theory-spinning, Messerschmidt's affidavit in fact characterized the violent assault only as a domestic dispute, not as a gang-related one. . . . And that description is consistent with the most natural understanding of the events. The warrant application thus had a hole at its very center: It lacked any explanation of how gang items would (or even might) provide evidence of the domestic assault the police were investigating."

JUSTICE SOTOMAYOR, with whom JUSTICE GINSBURG joins, dissenting

. . . .

The Court nonetheless concludes that the officers are entitled to qualified immunity because their conduct was "objectively reasonable." I could not disagree more. All 13 federal judges who previously considered this case had little difficulty concluding that the police officers' search for any gang-related material violated the Fourth Amendment. And a substantial majority agreed that the police's search for both gang-related material and all firearms not only violated the Fourth Amendment, but was objectively unreasonable. Like them, I believe that any "reasonably well-trained officer in petitioner's position would have known that his affidavit failed to establish probable cause."

We have repeatedly and recently warned appellate courts, "far removed from the scene," against second-guessing the judgments made by the police or reweighing the facts as they stood before the district court. The majority's decision today is totally inconsistent with those principles.

The inquiry our precedents demand is not whether different conclusions might conceivably be drawn from the crime scene. Rather, it is whether "a reasonably well-trained officer in petitioner's position would have known that his affidavit failed to establish probable cause." The operative question in this case, therefore, is whether — given that, as petitioners comprehended, the crime itself was not gang related — a reasonable officer nonetheless could have believed he had probable cause to seek a warrant to search the suspect's residence for all evidence of affiliation not only with the suspect's street gang, but "any Street Gang." He could not.

The Court offers two secondary explanations for why a search for gang-related items might have been justified, but they are equally unpersuasive. First, the majority suggests that such evidence hypothetically "might prove helpful in impeaching Bowen or rebutting various defenses he could raise at trial." That is a non-starter. The Fourth Amendment does not permit the police to search for evidence solely because it could be admissible for impeachment or rebuttal purposes. If it did, the police would be equally entitled to obtain warrants to rifle through the papers of anyone reasonably suspected of a crime for all evidence of his bad character, or any evidence of any "crime, wrong, or other act" that might prove the defendant's "motive, opportunity, intent, preparation, plan, knowledge, identity, absence of mistake, or lack of accident," . . . Indeed, the majority's rationale presumably would authorize the police to search the residence of every member of Bowen's street gang for similar weapons — which likewise "might [have] prove[d] helpful in impeaching Bowen or rebutting various defenses he could raise at trial." It has long been the case, however, that such general searches, detached from probable cause, are impermissible. By their own admission, however, the officers were not searching for gang-related indicia to bolster some hypothetical impeachment theory, but for other reasons: because "photos sought re gang membership could be linked with other gang members, evidencing criminal activity as gang affiliation is an enhancement to criminal charges." That kind of fishing expedition for evidence of unidentified criminal activity committed by unspecified persons was the very evil the Fourth Amendment was intended to prevent.

Simply finding gang-related paraphernalia, . . . would have done little to establish probable cause that particular evidence found in the home was connected to Bowen, rather than any of the several other active gang members who resided full time at the Millender home. Moreover, it would have done nothing to establish that Bowen had committed the non-gang-related crime specified in the warrant.

The Court also errs by concluding that petitioners could have reasonably concluded that they had probable cause to search for all firearms. ... It is small wonder that the District Court found these arguments "nonsensical and unpersuasive." It bears repeating that the Founders adopted the Fourth Amendment to protect against searches for evidence of unspecified crimes. And merely possessing other firearms is not a crime at all.

. . .

The warrant set forth no specific facts or particularized explanation establishing probable cause to believe that other guns found in the home were connected to the crime specified in the warrant or were otherwise illegal. While the Court hypothesizes that the police could have searched for all firearms to uncover evidence of yet unnamed crimes, the warrant specified that the police were investigating one particular crime — "an assault with a deadly weapon." And the police officers confirmed that their search was targeted to find the gun related to "the crime at issue."

MARYLAND v. GARRISON
480 U.S. 79 (1987)

JUSTICE STEVENS delivered the opinion of the Court.

[Facts Summarized:

Police entered Garrison's apartment while executing a search warrant and arrest warrant for McWebb and his residence. In getting the warrant, they did not realize there were two apartments on the third floor of McWebb's dwelling house. They found drugs in Garrison's apartment, and as soon as they discovered they were in the wrong place, they discontinued their search. The warrant authorized search of the premises known as 2036 Park Avenue, third floor apartment. The warrant was otherwise valid and supported by probable cause.]

. . . All of the officers reasonably believed that they were searching McWebb's apartment. No further search of respondent's apartment was made.

The matter on which there is a difference of opinion concerns the proper interpretation of the warrant. A literal reading of its plain language, as well as the language used in the application for the warrant, indicates that it was intended to authorize a search of the entire third floor. ...

In our view, the case presents two separate constitutional issues, one concerning the validity of the warrant and the other concerning the reasonableness of the manner in which it was executed. We shall discuss the questions separately.

The Warrant Clause of the Fourth Amendment categorically prohibits the issuance of any warrant except one "particularly describing the place to be searched and the persons or things to be seized." The manifest purpose of this particularity requirement was to prevent general searches. By limiting the authorization to search to the specific areas and things for which there is probable cause to search, the requirement ensures that the search will be

carefully tailored to its justifications, and will not take on the character of the wide-ranging exploratory searches the Framers intended to prohibit. Thus, the scope of a lawful search is "defined by the object of the search and the places in which there is probable cause to believe that it may be found. Just as probable cause to believe that a stolen lawnmower may be found in a garage will not support a warrant to search an upstairs bedroom, probable cause to believe that undocumented aliens are being transported in a van will not justify a warrantless search of a suitcase." In this case there is no claim that the "persons or things to be seized" were inadequately described or that there was no probable cause to believe that those things might be found in "the place to be searched" as it was described in the warrant. With the benefit of hindsight, however, we now know that the description of that place was broader than appropriate because it was based on the mistaken belief that there was only one apartment on the third floor of the building at 2036 Park Avenue. The question is whether that factual mistake invalidated a warrant that undoubtedly would have been valid if it had reflected a completely accurate understanding of the building's floor plan.

Plainly, if the officers had known, or even if they should have known, that there were two separate dwelling units on the third floor of 2036 Park Avenue, they would have been obligated to exclude respondent's apartment from the scope of the requested warrant. But we must judge the constitutionality of their conduct in light of the information available to them at the time they acted. Those items of evidence that emerge after the warrant is issued have no bearing on whether or not a warrant was validly issued. Just as the discovery of contraband cannot validate a warrant invalid when issued, so is it equally clear that the discovery of facts demonstrating that a valid warrant was unnecessarily broad does not retroactively invalidate the warrant. The validity of the warrant must be assessed on the basis of the information that the officers disclosed, or had a duty to discover and to disclose, to the issuing Magistrate. On the basis of that information, we agree with the conclusion of all three Maryland courts that the warrant, insofar as it authorized a search that turned out to be ambiguous in scope, was valid when it issued.

The question whether the execution of the warrant violated respondent's constitutional right to be secure in his home is somewhat less clear. We have no difficulty concluding that the officers' entry into the third-floor common area was legal; they carried a warrant for those premises, and they were accompanied by McWebb, who provided the key that they used to open the door giving access to the third-floor common area. If the officers had known, or should have known, that the third floor contained two apartments before they entered the living quarters on the third floor, and thus had been aware of the error in the warrant, they would have been obligated to limit their search to McWebb's apartment. Moreover, as the officers recognized, they were required to discontinue the search of respondent's apartment as soon as they discovered that there were two separate units on the third floor and therefore were put on notice of the risk that they might be in a unit erroneously included within the terms of the warrant. The officers' conduct and the limits of the search were based on the information available as the search proceeded. While the purposes justifying a police search strictly limit the permissible extent of the search, the Court has also recognized the need to allow some latitude for honest mistakes that are made by officers in the dangerous and difficult process of making arrests and executing search warrants.

[T]he validity of the search of respondent's apartment pursuant to a warrant authorizing the search of the entire third floor depends on whether the officers' failure to realize the overbreadth of the warrant was objectively understandable and reasonable. Here it unquestionably was. The objective facts available to the officers at the time suggested no distinction between McWebb's apartment and the third-floor premises.

For that reason, the officers properly responded to the command contained in a valid warrant even if the warrant is interpreted as authorizing a search limited to McWebb's apartment rather than the entire third floor. Prior to the officers' discovery of the factual mistake, they perceived McWebb's apartment and the third-floor premises as one and the same; therefore their execution of the warrant reasonably included the entire third floor. Under either interpretation of the warrant, the officers' conduct was consistent with a reasonable effort to ascertain and identify the place intended to be searched within the meaning of the Fourth Amendment. .

Neutral And Detached Magistrate

Although the Fourth Amendment doesn't specifically mention that the warrant be issued by a neutral and detached magistrate, case law makes clear that the magistrate must be neutral and detached. The term neutral and detached magistrate refers to two qualities: neutrality meaning unbiased, and detached meaning that the magistrate should not be part of the executive branch (nor closely intertwined) — nor be overly interested in the outcome of the case.

Other Cases: Neutral and Detached Magistrate

Coolidge v. New Hampshire, 403 US 43 (1971) Facts: see above:	The petitioner's first claim is that the warrant authorizing the seizure and subsequent search of his 1951 Pontiac automobile was invalid because not issued by a "neutral and detached magistrate." ... [W]e agree with the petitioner that the warrant was invalid for this reason ....

The classic statement of the policy underlying the warrant requirement of the Fourth Amendment is that of Mr. Justice Jackson, writing for the Court in *Johnson v. United States*,

"The point of the Fourth Amendment, which often is not grasped by zealous officers, is not that it denies law enforcement the support of the usual inferences which reasonable men draw from evidence. Its protection consists in requiring that those inferences be drawn by a neutral and detached magistrate instead of being judged by the officer engaged in the often competitive enterprise of ferreting out crime. Any assumption that evidence sufficient to support a magistrate's disinterested determination to issue a search warrant will justify the officers in making a search without a warrant would reduce the Amendment to a nullity and leave the people's homes secure only in the discretion of police officers. . . . When the right of privacy must reasonably yield to the right of search is, as a rule, to be decided by a judicial officer, not by a policeman or government enforcement agent."

In this case, the determination of probable cause was made by the chief "government enforcement agent" of the State - the Attorney General - who was actively in charge of the investigation and later was to be chief prosecutor at the trial. …[T]he State argues that the Attorney General, who was unquestionably authorized as a justice of the peace to issue warrants under then-existing state law, did in fact act as a "neutral and detached magistrate." Further, the State claims that any magistrate, confronted with the showing of probable cause made by the Manchester chief of police, would have issued the warrant in question. To the first proposition it is enough to answer that there could hardly be a more appropriate setting than this for a per se rule of disqualification rather than a case-by-case evaluation of all the circumstances. Without disrespect to the state law enforcement agent here involved, the whole point of the basic rule so well expressed by Mr. Justice Jackson is that prosecutors and policemen simply cannot be asked to maintain the requisite neutrality with regard to their own investigations - the "competitive enterprise" that must rightly engage their single-minded attention As for the proposition that the existence of probable cause renders noncompliance with the warrant procedure an irrelevance, it is enough to cite *Agnello v. United States*:

"Belief, however well founded, that an article sought is concealed in a dwelling house furnishes no justification for a search of that place without a warrant. And such searches are held unlawful notwithstanding facts unquestionably showing probable cause."

But the New Hampshire Supreme Court, in upholding the conviction . . . [erroneously] . . . relied upon the theory that even if the warrant procedure here in issue would clearly violate the standards imposed on the Federal Government by the Fourth Amendment, it is not forbidden the States under the Fourteenth.

. . .

But it is too plain for extensive discussion that this now abandoned New Hampshire method of issuing "search warrants" violated a fundamental premise of both the Fourth and Fourteenth Amendments. We find no escape from the conclusion that the seizure and search of the Pontiac automobile cannot constitutionally rest upon the warrant issued by the state official who was the chief investigator and prosecutor in this case. Since he was not the neutral and detached magistrate required by the Constitution, the search stands on no firmer ground than if there had been no warrant at all. . . .

Connally v. Georgia, 429 US 245 (1977)

SUMMARY: The magistrate received five dollars for each warrant issued, but nothing if the warrant was denied. The Court held that the mere possibility of financial gain was sufficient to violate due process and the Fourth Amendment rights of suspects.

Lo-Ji Sales, Inc. v. New York, 442 US 319 (1979)

SUMMARY: The Court found that an overly helpful town judge who joined in on the search and raid of an adult bookstore and was there on hand to determine whether there was probable cause to seize various materials violated the requirement that a magistrate be detached. The Court stated, "The Town Justice did not manifest that neutrality and detachment demanded of a judicial officer when presented with a warrant application for a search and seizure." The loss of detachment could be inferred from the objective fact that the town justice "allowed himself to become a member, if not the leader, of the search party which was essentially a police operation."

Shadwick v. City of Tampa, 429 US 245 (1972)

SUMMARY: The Court upheld a law which allowed a municipal court clerk to issue arrest warrants for municipal ordinance violations. The clerk, under this law, was not subject to the authority of the prosecutor or police but worked for the judicial branch and was under the supervision of a municipal judge and that the clerk was charged with determining and was capable of determining whether probable cause existed to believe a municipal ordinance had been violated.

ISSUES IN SEEKING A WARRANT

Securing A Premise Or Automobile While A Warrant Is Obtained — Freezing The Scene

"[S]ecuring a dwelling, on the basis of probable cause, to prevent the destruction or removal of evidence while a search warrant is being sought is not itself an unreasonable seizure of either the dwelling or its contents." *Segura v. United States*, 468 U.S. 796 (1984). Securing a residence involves police stationed outside a residence keeping people from entering it. Securing a residence does not involve the police entering the residence, and a warrantless entry into a dwelling without exigent circumstances is generally an illegal search under the Fourth Amendment. In *Illinois v. McArthur*, 531 U.S. 326 (2001), the Court found that the actions of police officers in securing defendant's residence for two hours while they sought a search warrant did not violate the Fourth Amendment because police had probable cause to believe that the residence contained illegal drugs and reasonably feared that defendant might destroy evidence inside the house if he was allowed in. The Court similarly found it reasonable to secure or "seize and impound an automobile, on the basis of probable cause, for whatever period is necessary to obtain a warrant for the search." *Chambers v. Maroney*, 399 U.S. 42, 51 (1970). In *Riley v. California*, 573 U.S. 373 (2014), the Court extended the reasoning in *McArthur* and noted in dicta[61] that the Fourth Amendment would allow police to secure a cell phone until they could obtain a warrant allowing them to search its contents.

Special Warrants For Electronic Surveillance

If police are interested in doing a wiretap or electronic surveillance of an individual, they must apply for a special warrant. Title III of the Omnibus Crime Control and Safe Streets Act of 1968 relating to wiretapping and electronic surveillance sets forth the special application process and limitations of a wiretap order. This act provided the most protection for individual privacy by placing a general ban on the interception of "wire, oral, or electronic communications" while they were taking place (§2511). However, the ban contained a serious crime exception. Serious crimes were those punishable by death or more than one year in prison. Under the Act, the U.S. Attorney General or other senior Department of Justice official had to approve a law enforcement officer's application to a

---

[61] "Dicta" is a term describing those parts of a court opinion that are not necessarily essential or key to the holding of the case. In Riley, the issue presented was whether a search incident to a lawful arrest exception to the warrant requirement allows police to automatically search a phone found on someone they are arresting. The "dicta" was along the lines . . . well, of course if they have probable cause to believe it contains evidence of a crime, they nevertheless can secure the phone (keep it away from the owner) and go and get a warrant.

federal judge for a court order allowing the officer to secretly intercept and capture conversations. The application must include how long the interception was going to last.

The Uniting and Strengthening America by Providing Appropriate Tools Required to Intercept and Obstruct Terrorism Act of 2001 (Patriot Act) (PUB L.107-56 (2001)) reduced the restrictions on electronic surveillance, increased government power, and decreased privacy protection for individuals. The Patriot Act significantly expanded government surveillance power beyond the Omnibus Control and Safe streets Act of 1968. It allows the government to access stored "wire and electronic communications," such as voice and e-mail. The Patriot Act covers situations in which law enforcement is investigating acts of terrorism; it was not created to be used by law enforcement in the investigation of general criminal conduct. That said, the increased law enforcement power extends to "any criminal investigation," not just to serious crimes (assuming the overall investigation is tied in some way to terrorism). Officers still need to get a warrant based on probable cause to do the electronic surveillance. But, if the information has been stored for more than six months, the government doesn't have to tell subscribers about the warrant for 90 days if doing so would jeopardize the investigation. The Patriot Act also allows "trap and trace" devices and pen registers which can be used to investigate any crime without court approval and without officers' ever notifying subscribers they have it or what they learn from it. Officers are limited in getting and using the secret caller IDs only by having to get approval of a department senior official. Finally, the Patriot Act has expanded governmental authority by allowing sneak and peek warrants (§ 213). Sneak and peek warrants allow officers to enter private places without the owner or occupant consenting or even knowing about it. In order to issue a sneak and peek warrant the judge must find: reasonable cause to believe that providing immediate notification of the execution of the warrant may have an adverse effect, reasonable necessity for the seizure, and notice was given within a reasonable time of the execution of the warrant unless there is good cause shown.

WAS THE WARRANT EXECUTED PROPERLY?

The defendant can challenge both the validity of the warrant and irregularities in the execution of the warrant. Several cases discuss proper procedures in executing a validly obtained warrant, and from them we see that improperly executing an otherwise valid warrant does not necessarily require the suppression of evidence found. See, *Hudson v. Michigan*, 547 U.S. 586 (2006).

Irregularities In Execution Of The Warrant.

But what is an improper manner of execution? In one case, the court found that it was a violation of the Fourth Amendment for police officers to bring members of the media or other third parties into a home during the execution of a search warrant when the presence of the third parties is not in aid of the execution of the warrant. *Wilson v. Layne*, 526 U.S. 603 (1999). Generally, unless the police obtain a special "night time warrant" it is improper for warrants to be executed at night. The judge may authorize execution of the warrant at any time of the day or night under state laws, but generally, the search warrant affidavit must specify the special circumstances justifying a nighttime search. (For example, consider the warrant Messerschmidt sought for Bowen in *Messerchmidt v. Millender*, above).

Staleness

Just like waiting to seek a warrant may make the information stale and negate probable cause, waiting to execute a warrant may make it stale. To that end, states generally have a time period within which officers must execute and "return" the warrant. The judge may also set the time period within which it must be executed on the face of the warrant. Failure to execute the warrant within a statutory time requirement or within the period set forth on the face of the warrant, is the same as proceeding without a warrant. Assuming there is no statutory period, nor a time set by the magistrate, police should nevertheless make sure they execute the warrant in a timely fashion, or else the defendant can claim it was "stale" As discussed above, information contained in an affidavit must be sufficiently "fresh" to justify the conclusion that the seizable evidence is present at the location to be searched ant the time that application for the warrant is made. If the affidavit contains facts that show it is more probable than not that the items sought are still at the location to be searched, then the information is not stale. The warrant return must be filed within a certain time period, but that seems to relate to when the warrant was executed and not necessarily from the time it was obtained.

In determining whether a warrant is stale courts will consider: the totality of the circumstances. Factors include the length of time delay in executing the warrant after it has been issued, the character of the crime and the thing to be seized (for example, if there is a commercial quantity of drugs rather than a personal use quantity of drugs-- seeing three pounds of marijuana at the house two days before the warrant issued made the execution not stale), the durable quality of the items sought (things not readily discarded or consumed are more likely to be there longer and thus the warrant is less likely to be stale), the fact that the item is not contraband (people will be less likely to destroy, move, or hide evidence that is not considered contraband[62]), whether the evidence concerns ongoing criminal activity (this increases the likelihood that even after the passage of time, items subject to seizure will remain in the location to be searched), any admissions regarding expectation of continuing presence of seizable evidence, and any prior criminal activity.

Knock And Announce

Most case law concerning improperly executed warrants involves situations where police failed to knock and announce their presence when entering a residence (or building closed to the public). In *Wilson v. Arkansas*, 514 U.S. 927, 936 (1995), the Court held that the knock-and-announce requirement is an element of the Fourth Amendment "reasonableness" inquiry and that the "search and seizure of a dwelling might be constitutionally defective if police officers entered without prior announcement." In *Richards v. Wisconsin*, 520 U.S. 385 (1997), the Court noted that, in appropriate circumstances, it would be reasonable under the Fourth Amendment for the issuing magistrate to authorize a no-knock entry on the face of the warrant. *Richards* indicated that police need not knock and announce when doing so could enable the occupants to destroy the evidence. Although the Fourth Amendment allows exceptions to the knock and announce rule, it does not permit a blanket exception to the knock-and-announce requirement for all felony drug investigations; instead, the officers' actions must be evaluated based on the circumstances at the time of the entry.

HUDSON v. MICHIGAN
547 U.S. 586 (2006)

JUSTICE SCALIA delivered the opinion of the Court, except as to Part IV.

We decide whether violation of the "knock-and-announce" rule requires the suppression of all evidence found in the search.

Police obtained a warrant authorizing a search for drugs and firearms at the home of petitioner Booker Hudson. They discovered both. Large quantities of drugs were found,

including cocaine rocks in Hudson's pocket. A loaded gun was lodged between the cushion and armrest of the chair in which he was sitting. Hudson was charged under Michigan law with unlawful drug and firearm possession.

This case is before us only because of the method of entry into the house. When the police arrived to execute the warrant, they announced their presence, but waited only a

---

[62] "Contraband" is the term used for objects that are criminally possessed.

short time — perhaps "three to five seconds," — before turning the knob of the unlocked front door and entering Hudson's home. Hudson moved to suppress all the inculpatory evidence, arguing that the premature entry violated his Fourth Amendment rights.

The common-law principle that law enforcement officers must announce their presence and provide residents an opportunity to open the door is an ancient one. ... In *Wilson*, ... [we held that it was also a command of the Fourth Amendment.].

We recognized that the new constitutional rule we had announced is not easily applied. *Wilson* and cases following it have noted the many situations in which it is not necessary to knock and announce. ...

When the knock-and-announce rule does apply, it is not easy to determine precisely what officers must do. ...Happily, these issues do not confront us here. From the trial level onward, Michigan has conceded that the entry was a knock-and-announce violation. The issue here is remedy. *Wilson* specifically declined to decide whether the exclusionary rule is appropriate for violation of the knock-and-announce requirement. ... That question is squarely before us now.

. . . Cases excluding the fruits of unlawful warrantless searches . . . say nothing about the appropriateness of exclusion to vindicate the interests protected by the knock-and-announce requirement. Until a valid warrant has issued, citizens are entitled to shield "their persons, houses, papers, and effects," ... from the government's scrutiny. Exclusion of the evidence obtained by a warrantless search vindicates that entitlement. The interests protected by the knock-and-announce requirement are quite different — and do not include the shielding of potential evidence from the government's eyes.

One of those interests is the protection of human life and limb, because an unannounced entry may provoke violence in supposed self-defense by the surprised resident. ... Another interest is the protection of property. Breaking a house (as the old cases typically put it) absent an announcement would penalize someone who " 'did not know of the process, of which, if he had notice, it is to be presumed that he would obey it. ... ' " ... The knock-and-announce rule gives individuals "the opportunity to comply with the law and to avoid the destruction of property occasioned by a forcible entry." ...And thirdly, the knock-and-announce rule protects those elements of privacy and dignity that can be destroyed by a sudden entrance. It gives residents the "opportunity to prepare themselves for" the entry of the police. ..."The brief interlude between announcement and entry with a warrant may be the opportunity that an individual has to pull on clothes or get out of bed." ... In other words, it assures the opportunity to collect oneself before answering the door.

What the knock-and-announce rule has never protected, however, is one's interest in preventing the government from seeing or taking evidence described in a warrant. Since the interests that were violated in this case have nothing to do with the seizure of the evidence, the exclusionary rule is inapplicable.

. . .[T]he exclusionary rule has never been applied except "where its deterrence benefits outweigh its 'substantial social costs,' " .... The costs here are considerable. In addition to the grave adverse consequence that exclusion of relevant incriminating evidence always entails (viz., the risk of releasing dangerous criminals into society), imposing that massive remedy for a knock-and-announce violation would generate a constant flood of alleged failures to observe the rule. ...

Another consequence of the incongruent remedy Hudson proposes would be police officers' refraining from timely entry after knocking and announcing. As we have observed, the amount of time they must wait is necessarily uncertain. If the consequences of running afoul of the rule were so massive, officers would be inclined to wait longer than the law requires — producing preventable violence against officers in some cases, and the destruction of evidence in many others. ...

Next to these "substantial social costs" we must consider the deterrence benefits, existence of which is a necessary condition for exclusion. ... Violation of the warrant requirement sometimes produces incriminating evidence that could not otherwise be obtained. But ignoring knock-and-announce can realistically be expected to achieve absolutely nothing except the prevention of destruction of evidence and the avoidance of life-threatening resistance by occupants of the premises — dangers which, if there is even "reasonable suspicion" of their existence, suspend the knock-and-announce requirement anyway. Massive deterrence is hardly required.

In sum, the social costs of applying the exclusionary rule to knock-and-announce violations are considerable; the incentive to such violations is minimal to begin with, and the extant deterrences against them are substantial ... Resort to the massive remedy of suppressing evidence of guilt is unjustified.

Like today's case, *Segura v. United States* involved a concededly illegal entry. Police conducting a drug crime investigation waited for Segura outside an apartment building; when he arrived, he denied living there. The police arrested him and brought him to the apartment where they suspected illegal activity. An officer knocked. When someone inside opened the door, the police entered, taking Segura with them. They had neither a warrant nor consent to enter, and they did not announce themselves as police — an entry as illegal as can be. Officers then stayed in the apartment for 19 hours awaiting a search warrant . ... Once alerted that the search warrant had been obtained, the police — still inside, having secured the premises so that no evidence could be removed — conducted a search. We refused to exclude the resulting evidence. We recognized that only the evidence gained from the particular violation could be excluded, ... , and therefore distinguished the effects of the illegal entry from the effects of the legal search: "None of the information on which the warrant was secured was derived from or related in any

way to the initial entry into petitioners' apartment. ... It was therefore "beyond dispute that the information possessed by the agents before they entered the apartment constituted an independent source for the discovery and seizure of the evidence now challenged." ...

If the search in *Segura* could be "wholly unrelated to the prior entry," when the only entry was warrantless, it would be bizarre to treat more harshly the actions in this case, where the only entry was with a warrant. If the probable cause backing a warrant that was issued later in time could be an "independent source" for a search that proceeded after the officers illegally entered and waited, a search warrant obtained before going in must have at least this much effect.

In . . . *Harris*, the police violated the defendant's Fourth Amendment rights by arresting him at home without a warrant. ... Once taken to the station house, he gave an incriminating statement. ... We refused to exclude it. Like the illegal entry which led to discovery of the evidence in today's case, the illegal arrest in *Harris* began a process that culminated in acquisition of the evidence sought to be excluded. While Harris's statement was "the product of an arrest and being in custody," it "was not the fruit of the fact that the arrest was made in the house rather than someplace else." . . .

United States v. Ramirez . . . involved a claim that police entry violated the Fourth Amendment because it was effected by breaking a window. We ultimately concluded that the property destruction was, under all the circumstances, reasonable, but in the course of our discussion we unanimously said the following: "[D]estruction of property in the course of a search may violate the Fourth Amendment, even though the entry itself is lawful and the fruits of the search are not subject to suppression." ... Had the breaking of the window been unreasonable, the Court said, it would have been necessary to determine whether there had been a "sufficient causal relationship between the breaking of the window and the discovery of the guns to warrant suppression of the evidence." . . . . What clearer expression could there be of the proposition that an impermissible manner of entry does not necessarily trigger the exclusionary rule?

Other Case: Knock and Announce

Wilson v. Arkansas, 514 U.S. 927 (1995)

SUMMARY: Wilson made narcotic sales to police informants. During one of these sales Wilson produced a pistol and waved it in the informant's face threatening to kill her if she was working for the police. Police obtained a warrant to search Wilson's house and arrest her and another, Jacobs. In the warrant affidavit, it was noted that Jacobs had convictions for arson and firebombing. When police went to execute the warrant, they found the main door open, and as they entered an unlocked screen door, they then first identified themselves as police with a w arrant. They found drugs, drug paraphernalia, a gun and ammunition. Wilson was in the bathroom flushing marijuana down the toilet.

Before trial Wilson filed a motion to suppress the evidence found during the search asserting, among other things that he search was illegal because officers had failed to knock and announce their presence before entering her home. The trial court denied the motion, Wilson was convicted of all charges, and the case wound its way up to the Supreme Court by writ of a petition of certiorari]

OPINION: We granted certiorari to resolve the conflict among the lower courts as to whether the common-law knock-and-announce principle forms a part of the Fourth Amendment reasonableness inquiry. ... We hold that it does.

...

Our ... cases have acknowledged that the common-law principle of announcement is "embedded in Anglo-American law," ...but we have never squarely held that this principle is an element of the reasonableness inquiry under the Fourth Amendment. We now so hold. .... Contrary to the decision below, we hold that in some circumstances an officer's unannounced entry into a home might be unreasonable under the Fourth Amendment.

...

We need not attempt a comprehensive catalog of the relevant countervailing factors here. For now, we leave to the lower courts the task of determining the circumstances under which an unannounced entry is reasonable under the Fourth Amendment. We simply hold that although a search or seizure of a dwelling might be constitutionally defective if police officers enter without prior announcement, law enforcement interests may also establish the reasonableness of an unannounced entry. .

Protective Sweep During Execution Of Arrest Warrant

The Courts have allowed a protective sweep of a residence when an officer, armed with an arrest warrant go to the suspect's home and arrest him.

MARYLAND v. BUIE
484 U.S. 325 (1990)

JUSTICE WHITE delivered the opinion of the Court.

On February 3, 1986, two men committed an armed robbery of a Godfather's Pizza restaurant in Prince George's County, Maryland. One of the robbers was wearing a red running suit. That same day, Prince George's County police obtained arrest warrants for respondent Jerome Edward Buie and his suspected accomplice in the robbery, Lloyd Allen. Buie's house was placed under police surveillance.

On February 5, the police executed the arrest warrant for Buie. They first had a police department secretary telephone Buie's house to verify that he was home. The secretary spoke to a female first, then to Buie himself. Six or seven officers proceeded to Buie's house. Once inside, the officers fanned out through the first and second floors. Corporal James Rozar announced that he would "freeze" the basement so that no one could come up and surprise the officers. With his service revolver drawn, Rozar twice shouted into the basement, ordering anyone down there to come out. When a voice asked who was calling, Rozar announced three times: "this is the police, show me your hands." Eventually, a pair of hands appeared around the bottom of the stairwell and Buie emerged from the basement. He was arrested, searched, and handcuffed by Rozar. Thereafter, Detective Joseph Frolich entered the basement "in case there was someone else" down there. He noticed a red running suit lying in plain view on a stack of clothing and seized it.

The trial court denied Buie's motion to suppress the running suit, stating in part: "The man comes out from a basement, the police don't know how many other people are down there. He is charged with a serious offense." The State introduced the running suit into evidence at Buie's trial. A jury convicted Buie of robbery with a deadly weapon and using a handgun in the commission of a felony.

…

It is not disputed that until the point of Buie's arrest the police had the right, based on the authority of the arrest warrant, to search anywhere in the house that Buie might have been found, including the basement. "If there is sufficient evidence of a citizen's participation in a felony to persuade a judicial officer that his arrest is justified, it is constitutionally reasonable to require him to open his doors to the officers of the law." *Payton v. New York*, 445 U.S. 573, 602 -603 (1980). There is also no dispute that if Detective Frolich's entry into the basement was lawful, the seizure of the red running suit, which was in plain view and which the officer had probable cause to believe was evidence of a crime, was also lawful under the Fourth Amendment. The issue in this case is what level of justification the Fourth Amendment required before Detective Frolich could legally enter the basement to see if someone else was there.

[T]he Fourth Amendment bars only unreasonable searches and seizures. … [I]n determining reasonableness, we have balanced the intrusion on the individual's Fourth Amendment interests against its promotion of legitimate governmental interests. Under this test, a search of the house or office is generally not reasonable without a warrant issued on probable cause. There are other contexts, however, where the public interest is such that neither a warrant nor probable cause is required.

The *Terry* case is most instructive for present purposes. There we held that an on-the-street "frisk" for weapons must be tested by the Fourth Amendment's general proscription against unreasonable searches because such a frisk involves "an entire rubric of police conduct - necessarily swift action predicated upon the on-the-spot observations of the officer on the beat - which historically has not been, and as a practical matter could not be, subjected to the warrant procedure." We stated that there is "`no ready test for determining reasonableness other than by balancing the need to search . . . against the invasion which the search . . . entails.'" Applying that balancing test, it was held that although a frisk for weapons "constitutes a severe, though brief, intrusion upon cherished personal security," such a frisk is reasonable when weighed against the "need for law enforcement officers to protect themselves and other prospective victims of violence in situations where they may lack probable cause for an arrest." We therefore authorized a limited patdown for weapons where a reasonably prudent officer would be warranted in the belief, based on "specific and articulable facts," and not on a mere "inchoate and unparticularized suspicion or `hunch,'" … "that he is dealing with an armed and dangerous individual,". …

In *Michigan v. Long,* the principles of Terry were applied in the context of a roadside encounter: "[T]he search of the passenger compartment of an automobile, limited to those areas in which a weapon may be placed or hidden, is permissible if the police officer possesses a reasonable belief based on `specific and articulable facts which, taken together with the rational inferences from those facts, reasonably warrant' the officer in believing that the suspect is dangerous and the suspect may gain immediate control of weapons. The *Long* Court expressly rejected the contention that *Terry* restricted preventative searches to the person of a detained suspect. In a sense, *Long* authorized a "frisk" of an automobile for weapons.

The ingredients to apply the balance struck in *Terry* and *Long* are present in this case. Possessing an arrest warrant and probable cause to believe Buie was in his home, the officer were entitled to enter and to search anywhere in the house in which Buie might be found. Once he was found, however, the search for him was over, and there was no longer that particular justification for entering any rooms that had not yet been searched.

That Buie had an expectation of privacy in those remaining areas of his house, however, does not mean such rooms were immune from entry. In *Terry* and *Long* we were concerned with the immediate interest of the police officers in taking steps to assure themselves that the persons with whom they were dealing were not armed with, or able to gain immediate control of, a weapon that could unexpectedly and fatally be used against them. In the instant case, there is an analogous interest of the officers in taking steps to assure themselves that the house in which a suspect is being, or has just been, arrested is not harboring other persons who are dangerous and who could unexpectedly launch an attack. The risk of danger in the context of an arrest in the home is as great as, if not greater than, it is in an on-the-street or roadside investigatory encounter. A *Terry* or *Long* frisk occurs before a police-citizen confrontation has escalated to

the point of arrest. A protective sweep, in contrast, occurs as an adjunct to the serious step of taking a person into custody for the purpose of prosecuting him for a crime. Moreover, unlike an encounter on the street or along a highway, an in-home arrest puts the officer at the disadvantage of being on his adversary's "turf." An ambush in a confined setting of unknown configuration is more to be feared than it is in open, more familiar surroundings.

[A]rresting officers are permitted in such circumstances to take reasonable steps to ensure their safety after, and while making, the arrest. That interest is sufficient to outweigh the intrusion such procedures may entail.

We agree with the State . . . that a warrant was not required. We also hold that as an incident to the arrest the officers could, as a precautionary matter and without probable cause or reasonable suspicion, look in closets and other spaces immediately adjoining the place of arrest from which an attack could be immediately launched. Beyond that, however, we hold that there must be articulable facts which, taken together with the rational inferences from those facts, would warrant a reasonably prudent officer in believing that the area to be swept harbors an individual posing a danger to those on the arrest scene. . . .

We should emphasize that such a protective sweep, aimed at protecting the arresting officers, if justified by the circumstances, is nevertheless not a full search of the premises, but may extend only to a cursory inspection of those spaces where a person may be found. The sweep lasts no longer than is necessary to dispel the reasonable suspicion of danger and in any event no longer than it takes to complete the arrest and depart the premises.

The Fourth Amendment permits a properly limited protective sweep in conjunction with an in-home arrest when the searching officer possesses a reasonable belief based on specific and articulable facts that the area to be swept harbors an individual posing a danger to those on the arrest scene. …

Detaining And Searching Persons At A Search Scene

Absent probable cause or reasonable officer-safety concerns, police may not search people who are not named in a search warrant just because they happen to be present during the execution of the search warrant. Frisk searches conducted during the execution of a search warrant must be based on reasonable suspicion to believe the particular person is armed or dangerous. *Ybarra v. Illinois*, 444 U.S. 85 (1979). The cases of *Muehler v. Mena*, 544 U.S. 93 (2005) and *Bailey v. United States, 568 U.S. 186 (2013)*, discuss the seminal case of *Michigan v. Summers*, 452 U.S. 692 (1981). All three of those cases concern police officer behavior when executing a search warrant.

YBARRA v. ILLINOIS
444 U.S. 85 (1979)

JUSTICE STEWART delivered the opinion of the Court.

An Illinois statute authorizes law enforcement officers to detain and search any person found on premises being searched pursuant to a search warrant, to protect themselves from attack or to prevent the disposal or concealment of anything described in the warrant. The question before us is whether the application of this statute to the facts of the present case violated the Fourth and Fourteenth Amendments.

On March 1, 1976, a special agent of the Illinois Bureau of Investigation presented a "Complaint for Search Warrant" to a judge of an Illinois Circuit Court. The complaint recited that the agent had spoken with an informant known to the police to be reliable and:

> "3. The informant related … that over the weekend of 28 and 29 February he was in the [Aurora Tap Tavern, located in the city of Aurora, Ill.] and observed fifteen to twenty-five tin-foil packets on the person of the bartender `Greg' and behind the bar. He also has been in the tavern on at least ten other occasions and has observed tin-foil packets on `Greg' and in a drawer behind the bar. The informant has used heroin in the past and knows that tin-foil packets are a common method of packaging heroin.

> "4. The informant advised . . . that over the weekend of 28 and 29 February he had a conversation with `Greg' and was advised that `Greg' would have heroin for sale on Monday, March 1, 1976. This conversation took place in the tavern described."

On the strength of this complaint, the judge issued a warrant authorizing the search of "the following person or place: . . . [T]he Aurora Tap Tavern. … Also the person of `Greg', the bartender, a male white with blondish hair appx. 25 years." The warrant authorized the police to search for "evidence of the offense of possession of a controlled substance," to wit, "[h]eroin, contraband, other controlled substances, money, instrumentalities and narcotics, paraphernalia used in the manufacture, processing and distribution of controlled substances."

In the late afternoon of that day, seven or eight officers proceeded to the tavern. Upon entering it, the officers announced their purpose and advised all those present that they were going to conduct a "cursory search for weapons." One of the officers then proceeded to pat down each of the 9 to 13 customers present in the tavern, while the remaining officers engaged in an extensive search of the premises.

The police officer who frisked the patrons found the appellant, Ventura Ybarra, in front of the bar standing by a pinball machine. In his first patdown of Ybarra, the officer felt what he described as "a cigarette pack with objects in it." He did not remove this pack from Ybarra's pocket. Instead, he moved on and proceeded to pat down other customers. After completing this process the officer returned to Ybarra and frisked him once again. This second search of Ybarra took place approximately 2 to 10 minutes after the first. The officer relocated and retrieved the cigarette pack from Ybarra's pants pocket. Inside the pack he found six tinfoil packets containing a brown powdery substance which later turned out to be heroin.

The case proceeded to trial before the court sitting without a jury, and Ybarra was found guilty of the possession of heroin.

...

There is no reason to suppose that, when the search warrant was issued on March 1, 1976, the authorities had probable cause to believe that any person found on the premises of the Aurora Tap Tavern, aside from "Greg," would be violating the law. The search warrant complaint did not allege that the bar was frequented by persons illegally purchasing drugs. It did not state that the informant had ever seen a patron of the tavern purchase drugs from "Greg" or from any other person. Nowhere, in fact, did the complaint even mention the patrons of the Aurora Tap Tavern.

Not only was probable cause to search Ybarra absent at the time the warrant was issued, it was still absent when the police executed the warrant. Upon entering the tavern, the police did not recognize Ybarra and had no reason to believe that he had committed, was committing, or was about to commit any offense under state or federal law. Ybarra made no gestures indicative of criminal conduct, made no movements that might suggest an attempt to conceal contraband, and said nothing of a suspicious nature to the police officers. In short, the agents knew nothing in particular about Ybarra, except that he was present, along with several other customers, in a public tavern at a time when the police had reason to believe that the bartender would have heroin for sale.

It is true that the police possessed a warrant based on probable cause to search the tavern in which Ybarra happened to be at the time the warrant was executed. But, a person's mere propinquity to others independently suspected of criminal activity does not, without more, give rise to probable cause to search that person. *Sibron v. New York*,. Where the standard is probable cause, a search or seizure of a person must be supported by probable cause particularized with respect to that person. This requirement cannot be undercut or avoided by simply pointing to the fact that coincidentally there exists probable cause to search or seizure another or to search the premises where the person may happen to be. The Fourth and Fourteenth Amendments protect the "legitimate expectations of privacy" of persons, not places.

Each patron who walked into the Aurora Tap Tavern on March 1, 1976, was clothed with constitutional protection against an unreasonable search or an unreasonable seizure. That individualized protection was separate and distinct from the Fourth and Fourteenth Amendment protection possessed by the proprietor of the tavern or by "Greg." Although the search warrant, issued upon probable cause, gave the officers authority to search the premises and to search "Greg," it gave them no authority whatever to invade the constitutional protections possessed individually by the tavern's customers.

Notwithstanding the absence of probable cause to search Ybarra, the State argues that the action of the police in searching him and seizing what was found in his pocket was nonetheless constitutionally permissible. We are asked to find that the first patdown search of Ybarra constituted a reasonable frisk for weapons under the doctrine of *Terry v. Ohio*. If this finding is made, it is then possible to conclude, the State argues, that the second search of Ybarra was constitutionally justified. The argument is that the patdown yielded probable cause to believe that Ybarra was carrying narcotics, and that this probable cause constitutionally supported the second search, no warrant being required in light of the exigencies of the situation coupled with the ease with which Ybarra could have disposed of the illegal substance.

We are unable to take even the first step required by this argument. The initial frisk of Ybarra was simply not supported by a reasonable belief that he was armed and presently dangerous, a belief which this Court has invariably held must form the predicate to a patdown of a person for weapons. When the police entered the Aurora Tap Tavern on March 1, 1976, the lighting was sufficient for them to observe the customers. Upon seeing Ybarra, they neither recognized him as a person with a criminal history nor had any particular reason to believe that he might be inclined to assault them. Moreover, as Police Agent Johnson later testified, Ybarra, whose hands were empty, gave no indication of possessing a weapon, made no gestures or other actions indicative of an intent to commit an assault, and acted generally in a manner that was not threatening. At the suppression hearing, the most Agent Johnson could point to was that Ybarra was wearing a 3/4-length lumber jacket, clothing which the State admits could be expected on almost any tavern patron in Illinois in early March. In short, the State is unable to articulate any specific fact that would have justified a police officer at the scene in even suspecting that Ybarra was armed and dangerous.

The *Terry* case created an exception to the requirement of probable cause, an exception whose "narrow scope" this Court "has been careful to maintain." Under that doctrine a law enforcement officer, for his own protection and safety, may conduct a patdown to find weapons that he reasonably believes or suspects are then in the possession of the person he has accosted. … Nothing in *Terry* can be understood to allow a generalized "cursory search for weapons" or, indeed, any search whatever for anything but weapons. The "narrow scope" of the *Terry* exception does not permit a frisk for weapons on less than reasonable belief or suspicion directed at the person to be frisked, even though that person happens to be on premises where an authorized narcotics search is taking place.

What has been said largely disposes of the State's second and alternative argument in this case. Emphasizing the important governmental interest "in effectively controlling traffic in dangerous, hard drugs" and the ease with which the evidence of narcotics possession may be concealed or moved around from person to person, the State contends that the *Terry* "reasonable belief or suspicion" standard should be made applicable to aid the evidence-gathering function of the search warrant. More precisely, we are asked to construe the Fourth and Fourteenth Amendments to permit evidence searches of persons who, at the commencement of the search, are on "compact" premises subject to a search warrant, at least where the police have a "reasonable belief" that such persons "are connected with" drug trafficking and "may be concealing or carrying away the contraband."

Over 30 years ago, the Court rejected a similar argument in *United States v. Di Re*. In that case, a federal investigator had been told by an informant that a transaction in counterfeit gasoline ration coupons was going to occur at a particular place. The investigator went to that location at the appointed time and saw the car of one of the suspected parties to the illegal transaction. The investigator went over to the car and observed a man in the driver's seat, another man (Di Re) in the passenger's seat, and the informant in the back. The informant told the investigator that the person in the driver's seat had given him counterfeit coupons. Thereupon, all three men were arrested and searched. Among the arguments unsuccessfully advanced by the Government to support the constitutionality of the search of Di Re was the contention that the investigator could lawfully have searched the car, since he had reasonable cause to believe that it contained contraband, and correspondingly could have searched any occupant of the car because the contraband sought was of the sort "which could easily be concealed on the person." Not deciding whether or not under the Fourth Amendment the car could have been searched, the Court held that it was "not convinced that a person, by mere presence in a suspected car, loses immunities from search of his person to which he would otherwise be entitled."

For these reasons, we conclude that the searches of Ybarra and the seizure of what was in his pocket contravened the Fourth and Fourteenth Amendments.

MUEHLER v. MENA
544 U.S. 93 (2005)

CHIEF JUSTICE REHNQUIST delivered the opinion of the Court.

Respondent Iris Mena was detained in handcuffs during a search of the premises that she and several others occupied. Petitioners were lead members of a police detachment executing a search warrant of these premises. She sued the officers and the District Court found in her favor. The Court of Appeals affirmed the judgment, holding that the use of handcuffs to detain Mena during the search violated the Fourth Amendment and that the officers' questioning of Mena about her immigration status during the detention constituted an independent Fourth Amendment violation. . . . We hold that Mena's detention in handcuffs for the length of the search was consistent with our opinion in *Michigan v. Summers*, (1981), and that the officers' questioning during that detention did not violate her Fourth Amendment rights.

Based on information gleaned from the investigation of a gang-related, driveby shooting, petitioners Muehler and Brill had reason to believe at least one member of a gang — the West Side Locos — lived at 1363 Patricia Avenue. They also suspected that the individual was armed and dangerous, since he had recently been involved in the driveby shooting. As a result, Muehler obtained a search warrant for 1363 Patricia Avenue that authorized a broad search of the house and premises for, among other things, deadly weapons and evidence of gang membership. In light of the high degree of risk involved in searching a house suspected of housing at least one, and perhaps multiple, armed gang members, a Special Weapons and Tactics (SWAT) team was used to secure the residence and grounds before the search.

At 7 a.m. on February 3, 1998, petitioners, along with the SWAT team and other officers, executed the warrant. Mena was asleep in her bed when the SWAT team, clad in helmets and black vests adorned with badges and the word "POLICE," entered her bedroom and placed her in handcuffs at gunpoint. The SWAT team also handcuffed three other individuals found on the property. The SWAT team then took those individuals and Mena into a converted garage, which contained several beds and some other bedroom furniture. While the search proceeded, one or two officers guarded the four detainees, who were allowed to move around the garage but remained in handcuffs.

In her §1983 suit against the officers she alleged that she was detained "for an unreasonable time and in an unreasonable manner" in violation of the Fourth Amendment. In addition, she claimed that the warrant and its execution were overbroad, that the officers failed to comply with the "knock and announce" rule, and that the officers had needlessly destroyed property during the search. The officers moved for summary judgment, asserting that they were entitled to qualified immunity, but the District Court denied their motion. . . . After a trial, a jury, pursuant to a special verdict form, found that Officers Muehler and Brill violated Mena's Fourth Amendment right to be free from unreasonable seizures by detaining her both with force greater than that which was reasonable and for a longer period than that which was reasonable. The jury awarded Mena $10,000 in actual damages and $20,000 in punitive damages against each petitioner for a total of $60,000.

In *Michigan v. Summers*, (1981), we held that officers executing a search warrant for contraband have the authority "to detain the occupants of the premises while a proper search is conducted." Such detentions are appropriate, we explained, because the character of the additional intrusion caused by detention is slight and because the justifications for detention are substantial. We made clear that the detention of an occupant is "surely less intrusive than the search itself," and the presence of a warrant assures that a neutral magistrate has determined that probable cause exists to search the home. . . . Against this incremental intrusion, we posited three legitimate law enforcement interests that provide substantial justification for detaining an occupant: "preventing flight in the event that incriminating evidence is found"; "minimizing the risk of harm to the officers"; and facilitating "the orderly completion of the search," as detainees' "self-interest may induce them to open locked doors or locked containers to avoid the use of force."

Mena's detention was, under *Summers*, plainly permissible. An officer's authority to detain incident to a search is categorical; it does not depend on the "quantum of proof justifying detention or the extent of the intrusion to be imposed by the seizure." Thus, Mena's detention for the duration of the search was reasonable under Summers because a warrant existed to search 1363 Patricia Avenue and she was an occupant of that address at the time of the search.

…

The officers' use of force in the form of handcuffs to effectuate Mena's detention in the garage, as well as the detention of the three other occupants, was reasonable because the governmental interests outweigh the marginal intrusion. … The imposition of correctly applied handcuffs on Mena, who was already being lawfully detained during a search of the house, was undoubtedly a separate intrusion in addition to detention in the converted garage. The detention was thus more intrusive than that which we upheld in *Summers*. …

But this was no ordinary search. The governmental interests in not only detaining, but using handcuffs, are at their maximum when, as here, a warrant authorizes a search for weapons and a wanted gang member resides on the premises. In such inherently dangerous situations, the use of handcuffs minimizes the risk of harm to both officers and occupants. . . . Though this safety risk inherent in executing a search warrant for weapons was sufficient to justify the use of handcuffs, the need to detain multiple occupants made the use of handcuffs all the more reasonable. . . .

Mena argues that, even if the use of handcuffs to detain her in the garage was reasonable as an initial matter, the duration of the use of handcuffs made the detention unreasonable. The duration of a detention can, of course, affect the balance of interests under *Graham*. However, the 2- to 3- hour detention in handcuffs in this case does not outweigh the government's continuing safety interests. As we have noted, this case involved the detention of four detainees by two officers during a search of a gang house for dangerous weapons. We conclude that the detention of Mena in handcuffs during the search was reasonable.

JUSTICE KENNEDY, *concurring.*

I concur in the judgment and in the opinion of the Court. It does seem important to add this brief statement to help ensure that police handcuffing during searches becomes neither routine nor unduly prolonged.

The safety of the officers and the efficacy of the search are matters of first concern, but so too is it a matter of first concern that excessive force is not used on the persons detained, especially when these persons, though lawfully detained under *Michigan v. Summers*, (1981), are not themselves suspected of any involvement in criminal activity. The use of handcuffs is the use of force, and such force must be objectively reasonable under the circumstances.

If the search extends to the point when the handcuffs can cause real pain or serious discomfort, provision must be made to alter the conditions of detention at least long enough to attend to the needs of the detainee. This is so even if there is no question that the initial handcuffing was objectively reasonable. The restraint should also be removed if, at any point during the search, it would be readily apparent to any objectively reasonable officer that removing the handcuffs would not compromise the officers' safety or risk interference or substantial delay in the execution of the search. The time spent in the search here, some two to three hours, certainly approaches, and may well exceed, the time beyond which a detainee's Fourth Amendment interests require revisiting the necessity of handcuffing in order to ensure the restraint, even if permissible as an initial matter, has not become excessive.

That said, under these circumstances I do not think handcuffing the detainees for the duration of the search was objectively unreasonable . . . [And b]ecause on this record it does not appear the restraints were excessive, I join the opinion of the Court.

JUSTICE STEVENS, with whom JUSTICE SOUTER, JUSTICE GINSBURG, and JUSTICE BREYER join, concurring in the judgment.

[I]t is clear that the SWAT team's initial actions were reasonable. …

A jury could reasonably have found a number of facts supporting a conclusion that the prolonged handcuffing was unreasonable. No contraband was found in Iris' room or on her person. There were no indications suggesting she was or ever had been a gang member, which was consistent with the fact that during the police officers' last visit to the home, no gang members were present. She fully cooperated with the officers and the INS agent, answering all their questions. She was unarmed, and given her small size, was clearly no match for either of the two armed officers who were guarding her. In sum, there was no evidence that Mena posed any threat to the officers or anyone else.

…

In short, under the factors listed in *Graham* and those validly presented to the jury in the jury instructions, a jury could have reasonably found from the evidence that there was no apparent need to handcuff Iris for the entire duration of the search and that she was detained for an unreasonably prolonged period. She posed no threat whatsoever to the officers at the scene. She was not suspected of any crime and was not a person targeted by the search warrant. She had no reason to flee the scene and gave no indication that she desired to do so. Viewing the facts in the light most favorable to the jury's verdict, as we are required to do, there is certainly no obvious factual basis for rejecting the jury's verdict that the officers acted unreasonably, and no obvious basis for rejecting the conclusion that, on these facts, the quantum of force used was unreasonable as a matter of law.

BAILEY v. UNITED STATES
568 U.S. 186 (2013)

Justice Kennedy delivered the opinion of the Court.

The instant case involves the search of a place (an apartment dwelling) and the seizure of a person. But here, though it is acknowledged that the search was lawful, it does not follow that the seizure was lawful as well. The seizure of the person is quite in question. The issue to be resolved is whether the seizure of the person was reasonable when he was stopped and detained at some distance away from the premises to be searched when the only justification for the detention was to ensure the safety and efficacy of the search.

I

A

[Facts summarized: Defendant was seized about 1 mile from an apartment they were searching pursuant to a warrant. He denied it was his apartment and that he was connected in any way to the was being searched, but after seizing him, they searched him incident to arrest and found a key that fit the door of the basement apartment.]

B

Bailey was charged with three federal offenses: possession of cocaine with intent to distribute, possession of a firearm by a felon, and possession of a firearm in furtherance of a drug-trafficking offense. At trial Bailey moved to suppress the apartment key and the statements he made when stopped by Detectives Sneider and Gorbecki. That evidence, Bailey argued, derived from an unreasonable seizure. After an evidentiary hearing . . . the District Court held that Bailey's detention was permissible under *Michigan* v. *Summers* (1981), as a detention incident to the execution of a search warrant. . . .

The Court of Appeals for the Second Circuit ruled that Bailey's detention was proper and affirmed denial of the suppression motion. It interpreted this Court's decision in *Summers* to "authoriz[e] law enforcement to detain the occupant of premises subject to a valid search warrant when that person is seen leaving those premises and the detention is effected *as soon as reasonably practicable*." . . .

The Federal Courts of Appeals have reached differing conclusions as to whether *Michigan* v. *Summers* justifies the detention of occupants beyond the immediate vicinity of the premises covered by a search warrant. This Court granted certiorari to address the question. 566 U. S. ___ (2012).

II

. . . .

In *Summers*, the Court . . . permitted officers executing a search warrant "to detain the occupants of the premises while a proper search is conducted." The rule in *Summers* extends farther than some earlier exceptions because it does not require law enforcement to have particular suspicion that an individual is involved in criminal activity or poses a specific danger to the officers. In *Muehler*, applying the rule in *Summers*, the Court stated: "An officer's authority to detain incident to a search is categorical; it does not depend on the 'quantum of proof justifying detention or the extent of the intrusion to be imposed by the seizure.' " The rule announced in *Summers* allows detention incident to the execution of a search warrant "because the character of the additional intrusion caused by detention is slight and because the justifications for detention are substantial." *Muehler.*

In *Summers* and later cases the occupants detained were found within or immediately outside a residence at the moment the police officers executed the search warrant. In *Summers*, the defendant was detained on a walk leading down from the front steps of the house. . . . Here, however, petitioner left the apartment before the search began; and the police officers waited to detain him until he was almost a mile away. The issue is whether the reasoning in *Summers* can justify detentions beyond the immediate vicinity of the premises being searched. An exception to the Fourth Amendment rule prohibiting detention absent probable cause must not diverge from its purpose and rationale. . . . It is necessary, then, to discuss the reasons for the rule explained in *Summers* to determine if its rationale extends to a detention like the one here.

A

In *Summers*, the Court recognized three important law enforcement interests that, taken together, justify the detention of an occupant who is on the premises during the execution of a search warrant: officer safety, facilitating the completion of the search, and preventing flight.

1

The first interest identified in *Summers* was "the interest in minimizing the risk of harm to the officers." There the Court held that "the execution of a warrant to search for narcotics is the kind of transaction that may give rise to sudden violence or frantic efforts to conceal or destroy evidence," and "[t]he risk of harm to both the police and the occupants is minimized if the officers routinely exercise unquestioned command of the situation."

When law enforcement officers execute a search warrant, safety considerations require that they secure the premises, which may include detaining current occupants. By taking "unquestioned command of the situation," the officers can search without fear that occupants, who are on the premises and able to observe the course of the search, will become disruptive, dangerous, or otherwise frustrate the search.

[In *Muehler*] . . . the person detained and held in handcuffs was not suspected of the criminal activity being investigated; but, the Court held, she could be detained nonetheless, to secure the premises while the search was underway. The "safety risk inherent in executing a search warrant for weapons was sufficient to justify the use of handcuffs, [and] the need to detain multiple occupants made the use of handcuffs all the more reasonable." While the Court in *Muehler* did remand for consideration of whether the detention there — alleged to have been two or three hours — was necessary in light of all the circumstances, the fact that so prolonged a detention indeed might have been permitted illustrates the far-reaching authority the police have when the detention is made at the scene of the search. This in turn counsels caution before extending the power to detain persons stopped or apprehended away from the premises where the search is being conducted.

It is likely, indeed almost inevitable in the case of a resident, that an occupant will return to the premises at some point; and this might occur when the officers are still conducting the search. Officers can and do mitigate that risk, however, by taking routine precautions, for instance by erecting barricades or posting someone on the perimeter or at the door. In the instant case Bailey had left the premises, apparently without knowledge of the search. He posed little risk to the officers at the scene. If Bailey had rushed back to his apartment, the police could have apprehended and detained him under *Summers*. There is no established principle, however, that allows the arrest of anyone away from the premises who is likely to return.

The risk, furthermore, that someone could return home during the execution of a search warrant is not limited to occupants who depart shortly before the start of a search. The risk that a resident might return home, either for reasons unrelated to the search or after being alerted by someone at the scene, exists whether he left five minutes or five hours earlier. . . .

. . . Although the danger of alerting occupants who remain inside may be of real concern in some instances, as in the case when a no-knock warrant has been issued, this safety rationale rests on the false premise that a detention must take place. If the officers find that it would be dangerous to detain a departing individual in front of a residence, they are not required to stop him. And, where there are grounds to believe the departing occupant is dangerous, or involved in criminal activity, police will generally not need *Summers* to detain him at least for brief questioning, as they can rely instead on *Terry*.

The risk that a departing occupant might notice the police surveillance and alert others still inside the residence is also an insufficient safety rationale to justify expanding the existing categorical authority to detain so that it extends beyond the immediate vicinity of the premises to be searched. . . .

2

The second law enforcement interest relied on in *Summers* was that "the orderly completion of the search may be facilitated if the occupants of the premises are present." This interest in efficiency derives from distinct, but related, concerns.

If occupants are permitted to wander around the premises, there is the potential for interference with the execution of the search warrant. They can hide or destroy evidence, seek to distract the officers, or simply get in the way. Those risks are not presented by an occupant who departs beforehand. So, in this case, after Bailey drove away from the Lake Drive apartment, he was not a threat to the proper execution of the search. Had he returned, officers would have been free to detain him at that point. A general interest in avoiding obstruction of a search, however, cannot justify detention beyond the vicinity of the premises to be searched.

. . . Here, it appears the police officers decided to wait until Bailey had left the vicinity of the search before detaining him. In any event it later became clear to the officers that Bailey did not wish to cooperate. ("I don't live there. Anything you find there ain't mine, and I'm not cooperating with your investigation"). And, by the time the officers brought Bailey back to the apartment, the search team had discovered contraband. Bailey's detention thus served no purpose in ensuring the efficient completion of the search.

3

The third law enforcement interest addressed in *Summers* was the "the legitimate law enforcement interest in preventing flight in the event that incriminating evidence is found." . . . As with the other interests identified in *Summers*, this justification serves to preserve the integrity of the search by controlling those persons who are on the scene. If police officers are concerned about flight, and have to keep close supervision of occupants who are not restrained, they might rush the search, causing unnecessary damage to property or compromising its careful execution. Allowing officers to secure the scene by detaining those present also prevents the search from being impeded by occupants leaving with the evidence being sought or the means to find it.

The concern over flight is not because of the danger of flight itself but because of the damage that potential flight can cause to the integrity of the search. This interest does not independently justify detention of an occupant beyond the immediate vicinity of the premises to be searched. The need to prevent flight, if unbounded, might be used to argue for detention, while a search is underway, of any regular occupant regardless of his or her location at the time of the search. If not circumscribed, the rationale of preventing flight would justify, for instance, detaining a suspect who is 10 miles away, ready to board a plane. The interest in preventing escape from police cannot extend this far without undermining the usual rules for arrest based on probable cause or a brief stop for questioning under standards derived from *Terry*. Even if the detention of a former occupant away from the premises could facilitate a later arrest should incriminating evidence be discovered, "the mere fact that law enforcement may be made more efficient can never by itself justify disregard of the Fourth Amendment." *Mincey v. Arizona* (1978).

In sum, of the three law enforcement interests identified to justify the detention in *Summers*, none applies with the same or similar force to the detention of recent occupants beyond the immediate vicinity of the premises to be searched. Any of the individual interests is also insufficient, on its own, to justify an expansion of the rule in *Summers* to permit the detention of a former occupant, wherever he may be found away from the scene of the search. This would give officers too much discretion. The categorical authority to detain incident to the execution of a search warrant must be limited to the immediate vicinity of the premises to be searched.

B

In *Summers*, the Court recognized . . . [that when] . . . detention occurs in the individual's own home, "it could add only minimally to the public stigma associated with the search itself and would involve neither the inconvenience nor the indignity associated with a compelled visit to the police station.".

Where officers arrest an individual away from his home, however, there is an additional level of intrusiveness. . . . The detention here was more intrusive than a usual detention at the search scene. Bailey's car was stopped; he was ordered to step out and was detained in full public view; he was handcuffed, transported in a marked patrol car, and detained further outside the apartment. These facts illustrate that detention away from a premises where police are already present often will be more intrusive than detentions at the scene.

C

Summers recognized that a rule permitting the detention of occupants on the premises during the execution of a search warrant, even absent individualized suspicion, was reasonable and necessary in light of the law enforcement interests in conducting a safe and efficient search. Because this exception grants substantial authority to police officers to detain outside of the traditional rules of the Fourth Amendment, it must be circumscribed.

. . . Once an occupant is beyond the immediate vicinity of the premises to be searched, the search-related law enforcement interests are diminished and the intrusiveness of the detention is more severe.

Here, petitioner was detained at a point beyond any reasonable understanding of the immediate vicinity of the premises in question; and so this case presents neither the necessity nor the occasion to further define the meaning of immediate vicinity. In closer cases courts can consider a number of factors to determine whether an occupant was detained within the immediate vicinity of the premises to be searched, including the lawful limits of the premises, whether the occupant was within the line of sight of his dwelling, the ease of reentry from the occupant's location, and other relevant factors.

Confining an officer's authority to detain under *Summers* to the immediate vicinity of a premises to be searched is a proper limit because it accords with the rationale of the rule. . . . If officers elect to defer the detention until the suspect or departing occupant leaves the immediate vicinity, the lawfulness of detention is controlled by other standards, including, of course, a brief stop for questioning based on reasonable suspicion under *Terry* or an arrest based on probable cause. A suspect's particular actions in leaving the scene, including whether he appears to be armed or fleeing with the evidence sought, and any information the officers acquire from those who are conducting the search, including information that incriminating evidence has been discovered, will bear, of course, on the lawfulness of a later stop or detention. For example, had the search team radioed Detectives Sneider and Gorbecki about the gun and drugs discovered in the Lake Drive apartment as the officers stopped Bailey and Middleton, this may have provided them with probable cause for an arrest.

III

Detentions incident to the execution of a search warrant are reasonable under the Fourth Amendment because the limited intrusion on personal liberty is outweighed by the special law enforcement interests at stake. Once an individual has left the immediate vicinity of a premises to be searched, however, detentions must be justified by some other rationale.

The judgment of the Court of Appeals is reversed, and the case is remanded for further proceedings consistent with this opinion.

Other Cases: Securing People at Scene of Search Warrant Execution

Los Angeles v. Rettele, 550 U.S. 609 (2007),

SUMMARY: The Rettele's sued police under 42 U.S.C. Section 1983, after the police ordered them out of bed during the execution of a search warrant. Police had them stand for a brief period of time while still naked, despite the fact that the suspects being sought were of a different race. The court determined that the orders by the police to the occupants, in the context of the lawful search in this case, were permissible, and perhaps necessary, to protect the safety of the deputies.

OPINION: In executing a search warrant officers may take reasonable action to secure the premises and to ensure their own safety and the efficacy of the search. The test of reasonableness under the Fourth Amendment is an objective one. . . . Unreasonable actions include the use of excessive force or restraints that cause unnecessary pain or are imposed for a prolonged and unnecessary period of time.

The orders by the police to the occupants, in the context of this lawful search, were permissible, and perhaps necessary, to protect the safety of the deputies. Blankets and bedding can conceal a weapon, and one of the suspects was known to own a firearm, factors which underscore this point. The Constitution does not require an officer to ignore the possibility that an armed suspect may sleep with a weapon within reach. …

The deputies needed a moment to secure the room and ensure that other persons were not close by or did not present a danger. Deputies were not required to turn their backs to allow Rettele and Sadler to retrieve clothing or to cover themselves with the sheets. Rather, "[t]he risk of harm to both the police and the occupants is minimized if the officers routinely exercise unquestioned command of the situation."

This is not to say, of course, that the deputies were free to force Rettele and Sadler to remain motionless and standing for any longer than necessary. We have recognized that "special circumstances, or possibly a prolonged detention" might render a search unreasonable. There is no accusation that the detention here was prolonged. The deputies left the home less than 15 minutes after arriving. The detention was shorter and less restrictive than the 2- to 3-hour handcuff detention upheld in Mena. …And there is no allegation that the deputies prevented Sadler and Rettele from dressing longer than necessary to protect their safety. Sadler was unclothed for no more than two minutes, and Rettele for only slightly more time than that. Sadler testified that once the police were satisfied that no immediate threat was presented, "they wanted us to get dressed and they were pressing us really fast to hurry up and get some clothes on."

Officers executing search warrants on occasion enter a house when residents are engaged in private activity; and the resulting frustration, embarrassment, and humiliation may be real, as was true here. When officers execute a valid warrant and act in a reasonable manner to protect themselves from harm, however, the Fourth Amendment is not violated.

SCOPE OF SEARCH WITH A WARRANT

Where can police search when they have a warrant? When police have a search warrant authorizing them to search for particular items, they can only look where those items may possibly be found. The scope of their search is limited by the character of the things mentioned in the search warrant. In *Arizona v. Hicks*, 480 U.S. 321 (1987), for example, the Court said the police could not permissibly move a stereo to examine serial numbers when the basis for their search was the investigation of a shooting.

There are two recognized tests for determining whether an officer executing a warrant to search premises may search the personal property of a person who is present but not mentioned in the warrant. Under the physical possession test, an officer executing a warrant may search all items that could contain articles identified in the warrant except those that are in the actual physical possession of a person not subject to the warrant. Under the actual notice test, the officer may search any items on the premises unless the officer has actual notice that the property belongs to a nonresident. The premise of the actual notice test is that a magistrate issuing a premises-wide warrant does not intend to authorize a search of the effects of "mere visitors" to the property; however, the requirement of actual notice provides some guidance to the officer executing the warrant.

Things Seen In Plain View During A Search

The plain view doctrine is applicable when police come upon evidence of a crime in a place they are lawfully present (for example, in a residence when executing a search warrant), and they see with their unaided senses, evidence of a crime that is immediately apparent (contraband, an instrumentality of a crime, etc). Under the plain view doctrine, police can seize that evidence without stopping and getting a warrant. (The plain view doctrine, at its core is really about allowing seizures without a warrant, as opposed to whether the evidence is the product of a search).

Coolidge v. New Hampshire, 403 U.S. 433 (1971) discussed the plain view doctrine in considering one of the state's theories why the court should not suppress physical evidence found in Coolidge's car which tied him to a murder. In Coolidge, there was a warrant, but it was invalid because it was not approved of by a neutral and detached magistrate but rather by the attorney general who was leading the investigation (see below). The Court, proceeding as if there was no warrant, stated,

> "The State's third theory in support of the warrantless seizure and search of the Pontiac car is that the car itself was an "instrumentality of the crime," and as such might be seized by the police on Coolidge's property because it was in plain view. ... But, for the reasons that follow, we hold that the "plain view" exception to the warrant requirement is inapplicable to this case.

> It is well established that under certain circumstances the police may seize evidence in plain view without a warrant. But it is important to keep in mind that, in the vast majority of cases, any evidence seized by the police will be in plain view, at least at the moment of seizure.

> An example of the applicability of the "plain view" doctrine is the situation in which the police have a warrant to search a given area for specified objects, and in the course of the search come across some other article of incriminating character. Where the initial intrusion that brings the police within plain view of such an article is supported, not by a warrant, but by one of the recognized exceptions to the warrant requirement, the seizure is also legitimate. Thus the police may inadvertently come across evidence while in "hot pursuit" of a fleeing suspect. And an object that comes into view during a search incident to arrest that is appropriately limited in scope under existing law may be seized without a warrant. Finally, the "plain view" doctrine has been applied where a police officer is not searching for evidence against the accused, but nonetheless inadvertently comes across an incriminating object.

> What the "plain view" cases have in common is that the police officer in each of them had a prior justification for an intrusion in the course of which he came inadvertently across a piece of evidence incriminating the accused. The doctrine serves to supplement the prior justification - whether it be a warrant for another object, hot pursuit, search incident to lawful arrest, or some other legitimate reason for being present unconnected with a search directed against the accused - and permits the warrantless seizure. Of course, the extension of the original justification is legitimate only where it is immediately apparent to the police that they have evidence before them

> ...

> ...As against the minor peril to Fourth Amendment protections, there is a major gain in effective law enforcement. Where, once an otherwise lawful search is in progress, the police inadvertently come upon a piece of evidence, it would often be a needless inconvenience, and sometimes dangerous - to the evidence or to the police themselves - to require them to ignore it until they have obtained a warrant particularly describing it.

> ...[T]he discovery of evidence in plain view must be inadvertent. The rationale of the exception to the warrant requirement ... is that a plain-view seizure will not turn an initially valid (and therefore limited) search into a "general" one, while the inconvenience of procuring a warrant to cover an inadvertent discovery is great. But where the discovery is anticipated, where the police know in advance the location of the evidence and intend to seize

it, the situation is altogether different. The requirement of a warrant to seize imposes no inconvenience whatever, or at least none which is constitutionally cognizable in a legal system that regards warrantless searches as "per se unreasonable" in the absence of "exigent circumstances."

If the initial intrusion is bottomed upon a warrant that fails to mention a particular object, though the police know its location and intend to seize it, then there is a violation of the express constitutional requirement of "Warrants . . . particularly describing . . . [the] things to be seized." The initial intrusion may, of course, be legitimated not by a warrant but by one of the exceptions to the warrant requirement, such as hot pursuit or search incident to lawful arrest. But to extend the scope of such an intrusion to the seizure of objects - not contraband nor stolen nor dangerous in themselves - which the police know in advance they will find in plain view and intend to seize, would fly in the face of the basic rule that no amount of probable cause can justify a warrantless seizure.

In the light of what has been said, it is apparent that the "plain view" exception cannot justify the police seizure of the Pontiac car in this case. The police had ample opportunity to obtain a valid warrant; they knew the automobile's exact description and location well in advance; they intended to seize it when they came upon Coolidge's property. And this is not a case involving contraband or stolen goods or objects dangerous in themselves.

The seizure was therefore unconstitutional, and so was the subsequent search at the station house. Since evidence obtained in the course of the search was admitted at Coolidge's trial, the judgment must be reversed and the case remanded to the New Hampshire Supreme Court."

In the case of *Texas v. Brown*, 460 U.S 730 (1983), the Court discussed at length the intended meaning of the "immediately apparent" requirement. The facts of the case involved an officer who saw defendant holding a green balloon as he shined his flashlight in the driver's car while doing a license check. The Court unanimously concluded that the search (shining the flashlight) was lawful, but grappled with whether the officer had to immediately know that the balloon held drugs. The Court seemed to back off the requirement of "immediately apparent" as part of the plain view analysis, and agreed that at least under those circumstances, the officers had probable cause to believe the balloon contained contraband.

In 1990 the Court abandoned the "inadvertent discovery" limitation—thus modifying *Coolidge*. In *Horton v. California,* 496 U.S. 128 (1990) the Court concluded that the Fourth Amendment does not prohibit a warrantless seizure of an item an officer finds in plain view during a lawful search of premises for different items, even though the officer's discovery of the seized item was not inadvertent (or "by chance"). Provided that the officer's presence on the premises was otherwise lawful, the Court determined that no logical reason justified suppression simply because the officer expected to find the items that were seized in plain view.

Plain Feel

In *Minnesota v. Dickerson*, 508 U.S. 366 (1993), the Court extended the "plain view" doctrine to include "plain touch." In Dickerson, the police were on patrol and had previously responded to complaints of drug sales in the hallways of a building (and had executed several search warrants on the premises of this notorious crack house.). Dickerson was walking towards the police, caught their eye, abruptly halted and began walking the other direction. Officer, now suspicious because of Dickerson's coming from a known drug house and his evasive actions, decided to stop him and investigate. Officers pulled their squad car into the alley, ordered Dickerson to stop and submit to a pat down search. They didn't find any weapons, but the felt a small lump in his nylon jacket. The officer said "I examined it with my fingers and it slid and it felt to be a lump of crack cocaine in cellophane." The officer then reached into Dickerson's pocket and pulled out a small plastic bag containing $1/5^{th}$ gram of cocaine (28 grams = 1 ounce, so $1/5^{th}$ gram is $1/140^{th}$ of an ounce of cocaine). The *Dickerson* Court held that there is a plain feel exception to the warrant requirement which is analogous to the plain view doctrine, but ultimately decided the case on whether the police should have been doing a frisk in the first place.

...The question presented today is whether police officers may seize nonthreatening contraband detected during a protective pat down search of the sort permitted by Terry. We think the answer is clearly that they may, so long as the officer's search stays within the bounds marked by Terry.

We have already held that police officers, at least under certain circumstances, may seize contraband detected during the lawful execution of a Terry search. In *Michigan v. Long* [1983], for example, police approached a man who had driven his car into a ditch and who appeared to be under the influence of some intoxicant. As the man moved to reenter the car from the roadside, police spotted a knife on the floorboard. The officers stopped the man, subjected him to a pat down search, and then inspected the interior of the vehicle for other weapons. During the search of the passenger compartment, the police discovered an open pouch containing marijuana and seized it. This Court upheld the validity of the search and seizure under Terry. The Court held first that, in the context of a roadside encounter, where police have reasonable suspicion based on specific and articulable facts to believe that a driver may be armed and dangerous, they may conduct a protective search for weapons not only of the driver's person but also of the passenger compartment of the automobile. Of course, the protective search of the vehicle, being justified solely by the danger that weapons stored there could be used against the officers or bystanders, must be "limited to those areas in which a weapon may be placed or hidden." ...The Court then held: "If, while conducting a legitimate Terry search of the interior of the automobile, the officer should, as here, discover contraband other than weapons, he clearly cannot be required to ignore the contraband, and the Fourth Amendment does not require its suppression in such circumstances." ...

The Court in Long justified this latter holding by reference to our cases under the "plain-view" doctrine. ...

We think that this doctrine has an obvious application by analogy to cases in which an officer discovers contraband through the sense of touch during an otherwise lawful search. The rationale of the plain view doctrine is that if contraband is left in open view and is observed by a police officer from a lawful vantage point, there has been no invasion of a legitimate expectation of privacy and thus no "search" within the meaning of the Fourth Amendment — or at least no search independent of the initial intrusion that gave the officers their vantage point. ... The warrantless seizure of contraband that presents itself in this manner is deemed justified by the realization that resort to a neutral magistrate under such circumstances would often be impracticable and would do little to promote the objectives of the Fourth Amendment. .... The same can be said of tactile discoveries of contraband. If a police officer lawfully pats down a suspect's outer clothing and feels an object whose contour or mass makes its identity immediately apparent, there has been no invasion of the suspect's privacy beyond that already authorized by the officer's search for weapons; if the object is contraband, its warrantless seizure would be justified by the same practical considerations that inhere in the plain view context.

...

Regardless of whether the officer detects the contraband by sight or by touch, however, the Fourth Amendment's requirement that the officer have probable cause to believe that the item is contraband before seizing it ensures against excessively speculative seizures.

...

It remains to apply these principles to the facts of this case. ... The dispositive question before this Court is whether the officer who conducted the search was acting within the lawful bounds marked by Terry at the time he gained probable cause to believe that the lump in respondent's jacket was contraband.

...[T]he court was correct in holding that the police officer in this case overstepped the bounds of the "strictly circumscribed" search for weapons allowed under Terry. ...Here, the officer's continued exploration of respondent's pocket after having concluded that it contained no weapon was unrelated to "[t]he sole justification of the search [under Terry]: ...the protection of the police officer and others nearby." ... It therefore amounted to the sort of evidentiary search that Terry expressly refused to authorize, and that we have condemned in subsequent cases. ...

Once again, the analogy to the plain-view doctrine is apt. In Arizona v. Hicks . . .(1987), this Court held invalid the seizure of stolen stereo equipment found by police while executing a valid search warrant for other evidence. Although the police were lawfully on the premises pursuant to the search warrant, they obtained probable cause to believe that the stereo equipment was contraband only after moving the equipment to permit officers to read its serial numbers. The subsequent seizure of the equipment could not be justified by the plain-view doctrine, this Court explained, because the incriminating character of the stereo equipment was not immediately apparent; rather, probable cause to believe that the equipment was stolen arose only as a result of a further search — the moving of the equipment — that was not authorized by the search warrant or by any exception to the warrant requirement. The facts of this case are very similar. Although the officer was lawfully in a position to feel the lump in respondent's pocket, because Terry entitled him to place his hands upon respondent's jacket, the court below determined that the incriminating character of the object was not immediately apparent to him. Rather, the officer determined that the item was contraband only after conducting a further search, one not authorized by Terry or by any other exception to the warrant requirement. Because this further search of respondent's pocket was constitutionally invalid, the seizure of the cocaine that followed is likewise unconstitutional. . . .

AFTER THE WARRANT IS EXECUTED

Generally, police must provide a receipt to the person from whom items were taken (or to the person in apparent control of the premises or vehicle) with a list of what items were seized. State laws generally require that the officer who has executed a search warrant shall, as soon as reasonably possible, return the warrant to the issuing judge together with a list of things seized and the date and time of the search. The return and warrant are then filed with the original affidavit. The time frame by which to return the warrant varies. In Oregon, for example the warrant return must be filed within five days (unless specifically authorized by the court), but under federal rules, the warrant must be returned in ten days. Defects in the warrant return do not generally lead to suppression of the evidence seized. Until the search warrant is executed, police must maintain secrecy about the search warrant proceeding. Federal court cases hold that federal trial courts have inherent authority to issue orders to seal search warrants in appropriate cases -- courts have rejected claims that the sealing of a search warrant violates the publics' right of access or the common law right of access.

Chapter Five: Exceptions To The Warrant Requirement

WAS THE SEIZURE REASONABLE EVEN WITHOUT A WARRANT?

In Chapter Three you saw that sometimes governmental action does not meet the Court's definition of a "search" or "seizure." (For example, when police see objects in public view, in open fields, or from the sky; or when items are abandoned or thrown away). Chapter Four explores the components of a valid warrant and what constitutes permissible governmental action during the executing a warrant. Although the Fourth Amendment requires police to have a warrant before conducting a search or a seizure, the Court has repeatedly recognized that reasonableness is the touchstone of the Fourth Amendment, and searches and seizures may be done without a warrant if they are conducted pursuant to a well-established exception to the warrant requirement. We will first examine the reasonableness of seizures done without a warrant and then address searches.

Arrests

An arrest is more than just a temporary or brief detention of a person (what we now call a "stop"). To justify an arrest, officers must have probable cause to believe that a crime has been committed and that the person arrested committed it. Although the Fourth Amendment seems to require police obtain a warrant before they seize an individual, the Court has carved out significant exceptions that, for all practical purposes, allow most arrests to be made without a warrant.

First, the Court in *United States v. Santana*, 427 U.S. 38 (1975), decided that a warrantless arrest of a suspect in a public place was valid if the suspect retreated from the public place into a private place. In *Santana* an undercover police officer bought heroin from McCafferty. He then drove her to Santana's house where she took the officer's money, went in to Santana's home, and came out with several envelopes of heroin. The officer arrested McCafferty and asked her where the money was. McCafferty indicated that Santana had it. While one officer transported McCafferty to the police station, other officers went to Santana's home and saw her standing in the doorway with a brown paper bag in her hand. They identified themselves as police officers, and Santana attempted to escape into her house. The officers chased and caught her. During the scuffle, two bundles of heroin fell to the floor. Police told Santana to empty her pockets, and she produced $135.00, of which $70.00 was the undercover officer's money. The court held that the warrantless arrest was not a violation of the Fourth Amendment because a warrantless arrest that begins in a public place is valid even if the suspect retreats into a private place and is arrested there.

"While it may be true under common law of property that the threshold of one's dwelling is 'private' place . . . not in an area where she had any expectation of privacy. . . She was not merely visible to the public but was exposed to public view, speech, hearing, and touch as if she had been standing completely outside her house. The police, therefore, had probable cause to arrest her and did so in the proper manner. Santana could not, furthermore, thwart her arrest by retreating into her private home. The District Court was correct in concluding that 'hot pursuit' means some sort of a chase but it need not be extended hue and cry 'in and about public streets.' The fact that the pursuit ended almost as soon as it began did not render it any less a 'hot pursuit' sufficient to justify the warrantless entry into Santana's house."

The Court justified Santana's arrest by relying on the hot pursuit rationale, but one year later, in *United States v. Watson*, 423 U.S. 411 (1976), the Court found that the police could lawfully conduct a warrantless arrest in public — even when they had the opportunity to get a warrant but did not do so (as long as it was permissible by state law or agency policy). In *Watson*, a reliable informant telephoned the postal inspector and informed him that he was in possession of a stolen credit card provided by Watson and that Watson had agreed to furnish the informant with additional cards. The informant agreed to meet with Watson and give a signal if he had additional stolen cards. When the signal was given, officers arrested Watson and took him from a restaurant where he was sitting to the street where he was Mirandized. When a search revealed no credit cards on Watson, the postal inspector asked if he could look inside Watson's car. The inspector told Watson that "if I find anything, it is going to go against you." Watson agreed to the search. Using keys furnished by Watson, the car was searched and an envelope containing stolen credit cards was found. Watson was charged and convicted with possession of stolen credit cards.

The Court decided whether the police, who had sufficient time to get an arrest warrant, could nevertheless conduct a warrantless arrest of Watson in a public place. The Court held that they could. *Watson* creates a general "public place" exception to the warrant requirement regardless of the severity of the crime.

Four years after *Watson*, in *Payton v. New York*, 445 U.S. 573 (1980), the Court decided that the public place exception does not extend to the home. It concluded, "In terms that apply equally to seizures of property and to seizures of persons, the Fourth Amendment has drawn a firm line at the entrance to the house. Absent exigent circumstances, that threshold may not reasonably be crossed without a warrant."

In *Payton* police officers conducted a two-day intensive investigation and assembled sufficient evidence to establish probable cause to believe that Payton had murdered the manager of a gas station. Officers went to Payton's apartment to arrest him. They had no warrant, although they had time to obtain one. Light and music came from the apartment, but there was no response to the officers' knock on the metal door. Officers summoned emergency assistance and used crowbars to break open the door and enter the apartment. No one was present in the apartment, but police saw in plain view a .30-caliber shell casing, which they seized. Payton later surrendered to the police and was indicted for murder. In a motion to suppress the evidence, the trial court ruled that the search of the house was illegal and suppressed some evidence. The court, however, held that the shell casing was in plain view and allowed it to be admitted into evidence. Payton was ultimately convicted.

The Court held that the Fourth Amendment requires police to get an arrest warrant when they enter a person's home to make a routine felony arrest when there is time to obtain a warrant. Police have lawful authority under the Fourth Amendment to enter the residence of a person for whom they have an arrest warrant, provided that the officers reasonably believe that the person named in the warrant is present. "If there is sufficient evidence of a citizen's participation in a felony to persuade a judicial officer that his arrest is justified, it is constitutionally reasonable to require him to open his doors to the officers of the law. Thus, for Fourth Amendment purposes, an arrest warrant founded on probable cause implicitly carries with it the limited authority to enter a dwelling in which the suspect lives when there is reason to believe the suspect is within." *Payton*, 445 U.S., at 602-03.

After *Watson* and *Payton*, police can either wait for the suspect to be in public and arrest without a warrant, or obtain an arrest warrant, unless there is some other exception which would allow police to enter a home and arrest (for example, consent or the hot pursuit exception based on exigent circumstances.)

The next year, the Court decided *Steagold v. New York*, 451 U.S. 204 (1981) and held that an arrest warrant does not justify police entry into the residence of a third person (not the person named in the warrant) to conduct an arrest. Instead, police must seek a search warrant if they wish to arrest someone inside a third person's home (absent consent). The Court expressed concerned for the privacy of the third person rather than basing its decision on the liberty interest of the person mentioned in the warrant. Now, if the police enter the third person's dwelling unlawfully, they have standing to claim that their Fourth Amendment rights have been violated; note that the defendant who is arrested has no "standing" to complain on behalf of the homeowner.

Reasonable Manner Of Arrest[63]

Defendants can challenge an arrest on two grounds: 1) a lack of probable cause and 2) an unreasonable manner of arrest. Police may not use any more force than necessary (excessive force) to conduct an arrest. Historically, the courts have held that it was reasonable for a police officer to shoot a fleeing felon. In *Tennessee v. Garner*, 471 U.S. 1 (1985), the Court limited the use of deadly force by equating the shooting of a fleeing suspect to a seizure and thus required the reasonableness of the police action to be tested under the Fourth Amendment. After *Graham v. Connor*, 490 U.S. 396 (1989), courts are to evaluate challenges to the manner of arrest (use of force cases) not by looking at the subjective motivation of the officers (did they mean the arrestee ill-will) but rather at the objective reasonableness of their behavior.

TENNESSEE v. GARNER
471 U.S. 1 (1985)

JUSTICE WHITE delivered the opinion of the court.

At about 10:45 P.M. on October 3, 1974, Memphis Police Officers Elton Hymon and Leslie Wright were dispatched to answer a "prowler inside call." Upon arriving at the scene they saw a woman standing on her porch and gesturing toward the adjacent house. She told them she had heard glass breaking and that "they" or "someone" was breaking in next door. While Wright radioed the dispatcher to say that they were on the scene, Hymon went behind the house. He heard a door slam and saw someone run across the backyard. The fleeing suspect . . . Edward Garner, stopped at a 6-feet-high chain link fence at the edge of the yard. With the aid of a flashlight, Hymon was able to see Garner's face and hands. He saw no sign of a weapon, and, though not certain, was "reasonably sure" and "figured" that Garner was unarmed. . . . He thought Garner was 17 or 18 years old and about 5'5" or 5'7" tall. While Garner was

crouched at the base of the fence, Hymon called out "police, halt" and took a few steps toward him. Garner then began to climb over the fence. Convinced that if Garner made it over the fence he would elude capture, Hymon shot him. The bullet hit Garner in the back of the head. Garner was taken by ambulance to a hospital, where he died on the operating table. Ten dollars and a purse taken from the house were found on his body.

In using deadly force to prevent the escape, Hymon was acting under the authority of a Tennessee statute and pursuant to Police Department policy. The statute provides that "[i]f, after notice of the intention to arrest the defendant, he either flees or forcibly resists, the officer may use all the necessary means to effect the arrest." The Department policy was slightly more restrictive than the statute, but still allowed the use of deadly force in cases of burglary. . . . The incident was reviewed by the Memphis Police Firearm's Review Board

---

[63] On January 25, 2023 five Memphis Police officers were charged with second degree murder and other charges arising from the death of Tyre Nichols as a result of excessive force used in his seizure for purportedly driving in a reckless manner on January 7, 2023. As of this writing, January 31st, 2023 another officer was charged, the SCORPIAN unit for which they worked was disbanded, peaceful protests have occurred, and it was reported that four of the five former police officers who were indicted were previously suspended or received written reprimands. Additionally, "the police officers report written hours after officers beat Tyre Nichols was starkly at odds with what videos have since revealed, making no mention of the powerful kicks and punches on Mr. Nichols and instead claiming that he was violent. See, New York Times, 31 January, 2023, "Videos Contradict Initial Police Report on Tyre Nichols Arrest" and CNN, "First police report in Tyre Nichols case does not match video of deadly beating."

and presented to a grand jury. Neither took any action. . .

Garner's father then brought this action in the Federal District Court for the Western District of Tennessee, seeking damages under 42 USC Sec. 1983 for asserted violations of Garner's constitutional rights. The complaint alleged that the shooting violated the Fourth, Fifth, Sixth, Eighth, and Fourteenth Amendments of the United States Constitution. It named as defendants Officer Hymon, the Police Department, its Director, and the Mayor and city of Memphis. After a 3-day bench trial, the District Court entered judgment for all defendants. It dismissed the claims against the Mayor and the Director for lack of evidence. It then concluded that Hymon's actions were authorized by the Tennessee statute, which in turn was constitutional. Hymon had employed the only reasonable and practicable means of preventing Garner's escape. Garner had "recklessly and heedlessly attempted to vault over the fence to escape, thereby assuming the risk of being fired upon." . . .

The Court of Appeals reversed and remanded. . . . It reasoned that the killing of a fleeing suspect is a "seizure" under the Fourth Amendment, and is therefore constitutional only if "reasonable." The Tennessee statute failed as applied to this case because it did not adequately limit the use of deadly force by distinguishing between felonies of different magnitudes — "the facts, as found, did not justify the use of deadly force under the Fourth Amendment." . . . Officers cannot resort to deadly force unless they "have probable cause . . . to believe that the suspect [has committed a felony and] poses a threat to the safety of the officers or a danger to the community if left at large." . . .

Whenever an officer restrains the freedom of a person to walk away, he has seized that person. . . . While it is not always clear just when minimal police interference becomes a seizure . . . there can be no question that apprehension by the use of deadly force is a seizure subject to the reasonableness requirement of the Fourth Amendment.

A police officer may arrest a person if he has probable cause to believe that person committed a crime. . . . Petitioners and appellant argue that if this requirement is satisfied the Fourth Amendment has nothing to say about how that seizure is made. This submission ignores the many cases in which this Court, by balancing the extent of the intrusion against the need for it, has examined the reasonableness of the manner in which a search or seizure is conducted. . . .

Petitioners and appellant have not persuaded us that shooting nondangerous fleeing suspects is so vital as to outweigh the suspect's interest in his own life.

The use of deadly force to prevent the escape of all felony suspects, whatever the circumstances, is constitutionally unreasonable. It is not better that all felony suspects die than that they escape. Where the suspect poses no immediate threat to the officer and no threat to others, the harm resulting from failing to apprehend him does not justify the use of deadly force to do so. It is no doubt unfortunate when a suspect who is in sight escapes, but the fact that the police arrive a little late or are a little slower afoot does not always justify killing the suspect. A police officer may not seize an unarmed, nondangerous suspect by shooting him dead. The Tennessee statute is unconstitutional insofar as it authorizes the use of deadly force against such fleeing suspects.

It is not, however, unconstitutional on its face. Where the officer has probable cause to believe that the suspect poses a threat of serious physical harm, either to the officer or to others, it is not constitutionally unreasonable to prevent escape by using deadly force. Thus, if the suspect threatens the officer with a weapon or there is probable cause to believe that he has committed a crime involving the infliction or threatened infliction of serious physical harm, deadly force may be used if necessary to prevent escape, and if, where feasible, some warning has been given. As applied in such circumstances, the Tennessee statute would pass constitutional muster. . . .

...In reversing, the Court of Appeals accepted the District Court's factual conclusions and held that "the facts, as found, did not justify the use of deadly force." . . . We agree. . . .

GRAHAM V. CONNOR
490 U.S. 396 (1989)

CHIEF JUSTICE REHNQUIST delivered the opinion of the Court.

This case requires us to decide what constitutional standard governs a free citizen's claim that law enforcement officials used excessive force in the course of making an arrest, investigatory stop, or other "seizure" of his person. We hold that such claims are properly analyzed under the Fourth Amendment's "objective reasonableness" standard, rather than under a substantive due process standard.

In this action under 42 U.S.C. 1983, petitioner Dethorne Graham seeks to recover damages for injuries allegedly sustained when law enforcement officers used physical force against him during the course of an investigatory stop. ... On November 12, 1984, Graham, a diabetic, felt the onset of an insulin reaction. He asked a friend, William Berry, to drive him to a nearby convenience store so he could purchase some orange juice to counteract the reaction. Berry agreed, but when Graham entered the store, he saw a number of people ahead of him in the checkout line. Concerned about the delay, he hurried out of the store and asked Berry to drive him to a friend's house instead.

Respondent Connor, an officer of the Charlotte, North Carolina, Police Department, saw Graham hastily enter and leave the store. The officer became suspicious that something was amiss and followed Berry's car. About one-half mile from the store, he made an investigative stop. Although Berry told Connor that Graham was simply suffering from a "sugar reaction," the officer ordered Berry and Graham to wait while he found out what, if anything, had happened at the convenience store. When Officer Connor returned to his patrol car to call for backup assistance, Graham got out of the car, ran around it twice, and finally sat down on the curb, where he passed out briefly.

In the ensuing confusion, a number of other Charlotte police officers arrived on the scene in response to Officer Connor's request for backup. One of the officers rolled Graham over on the sidewalk and cuffed his hands tightly behind his back, ignoring Berry's pleas to get him some sugar. Another officer said: "I've seen a lot of people with sugar diabetes that never acted like this. Ain't nothing wrong with the M. F. but drunk. Lock the S. B. up." Several officers then lifted Graham up from behind, carried him over to Berry's car, and placed him face down on its hood. Regaining consciousness, Graham asked the officers to check in his wallet for a diabetic decal that he carried. In response, one of the officers told him to "shut up" and shoved his face down against the hood of the car. Four officers grabbed Graham and threw him headfirst into the police car. A friend of Graham's brought some orange juice to the car, but the officers refused to let him have it. Finally, Officer Connor received a report that Graham had done nothing wrong at the convenience store, and the officers drove him home and released him.

At some point during his encounter with the police, Graham sustained a broken foot, cuts on his wrists, a bruised forehead, and an injured shoulder; he also claims to have developed a loud ringing in his right ear that continues to this day. He commenced this action under 42 U.S.C. 1983 against the individual officers involved in the incident, all of whom are respondents here, alleging that they had used excessive force in making the investigatory stop, in violation of "rights secured to him under the Fourteenth Amendment to the United States Constitution and 42 U.S.C. 1983." The case was tried before a jury. At the close of petitioner's evidence, respondents moved for a directed verdict. . . . Finding that the amount of force used by the officers was "appropriate under the circumstances," that "[t]here was no discernable injury inflicted," and that the force used "was not applied maliciously or sadistically for the very purpose of causing harm," but in "a good faith effort to maintain or restore order in the face of a potentially explosive situation," the District Court granted respondents' motion for a directed verdict.

A divided panel of the Court of Appeals for the Fourth Circuit affirmed. . . . [T]he majority held that a reasonable jury applying the four-part test it had just endorsed to petitioner's evidence "could not find that the force applied was constitutionally excessive." The dissenting judge argued that this Court's decisions in *Terry v. Ohio* and *Tennessee v. Garner*, required that excessive force claims arising out of investigatory stops be analyzed under the Fourth Amendment's "objective reasonableness" standard. We granted certiorari and now reverse.

We reject this notion that all excessive force claims brought under 1983 are governed by a single generic standard. As we have said many times, 1983 "is not itself a source of substantive rights," but merely provides "a method for vindicating federal rights elsewhere conferred." *Baker v. McCollan.* In addressing an excessive force claim brought under 1983, analysis begins by identifying the specific constitutional right allegedly infringed by the challenged application of force. ("The first inquiry in any 1983 suit" is "to isolate the precise constitutional violation with which [the defendant] is charged"). In most instances, that will be either the Fourth Amendment's prohibition against unreasonable seizures of the person, or the Eighth Amendment's ban on cruel and unusual

punishments, which are the two primary sources of constitutional protection against physically abusive governmental conduct. The validity of the claim must then be judged by reference to the specific constitutional standard which governs that right, rather than to some generalized "excessive force" standard.

Where, as here, the excessive force claim arises in the context of an arrest or investigatory stop of a free citizen, it is most properly characterized as one invoking the protections of the Fourth Amendment . . . This much is clear from our decision in *Tennessee v. Garner*, supra. . . . Though the complaint alleged violations of both the Fourth Amendment and the Due Process Clause, we analyzed the constitutionality of the challenged application of force solely by reference to the Fourth Amendment's prohibition against unreasonable seizures of the person, holding that the "reasonableness" of a particular seizure depends not only on when it is made, but also on how it is carried out. Today we make explicit what was implicit in *Garner's* analysis, and hold that all claims that law enforcement officers have used excessive force - deadly or not - in the course of an arrest, investigatory stop, or other "seizure" of a free citizen should be analyzed under the Fourth Amendment and its "reasonableness" standard, rather than under a "substantive due process" approach.

Our Fourth Amendment jurisprudence has long recognized that the right to make an arrest or investigatory stop necessarily carries with it the right to use some degree of physical coercion or threat thereof to effect it. Because "[t]he test of reasonableness under the Fourth Amendment is not capable of precise definition or mechanical application," however, its proper application requires careful attention to the facts and circumstances of each particular case, including the severity of the crime at issue, whether the suspect poses an immediate threat to the safety of the officers or others, and whether he is actively resisting arrest or attempting to evade arrest by flight.

The "reasonableness" of a particular use of force must be judged from the perspective of a reasonable officer on the scene, rather than with the 20/20 vision of hindsight. … With respect to a claim of excessive force…[t]he calculus of reasonableness must embody allowance for the fact that police officers are often forced to make split-second judgments - in circumstances that are tense, uncertain, and rapidly evolving - about the amount of force that is necessary in a particular situation.

As in other Fourth Amendment contexts, however, the "reasonableness" inquiry in an excessive force case is an objective one: the question is whether the officers' actions are "objectively reasonable" in light of the facts and circumstances confronting them, without regard to their underlying intent or motivation. . . . An officer's evil intentions will not make a Fourth Amendment violation out of an objectively reasonable use of force; nor will an officer's good intentions make an objectively unreasonable use of force constitutional.

[The court remanded the case to the lower court to consider the claim under the Fourth Amendment analysis.]

Other Cases: Reasonable Use of Force in Seizure

Mullenix v. Luna, 577 U.S. ___ (2015)

SUMMARY: On the night of March 23, 2010, Sergeant Randy Baker of the Tulia, Texas Police Department followed Israel Leija, Jr., to a drive-in restaurant, with a warrant for his arrest. When Baker approached Leija's car and informed him that he was under arrest, Leija sped off, headed for Interstate 27. Baker gave chase and was quickly joined by Trooper Gabriel Rodriguez of the Texas Department of Public Safety (DPS).

Leija entered the interstate and led the officers on an 18-minute chase at speeds between 85 and 110 miles per hour. Twice during the chase, Leija called the Tulia Police dispatcher, claiming to have a gun and threatening to shoot at police officers if they did not abandon their pursuit. The dispatcher relayed Leija's threats, together with a report that Leija might be intoxicated, to all concerned officers.

As Baker and Rodriguez maintained their pursuit, other law enforcement officers set up tire spikes at three locations. Officer Troy Ducheneaux of the Canyon Police Department manned the spike strip at the first location Leija was expected to reach, beneath the overpass at Cemetery Road. Ducheneaux and the other officers had received training on the deployment of spike strips, including on how to take a defensive position so as to minimize the risk posed by the passing driver.

DPS Trooper Chadrin Mullenix also responded. He drove to the Cemetery Road overpass, initially intending to set up a spike strip there. Upon learning of the other spike strip positions, however, Mullenix began to consider another tactic: shooting at Leija's car in order to disable it. Mullenix had not received training in this tactic and had not attempted it before, but he radioed the idea to Rodriguez. Rodriguez responded "10-4," gave Mullenix his position, and said that Leija had slowed to 85 miles per hour. Mullenix then asked the DPS dispatcher to inform his supervisor, Sergeant Byrd, of his plan and ask if Byrd thought it was "worth doing." Before receiving Byrd's response, Mullenix exited his vehicle and, armed with his service rifle, took a shooting position on the overpass, 20 feet above I-27. Respondents allege that from this position, Mullenix still could hear Byrd's response to "stand by" and "see if the spikes work first."

As Mullenix waited for Leija to arrive, he and another officer, Randall County Sheriff's Deputy Tom Shipman, discussed whether Mullenix's plan would work and how and where to shoot the vehicle to best carry it out. Shipman also informed Mullenix that another officer was located beneath the overpass.

Approximately three minutes after Mullenix took up his shooting position, he spotted Leija's vehicle, with Rodriguez in pursuit. As Leija approached the overpass, Mullenix fired six shots. Leija's car continued forward beneath the overpass, where it engaged the spike strip, hit the median, and rolled two and a half times. It was later determined that Leija had been killed by Mullenix's shots, four of which struck his upper body. There was no evidence that any of Mullenix's shots hit the car's radiator, hood, or engine block.

Respondents sued Mullenix . . . alleging that he had violated the Fourth Amendment by using excessive force against Leija. Mullenix moved for summary judgment on the ground of qualified immunity, but the District Court denied his motion, finding that "[t]here are genuine issues of fact as to whether Trooper Mullenix acted recklessly, or acted as a reasonable, trained peace officer would have acted in the same or similar circumstances."

Mullenix appealed, and the Court of Appeals for the Fifth Circuit affirmed. The court agreed with the District Court that the "immediacy of the risk posed by Leija is a disputed fact that a reasonable jury could find either in the plaintiffs' favor or in the officer's favor, precluding us from concluding that Mullenix acted objectively reasonably as a matter of law."

. . . .

OPINION: We address only the qualified immunity question, not whether there was a Fourth Amendment violation in the first place, and now reverse.

The doctrine of qualified immunity shields officials from civil liability so long as their conduct " 'does not violate clearly established statutory or constitutional rights of which a reasonable person would have known.' " A clearly established right is one that is "sufficiently clear that every reasonable official would have understood that what he is doing violates that right." "We do not require a case directly on point, but existing precedent must have placed the statutory or constitutional question beyond debate." Put simply, qualified immunity protects "all but the plainly incompetent or those who knowingly violate the law."

…

…[E]xcessive force cases involving car chases reveal the hazy legal backdrop against which Mullenix acted. In Brosseau . . . the Court held that an officer did not violate clearly established law when she shot a fleeing suspect out of fear that he endangered "other officers on foot who [she] believed were in the immediate area," "the occupied vehicles in [his] path," and "any other citizens who might be in the area." …

This Court has considered excessive force claims in connection with high-speed chases on only two occasions since Brosseau. In *Scott v. Harris* the Court held that an officer did not violate the Fourth Amendment by ramming the car of a fugitive whose reckless driving "posed an actual and imminent threat to the lives of any pedestrians who might have been present, to other civilian motorists, and to the officers involved in the chase." And *Plumhoff v. Rickard* held] … that an officer acted reasonably when he fatally shot a fugitive who was "intent on resuming" a chase that "pose[d] a deadly threat for others on the road." The Court has thus never found the use of deadly force in connection with a dangerous car chase to violate the Fourth Amendment, let alone to be a basis for denying qualified immunity.

…

JUSTICE SCALIA, concurring in the judgment, Omitted.

JUSTICE SOTOMAYOR, dissenting.

Chadrin Mullenix fired six rounds in the dark at a car traveling 85 miles per hour. He did so without any training in that tactic, against the wait order of his superior officer, and less than a second before the car hit spike strips deployed to stop it. Mullenix's rogue conduct killed the driver, Israel Leija, Jr. Because it was clearly established under the Fourth Amendment that an officer in Mullenix's position should not have fired the shots, I respectfully dissent from the grant of summary reversal.

I

Resolving all factual disputes in favor of plaintiffs, as the Court must on a motion for summary judgment, Mullenix knew the following facts before he shot at Leija's engine block: Leija had led police officers on an 18-minute car chase, at speeds ranging from 85 to 110 miles per hour. Leija had twice called the police dispatcher threatening to shoot at officers if they did not cease the pursuit. Police officers were deploying three sets of spike strips in order to stop Leija's flight. The officers were trained to stop a car using spike strips. This training included how to take a defensive position to minimize the risk of danger from the target car. Mullenix knew that spike strips were being set up directly beneath the overpass where he was stationed. There is no evidence below that any of the officers with whom Mullenix was in communication — including Officer Troy Ducheneaux, whom Mullenix believed to be below the overpass — had expressed any concern for their safety.

Mullenix had no training in shooting to disable a moving vehicle and had never seen the tactic done before. He also lacked permission to take the shots: When Mullenix relayed his plan to his superior officer, Robert Byrd, Byrd responded "stand by" and "see if the spikes work first." Three minutes after arriving at the overpass, Mullenix fired six rounds at Leija's car. None hit the car's engine block; at least four struck Leija in the upper body, killing Leija.

II

When confronting a claim of qualified immunity, a court asks two questions. First, the court considers whether the officer in fact violated a constitutional right. Second, the court asks whether the contours of the right were "sufficiently clear that a reasonable official would [have understood] that what he is doing violates that right." This Court has rejected the idea that "an official action is protected by qualified immunity unless the very action in question has previously been held unlawful." Instead, the crux of the qualified immunity test is whether officers have "fair notice" that they are acting unconstitutionally.

Respondents here allege that Mullenix violated the Fourth Amendment's prohibition on unreasonable seizures by using deadly force to apprehend Leija. This Court's precedents clearly establish that the Fourth Amendment is violated unless the " 'governmental interests' " in effectuating a particular kind of seizure outweigh the " 'nature and quality of the intrusion on the individual's Fourth Amendment interests.' " There must be a "governmental interes[t]" not only in effectuating a seizure, but also in "how [the seizure] is carried out."

Balancing a particular governmental interest in the use of deadly force against the intrusion occasioned by the use of that force is inherently a fact-specific inquiry, not susceptible to bright lines. But it is clearly established that the government must have some interest in using deadly force over other kinds of force.

Here, then, the clearly established legal question — the question a reasonable officer would have asked — is whether, under all the circumstances as known to Mullenix, there was a governmental interest in shooting at the car rather than waiting for it to run over spike strips.

The majority does not point to any such interest here. It claims that Mullenix's goal was not merely to stop the car, but to stop the car "in a manner that avoided the risks" of relying on spike strips. But there is no evidence in the record that shooting at Leija's engine block would stop the car in such a manner.

. . . .

[N]either petitioner nor the majority can point to any possible marginal gain in shooting at the car over using the spike strips already in place. It is clearly established that there must be some governmental interest that necessitates deadly force. . . .

Under the circumstances known to him at the time, Mullenix puts forth no plausible reason to choose shooting at Leija's engine block over waiting for the results of the spike strips. I would thus hold that Mullenix violated Leija's clearly established right to be free of intrusion absent some governmental interest.

III

The majority largely evades this key legal question by focusing primarily on the governmental interest in whether the car should be stopped rather than the dispositive question of how the car should be stopped. But even assuming that Leija posed a "sufficient" or "immediate" threat, Mullenix did not face a "choice between two evils" of shooting at a suspect's car or letting him go. Instead, Mullenix chose to employ a potentially lethal tactic (shooting at Leija's engine block) in addition to a tactic specifically designed to accomplish the same result (spike strips). By granting Mullenix qualified immunity, this Court goes a step further than our previous cases and does so without full briefing or argument.

When Mullenix confronted his superior officer after the shooting, his first words were, "How's that for proactive?" (Mullenix was apparently referencing an earlier counseling session in which Byrd suggested that he was not enterprising enough.) The glib comment does not impact our legal analysis; an officer's actual intentions are irrelevant to the Fourth

Amendment's "objectively reasonable" inquiry. But the comment seems to me revealing of the culture this Court's decision supports when it calls it reasonable — or even reasonably reasonable — to use deadly force for no discernible gain and over a supervisor's express order to "stand by." By sanctioning a "shoot first, think later" approach to policing, the Court renders the protections of the Fourth Amendment hollow.

For the reasons discussed, I would deny Mullenix's petition for a writ of certiorari. I thus respectfully dissent

County of Sacramento v. Lewis, 520 U.S. 397 (1998)

SUMMARY: Brown and her husband approached a police checkpoint and then turned around to avoid it. Deputy Morrison and Reserve Deputy Burns pursued the vehicle for more than four miles at speeds of excess of 100 miles per hour. When the Browns stopped, Morrison pointed his gun at the truck and ordered them to raise their hands. Burns, who was unarmed, went to the passenger side of the truck and ordered Brown out of the vehicle. When Brown did not respond after the second request, Burns pulled Brown from the truck by the arm and swung her to the ground. The fall caused severe injuries to Brown's knees, possibly requiring knee replacement. Brown sued Burns, the county sheriff, and the county for her injuries claiming that they failed to adequately review Burn's background (he had a history of assault and battery, resisting arrest, driving while intoxicated, etc.)

The Court held the county could not be liable for a case involving excessive use of force for a single hiring decision made by a county official.

Scott v. Harris, 550 U.S. 372 (2007),

SUMMARY: The Court examined whether an officer ramming defendant's car with a police patrol car was a reasonable (or excessive) use of force and whether the officer had immunity when Harris sued him.

As part of its review, the Court, for the first time, examined video evidence of the actual chase. The members of the majority characterized

Harris' driving as "shockingly fast" "swerving around more than a dozen cars" "forcing cars to their respective shoulders in order to avoid being hit." The majority thus concluded that Scott should not be liable for the serious injuries Harris suffered when he rammed Harris' car with his patrol car causing Harris to lose control of his vehicle, leave the roadway, drive down an embankment and crash.

(MAJORITY) OPINION:

> "A police officer's attempt to terminate a dangerous high-speed car chase that threatens the lives of innocent bystanders does not violate the Fourth Amendment, even when it places the fleeing motorist at risk of serious injury or death.

> The car chase that respondent initiated in this case posed a substantial and immediate risk of serious physical injury to others; no reasonable jury could conclude otherwise. Scott's attempt to terminate the chase by forcing respondent off the road was reasonable. . . ."

Justice Stevens' saw things quite differently. He opined that the Court of Appeals did not err when it concluded that there was "no evidence that [Harris] ever lost control of his vehicle, that the incident in the shopping center parking lot did not create any risk to pedestrians or other vehicles because the chase occurred just before 11 p.m. on a weekday night and the center was closed." He added, "the video showed no pedestrians, parked cars, sidewalks or residences visible at any time during the chase."

> "If two groups of judges can disagree so vehemently about the nature of the pursuit and the circumstances surrounding that pursuit, it seems eminently likely that a reasonable juror could disagree with this Court's characterization of events. Moreover, under the standard set forth in *Garner*, it is certainly possible that "a jury could conclude that Scott unreasonably used deadly force to seize Harris by ramming him off the road under the instant circumstances."

Not only does . . . [the majority] rule fly in the face of the flexible and case-by-case "reasonableness" approach applied in *Garner* and *Graham v. Connor*, but it is also arguably inapplicable to the case at hand, given that it is not clear that this chase threatened the life of any "innocent bystande[r]." In my view, the risks inherent in justifying unwarranted police conduct on the basis of unfounded assumptions are unacceptable, particularly when less drastic measures — in this case, the use of stop sticks . . . or a simple warning issued from a loudspeaker — could have avoided such a tragic result. In my judgment, jurors in Georgia should be allowed to evaluate the reasonableness of the decision to ram respondent's speeding vehicle in a manner that created an obvious risk of death and has in fact made him a quadriplegic at the age of 19."

Arrests For Minor Crimes

The next question explores whether it is reasonable to arrest someone for a minor infraction.

ATWATER v. CITY OF LAGO VISTA
532 U.S. 318 (2001)

JUSTICE SOUTER delivered the opinion of the Court.

The question is whether the Fourth Amendment forbids a warrantless arrest for a minor criminal offense, such as a misdemeanor seatbelt violation punishable only by a fine. We hold that it does not.

[Facts of case are seen in the dissent, but essentially, Atwater was stopped for failing to wear a seatbelt and to have her children seatbelted. She was arrested in their presence, taken to jail, remained detained for one hour before she appeared before a magistrate and was released on $310 bond. She was charged with various minor crimes and ultimately plead to one charge and paid a $50.00 fine. In each of the offenses for which she was charged, the officer had discretion to issue a citation rather than arrest her.]

"[T]here is no historical evidence that the Framers or proponents of the Fourth Amendment, outspokenly opposed to the infamous general warrants and writs of assistance, were at all concerned about warrantless arrests by local constables and other peace officers." We simply cannot conclude that the Fourth Amendment, as originally understood, forbade peace officers to arrest without a warrant for misdemeanors not amounting to or involving breach of the peace.

Atwater . . . argues for a modern arrest rule, one not necessarily requiring violent breach of the peace, but nonetheless forbidding custodial arrest, even upon probable cause, when conviction could not ultimately carry any jail time and when the government shows no compelling need for immediate detention.

. . .

Accordingly, we confirm today what our prior cases have intimated: the standard of probable cause "applie[s] to all arrests, without the need to `balance' the interests and circumstances involved in particular situations." If an officer has probable cause to believe that an individual has committed even a very minor criminal offense in his presence, he may, without violating the Fourth Amendment, arrest the offender.

Atwater's arrest satisfied constitutional requirements. There is no dispute that Officer Turek had probable cause to believe that Atwater had committed a crime in his presence. She admits that neither she nor her children were wearing seat belts, as required by Tex. Tran. Code Ann. Turek was accordingly authorized (not required, but authorized) to make a custodial arrest without balancing costs and benefits or determining whether or not Atwater's arrest was in some sense necessary.

Nor was the arrest made in an "extraordinary manner, unusually harmful to [her] privacy or . . . physical interests."

Atwater's arrest was surely "humiliating," as she says in her brief, but it was no more "harmful to . . . privacy or . . . physical interests" than the normal custodial arrest. . . . The arrest and booking were inconvenient and embarrassing to Atwater, but not so extraordinary as to violate the Fourth Amendment.

JUSTICE O'CONNOR, with whom JUSTICE STEVENS, JUSTICE GINSBURG, and JUSTICE BREYER join, dissenting.

The Fourth Amendment guarantees the right to be free from "unreasonable searches and seizures." The Court recognizes that the arrest of Gail Atwater was a "pointless indignity" that served no discernible state interest, and yet holds that her arrest was constitutionally permissible. Because the Court's position is inconsistent with the explicit guarantee of the Fourth Amendment, I dissent.

A full custodial arrest, such as the one to which Ms. Atwater was subjected, is the quintessential seizure. When a full custodial arrest is effected without a warrant, the plain language of the Fourth Amendment requires that the arrest be reasonable. It is beyond cavil that "[t]he touchstone of our analysis under the Fourth Amendment is always 'the reasonableness in all the circumstances of the particular governmental invasion of a citizen's personal security.' "

. . . .

The Court's thorough exegesis makes it abundantly clear that warrantless misdemeanor arrests were not the subject of a clear and consistently applied rule at common law.

We therefore must engage in the balancing test required by the Fourth Amendment While probable cause is surely a necessary condition for warrantless arrests for fine-only offenses, any realistic assessment of the interests implicated by such arrests demonstrates that probable cause alone is not a sufficient condition.

A custodial arrest exacts an obvious toll on an individual's liberty and privacy, even when the period of custody is relatively brief. The arrestee is subject to a full search of her person and confiscation of her possessions. *United States v. Robinson.* If the arrestee is the occupant of a car, the entire passenger compartment of the car, including packages therein, is subject to search as well. The arrestee may be detained for up to 48 hours without having a magistrate determine whether there in fact was probable cause for the arrest. Because people arrested for all types of violent and nonviolent offenses may be housed together awaiting such review, this detention period is potentially dangerous.

A full custodial arrest may on occasion vindicate legitimate state interests, even if the crime is punishable only by fine. Arrest is the surest way to abate criminal conduct. It may also allow the police to verify the offender's identity and, if the offender poses a flight risk, to ensure her appearance at trial. But when such considerations are not present, a citation or summons may serve the State's remaining law enforcement interests every bit as effectively as an arrest.

Because a full custodial arrest is such a severe intrusion on an individual's liberty, its reasonableness hinges on "the degree to which it is needed for the promotion of legitimate governmental interests." *Wyoming v. Houghton.* In light of the availability of citations to promote a State's interests when a fine-only offense has been committed, I cannot concur in a rule which deems a full custodial arrest to be reasonable in every circumstance. Giving police officers constitutional carte blanche to effect an arrest whenever there is probable cause to believe a fine-only misdemeanor has been committed is irreconcilable with the Fourth Amendment's command that seizures be reasonable. Instead, I would require that when there is probable cause to believe that a fine-only offense has been committed, the police officer should issue a citation unless the officer is "able to point to specific and articulable facts which, taken together with rational inferences from those facts, reasonably warrant [the additional] intrusion" of a full custodial arrest.

. . . .

The officer's actions cannot sensibly be viewed as a permissible means of balancing Atwater's Fourth Amendment interests with the State's own legitimate interests.

There is no question that Officer Turek's actions severely infringed Atwater's liberty and privacy. Turek was loud and accusatory from the moment he approached Atwater's car. Atwater's young children were terrified and hysterical. Yet when Atwater asked Turek to lower his voice because he was scaring the children, he responded by jabbing his finger in Atwater's face and saying, "You're going to jail." . . . Having made the decision to arrest, Turek did not inform Atwater of her right to remain silent. He instead asked for her license and insurance information.

Atwater asked if she could at least take her children to a friend's house down the street before going to the police station. But Turek — who had just castigated Atwater for not caring for her children — refused and said he would take the children into custody as well. Only the intervention of neighborhood children who had witnessed the scene and summoned one of Atwater's friends saved the children from being hauled to jail with their mother.

With the children gone, Officer Turek handcuffed Ms. Atwater with her hands behind her back, placed her in the police car, and drove her to the police station.. Ironically, Turek did not secure Atwater in a seat belt for the drive. At the station, Atwater was forced to remove her shoes, relinquish her possessions, and wait in a holding cell for about an hour. A judge finally informed Atwater of her rights and the charges against her, and released her when she posted bond. Atwater returned to the scene of the arrest, only to find that her car had been towed.

Ms. Atwater ultimately pleaded no contest to violating the seatbelt law and was fined $50. Even though that fine was the maximum penalty for her crime, and even though Officer Turek has never articulated any justification for his actions, the city contends that arresting Atwater was constitutionally reasonable because it advanced two legitimate interests: "the enforcement of child safety laws and encouraging [Atwater] to appear for trial."

It is difficult to see how arresting Atwater served either of these goals any more effectively than the issuance of a citation. With respect to the goal of law enforcement generally, Atwater did not pose a great danger to the community. She had been driving very slowly — approximately 15 miles per hour — in broad daylight on a residential street that had no other traffic. Nor was she a repeat offender; until that day, she had received one traffic citation in her life — a ticket, more than 10 years earlier, for failure to signal a lane change. Although Officer Turek had stopped Atwater approximately three months earlier because he thought that Atwater's son was not wearing a seatbelt, Turek had been mistaken. Moreover, Atwater immediately accepted responsibility and apologized for her conduct. Thus, there was every indication that Atwater would have buckled herself and her children in had she been cited and allowed to leave.

With respect to the related goal of child welfare, the decision to arrest Atwater was nothing short of counterproductive. Atwater's children witnessed Officer Turek yell at their mother and threaten to take them all into custody. Ultimately, they were forced to leave her behind with Turek, knowing that she was being taken to jail. Understandably, the 3-year-old boy was "very, very, very traumatized." After the incident, he had to see a child psychologist regularly, who reported that the boy "felt very guilty that he couldn't stop this horrible thing ... he was powerless to help his mother or sister.". Both of Atwater's children are now terrified at the sight of any police car. According to Atwater, the arrest "just never leaves us. It's a conversation we have every other day, once a week, and it's — it raises its head constantly in our lives."

Citing Atwater surely would have served the children's interests well. It would have taught Atwater to ensure that her children were buckled up in the future. It also would have taught the children an important lesson in accepting responsibility and obeying the law. Arresting Atwater, though, taught the children an entirely different lesson: that "the bad person could just as easily be the policeman as it could be the most horrible person they could imagine."

Respondents also contend that the arrest was necessary to ensure Atwater's appearance in court. Atwater, however, was far from a flight risk. A 16-year resident of Lago Vista, population 2,486, Atwater was not likely to abscond. Although she was unable to produce her driver's license because it had been stolen, she gave Officer Turek her license number and address. In addition, Officer Turek knew from their previous encounter that Atwater was a local resident.

The city's justifications fall far short of rationalizing the extraordinary intrusion on Gail Atwater and her children. Measuring "the degree to which [Atwater's custodial arrest was] needed for the promotion of legitimate governmental interests," against "the degree to which it intrud[ed] upon [her] privacy,"... it can hardly be doubted that Turek's actions were disproportionate to Atwater's crime. The majority's assessment that "Atwater's claim to live free of pointless indignity and confinement clearly outweighs anything the City can raise against it specific to her case," is quite correct. In my view, the Fourth Amendment inquiry ends there.

Seizing Occupants Of Cars

At what point do police "stop" a person when they pull over a vehicle? Does the officer's motivation for the stop matter? In some cases, the Court looked at the officer's intent to determine whether a stop occurred (see, e.g., *Illinois v. Lidster,* 540 U.S. 419 (2003) ("The stop's primary law enforcement purpose was not to determine whether a vehicle's occupants were committing a crime, but to ask vehicle occupants, as members of the public, for their help in providing information about a crime in all likelihood committed by others. The police expected the information elicited to help them apprehend, not the vehicle's occupants, but other individuals."). But, in other cases the court held that test is objective and the officer's underlying intent was immaterial (see e.g., *Brendlin v. California,* 551 U.S. 249 (2007) (above) and *Whren v. United States,* 517 U.S. 806 (1996) (below)) The following cases explore the reasonableness of conducting vehicle stops (and their occupants) without a warrant in a variety of contexts.

WHREN v. UNITED STATES
517 U.S. 806 (1996)

JUSTICE SCALIA delivered the opinion of the Court

...

On the evening of June 10, 1993, plainclothes vice-squad officers of the District of Columbia Metropolitan Police Department were patrolling a "high drug area" of the city in an unmarked car. Their suspicions were aroused when they passed a dark Pathfinder truck with temporary license plates and youthful occupants waiting at a stop sign, the driver looking down into the lap of the passenger at his right. The truck remained stopped at the intersection for what seemed an unusually long time — more than 20 seconds. When the police car executed a U-turn in order to head back toward the truck, the Pathfinder turned suddenly to its right, without signalling, and sped off at an "unreasonable" speed. The policemen followed, and in a short while overtook the Pathfinder when it stopped behind other traffic at a red light. They pulled up alongside, and Officer Ephraim Soto stepped out and approached the driver's door, identifying himself as a police officer and directing the driver, petitioner Brown, to put the vehicle in park. When Soto drew up to the driver's window, he immediately observed two large plastic bags of what appeared to be crack cocaine in petitioner Whren's hands. Petitioners were arrested, and quantities of several types of illegal drugs were retrieved from the vehicle.

Petitioners . . . challenged the legality of the stop and the resulting seizure of the drugs. They argued that the stop had not been justified by probable cause to believe, or even reasonable suspicion, that petitioners were engaged in illegal drug-dealing activity; and that Officer Soto's asserted ground for approaching the vehicle — to give the driver a warning concerning traffic violations — was pretextual. The District Court denied the suppression motion. ...

...

Temporary detention of individuals during the stop of an automobile by the police, even if only for a brief period and for a limited purpose, constitutes a "seizure" of "persons." ... An automobile stop is thus subject to the constitutional imperative that it not be "unreasonable" under the circumstances. As a general matter, the decision to stop an automobile is reasonable where the police have probable cause to believe that a traffic violation has occurred.

Petitioners accept that Officer Soto had probable cause to believe that various provisions of the District of Columbia traffic code had been violated. They argue, however, that "in the unique context of civil traffic regulations" probable cause is not enough.

Since, they contend, the use of automobiles is so heavily and minutely regulated that total compliance with traffic and safety rules is nearly impossible, a police officer will almost invariably be able to catch any given motorist in a technical violation. This creates the temptation to use traffic stops as a means of investigating other law violations, as to which no probable cause or even articulable suspicion exists. Petitioners, who are both black, further contend that police officers might decide which motorists to stop based on decidedly impermissible factors, such as the race of the car's occupants. To avoid this danger, they say, the Fourth Amendment test for traffic stops should be, not the normal one (applied by the Court of Appeals) of whether probable cause existed to justify the stop; but rather, whether a police officer, acting reasonably, would have made the stop for the reason given.

[The Court discussed several cases that dealt with ulterior motives of police officers in making arrests, then asserts that these didn't really mean what the court had seemed to mean in those decisions, but instead characterizing all of those cases as ones in which probable cause did not exist.]

We think these cases foreclose any argument that the constitutional reasonableness of traffic stops depends on the actual motivations of the individual officers involved. We of course agree with petitioners that the Constitution prohibits selective enforcement of the law based on considerations such as race. But the constitutional basis for objecting to intentionally discriminatory application of laws is the Equal Protection Clause, not the Fourth Amendment. Subjective intentions play no role in ordinary, probable-cause Fourth Amendment analysis.

[The Court declined to adopt Whren's assertion that their proposed standard (requiring the courts to decide whether other reasonable officers would have made the stop for the reasons given by the officer) IS an objective one. And they also ask the Court to do a balancing and weighing test.]

It is of course true that in principle every Fourth Amendment case, since it turns upon a "reasonableness" determination, involves a balancing of all relevant factors. With rare exceptions not applicable here, however, the result of that balancing is not in doubt where the search or seizure is based upon probable cause. . . .

Where probable cause has existed, the only cases in which we have found it necessary actually to perform the "balancing" analysis involved searches or seizures conducted in an extraordinary manner, unusually harmful to an individual's privacy or even physical interests — such as, for example, seizure by means of deadly force, unannounced entry into a home, entry into a home without a warrant, or physical penetration of the body. The making of a traffic stop out-of-uniform does not remotely qualify as such an extreme practice, and so is governed by the usual rule that probable cause to believe the law has been broken "outbalances" private interest in avoiding police contact.

Petitioners urge as an extraordinary factor in this case that the "multitude of applicable traffic and equipment regulations" is so large and so difficult to obey perfectly that virtually everyone is guilty of violation, permitting the police to single out almost whomever they wish for a stop. But we are aware of no principle that would allow us to decide at what point a code of law becomes so expansive and so commonly violated that infraction itself can no longer be the ordinary measure of the lawfulness of enforcement. And even if we could identify such exorbitant codes, we do not know by what standard (or what right) we would decide, as petitioners would have us do, which particular provisions are sufficiently important to merit enforcement.

For the run-of-the-mine case, which this surely is, we think there is no realistic alternative to the traditional common-law rule that probable cause justifies a search and seizure. Here the District Court found that the officers had probable cause to believe that petitioners had violated the traffic code. That rendered the stop reasonable under the Fourth Amendment. …

HEIEN v. NORTH CAROLINA
574 U.S. ___ (2014)

CHIEF JUSTICE ROBERTS delivered the opinion of the Court.

The Fourth Amendment prohibits "unreasonable searches and seizures." Under this standard, a search or seizure may be permissible even though the justification for the action includes a reasonable factual mistake. An officer might, for example, stop a motorist for traveling alone in a high-occupancy vehicle lane, only to discover upon approaching the car that two children are slumped over asleep in the back seat. The driver has not violated the law, but neither has the officer violated the Fourth Amendment.

But what if the police officer's reasonable mistake is not one of fact but of law? In this case, an officer stopped a vehicle because one of its two brake lights was out, but a court later determined that a single working brake light was all the law required. The question presented is whether such a mistake of law can nonetheless give rise to the reasonable suspicion necessary to uphold the seizure under the Fourth Amendment. We hold that it can. Because the officer's mistake about the brake-light law was reasonable, the stop in this case was lawful under the Fourth Amendment.

I

[Summary of Facts and Procedural History:

Heien was a passenger in a car driven by Vasquez who, as they travelled by, raised the suspicion of Sergeant Dariss who was on patrol in North Carolina. Darisse pulled the car over for a faulty brake light (only one brake light worked). The stop resulted in the search of the car and the discovery of cocaine. Heien was charged and moved to suppress the drugs claiming that the stop violated his Fourth Amendment rights. At the hearing, officer testified that the brake lights had given reasonable suspicion to make the stop, even though it turns out he was mistaken and that North Carolina law does not require two brake lights. The trial court agreed, and Heien plead guilty and reserved the right to appeal. The North Carolina Court of Appeals reversed the conviction because the stop was not valid because it was not based on a violation of North Carolina Law. Thus, it held, the stop was objectively unreasonable. The North Carolina Supreme Court reversed that, and said that although it was not a violation of N.C. law, it was reasonable for the officer to think that it was, and therefore it was a mistake of law. The U.S. Supreme Court granted certiorari.]

II

A traffic stop for a suspected violation of law is a "seizure" of the occupants of the vehicle and therefore must be conducted in accordance with the Fourth Amendment. All parties agree that to justify this type of seizure, officers need only "reasonable suspicion" — that is, "a particularized and objective basis for suspecting the particular person stopped" of breaking the law. The question here is whether reasonable suspicion can rest on a mistaken understanding of the scope of a legal prohibition. We hold that it can.

As the text indicates and we have repeatedly affirmed, "the ultimate touchstone of the Fourth Amendment is 'reasonableness.' " To be reasonable is not to be perfect, and so the Fourth Amendment allows for some mistakes on the part of government officials, giving them "fair leeway for enforcing the law in the community's protection." We have recognized that searches and seizures based on mistakes of fact can be reasonable. The warrantless

search of a home, for instance, is reasonable if undertaken with the consent of a resident, and remains lawful when officers obtain the consent of someone who reasonably appears to be but is not in fact a resident. By the same token, if officers with probable cause to arrest a suspect mistakenly arrest an individual matching the suspect's description, neither the seizure nor an accompanying search of the arrestee would be unlawful. The limit is that "the mistakes must be those of reasonable men."

But reasonable men make mistakes of law, too, and such mistakes are no less compatible with the concept of reasonable suspicion. Reasonable suspicion arises from the combination of an officer's understanding of the facts and his understanding of the relevant law. The officer may be reasonably mistaken on either ground. Whether the facts turn out to be not what was thought, or the law turns out to be not what was thought, the result is the same: the facts are outside the scope of the law. There is no reason, under the text of the Fourth Amendment or our precedents, why this same result should be acceptable when reached by way of a reasonable mistake of fact, but not when reached by way of a similarly reasonable mistake of law.

…

… In *Michigan v.DeFillippo*, . . . we addressed the validity of an arrest made under a criminal law later declared unconstitutional. A Detroit ordinance that authorized police officers to stop and question individuals suspected of criminal activity also made it an offense for such an individual "to refuse to identify himself and produce evidence of his identity." Detroit police officers sent to investigate a report of public intoxication arrested Gary DeFillippo after he failed to identify himself. A search incident to arrest uncovered drugs, and DeFillippo was charged with possession of a controlled substance. The Michigan Court of Appeals ordered the suppression of the drugs, concluding that the identification ordinance was unconstitutionally vague and that DeFillippo's arrest was therefore invalid.

Accepting the unconstitutionality of the ordinance as a given, we nonetheless reversed. At the time the officers arrested DeFillippo, we explained, "there was no controlling precedent that this ordinance was or was not constitutional, and hence the conduct observed violated a presumptively valid ordinance." Acknowledging that the outcome might have been different had the ordinance been "grossly and flagrantly unconstitutional," we concluded that under the circumstances "there was abundant probable cause to satisfy the constitutional prerequisite for an arrest."

The officers were wrong in concluding that DeFillippo was guilty of a criminal offense when he declined to identify himself. That a court later declared the ordinance unconstitutional does not change the fact that DeFillippo's conduct was lawful when the officers observed it. But the officers' assumption that the law was valid was reasonable, and their observations gave them "abundant probable cause" to arrest DeFillippo. Although DeFillippo could not be prosecuted under the identification ordinance, the search that turned up the drugs was constitutional.

. . . .

Heien is correct that in a number of decisions we have looked to the reasonableness of an officer's legal error in the course of considering the appropriate remedy for a constitutional violation, instead of whether there was a violation at all. . . . Any consideration of the reasonableness of an officer's mistake was therefore limited to the separate matter of remedy.

Here, by contrast, the mistake of law relates to the antecedent question of whether it was reasonable for an officer to suspect that the defendant's conduct was illegal. If so, there was no violation of the Fourth Amendment in the first place. None of the cases Heien or the dissent cites precludes a court from

considering a reasonable mistake of law in addressing that question.

Heien also contends that the reasons the Fourth Amendment allows some errors of fact do not extend to errors of law. Officers in the field must make factual assessments on the fly, Heien notes, and so deserve a margin of error. In Heien's view, no such margin is appropriate for questions of law: The statute here either requires one working brake light or two, and the answer does not turn on anything "an officer might suddenly confront in the field." But Heien's point does not consider the reality that an officer may "suddenly confront" a situation in the field as to which the application of a statute is unclear — however clear it may later become. A law prohibiting "vehicles" in the park either covers Segways or not, . . . but an officer will nevertheless have to make a quick decision on the law the first time one whizzes by.

[O]ur decision does not discourage officers from learning the law. The Fourth Amendment tolerates only reasonable mistakes, and those mistakes — whether of fact or of law — must be objectively reasonable. We do not examine the subjective understanding of the particular officer involved. And the inquiry is not as forgiving as the one employed in the distinct context of deciding whether an officer is entitled to qualified immunity for a constitutional or statutory violation. Thus, an officer can gain no Fourth Amendment advantage through a sloppy study of the laws he is duty-bound to enforce.

Finally, Heien and amici point to the well-known maxim, "Ignorance of the law is no excuse," and contend that it is fundamentally unfair to let police officers get away with mistakes of law when the citizenry is accorded no such leeway. Though this argument has a certain rhetorical appeal, it misconceives the implication of the maxim. The true symmetry is this: Just as an individual generally cannot escape criminal liability based on a mistaken understanding of the law, so too the government cannot impose criminal liability based on a mistaken understanding of the law. If the law required two working brake lights,

Heien could not escape a ticket by claiming he reasonably thought he needed only one; if the law required only one, Sergeant Darisse could not issue a valid ticket by claiming he reasonably thought drivers needed two. But just because mistakes of law cannot justify either the imposition or the avoidance of criminal liability, it does not follow that they cannot justify an investigatory stop. And Heien is not appealing a brake-light ticket; he is appealing a cocaine-trafficking conviction as to which there is no asserted mistake of fact or law.

III

Here we have little difficulty concluding that the officer's error of law was reasonable. . . .

It was thus objectively reasonable for an officer in Sergeant Darisse's position to think that Heien's faulty right brake light was a violation of North Carolina law. And because the mistake of law was reasonable, there was reasonable suspicion justifying the stop.

JUSTICE KAGAN, with whom JUSTICE GINSBURG joins, concurring.

I concur in full in the Court's opinion, which explains why certain mistakes of law can support the reasonable suspicion needed to stop a vehicle under the Fourth Amendment. In doing so, the Court correctly emphasizes that the "Fourth Amendment tolerates only . . . objectively reasonable" mistakes of law. And the Court makes clear that the inquiry into whether an officer's mistake of law counts as objectively reasonable "is not as forgiving as the one employed in the distinct context of deciding whether an officer is entitled to qualified immunity." I write separately to elaborate briefly on those important limitations.

. . .

A court tasked with deciding whether an officer's mistake of law can support a seizure thus faces a straightforward question of statutory construction. If the statute is genuinely ambiguous, such that overturning the officer's judgment requires hard interpretive work, then the officer has made a reasonable mistake. But if not, not. As the Solicitor General made the point at oral argument, the statute must pose a "really difficult" or "very hard question of statutory interpretation." And indeed, both North Carolina and the Solicitor General agreed that such cases will be "exceedingly rare."

The Court's analysis of Sergeant Darisse's interpretation of the North Carolina law at issue here appropriately reflects these principles. . . . The critical point is that the statute poses a quite difficult question of interpretation, and Sergeant Darisse's judgment, although overturned, had much to recommend it. I therefore agree with the Court that the traffic stop he conducted did not violate the Fourth Amendment.

JUSTICE SOTOMAYOR, dissenting.

. . . .

To my mind, the more administrable approach — and the one more consistent with our precedents and principles — would be to hold that an officer's mistake of law, no matter how reasonable, cannot support the individualized suspicion necessary to justify a seizure under the Fourth Amendment. I respectfully dissent.

In Brendlin v. California, 551 US 249 (2007), (Chapter Three, above) the Court held that stopping a car is a seizure of all the occupants. In the following case, *Arizona v. Johnson*, 555 U.S. 323 (2009), the Court had to decide whether it was reasonable for an officer to conduct a Terry pat-down search of a passenger who was riding in a car which was stopped for a citable but not arrestable vehicle infraction. In deciding *Johnson*, the Court relied on precedent established in *Pennsylvania v. Mimms* and *Maryland v. Wilson*. Those cases evaluated the reasonableness of the officer's actions in requiring the driver or passengers out of the car.

ARIZONA v. JOHNSON
555 U.S. 323 (2009)

JUSTICE GINSBURG delivered the opinion of the Court.

This case concerns the authority of police officers to "stop and frisk" a passenger in a motor vehicle temporarily seized upon police detection of a traffic infraction. In a pathmarking decision, *Terry* v. *Ohio*, 392 U. S. 1 (1968), the Court considered whether an investigatory stop (temporary detention) and frisk (patdown for weapons) may be conducted without violating the Fourth Amendment's ban on unreasonable searches and seizures. The Court upheld "stop and frisk" as constitutionally permissible if two conditions are met. First, the investigatory stop must be lawful. That requirement is met in an on-the-street encounter, *Terry* determined, when the police officer reasonably suspects that the person apprehended is committing or has committed a criminal offense. Second, to proceed from a stop to a frisk, the police officer must reasonably suspect that the person stopped is armed and dangerous.

For the duration of a traffic stop, we recently confirmed, a police officer effectively seizes "everyone in the vehicle," the driver and all passengers. *Brendlin* v. *California*. Accordingly, we hold that, in a traffic-stop setting, the first *Terry* condition — a lawful investigatory stop — is met whenever it is lawful for police to detain an automobile and its occupants pending inquiry into a vehicular violation. The police need not have, in addition, cause to believe any occupant of the vehicle is involved in criminal activity. To justify a patdown of the driver or a passenger during a traffic stop, however, just as in the case of a pedestrian reasonably suspected of criminal activity, the police must harbor reasonable suspicion that the person subjected to the frisk is armed and dangerous.

On April 19, 2002, Officer Maria Trevizo and Detectives Machado and Gittings, all members of Arizona's gang task force, were on patrol in

Tucson near a neighborhood associated with the Crips gang. At approximately 9 p.m., the officers pulled over an automobile after a license plate check revealed that the vehicle's registration had been suspended for an insurance-related violation. Under Arizona law, the violation for which the vehicle was stopped constituted a civil infraction warranting a citation. At the time of the stop, the vehicle had three occupants — the driver, a front-seat passenger, and a passenger in the back seat, Lemon Montrea Johnson, the respondent here. In making the stop the officers had no reason to suspect anyone in the vehicle of criminal activity.

The three officers left their patrol car and approached the stopped vehicle. Machado instructed all of the occupants to keep their hands visible. He asked whether there were any weapons in the vehicle; all responded no. Machado then directed the driver to get out of the car. Gittings dealt with the front-seat passenger, who stayed in the vehicle throughout the stop. While Machado was getting the driver's license and information about the vehicle's registration and insurance, Trevizo attended to Johnson.

Trevizo noticed that, as the police approached, Johnson looked back and kept his eyes on the officers. When she drew near, she observed that Johnson was wearing clothing, including a blue bandana, that she considered consistent with Crips membership. She also noticed a scanner in Johnson's jacket pocket, which "struck [her] as highly unusual and cause [for] concern," because "most people" would not carry around a scanner that way "unless they're going to be involved in some kind of criminal activity or [are] going to try to evade the police by listening to the scanner." In response to Trevizo's questions, Johnson provided his name and date of birth but said he had no identification with him. He volunteered that he was from Eloy, Arizona, a place Trevizo knew was home to a Crips gang. Johnson further told Trevizo that he had served time in prison for burglary and had been out for about a year.

Trevizo wanted to question Johnson away from the front-seat passenger to gain "intelligence about the gang [Johnson] might be in." For that reason, she asked him to get out of the car. Johnson complied. Based on Trevizo's observations and Johnson's answers to her questions while he was still seated in the car, Trevizo suspected that "he might have a weapon on him." When he exited the vehicle, she therefore "patted him down for officer safety." During the patdown, Trevizo felt the butt of a gun near Johnson's waist. At that point Johnson began to struggle, and Trevizo placed him in handcuffs.

. . . .

Terry established the legitimacy of an investigatory stop "in situations where [the police] may lack probable cause for an arrest." When the stop is justified by suspicion (reasonably grounded, but short of probable cause) that criminal activity is afoot, the Court explained, the police officer must be positioned to act instantly on reasonable suspicion that the persons temporarily detained are armed and dangerous. Recognizing that a limited search of outer clothing for weapons serves to protect both the officer and the public, the Court held the patdown reasonable under the Fourth Amendment.

"[M]ost traffic stops," this Court has observed, "resemble, in duration and atmosphere, the kind of brief detention authorized in *Terry*." *Berkemer* v. *McCarty*. Furthermore, the Court has recognized that traffic stops are "especially fraught with danger to police officers." *Michigan* v. *Long*. " 'The risk of harm to both the police and the occupants [of a stopped vehicle] is minimized,' " we have stressed, " 'if the officers routinely exercise unquestioned command of the situation.' " *Maryland* v. *Wilson*, Three decisions cumulatively portray *Terry*'s application in a traffic-stop setting: *Pennsylvania* v. *Mimms; Maryland* v. *Wilson*; and *Brendlin* v. *California.*

In *Mimms*, the Court held that "once a motor vehicle has been lawfully detained for a traffic violation, the police officers may order the driver to get out of the vehicle without violating the Fourth Amendment's proscription of unreasonable searches and seizures." The government's "legitimate and weighty" interest in officer safety, the Court said, outweighs the "*de minimis*" additional intrusion of requiring a driver, already lawfully stopped, to exit the vehicle. Citing *Terry* as controlling, the Court further held that a driver, once outside the stopped vehicle, may be patted down for weapons if the officer reasonably concludes that the driver "might be armed and presently dangerous."

Wilson held that the *Mimms* rule applied to passengers as well as to drivers. Specifically, the Court instructed that "an officer making a traffic stop may order passengers to get out of the car pending completion of the stop . "[T]he same weighty interest in officer safety," the Court observed, "is present regardless of whether the occupant of the stopped car is a driver or passenger."

It is true, the Court acknowledged, that in a lawful traffic stop, "[t]here is probable cause to believe that the driver has committed a minor vehicular offense," but "there is no such reason to stop or detain the passengers.". On the other hand, the Court emphasized, the risk of a violent encounter in a traffic-stop setting "stems not from the ordinary reaction of a motorist stopped for a speeding violation, but from the fact that evidence of a more serious crime might be uncovered during the stop." "[T]he motivation of a passenger to employ violence to prevent apprehension of such a crime," the Court stated, "is every bit as great as that of the driver." Moreover, the Court noted, "as a practical matter, the passengers are already stopped by virtue of the stop of the vehicle," so "the additional intrusion on the passenger is minimal,"

Completing the picture, *Brendlin* held that a passenger is seized, just as the driver is, "from the moment [a car stopped by the police comes] to a halt on the side of the road." A passenger therefore has standing to challenge a stop's constitutionality.

…

A lawful roadside stop begins when a vehicle is pulled over for investigation of a traffic violation. The temporary seizure of driver and passengers ordinarily continues, and remains reasonable, for the duration of the stop. Normally, the stop ends when the police have no further need to control the scene, and inform the driver and passengers they are free to leave. See *Brendlin*. An officer's inquiries into matters unrelated to the justification for the traffic stop, this Court has made plain, do not convert the encounter into something other than a lawful seizure, so long as those inquiries do not measurably extend the duration of the stop.

In sum . . . a traffic stop of a car communicates to a reasonable passenger that he or she is not free to terminate the encounter with the police and move about at will. Nothing occurred in this case that would have conveyed to Johnson that, prior to the frisk, the traffic stop had ended or that he was otherwise free "to depart without police permission." Officer Trevizo surely was not constitutionally required to give Johnson an opportunity to depart the scene after he exited the vehicle without first ensuring that, in so doing, she was not permitting a dangerous person to get behind her

Roving Patrols, Checkpoints, And Roadblocks

The Court distinguishes between roving patrols (mobile patrols stopping vehicles near the international border), checkpoints (fixed checkpoints near the border), and roadblocks (stops temporarily set up along major thoroughfares). The following cases discuss whether these seizures are reasonable without a warrant and the level objective basis needed to justify the seizure.

Roving Patrols

UNITED STATES v. BRIGNONI-PONCE
422 U.S. 873 (1975)

JUSTICE POWELL delivered the opinion of the Court.

The only issue presented for decision is whether a roving patrol may stop a vehicle in an area near the border and question its occupants when the only ground for suspicion is that the occupants appear to be of Mexican ancestry. …

The Fourth Amendment applies to all seizures of the person, including seizures that involve only a brief detention short of traditional arrest. …As with other categories of police action subject to Fourth Amendment constraints, the reasonableness of such seizures depends on a balance between the public interest and the individual's right to personal security free from arbitrary interference by law officers.

The Government makes a convincing demonstration that the public interest demands effective measures to prevent the illegal entry of aliens at the Mexican border. Estimates of the number of illegal immigrants in the United States vary widely. A conservative estimate in 1972 produced a figure of about one million, but the INS now suggests there may be as many as 10 or 12 million aliens illegally in the country. Whatever the number, these aliens create significant economic and social problems, competing with citizens and legal resident aliens for jobs, and generating extra demand for social services. The aliens themselves are vulnerable to exploitation because they cannot complain of substandard working conditions without risking deportation.

The Mexican border is almost 2,000 miles long, and even a vastly reinforced Border Patrol would find it impossible to prevent illegal border crossings. Many aliens cross the Mexican border on foot, miles away from patrolled areas, and then purchase transportation from the border area to inland cities, where they find jobs and elude the immigration authorities. Others gain entry on valid temporary border-crossing permits, but then violate the conditions of their entry. Most of these aliens leave the border area in private vehicles, often assisted by professional "alien smugglers." The Border Patrol's traffic-checking operations are designed to prevent this inland movement. They succeed in apprehending some illegal entrants and smugglers, and they deter the movement of others by threatening apprehension and increasing the cost of illegal transportation.

Against this valid public interest we must weigh the interference with individual liberty that results when an officer stops an automobile and questions its occupants. The intrusion is modest. The Government tells us that a stop by a roving patrol "usually consumes no more than a minute." There is no search of the vehicle or its occupants, and the visual inspection is limited to those parts of the vehicle that can be seen by anyone standing alongside. According to the Government, "[a]ll that is required of the vehicle's occupants is a response to a brief question or two and possibly the production of a document evidencing a right to be in the United States."

Because of the limited nature of the intrusion, stops of this sort may be justified on facts that do not amount to the probable cause required for an arrest. ...Because of the importance of the governmental interest at stake, the minimal intrusion of a brief stop, and the absence of practical alternatives for policing the border, we hold that when an officer's observations lead him reasonably to suspect that a particular vehicle may contain aliens who are illegally in the country, he may stop the car briefly and investigate the circumstances that provoke suspicion. As in Terry, the stop and inquiry must be "reasonably related in scope to the justification for their initiation." The officer may question the driver and passengers about their citizenship and immigration status, and he may ask them to explain suspicious circumstances, but any further detention or search must be based on consent or probable cause.

We are unwilling to let the Border Patrol dispense entirely with the requirement that officers must have a reasonable suspicion to justify roving-patrol stops. In the context of border area stops, the reasonableness requirement of the Fourth Amendment demands something more than the broad and unlimited discretion sought by the Government. Roads near the border carry not only aliens seeking to enter the country illegally, but a large volume of legitimate traffic as well. ...We are confident that substantially all of the traffic in these cities is lawful and that relatively few of their residents have any connection with the illegal entry and transportation of aliens. To approve roving-patrol stops of all vehicles in the border area, without any suspicion that a particular vehicle is carrying illegal immigrants, would subject the residents of these and other areas to potentially unlimited interference with their use of the highways, solely at the discretion of Border Patrol officers. (.

We are not convinced that the legitimate needs of law enforcement require this degree of interference with lawful traffic. . . . [T]he nature of illegal alien traffic and the characteristics of smuggling operations tend to generate articulable grounds for identifying violators. Consequently, a requirement of reasonable suspicion for stops allows the Government adequate means of guarding the public interest and also protects residents of the border areas from indiscriminate official interference. Under the circumstances, and even though the intrusion incident to a stop is modest, we conclude that it is not "reasonable" under the Fourth Amendment to make such stops on a random basis.

...

...Except at the border and its functional equivalents, officers on roving patrol may stop vehicles only if they are aware of specific articulable facts, together with rational inferences from those facts, that reasonably warrant suspicion that the vehicles contain aliens who may be illegally in the country.

In deciding whether there is reasonable suspicion to stop a car in the border area. Officers may consider the characteristics of the area in which they encounter a vehicle. Its proximity to the border, the usual patterns of traffic on the particular road, and previous experience with alien traffic are all relevant. ...They also may consider information about recent illegal border crossings in the area. The driver's behavior may be relevant, as erratic driving or obvious attempts to evade officers can support a reasonable suspicion. ... Aspects of the vehicle itself may justify suspicion. For instance, officers say that certain station wagons, with large compartments for fold-down seats or spare tires, are frequently used for transporting concealed aliens. The vehicle may appear to be heavily loaded, it may have an extraordinary number of passengers, or the officers may observe persons trying to hide.

...

In this case the officers relied on a single factor to justify stopping respondent's car: the apparent Mexican ancestry of the occupants. We cannot conclude that this furnished reasonable grounds to believe that the three occupants were aliens. ...

Large numbers of native-born and naturalized citizens have the physical characteristics identified with Mexican ancestry, and even in the border area a relatively small proportion of them are aliens. The likelihood that any given person of Mexican ancestry is an alien is high enough to make Mexican appearance a relevant factor, but standing alone it does not justify stopping all Mexican-Americans to ask if they are aliens.

JUSTICE DOUGLAS, concurring in the judgment. Omitted.

Checkpoints

UNITED STATES v. MARTINEZ-FUERTE
428 U.S. 543 (1976)

JUSTICE POWELL delivered the opinion of the Court.

[This case involved three different cases from the Ninth Circuit and one case from the Fifth Circuit. The question presented was whether stops at permanent checkpoints within the United States whose purpose was to look for illegal immigrants violated the Fourth Amendment.]

. . . It is agreed that checkpoint stops are "seizures" within the meaning of the Fourth Amendment. The defendants [in this case] contend primarily that the routine stopping of vehicles at a checkpoint is invalid because Brignoni-Ponce must be read as proscribing any stops in the absence of reasonable suspicion. . . . [W]e turn first to whether reasonable suspicion is a prerequisite to a valid stop, a question to be resolved by balancing the interests at stake.

...

While the need to make routine checkpoint stops is great, the consequent intrusion on Fourth Amendment interests is quite limited. The stop does intrude to a limited extent on motorists' right to "free passage without interruption," and arguably on their right to personal security. But it involves only a brief detention of travelers during which

> "`[a]ll that is required of the vehicle's occupants is a response to a brief question or two and possibly the production of a document evidencing a right to be in the United States.'"

Neither the vehicle nor its occupants are searched, and visual inspection of the vehicle is limited to what can be seen without a search. This objective intrusion - the stop itself, the questioning, and the visual inspection - also existed in roving-patrol stops. But we view checkpoint stops in a different light because the subjective intrusion - the generating of concern or even fright on the part of lawful travelers - is appreciably less in the case of a checkpoint stop. In *Ortiz*, we noted:

> "[T]he circumstances surrounding a checkpoint stop and search are far less intrusive than those attending a roving-patrol stop. Roving patrols often operate at night on seldom-traveled roads, and their approach may frighten motorists. At traffic checkpoints the motorist can see that other vehicles are being stopped, he can see visible signs of the officers' authority, and he is much less likely to be frightened or annoyed by the intrusion." 422 U.S., at 894-895.

Routine checkpoint stops do not intrude similarly on the motoring public. First, the potential interference with legitimate traffic is minimal. Motorists using these highways are not taken by surprise as they know, or may obtain knowledge of, the location of the checkpoints and will not be stopped elsewhere. Second, checkpoint operations both appear to and actually involve less discretionary enforcement activity. The regularized manner in which established checkpoints are operated is visible evidence, reassuring to law-abiding motorists, that the stops are duly authorized and believed to serve the public interest. The location of a fixed checkpoint is not chosen by officers in the field, but by officials responsible for making overall decisions as to the most effective allocation of limited enforcement resources.
…

… [T]he reasonableness of the procedures followed in making these checkpoint stops makes the resulting intrusion on the interests of motorists minimal. On the other hand, the purpose of the stops is legitimate and in the public interest, and the need for this enforcement technique is demonstrated by the records in the cases before us. Accordingly, we hold that the stops and questioning at issue may be made in the absence of any individualized suspicion at reasonably located checkpoints.

We further believe that it is constitutional to refer motorists selectively to the secondary inspection area . . . on the basis of criteria that would not sustain a roving-patrol stop. Thus, even if it be assumed that such referrals are made largely on the basis of apparent Mexican ancestry we perceive no constitutional violation. As the intrusion here is sufficiently minimal that no particularized reason need exist to justify it, we think it follows that the Border Patrol officers must have wide discretion in selecting the motorists to be diverted for the brief questioning involved.

In summary, we hold that stops for brief questioning routinely conducted at permanent checkpoints are consistent with the Fourth Amendment and need not be authorized by warrant. The principal protection of Fourth Amendment rights at checkpoints lies in appropriate limitations on the scope of the stop. We have held that checkpoint searches are constitutional only if justified by consent or probable cause to search. And our holding today is limited to the type of stops described in this opinion. "[A]ny further detention . . . must be based on consent or probable cause.". None of the defendants in these cases argues that the stopping officers exceeded these limitations.

JUSTICE BRENNAN, with whom JUSTICE MARSHALL joins, dissenting.

Today's decision is the ninth this Term marking the continuing evisceration of Fourth Amendment protections against unreasonable searches and seizures. Early in the Term, *Texas v. White*, (1975), permitted the warrantless search of an automobile in police custody despite the unreasonableness of the custody and opportunity to obtain a warrant. *United States v. Watson*, (1976), held that regardless of whether opportunity exists to obtain a warrant, an arrest in a public place for a previously committed felony never requires a warrant, a result certainly not fairly supported by either history or precedent. *United States v. Santana* (1976), went further and approved the warrantless arrest for a felony of a person standing on the front porch of her residence. *United States v. Miller*, (1976), narrowed the Fourth Amendment's protection of privacy by denying the existence of a protectible interest in the compilation of checks, deposit slips, and other records pertaining to an individual's bank account. *Stone v. Powell* precluded the assertion of Fourth Amendment claims in federal collateral relief proceedings. *United States v. Janis* held that evidence unconstitutionally seized by a state officer is admissible in a civil proceeding by or against the *United States. South Dakota v. Opperman*, approved sweeping inventory searches of automobiles in police custody irrespective of the particular circumstances of the case. Finally, in *Andresen v. Maryland*, (1976), the Court, in practical effect, weakened the Fourth Amendment prohibition against general warrants.

Consistent with this purpose to debilitate Fourth Amendment protections, the Court's decision today virtually empties the Amendment of its reasonableness requirement by holding that law enforcement officials manning fixed checkpoint stations who make standardless seizures of persons do not violate the Amendment. This holding cannot be squared with this Court's recent decisions. . . . I dissent.

. . . .

As the Court concedes, the checkpoint stop involves essentially the same intrusions as a roving-patrol stop, yet the Court provides no principled basis for distinguishing checkpoint stops.

In abandoning any requirement of a minimum of reasonable suspicion, or even articulable suspicion, the Court in every practical sense renders meaningless, as applied to checkpoint stops, the *Brignoni-Ponce* holding that "standing alone [Mexican appearance] does not justify stopping all Mexican-Americans to ask if they are aliens." Since the objective is almost entirely the Mexican illegally in the country, checkpoint officials, uninhibited by any objective standards and therefore free to stop any or all motorists without explanation or excuse, wholly on whim, will perforce target motorists of Mexican appearance. The process will then inescapably discriminate against citizens of Mexican ancestry and Mexican aliens lawfully in this country for no other reason than that they unavoidably possess the same "suspicious" physical and grooming characteristics of illegal Mexican aliens.

Every American citizen of Mexican ancestry and every Mexican alien lawfully in this country must know after today's decision that he travels the fixed checkpoint highways at the risk of being subjected not only to a stop, but also to detention and interrogation, both prolonged and to an extent far more than for non-Mexican appearing motorists. To be singled out for referral and to be detained and interrogated must be upsetting to any motorist. One wonders what actual experience supports my Brethren's conclusion that referrals "should not be frightening or offensive because of their public and relatively routine nature." In point of fact, referrals, viewed in context, are not relatively routine; thousands are otherwise permitted to pass. But for the arbitrarily selected motorists who must suffer the delay and humiliation of detention and interrogation, the experience can obviously be upsetting. And that experience is particularly vexing for the motorist of Mexican ancestry who is selectively referred, knowing that the officers' target is the Mexican alien. That deep resentment will be stirred by a sense of unfair discrimination is not difficult to foresee. In short, if a balancing process is required, the balance should be struck, as in *Brignoni-Ponce*, to require that Border Patrolofficers act upon at least reasonable suspicion in making checkpoint stops. In any event, even if a different balance were struck, the Court cannot, without ignoring the Fourth Amendment requirement of reasonableness, justify wholly unguided seizures by officials manning the checkpoints. . . .

There is no principle in the jurisprudence of fundamental rights which permits constitutional limitations to be dispensed with merely because they cannot be conveniently satisfied. Dispensing with reasonable suspicion as a prerequisite to stopping and inspecting motorists because the inconvenience of such a requirement would make it impossible to identify a given car as a possible carrier of aliens is no more justifiable than dispensing with probable cause as prerequisite to the search of an individual because the inconvenience of such a requirement would make it impossible to identify a given person in a high-crime area as a possible carrier of concealed weapons. "The needs of law enforcement stand in constant tension with the Constitution's protections of the individual against certain exercises of official power. It is precisely the predictability of these pressures that counsels a resolute loyalty to constitutional safeguards." *Almeida-Sanchez v. United States.*

Roadblocks

In *Brown v. Texas*, 443 U.S. 47 (1979), the Court enunciated a three-step balancing test to judge the reasonableness of a suspicionless seizure. This standard has been applied to roadblocks. *Delaware v. Prouse*, 440 U.S. 648 (1989), held that, in the absence of articulable facts justifying reasonable suspicion that the vehicle or the operator was unlicensed, a "random" stop of an automobile for the purpose of checking the vehicle registration and the operator's license violated the Fourth Amendment. *Prouse* noted, however that if all traffic is stopped in roadblock fashion, it is not a violation of the Fourth Amendment. The next year the Court decided *Michigan Dept. State Police v. Sitz,* 496 U.S. 444 (1990*).* This case involved Michigan motorists suing to ask the Court to declare that proposed drunk driving detection roadblocks in that Michigan unconstitutional. In *City of Indianapolis v. Edmond*, 531 U.S. 32, (2000) the Court reviewed a highway checkpoint program whose primary purpose is the discovery and interdiction of illegal narcotics violated the Fourth Amendment, and in *Illinois v. Lidster*, 540 U.S. 419 (2003), the Court decided whether a roadblock established to get information about a hit and run fatality one week prior violated the Fourth Amendment.

BROWN V. TEXAS
443 U.S. 47 (1979)

CHIEF JUSTICE BURGER delivered the opinion of the Court.

This appeal presents the question whether appellant was validly convicted for refusing to comply with a policeman's demand that he identify himself pursuant to a provision of Texas Penal Code which makes it a crime to refuse such identification on request.

I

At 12:45 in the afternoon of December 9, 1977, Officers Venegas and Sotelo of the El Paso Police Department were cruising in a patrol car. They observed appellant and another man walking in opposite directions away from one another in an alley. Although the two men were a few feet apart when they first were seen, Officer Venegas later testified that both officers believed the two had been together or were about to meet until the patrol car appeared.

The car entered the alley, and Officer Venegas got out and asked appellant to identify himself and explain what he was doing there. The other man was not questioned or detained. The officer testified that he stopped appellant because the situation "looked suspicious and we had never seen that subject in that area before." The area of El Paso where appellant was stopped has a high incidence of drug traffic. However, the officers did not claim to suspect appellant of any specific misconduct, nor did they have any reason to believe that he was armed.

Appellant refused to identify himself and angrily asserted that the officers had no right to stop him. Officer Venegas replied that he was in a "high drug problem area"; Officer Sotelo then "frisked" appellant, but found nothing.

When appellant continued to refuse to identify himself, he was arrested for violation of Tex. Penal Code . . . which makes it a criminal act for a person to refuse to give his name and address to an officer "who has lawfully stopped him and requested the information." Following the arrest the officers searched appellant; nothing untoward was found.

While being taken to the El Paso County Jail appellant identified himself. Nonetheless, he was held in custody and charged. ...When he was booked, he was routinely searched a third time. Appellant was convicted in the El Paso Municipal Court and fined $20 plus court costs. ... He then exercised his right under Texas law to a trial *de novo* in the El Paso County Court. There, he moved to set aside the information on the ground that § 38.02 (a) of the Texas Penal Code violated the First, Fourth, and Fifth Amendments and was unconstitutionally vague in violation of the Fourteenth Amendment. The motion was denied. Appellant waived a jury, and the court convicted him and imposed a fine of $45 plus court costs.

II

When the officers detained appellant for the purpose of requiring him to identify himself, they performed a seizure of his person subject to the requirements of the Fourth Amendment. In convicting appellant, the County Court necessarily found as a matter of fact that the officers "lawfully stopped" appellant. . . . The Fourth Amendment, of course, "applies to all seizures of the person, including seizures that involve only a brief detention short of traditional arrest. ...

The reasonableness of seizures that are less intrusive than a traditional arrest . . . depends

"on a balance between the public interest and the individual's right to personal security free from arbitrary interference by law officers." Consideration of the constitutionality of such seizures involves a weighing of the gravity of the public concerns served by the seizure, the degree to which the seizure advances the public interest, and the severity of the interference with individual liberty.

A central concern in balancing these competing considerations in a variety of settings has been to assure that an individual's reasonable expectation of privacy is not subject to arbitrary invasions solely at the unfettered discretion of officers in the field. To this end, the Fourth Amendment requires that a seizure must be based on specific, objective facts indicating that society's legitimate interests require the seizure of the particular individual, or that the seizure must be carried out pursuant to a plan embodying explicit, neutral limitations on the conduct of individual officers.

The State does not contend that appellant was stopped pursuant to a practice embodying neutral criteria, but rather maintains that the officers were justified in stopping appellant because they had a "reasonable, articulable suspicion that a crime had just been, was being, or was about to be committed." We have recognized that in some circumstances an officer may detain a suspect briefly for questioning although he does not have "probable cause" to believe that the suspect is involved in criminal activity, as is required for a traditional arrest. However, we have required the officers to have a reasonable suspicion, based on objective facts, that the individual is involved in criminal activity.

The flaw in the State's case is that none of the circumstances preceding the officers' detention of appellant justified a reasonable suspicion that he was involved in criminal conduct. Officer Venegas testified at appellant's trial that the situation in the alley "looked suspicious," but he was unable to point to any facts supporting that conclusion. There is no indication in the record that it was unusual for people to be in the alley. The fact that appellant was in a neighborhood frequented by drug users, standing alone, is not a basis for concluding that appellant himself was engaged in criminal conduct. In short, the appellant's activity was no different from the activity of other pedestrians in that neighborhood. When pressed, Officer Venegas acknowledged that the only reason he stopped appellant was to ascertain his identity. The record suggests an understandable desire to assert a police presence; however, that purpose does not negate Fourth Amendment guarantees.

In the absence of any basis for suspecting appellant of misconduct, the balance between the public interest and appellant's right to personal security and privacy tilts in favor of freedom from police interference. The Texas statute under which appellant was stopped and required to identify himself is designed to advance a weighty social objective in large metropolitan centers: prevention of crime. But even assuming that purpose is served to some degree by stopping and demanding identification from an individual without any specific basis for believing he is involved in criminal activity, the guarantees of the Fourth Amendment do not allow it. When such a stop is not based on objective criteria, the risk of arbitrary and abusive police practices exceeds tolerable limits.

The application of Tex. Penal Code ... to detain appellant and require him to identify himself violated the Fourth Amendment because the officers lacked any reasonable suspicion to believe appellant was engaged or had engaged in criminal conduct. Accordingly, appellant may not be punished for refusing to identify himself, and the conviction is *Reversed.*

MICHIGAN DEPT. STATE POLICE v. SITZ
496 U.S. 444 (1990)

CHIEF JUSTICE REHNQUIST delivered the opinion of the Court.

This case poses the question whether a State's use of highway sobriety checkpoints violates the Fourth and Fourteenth Amendments to the United States Constitution. We hold that it does not and therefore reverse the contrary holding of the Court of Appeals of Michigan.

Petitioners, the Michigan Department of State Police and its director, established a sobriety checkpoint pilot program in early 1986. The director appointed a Sobriety Checkpoint Advisory Committee comprising representatives of the State Police force, local police forces, state prosecutors, and the University of Michigan Transportation Research Institute. Pursuant to its charge, the advisory committee created guidelines setting forth procedures governing checkpoint operations, site selection, and publicity.

Under the guidelines, checkpoints would be set up at selected sites along state roads. All vehicles passing through a checkpoint would be stopped and their drivers briefly examined for signs of intoxication. In cases where a checkpoint officer detected signs of intoxication, the motorist would be directed to a location out of the traffic flow where an officer would check the motorist's driver's license and car registration and, if warranted, conduct further sobriety tests. Should the field tests and the officer's observations suggest that the driver was intoxicated, an arrest would be made. All other drivers would be permitted to resume their journey immediately.

The first — and to date the only — sobriety checkpoint operated under the program was conducted in Saginaw County with the assistance of the Saginaw County Sheriff's Department. During the 75-minute duration of the checkpoint's operation, 126 vehicles passed through the checkpoint. The average delay for each vehicle was approximately 25 seconds. Two drivers were detained for field sobriety testing, and one of the two was arrested for driving under the influence of alcohol. A third driver who drove through without stopping was pulled over by an officer in an observation vehicle and arrested for driving under the influence.

...

To decide this case the trial court performed a balancing test derived from our opinion in *Brown v. Texas* (1979). As described by the Court of Appeals, the test involved "balancing the state's interest in preventing accidents caused by drunk drivers, the effectiveness of sobriety checkpoints in achieving that goal, and the level of intrusion on an individual's privacy caused by the checkpoints." The Court of Appeals agreed that "the *Brown* three-prong balancing test was the correct test to be used to determine the constitutionality of the sobriety checkpoint plan."

As characterized by the Court of Appeals, the trial court's findings with respect to the balancing factors were that the State has "a grave and legitimate" interest in curbing drunken driving; that sobriety checkpoint programs are generally "ineffective" and, therefore, do not significantly further that interest; and that the checkpoints' "subjective intrusion" on individual liberties is substantial. According to the court, the record disclosed no basis for disturbing the trial court's findings, which were made within the context of an analytical framework prescribed by this Court for determining the constitutionality of seizures less intrusive than traditional arrests.

[R]espondents seek to defend the judgment in their favor by insisting that the balancing test derived from *Brown v. Texas*, was not the proper method of analysis. Respondents maintain that the analysis must proceed from a basis of probable cause or reasonable suspicion, and rely for support on language from our decision last Term in *Treasury Employees v. Von Raab*, (1989). We said in *Von Raab*:

> "[W]here a Fourth Amendment intrusion serves special governmental needs, beyond the normal need for law enforcement, it is necessary to balance the individual's privacy expectations against the Government's interests to determine whether it is impractical to require a warrant or some level of individualized suspicion in the particular context."

Respondents argue that there must be a showing of some special governmental need "beyond the normal need" for criminal law enforcement before a balancing analysis is appropriate, and that petitioners have demonstrated no such special need."

Von Raab ... was in no way designed to repudiate our prior cases dealing with police stops of motorists on public highways....

Petitioners concede ... that a Fourth Amendment "seizure" occurs when a vehicle is stopped at a checkpoint. ...The question thus becomes whether such seizures are "reasonable" under the Fourth Amendment.

[T]he instant action challenges only the use of sobriety checkpoints generally. We address only the initial stop of each motorist passing through a checkpoint and the associated preliminary questioning and observation by checkpoint officers. Detention of particular motorists for more extensive field sobriety testing may require satisfaction of an individualized suspicion standard.

No one can seriously dispute the magnitude of the drunken driving problem or the States' interest in eradicating it. ...

Conversely, the weight bearing on the other scale - the measure of the intrusion on motorists stopped briefly at sobriety checkpoints - is slight. ...The trial court and the Court of Appeals, thus, accurately gauged the "objective" intrusion, measured by the duration of the seizure and the intensity of the investigation, as minimal.

With respect to what it perceived to be the "subjective" intrusion on motorists, however, the Court of Appeals found such intrusion substantial. The court first affirmed the trial court's finding that the guidelines governing checkpoint operation minimize the discretion of the officers on the scene. But the court also agreed with the trial court's conclusion that the checkpoints have the potential to generate fear and surprise in motorists. This was so because the record failed to demonstrate that approaching motorists would be aware of their option to make U-turns or turnoffs to avoid the checkpoints. On that basis, the court deemed the subjective intrusion from the checkpoints unreasonable.

We believe the Michigan courts misread our cases concerning the degree of "subjective intrusion" and the potential for generating fear and surprise. The "fear and surprise" to be considered are not the natural fear of one who has been drinking over the prospect of being stopped at a sobriety checkpoint but, rather, the fear and surprise engendered in law-abiding motorists by the nature of the stop. This was made clear in *Martinez-Fuerte*. Comparing checkpoint stops to roving patrol stops considered in prior cases, we said:

"[W]e view checkpoint stops in a different light because the subjective intrusion — the generating of concern or even fright on the part of lawful travelers — is appreciably less in the case of a checkpoint stop. . . .

Here, checkpoints are selected pursuant to the guidelines, and uniformed police officers stop every approaching vehicle. The intrusion resulting from the brief stop at the sobriety checkpoint is for constitutional purposes indistinguishable from the checkpoint stops we upheld in *Martinez-Fuerte*.

The Court of Appeals went on to consider as part of the balancing analysis the "effectiveness" of the proposed checkpoint program. Based on extensive testimony in the trial record, the court concluded that the checkpoint program failed the "effectiveness" part of the test, and that this failure materially discounted petitioners' strong interest in implementing the program. We think the Court of Appeals was wrong on this point as well.

The actual language from *Brown v. Texas*, upon which the Michigan courts based their evaluation of "effectiveness," describes the balancing factor as "the degree to which the

seizure advances the public interest." This passage from *Brown* was not meant to transfer from politically accountable officials to the courts the decision as to which among reasonable alternative law enforcement techniques should be employed to deal with a serious public danger. Experts in police science might disagree over which of several methods of apprehending drunken drivers is preferable as an ideal. But for purposes of Fourth Amendment analysis, the choice among such reasonable alternatives remains with the governmental officials who have a unique understanding of, and a responsibility for, limited public resources, including a finite number of police officers. Brown's rather general reference to "the degree to which the seizure advances the public interest" was derived, as the opinion makes clear, from the line of cases culminating in *Martinez-Fuerte*. Neither *Martinez-Fuerte* nor *Delaware v. Prouse* (1979), however, the two cases cited by the Court of Appeals as providing the basis for its "effectiveness" review, supports the searching examination of "effectiveness" undertaken by the Michigan court.

In *Delaware v. Prouse*, we disapproved random stops made by Delaware Highway Patrol officers in an effort to apprehend unlicensed drivers and unsafe vehicles. We observed that no empirical evidence indicated that such stops would be an effective means of promoting roadway safety and said that "[i]t seems common sense that the percentage of all drivers on the road who are driving without a license is very small and that the number of licensed drivers who will be stopped in order to find one unlicensed operator will be large indeed." We observed that the random stops involved the "kind of standardless and unconstrained discretion [which] is the evil the Court has discerned when in previous cases it has insisted that the discretion of the official in the field be circumscribed, at least to some extent." We went on to state that our holding did not "cast doubt on the permissibility of roadside truck weigh-stations and inspection checkpoints, at which some vehicles may be subject to further detention for safety and regulatory inspection than are others."

Unlike *Prouse*, this case involves neither a complete absence of empirical data nor a challenge to random highway stops. During the operation of the Saginaw County checkpoint, the detention of the 126 vehicles that entered the checkpoint resulted in the arrest of two drunken drivers. Stated as a percentage, approximately 1.6 percent of the drivers passing through the checkpoint were arrested for alcohol impairment. In addition, an expert witness testified at the trial that experience in other States demonstrated that, on the whole, sobriety checkpoints resulted in drunken driving arrests of around 1 percent of all motorists stopped

In sum, the balance of the State's interest in preventing drunken driving, the extent to which this system can reasonably be said to advance that interest, and the degree of intrusion upon individual motorists who are briefly stopped, weighs in favor of the state program. We therefore hold that it is consistent with the Fourth Amendment.

JUSTICE BRENNAN, with whom JUSTICE MARSHALL joins, dissenting.

Today, the Court rejects a Fourth Amendment challenge to a sobriety checkpoint policy in which police stop all cars and inspect all drivers for signs of intoxication without any individualized suspicion that a specific driver is intoxicated. The Court does so by balancing "the State's interest in preventing drunken driving, the extent to which this system can reasonably be said to advance that interest, and the degree of intrusion upon individual motorists who are briefly stopped." . . . I agree that the Court misapplies that test by undervaluing the nature of the intrusion and exaggerating the law enforcement need to use the roadblocks to prevent drunken driving. ...I write separately to express a few additional points.

The majority opinion creates the impression that the Court generally engages in a balancing test in order to determine the constitutionality of all seizures, or at least those "dealing with police stops of motorists on public highways." This is not the case. In most cases, the police must possess probable cause for a seizure to be judged reasonable. Only when a seizure is "substantially less intrusive," than a typical arrest is the general rule replaced by a balancing test. I agree with the Court that the initial stop of a car at a roadblock under the Michigan State Police sobriety checkpoint policy is sufficiently less intrusive than an arrest so that the reasonableness of the seizure may be judged, not by the presence of probable cause, but by balancing "the gravity of the public concerns served by the seizure, the degree to which the seizure advances the public interest, and the severity of the interference with individual liberty." *Brown v. Texas*,(1979). But one searches the majority opinion in vain for any acknowledgment that the reason for employing the balancing test is that the seizure is minimally intrusive.

Indeed, the opinion reads as if the minimal nature of the seizure ends rather than begins the inquiry into reasonableness. Once the Court establishes that the seizure is "slight," it asserts without explanation that the balance "weighs in favor of the state program." The Court ignores the fact that in this class of minimally intrusive searches, we have generally required the government to prove that it had reasonable suspicion for a minimally intrusive seizure to be considered reasonable. Some level of individualized suspicion is a core component of the protection the Fourth Amendment provides against arbitrary government action. ... By holding that no level of suspicion is necessary before the police may stop a car for the purpose of preventing drunken driving, the Court potentially subjects the general public to arbitrary or harassing conduct by the police.

. . .There has been no showing in this case that there is a similar difficulty in detecting individuals who are driving under the influence of alcohol, nor is it intuitively obvious that such a difficulty exists. That stopping every car might make it easier to prevent drunken driving, is an insufficient justification for abandoning the requirement of individualized suspicion. ... Without proof that the police cannot develop individualized suspicion that a person is driving while impaired by alcohol, I believe the constitutional balance must be struck in favor of protecting the public against even the "minimally intrusive" seizures involved in this case.

I do not dispute the immense social cost caused by drunken drivers, nor do I slight the government's efforts to prevent such tragic losses. Indeed, I would hazard a guess that today's opinion will be received favorably by a majority of our society, who would willingly suffer the minimal intrusion of a sobriety checkpoint stop in order to prevent drunken driving. But consensus that a particular law enforcement technique serves a laudable purpose has never been the touchstone of constitutional analysis.

In the face of the "momentary evil" of drunken driving, the Court today abdicates its role as the protector of that fundamental right. I respectfully dissent.

JUSTICE STEVENS, with whom JUSTICE BRENNAN and JUSTICE MARSHALL join as to Parts I and II, dissenting.

[T]he findings of the trial court, based on an extensive record and affirmed by the Michigan Court of Appeals, indicate that the net effect of sobriety checkpoints on traffic safety is infinitesimal and possibly negative.

Indeed, the record in this case makes clear that a decision holding these suspicionless seizures unconstitutional would not impede the law enforcement community's remarkable progress in reducing the death toll on our highways. ... The number of man-hours devoted to these operations is not in the record, but it seems inconceivable that a higher arrest rate could not have been achieved by more conventional means. . . .

Any relationship between sobriety checkpoints and an actual reduction in highway fatalities is even less substantial than the minimal impact on arrest rates.

In light of these considerations, it seems evident that the Court today misapplies the

balancing test announced in *Brown v. Texas*, (1979). The Court overvalues the law enforcement interest in using sobriety checkpoints, undervalues the citizen's interest in freedom from random, announced investigatory seizures, and mistakenly assumes that there is "virtually no difference" between a routine stop at a permanent, fixed checkpoint and a surprise stop at a sobriety checkpoint. I believe this case is controlled by our several precedents condemning suspicionless random stops of motorists for investigatory purposes.

There is a critical difference between a seizure that is preceded by fair notice and one that is effected by surprise. That is one reason why a border search, or indeed any search at a permanent and fixed checkpoint, is much less intrusive than a random stop. A motorist with advance notice of the location of a permanent checkpoint has an opportunity to avoid the search entirely, or at least to prepare for, and limit, the intrusion on her privacy.

. . .

The evidence in this case indicates that sobriety checkpoints result in the arrest of a fraction of one percent of the drivers who are stopped, but there is absolutely no evidence that this figure represents an increase over the number of arrests that would have been made by using the same law enforcement resources in conventional patrols. Thus, although the gross number of arrests is more than zero, there is a complete failure of proof on the question whether the wholesale seizures have produced any net advance in the public interest in arresting intoxicated drivers.

Drunken driving, unlike smuggling, may thus be detected absent any checkpoints. A program that produces thousands of otherwise impossible arrests is not a relevant precedent for a program that produces only a handful of arrests which would be more easily obtained without resort to suspicionless seizures of hundreds of innocent citizens.

. . .Random, suspicionless seizures designed to search for evidence of firearms, drugs, or intoxication belong, however, in a fundamentally different category. These seizures play upon the detained individual's reasonable expectations of privacy, injecting a suspicionless search into a context where none would normally occur. The imposition that seems diaphanous today may be intolerable tomorrow.

Second, sobriety checkpoints are elaborate, and disquieting, publicity stunts. The possibility that anybody, no matter how innocent, may be stopped for police inspection is nothing if not attention getting. The shock value of the checkpoint program may be its most effective feature. . . .

This is a case that is driven by nothing more than symbolic state action - an insufficient justification for an otherwise unreasonable program of random seizures. Unfortunately, the Court is transfixed by the wrong symbol - the illusory prospect of punishing countless intoxicated motorists - when it should keep its eyes on the road plainly marked by the Constitution.

I respectfully dissent.

[Note, this case was sent back to the Michigan Supreme Court to decide whether these roadblocks were permitted under Michigan's Constitution. They are not.

CITY OF INDIANAPOLIS v. EDMOND 531 U.S. 32 (2000)

JUSTICE O'CONNOR delivered the opinion of the Court.

In *Michigan Dept. State Police* v. *Sitz,* and *United States* v. *Martinez-Fuerte* we held that brief, suspicionless seizures at highway checkpoints for the purposes of combating drunk driving and intercepting illegal immigrants were constitutional. We now consider the constitutionality of a highway checkpoint program whose primary purpose is the discovery and interdiction of illegal narcotics.

I

In August 1998, the city of Indianapolis began to operate vehicle checkpoints on Indianapolis roads in an effort to interdict unlawful drugs. The city conducted six such roadblocks between August and November that year, stopping 1,161 vehicles and arresting 104 motorists. Fifty-five arrests were for drug-related crimes, while 49 were for offenses unrelated to drugs. . . .The overall "hit rate" of the program was thus approximately nine percent.

Pursuant to written directives issued by the chief of police, at least one officer approaches the vehicle, advises the driver that he or she is being stopped briefly at a drug checkpoint, and asks the driver to produce a license and registration. The officer also looks for signs of impairment and conducts an open-view examination of the vehicle from the outside. A narcotics-detection dog walks around the outside of each stopped vehicle.

The directives instruct the officers that they may conduct a search only by consent or based on the appropriate quantum of particularized suspicion. The officers must conduct each stop in the same manner until particularized suspicion develops, and the officers have no discretion to stop any vehicle out of sequence. The city agreed in the stipulation to operate the checkpoints in such a way as to ensure that the total duration of each stop, absent reasonable suspicion or probable cause, would be five minutes or less.

[C]heckpoint locations are selected weeks in advance based on such considerations as area crime statistics and traffic flow. The checkpoints are generally operated during daylight hours and are identified with lighted signs reading, "NARCOTICS CHECKPOINT ___ MILE AHEAD, NARCOTICS K-9 IN USE, BE PREPARED TO STOP." . . . Once a group of cars has been stopped, other traffic proceeds without interruption until all the stopped cars have been processed or diverted for further processing. . . . [T]he average stop for a vehicle not subject to further processing lasts two to three minutes or less.

Respondents James Edmond and Joell Palmer were each stopped at a narcotics checkpoint in late September 1998. Respondents then filed a lawsuit on behalf of themselves and the class of all motorists who had been stopped or were subject to being stopped in the future at the Indianapolis drug checkpoints. Respondents claimed that the roadblocks violated the Fourth Amendment of the United States Constitution and the search and seizure provision of the Indiana Constitution.

[W]e have upheld certain regimes of suspicionless searches where the program was designed to serve "special needs, beyond the normal need for law enforcement." . . . We have also allowed searches for certain administrative purposes without particularized suspicion of misconduct, provided that those searches are appropriately limited. . . .

We have also upheld brief, suspicionless seizures of motorists at a fixed Border Patrol checkpoint designed to intercept illegal aliens, and at a sobriety checkpoint aimed at removing drunk drivers from the road. In addition, in *Delaware* v. *Prouse,* 440 U. S. 648, 663 (1979), we suggested that a similar type of roadblock with the purpose of verifying drivers' licenses and vehicle registrations would be permissible. In none of these cases, however, did we indicate approval of a checkpoint program whose primary purpose was to detect evidence of ordinary criminal wrongdoing.

In *Prouse,* we invalidated a discretionary, suspicionless stop for a spot check of a motorist's driver's license and vehicle registration. The officer's conduct in that case was unconstitutional primarily on account of his exercise of "standardless and unconstrained discretion." . . .We nonetheless acknowledged the States' "vital interest in ensuring that only those qualified to do so are permitted to operate motor vehicles, that these

vehicles are fit for safe operation, and hence that licensing, registration, and vehicle inspection requirements are being observed." . . . Accordingly, we suggested that "[q]uestioning of all oncoming traffic at roadblock-type stops" would be a lawful means of serving this interest in highway safety. . . .

We further indicated in *Prouse* that we considered the purposes of such a hypothetical roadblock to be distinct from a general purpose of investigating crime. The State proffered the additional interests of "the apprehension of stolen motor vehicles and of drivers under the influence of alcohol or narcotics" in its effort to justify the discretionary spot check. . . . We attributed the entirety of the latter interest to the State's interest in roadway safety. . . . We also noted that the interest in apprehending stolen vehicles may be partly subsumed by the interest in roadway safety. *Ibid.* We observed, however, that "[t]he remaining governmental interest in controlling automobile thefts is not distinguishable from the general interest in crime control." *Ibid.* Not only does the common thread of highway safety thus run through *Sitz* and *Prouse,* but *Prouse* itself reveals a difference in the Fourth Amendment significance of highway safety interests and the general interest in crime control.

It is well established that a vehicle stop at a highway checkpoint effectuates a seizure within the meaning of the Fourth Amendment. …The fact that officers walk a narcotics-detection dog around the exterior of each car at the Indianapolis checkpoints does not transform the seizure into a search. … [W]hat principally distinguishes these checkpoints from those we have previously approved is their primary purpose.

As petitioners concede, the Indianapolis checkpoint program unquestionably has the primary purpose of interdicting illegal narcotics. …

We have never approved a checkpoint program whose primary purpose was to detect evidence of ordinary criminal wrongdoing.

Rather, our checkpoint cases have recognized only limited exceptions to the general rule that a seizure must be accompanied by some measure of individualized suspicion. We suggested in *Prouse* that we would not credit the "general interest in crime control" as justification for a regime of suspicionless stops. ...Consistent with this suggestion, each of the checkpoint programs that we have approved was designed primarily to serve purposes closely related to the problems of policing the border or the necessity of ensuring roadway safety. Because the primary purpose of the Indianapolis narcotics checkpoint program is to uncover evidence of ordinary criminal wrongdoing, the program contravenes the Fourth Amendment.

Petitioners also emphasize the severe and intractable nature of the drug problem as justification for the checkpoint program. ...There is no doubt that traffic in illegal narcotics creates social harms of the first magnitude. ... The law enforcement problems that the drug trade creates likewise remain daunting and complex, particularly in light of the myriad forms of spin-off crime that it spawns. ...The same can be said of various other illegal activities, if only to a lesser degree. But the gravity of the threat alone cannot be dispositive of questions concerning what means law enforcement officers may employ to pursue a given purpose. Rather, in determining whether individualized suspicion is required, we must consider the nature of the interests threatened and their connection to the particular law enforcement practices at issue. We are particularly reluctant to recognize exceptions to the general rule of individualized suspicion where governmental authorities primarily pursue their general crime control ends.

Nor can the narcotics-interdiction purpose of the checkpoints be rationalized in terms of a highway safety concern similar to that present in *Sitz*. The detection and punishment of almost any criminal offense serves broadly the safety of the community, and our streets would no doubt be safer but for the scourge of illegal drugs. Only with respect to a smaller class of offenses, howevers society confronted with the type of immediate, vehicle-bound threat to life and limb that the sobriety checkpoint in *Sitz* was designed to eliminate.

Petitioners also liken the anticontraband agenda of the Indianapolis checkpoints to the antismuggling purpose of the checkpoints in *Martinez-Fuerte*. ...The problem with this argument is that the same logic prevails any time a vehicle is employed to conceal contraband or other evidence of a crime. This type of connection to the roadway is very different from the close connection to roadway safety that was present in *Sitz* and *Prouse*. Further, the Indianapolis checkpoints are far removed from the border context that was crucial in *Martinez-Fuerte*. ...[W]e must look more closely at the nature of the public interests that such a regime is designed principally to serve.

The primary purpose of the Indianapolis narcotics checkpoints is in the end to advance "the general interest in crime control."...We decline to suspend the usual requirement of individualized suspicion where the police seek to employ a checkpoint primarily for the ordinary enterprise of investigating crimes. We cannot sanction stops justified only by the generalized and ever-present possibility that interrogation and inspection may reveal that any given motorist has committed some crime.

Of course, there are circumstances that may justify a law enforcement checkpoint where the primary purpose would otherwise, but for some emergency, relate to ordinary crime control. For example, . . . the Fourth Amendment would almost certainly permit an appropriately tailored roadblock set up to thwart an imminent terrorist attack or to catch a dangerous criminal who is likely to flee by way of a particular route. The exigencies created by these scenarios are far removed from the circumstances under which authorities might simply stop cars as a matter of course to see if there just happens to be a felon leaving the jurisdiction. While we do not limit the purposes that may justify a checkpoint program to any rigid set of categories, we decline to approve a program whose primary purpose is ultimately indistinguishable from the general interest in crime control. …

It goes without saying that our holding today does nothing to alter the constitutional status of the sobriety and border checkpoints that we approved in *Sitz* and *Martinez-Fuerte*, or of the type of traffic checkpoint that we suggested would be lawful in *Prouse*. The constitutionality of such checkpoint programs still depends on a balancing of the competing interests at stake and the effectiveness of the program. …When law enforcement authorities pursue primarily general crime control purposes at checkpoints such as here, however, stops can only be justified by some quantum of individualized suspicion.

Our holding also does not affect the validity of border searches or searches at places like airports and government buildings, where the need for such measures to ensure public safety can be particularly acute. Nor does our opinion speak to other intrusions aimed primarily at purposes beyond the general interest in crime control. Our holding also does not impair the ability of police officers to act appropriately upon information that they properly learn during a checkpoint stop justified by a lawful primary purpose, even where such action may result in the arrest of a motorist for an offense unrelated to that purpose. Finally, we caution that the purpose inquiry in this context is to be conducted only at the programmatic level and is not an invitation to probe the minds of individual officers acting at the scene. …

Because the primary purpose of the Indianapolis checkpoint program is ultimately indistinguishable from the general interest in crime control, the checkpoints violate the Fourth Amendment.

LLINOIS v. LIDSTER
540 U.S. 419 (2004)

JUSTICE BREYER delivered the opinion of the Court

This Fourth Amendment case focuses upon a highway checkpoint where police stopped motorists to ask them for information about a recent hit-and-run accident. We hold that the police stops were reasonable, hence, constitutional.

The relevant background is as follows: On Saturday, August 23, 1997, just after midnight, an unknown motorist traveling eastbound on a highway in Lombard, Illinois, struck and killed a 70-year-old bicyclist. The motorist drove off without identifying himself. About one week later at about the same time of night and at about the same place, local police set up a highway checkpoint designed to obtain more information about the accident from the motoring public.

Police cars with flashing lights partially blocked the eastbound lanes of the highway. The blockage forced traffic to slow down, leading to lines of up to 15 cars in each lane. As each vehicle drew up to the checkpoint, an officer would stop it for 10 to 15 seconds, ask the occupants whether they had seen anything happen there the previous weekend, and hand each driver a flyer. The flyer said "ALERT . . .FATAL HIT & RUN ACCIDENT" and requested "assistance in identifying the vehicle and driver in this accident which killed a 70-year-old bicyclist.

Robert Lidster, the respondent, drove a minivan toward the checkpoint. As he approached the checkpoint, his van swerved, nearly hitting one of the officers. The officer smelled alcohol on Lidster's breath. He directed Lidster to a side street where another officer administered a sobriety test and then arrested Lidster. Lidster was tried and convicted in Illinois state court of driving under the influence of alcohol.

Lidster challenged the lawfulness of his arrest and conviction on the ground that the government had obtained much of the relevant evidence through use of a checkpoint stop that violated the Fourth Amendment.

Because lower courts have reached different conclusions about this matter, we granted certiorari. . . . We now reverse. . . .

The Illinois Supreme Court basically held that our decision in *Edmond* governs the outcome of this case. We do not agree. Edmond involved a checkpoint at which police stopped vehicles to look for evidence of drug crimes committed by occupants of those vehicles. . . . We found that police had set up this checkpoint primarily for general "crime control" purposes, **i.e.**, "to detect evidence of ordinary criminal wrongdoing." We noted that the stop was made without individualized suspicion. And we held that the Fourth Amendment forbids such a stop, in the absence of special circumstances.

The checkpoint stop here differs significantly from that in *Edmond*. The stop's primary law enforcement purpose was not to determine whether a vehicle's occupants were committing a crime, but to ask vehicle occupants, as members of the public, for their help in providing information about a crime in all likelihood committed by others. The police expected the information elicited to help them apprehend, not the vehicle's occupants, but other individuals.

Neither do we believe, *Edmond* aside, that the Fourth Amendment would have us apply an *Edmond*-type rule of automatic unconstitutionality to brief, information-seeking highway stops of the kind now before us. For one thing, the fact that such stops normally lack individualized suspicion cannot by itself determine the constitutional outcome. As in *Edmond*, the stop here at issue involves a motorist. The Fourth Amendment does not treat a motorist's car as his castle. . . . And special law enforcement concerns will sometimes justify highway stops without individualized suspicion. See *Michigan Dept. State Police v. Sitz*, (1990) (sobriety checkpoint); *Martinez-Fuerte* (Border Patrol checkpoint). Moreover, unlike *Edmond*, the context here (seeking information from the

public) is one in which, by definition, the concept of individualized suspicion has little role to play. Like certain other forms of police activity, say, crowd control or public safety, an information-seeking stop is not the kind of event that involves suspicion, or lack of suspicion, of the relevant individual.

For another thing, information-seeking highway stops are less likely to provoke anxiety or to prove intrusive. The stops are likely brief. The police are not likely to ask questions designed to elicit self-incriminating information. . . .

Further, the law ordinarily permits police to seek the voluntary cooperation of members of the public in the investigation of a crime. . . .

The importance of soliciting the public's assistance is offset to some degree by the need to stop a motorist to obtain that help — a need less likely present where a pedestrian, not a motorist, is involved. The difference is significant in light of our determinations that such an involuntary stop amounts to a "seizure" in Fourth Amendment terms. E.g., *Edmond*. That difference, however, is not important enough to justify an Edmond-type rule here. After all, as we have said, the motorist stop will likely be brief. Any accompanying traffic delay should prove no more onerous than many that typically accompany normal traffic congestion. And the resulting voluntary questioning of a motorist is as likely to prove important for police investigation as is the questioning of a pedestrian. . . .

Finally, we do not believe that an *Edmond*-type rule is needed to prevent an unreasonable proliferation of police checkpoints. . . . Practical considerations — namely, limited police resources and community hostility to related traffic tie-ups — seem likely to inhibit any such proliferation. . . . And, of course, the Fourth Amendment's normal insistence that the stop be reasonable in context will still provide an important legal limitation on police use of this kind of information-seeking checkpoint. These considerations, taken together, convince us that an *Edmond*-type presumptive rule of unconstitutionality does not apply here. That does not mean the stop is automatically, or even presumptively, constitutional. It simply means that we must judge its reasonableness, hence, its constitutionality, on the basis of the individual circumstances. And as this Court said in *Brown v. Texas*, (1979), in judging reasonableness, we look to "the gravity of the public concerns served by the seizure, the degree to which the seizure advances the public interest, and the severity of the interference with individual liberty." . . .

We now consider the reasonableness of the checkpoint stop before us in light of the factors just mentioned, an issue that, in our view, has been fully argued here. . . . We hold that the stop was constitutional.

The relevant public concern was grave. Police were investigating a crime that had resulted in a human death. . . .

The stop advanced this grave public concern to a significant degree. The police appropriately tailored their checkpoint stops to

fit important criminal investigatory needs. The stops took place about one week after the hit-and-run accident, on the same highway near the location of the accident, and at about the same time of night. And police used the stops to obtain information from drivers, some of whom might well have been in the vicinity of the crime at the time it occurred. . .

Most importantly, the stops interfered only minimally with liberty of the sort the Fourth Amendment seeks to protect. Viewed objectively, each stop required only a brief wait in line — a very few minutes at most. Contact with the police lasted only a few seconds. ... Police contact consisted simply of a request for information and the distribution of a flyer. ... Viewed subjectively, the contact provided little reason for anxiety or alarm. The police stopped all vehicles systematically. And there is no allegation here that the police acted in a discriminatory or otherwise unlawful manner while questioning motorists during stops.

For these reasons we conclude that the checkpoint stop was constitutional.

WAS THE SEARCH REASONABLE EVEN WITHOUT A WARRANT?

This next section explores situations where searches were done without a warrant but are found to be constitutional because the search falls under a "well-established exception to the warrant requirement.

Searches Incident To Arrest

The police's ability to conduct warrantless searches of individuals placed under arrest is well established. In *United States v. Robinson*, 414 U.S. 218 (1973) the Court noted that there are two historical rationales for the search-incident-to-arrest exception: (1) the need to disarm the suspect in order to take him into custody, and (2) the need to preserve evidence for later use at trial. In a series of cases the Court has examined the permissible scope of searches done incidental to an arrest, whether a search can be done when police are authorized to, but do not, arrest but rather issue a citation; whether a search done immediately prior to an arrest are "incidental"; how long after the arrest is conducted can the search take place and still be "incidental"; and whether a search incident to an arrest which turns out to be unlawful is still valid (you looked at that while reading about the exclusionary rule).

Scope Of Searches Incident To Arrest

Where can police search when they arrest a suspect? Can they search his or her person? Can they do a body-cavity/very intrusive search or just frisk? Can they search the arrestee's home or location where the arrest takes place? Can they search property found on or near the arrestee's person? What if the arrest arises out of a vehicle stop?

Generally, the scope of a search-incident-to-arrest is limited to the arrestee's person and the area within the arrestee's immediate control — the area from within which the arrestee might gain possession of a weapon or destructible evidence. *Chimel v. California* 385 U.S. 752 (1969), and *United States v. Robinson*, 414 U.S. 218 (1973), are both cases cited frequently. Under *Chimel,* the arrestee and everything the arrestee wears may be searched, but this does not include a full-blown search of the arrestee's entire home. You have read above that when executing an arrest warrant the Fourth Amendment allows officers to conduct a limited protective sweep in the course of an in-home arrest if they have a "reasonable belief based on specific and articulable facts that the area to be swept harbors an individual posing a danger to those on the arrest scene." *Maryland v. Buie*, 494 U.S. 325 (1990). A protective sweep is a "quick and limited search of premises, incident to an arrest and * * * narrowly confined to a cursory visual inspection of those places in which a person might be hiding." *Maryland v. Buie*, 494 U.S., at 327. Items in plain view may be seized during a protective sweep.

ARIZONA v. GANT
536 U.S. 332 (2009)

JUSTICE STEVENS delivered the opinion of the Court.

After Rodney Gant was arrested for driving with a suspended license, handcuffed, and locked in the back of a patrol car, police officers searched his car and discovered cocaine in the pocket of a jacket on the backseat. Because Gant could not have accessed his car to retrieve weapons or evidence at the time of the search, the Arizona Supreme Court held that the search-incident-to-arrest exception to the Fourth Amendment's warrant requirement, as defined in *Chimel v. California*, and applied to vehicle searches in *New York v. Belton*, did not justify the search in this case. We agree with that conclusion.

Under *Chimel*, police may search incident to arrest only the space within an arrestee's " 'immediate control,' " meaning "the area from within which he might gain possession of a weapon or destructible evidence." The safety and evidentiary justifications underlying *Chimel's* reaching-distance rule determine *Belton's* scope. Accordingly, we hold that *Belton* does not authorize a vehicle search incident to a recent occupant's arrest after the arrestee has been secured and cannot access

the interior of the vehicle. Consistent with the holding in *Thornton v. United States*, . . . we also conclude that circumstances unique to the automobile context justify a search incident to arrest when it is reasonable to believe that evidence of the offense of arrest might be found in the vehicle.

I

On August 25, 1999, acting on an anonymous tip that the residence at 2524 North Walnut Avenue was being used to sell drugs, Tucson police officers Griffith and Reed knocked on the front door and asked to speak to the owner. Gant answered the door and, after identifying himself, stated that he expected the owner to return later. The officers left the residence and conducted a records check, which revealed that Gant's driver's license had been suspended and there was an outstanding warrant for his arrest for driving with a suspended license.

When the officers returned to the house that evening, they found a man near the back of the house and a woman in a car parked in front of it. After a third officer arrived, they arrested the man for providing a false name and the woman for possessing drug paraphernalia.

Both arrestees were handcuffed and secured in separate patrol cars when Gant arrived. The officers recognized his car as it entered the driveway, and Officer Griffith confirmed that Gant was the driver by shining a flashlight into the car as it drove by him. Gant parked at the end of the driveway, got out of his car, and shut the door. Griffith, who was about 30 feet away, called to Gant, and they approached each other, meeting 10-to-12 feet from Gant's car. Griffith immediately arrested Gant and handcuffed him.

Because the other arrestees were secured in the only patrol cars at the scene, Griffith called for backup. When two more officers arrived, they locked Gant in the backseat of their vehicle. After Gant had been handcuffed and placed in the back of a patrol car, two officers searched his car: One of them found a gun, and the other discovered a bag of cocaine in the pocket of a jacket on the backseat.

Gant was charged with two offenses — possession of a narcotic drug for sale and possession of drug paraphernalia (i.e., the plastic bag in which the cocaine was found). He moved to suppress the evidence seized from his car on the ground that the warrantless search violated the Fourth Amendment. Among other things, Gant argued that *Belton* did not authorize the search of his vehicle because he posed no threat to the officers after he was handcuffed in the patrol car and because he was arrested for a traffic offense for which no evidence could be found in his vehicle. When asked at the suppression hearing why the search was conducted, Officer Griffith responded: "Because the law says we can do it."

The trial court rejected the State's contention that the officers had probable cause to search Gant's car for contraband when the search began, but it denied the motion to suppress. Relying on the fact that the police saw Gant commit the crime of driving without a license and apprehended him only shortly after he exited his car, the court held that the search was permissible as a search incident to arrest. A jury found Gant guilty on both drug counts,

and he was sentenced to a 3-year term of imprisonment.

. . . .

The chorus that has called for us to revisit *Belton* includes courts, scholars, and Members of this Court who have questioned that decision's clarity and its fidelity to Fourth Amendment principles. We therefore granted the State's petition for certiorari. 552 U. S. ___ (2008).

II

Consistent with our precedent, our analysis begins, as it should in every case addressing the reasonableness of a warrantless search, with the basic rule that "searches conducted outside the judicial process, without prior approval by judge or magistrate, are per se unreasonable under the Fourth Amendment — subject only to a few specifically established and well-delineated exceptions." Among the exceptions to the warrant requirement is a search incident to a lawful arrest. The exception derives from interests in officer safety and evidence preservation that are typically implicated in arrest situations.

In *Chimel*, we held that a search incident to arrest may only include "the arrestee's person and the area 'within his immediate control' — construing that phrase to mean the area from within which he might gain possession of a weapon or destructible evidence." That limitation, which continues to define the boundaries of the exception, ensures that the scope of a search incident to arrest is commensurate with its purposes of protecting arresting officers and safeguarding any evidence of the offense of arrest that an arrestee might conceal or destroy. . . . If there is no possibility that an arrestee could reach into the area that law enforcement officers seek to search, both justifications for the search-incident-to-arrest exception are absent and the rule does not apply.

In *Belton*, we considered *Chimel's* application to the automobile context. A lone police officer in that case stopped a speeding car in which Belton was one of four occupants.

While asking for the driver's license and registration, the officer smelled burnt marijuana and observed an envelope on the car floor marked "Supergold" — a name he associated with marijuana. Thus having probable cause to believe the occupants had committed a drug offense, the officer ordered them out of the vehicle, placed them under arrest, and patted them down. Without handcuffing the arrestees, the officer " 'split them up into four separate areas of the Thruway . . .so they would not be in physical touching area of each other' " and searched the vehicle, including the pocket of a jacket on the backseat, in which he found cocaine.

. . .

[In *Belton*] we held that when an officer lawfully arrests "the occupant of an automobile, he may, as a contemporaneous incident of that arrest, search the passenger compartment of the automobile" and any containers therein. That holding was based in large part on our assumption "that articles inside the relatively narrow compass of the passenger compartment of an automobile are in fact generally, even if not inevitably, within 'the area into which an arrestee might reach.' "

. . .

III

. . . [Reading of our *Belton*] opinion has been widely understood to allow a vehicle search incident to the arrest of a recent occupant even if there is no possibility the arrestee could gain access to the vehicle at the time of the search.

. . . .

Under this broad reading of *Belton*, a vehicle search would be authorized incident to every arrest of a recent occupant notwithstanding that in most cases the vehicle's passenger compartment will not be within the arrestee's reach at the time of the search. To read *Belton* as authorizing a vehicle search incident to every recent occupant's arrest would thus untether the rule from the justifications underlying the *Chimel* exception — a result clearly incompatible with our statement in

Belton that it "in no way alters the fundamental principles established in the *Chimel* case regarding the basic scope of searches incident to lawful custodial arrests." Accordingly, we reject this reading of *Belton* and hold that the *Chimel* rationale authorizes police to search a vehicle incident to a recent occupant's arrest only when the arrestee is unsecured and within reaching distance of the passenger compartment at the time of the search.

Although it does not follow from *Chimel*, we also conclude that circumstances unique to the vehicle context justify a search incident to a lawful arrest when it is "reasonable to believe evidence relevant to the crime of arrest might be found in the vehicle." In many cases, as when a recent occupant is arrested for a traffic violation, there will be no reasonable basis to believe the vehicle contains relevant evidence. But in others . . . the offense of arrest will supply a basis for searching the passenger compartment of an arrestee's vehicle and any containers therein.

Neither the possibility of access nor the likelihood of discovering offense-related evidence authorized the search in this case. . . . Under those circumstances, Gant clearly was not within reaching distance of his car at the time of the search. An evidentiary basis for the search was also lacking in this case. . . .Gant was arrested for driving with a suspended license — an offense for which police could not expect to find evidence in the passenger compartment of Gant's car. Because police could not reasonably have believed either that Gant could have accessed his car at the time of the search or that evidence of the offense for which he was arrested might have been found therein, the search in this case was unreasonable.

. . .

Although it appears that the State's reading of *Belton* has been widely taught in police academies and that law enforcement officers have relied on the rule in conducting vehicle searches during the past 28 years, many of these searches were not justified by the reasons underlying the *Chimel* exception. Countless individuals guilty of nothing more serious than a traffic violation have had their constitutional right to the security of their private effects violated as a result. The fact that the law enforcement community may view the State's version of the *Belton* rule as an entitlement does not establish the sort of reliance interest that could outweigh the countervailing interest that all individuals share in having their constitutional rights fully protected. If it is clear that a practice is unlawful, individuals' interest in its discontinuance clearly outweighs any law enforcement "entitlement" to its persistence. …

VI

Police may search a vehicle incident to a recent occupant's arrest only if the arrestee is within reaching distance of the passenger compartment at the time of the search or it is reasonable to believe the vehicle contains evidence of the offense of arrest. When these justifications are absent, a search of an arrestee's vehicle will be unreasonable unless police obtain a warrant or show that another exception to the warrant requirement applies. The Arizona Supreme Court correctly held that this case involved an unreasonable search. Accordingly, the judgment of the State Supreme Court is affirmed.

JUSTICE SCALIA, concurring. Omitted.

JUSTICE BREYER, dissenting. Omitted.

JUSTICE ALITO, with whom THE CHIEF JUSTICE and JUSTICE KENNEDY join, and with whom JUSTICE BREYER joins except as to Part II-E, dissenting. Omitted.

. . . .

RILEY v. CALIFORNIA
573 U.S. 373 (2014)

Chief Justice Roberts delivered the opinion of the Court.

These two cases raise a common question: whether the police may, without a warrant, search digital information on a cell phone seized from an individual who has been arrested.

I
A

In the first case, petitioner David Riley was stopped by a police officer for driving with expired registration tags. In the course of the stop, the officer also learned that Riley's license had been suspended. The officer impounded Riley's car, pursuant to department policy, and another officer conducted an inventory search of the car. Riley was arrested for possession of concealed and loaded firearms when that search turned up two handguns under the car's hood.

An officer searched Riley incident to the arrest and found items associated with the "Bloods" street gang. He also seized a cell phone from Riley's pants pocket. According to Riley's uncontradicted assertion, the phone was a "smart phone," a cell phone with a broad range of other functions based on advanced computing capability, large storage capacity, and Internet connectivity. The officer accessed information on the phone and noticed that some words (presumably in text messages or a contacts list) were preceded by the letters "CK" — a label that, he believed, stood for "Crip Killers," a slang term for members of the Bloods gang.

At the police station about two hours after the arrest, a detective specializing in gangs further examined the contents of the phone. The detective testified that he "went through" Riley's phone "looking for evidence, because . . . gang members will often video themselves with guns or take pictures of themselves with the guns." Although there was "a lot of stuff" on the phone, particular files that "caught [the detective's] eye" included videos of young men sparring while someone yelled encouragement using the moniker "Blood." The police also found photographs of Riley standing in front of a car they suspected had been involved in a shooting a few weeks earlier.

Riley was ultimately charged, in connection with that earlier shooting, with firing at an occupied vehicle, assault with a semiautomatic firearm, and attempted murder. The State alleged that Riley had committed those crimes for the benefit of a criminal street gang, an aggravating factor that carries an enhanced sentence. Prior to trial, Riley moved to suppress all evidence that the police had obtained from his cell phone. He contended that the searches of his phone violated the Fourth Amendment, because they had been performed without a warrant and were not otherwise justified by exigent circumstances. The trial court rejected that argument. At Riley's trial, police officers testified about the photographs and videos found on the phone, and some of the photographs were admitted into evidence. Riley was convicted on all three counts and received an enhanced sentence of 15 years to life in prison.

The California Court of Appeal affirmed. . . . The court relied on the California Supreme Court's decision in *People v. Diaz*, 51 Cal. 4th 84, 244 P. 3d 501 (2011), which held that the Fourth Amendment permits a warrantless search of cell phone data incident to an arrest, so long as the cell phone was immediately associated with the arrestee's person.

The California Supreme Court denied Riley's petition for review, and we granted certiorari.

B

In the second case, a police officer performing routine surveillance observed respondent Brima Wurie make an apparent drug sale from a car. Officers subsequently arrested Wurie and took him to the police station. At the station, the officers seized two cell phones from Wurie's person. The one at issue here was a "flip phone," a kind of phone that is flipped open for use and that generally has a smaller range of features than a smart phone. Five to ten minutes after arriving at the station, the officers noticed that the phone was repeatedly receiving calls from a source identified as "my house" on the phone's external screen. A few minutes later, they opened the phone and saw a photograph of a woman and a baby set as the phone's wallpaper. They pressed one button on the phone to access its call log, then another button to determine the phone number associated with the "my house" label. They next used an online phone directory to trace that phone number to an apartment building.

When the officers went to the building, they saw Wurie's name on a mailbox and observed through a window a woman who resembled the woman in the photograph on Wurie's phone. They secured the apartment while obtaining a search warrant and, upon later executing the warrant, found and seized 215 grams of crack cocaine, marijuana, drug paraphernalia, a firearm and ammunition, and cash.

Wurie was charged with distributing crack cocaine, possessing crack cocaine with intent to distribute, and being a felon in possession of a firearm and ammunition. He moved to suppress the evidence obtained from the search of the apartment, arguing that it was the fruit of an unconstitutional search of his cell phone. The District Court denied the motion. Wurie was convicted on all three counts and sentenced to 262 months in prison.

A divided panel of the First Circuit reversed the denial of Wurie's motion to suppress and vacated Wurie's convictions for possession with intent to distribute and possession of a firearm as a felon. The court held that cell phones are distinct from other physical possessions that may be searched incident to arrest without a warrant, because of the amount of personal data cell phones contain and the negligible threat they pose to law enforcement interests.

We granted certiorari.

II

"[T]he ultimate touchstone of the Fourth Amendment is 'reasonableness.' " *Brigham City, Utah v. Stuart* (2006). Our cases have determined that "[w]here a search is undertaken by law enforcement officials to discover evidence of criminal wrongdoing, . . . reasonableness generally requires the obtaining of a judicial warrant." *Vernonia School Dist, 47J v. Acton* (1995). Such a warrant ensures that the inferences to support a search are "drawn by a neutral and detached magistrate instead of being judged by the officer engaged in the often competitive enterprise of ferreting out crime." *Johnson v. United States* (1948). In the absence of a warrant, a search is reasonable only if it falls within a specific exception to the warrant requirement.

The two cases before us concern the reasonableness of a warrantless search incident to a lawful arrest.

Although the existence of the exception for such searches has been recognized for a century, its scope has been debated for nearly as long. That debate has focused on the extent to which officers may search property found on or near the arrestee. Three related precedents set forth the rules governing such searches:

The first, *Chimel v. California* (1969), laid the groundwork for most of the existing search incident to arrest doctrine. Police officers in that case arrested Chimel inside his home and proceeded to search his entire three-bedroom house, including the attic and garage. In particular rooms, they also looked through the contents of drawers.

The Court crafted the following rule for assessing the reasonableness of a search incident to arrest:

> "When an arrest is made, it is reasonable for the arresting officer to search the person arrested in order to remove any weapons that the latter might seek to use in order to resist arrest or effect his escape. Otherwise, the officer's safety might well be endangered, and the arrest itself frustrated. In addition, it is entirely reasonable for the arresting officer to search for and seize any evidence on the

arrestee's person in order to prevent its concealment or destruction. . . . There is ample justification, therefore, for a search of the arrestee's person and the area 'within his immediate control' — construing that phrase to mean the area from within which he might gain possession of a weapon or destructible evidence."

The extensive warrantless search of Chimel's home did not fit within this exception, because it was not needed to protect officer safety or to preserve evidence.

Four years later, in *United States v. Robinson* (1973), the Court applied the *Chimel* analysis in the context of a search of the arrestee's person. A police officer had arrested Robinson for driving with a revoked license. The officer conducted a patdown search and felt an object that he could not identify in Robinson's coat pocket. He removed the object, which turned out to be a crumpled cigarette package, and opened it. Inside were 14 capsules of heroin.

The Court of Appeals concluded that the search was unreasonable because Robinson was unlikely to have evidence of the crime of arrest on his person, and because it believed that extracting the cigarette package and opening it could not be justified as part of a protective search for weapons. This Court reversed. . . . [T]he Court explained, "[t]he authority to search the person incident to a lawful custodial arrest, while based upon the need to disarm and to discover evidence, does not depend on what a court may later decide was the probability in a particular arrest situation that weapons or evidence would in fact be found upon the person of the suspect." Instead, a "custodial arrest of a suspect based on probable cause is a reasonable intrusion under the Fourth Amendment; that intrusion being lawful, a search incident to the arrest requires no additional justification."

The Court thus concluded that the search of Robinson was reasonable even though there was no concern about the loss of evidence, and the arresting officer had no specific concern that Robinson might be armed. In doing so, the Court did not draw a line between a search of Robinson's person and a further examination of the cigarette pack found during that search. It merely noted that, "[h]aving in the course of a lawful search come upon the crumpled package of cigarettes, [the officer] was entitled to inspect it." A few years later, the Court clarified that this exception was limited to "personal property . . . immediately associated with the person of the arrestee."

The search incident to arrest trilogy concludes with *Gant*, which analyzed searches of an arrestee's vehicle. *Gant*, like *Robinson*, recognized that the *Chimel* concerns for officer safety and evidence preservation underlie the search incident to arrest exception. As a result, the Court concluded that *Chimel* could authorize police to search a vehicle "only when the arrestee is unsecured and within reaching distance of the passenger compartment at the time of the search." *Gant* added, however, an independent exception for a warrantless search of a vehicle's passenger compartment "when it is 'reasonable to believe evidence relevant to the crime of arrest might be found in the vehicle.'" That exception stems not from *Chimel*, the Court explained, but from "circumstances unique to the vehicle context."

III

These cases require us to decide how the search incident to arrest doctrine applies to modern cell phones, which are now such a pervasive and insistent part of daily life that the proverbial visitor from Mars might conclude they were an important feature of human anatomy. A smart phone of the sort taken from Riley was unheard of ten years ago; a significant majority of American adults now own such phones. Even less sophisticated phones like Wurie's, which have already faded in popularity since Wurie was arrested in 2007, have been around for less than 15 years. Both phones are based on technology nearly inconceivable just a few decades ago, when *Chimel* and *Robinson* were decided.

Absent more precise guidance from the founding era, we generally determine whether to exempt a given type of search from the warrant requirement "by assessing, on the one hand, the degree to which it intrudes upon an individual's privacy and, on the other, the degree to which it is needed for the promotion of legitimate governmental interests." Such a balancing of interests supported the search incident to arrest exception in *Robinson*, and a mechanical application of *Robinson* might well support the warrantless searches at issue here.

But while *Robinson's* categorical rule strikes the appropriate balance in the context of physical objects, neither of its rationales has much force with respect to digital content on cell phones. On the government interest side, Robinson concluded that the two risks identified in *Chimel* — harm to officers and destruction of evidence — are present in all custodial arrests. There are no comparable risks when the search is of digital data. In addition, *Robinson* regarded any privacy interests retained by an individual after arrest as significantly diminished by the fact of the arrest itself. Cell phones, however, place vast quantities of personal information literally in the hands of individuals. A search of the information on a cell phone bears little resemblance to the type of brief physical search considered in *Robinson*.

We therefore decline to extend *Robinson* to searches of data on cell phones, and hold instead that officers must generally secure a warrant before conducting such a search.

A

[W]e ask . . . whether application of the search incident to arrest doctrine to this particular category of effects would "untether the rule from the justifications underlying the *Chimel* exception" . . . .

1

Digital data stored on a cell phone cannot itself be used as a weapon to harm an arresting officer or to effectuate the arrestee's escape. Law enforcement officers remain free to examine the physical aspects of a phone to ensure that it will not be used as a weapon — say, to determine whether there is a razor blade hidden between the phone and its case. Once an officer has secured a phone and eliminated any potential physical threats, however, data on the phone can endanger no one.

...

The United States and California both suggest that a search of cell phone data might help ensure officer safety in more indirect ways, for example by alerting officers that confederates of the arrestee are headed to the scene. ...To the extent dangers to arresting officers may be implicated in a particular way in a particular case, they are better addressed through consideration of case-specific exceptions to the warrant requirement, such as the one for exigent circumstances. . . .

2

The United States and California focus primarily on the second *Chimel* rationale: preventing the destruction of evidence.

Both Riley and Wurie concede that officers could have seized and secured their cell phones to prevent destruction of evidence while seeking a warrant. That is a sensible concession. And once law enforcement officers have secured a cell phone, there is no longer any risk that the arrestee himself will be able to delete incriminating data from the phone.

The United States and California argue that information on a cell phone may nevertheless be vulnerable to two types of evidence destruction unique to digital data — remote wiping and data encryption. Remote wiping occurs when a phone, connected to a wireless network, receives a signal that erases stored data. This can happen when a third party sends a remote signal or when a phone is preprogrammed to delete data upon entering or leaving certain geographic areas (so-called "geofencing"). Encryption is a security feature that some modern cell phones use in addition to password protection. When such

phones lock, data becomes protected by sophisticated encryption that renders a phone all but "unbreakable" unless police know the password.

. . . .

[The Court dismissed the State's arguments about the destruction of evidence through remote-wiping and data encryption]

. . . .

To the extent that law enforcement still has specific concerns about the potential loss of evidence in a particular case, there remain more targeted ways to address those concerns. If "the police are truly confronted with a 'now or never' situation," — for example, circumstances suggesting that a defendant's phone will be the target of an imminent remote-wipe attempt — they may be able to rely on exigent circumstances to search the phone immediately. Or, if officers happen to seize a phone in an unlocked state, they may be able to disable a phone's automatic-lock feature in order to prevent the phone from locking and encrypting data. Such a preventive measure could be analyzed under the principles set forth in our decision in *McArthur* which approved officers' reasonable steps to secure a scene to preserve evidence while they awaited a warrant.

B

The search incident to arrest exception rests not only on the heightened government interests at stake in a volatile arrest situation, but also on an arrestee's reduced privacy interests upon being taken into police custody.

The fact that an arrestee has diminished privacy interests does not mean that the Fourth Amendment falls out of the picture entirely. Not every search "is acceptable solely because a person is in custody." To the contrary, when "privacy-related concerns are weighty enough" a "search may require a warrant, notwithstanding the diminished expectations of privacy of the arrestee." One such example, of course, is *Chimel. Chimel* refused to "characteriz[e] the invasion of privacy that results from a top-to-bottom search of a man's house as 'minor.' " Because a search of the arrestee's entire house was a substantial invasion beyond the arrest itself, the Court concluded that a warrant was required.

Robinson is the only decision from this Court applying *Chimel* to a search of the contents of an item found on an arrestee's person. . . . Lower courts applying *Robinson* and *Chimel*, however, have approved searches of a variety of personal items carried by an arrestee.

The United States asserts that a search of all data stored on a cell phone is "materially indistinguishable" from searches of these sorts of physical items. That is like saying a ride on horseback is materially indistinguishable from a flight to the moon. Both are ways of getting from point A to point B, but little else justifies lumping them together. Modern cell phones, as a category, implicate privacy concerns far beyond those implicated by the search of a cigarette pack, a wallet, or a purse. A conclusion that inspecting the contents of an arrestee's pockets works no substantial additional intrusion on privacy beyond the arrest itself may make sense as applied to physical items, but any extension of that reasoning to digital data has to rest on its own bottom.

1

Cell phones differ in both a quantitative and a qualitative sense from other objects that might be kept on an arrestee's person....

[The court opinion then discusses in several pages all the awesomeness of cell phones that they were "wowed" about in 2014 that we now take for granted in 2023 (and beyond). That awesomeness includes all the different functions a cell phone provides (camera, video player, library, diaries, photo albums, etc); the qualitative different than other things individuals carry on their persons; that almost everyone now has a cell phone; that people store things not only on their phones but also "in the cloud". The court noted the qualitative difference between cell phones as well as other items that could be on a person when

they are arrested, for example, their browsing history (showing their personal interests or concerns) and historic location information.]

...

...[I]t is "a totally different thing to search a man's pockets and use against him what they contain, from ransacking his house for everything which may incriminate him." If his pockets contain a cell phone, however, that is no longer true. Indeed, a cell phone search would typically expose to the government far more than the most exhaustive search of a house: A phone not only contains in digital form many sensitive records previously found in the home; it also contains a broad array of private information never found in a home in any form — unless the phone is.

The possibility that a search might extend well beyond papers and effects in the physical proximity of an arrestee is yet another reason that the privacy interests here dwarf those in *Robinson*.

C

[The Court goes through each of the government's proposed rules that would restrict the scope of the cell phone search but still allow it. The government suggested the Court follow the rationale in *Gant* and allow a search of the phone for evidence of the crime for which the suspect is being arrested. The Court declined. The "United States also proposes a rule that would restrict the scope of a cell phone search to those areas of the phone where an officer reasonably believes that information relevant to the crime, the arrestee's identity, or officer safety will be discovered." The Court declined. Finally, the government suggested that it should always be able to search a phone or the call log (relying on the case of *Smith v. Maryland*, which you read above). The Court declined this approach as well.

IV

We cannot deny that our decision today will have an impact on the ability of law enforcement to combat crime. Cell phones have become important tools in facilitating coordination and communication among members of criminal enterprises, and can provide valuable incriminating information about dangerous criminals. Privacy comes at a cost.

Our holding, of course, is not that the information on a cell phone is immune from search; it is instead that a warrant is generally required before such a search, even when a cell phone is seized incident to arrest. Our cases have historically recognized that the warrant requirement is "an important working part of our machinery of government," not merely "an inconvenience to be somehow 'weighed' against the claims of police efficiency. Recent technological advances similar to those discussed here have, in addition, made the process of obtaining a warrant itself more efficient.

Moreover, even though the search incident to arrest exception does not apply to cell phones, other case-specific exceptions may still justify a warrantless search of a particular phone. "One well-recognized exception applies when ' "the exigencies of the situation" make the needs of law enforcement so compelling that

[a] warrantless search is objectively reasonable under the Fourth Amendment.' " Such exigencies could include the need to prevent the imminent destruction of evidence in individual cases, to pursue a fleeing suspect, and to assist persons who are seriously injured or are threatened with imminent injury. . . .

The defendants here recognize. . . that such fact-specific threats may justify a warrantless search of cell phone data. The critical point is that, unlike the search incident to arrest exception, the exigent circumstances exception requires a court to examine whether an emergency justified a warrantless search in each particular case.

Modern cell phones are not just another technological convenience. With all they contain and all they may reveal, they hold for many Americans "the privacies of life," The fact that technology now allows an individual to carry such information in his hand does not make the information any less worthy of the protection for which the Founders fought. Our answer to the question of what police must do before searching a cell phone seized incident to an arrest is accordingly simple — get a warrant.

Other Cases: Searches Incident to Lawful Arrest

Birchfield v. North Dakota, 579 U.S. ___ (2016)

SUMMARY: This case involved three defendants who were arrested for driving while intoxicated and who either had their breath or blood searched incident to their arrest or were threatened with having their blood searched incident to their arrest. The majority opinion discusses the development of "implied consent laws" throughout the states and how some states have toughened their drunk driving laws by criminalizing the refusal to undergo testing. One defendant was arrested and then refused a blood test. He was then charged with a crime. One defendant was arrested and refused to take the breath test. He was charged with "test refusal in the first degree." The final defendant was arrested, taken to a hospital and warned that test

refusal was a crime in and of itself; he thereupon agreed to have his blood drawn.

The Court had to decide whether breath and blood tests were permissible searches incident to a lawful arrest under the Fourth Amendment.

The majority opinion written by Justice Alito engaged in a balancing between privacy interests of individuals subjected to breath and blood testing. It weighed those interests against the government's interest in preserving public highway safety and the compelling interest to deter drunken driving and prevent traffic fatalities and injuries. It drew the balance against the state with regard to blood testing but in favor of the state with regard to breath testing.

The Court held that the Fourth Amendment permits warrantless breath tests incident to arrests for drunk driving but not warrantless blood tests.

Justice Sotomayor wrote an opinion agreeing that blood testing is not constitutionally permissible under the Fourth Amendment under the search incident to the arrest exception to the warrant requirement.

> Because no governmental interest categorically makes it impractical for an officer to obtain a warrant before measuring a driver's alcohol level, the Fourth Amendment prohibits such searches without a warrant, unless exigent circumstances exist in a particular case.

Justice Thomas wrote an opinion arguing that both blood and breath testing should be permitted as exigent circumstance searches (citing an earlier decision where he had dissented that blood alcohol levels dissipating were emergency circumstances and thus there would be no need to analyze these searches under search incident to arrest exceptions.

> The compromise the Court reaches today is not a good one. By deciding that some (but not all) warrantless tests revealing the blood alcohol concentration (BAC) of an arrested driver are constitutional, the Court contorts the search-incident-to-arrest exception to the Fourth Amendment's warrant requirement. The far simpler answer to the question presented is the one rejected in *Missouri v. McNeely*. Here, the tests revealing the BAC of a driver suspected of driving drunk are constitutional under the exigent-circumstances exception to the warrant requirement.

"Incident To" A Lawful Arrest?

When is a search "incident to" an arrest? Generally, searches incident to arrest are done immediately prior to or after taking the defendant into custody, but the circumstances surrounding a particular arrest can justify substantial delay. To search incident to arrest, police must first have probable cause to make an arrest *before the search* is conducted. If the police only obtained probable cause for the arrest due to evidence they discovered during the search after the arrest, the search will not "fit" into this exception. See, *Smith v. Ohio*, 494 U.S. 541 (1990).

UNITED STATES v. EDWARDS
415 U.S. 800 (1974)

MR. JUSTICE WHITE delivered the opinion of the Court.

The question here is whether the Fourth Amendment should be extended to exclude from evidence certain clothing taken from respondent Edwards while he was in custody at the city jail approximately 10 hours after his arrest.

[Facts and Procedural History Summarized:

The police lawfully arrested defendant on the streets of Lebanon, Ohio and charged him with attempting to break in to the city post office. He was taken and lodged in the city jail, and about that time investigation revealed that pain/wood chips from the scene of the attempted entry were likely to be found on Edward's clothing. It wasn't until the next morning that jail staff could purchase and provide Edwards substitute clothing for those he wore when arrested. They took his clothes about ten hours after his arrest as evidence and ultimately sent them off to be processed. Edwards moved to suppress the evidence from his clothes as a violation of his Fourth Amendment rights as they were not seized and searched with a warrant. The trial court denied the motion, but the Circuit Court reversed. Its reversal was inconsistent with a position taken in other circuits. The Supreme Court granted certiorari to resolve the matter.

The Court, cited Abel v. United States (1960) in which it held that police's search of Abel's belongings that he took with him to the detention without a warrant was appropriate as incident to a lawful arrest. The Abel Court noted that a valid search of the property could have been made at the place of arrest and perceived little difference when the accused took the property with him.]

Opinion:

The courts of appeals have followed this same rule, holding that both the person and the property in his immediate possession may be searched at the station house after the arrest has occurred at another place and if evidence of crime is discovered, it may be seized and admitted in evidence. Nor is there any doubt that clothing or other belongings may be seized upon arrival of the accused at the place of detention and later subjected to laboratory analysis or that the test results are admissible at trial. ...

[The Court disagreed with the Court of Appeals that searches incident to a lawful arrest justification ceases as soon as the administrative process and mechanics of arrest have come to a halt.]

...This was no more than taking from respondent the effects in his immediate possession that constituted evidence of crime. This was and is a normal incident of a custodial arrest, and reasonable delay in effectuating it does not change the fact that Edwards was no more imposed upon than he could have been at the time and place of the arrest or immediately upon arrival at the place of detention. The police did no more on June 1 than they were entitled to do incident to the usual custodial arrest and incarceration.

Other closely related considerations sustain the examination of the clothing in this case. It must be remembered that on both May 31 and June 1 the police had lawful custody of Edwards and necessarily of the clothing he wore. When it became apparent that the articles of clothing were evidence of the crime for which Edwards was being held, the police were entitled to take, examine, and preserve them for use as evidence, just as they are normally permitted to seize evidence of crime when it is lawfully encountered. Surely, the clothes could have been brushed down and vacuumed while Edwards had them on in the cell, and it was similarly reasonable to take and examine them as the police did, particularly in view of the existence of probable cause linking the clothes to the crime. Indeed, it is difficult to perceive what is unreasonable about the police's examining and holding as evidence those personal effects of the accused that they already have in their lawful custody as the result of a lawful arrest.

. . . [In] ... United States v. Caruso, ... defendant's clothes were not taken until six hours after his arrival at a place of detention. The Court of Appeals properly held that no warrant was required:

"He and his clothes were constantly in custody from the moment of his arrest, and the inspection of his clothes and the holding of them for use in evidence were, under the circumstances, reasonable and proper."

...

In upholding this search and seizure, we do not conclude that the Warrant Clause of the Fourth Amendment is never applicable to postarrest seizures of the effects of an arrestee. But we do think that the Court of Appeals for the First Circuit captured the essence of situations like this when it said in United States v. DeLeo:

"While the legal arrest of a person should not destroy the privacy of his premises, it does - for at least a reasonable time and to a reasonable extent - take his own privacy out of the realm of protection from police interest in weapons, means of escape, and evidence."

JUSTICE STEWART dissenting. Omitted.

Searching Incident To Issuance Of A Citation

It is a fairly common practice for police to issue the suspect a citation to appear in court rather than taking the time to make an arrest—particularly if the jail is at capacity This raises the question, then, of whether police may search a person when they issue a citation rather than do a full custodial arrest. *Knowles v. Iowa* answers that question

---

KNOWLES v. IOWA
525 U.S. 113 (1998)

CHIEF JUSTICE REHNQUIST delivered the opinion of the Court.

An Iowa police officer stopped petitioner Knowles for speeding, but issued him a citation rather than arresting him. The question presented is whether such a procedure authorizes the officer, consistently with the Fourth Amendment, to conduct a full search of the car. We answer this question "no."

...

In *Robinson* we noted the two historical rationales for the "search incident to arrest" exception: (1) the need to disarm the suspect in order to take him into custody, and (2) the need to preserve evidence for later use at trial. . . . But neither of these underlying rationales for the search incident to arrest exception is sufficient to justify the search in the present case.

We have recognized that the first rationale — officer safety — is "'both legitimate and weighty.'" . . . The threat to officer safety from issuing a traffic citation, however, is a good deal less than in the case of a custodial arrest. In *Robinson*, we stated that a custodial arrest involves "danger to an officer" because of "the extended exposure which follows the taking of a suspect into custody and transporting him to the police station." . . . We recognized that "[t]he danger to the police officer flows from the fact of the arrest, and its attendant proximity, stress, and uncertainty, and not from the grounds for arrest." . . . A routine traffic stop, on the other hand, is a relatively brief encounter and "is more analogous to a so-called '*Terry* stop' . . .than to a formal arrest." . . .

This is not to say that the concern for officer safety is absent in the case of a routine traffic stop. It plainly is not. . . . But while the concern for officer safety in this context may justify the "minimal" additional intrusion of ordering a driver and passengers out of the car, it does not by itself justify the often considerably greater intrusion attending a full field-type search. . . .

Nor has Iowa shown the second justification for the authority to search incident to arrest — the need to discover and preserve evidence. Once Knowles was stopped for speeding and issued a citation, all the evidence necessary to prosecute that offense had been obtained. No further evidence of excessive speed was going to be found either on the person of the offender or in the passenger compartment of the car.

Iowa nevertheless argues that a "search incident to citation" is justified because a suspect who is subject to a routine traffic stop may attempt to hide or destroy evidence related to his identity (e. g., a driver's license or vehicle registration), or destroy evidence of another, as yet undetected crime. As for the destruction of evidence relating to identity, if a police officer is not satisfied with the identification furnished by the driver, this may be a basis for arresting him rather than merely issuing a citation. As for destroying evidence of other crimes, the possibility that an officer would stumble onto evidence wholly unrelated to the speeding offense seems remote.

In *Robinson*, we held that the authority to conduct a full field search as incident to an arrest was a "bright-line rule," which was based on the concern for officer safety and destruction or loss of evidence, but which did not depend in every case upon the existence of either concern. Here we are asked to extend that "bright-line rule" to a situation where the concern for officer safety is not present to the same extent and the concern for destruction or loss of evidence is not present at all. We decline to do so.

Lawfulness Of Arrest

In *Virginia v. Moore 552 U.S. 164 (2008)*, the Court examined whether an arrest which violated state law nevertheless justified a Fourth Amendment warrantless search. Moore was stopped for the misdemeanor charge of driving with a suspended license. Police had probable cause to believe that Moore had committed a crime, and arrested him rather than citing him. Virginia state law required he be cited and not arrested. In the subsequent search, police found 16 grams of crack cocaine and $516 in cash in his pants pocket. Moore moved to suppress the drug evidence, arguing that the search violated his Fourth Amendment rights. At the U.S. Supreme Court, the state argued that Moore's arrest and subsequent search did not violate the Fourth Amendment, even though it admittedly violated Virginia state law. Other states filed amicus curiae (friend of the court) briefs arguing that it is a state's responsibility to regulate how arrests are made and, if there is a violation of the state regulation (as opposed to a Fourth Amendment violation), the state should be able to define its own remedies.

The Court agreed.

"In *Cooper v. California,* we . . . concluded that whether state law authorized the search was irrelevant. States, we said, remained free "to impose higher standards on searches and seizures than required by the Federal Constitution," but regardless of state rules, police could search a lawfully seized vehicle as a matter of federal constitutional law.

In *California v. Greenwood*, we held that search of an individual's garbage forbidden by California's Constitution was not forbidden by the Fourth Amendment. "[W]hether or not a search is reasonable within the meaning of the Fourth Amendment," we said, has never "depend[ed]" on the law of the particular State in which the search occurs." While "[i]ndividual States may surely construe their own constitutions as imposing more stringent constraints on police conduct than does the Federal Constitution," state law did not alter the content of the Fourth Amendment. . . .

[O]fficers may perform searches incident to constitutionally permissible arrests in order to ensure their safety and safeguard evidence. . . .We have described this rule as covering any "lawful arrest," with constitutional law as the reference point. That is to say, we have equated a lawful arrest with an arrest based on probable cause: "A custodial arrest of a suspect based on probable cause is a reasonable intrusion under the Fourth Amendment; *that intrusion being lawful,* a search incident to the arrest requires no additional justification." But it is not surprising that States have used "lawful" as shorthand for compliance with state law, while our constitutional decision in *Robinson* used "lawful" as shorthand for compliance with constitutional constraints.

The interests justifying search are present whenever an officer makes an arrest. A search enables officers to safeguard evidence, and, most critically, to ensure their safety during "the extended exposure which follows the taking of a suspect into custody and transporting him to the police station." *Robinson.* Officers issuing citations do not face the same danger, and we therefore held in *Knowles v. Iowa,* 525 U. S. 113 (1998), that they do not have the same authority to search."

Exigent Circumstance Searches

Emergency situations (known as exigent circumstances) have compelled the courts to relax the warrant requirement.

"The exigent circumstances exception is a general catchall category that encompasses a number of diverse situations. What they have in common is some kind of emergency that makes obtaining a search warrant impractical, useless, dangerous, or unnecessary. Among these situations are the danger of physical harm to the officer or destruction of evidence, searches in hot pursuit, danger to a third person, and driving while intoxicated." [64]

The Court has repeatedly held that the Fourth Amendment permits a warrantless entry and search if exigent circumstances justify the intrusion. "Exigent circumstances exist when there is probable cause for a search or seizure and either the evidence sought is in imminent danger of destruction, the safety of law enforcement officers or the general public is threatened, the police are in hot pursuit of a suspect, or a suspect is likely to flee before the pursuing officer can obtain a warrant." *Thirty Fifth Annual Review of Criminal Procedure*, 35 Geo. L.J. Ann. Rev. Crim. Proc. 94 (2006). In addition to showing exigent circumstances and probable cause, the government must also demonstrate that the search was conducted in a reasonable manner. The government may need to prove that a warrant, even a telephonic warrant, was unavailable or impractical.

Under certain circumstances police may be able to secure ("seize") a home (and not enter it) while they await a warrant. Under the Fourth Amendment, securing a dwelling on the basis of probable cause, to prevent the destruction or removal of evidence while a search warrant is being sought is not itself an unreasonable seizure of either the dwelling or its contents. *Segura v. United States*, 468 U.S. 796 (1984). In *Illinois v. McArthur*, 531 U.S. 326 (2001) the Court found that a two-hour seizure of the defendant's home while police obtained a warrant did not violate the Fourth Amendment because the police reasonably feared that the defendant would destroy evidence if allowed to enter the home unaccompanied by an officer.

Exigent Circumstances -- Automobile Searches

Police may search an automobile without a warrant under a variety of exceptions to the warrant requirement. In addition to searching a car after getting consent, or searching it as incident to arrest under the parameters established in *Gant*, police may search a car without getting a warrant when emergency circumstances justify it (probable cause to believe the car contains evidence of a crime, and the car is mobile).

In *Carroll v. United States*, 267 U.S. 132 (1925) the Supreme Court created the "automobile exception" when it upheld a warrantless search of a motor vehicle that police believed was carrying contraband. The Court justified the search without a warrant based on exigency presented by a mobile car. "If a car is readily mobile and probable cause exists to believe it contains contraband, the Fourth Amendment * * * permits police to search the vehicle without more." *Maryland v. Dyson*, 527 U.S. 465 (1999). So, as with other exigent circumstance exceptions, police must show probable cause that a crime has been committed and evidence of the crime will be found in the car plus exigency.

---

[64] Del Carmen, R., Criminal Procedure: Law and Practice, Thomson Wadsworth, 7th ed. 2007, p. 248.

COLLINS v. VIRGINIA
584 U.S. 1 (2018)

JUSTICE SOTOMAYOR delivered the opinion of the Court.

This case presents the question whether the automobile exception to the Fourth Amendment permits a police officer, uninvited and without a warrant, to enter the curtilage of a home in order to search a vehicle parked therein. It does not.

I

[Facts and Procedural History Summarized:

Two Virginia law enforcement officers on two separate occasions saw someone on an orange and black motorcycle speeding. Both times, the cycle and driver were able to elude their attempts to stop him. They learned that the cycle was likely stole by, and in the possession of, Ryan Collins. Investigation (including reviewing his facebook posts) revealed that the cycle was at the top of a driveway of a home where Collin's girlfriend lived and he frequently stayed. Officer Rhodes went to the address, parked on the street, saw a motorcycle covered with tarp parked at an angle and in the same location as on the facebook post. Without a warrant Rhodes went toward the house, took a picture of the covered cycle from the sidewalk, then walked onto the property where the cycle was parked. To investigate further, he pulled the tarp off, saw a motorcycle like the speeding one, ran a search of the license plate and vin number. Rhodes confirmed that the motorcycle was stole. He took pictures of the untarped cycle, then put the tarp back on and waited in his car for Collins to return home. When he did so, Rhodes went to the door and spoke with Collins who said he bought the care without title. Collins ws charged and filed a motion to suppress. It was denied, and Collins appealed. The case made its way to the U.S. Supreme Court].

We granted certiorari, 582 U. S. ___ (2017), and now reverse.

II

The Fourth Amendment provides in relevant part that the "right of the people to be secure in their persons, houses, papers, and effects, against unreasonable searches and seizures, shall not be violated." This case arises at the intersection of two components of the Court's Fourth Amendment jurisprudence: the automobile exception to the warrant requirement and the protection extended to the curtilage of a home.

A

1

The Court has held that the search of an automobile can be reasonable without a warrant. The Court first articulated the so-called automobile exception in *Carroll* v. *United States* (1925). In that case, law enforcement officers had probable cause to believe that a car they observed traveling on the road contained illegal liquor. They stopped and searched the car, discovered and seized the illegal liquor, and arrested the occupants. The Court upheld the warrantless search and seizure, explaining that a "necessary difference" exists between searching "a store, dwelling house or other structure" and searching "a ship, motor boat, wagon or automobile" because a "vehicle can be quickly moved out of the locality or jurisdiction in which the warrant must be sought."

The "ready mobility" of vehicles served as the core justification for the automobile exception for many years. Later cases then introduced an additional rationale based on "the pervasive regulation of vehicles capable of traveling on the public highways." As the Court explained in *South Dakota* v. *Opperman*, (1976):

> "Automobiles, unlike homes, are subjected to pervasive and continuing governmental regulation and controls, including periodic inspection and

licensing requirements. As an everyday occurrence, police stop and examine vehicles when license plates or inspection stickers have expired, or if other violations, such as exhaust fumes or excessive noise, are noted, or if headlights or other safety equipment are not in proper working order."

In announcing each of these two justifications, the Court took care to emphasize that the rationales applied only to automobiles and not to houses, and therefore supported "treating automobiles differently from houses" as a constitutional matter. *Cady* v. *Dombrowski* (1973).

When these justifications for the automobile exception "come into play," officers may search an automobile without having obtained a warrant so long as they have probable cause to do so.

2

Like the automobile exception, the Fourth Amendment's protection of curtilage has long been black letter law. "[W]hen it comes to the Fourth Amendment, the home is first among equals." *Florida* v. *Jardines*, (2013). "At the Amendment's 'very core' stands 'the right of a man to retreat into his own home and there be free from unreasonable governmental intrusion.' " To give full practical effect to that right, the Court considers curtilage . . . to be " 'part of the home itself. . . . "The protection afforded the curtilage is essentially a protection of families and personal privacy in an area intimately linked to the home, both physically and psychologically, where privacy expectations are most heightened." *California* v. *Ciraolo* (1986).

When a law enforcement officer physically intrudes on the curtilage to gather evidence, a search within the meaning of Fourth Amendment has occurred. *Jardines*. Such conduct thus is presumptively unreasonable absent a warrant.

B

1

With this background in mind, we turn to the application of these doctrines in the instant case. As an initial matter, we decide whether the part of the driveway where Collins' motorcycle was parked and subsequently searched is curtilage. [The Court concluded that it was.]

. . . .

2

In physically intruding on the curtilage of Collins' home to search the motorcycle, Officer Rhodes not only invaded Collins' Fourth Amendment interest in the item searched, *i.e.,* the motorcycle, but also invaded Collins' Fourth Amendment interest in the curtilage of his home. The question before the Court is whether the automobile exception justifies the invasion of the curtilage. The answer is no.

Applying the relevant legal principles to a slightly different factual scenario confirms that this is an easy case. Imagine a motorcycle parked inside the living room of a house, visible through a window to a passerby on the street. Imagine further that an officer has probable cause to believe that the motorcycle was involved in a traffic infraction. Can the officer, acting without a warrant, enter the house to search the motorcycle and confirm whether it is the right one? Surely not.

The reason is that the scope of the automobile exception extends no further than the automobile itself. Virginia asks the Court to expand the scope of the automobile exception to permit police to invade any space outside an automobile even if the Fourth Amendment protects that space. Nothing in our case law, however, suggests that the automobile exception gives an officer the right to enter a home or its curtilage to access a vehicle without a warrant. Expanding the scope of the automobile exception in this way would both undervalue the core Fourth Amendment protection afforded to the home and its curtilage and " 'untether' " the automobile exception " 'from the justifications underlying' " it.

The Court already has declined to expand the scope of other exceptions to the warrant requirement to permit warrantless entry into the home. The reasoning behind those decisions applies equally well in this context. For instance, under the plain-view doctrine, "any valid warrantless seizure of incriminating evidence" requires that the officer "have a lawful right of access to the object itself." A plain-view seizure thus cannot be justified if it is effectuated "by unlawful trespass." *Soldal* v. *Cook County* (1992). Had Officer Rhodes seen illegal drugs through the window of Collins' house, for example, assuming no other warrant exception applied, he could not have entered the house to seize them without first obtaining a warrant.

Similarly, it is a "settled rule that warrantless arrests in public places are valid," but, absent another exception such as exigent circumstances, officers may not enter a home to make an arrest without a warrant, even when they have probable cause. *Payton* v. *New York* (1980). That is because being " 'arrested in the home involves not only the invasion attendant to all arrests but also an invasion of the sanctity of the home.' " Likewise, searching a vehicle parked in the curtilage involves not only the invasion of Fourth Amendment interest in the vehicle but also an invasion of the sanctity of the curtilage.

Just as an officer must have a lawful right of access to any contraband he discovers in plain view in order to seize it without a warrant, and just as an officer must have a lawful right of access in order to arrest a person in his home, so, too, an officer must have a lawful right of access to a vehicle in order to search it pursuant to the automobile exception. The automobile exception does not afford the necessary lawful right of access to search a vehicle parked within a home or its curtilage because it does not justify an intrusion on a person's separate and substantial Fourth Amendment interest in his home and curtilage.

. . . To allow an officer to rely on the automobile exception to gain entry into a house or its curtilage for the purpose of conducting a vehicle search would unmoor the exception from its justifications, render hollow the Fourth Amendment protection the Constitution extends to the house and its curtilage, and transform what was meant to be an exception into a tool with far broader application. Indeed, its name alone should make all this clear enough: It is, after all, an exception for automobiles.[3]

Given the centrality of the Fourth Amendment interest in the home and its curtilage and the disconnect between that interest and the justifications behind the automobile exception, we decline Virginia's invitation to extend the automobile exception to permit a warrantless intrusion on a home or its curtilage.

CALIFORNIA v. CARNEY
471 U.S. 386 (1985)

CHIEF JUSTICE BURGER delivered the opinion of the Court.

[Facts Summarized:

Defendant was using a dodge mini motor home as a place to exchange marijuana for sex. Police heard about it, did surveillance, and got information from a youth they saw leaving the motorhome. Youth stated he had

received drugs for sex. Youth returned to the motorhome with the agents and knocked on the door; he got Carney to come outside. Agents without a warrant or consent entered the motorhome and searched. The Court had to decide whether the search, which was based on probable cause, was reasonable without a warrant—and as a part of that inquiry they needed to evaluate whether the motorhome ws more like a home or more like a car subject to the automobile exception.].

. . .

. . . [I]n *Carroll v. United States*, (1925) . . . the Court recognized that the privacy interests in an automobile are constitutionally protected; however, it held that the ready mobility of the automobile justifies a lesser degree of protection of those interests. The Court rested this exception on a long-recognized distinction between stationary structures and vehicles.

The capacity to be "quickly moved" was clearly the basis of the holding in *Carroll*, and our cases have consistently recognized ready mobility as one of the principal bases of the automobile exception. . . . In *Chambers*, for example, commenting on the rationale for the vehicle exception, we noted that "the opportunity to search is fleeting since a car is readily movable. More recently, in *United States v. Ross* (1982), we once again emphasized that "an immediate intrusion is necessary" because of "the nature of an automobile in transit. . . ." The mobility of automobiles, we have observed, "creates circumstances of such exigency that, as a practical necessity, rigorous enforcement of the warrant requirement is impossible."

. . . [O]ur later cases have made clear that ready mobility is not the only basis for the exception. The reasons for the vehicle exception, we have said, are twofold. "Besides the element of mobility, less rigorous warrant requirements govern because the expectation of privacy with respect to one's automobile is significantly less than that relating to one's home or office."

[R]educed expectations of privacy derive not from the fact that the area to be searched is in plain view, but from the pervasive regulation of vehicles capable of traveling on the public highways. As we explained in *South Dakota v. Opperman*, an inventory search case:

"Automobiles, unlike homes, are subjected to pervasive and continuing governmental regulation and controls, including periodic inspection and licensing requirements. As an everyday occurrence, police stop and examine vehicles when license plates or inspection stickers have expired, or if other violations, such as exhaust fumes or excessive noise, are noted, or if headlights or other safety equipment are not in proper working order."

When a vehicle is being used on the highways, or if it is readily capable of such use and is found stationary in a place not regularly used for residential purposes - temporary or otherwise - the two justifications for the vehicle exception come into play. First, the vehicle is obviously readily mobile by the turn of an ignition key, if not actually moving. Second, there is a reduced expectation of privacy stemming from its use as a licensed motor vehicle subject to a range of police regulation inapplicable to a fixed dwelling. At least in these circumstances, the overriding societal interests in effective law enforcement justify an immediate search before the vehicle and its occupants become unavailable.

While it is true that respondent's vehicle possessed some, if not many of the attributes of a home, it is equally clear that the vehicle falls clearly within the scope of the automobile exception Like the automobile in Carroll, respondent's motor home was readily mobile. Absent the prompt search and seizure, it could readily have been moved beyond the reach of the police. Furthermore, the vehicle was licensed to "operate on public streets; [was] serviced in public places; . . . and [was] subject to extensive regulation and inspection." And the vehicle was so situated that an objective observer would conclude that it was being used not as a residence, but as a vehicle.

Respondent urges us to distinguish his vehicle from other vehicles within the exception because it was capable of functioning as a home. In our increasingly mobile society, many vehicles used for transportation can be and are being used not only for transportation but for shelter, i. e., as a "home" or "residence." To distinguish between respondent's motor home and an ordinary sedan for purposes of the vehicle exception would require that we apply the exception depending upon the size of the vehicle and the quality of its appointments. Moreover, to fail to apply the exception to vehicles such as a motor home ignores the fact that a motor home lends itself easily to use as an instrument of illicit drug traffic and other illegal activity. . . . We decline today to distinguish between "worthy" and "unworthy" vehicles which are either on the public roads and highways, or situated such that it is reasonable to conclude that the vehicle is not being used as a residence.

Our application of the vehicle exception has never turned on the other uses to which a vehicle might be put. The exception has historically turned on the ready mobility of the vehicle, and on the presence of the vehicle in a setting that objectively indicates that the vehicle is being used for transportation. These two requirements for application of the exception ensure that law enforcement officials are not unnecessarily hamstrung in their efforts to detect and prosecute criminal activity, and that the legitimate privacy interests of the public are protected.

Other Cases: Automobile Exception

Chambers v. Maroney, 399 U.S. 42 (1970)

SUMMARY: Police stopped a car at night because it, and its occupants, fit the description of a car recently involved in a gas station robbery. The passengers were arrested, and the car was transported to the police station where the police searched it (without a warrant) and found incriminating evidence.

HOLDING AND OPINION: The Court upheld the search under the automobile exception.

. . .[T]he search that produced the incriminating evidence was made at the police station some time after the arrest and cannot be justified as a search incident to an arrest: "Once an accused is under arrest and in custody, then a search made at another place, without a warrant, is simply not incident to the arrest." . . .

There are, however, alternative grounds arguably justifying the search of the car in this case. Here . . . the police had probable cause to believe that the robbers, carrying guns and the fruits of the crime, had fled the scene in a light blue compact station wagon which would be carrying four men, one wearing a green sweater and another wearing a trench coat. . . . [T]here was probable cause to arrest the occupants of the station wagon that the officers stopped; just as obviously was there probable cause to search the car for guns and stolen money.

In terms of the circumstances justifying a warrantless search, the Court has long distinguished between an automobile and a home or office. [In Carroll]. . . the Court held that automobiles and other conveyances may be searched without a warrant in circumstances that would not justify the search without a warrant of a house or an office, provided that there is probable cause to believe that the car contains articles that the officers are entitled to seize.

The Court also noted that the search of an auto on probable cause proceeds on a theory wholly different from that justifying the search incident to an arrest:

"The right to search and the validity of the seizure are not dependent on the right to arrest. They are dependent on the reasonable cause the seizing officer has for belief that the contents of the automobile offend against the law."

. . .

[The Court analyzed the automobile exception and said that it applied under these facts (there was probable cause and the car had been mobile]

. . .

For constitutional purposes, we see no difference between on the one hand seizing and holding a car before presenting the probable cause issue to a magistrate and on the other hand carrying out an immediate search without a warrant. Given probable cause to search, either course is reasonable under the Fourth Amendment.

On the facts before us, the blue station wagon could have been searched on the spot when it was stopped since there was probable cause to search and it was a fleeting target for a search. The probable-cause factor still obtained at the station house and so did the mobility of the car unless the Fourth Amendment permits a warrantless seizure of the car and the denial of its use to anyone until a warrant is secured. In that event there is little to choose in terms of practical consequences between an immediate search without a warrant and the car's immobilization until a warrant is obtained." JUSTICE HARLAN, concurring in part and dissenting in part.

…

…Because the officers might be deprived of valuable evidence if required to obtain a warrant before effecting any search or seizure, I agree with the Court that they should be permitted to take the steps necessary to preserve evidence and to make a search possible. The Court holds that those steps include making a warrantless search

of the entire vehicle on the highway - a conclusion reached by the Court in *Carroll* without discussion - and indeed appears to go further and to condone the removal of the car to the police station for a warrantless search there at the convenience of the police. I cannot agree that this result is consistent with our insistence in other areas that departures from the warrant requirement strictly conform to the exigency presented.

Coolidge v. New Hampshire,

HOLDING: The Court ruled that the search of the automobile conducted two-and-a-half weeks after it was impounded was found to be unconstitutional because it was done without a warrant when the car was clearly not mobile.

Searching Containers In Cars Under The Automobile Exception

United States v. Ross, 456 U.S. 798 (1982), is the seminal case on searching containers in cars under the automobile exception.

UNITED STATES v. ROSS
456 U.S. 798 (1982)

JUSTICE STEVENS delivered the opinion of the Court.

SUMMARY: An informant told D.C. Police Department detectives that Ross was selling drugs which he kept in the trunk of a car. Detectives went to the address where the informant said he had just seen a drug transaction. They observed the driver and a car matching the informant's description. They stopped the car, got Ross out of the car, found a bullet on the seat of the car and pistol in the glove compartment. They arrested Ross and then took his keys and opened the trunk. In the trunk detective Cassidy found a closed brown paper bag which he opened. In the bag he discovered a number of glassine bags containing white powder. He replaced the bag, close the trunk and drove the car to headquarters. At the station, a thorough search was done and a red leather pouch was found. Cassidy unzipped the pouch and discovered $3200. Further testing of the white

powder determined it was heroin. Ross was charged, filed a motion to suppress the drugs and money. Motion was denied; Ross was convicted at trial, and on appeal, Ross' conviction was reversed on the grounds that the warrantless search of the containers in the trunk was unreasonable. Case made its way to the U.S. Supreme Court

OPINION: In this case, we consider the extent to which police officers — who have legitimately stopped an automobile and who have probable cause to believe that contraband is concealed somewhere within it — may conduct a probing search of compartments and containers within the vehicle whose contents are not in plain view. We hold that they may conduct a search of the vehicle that is as thorough as a magistrate could authorize in a warrant "particularly describing the place to be searched."

…

The rationale justifying a warrantless search of an automobile that is believed to be transporting contraband arguably applies with equal force to any movable container that is believed to be carrying an illicit substance. . . .

[T]he practical consequences of the *Carroll* decision would be largely nullified if the permissible scope of a warrantless search of an automobile did not include containers and packages found inside the vehicle. Contraband goods are rarely strewn across the trunk or floor of a car; since by their very nature such goods must be withheld from public view, they rarely can be placed in an automobile unless they are enclosed within some form of container. . . .

A lawful search of fixed premises generally extends to the entire area in which the object of the search may be found and is not limited by the possibility that separate acts of entry or opening may be required to complete the search. . . . A warrant to open a footlocker to search for marihuana would also authorize the opening of packages found inside. A warrant to search a vehicle would support a search of every part of the vehicle that might contain the object of the search. When a legitimate search is under way, and when its purpose and its limits have been precisely defined, nice distinctions between closets, drawers and containers, in the case of a home, or between glove compartments, upholstered seats, trunks and wrapped packages, in the case of a

vehicle, must give way to the interest in the prompt and efficient completion of the task at hand.

This rule applies equally to all containers, as indeed we believe it must. . . .

The scope of a warrantless search of an automobile thus is not defined by the nature of the container in which the contraband is secreted. … Rather, it is defined by the object of the search and the places where there is probable cause to believe it may be found. . . . Probable cause to believe that a container placed in the trunk of a taxi contains contraband or evidence does not justify search of the entire cab. . . .

The [automobile] exception recognized in *Carroll* is unquestionably one that is "specifically established and well delineated." …We hold that the scope of a warrantless search authorized by that exception is no broader and no narrower than a magistrate could legitimately authorize by warrant. If probable cause justifies the search of a lawfully stopped vehicle, it justifies the search of every part of the vehicle that may contain the object of the search. …

JUSTICE MARSHALL, with whom JUSTICE BRENNAN joins, dissenting, omitted.

Other Cases: Closed Containers, Automobile Exception

Wyoming v. Houghton, 526 U.S. 295 (1999)

This case presents the question whether police officers violate the Fourth Amendment when they search a passenger's personal belongings inside an automobile that they have probable cause to believe contains contraband.

In the early morning hours of July 23, 1995, a Wyoming Highway Patrol officer stopped an automobile for speeding and driving with a faulty brake light. There were three passengers in the front seat of the car: David Young (the driver), his girlfriend, and respondent. While questioning Young, the officer noticed a

hypodermic syringe in Young's shirt pocket. He left the occupants under the supervision of two backup officers as he went to get gloves from his patrol car. Upon his return, he instructed Young to step out of the car and place the syringe on the hood. The officer then asked Young why he had a syringe; with refreshing candor, Young replied that he used it to take drugs.

At this point, the backup officers ordered the two female passengers out of the car and asked them for identification. Respondent falsely identified herself as "Sandra James" and stated that she did not have any identification. Meanwhile, in light of Young's admission, the officer searched the passenger compartment of the car for contraband. On the back seat, he found a purse, which respondent claimed as hers. He removed from the purse a wallet containing respondent's driver's license, identifying her properly as Sandra K. Houghton. When the officer asked her why she had lied about her name, she replied: "In case things went bad."

Continuing his search of the purse, the officer found a brown pouch and a black wallet-type container. Respondent denied that the former was hers, and claimed ignorance of how it came to be there; it was found to contain drug paraphernalia and a syringe with 60 ccs of methamphetamine. Respondent admitted ownership of the black container, which was also found to contain drug paraphernalia, and a syringe (which respondent acknowledged was hers) with 10 ccs of methamphetamine — an amount insufficient to support the felony conviction at issue in this case. The officer also found fresh needle-track marks on respondent's arms. He placed her under arrest.

… It is uncontested in the present case that the police officers had probable cause to believe there were illegal drugs in the car. Thus, the Court held that "contraband goods concealed and illegally transported in an automobile or other vehicle may be searched for without a warrant" where probable cause exists.

[Court discussed Ross's holding and stated,

[Our] … later cases describing *Ross* have characterized it as applying broadly to *all* containers within a car, without qualification as to ownership. See, *e.g.* , *California* v. *Acevedo* , (1991).

To be sure, there was no passenger in *Ross*, and it was not claimed that the package in the trunk belonged to anyone other than the driver. Even so, if the rule of law that *Ross* announced were limited to contents belonging to the driver, or contents other than those belonging to passengers, one would have expected that substantial limitation to be expressed. And, more importantly, one would have expected that limitation to be apparent in the historical evidence that formed the basis for *Ross'*s holding. …

… In sum, neither *Ross* itself nor the historical evidence it relied upon admits of a distinction among packages or containers based on ownership. When there is probable cause to search for contraband in a car, it is reasonable for police officers … to examine packages and containers without a showing of individualized probable cause for each one. A passenger's personal belongings, just like the driver's belongings or containers attached to the car like a glove compartment, are "in" the car, and the officer has probable cause to search for contraband *in* the car.

United States v. *Di Re*, (1948), held that probable cause to search a car did not justify a body search of a passenger. And *Ybarra* v. *Illinois*, (1979), held that a search warrant for a tavern and its bartender did not permit body searches of all the bar's patrons. These cases turned on the unique, significantly heightened protection afforded against searches of one's person. "Even a limited search of the outer clothing . . .constitutes a severe, though brief, intrusion upon cherished personal security, and it must surely be an annoying, frightening, and perhaps humiliating experience." *Terry* v. *Ohio,* (1968). Such traumatic consequences are not to be expected when the police examine an item of personal property found in a car.

Whereas the passenger's privacy expectations are, as we have described, considerably diminished, the governmental interests at stake are substantial. Effective law enforcement would be appreciably impaired without the ability to search a passenger's personal belongings when there is reason to believe contraband or evidence of criminal wrongdoing is hidden in the car. As in all car-search cases, the "ready mobility" of an automobile creates a risk that the evidence or contraband will be permanently lost while a warrant is obtained. In addition, a car passenger — unlike the unwitting tavern patron in *Ybarra* — will often be engaged in a common enterprise with the driver, and have the same interest in concealing the fruits or the evidence of their wrongdoing. A criminal might be able to hide contraband in a passenger's belongings as readily as in other containers in the car, perhaps even surreptitiously, without the passenger's knowledge or permission. (This last possibility provided the basis for respondent's defense at trial; she testified that most of the seized contraband must have been placed in her purse by her traveling companions at one or another of various times, including the time she was "half asleep" in the car.)

... We hold that police officers with probable cause to search a car may inspect passengers' belongings found in the car that are capable of concealing the object of the search. ...

JUSTICE BREYER, concurring.

...[Given]...this Court's prior cases, I cannot argue that the fact that the container was a purse *automatically* makes a legal difference, for the Court has warned against trying to make that kind of distinction. But I can say that it would matter if a woman's purse, like a man's billfold, were attached to her person. It might then amount to a kind of "outer clothing," which under the Court's cases would properly receive increased protection. In this case, the purse was separate from the person, and no one has claimed that, under those circumstances, the type of container makes a difference. For that reason, I join the Court's opinion.

JUSTICE STEVENS , with whom JUSTICE SOUTER and JUSTICE GINSBURG join, dissenting.

...[U]nlike the Court, I think it quite plain that the search of a passenger's purse or briefcase involves an intrusion on privacy that may be just as serious as was the intrusion in *Di Re* ... I [am not] persuaded that the mere spatial association between a passenger and a driver provides an acceptable basis for presuming that they are partners in crime or for ignoring privacy interests in a purse. Whether or not the Fourth Amendment required a warrant to search Houghton's purse, at the very least the trooper in this case had to have probable cause to believe that her purse contained contraband. The Wyoming Supreme Court concluded that he did not.

Finally, in my view, the State's legitimate interest in effective law enforcement does not outweigh the privacy concerns at issue. I am as confident in a police officer's ability to apply a rule requiring a warrant or individualized probable cause to search belongings that are — as in this case — obviously owned by and in the custody of a passenger as is the Court in a "passenger-confederate[']s" ability to circumvent the rule. Certainly the ostensible clarity of the Court's rule is attractive. But that virtue is insufficient justification for its adoption. Moreover, a rule requiring a warrant or individualized probable cause to search passenger belongings is every bit as simple as the Court's rule; it simply protects more privacy.

California v. Acevedo, 500 U.S. 565 (1991)

SUMMARY: Police saw Acevedo leave an apartment with brown paper bags the size of the packages of marijuana they had seen earlier in the apartment. Acevedo put the bags into his trunk, got into the car, and drove away. The police stopped him, opened the trunk, found and opened the bags, found the marijuana and arrested him. The California courts, following an earlier Court opinion, held that the marijuana should be suppressed, because police had no probable cause to suspect that the car contained contraband, despite the fact that the bags contained contraband.

U.S. Supreme Court stated,

"[W]e see no principled distinction in terms of either the privacy expectation or the exigent circumstances between the paper bag found by the police in United States v. Ross and the paper bag found by the police here. Furthermore, by attempting to distinguish between a container for which the police are specifically searching and a container which they have come across in a car, we have provided only minimal protection for privacy and have impeded effective law enforcement."

Court held that Police are allowed to search a closed container in a car under the automobile exception.

The Court reasoned that that since the motorist was lawfully stopped, requiring a warrant for the container would offer little additional constitutional protection in that the container could just be held until the warrant was procured. The Court noted that a bright-line rule was important for efficient law enforcement.

Exigent Circumstances - Hot Pursuit

Hot pursuit is one form of exigent circumstance. Under the exigency exception commonly known as "hot pursuit," officers may conduct a warrantless search where: 1) the officer has probable cause to arrest the suspect; 2) the officer has probable cause to believe the suspect is in particular premises; and 3) there is an urgent need for immediate police action because delay would increase the risk of harm or escape. In *Warden v. Hayden*, 387 U.S. 294 (1967) the Court held that when police were in hot pursuit of an armed robber and followed him into a house, it would have been unreasonable to require the police to halt their investigation until a warrant was obtained. In *United States v. Santana*, 427 U.S. 38 (1976) the Court found that the fact that the pursuit ended almost as soon as it began did not make it less than a "hot pursuit." (The suspect attempted to avoid arrest by retreating from a doorway into the house as officers initiated an arrest.)

WARDEN v. HAYDEN
387 U.S. 294 (1967)

JUSTICE BRENNAN delivered the opinion of the court.

About 8 a. m. on March 17, 1962, an armed robber entered the business premises of the Diamond Cab Company in Baltimore, Maryland. He took some $363 and ran. Two cab drivers in the vicinity, attracted by shouts of "Holdup," followed the man to 2111 Cocoa Lane. One driver notified the company dispatcher by radio that the man was a Negro about 5'8" tall, wearing a light cap and dark jacket, and that he had entered the house on Cocoa Lane. The dispatcher relayed the information to police who were proceeding to the scene of the robbery. Within minutes, police arrived at the house in a number of patrol cars. An officer knocked and announced their presence. Mrs. Hayden answered, and the officers told her they believed that a robber had entered the house, and asked to search the house. She offered no objection.

The officers spread out through the first and second floors and the cellar in search of the robber. Hayden was found in an upstairs bedroom feigning sleep. He was arrested when the officers on the first floor and in the cellar reported that no other man was in the house. Meanwhile an officer was attracted to an adjoining bathroom by the noise of running water, and discovered a shotgun and a pistol in a flush tank; another officer who, according to the District Court, "was searching the cellar

for a man or the money" found in a washing machine a jacket and trousers of the type the fleeing man was said to have worn. A clip of ammunition for the pistol and a cap were found under the mattress of Hayden's bed, and ammunition for the shotgun was found in a bureau drawer in Hayden's room. All these items of evidence were introduced against respondent at his trial.

We agree with the Court of Appeals that neither the entry without warrant to search for the robber, nor the search for him without warrant was invalid. Under the circumstances of this case, "the exigencies of the situation made that course imperative." The police were informed that an armed robbery had taken place, and that the suspect had entered 2111 Cocoa Lane less than five minutes before they reached it. They acted reasonably when they entered the house and began to search for a man of the description they had been given and for weapons which he had used in the robbery or might use against them. The Fourth Amendment does not require police officers to delay in the course of an investigation if to do so would gravely endanger their lives or the lives of others. Speed here was essential, and only a thorough search of the house for persons and weapons could have insured that Hayden was the only man present and that the police had control of all weapons which could be used against them or to effect an escape.

Here, the seizures occurred prior to or immediately contemporaneous with Hayden's arrest, as part of an effort to find a suspected felon, armed, within the house into which he had run only minutes before the police arrived. The permissible scope of search must, therefore, at the least, be as broad as may reasonably be necessary to prevent the dangers that the suspect at large in the house may resist or escape.

It is argued that, while the weapons, ammunition, and cap may have been seized in the course of a search for weapons, the officer who seized the clothing was searching neither for the suspect nor for weapons when he looked into the washing machine in which he found the clothing. But even if we assume, although we do not decide, that the exigent circumstances in this case made lawful a search without warrant only for the suspect or his weapons, it cannot be said on this record that the officer who found the clothes in the washing machine was not searching for weapons. He testified that he was searching for the man or the money, but his failure to state explicitly that he was searching for weapons, in the absence of a specific question to that effect, can hardly be accorded controlling weight. He knew that the robber was armed and he did not know that some weapons had been found at the time he opened the machine. In these circumstances the inference that he was in fact also looking for weapons is fully justified.

Nothing in the language of the Fourth Amendment supports the distinction between "mere evidence" and instrumentalities, fruits of crime, or contraband. . . .

WELSH v. WISCONSIN
466 U.S. 740 (1984)

JUSTICE BRENNAN delivered the opinion of the court.

Shortly before 9 o'clock on the rainy night of April 24, 1978, a lone witness, Randy Jablonic, observed a car being driven erratically. After changing speeds and veering from side to side, the car eventually swerved off the road and came to a stop in an open field. No damage to any person or property occurred. Concerned about the driver and fearing that the car would get back on the highway, Jablonic drove his truck up behind the car so as to block it from returning to the road. Another passerby also stopped at the scene, and Jablonic asked her to call the police. Before the police arrived, however, the driver of the car emerged from his vehicle, approached Jablonic's truck, and asked Jablonic for a ride home. Jablonic instead suggested that they wait for assistance in removing or repairing the car. Ignoring Jablonic's suggestion, the driver walked away from the scene.

A few minutes later, the police arrived and questioned Jablonic. He told one officer what he had seen, specifically noting that the driver was either very inebriated or very sick. The officer checked the motor vehicle registration of the abandoned car and learned that it was registered to the petitioner, Edward G. Welsh. In addition, the officer noted that the petitioner's residence was a short distance from the scene, and therefore easily within walking distance.

Without securing any type of warrant, the police proceeded to the petitioner's home, arriving about 9 p.m. When the petitioner's stepdaughter answered the door, the police gained entry into the house. Proceeding upstairs to the petitioner's bedroom, they found him lying naked in bed. At this point, the petitioner was placed under arrest for driving or operating a motor vehicle while under the influence of an intoxicant. . . . The petitioner was taken to the police station, where he refused to submit to a breath-analysis test.

[Trial court found probable cause and exigent circumstances, and defendant was convicted. Appellate court found violation of the Fourth Amendment, since although there was probable cause there were no exigent circumstances. Supreme Court of Wisconsin reversed appellate court finding exigent circumstances (hot pursuit, need to prevent physical harm to offender and public, and need to prevent destruction of evidence.]

Because of the important Fourth Amendment implications of the decision below, we granted certiorari.

It is not surprising . . . that the Court has recognized, as "a `basic principle of Fourth Amendment law[,]' that searches and seizures inside a home without a warrant are presumptively unreasonable." Consistently with these long-recognized principles, the Court decided in *Payton v. New York*, supra, that warrantless felony arrests in the home are prohibited by the Fourth Amendment, absent probable cause and exigent circumstances. At the same time, the Court declined to consider the scope of any exception for exigent circumstances that might justify warrantless home arrests, thereby leaving to the lower courts the initial application of the exigent-circumstances exception. Prior decisions of this Court, however, have emphasized that exceptions to the warrant requirement are "few in number and carefully delineated," and that the police bear a heavy burden when attempting to demonstrate an urgent need that might justify warrantless searches or arrests. Indeed, the Court has recognized only a few such emergency conditions and has actually applied only the "hot pursuit" doctrine to arrests in the home.

Our hesitation in finding exigent circumstances, especially when warrantless arrests in the home are at issue, is particularly appropriate when the underlying offense for which there is probable cause to arrest is relatively minor. Before agents of the government may invade the sanctity of the home, the burden is on the government to demonstrate exigent circumstances that overcome the presumption of

unreasonableness that attaches to all warrantless home entries. When the government's interest is only to arrest for a minor offense, _that presumption of unreasonableness is difficult to rebut, and the government usually should be allowed to make such arrests only with a warrant issued upon probable cause by a neutral and detached magistrate.

We therefore conclude that the common-sense approach utilized by most lower courts is required by the Fourth Amendment prohibition on "unreasonable searches and seizures," and hold that an important factor to be considered when determining whether any exigency exists is the gravity of the underlying offense for which the arrest is being made. …[A]pplication of the exigent-circumstances exception in the context of a home entry should rarely be sanctioned when there is probable cause to believe that only a minor offense, such as the kind at issue in this case, has been committed.

… The petitioner was arrested in the privacy of his own bedroom for a noncriminal, traffic offense. The State attempts to justify the arrest by relying on the hot-pursuit doctrine, on the threat to public safety, and on the need to preserve evidence of the petitioner's blood-alcohol level. On the facts of this case, however, the claim of hot pursuit is unconvincing because there was no immediate or continuous pursuit of the petitioner from the scene of a crime. Moreover, because the petitioner had already arrived home, and had abandoned his car at the scene of the accident, there was little remaining threat to the public safety. Hence, the only potential emergency claimed by the State was the need to ascertain the petitioner's blood-alcohol level.

Even assuming, however, that the underlying facts would support a finding of this exigent circumstance, mere similarity to other cases involving the imminent destruction of evidence is not sufficient. The State of Wisconsin has chosen to classify the first offense for driving while intoxicated as a noncriminal, civil forfeiture offense for which no imprisonment is possible. . . . Given this expression of the State's interest, a warrantless home arrest cannot be upheld simply because evidence of the petitioner's blood-alcohol level might have dissipated while the police obtained a warrant. _To allow a warrantless home entry on these facts would be to approve unreasonable police behavior that the principles of the Fourth Amendment will not sanction.

The Supreme Court of Wisconsin let stand a warrantless, nighttime entry into the petitioner's home to arrest him for a civil traffic offense. Such an arrest, however, is clearly prohibited by the special protection afforded the individual in his home by the Fourth Amendment.

JUSTICE WHITE, with whom JUSTICE REHNQUIST joins, dissenting. Omitted.

Other Cases: Hot Pursuit

Lange v. California, 594 U.S. 2021

SUMMARY: Lange drove by a CHP officer while playing loud music and honking his horn. The officer followed him and attempted to pull him over by activating overhead lights. Rather than stopping, Lange pulled into his driveway and entered into his attached garage. The officer followed Lange into the garage, formed the opinion that Lange was intoxicated, and performed field sobriety tests on Lange. Lange's blood alcohol content turned out to be three times the legal limit. He was charged with misdemeanor driving under the influence of intoxicants and moved to suppress the evidence (officer's observations in the garage) arguing that the warrantless entry violated his Fourth Amendment rights.

The California courts found that the officer had probable cause to pull Lange over and that the pursuit of a misdemeanant is always permissible under the exigent circumstance exception. The Government urged the Court to adopt this per se rule (always allowing pursuit of a misdemeanant). But the Court declined to do so. It held that a case-by-case approach was better

"Misdemeanors run the gamut of seriousness, and they may be minor. … The Court has held that when a minor offense (and no flight) is involved, police officers do not usually face the kind of emergency that can justify a warrantless home entry . . . but not enough to justify a categorical rule. In many cases, flight creates a need for police to act swiftly. But no evidence suggests that every case of misdemeanor flight creates such a need.

The Court's Fourth Amendment precedents thus point toward assessing case by case the exigencies arising from misdemeanants' flight. When the totality of circumstances shows an emergency—a need to act before it is possible to get a warrant—the police may act without waiting. Those circumstances include the flight itself. But pursuit of a misdemeanant does not trigger a categorical rule allowing a warrantless home entry."

Exigent Circumstances -- Preventing Escape

Minnesota v. Olson, 495 U.S. 91 (1990), held that simply being wanted for a serious felony does not in itself create an exigency which would allow police to enter a home without a warrant. In that case, police suspected that murder suspect Olson was in a house, so they entered without a warrant to arrest him and prevent his escape. Although the state argued that their warrantless entry was justified by hot pursuit, the Court disagreed, stating,

"In *Payton v. New York*, the Court had no occasion to "consider the sort of emergency or dangerous situation, described in our cases as 'exigent circumstances,' that would justify a warrantless entry into a home for the purpose of either arrest or search," 445 U.S., at 583. This case requires us to determine whether the Minnesota Supreme Court was correct in holding that there were no exigent circumstances that justified the warrantless entry into the house to make the arrest.

The Minnesota Supreme Court applied essentially the correct standard in determining whether exigent circumstances existed. The court observed that "a warrantless intrusion may be justified by hot pursuit of a fleeing felon, or imminent destruction of evidence, . . . or the need to prevent a suspect's escape, or the risk of danger to the police or to other persons inside or outside the dwelling." The court also apparently thought that in the absence of hot pursuit there must be at least probable cause to believe that one or more of the other factors justifying the entry were present and that in assessing the risk of danger, the gravity of the crime and likelihood that the suspect is armed should be considered. Applying this standard, the state court determined that exigent circumstances did not exist.

We are not inclined to disagree with this fact-specific application of the proper legal standard. The [Minnesota Supreme] court pointed out that although a grave crime was involved, respondent "was known not to be the murderer but thought to be the driver of the getaway car," and that the police had already recovered the murder weapon. "The police knew that Louanne and Julie were with the suspect in the upstairs duplex with no suggestion of danger to them. Three or four Minneapolis police squads surrounded the house. The time was 3 p.m., Sunday. . . . It was evident the suspect was going nowhere. If he came out of the house he would have been promptly apprehended." We do not disturb the state court's judgment that these facts do not add up to exigent circumstances."

Exigent Circumstances -- Destruction Or Loss Of Evidence

Police may conduct a warrantless search or seizure in order to preserve evidence when they reasonably believe that the evidence sought is in immediate danger of being removed or destroyed. For example, in *Cupp v. Murphy*, 412 U.S. 291 (1973), the Court found exigent circumstances justified warrantless search of fingernail trace evidence related to a strangling when there was probable cause to arrest and there was danger that evidence would be destroyed. Exigent circumstances also justified warrantless entry of an apartment to search for drugs where police had probable cause to arrest and there was danger that evidence would be destroyed. *Ker v. California* 374 U.S. 23 (1963). On the other hand, the Court invalidated a warrantless search when it found only a mere possibility that the evidence would be destroyed. *Vale v. Louisiana*, 399 U.S. 30 (1970). The threat of danger or destruction to the evidence must be real or imminent. Police are not justified in searching a crime scene without a warrant absent an "indication that the evidence would be lost, destroyed, or removed during the time required to obtain a search warrant . . .[when]. . . there [was] no suggestion that a warrant could not easily and conveniently have been obtained." *Mincey v. Arizona*, 437 U.S. 385 (1978). Thus, the Court has refused to adopt either a general "murder scene exception" or a general "crime scene exception" to the warrant requirement. (See, *Mincey* and *Flippo v. West Virginia*, 528 U.S. 11 (1999)). More recently, the Court dealt with whether police permissibly created their own emergency by alerting residents to their presence rather than getting a warrant first. See *Kentucky v. King*, below.

Blood Alcohol/Controlled Substance Dissipation

Because blood alcohol levels dissipate with time, the courts allow police to take blood samples (by force, if necessary) from individuals suspected of drunk driving without first obtaining a search warrant. Exigent circumstances exist because alcohol in the suspect's bloodstream might disappear in the time required to obtain a warrant. In *Birchfield*, above, the Court analyzed the withdrawal of blood as part of an investigation into intoxicated driving, but analyzed it as a search incident to lawful arrest. Dissenting, Justice Thomas determined the issues could have been more easily settled by application of the exigent circumstance search exception. He would have found that the blood draws were constitutional in that the natural metabolization of the blood alcohol in the system creates an exigency.

Exigent Circumstances -- Protecting the Public

Case law allows police to enter residences without search warrants under exigent circumstance rationales when necessary to protect the public when taking time to obtain a warrant would endanger the public.

BRIGHAM CITY, UTAH v. STUART
547 U.S. 398 (2006)

CHIEF JUSTICE ROBERTS delivered the opinion of the Court.

In this case we consider whether police may enter a home without a warrant when they have an objectively reasonable basis for believing that an occupant is seriously injured or imminently threatened with such injury. We conclude that they may.

This case arises out of a melee that occurred in a Brigham City, Utah, home in the early morning hours of July 23, 2000. At about 3 a.m., four police officers responded to a call regarding a loud party at a residence. Upon arriving at the house, they heard shouting from inside, and proceeded down the driveway to investigate. There, they observed two juveniles drinking beer in the backyard. They entered the backyard, and saw — through a screen door and windows — an altercation taking place in the kitchen of the home. According to the testimony of one of the officers, four adults were attempting, with some difficulty, to restrain a juvenile. The juvenile eventually "broke free, swung a fist and struck one of the adults in the face." The officer testified that he observed the victim of the blow spitting blood into a nearby sink. The other adults continued to try to restrain the juvenile, pressing him up against a refrigerator with such force that the refrigerator began moving across the floor. At this point, an officer opened the screen door and announced the officers' presence. Amid the tumult, nobody noticed. The officer entered the kitchen and again cried out, and as the occupants slowly became aware that the police were on the scene, the altercation ceased.

. . . .

We granted certiorari . . . in light of differences among state courts and the Courts of Appeals concerning the appropriate Fourth Amendment standard governing warrantless entry by law enforcement in an emergency situation.

It is a "'basic principle of Fourth Amendment law that searches and seizures inside a home without a warrant are presumptively unreasonable.'" Nevertheless, because the ultimate touchstone of the Fourth Amendment is "reasonableness," the warrant requirement is subject to certain exceptions. We have held, for example, that law enforcement officers may make a warrantless entry onto private property to fight a fire and investigate its cause, to prevent the imminent destruction of evidence, or to engage in "hot pursuit" of a fleeing suspect." [W]arrants are generally required to search a person's home or his person unless 'the exigencies of the situation' make the needs of law enforcement so compelling that the warrantless search is objectively reasonable under the Fourth Amendment." *Mincey v. Arizona,* (1978).

One exigency obviating the requirement of a warrant is the need to assist persons who are seriously injured or threatened with such injury. " 'The need to protect or preserve life or avoid serious injury is justification for what would be otherwise illegal absent an exigency or emergency.' " Accordingly, law enforcement officers may enter a home without a warrant to render emergency assistance to an injured occupant or to protect an occupant from imminent injury.

Respondents do not take issue with these principles, but instead advance two reasons why the officers' entry here was unreasonable.

First, they argue that the officers were more interested in making arrests than quelling violence. They urge us to consider, in assessing the reasonableness of the entry, whether the officers were "indeed motivated primarily by a desire to save lives and property." The Utah Supreme Court also considered the officers' subjective motivations relevant.

Our cases have repeatedly rejected this approach. An action is "reasonable" under the Fourth Amendment, regardless of the individual officer's state of mind, "as long as the circumstances, viewed objectively, justify [the] action.". The officer's subjective motivation is irrelevant. . . . It therefore does not matter here — even if their subjective motives could be so neatly unraveled — whether the officers entered the kitchen to arrest respondents and gather evidence against them or to assist the injured and prevent further violence.

. . . .

Respondents . . . contend that their conduct was not serious enough to justify the officers' intrusion into the home. They rely on *Welsh v. Wisconsin*, (1984), in which we held that "an important factor to be considered when determining whether any exigency exists is the gravity of the underlying offense for which the arrest is being made." This contention, too, is misplaced. Welsh involved a warrantless entry by officers to arrest a suspect for driving while intoxicated. There, the "only potential emergency" confronting the officers was the need to preserve evidence (**i.e.,** the suspect's blood-alcohol level) — an exigency that we held insufficient under the circumstances to justify entry into the suspect's home. Here, the officers were confronted with ongoing violence occurring within the home. Welsh did not address such a situation.

…

[T]he officers had an objectively reasonable basis for believing both that the injured adult might need help and that the violence in the kitchen was just beginning. Nothing in the Fourth Amendment required them to wait until another blow rendered someone "unconscious" or "semi-conscious" or worse before entering.

…

The manner of the officers' entry was also reasonable. After witnessing the punch, one of the officers opened the screen door and yelled in "police." When nobody heard him, he stepped into the kitchen and announced himself again. Only then did the tumult subside. … Under these circumstances, there was no violation of the Fourth Amendment's knock-and-announce rule. Furthermore, once the announcement was made, the officers were free to enter; it would serve no purpose to require them to stand dumbly at the door awaiting a response while those within brawled on, oblivious to their presence.

. . .

JUSTICE STEVENS, concurring.

This is an odd flyspeck of a case. The charges that have been pending against respondents for the past six years are minor offenses — intoxication, contributing to the delinquency of a minor, and disorderly conduct — two of which could have been proved by evidence that was gathered by the responding officers before they entered the home. The maximum punishment for these crimes ranges between 90 days and 6 months in jail. And the Court's unanimous opinion restating well-settled rules of federal law is so clearly persuasive that it is hard to imagine the outcome was ever in doubt.

Under these circumstances, the only difficult question is which of the following is the most peculiar: (1) that the Utah trial judge, the intermediate state appellate court, and the Utah Supreme Court all found a Fourth Amendment violation on these facts; (2) that the prosecution chose to pursue this matter all the way to the United States Supreme Court; or (3) that this Court voted to grant the petition for a writ of certiorari.

Michigan v. Fisher, 588 U.S. 45(2009)

Police officers responded to a complaint of a disturbance near Allen Road in Brownstown, Michigan. Officer Christopher Goolsby later testified that, as he and his partner approached the area, a couple directed them to a residence where a man was "going crazy." Upon their arrival, the officers found a household in considerable chaos: a pickup truck in the driveway with its front smashed, damaged fence posts along the side of the property, and three broken house windows, the glass still on the ground outside. The officers also noticed blood on the hood of the pickup and on clothes inside of it, as well as on one of the doors to the house. (It is disputed whether they noticed this immediately upon reaching the house, but undisputed that they noticed it before the allegedly unconstitutional entry.) Through a window, the officers could see respondent, Jeremy Fisher, inside the house, screaming and throwing things. The back door was locked, and a couch had been placed to block the front door.

The officers knocked, but Fisher refused to answer. They saw that Fisher had a cut on his hand, and they asked him whether he needed medical attention. Fisher ignored these questions and demanded, with accompanying profanity, that the officers go to get a search warrant. Officer Goolsby then pushed the front door partway open and ventured into the house. Through the window of the open door he saw Fisher pointing a long gun at him. Officer Goolsby withdrew.

. . . .

...[T]he exigencies of the situation [may] make the needs of law enforcement so compelling that the warrantless search is objectively reasonable."

… This "emergency aid exception" does not depend on the officers' subjective intent or the seriousness of any crime they are investigating when the emergency arises. It requires only "an objectively reasonable basis for believing that "a person within [the house] is in need of immediate aid."

A straightforward application of the emergency aid exception, . . . dictates that the officer's entry was reasonable. Just as in *Brigham City*, the

police officers here were responding to a report of a disturbance. Just as in *Brigham City*, when they arrived on the scene they encountered a tumultuous situation in the house — and here they also found signs of a recent injury, perhaps from a car accident, outside. And just as in *Brigham City*, the officers could see violent behavior inside. Although Officer Goolsby and his partner did not see punches thrown, as did the officers in *Brigham City*, they did see Fisher screaming and throwing things. It would be objectively reasonable to believe that Fisher's projectiles might have a human target (perhaps a spouse or a child), or that Fisher would hurt himself in the course of his rage. In short, we find it as plain here as we did in Brigham City that the officer's entry was reasonable under the Fourth Amendment.

. . . .

It does not meet the needs of law enforcement or the demands of public safety to require officers to walk away from a situation like the one they encountered here. Only when an apparent threat has become an actual harm can officers rule out innocuous explanations for ominous circumstances. But "[t]he role of a peace officer includes preventing violence and restoring order, not simply rendering first aid to casualties." It sufficed to invoke the emergency aid exception that it was reasonable to believe that Fisher had hurt himself (albeit nonfatally) and needed treatment that in his rage he was unable to provide, or that Fisher was about to hurt, or had already hurt, someone else. . . .

JUSTICE STEVENS, with whom JUSTICE SOTOMAYOR joins, dissenting

[The state courts applied the proper state and Fourth Amendment law. The trial court determined that under the facts, the entry was illegal and not reasonable.]

Today, without having heard Officer Goolsby's testimony, this Court decides that the trial judge got it wrong. I am not persuaded that he did, but even if we make that assumption, it is hard to see how the Court is justified in micromanaging the day-to-day business of state tribunals making fact-intensive decisions of this kind. We ought not usurp the role of the factfinder when faced with a close question of the reasonableness of an officer's actions, particularly in a case tried in a state court. I therefore respectfully dissent.

Kentucky v. King, 563 U.S. 452 (2011)

[Official Summary]

Police officers in Lexington, Kentucky, followed a suspected drug dealer to an apartment complex. They smelled marijuana outside an apartment door, knocked loudly, and announced their presence. As soon as the officers began knocking, they heard noises coming from the apartment; the officers believed that these noises were consistent with the destruction of evidence. The officers announced their intent to enter the apartment, kicked in the door, and found respondent and others. They saw drugs in plain view during a protective sweep of the apartment and found additional evidence during a subsequent search. The Circuit Court denied respondent's motion to suppress the evidence, holding that exigent circumstances—the need to prevent destruction of evidence—justified the warrantless entry. Respondent entered a conditional guilty plea, reserving his right to appeal the suppression ruling, and the Kentucky Court of Appeals affirmed. The Supreme Court of Kentucky reversed. The court assumed that exigent circumstances existed, but it nonetheless invalidated the search. The exigent circumstances rule did not apply, the court held, because the police should have foreseen that their conduct would prompt the occupants to attempt to destroy evidence.

The U.S. Supreme Court majority opinion looked at lower courts "police-created emergency doctrine and stated that the "proper test is that warrantless searches are allowed when the circumstances make it reasonable . . . to dispense with the warrant requirement. Thus, a warrantless entry based on exigent circumstances is reasonable when the police did not create the exigency by engaging or threatening to engage in conduct violating the Fourth Amendment."

The Court declined to follow the approach proposed by Respondent . . . that "an exigency is impermissibly created when officers engage in conduct that would cause a reasonable person to believe that entry was imminent and inevitable" finding that approach is … flawed. "The ability of officers to respond to an exigency cannot turn on such subtleties as the officers' tone of voice in announcing their presence and the forcefulness of their knocks. A forceful knock may be necessary to alert the occupants that someone is at the door, and unless officers identify themselves loudly enough, occupants may not know who is at their doorstep. Respondent's test would make it extremely difficult for officers to know how loudly they may announce their presence or how forcefully they may knock without running afoul of the police-created exigency rule. And in most cases, it would be nearly impossible for a court to determine whether that threshold had been passed."

Assuming an emergency existed, the Court saw no evidence that the officers "either violated the Fourth Amendment or threatened to do so prior to the point when they entered the apartment." But they remanded the case back to Kentucky to see if there an exigency existed but noted, "Assuming an exigency did exist, the officers' conduct—banging on the door and announcing their presence—was entirely consistent with the Fourth Amendment." . . .

JUSTICE GINSBURG, dissenting.

The Court today arms the police with a way routinely to dishonor the Fourth Amendment's warrant requirement in drug cases. In lieu of presenting their evidence to a neutral magistrate, police officers may now knock, listen, then break the door down, nevermind that they had ample time to obtain a warrant….

. . . .

This case involves a principal exception to the warrant requirement, the exception applicable in "exigent circumstances." "[C]arefully delineated," the exception should govern only in genuine emergency situations. Circumstances qualify as "exigent" when there is an imminent risk of death or serious injury, or danger that evidence will be immediately destroyed, or that a suspect will escape. The question presented: May police, who could pause to gain the approval of a neutral magistrate, dispense with the need to get a warrant by themselves creating exigent circumstances? I would answer no, as did the Kentucky Supreme Court. The urgency must exist, I would rule, when the police come on the scene, not subsequent to their arrival, prompted by their own conduct

Community Caretaking

Haven't seen your neighbor for some time? Are you concerned about his welfare and suspect that he may have fallen and he cannot get up? If you call the police and have them do a "welfare check" on your neighbor, they are performing a community caretaking function. The Court first identified a police community caretaking function that may not implicate the Fourth Amendment in *Cady v. Dombrowski*, 413 U.S. 433 (1973). The Court noted, "local law enforcement officials frequently investigate motor vehicle accidents and engage in community caretaking functions, totally divorced from the detection, investigation, or acquisition of evidence relating to the violation of a criminal statute." Community caretaking searches are motivated by the desire to render aid not to investigate a crime, and police will probably not even have formed a reasonable suspicion that a crime has been committed when engaging in a community caretaking function. Community caretaking searches differ from exigent circumstance circumstances in two regards. First, community caretaking searches are not necessarily emergency situations where the police are concerned with the destruction of evidence. In fact, community caretaking functions are those that have no criminal law enforcement purpose. Second, unlike exigent circumstance searches which require probable cause to believe that evidence of a crime will be jeopardized without a prompt (warrantless) search or seizure, police need no probable cause to do a community caretaking search. In these circumstances, the police presence in the home without a warrant is entirely reasonable.

Administrative Searches

Afraid that your favorite bar is a fire-trap? Anxious that your best friend's stairwell is on the verge of collapsing and putting you at risk when you visit? If you call the building department and they want to go and do an inspection, they are conducting an administrative search. *Camara v. Municipal Court*, 387 U.S. 523 (1967) held that the Fourth Amendment applies to every governmental agent who might violate a person's expectation of privacy including administrative agencies. After *Camara,* the Court applied the administrative search doctrine and "area warrant" requirements to commercial businesses inspections. See, *See v. Seattle*, 387 U.S. 541 (1967). That said, by 1970, the Court relaxed the area warrant requirement for inspections of businesses in *pervasively regulated industries* such as liquor stores or gun dealerships, as long as they did so during normal business hours and did not use force. Dealers who refused inspections could lose their licenses. Safety inspections of mines was allowed without warrants under the Mine Safety and Health Act because all mine owners were required to know the law and it was presumed to be a constitutionally adequate substitute for the warrant requirement. The Court has not completely done away with area warrants and still requires them for worker safety inspections by the Occupational Safety and Health Authority (OSHA) holding that simply requiring safety and health inspections of an industry does not make it a pervasively regulated industry. The Court has also merged the administrative search with the concept of "special needs" searches (see below) in *New York v. Burger*, 482 U.S. 691(1987)(search of an automobile junk shop), and *O'Connor v. Ortega*, 480 U.S. 709 (1987) (search of an employee's desk, filing cabinet, and his office at a state hospital)--the plurality decision in *O'Connor* balanced Dr. Ortega's expectation of privacy in his office against the governmental interest and "special need" to protect others against sexual harassment.

CAMARA v. MUNICIPAL COURT
387 U.S. 523 (1967)

JUSTICE WHITE delivered the opinion of the court.

Appellant brought this action in a California Superior Court alleging that he was awaiting trial on a criminal charge of violating the San Francisco Housing Code by refusing to permit a warrantless inspection of his residence,

. . . .

Appellant has argued throughout this litigation that . . . [the Code] . . . is contrary to the Fourth and Fourteenth Amendments in that it authorizes municipal officials to enter a private dwelling without a search warrant and without probable cause to believe that a violation of the Housing Code exists therein. Consequently, appellant contends, he may not be prosecuted . . . for refusing to permit an inspection unconstitutionally authorized. ... [T]he District Court of Appeal held that ... [the Code] . . . does not violate Fourth Amendment rights because it "is part of a regulatory scheme which is essentially civil rather than criminal in nature, inasmuch as that section creates a right of inspection which is limited in scope and may not be exercised under unreasonable conditions.". . .

...

We may agree that a routine inspection of the physical condition of private property is a less hostile intrusion than the typical policeman's search for the fruits and instrumentalities of crime. ... But we cannot agree that the Fourth Amendment interests at stake in these inspection cases are merely "peripheral." It is surely anomalous to say that the individual and his private property are fully protected by the Fourth Amendment only when the individual is suspected of criminal behavior.

. . . .

Like most regulatory laws, fire, health, and housing codes are enforced by criminal

processes. In some cities, discovery of a violation by the inspector leads to a criminal complaint. Even in cities where discovery of a violation produces only an administrative compliance order, refusal to comply is a criminal offense, and the fact of compliance is verified by a second inspection, again without a warrant. Finally, as this case demonstrates, refusal to permit an inspection is itself a crime, punishable by fine or even by jail sentence.

In summary, we hold that administrative searches of the kind at issue here are significant intrusions upon the interests protected by the Fourth Amendment, that such searches when authorized and conducted without a warrant procedure lack the traditional safeguards which the Fourth Amendment guarantees to the individual, and that the reasons put forth in *Frank v. Maryland* and in other cases for upholding these warrantless searches are insufficient to justify so substantial a weakening of the Fourth Amendment's protections. Because of the nature of the municipal programs under consideration, however, these conclusions must be the beginning, not the end, of our inquiry. . . .

Unlike the search pursuant to a criminal investigation, the inspection programs at issue here are aimed at securing city-wide compliance with minimum physical standards for private property. The primary governmental interest at stake is to prevent even the unintentional development of conditions which are hazardous to public health and safety. Because fires and epidemics may ravage large urban areas, because unsightly conditions adversely affect the economic values of neighboring structures, numerous courts have upheld the police power of municipalities to impose and enforce such minimum standards even upon existing structures. In determining whether a particular inspection is reasonable - and thus in determining whether there is probable cause to issue a warrant for that inspection - the need for the inspection must be weighed in terms of these reasonable goals of code enforcement.

There is unanimous agreement among those most familiar with this field that the only effective way to seek universal compliance with the minimum standards required by municipal codes is through routine periodic inspections of all structures. It is here that the probable cause debate is focused, for the agency's decision to conduct an area inspection is unavoidably based on its appraisal of conditions in the area as a whole, not on its knowledge of conditions in each particular building. Appellee contends that, if the probable cause standard urged by appellant is adopted, the area inspection will be eliminated as a means of seeking compliance with code standards and the reasonable goals of code enforcement will be dealt a crushing blow.

. . . It has been suggested to vary the probable cause test from the standard applied in criminal cases would be to authorize a "synthetic search warrant" and thereby to lessen the overall protections of the Fourth Amendment. But we do not agree. The warrant procedure is designed to guarantee that a decision to search private property is justified by a reasonable governmental interest. But reasonableness is still the ultimate standard. If a valid public interest justifies the intrusion contemplated, then there is probable cause to issue a suitably restricted search warrant. Such an approach neither endangers time-honored doctrines applicable to criminal investigations nor makes a nullity of the probable cause requirement in this area. It merely gives full recognition to the competing public and private interests here at stake and, in so doing, best fulfills the historic purpose behind the constitutional right to be free from unreasonable government invasions of privacy.

III

Since our holding emphasizes the controlling standard of reasonableness, nothing we say today is intended to foreclose prompt inspections, even without a warrant, that the law has traditionally upheld in emergency situations. On the other hand, in the case of most routine area inspections, there is no compelling urgency to inspect at a particular time or on a particular day. Moreover, most citizens allow inspections of their property without a warrant. Thus, as a practical matter and in light of the Fourth Amendment's requirement that a warrant specify the property to be searched, it seems likely that warrants should normally be sought only after entry is refused unless there has been a citizen complaint or there is other satisfactory reason for securing immediate entry. Similarly, the requirement of a warrant procedure does not suggest any change in what seems to be the prevailing local policy, in most situations, of authorizing entry, but not entry by force, to inspect.

IV.

In this case, appellant has been charged with a crime for his refusal to permit housing inspectors to enter his leasehold without a warrant. There was no emergency demanding immediate access; in fact, the inspectors made three trips to the building in an attempt to obtain appellant's consent to search. Yet no warrant was obtained and thus appellant was unable to verify either the need for or the appropriate limits of the inspection. No doubt, the inspectors entered the public portion of the building with the consent of the landlord, through the building's manager, but appellee does not contend that such consent was sufficient to authorize inspection of appellant's premises. Assuming the facts to be as the parties have alleged, we therefore conclude that appellant had a constitutional right to insist that the inspectors obtain a warrant to search and that appellant may not constitutionally be convicted for refusing to consent to the inspection. It appears from the opinion of the District Court of Appeal that under these circumstances a writ of prohibition will issue to the criminal court under California law.

International Border Searches

Customs officials do not need a warrant when conducting searches at international borders. The justification for warrantless border searches stems from the executive branch's expansive authority to prevent the introduction of contraband into this country. Routine border inspections include the authority to remove and disassemble a vehicle's fuel tank-- interference with the motorist's possessory interest is justified by the government's paramount interest in protecting the border. *United States v. Flores-Montano*, 541 U.S. 149 (2004). An "international border" includes more than just geographical borders between two countries, and the international border exception to the warrant requirement extends to searches conducted at the "functional equivalent" of the border. See, *Almeida-Sanchez v. United.*, 413 U.S. 266 (1973). The rationale for the border exception also applies to persons or objects leaving the country. *California Bankers Association v. Schultz*, 416 U.S. 21 (1974).

UNITED STATES v. RAMSEY
431 U.S 606 (1977)

JUSTICE REHNQUIST delivered the opinion of the Court.

[Facts Summarized:

Ramsey and Kelly were involved in international heroin-by-mail trade. They were working with Bailey and Ward who worked out of West Germany and Thailand. West German authorities alerted Thailand of Ward and Bailey's presence who then placed them under surveillance. They were seen mailing letter-sized envelopes from Thailand to Washington D.C. Ward and Bailey were arrested by Thai officials and eleven heroinfilled envelopes addressed to Washington D.C. area (connected to Ramsey and Kelly) were seized.

In New Yorkd City, Custom Inspector Kallnischkies, unaware of the events in Thailand and Germany, inspected a sack of incoming international mail from Thailand, he intercepted several envelopes which appeared to be from same typewriter directed at four different D.C. addresses. They were bulky and he believed the envelopes might contain merchandise or contraband and not correspondence. He opened one of them, discovered it contained powdered substance, did a field test on the drugs, and as he suspected, the test showed a positive reaction to heroin. He opened the others; they also contained heroin; he contacted DEA agents in

D.C. and sent them the envelopes in a locked pouch. DEA agents obtained a warrant, and they opened the envelopes and removed most of the heroin. They resealed six of the envelopes and delivered them under surveillance. Kelly and Ramsey opened them and they were arrested. DEA agents received warrant and they searched Ramsey's home and found two pistols.

Ramsey, Kelly, Bailey, and Ward were all indicted. They moved to suppress the drugs and the guns. That motion was denied, and there was a stipulated bench trial, and they were found guilty and sentenced to a term of 10 to 30 years. On appeal, the Court of Appeals for District of Columbia reversed the conviction holding that the border search exception to the warrant requirement did not apply to routine opening of international letter mail, and that the opening required probable cause and a warrant signed by a neutral magistrate. U.S. Supreme Court accepted review, and disagreed.]

That searches made at the border, pursuant to the longstanding right of the sovereign to protect itself by stopping and examining persons and property crossing into this country, are reasonable simply by virtue of the fact that they occur at the border, should, by now, require no extended demonstration.

This interpretation, that border searches were not subject to the warrant provisions of the Fourth Amendment and were "reasonable" within the meaning of that Amendment, has been faithfully adhered to by this Court. . . .

> "Travellers may be . . . stopped in crossing an international boundary because of national self protection reasonably requiring one entering the country to identify himself as entitled to come in, and his belongings as effects which may be lawfully brought in."

Border searches . . . from before the adoption of the Fourth Amendment, have been considered to be "reasonable" by the single fact that the person or item in question had entered into our country from outside. There has never been any additional requirement that the reasonableness of a border search depended on the existence of probable cause. This longstanding recognition that searches at our borders without probable cause and without a warrant are nonetheless "reasonable" has a history as old as the Fourth Amendment itself. We reaffirm it now.

Respondents urge upon us, however, the position that mailed letters are somehow different, and, whatever may be the normal rule with respect to border searches, different considerations, requiring the full panoply of Fourth Amendment protections, apply to international mail. ... We do not agree that this inclusion of letters within the border-search exception represents any "extension" of that exception.

The border-search exception is grounded in the recognized right of the sovereign to control, subject to substantive limitations imposed by the Constitution, who and what may enter the country. It is clear that there is nothing in the rationale behind the border-search exception which suggests that the mode of entry will be critical. It was conceded at oral argument that customs officials could search, without probable cause and without a warrant, envelopes carried by an entering traveler, whether in his luggage or on his person. Surely no different constitutional standard should apply simply because the envelopes were mailed, not carried. The critical fact is that the envelopes cross the border and enter this country, not that they are brought in by one mode of transportation rather than another. It is their entry into this country from without it that makes a resulting search "reasonable."

[T]he existing system of border searches has not been shown to invade protected First Amendment rights, and hence there is no reason to think that the potential presence of correspondence makes the otherwise constitutionally reasonable search unreasonable....

UNITED STATES v. MONTOYA DE HERNANDEZ
473 U.S 531 (1985)

Upon her arrival at Los Angeles International Airport on a flight from Bogota, Colombia, respondent was detained by customs officials when, after examination of her passport and the contents of her valise and questioning by the officials, she was suspected of being a "balloon swallower," i. e., one who attempts to smuggle narcotics into this country hidden in her alimentary canal. She was detained incommunicado for almost 16 hours before the officials sought a court order authorizing a pregnancy test (she having claimed to be pregnant), an x ray, and a rectal examination.

During those 16 hours she was given the option of returning to Colombia on the next available flight, agreeing to an x ray, or remaining in detention until she produced a monitored bowel movement. She chose the first option, but the officials were unable to place her on the next flight, and she refused to use the toilet facilities. Pursuant to the court order, a pregnancy test was conducted at a hospital and proved negative, and a rectal examination resulted in the obtaining of 88 cocaine-filled balloons that had been smuggled in her alimentary canal.

Subsequently, after a suppression hearing, the District Court admitted the cocaine in evidence against respondent, and she was convicted of various federal narcotics offenses. The Court of Appeals reversed, holding that respondent's detention violated the Fourth Amendment because the customs officials did not have a "clear indication" of alimentary canal smuggling at the time respondent was detained.

The detention of a traveler at the border, beyond the scope of a routine customs search and inspection, is justified at its inception if customs agents, considering all the facts surrounding the traveler and her trip, reasonably suspect that the traveler is smuggling contraband in her alimentary canal; here, the facts, and their rational inferences, known to the customs officials clearly supported a reasonable suspicion that respondent was an alimentary canal smuggler.

. . . .

The "reasonable suspicion" standard effects a needed balance between private and public interests when law enforcement officials must make a limited intrusion on less than probable cause. It thus fits well into situations involving alimentary canal smuggling at the border: this type of smuggling gives no external signs, and inspectors will rarely possess probable cause to arrest or search, yet governmental interests in stopping smuggling at the border are high.

Under the circumstances, respondent's detention, while long, uncomfortable, and humiliating, was not unreasonably long. Alimentary canal smuggling cannot be detected in the amount of time in which other illegal activity may be investigated through brief stops. When respondent refused an x ray as an alternative to simply awaiting her bowel movement, the customs inspectors were left with only two practical alternatives: detain her for such time as necessary to confirm their suspicions or turn her loose into the interior of the country carrying the reasonably suspected contraband drugs. Moreover, both the length of respondent's detention and its discomfort resulted solely from the method that she chose to smuggle illicit drugs into this country. And in the presence of an articulable suspicion of alimentary canal smuggling, the customs officials were not required by the Fourth Amendment to pass respondent and her cocaine-filled balloons into the interior.

Inventory Searches

Local and state laws generally authorize the police to impound vehicles for certain reasons — to remove vehicles in accidents, to permit the flow of traffic, to preserve evidence, to remove damaged vehicles from the highways, to tow vehicles which are unlawfully parked, to remove the vehicle after the driver has been arrested, etc. The inventory search of an impounded vehicle is an administrative search and is considered reasonable under the Fourth Amendment as part of routine caretaking functions. Police officers do not conduct inventory searches to obtain evidence of criminal wrongdoing, but any evidence discovered the inventory falls within the plain view doctrine and is admissible despite the lack of a valid warrant.

Law enforcement officers also perform inventory searches of individuals before lodging them in the jail. All inventory searches are justified by the need to protect property and the custodians of the property. The Court requires inventory searches to be conducted under standardized procedures so that each inventory search is as similar to all other searches as possible. The scope of inventory searches is broad, and the search can be very thorough.

COLORADO v. BERTINE
479 U.S. 367 (1987)

CHIEF JUSTICE REHNQUIST delivered the opinion of the Court.

On February 10, 1984, a police officer in Boulder, Colorado, arrested respondent Steven Lee Bertine for driving while under the influence of alcohol. After Bertine was taken into custody and before the arrival of a tow truck to take Bertine's van to an impoundment lot, a backup officer inventoried the contents of the van. The officer opened a closed backpack in which he found controlled substances, cocaine paraphernalia, and a large amount of cash. Bertine was subsequently charged with driving while under the influence of alcohol, unlawful possession of cocaine with intent to dispense, sell, and distribute, and unlawful possession of methaqualone. We are asked to decide whether the Fourth Amendment prohibits the State from proving these charges with the evidence discovered during the inventory of Bertine's van. We hold that it does not.

The backup officer inventoried the van in accordance with local police procedures, which require a detailed inspection and inventory of impounded vehicles. He found the backpack directly behind the front seat of the van. Inside the pack, the officer observed a nylon bag containing metal canisters. Opening the canisters, the officer discovered that they contained cocaine, methaqualone tablets, cocaine paraphernalia, and $700 in cash. In an outside zippered pouch of the backpack, he also found $210 in cash in a sealed envelope. After completing the inventory of the van, the officer had the van towed to an impound lot and brought the backpack, money, and contraband to the police station.

After Bertine was charged with the offenses described above, he moved to suppress the evidence found during the inventory search on the ground, inter alia, that the search of the closed backpack and containers exceeded the permissible scope of such a search under the Fourth Amendment. The Colorado trial court ruled that probable cause supported Bertine's arrest and that the police officers had made the decisions to impound the vehicle and to conduct a thorough inventory search in good faith. Although noting that the inventory of the vehicle was performed in a "somewhat slipshod" manner, the District Court concluded that "the search of the backpack was done for the purpose of protecting the owner's property, protection of the police from subsequent claims of loss or stolen property, and the protection of the police from dangerous instrumentalities." The court observed that the standard procedures for impounding vehicles mandated a "detailed inventory involving the opening of containers and the listing of [their] contents." Based on these findings, the court determined that the inventory search did not violate Bertine's rights under the Fourth Amendment of the United States Constitution. The court, nevertheless, granted Bertine's motion to suppress, holding that the inventory search violated the Colorado Constitution.

We granted certiorari to consider the important and recurring question of federal law . . . [I]nventory searches are now a well-defined exception to the warrant requirement of the Fourth Amendment. The policies behind the warrant requirement are not implicated in an inventory search, nor is the related concept of probable cause:

> "The standard of probable cause is peculiarly related to criminal investigations, not routine, noncriminal procedures. . . . The probable-cause approach is unhelpful when analysis centers upon the reasonableness of routine administrative caretaking functions, particularly when no claim is made that the protective procedures are a subterfuge for criminal investigations."

[A]n inventory search may be "reasonable" under the Fourth Amendment even though it is not conducted pursuant to a warrant based upon probable cause. In *Opperman*, this Court assessed the reasonableness of an inventory search of the glove compartment in an abandoned automobile impounded by the police. We found that inventory procedures serve to protect an owner's property while it is in the custody of the police, to insure against claims of lost, stolen, or vandalized property, and to guard the police from danger. In light of these strong governmental interests and the diminished expectation of privacy in an automobile, we upheld the search. In reaching this decision, we observed that our cases accorded deference to police caretaking procedures designed to secure and protect vehicles and their contents within police custody.

In our more recent decision, *Lafayette*, a police officer conducted an inventory search of the contents of a shoulder bag in the possession of an individual being taken into custody. In deciding whether this search was reasonable, we recognized that the search served legitimate governmental interests similar to those identified in *Opperman*. We determined that those interests outweighed the individual's Fourth Amendment interests and upheld the search.

In the present case, as in *Opperman* and *Lafayette*, there was no showing that the police, who were following standardized procedures, acted in bad faith or for the sole purpose of investigation. In addition, the governmental interests justifying the inventory searches in *Opperman* and *Lafayette* are nearly the same as those which obtain here. In each case, the police were potentially responsible for the property taken into their custody. By securing the property, the police protected the property from unauthorized interference. Knowledge of the precise nature of the property helped guard against claims of theft, vandalism, or negligence. Such knowledge also helped to avert any danger to police or others that may have been posed by the property.

[T]he security of the storage facility does not completely eliminate the need for inventorying; the police may still wish to protect themselves or the owners of the lot against false claims of theft or dangerous instrumentalities. And while giving Bertine an opportunity to make alternative arrangements would undoubtedly have been possible, we said in *Lafayette*:

> "[T]he real question is not what `could have been achieved,' but whether the Fourth Amendment requires such steps . . . .

> "The reasonableness of any particular governmental activity does not necessarily or invariably turn on the existence of alternative `less intrusive' means."

We conclude that here. . . reasonable police regulations relating to inventory procedures administered in good faith satisfy the Fourth Amendment, even though courts might as a matter of hindsight be able to devise equally reasonable rules requiring a different procedure.

. . . .

Bertine . . . argues that the inventory search of his van was unconstitutional because departmental regulations gave the police officers discretion to choose between impounding his van and parking and locking it in a public parking place. . . . [We reject this argument]. Nothing in *Opperman* or *Lafayette* prohibits the exercise of police discretion so long as that discretion is exercised according to standard criteria and on the basis of something other than suspicion of evidence of criminal activity. Here, the discretion afforded the Boulder police was exercised in light to standardized criteria, related to the feasibility and appropriateness of parking and locking a vehicle rather than impounding it. There was no showing that the police chose to impound Bertine's van in order to investigate suspected criminal activity.

JUSTICE BLACKMUN, with whom JUSTICE POWELL and JUSTICE O'CONNOR join, concurring.

I join the Court's opinion, but write separately to underscore the importance of having such inventories conducted only pursuant to standardized police procedures. The underlying rationale for allowing an inventory exception to the Fourth Amendment warrant rule is that police officers are not vested with discretion to determine the scope of the inventory search. This absence of discretion ensures that inventory searches will not be used as a purposeful and general means of discovering evidence of crime. Thus, it is permissible for police officers to open closed containers in an inventory search only if they are following standard police procedures that mandate the opening of such containers in every impounded vehicle. . . .

JUSTICE MARSHALL, with whom JUSTICE BRENNAN joins, dissenting. Omitted.

Even if inventory was proper for the car, it shouldn't extend to the backpack.

Fire Inspections

When fire fighters enter a burning building, they are government agents who are intruding on a business or homeowners expectation of privacy, but we certainly don't expect them to get a warrant before they can enter to put out the fire. However, firefighters don't just put out fires, they look for the source of the fire and investigate possible arson — a crime. The Court in two Michigan cases, *Michigan v. Tyler*, 436 U.S. 499 (1978) and *Michigan v. Clifford*, 464 U.S 287 (1984), announced administrative search and criminal search rules in the fire inspection context.

Michigan v. Tyler involved firefighters entering a furniture store at midnight. Two hours later the inspector arrived to determine the cause of the fire — about the same time as the firefighters were watering down the embers. By 3:30 a.m., a police detective was at the scene taking pictures of the suspected arson and he left shortly afterwards because the darkness and smoke made further inspection impossible. At 8:00 a.m. fire inspectors returned after the fire was completely extinguished and the building was empty. They left and then again returned at 9:30 with the police investigator and conducted a search in which they discovered more evidence of arson. The investigators left to get tools to seize the incriminating evidence. Three weeks later, a state police arson inspector returned to take pictures. All the entries were made without consent or warrants. The Court held that the Fourth Amendment applied to the postfire searches. Accordingly, the court found that the searches before and including the 9:30 search were continuations of the valid search that began in the middle of the night. All of the searches and entries after the 9:30 search were separate searches and a warrant was needed. The court held that the photographs by the state police arson inspector were not admissible without a warrant as too much time had elapsed.

Michigan v. Clifford involved fire fighters responding to a house fire at 5:40 a.m. By 7:00 a.m. they had put out the blaze and left the scene. By 8:00 a.m. the fire inspector received an order to investigate, but because he had other cases he didn't get to the scene until 1:00 p.m. When he got there, he found that the owner had hired a work crew to board up the house and pump out the water. (Clifford was away on vacation but communicating through his neighbor and insurance agent). When the work crew left, the investigators entered the basement and found evidence of an arson. The evidence was seized. The Court held that the seizure was a violation of the Fourth Amendment. It found that by hiring a crew to board up and pump out the house, the owner manifested his expectation of privacy in his home and the officer should have obtained an administrative search warrant before entering. The time lapse demonstrated there was no emergency, and once the officers found incriminating items in the basement, it was necessary to halt the search and take the evidence to a magistrate to seek a criminal search warrant.

School Searches

The Court's first school search case was *New Jersey v. T.L.O.,* 469 U.S. 325 (1985). *T.L.O.* is important for several reasons. First, in it, the Court established the "special needs doctrine" which it has applied in other contexts. Second, the court balanced the needs of schools against the students' privacy interests. Third, although holding that schools, to some extent, do act *in loco parentis* (school administrators are substitute parents while students are in school), students nevertheless enjoy the protections of the Bill of Rights even while they are in school.

In *T.L.O,* a teacher had discovered a 14-year-old freshman smoking in the bathroom in violation of a school rule. She was brought into the principal's office and questioned by an assistant vice principal. She denied that she had been smoking and claimed that she did not smoke. The assistant vice principal demanded to see her purse, opened the purse, found a package of cigarettes, removed the cigarettes and noticed a package of rolling papers. He searched the purse more thoroughly and found marijuana, a pipe, plastic bags, and a substantial quantity of money in one-dollar bills, an index card containing a list of those students who owed T.L.O. money and two letters that implicated her in marijuana dealing. The state brought delinquency charges, adjudicated T.L.O. as delinquent, and she received a one-year probation sentence. She appealed.

The Court held that the Fourth Amendment applied to searches by school officials but that this particular search was reasonable. Justice White's opined that T.L.O. retained a Fourth Amendment privacy interest in her person and "there is no reason to conclude that students have necessarily waived all rights to privacy in such items (the court noted High School students may carry keys, money, necessaries of personal hygiene and grooming in purses and book bags and might also carry "highly personal items" such as photographs, letters and diaries.) merely by bringing them onto school grounds." The Court disagreed with the state's argument that public school students have no reasonable expectation of privacy in school. The Fourth Amendment's ban on unreasonable searches and seizures applies to searches conducted by public schools, and the school can't escape the commands of the Fourth Amendment because of their authority over school children. When schools search students, they aren't acting *in loco parentis,* and students have a reasonable expectation of privacy.

In analyzing whether the search of T.L.O. was reasonable, the Court noted that there was no warrant and no probable cause to believe the minor study was carrying drugs. The Striking a balance between the student's reasonable expectation of privacy and the schools legitimate need to maintain a healthy learning environment by enforcing school rules such as the ban on smoking, the Court found that a "warrant requirement, in particular, is unsuited to the school environment: requiring a teacher to obtain a warrant before searching a child suspected of an infraction of school rules (or of the criminal law) would unduly interfere with the maintenance of the swift and informal disciplinary procedures needed in the schools."

The majority and dissent disagreed on the standard of evidence needed for a warrantless school search by a teacher or administrator in a public school setting. The majority believed that reasonable suspicion sufficed, but the dissent would have required probable cause. Because T.L.O. denied smoking after being caught, it was reasonable for the vice principal to resolve the dispute by inspecting her purse to determine if she carried cigarettes. When the vice principal saw rolling papers, he had some suspicion that she might be in possession of marijuana. The observation of the rolling papers did not give rise to probable cause, however. The majority concluded the vice principal had reasonable suspicion sufficient to justify the warrantless search. The dissenters agreed that the school need not have obtained a warrant, but found that under these facts the search was not reasonable because the administrators lacked probable cause.

Justice White wrote that "the special needs of the school environment require assessment of the legality of such searches against a standard less exacting than that of probable cause." Justice

Blackmun wrote, "Only in those exceptional circumstances in which *special needs*, beyond the normal need for law enforcement, make the warrant and probable-cause requirement impracticable, is a court entitled to substitute its balancing of interests for that of the Framers." Later cases applied this reasoning from *T.L.O* and its formulation of a "special needs doctrine."

In *Stafford School District #1 v Redding* the Court examined whether the school district was entitled to immunity in a civil suit filed by the student after she was strip-searched at school (a more intrusive search than what occurred in *T.L.O.*).

STAFFORD UNIFIED SCHOOL DISTRICT #1 v. REDDING
557 U.S. 364 (2009)

JUSTICE SOUTER delivered the opinion of the Court.

SUMMARY: 13-year-old Savana Redding was subject to what the Court characterized as a strip search. School officials had searched her bra and underpants in their quest to find prescription-strength ibuprofen they had reasonable suspicion to believe she possessed at school. The school had policies strictly prohibiting the use or possession of any drug, including prescription or over-the-counter-drugs, and they first searched her backpack without finding the drugs.

After the search, Savana's mother sued the school and the school officials alleging they violated Savana's Fourth Amendment rights. The assistant principle, Wilson, the administrative assistant, Romero, and the school nurse, Schwalllier, all claimed that the search met the requirements of T.L.O, and in any event, they had qualified immunity for their actions.

The Court had to decide whether reasonable suspicion required to conduct at school which was announced in T.L.O sufficed for the more intrusive strip search. The Court balanced Savana's heightened expectation of privacy in a strip search (embarrassing, frightening, humiliating for a 13 year old) against the schools need to keep drugs (of any kind) off campus. The Court seemingly acknowledged that the reasonableness of the search in this context was colored by the balance of non-dangerous contraband against the extreme intrusiveness of the search.

OPINION: "The indignity of the search does not, of course, outlaw it, but it does implicate the rule of reasonableness as stated in *T. L. O.* that "the search as actually conducted [be] reasonably related in scope to the circumstances which justified the interference in the first place." The scope will be permissible, that is, when it is "not excessively intrusive in light of the age and sex of the student and the nature of the infraction."

Here, the content of the suspicion failed to match the degree of intrusion. ...

...[There is a] . . . quantum leap from outer clothes and backpacks to exposure of intimate parts. The meaning of such a search, and the degradation its subject may reasonably feel, place a search that intrusive in a category of its own demanding its own specific suspicions.

T. L. O. directed school officials to limit the intrusiveness of a search, "in light of the age and sex of the student and the nature of the infraction," and as we have just said at some length, the intrusiveness of the strip search here cannot be seen as justifiably related to the circumstances. But we realize that the lower courts have reached divergent conclusions regarding how the *T. L. O.* standard applies to such searches.

The strip search of Savana Redding was unreasonable and a violation of the Fourth Amendment, but petitioners Wilson, Romero, and Schwallier are nevertheless protected from liability through qualified immunity." . . .

JUSTICE STEVENS, with whom JUSTICE GINSBURG joins, concurring in part and dissenting in part.

In *New Jersey v. T. L. O.*, 469 U. S. 325 (1985), the Court established a two-step inquiry for determining the reasonableness of a school official's decision to search a student. First, the Court explained, the search must be " 'justified at its inception' " by the presence of "reasonable grounds for suspecting that the search will turn up evidence that the student has violated or is violating either the law or the rules of the school." Second, the search must be "permissible in its scope," which is achieved "when the measures adopted are reasonably related to the objectives of the search and not excessively intrusive in light of the age and sex of the student and the nature of the infraction."

Nothing the Court decides today alters this basic framework. It simply applies *T. L. O.* to declare unconstitutional a strip search of a 13-year-old honors student that was based on a groundless suspicion that she might be hiding medicine in her underwear. This is, in essence, a case in which clearly established law meets clearly outrageous conduct. I have long believed that " '[i]t does not require a constitutional scholar to conclude that a nude search of a 13-year-old child is an invasion of constitutional rights of some magnitude.' " The strip search of Savana Redding in this case was both more intrusive and less justified than the search of the student's purse in *T. L. O.* . . . .

JUSTICE GINSBURG, concurring in part and dissenting in part.

Any reasonable search for the pills would have ended when inspection of Redding's backpack and jacket pockets yielded nothing. Wilson had no cause to suspect, based on prior experience at the school or clues in this case, that Redding had hidden pills — containing the equivalent of two Advils or one Aleve — in her underwear or body. To make matters worse, Wilson did not release Redding, to return to class or to go home, after the search. Instead, he made her sit on a chair outside his office for over two hours. At no point did he

attempt to call her parent. Abuse of authority of that order should not be shielded by official immunity.

In contrast to *T. L. O.*, where a teacher discovered a student smoking in the lavatory, and where the search was confined to the student's purse, the search of Redding involved her body and rested on the bare accusation of another student whose reliability the Assistant Principal had no reason to trust. The Court's opinion in *T. L. O.* plainly stated the controlling Fourth Amendment law: A search ordered by a school official, even if "justified at its inception," crosses the constitutional boundary if it becomes "excessively intrusive in light of the age and sex of the student and the nature of the infraction."

Here, "the nature of the [supposed] infraction," the slim basis for suspecting Savana Redding, and her "age and sex," establish beyond doubt that Assistant Principal Wilson's order cannot be reconciled with this Court's opinion in *T. L. O.* Wilson's treatment of Redding was abusive and it was not reasonable for him to believe that the law permitted it. I join Justice Stevens in dissenting from the Court's acceptance of Wilson's qualified immunity plea, and would affirm the Court of Appeals' judgment in all respects.

JUSTICE THOMAS, concurring in the judgment in part and dissenting in part.

I would hold that the search of Savana Redding did not violate the Fourth Amendment. The majority imposes a vague and amorphous standard on school administrators. It also grants judges sweeping authority to second-guess the measures that these officials take to maintain discipline in their schools and ensure the health and safety of the students in their charge. This deep intrusion into the administration of public schools exemplifies why the Court should return to the common-law doctrine of in loco parentis under which "the judiciary was reluctant to interfere in the routine business of school administration, allowing schools and teachers to set and enforce rules and to maintain order." But even under the prevailing Fourth Amendment test established by *New Jersey v. T. L. O.*, 469 U. S. 325 (1985), all petitioners, including the school district, are entitled to judgment as a matter of law in their favor.

. . .

Here, petitioners had reasonable grounds to suspect that Redding was in possession of prescription and nonprescription drugs in violation of the school's prohibition of the "non-medical use, possession, or sale of a drug" on school property or at school events. . . . Fourth Amendment searches do not occur in a vacuum; rather, context must inform the judicial inquiry. In this instance, the suspicion of drug possession arose at a

middle school that had "a history of problems with students using and distributing prohibited and illegal substances on campus."

. . .

In determining whether the search's scope was reasonable under the Fourth Amendment, it is therefore irrelevant whether officials suspected Redding of possessing prescription-strength Ibuprofen, nonprescription-strength Naproxen, or some harder street drug. Safford prohibited its possession on school property. Reasonable suspicion that Redding was in possession of drugs in violation of these policies, therefore, justified a search extending to any area where small pills could be concealed. The search did not violate the Fourth Amendment.

Special Needs: Drug Tests

The second major school search case that the Court decided involved drug testing of high school students involved in athletics. In *Vernonia School District 47J v. Acton*, 515 U.S. 646 (1995), the high school in Vernonia, Oregon had enacted mandatory, random urinalysis testing of all students involved in interscholastic athletic programs. James Acton (a 14-year-old junior highschooler) sought a preliminary injunction against this policy. Whereas *T.L.O.* involved individualized suspicion, the search in *Acton* was suspicionless.

Vernonia refers to two important drug testing cases also decided under the "special needs doctrine" — *Skinner v. Railway Labor Executives' Assn.* (1989) and *National Treasury Employees Union v. Von Raab* (1989). In Skinner the court upheld a federal law that mandated drug testing of all on-site employees after a major train accident, whether the employees worked for a private railroad company line or a line run by the government. In *Van Raab*, U.S. Customs Service required automatic drug testing for the hiring or promotion of all officers who (1) are directly involved in drug law enforcement, (2) must carry firearms, or (3) handle classified material that drug smugglers could get by bribing or blackmailing drug-dependent employees. The program was not designed to prevent on-the-job impairment but to ensure that customs officers in drug enforcement would lead drug-free lives. The Court upheld drug testing for agents involved in drug law enforcement and those who carried firearms but could not agree on the reasonableness of testing agents handling classified information (and sent it back for further fact-finding).

VERNONIA SCHOOL DISTRICT 47J v. ACTON
515 U.S. 646 (1995)

JUSTICE SCALIA delivered the opinion of the Court.

The Student Athlete Drug Policy adopted by School District 47J in the town of Vernonia, Oregon, authorizes random urinalysis drug testing of students who participate in the

District's school athletics programs. We granted certiorari to decide whether this violates the Fourth and Fourteenth Amendments to the United States Constitution.

Petitioner Vernonia School District 47J (District) operates one high school and three grade schools in the logging community of Vernonia, Oregon. As elsewhere in small-town America, school sports play a prominent role in the town's life, and student athletes are admired in their schools and in the community.

Drugs had not been a major problem in Vernonia schools. In the mid-to-late 1980's, however, teachers and administrators observed a sharp increase in drug use. Students began to speak out about their attraction to the drug culture, and to boast that there was nothing the school could do about it. Along with more drugs came more disciplinary problems. Between 1988 and 1989 the number of disciplinary referrals in Vernonia schools rose to more than twice the number reported in the early 1980's, and several students were suspended. Students became increasingly rude during class; outbursts of profane language became common.

Not only were student athletes included among the drug users but, as the District Court found, athletes were the leaders of the drug culture. This caused the District's administrators particular concern, since drug use increases the risk of sports-related injury. Expert testimony at the trial confirmed the deleterious effects of drugs on motivation, memory, judgment, reaction, coordination, and performance. The high school football and wrestling coach witnessed a severe sternum injury suffered by a wrestler, and various omissions of safety procedures and misexecutions by football players, all attributable in his belief to the effects of drug use.

Initially, the District responded to the drug problem by offering special classes, speakers, and presentations designed to deter drug use. It even brought in a specially trained dog to detect drugs, but the drug problem persisted. According to the District Court:

"[T]he administration was at its wits end and . . . a large segment of the student body, particularly those involved in

interscholastic athletics, was in a state of rebellion. Disciplinary problems had reached `epidemic proportions.' The coincidence of an almost three-fold increase in classroom disruptions and disciplinary reports along with the staff's direct observations of students using drugs or glamorizing drug and alcohol use led the administration to the inescapable conclusion that the rebellion was being fueled by alcohol and drug abuse as well as the student's misperceptions about the drug culture."

At that point, District officials began considering a drug-testing program. They held a parent "input night" to discuss the proposed Student Athlete Drug Policy (Policy), and the parents in attendance gave their unanimous approval. The school board approved the Policy for implementation in the fall of 1989. Its expressed purpose is to prevent student athletes from using drugs, to protect their health and safety, and to provide drug users with assistance programs.

The Policy applies to all students participating in interscholastic athletics. Students wishing to play sports must sign a form consenting to the testing and must obtain the written consent of their parents. Athletes are tested at the beginning of the season for their sport. In addition, once each week of the season the names of the athletes are placed in a "pool" from which a student, with the supervision of two adults, blindly draws the names of 10% of the athletes for random testing. Those selected are notified and tested that same day, if possible.

The student to be tested completes a specimen control form which bears an assigned number. Prescription medications that the student is taking must be identified by providing a copy of the prescription or a doctor's authorization. The student then enters an empty locker room accompanied by an adult monitor of the same sex. Each boy selected produces a sample at a urinal, remaining fully clothed with his back to the monitor, who stands approximately 12 to 15 feet behind the student. Monitors may (though do not always) watch the student while he produces the sample, and they listen for normal sounds of urination. Girls produce samples in an enclosed bathroom stall, so that they can be heard but not observed. After the sample is produced, it is given to the monitor, who checks it for temperature and tampering and then transfers it to a vial.

The samples are sent to an independent laboratory, which routinely tests them for amphetamines, cocaine, and marijuana. Other drugs, such as LSD, may be screened at the request of the District, but the identity of a particular student does not determine which drugs will be tested. The laboratory's procedures are 99.94% accurate. The District follows strict procedures regarding the chain of custody and access to test results. The laboratory does not know the identity of the students whose samples it tests. It is authorized to mail written test reports only to the superintendent and to provide test results to District personnel by telephone only after the requesting official recites a code confirming his authority. Only the superintendent, principals, vice-principals, and athletic directors have access to test results, and the results are not kept for more than one year.

If a sample tests positive, a second test is administered as soon as possible to confirm the result. If the second test is negative, no further action is taken. If the second test is positive, the athlete's parents are notified, and the school principal convenes a meeting with the student and his parents, at which the student is given the option of (1) participating for six weeks in an assistance program that includes weekly urinalysis, or (2) suffering suspension from athletics for the remainder of the current season and the next athletic season. The student is then retested prior to the start of the next athletic season for which he or she is eligible. The Policy states that a second offense results in automatic imposition of option (2); a third offense in suspension for the remainder of the current season and the next two athletic seasons.

In the fall of 1991, respondent James Acton, then a seventh-grader, signed up to play football at one of the District's grade schools. He was denied participation, however, because he and his parents refused to sign the testing consent forms. The Actons filed suit, seeking declaratory and injunctive relief from enforcement of the Policy on the grounds that it violated the Fourth and Fourteenth Amendments to the United States Constitution and Article I § 9, of the Oregon Constitution.

. . .We have held that the Fourteenth Amendment extends this constitutional guarantee to searches and seizures by state officers, including public school officials, *New Jersey v. T. L. O.*, (1985). In *Skinner v. Railway Labor Executives' Assn.* , we held that state-compelled collection and testing of urine, such as that required by the Student Athlete Drug Policy, constitutes a "search" subject to the demands of the Fourth Amendment.

As the text of the Fourth Amendment indicates, the ultimate measure of the constitutionality of a governmental search is "reasonableness." At least in a case such as this, where there was no clear practice, either approving or disapproving the type of search at issue, at the time the constitutional provision was enacted, whether a particular search meets the reasonableness standard "`is judged by balancing its intrusion on the individual's Fourth Amendment interests against its promotion of legitimate governmental interests.'" Where a search is undertaken by law enforcement officials to discover evidence of criminal wrongdoing, this Court has said that reasonableness generally requires the obtaining of a judicial warrant. Warrants cannot be issued, of course, without the showing of probable cause required by the Warrant Clause. But a warrant is not required to establish the reasonableness of all government searches; and when a warrant is not required (and the Warrant Clause therefore not applicable), probable cause is not invariably required either. A search unsupported by probable cause can be constitutional, we have said, "when special needs, beyond the normal need for law enforcement, make the warrant and probable-cause requirement impracticable."

We have found such "special needs" to exist in the public-school context. There, the warrant requirement "would unduly interfere with the maintenance of the swift and informal disciplinary procedures [that are] needed," and "strict adherence to the requirement that searches be based upon probable cause" would undercut "the substantial need of teachers and administrators for freedom to maintain order in the schools." The school search we approved in *T. L. O.*, while not based on probable cause, was based on individualized suspicion of wrongdoing. We have upheld suspicionless searches and seizures to conduct drug testing of railroad personnel involved in train accidents; to conduct random drug testing of federal customs officers who carry arms or are involved in drug interdiction; and to maintain automobile checkpoints looking for illegal immigrants and contraband.

The first factor to be considered is the nature of the privacy interest upon which the search here at issue intrudes. The Fourth Amendment does not protect all subjective expectations of privacy, but only those that society recognizes as "legitimate." What expectations are legitimate varies, of course, with context, depending, for example, upon whether the individual asserting the privacy interest is at home, at work, in a car, or in a public park. . . .

. . . School sports are not for the bashful. They require "suiting up" before each practice or event, and showering and changing afterwards. Public school locker rooms, the usual sites for these activities, are not notable for the privacy they afford. The locker rooms in Vernonia are typical: no individual dressing rooms are provided; shower heads are lined up along a wall, unseparated by any sort of partition or curtain; not even all the toilet stalls have doors. . . . [T]here is "an element of `communal undress' inherent in athletic participation."

There is an additional respect in which school athletes have a reduced expectation of privacy. By choosing to "go out for the team," they voluntarily subject themselves to a degree of regulation even higher than that imposed on students generally. In Vernonia's public schools, they must submit to a preseason physical exam (James testified that his included the giving of a urine sample), they must acquire adequate insurance coverage or sign an insurance waiver, maintain a minimum grade point average, and comply with any "rules of conduct, dress, training hours and related matters as may be established for each sport by the head coach and athletic director with the principal's approval." Somewhat like adults who choose to participate in a "closely regulated industry," students who voluntarily participate in school athletics have reason to expect intrusions upon normal rights and privileges, including privacy.

Having considered the scope of the legitimate expectation of privacy at issue here, we turn next to the character of the intrusion that is complained of. . . . [The] degree of intrusion depends upon the manner in which production of the urine sample is monitored. Under the District's Policy, male students produce samples at a urinal along a wall. They remain fully clothed and are only observed from behind, if at all. Female students produce samples in an enclosed stall, with a female monitor standing outside listening only for sounds of tampering. These conditions are nearly identical to those typically encountered in public restrooms, which men, women, and especially school children use daily. Under such conditions, the privacy interests compromised by the process of obtaining the urine sample are in our view negligible. The other privacy-invasive aspect of urinalysis is, of course, the information it discloses concerning the state of the subject's body, and the materials he has ingested. In this regard it is significant that the tests at issue here look only for drugs, and not for whether the student is, for example, epileptic, pregnant, or diabetic. Moreover, the drugs for which the samples are screened are standard, and do not vary according to the identity of the student. And finally, the results of the tests are disclosed only to a limited class of school personnel who have a need to know; and they are not turned over to law enforcement authorities or used for any internal disciplinary function.

Respondents argue, however, that the District's Policy is in fact more intrusive than this suggests, because it requires the students, if they are to avoid sanctions for a falsely positive test, to identify in advance prescription medications they are taking. We agree that this raises some cause for concern . . . . On the other hand, we have never indicated that requiring advance disclosure of medications is per se unreasonable. Indeed, in *Skinner* we held that it was not "a significant invasion of privacy." It can be argued that, in *Skinner*, the disclosure went only to the medical personnel taking the sample, and the Government personnel analyzing it, (railroad personnel responsible for forwarding the sample, and presumably accompanying information, to the Government's testing lab); and that disclosure to teachers and coaches - to persons who personally know the student - is a greater invasion of privacy. . . .

The General Authorization Form that respondents refused to sign, which refusal was the basis for James's exclusion from the sports program, said only (in relevant part): "I . . . authorize the Vernonia School District to conduct a test on a urine specimen which I provide to test for drugs and/or alcohol use. I also authorize the release of information concerning the results of such a test to the Vernonia School District and to the parents and/or guardians of the student." While the practice of the District seems to have been to have a school official take medication information from the student at the time of the test, that practice is not set forth in, or required by, the Policy, which says simply: "Student athletes who . . . are or have been taking prescription medication must provide verification (either by a copy of the prescription or by doctor's authorization) prior to being tested." It may well be that, if and when James was selected for random testing at a time that he was taking medication, the School District would have permitted him to provide the requested information in a confidential manner - for example, in a sealed envelope delivered to the testing lab. Nothing in the Policy contradicts that, and when

respondents choose, in effect, to challenge the Policy on its face, we will not assume the worst. Accordingly, we reach the same conclusion as in *Skinner*: that the invasion of privacy was not significant.

Finally, we turn to consider the nature and immediacy of the governmental concern at issue here, and the efficacy of this means for meeting it. In both *Skinner* and *Von Raab*, we characterized the government interest motivating the search as "compelling." *Skinner*, (interest in preventing railway accidents); *Von Raab*, (interest in insuring fitness of customs officials to interdict drugs and handle firearms). Relying on these cases, the District Court held that because the District's program also called for drug testing in the absence of individualized suspicion, the District "must demonstrate a `compelling need' for the program." The Court of Appeals appears to have agreed with this view. It is a mistake, however, to think that the phrase "compelling state interest," in the Fourth Amendment context, describes a fixed, minimum quantum of governmental concern, so that one can dispose of a case by answering in isolation the question: Is there a compelling state interest here? Rather, the phrase describes an interest which appears important enough to justify the particular search at hand, in light of other factors which show the search to be relatively intrusive upon a genuine expectation of privacy. Whether that relatively high degree of government concern is necessary in this case or not, we think it is met.

That the nature of the concern is important - indeed, perhaps compelling can hardly be doubted. Deterring drug use by our Nation's schoolchildren is at least as important as enhancing efficient enforcement of the Nation's laws against the importation of drugs, which was the governmental concern in *Von Raab*, or deterring drug use by engineers and trainmen, which was the governmental concern in *Skinner*. . . . Finally, it must not be lost sight of that this program is directed more narrowly to drug use by school athletes, where the risk of immediate physical harm to the drug user or those with whom he is playing his sport is particularly high. Apart from psychological effects, which include impairment of judgment, slow reaction time, and a lessening of the perception of pain, the particular drugs screened by the District's Policy have been demonstrated to pose substantial physical risks to athletes.

As for the immediacy of the District's concerns: We are not inclined to question - indeed, we could not possibly find clearly erroneous - the District Court's conclusion that "a large segment of the student body, particularly those involved in interscholastic athletics, was in a state of rebellion," that "[d]isciplinary actions had reached `epidemic proportions,'" and that "the rebellion was being fueled by alcohol and drug abuse as well as by the student's misperceptions about the drug culture." That is an immediate crisis of greater proportions than existed in *Skinner*, where we upheld the Government's drug testing program based on findings of drug use by railroad employees nationwide, without proof that a problem existed on the particular railroads whose employees were subject to the test. And of much greater proportions than existed in *Von Raab*, where there was no documented history of drug use by any customs officials.

As to the efficacy of this means for addressing the problem: It seems to us self-evident that a drug problem largely fueled by the "role model" effect of athletes' drug use, and of particular danger to athletes, is effectively addressed by making sure that athletes do not use drugs. Respondents argue that a "less intrusive means to the same end" was available, namely, "drug testing on suspicion of drug use." We have repeatedly refused to declare that only the "least intrusive" search practicable can be reasonable under the Fourth Amendment. . . . In many respects, we think, testing based on "suspicion" of drug use would not be better, but worse.

Taking into account all the factors we have considered above - the decreased expectation of privacy, the relative unobtrusiveness of the search, and the severity of the need met by the search - we conclude Vernonia's Policy is reasonable and hence constitutional.

We caution against the assumption that suspicionless drug testing will readily pass constitutional muster in other contexts. The most significant element in this case is the first we discussed: that the Policy was undertaken in furtherance of the government's responsibilities, under a public school system, as guardian and tutor of children entrusted to its care. . . . [W]hen the government acts as guardian and tutor the relevant question is whether the search is one that a reasonable guardian and tutor might undertake. Given the findings of need made by the District Court, we conclude that in the present case it is.

We may note that the primary guardians of Vernonia's schoolchildren appear to agree. The record shows no objection to this districtwide program by any parents other than the couple before us here - even though, as we have described, a public meeting was held to obtain parents' views. We find insufficient basis to contradict the judgment of Vernonia's parents, its school board, and the District Court, as to what was reasonably in the interest of these children under the circumstances.

[SUMMARY: Justice O'Connor dissented, criticizing the lack of individual suspicion. She stated, "[t]he Court's decision subjects millions of student athletes, the 'overwhelming majority' who have given school officials "no reason whatsoever to suspect they use drugs at school, to an intrusive bodily search." She noted that the costs of failure to drug test school athletes simply did not put the lives and safety of many people at risk. Therefore, she concluded, the school district cannot decide to discard individualized suspicion without specific and compelling reasons to show that eliminating individualized suspicion is reasonable.]

Board of Education of Independent School District No. 92 of Pottawatomie County v. Earls, 536 U.S. 822 (2002)

SUMMARY: The Court extended the rule of Vernonia to high school students engaged in any extracurricular activities. Although the *Earls* Court found no evidence of a widespread drug problem in the Tecumseh, Oklahoma schools, it did note some evidence that overall the drug problem had grown worse.

Justice Ginsburg dissented. She concluded that the two reasons justifying the drug tests in Vernonia— that drug use could be physically harmful for athletes and that athletes were leaders of an aggressive drug cult — did not apply to all extracurricular activities

"At the margins, of course, no policy of *random* drug testing is perfectly tailored to the harms it seeks to address. The School District cites the dangers faced by members of the band, who must "perform extremely precise routines with heavy equipment and instruments in close proximity to other students," and by Future Farmers of America, who "are required to individually control and restrain animals as large as 1500 pounds." For its part, the United States acknowledges that "the linebacker faces a greater risk of serious injury if he takes the field under the influence of drugs than the drummer in the halftime band," but parries that "the risk of injury to a student who is under the influence of drugs while playing golf, cross country, or volleyball (sports covered by the policy in *Vernonia*) is scarcely any greater than the risk of injury to a student . . .handling a 1500-pound steer (as [Future Farmers of America] members do) or working with cutlery or other sharp instruments (as [Future Homemakers of America] members do)." ... Notwithstanding nightmarish images of out-of-control flatware, livestock run amok, and colliding tubas disturbing the peace and quiet of Tecumseh, the great majority of students the School District seeks to test in truth are engaged in activities that are not safety sensitive to an unusual degree. There is a difference between imperfect tailoring and no tailoring at all.

To summarize, this case resembles *Vernonia* only in that the School Districts in both cases conditioned engagement in activities outside the obligatory curriculum on random subjection to urinalysis. The defining characteristics of the two programs, however, are entirely dissimilar. The Vernonia district sought to test a subpopulation of students distinguished by their reduced expectation of privacy, their special susceptibility to drug-related injury, and their heavy involvement with drug use. The Tecumseh district seeks to test a much larger population associated with none of these factors. It does so, moreover, without carefully safeguarding student confidentiality and without regard to the program's untoward effects. A program so sweeping is not sheltered by *Vernonia;* its unreasonable reach renders it impermissible under the Fourth Amendment."

Commonwealth v. Neilson, 423 Mass. 75 (1996)

NOTE: Searches of college dormitories are not exactly the same as a school search for a couple of reasons: there is no in loco parentis rationale, college students are generally adults. Moreover, dormitories generally have students sign residence hall contracts allowing consent to search to enforce college health and safety regulations. So, these searches may be justified under a consent rationale rather than a special needs rationale.

SUMMARY: In *Neilson*, the defendant was charged with illegal possession of marijuana after a maintenance worker heard a cat inside his dormitory suite. The worker reported the information to college officials, who visited the suite and informed one of the residents that the cat must be removed pursuant to university health and safety regulations. That afternoon a university official posted a notice on the suite informing students of a possible violation of college policy and notifying them that a door-to-door check would be conducted. That night officials returned; defendant was not present, and while searching the room, officials noticed a light emanating from the closet. Fearing a fire hazard, they opened the close and discovered two four-foot-tall marijuana plants, fertilizer, grow lights, etc. School officials stopped their investigation at this point, and called in the local campus police. They entered the room, observed the marijuana, took pictures, seized and removed all the contraband from the room — all without a warrant.

Neilson has signed a residence hall contract that provided, "residence life staff members will enter student rooms to inspect for hazards to health or personal safety." Accordingly, Neilson didn't argue that the initial entry by the residence hall staff was improper. He consented to reasonable searches to enforce college health and safety regulations and recognized that the search for the cat was within the scope of that consent. He did argue that his constitutional rights were violated when the campus police searched the room and seized the evidence. The court agreed,

> "The police entered the room without a warrant, consent, or exigent circumstances. This search was unreasonable and violated the defendant's Fourth Amendment rights. . . First, there was no consent to the police entry and search of the room. The defendant's consent was given not to police officials, but to the University and the latter cannot fragmentize, share, or delegate it. … Second, the plain view doctrine does not apply to the police seizure, where the officers were not lawfully present in the dormitory room when they made their plain view observations. While the college officials were legitimately present in the room to enforce a reasonable health and safety regulation, the sole purpose of the warrantless police entry into the dormitory room was to confiscate contraband for purposes of a criminal proceeding."

Probation And Parole Searches

In *Griffin v. Wisconsin*, 483 U.S. 868 (1987) the court extended the special needs doctrine to warrantless entry and search of a probationer's home by probation officers on reasonable grounds to believe that contraband was present. "Although a probationer had a Fourth Amendment reasonable expectation of privacy in his home, the existence of reasonable grounds to believe contraband is present creates a special need, beyond the normal need for law enforcement, to justify the warrantless search and seizure of the probationer's house."

In *Samson v. California*, 547 U.S. 843 (2006), the Court examined the suspicionless searches of individuals on parole in California. California law required every prisoner eligible for release on state parole to "agree in writing to be subject to search or seizure by a parole officer or other peace officer at any time of the day or night, with or without a search warrant and with or without cause." The Court stated,

> "Examining the totality of the circumstances pertaining to petitioner's status as a parolee, "an established variation on imprisonment," . . . including the plain terms of the parole search condition, we conclude that petitioner did not have an expectation of privacy that society would recognize as legitimate.

> The State's interest, by contrast, are substantial. This Court has repeatedly acknowledged that a State has an overwhelming interest in supervising parolees because "parolees. . . are more likely to commit future criminal offenses." Similarly, this Court has repeatedly acknowledged that a state's interests in reducing recidivism and thereby promoting reintegration and positive citizenship among probationers and parolees warrant privacy intrusions that would not otherwise be tolerated under the Fourth Amendment. . . .

Justice Stevens issued a strong dissent, stating:

"Not surprisingly, the majority does not seek to justify the search of petitioner on "special needs" grounds. Although the Court has in the past relied on special needs to uphold warrantless searches of probationers, . . . it has never gone so far as to hold that a probationer or parolee may be subjected to full search at the whim of any law enforcement officer he happens to encounter, whether or not the officer has reason to suspect him of wrongdoing. *Griffin*, after all, involved a search by a probation officer that was supported by reasonable suspicion. The special role of probation officers was critical to the analysis; "we deal with a situation," the Court explained, "in which there is an ongoing supervisory relationship — and one that is not, or at least not entirely, adversarial — between the object of the search and the decisionmaker." . . . The State's interest or "special need," as articulated in *Griffin*, was an interest in supervising the wayward probationer's reintegration into society — not, or at least not principally, the general law enforcement goal of detecting crime . . .

... [T]he Court for the first time upholds an entirely suspicionless search unsupported by any special need. And it goes further: In special needs cases we have at least insisted upon programmatic safeguards designed to ensure evenhandedness in application; if individualized suspicion is to be jettisoned, it must be replaced with measures to protect against the state actor's unfettered discretion. . . . Here, by contrast, there are no policies in place — no "standards, guidelines, or procedures," –to rein in officers and furnish a bulwark against the arbitrary exercise of discretion that is the height of unreasonableness. . . ."

Prison And Prisoner Searches

Historically, prisoners had no Fourth Amendment rights. *Lanza v. New York, 370 U.S. 139* (1962), held that a "jail shares none of the attributes of privacy of a home, automobile, an office or hotel room, . . . and official surveillance had traditionally been the rule of the day in prisons," 370 US, at 139. In *Hudson v. Palmer, 468 U.S. 517* (1984), the court conceded that prisoners may have some recognizable expectation of privacy and that "prisons are not beyond the reach of the Constitution." 468 U.S., at 523. The Court indicated that the reasonableness of prisoner searches depends on balancing the need to maintain prison and jail security, safety, and discipline against the invasion to prisoners' substantially reduced reasonable expectation of privacy. Applying this balancing approach, the Court concluded that an unannounced search of prisoners and their cells for weapons and contraband was not a search at all.

"Notwithstanding our caution in approaching claims that the Fourth Amendment is inapplicable in a given context, we hold that society is not prepared to recognize as legitimate any . . . expectation of privacy that a prisoner might have in his prison cell and that, accordingly, the Fourth Amendment proscription against unreasonable searches does not apply within the confines of the prison cell. The recognition of privacy rights for prisoners in their individual cells simply cannot be reconciled with the concept of incarceration and the needs and objectives of the penal institutions."

Justice Stevens wrote for a four-member dissent:

"The view once held than at inmate is a mere slave is now totally rejected.[65] The restraints and the punishment which a criminal conviction entails do not place the citizen beyond the ethical tradition that accords respect to the dignity and intrinsic worth of every individual. "Liberty" and "custody" are not mutually exclusive concepts." By telling prisoners, that no

---

[65] See, https://www.pewtrusts.org/en/research-and-analysis/blogs/stateline/2022/08/22/yes-slavery-is-on-the-ballot-in-these-states for a discussion survey of states (five of them, including Oregon) which had constitutional amendments prohibiting slavery on their ballots in 2022. These proposed state constitutional amendments were directed at prohibiting involuntary servitude including forced prison labor. Notwithstanding the Thirteenth Amendment prohibiting slavery, many state constitutions had an "exception clause" that allowed involuntary servitude as a punishment for crime.

aspect of their individuality, from a photo of a child to a letter from a wife, is entitled to constitutional protection, the Court breaks with the ethical tradition that I had thought was enshrined forever in our jurisprudence."

The Court treats body searches, strip searches, and body cavity searches of prisoners differently than cell searches. Still, these types of searches may be reasonable without warrants or probable cause, if, in the particular situation the need for security, safety or discipline outweigh prisoners' reasonable expectations of privacy. In *Bell v. Wolfish,* 441 U.S. 520 (1979), the Court held that it was reasonable to require jail inmates awaiting trial to expose their body cavities for visual inspection after every visit with a person from outside the jail. The Court focused on the need to maintain safety and order in the jail (and prevent contraband from coming into the facility). Highly intrusive prisoner searches require reasonable suspicion at a minimum. For example, in *Mary Beth G. v. City of Chicago*, 723 F.2d. 1263 (7th Cir. 1983), the U.S. Seventh Circuit Court of Appeals found Chicago's policy of strip-searching all women confined in the Cook County Jail was unreasonable. Similarly, *Kennedy v. Hardiman*, 684 F. Supp, 540 (U.S. District Court, N.D., Illinois Eastern Division 1988) found an extensive strip/body cavity search unreasonable when based on an anonymous tip. That said, in *Florence v. Board of Chosen Freeholders of County of Burlington,* 566 U.S. 318 (2012) the Court seemed to approve a strip search without reasonable, individualized, suspicion when a person is brought in from the outside to general population facility.

FLORENCE v. BOARD OF CHOSEN FREEHOLDERS OF COUNTY OF BURLINGTON
566 U.S. 318 (2012)

JUSTICE KENNEDY delivered the opinion of the Court, except as to Part IV.

This case presents the question of what rules, or limitations, the Constitution imposes on searches of arrested persons who are to be held in jail while their cases are being processed. The term "jail" is used here in a broad sense to include prisons and other detention facilities. The specific measures being challenged will be described in more detail; but, in broad terms, the controversy concerns whether every detainee who will be admitted to the general population may be required to undergo a close visual inspection while undressed.

[Based on an erroneously uncleared outstanding warrant in the County's computer system, the officer arrested Florence] and took him to the Burlington County Detention Center. He was held there for six days and then was transferred to the Essex County Correctional Facility. It is not the arrest or confinement but the search process at each jail that gives rise to the claims before the Court.

Burlington County jail procedures required every arrestee to shower with a delousing agent. Officers would check arrestees for scars, marks, gang tattoos, and contraband as they disrobed. Petitioner claims he was also instructed to open his mouth, lift his tongue, hold out his arms, turn around, and lift his genitals. (It is not clear whether this last step was part of the normal practice.)

The Essex County Correctional Facility, where petitioner was taken after six days, is the largest county jail in New Jersey. It admits more than 25,000 inmates each year and houses about 1,000 gang members at any given time. When petitioner was transferred there, all arriving detainees passed through a metal detector and waited in a group holding cell for a more thorough search. When they left the holding cell, they were instructed to remove their clothing while an officer looked for body markings, wounds, and contraband. Apparently without touching the detainees, an officer looked at their ears, nose, mouth, hair, scalp, fingers, hands, arms, armpits, and other body openings. This policy applied regardless of the circumstances of the arrest, the suspected offense, or the detainee's behavior, demeanor, or criminal history. Petitioner alleges he was required to lift his genitals, turn around, and cough in a squatting position as part of the process. After a mandatory shower, during which his clothes were inspected, petitioner was admitted to the facility. He was released the next day, when the charges against him were dismissed.

Petitioner sued the governmental entities that operated the jails, one of the wardens, and certain other defendants. . . . [He] maintained that persons arrested for a minor offense could not be required to remove their clothing and expose the most private areas of their bodies to close visual inspection as a routine part of the intake process. Rather, he contended, officials could conduct this kind of search only if they had reason to suspect a particular inmate of concealing a weapon, drugs, or other contraband. The District Court certified a class of individuals who were charged with a nonindictable offense under New Jersey law, processed at either the Burlington County or Essex County jail, and directed to strip naked even though an officer had not articulated any reasonable suspicion they were concealing contraband.

. . . .

The term … [strip search] …is imprecise. …In the instant case, the term does not include any touching of unclothed areas by the inspecting officer. There are no allegations that the detainees here were touched in any way as part of the searches.

The Federal Courts of Appeals have come to differing conclusions as to whether the Fourth Amendment requires correctional officials to exempt some detainees who will be admitted to a jail's general population from the searches here at issue. This Court granted certiorari to address the question.

The difficulties of operating a detention center must not be underestimated by the courts. . . . Maintaining safety and order at these institutions requires the expertise of correctional officials, who must have substantial discretion to devise reasonable solutions to the problems they face. The Court has confirmed the importance of deference to correctional officials and explained that a regulation impinging on an inmate's constitutional rights must be upheld "if it is reasonably related to legitimate penological interests." . . .

The Court's opinion in *Bell v. Wolfish* is the starting point for understanding how this framework applies to Fourth Amendment challenges. That case addressed a rule requiring pretrial detainees in any correctional facility run by the Federal Bureau of Prisons "to expose their body cavities for visual inspection as a part of a strip search conducted after every contact visit with a person from outside the institution." Inmates at the federal Metropolitan Correctional Center in New York City argued there was no security justification for these searches. Officers searched guests before they entered the visiting room, and the inmates were under constant surveillance during the visit. There had been but one instance in which an inmate attempted to sneak contraband back into the facility. The Court nonetheless upheld the search policy. It deferred to the judgment of correctional officials that the inspections served not only to discover but also to deter the smuggling of weapons, drugs, and other prohibited items inside. The Court explained that there is no mechanical way to determine whether intrusions on an inmate's privacy are reasonable. The need for a particular search must be balanced against the resulting invasion of personal rights.

…

The Court has also recognized that deterring the possession of contraband depends in part on the ability to conduct searches without predictable exceptions. In *Hudson v. Palmer* it addressed the question of whether prison officials could perform random searches of inmate lockers and cells even without reason to suspect a particular individual of concealing a prohibited item. The Court upheld the constitutionality of the practice, recognizing that " '[f]or one to advocate that prison searches must be conducted only pursuant to an enunciated general policy or when suspicion is directed at a particular inmate is to ignore the realities of prison operation.' " ...

[C]orrectional officials must be permitted to devise reasonable search policies to detect and deter the possession of contraband in their facilities. . . . The task of determining whether a policy is reasonably related to legitimate security interests is "peculiarly within the province and professional expertise of corrections officials." This Court has repeated the admonition that, " 'in the absence of substantial evidence in the record to indicate that the officials have exaggerated their response to these considerations courts should ordinarily defer to their expert judgment in such matters.' "

...

[The Court discussed extensively the need for security and the various threats jail and prisons pose to guards by gangs, contraband, contagious infections which can be introduced by new detainees brought into the detention facility and how seemingly innocuous, but nevertheless dangerous, contraband gets introduced into general population detention facilities]

...

Petitioner acknowledges that correctional officials must be allowed to conduct an effective search during the intake process and that this will require at least some detainees to lift their genitals or cough in a squatting position. These procedures, similar to the ones upheld in Bell, are designed to uncover contraband that can go undetected by a patdown, metal detector, and other less invasive searches. Petitioner maintains there is little benefit to conducting these more invasive steps on a new detainee who has not been arrested for a serious crime or for any offense involving a weapon or drugs. In his view these detainees should be exempt from this process unless they give officers a particular reason to suspect them of hiding contraband. It is reasonable, however, for correctional officials

to conclude this standard would be unworkable. The record provides evidence that the seriousness of an offense is a poor predictor of who has contraband andthat it would be difficult in practice to determine whether individual detainees fall within the proposed exemption.

People detained for minor offenses can turn out to be the most devious and dangerous criminals. ...[The Court discusses at length the problems in identifying minor offense detainees who aren't dangerous nor likely to sneak in contraband from those who will.]

...

This case does not require the Court to rule on the types of searches that would be reasonable in instances where, for example, a detainee will be held without assignment to the general jail population and without substantial contact with other detainees. . . .

Petitioner's amici raise concerns about instances of officers engaging in intentional humiliation and other abusive practices. . . . There also may be legitimate concerns about the invasiveness of searches that involve the touching of detainees. These issues are not implicated on the facts of this case, however, and it is unnecessary to consider them here.

Even assuming all the facts in favor of petitioner, the search procedures at the Burlington County Detention Center and the Essex County Correctional Facility struck a reasonable balance between inmate privacy and the needs of the institutions. The Fourth and Fourteenth Amendments do not require adoption of the framework of rules petitioner proposes.

CHIEF JUSTICE ROBERTS, concurring, omitted.

JUSTICE ALITO, concurring.

I join the opinion of the Court but emphasize the limits of today's holding. The Court holds that jail administrators may require all arrestees who are committed to the general population of a jail to undergo visual strip searches not involving physical contact by corrections officers. To perform the searches, officers may direct the arrestees to disrobe, shower, and submit to a visual inspection. As part of the inspection, the arrestees may be required to manipulate their bodies.

. . .

It is important to note . . . that the Court does not hold that it is always reasonable to conduct a full strip search of an arrestee whose detention has not been reviewed by a judicial officer and who could be held in available facilities apart from the general population. Most of those arrested for minor offenses are not dangerous, and most are released from custody prior to or at the time of their initial appearance before a magistrate. In some cases, the charges are dropped. In others, arrestees are released either on their own recognizance or on minimal bail. In the end, few are sentenced to incarceration. For these persons, admission to the general jail population, with the concomitant humiliation of a strip search, may not be reasonable, particularly if an alternative procedure is feasible. For example, the Federal Bureau of Prisons (BOP) and possibly even some local jails appear to segregate temporary detainees who are minor offenders from the general population.

JUSTICE BREYER, with whom JUSTICE GINSBURG, JUSTICE SOTOMAYOR, and JUSTICE KAGAN join, dissenting.

The petition for certiorari asks us to decide "[w]hether the Fourth Amendment permits a ... suspicionless strip search of every individual arrested for any minor offense. ..." This question is phrased more broadly than what is at issue. The case is limited to strip searches of those arrestees entering a jail's general population. . . . And the kind of strip search in question involves more than undressing and taking a shower (even if guards monitor the shower area for threatened disorder). Rather, the searches here involve close observation of the private areas of a person's body and for that reason constitute a far more serious invasion of that person's privacy.

. . . .

In my view, such a search of an individual arrested for a minor offense that does not involve drugs or violence — say a traffic offense, a regulatory offense, an essentially civil matter, or any other such misdemeanor — is an "unreasonable searc[h]" forbidden by the Fourth Amendment, unless prison authorities have reasonable suspicion to believe that the individual possesses drugs or other contraband. And I dissent from the Court's contrary determination.

A strip search that involves a stranger peering without consent at a naked individual, and in particular at the most private portions of that person's body, is a serious invasion of privacy. . . . The Courts of Appeals have more directly described the privacy interests at stake, writing, for example, that practices similar to those at issue here are "demeaning, dehumanizing, undignified, humiliating, terrifying, unpleasant, embarrassing, [and] repulsive, signifying degradation and submission." . . . These kinds of searches also gave this Court the "most pause" in *Bell* . . . (guards strip searched prisoners after they received outside visits). Even when carried out in a respectful manner, and even absent any physical touching, such searches are inherently harmful, humiliating, and degrading. And the harm to privacy interests would seem particularly acute where the person searched may well have no expectation of being subject to such a search, say, because she had simply received a traffic ticket for failing to buckle a seatbelt, because he had not previously paid a civil fine, or because she had been arrested for a minor trespass.

The petitioner, Albert W. Florence, states that his present arrest grew out of an (erroneous) report that he had failed to pay a minor civil fine previously assessed because he had hindered a prosecution (by fleeing police officers in his automobile). He alleges that he was held for six days in jail before being taken to a magistrate and that he was subjected to two strip searches of the kind in question.

[T] he "particular" invasion of interests must be " 'reasonably related' " to the justifying "penological interest" and the need must not be " 'exaggerated.' " It is at this point that I must part company with the majority. I have found no convincing reason indicating that, in the absence of reasonable suspicion, involuntary strip searches of those arrested for minor offenses are necessary in order to further the penal interests mentioned. And there are strong reasons to believe they are not justified.

The lack of justification is fairly obvious with respect to the first two penological interests advanced. The searches already employed at Essex and Burlington include: (a) pat-frisking all inmates; (b) making inmates go through metal detectors (including the Body Orifice Screening System (BOSS) chair used at Essex County Correctional Facility that identifies metal hidden within the body); (c) making inmates shower and use particular delousing agents or bathing supplies; and (d) searching inmates' clothing. In addition, petitioner concedes that detainees could be lawfully subject to being viewed in their undergarments by jail officers or during showering (for security purposes). ... No one here has offered any reason, example, or empirical evidence suggesting the inadequacy of such practices for detecting injuries, diseases, or tattoos. In particular, there is no connection between the genital lift and the "squat and cough" that Florence was allegedly subjected to and health or gang concerns.

The lack of justification for such a strip search is less obvious but no less real in respect to the third interest, namely that of detecting contraband. The information demonstrating the lack of justification is of three kinds. First, there are empirically based conclusions reached in specific cases. ... The New York Federal District Court ... conducted a study of 23,000 persons admitted to the Orange County correctional facility between 1999 and 2003. These 23,000 persons underwent a strip search of the kind described. . . . Of these 23,000 persons, the court wrote, "the County encountered three incidents of drugs recovered

from an inmate's anal cavity and two incidents of drugs falling from an inmate's underwear during the course of a strip search." The court added that in four of these five instances there may have been "reasonable suspicion" to search, leaving only one instance in 23,000 in which the strip search policy "arguably" detected additional contraband. The study is imperfect, for search standards changed during the time it was conducted. But the large number of inmates, the small number of "incidents," and the District Court's own conclusions make the study probative though not conclusive.

Similarly, in *Shain v. Ellison*, the court received data produced by the county jail showing that authorities conducted body-cavity strip searches, similar to those at issue here, of 75,000 new inmates over a period of five years. In 16 instances the searches led to the discovery of contraband. The record further showed that 13 of these 16 pieces of contraband would have been detected in a patdown or a search of shoes and outer-clothing. In the three instances in which contraband was found on the detainee's body or in a body cavity, there was a drug or felony history that would have justified a strip search on individualized reasonable suspicion.

Second, there is the plethora of recommendations of professional bodies, such as correctional associations, that have studied and thoughtfully considered the matter. The American Correctional Association (ACA) ... has promulgated a standard that forbids suspicionless strip searches. And it has done so after consultation with the American Jail Association, National Sheriff's Association, National Institute of Corrections of the Department of Justice, and Federal Bureau of Prisons. ...A standard desk reference for general information about sound correctional practices advises against suspicionless strip searches.

Moreover, many correctional facilities apply a reasonable suspicion standard before strip searching inmates entering the general jail population, including the U. S. Marshals Service, the Immigration and Customs

Service, and the Bureau of Indian Affairs. ... The Federal Bureau of Prisons (BOP) itself forbids suspicionless strip searches for minor offenders, though it houses separately (and does not admit to the general jail population) a person who does not consent to such a search.

Third, there is general experience in areas where the law has forbidden here-relevant suspicionless searches. Laws in at least 10 States prohibit suspicionless strip searches. ...

At the same time at least seven Courts of Appeals have considered the question and have required reasonable suspicion that an arrestee is concealing weapons or contraband before a strip search of one arrested for a minor offense can take place. ... Respondents have not presented convincing grounds to believe that administration of these legal standards has increased the smuggling of contraband into prison.

Indeed, neither the majority's opinion nor the briefs set forth any clear example of an instance in which contraband was smuggled into the general jail population during intake that could not have been discovered if the jail was employing a reasonable suspicion standard. ...

I am left without an example of any instance in which contraband was found on an individual through an inspection of their private parts or body cavities which could not have been found under a policy requiring reasonable suspicion. ...

Those arrested for minor offenses are often stopped and arrested unexpectedly. And they consequently will have had little opportunity to hide things in their body cavities. Thus, the widespread advocacy by prison experts and the widespread application in many States and federal circuits of "reasonable suspicion" requirements indicates an ability to apply such standards in practice without unduly interfering with the legitimate penal interest in preventing the smuggling of contraband.

Contrary to the majority's suggestion, . . . [Bell] does not provide precedent for the proposition that the word of prison officials (accompanied by a "single instance" of empirical example) is sufficient to support a strip search policy.

It is true that in *Bell* the Court found the prison justified in conducting postcontact searches even as to pre-trial detainees who had been brought before a magistrate, denied bail, and "committed to the detention facility only because no other less drastic means [could] reasonably assure [their] presence at trial." The Court recognized that those ordered detained by a magistrate were often those "charged with serious crimes, or who have prior records." For that reason, those detainees posed at least the same security risk as convicted inmates, if not "a greater risk to jail security and order," and a "greater risk of escape." And, of course, in *Bell*, both the inmates at issue and their visitors had the time to plan to smuggle contraband in that case, unlike those persons at issue here (imprisoned soon after an unexpected arrest).

The *Bell* Court had no occasion to focus upon those arrested for minor crimes, prior to a judicial officer's determination that they should be committed to prison. . . . In my view, it is highly questionable that officials would be justified, for instance, in admitting to the dangerous world of the general jail population and subjecting to a strip search someone with no criminal background arrested for jaywalking or another similarly minor crime. . . .

In an appropriate case, therefore, it remains open for the Court to consider whether it would be reasonable to admit an arrestee for a minor offense to the general jail population, and to subject her to the "humiliation of a strip search," prior to any review by a judicial officer.

For the reasons set forth, I cannot find justification for the strip search policy at issue here — a policy that would subject those arrested for minor offenses to serious invasions of their personal privacy. I consequently dissent.

EXCLUSIONARY RULE

Assuming there was no warrant, and no exception to the warrant requirement, what remedy is there when government violates constitutional prohibitions/guarantees? The Fourth Amendment does not provide a remedy when a search or seizure is unreasonable or done without a warrant. The first time the Court suppressed evidence obtained illegally by federal officers was in *Boyd v. United States,* 116 U.S. 616 (1896) (*Boyd* challenged an order directing him to turn over an invoice on cases of imported glass to determine whether he had paid customs taxes. The Court reviewed the order and found that it violated the Fourth and Fifth Amendments and suppressed the evidence.) The *Boyd* Court did not create a *per se* rule of exclusion, resulting in decades of court opinions adopting the case-by-case approach to applying the remedy, denying the remedy, expanding the remedy (derivative evidence rule), and contracting the remedy (exceptions to the exclusionary rule). The following cases show the historical development of what is known as the exclusionary rule, the standing requirement, and the exceptions to the exclusionary rule. Many of the cases you have already read (and many you still have to read) involve a motion to suppress or exclude evidence filed by defendants based upon their belief that their Fourth Amendment rights were violated. These motions to suppress are the legal process by which the exclusionary rule is implemented. These motions are filed prior to trial, and the judge deciding them aren't necessarily the trial judge. In fact, if the motion to suppress is successful and "dispositive" (meaning that after the evidence is excluded there is not enough evidence for the prosecution to go forward and prove its case beyond a reasonable doubt), there may never even be a trial. Alternately, after an unsuccessful motion to suppress, defendants may opt to enter a conditional plea of guilty and then appeal their case. Defendants may also file pretrial motions to exclude evidence for reasons other than search and seizure, such as improper interrogations or identification procedures. Thus, this section of material could also find a home in the chapter on interrogations and confessions, identification procedures, and pre-trial processes.

Standing[66]

The Court has limited the right to assert the exclusionary rule to defendants who have personally suffered a violation of his or her own constitutional right. Individuals must have "standing" to move to suppress evidence and cannot assert the remedy to bar evidence obtained through the violation of a right of some third party. For example, if Sam and Betty owned a home which was illegally searched and through the search the police came up with evidence against Joe, Joe would have no claim for suppression of the evidence, because his rights were not violated by the illegal search of Sam and Betty's. The key case on standing after the decision in *Katz* is *Rakas v. Illinois, 439 U.S. 128 (1978)* which featured prominently in *Byrd v. United States,* 584 U.S. ____ (2018).)[67]

---

[66] The most recent case involving "standing" does not involve the exclusionary rule being applied to either search and seizure claims or illegal interrogation claims. In *Carny v. Adams*, 592 U.S. ____ (2021) the issue of standing was before the Court when a Delaware attorney challenged a Delaware requirement that judgeship positions on certain courts could only be filled by Republican or Democrat judges (the State had a policy of balancing the judgeships so that neither would have a clear majority. Adams had been a Democrat, but had reregistered as "unaffiliated." He then filed a lawsuit arguing that he wanted to apply for a judgeship but was unable to do so. The Court unanimously held that since Adams was not actually "able and ready" to apply for a position, and he was not able to show "injury in fact" that was "concrete and particularized" and "actual or imminent," he did not have standing to raise the complaint. Justice Breyer's opinion noted that Adams's suit was more of an abstract generalized grievance, not an actual desire to become a judge, and that there was no evidence that he had applied for any of the numerous vacancies when he was registered as a Democrat.

[67] According to Justicia on Standing: The Court for a long period followed a rule of "standing" by which it determined whether a party was the appropriate person to move to suppress allegedly illegal evidence. Under that rule, one could ordinarily contest only those government actions that harm him. The standing principle in

Byrd involved the search of a rental car driven by Byrd who was not on the rental contract. The key features of *Rakas* that the Byrd Court pointed to was that legal standing (the right to gripe) is based on having a legitimate expectation of privacy in the property or premises to be searched; common law rules concerning property are a factor to be considered, but they are not controlling when deciding whether a person has a reasonable expectation of privacy; lawful presence on the premise or place searched is not enough, by itself, to establish standing but this didn't mean that a passenger lawfully in a car couldn't have standing to exclude unless he was the owner or had a possessory interest in the car. Finally, the Court noted that, unlike with Byrd, Rakas had not claimed a legitimate interest in privacy in the car. The Byrd Court discussed other differences between the facts in *Byrd* and the facts in *Rakas*.

> "[Moreover] . . . this case does not involve a passenger at all but instead the driver and sole occupant of a rental car. As Justice Powell observed . . . a 'distinction . . . may be made in some circumstances between the Fourth Amendment rights of passengers and the rights of an individual who has exclusive control of an automobile or of its locked compartments.' . . . '[O]ne who owns or lawfully possesses or controls property will in all likelihood have a legitimate expectation of privacy by virtue of [the] right to exclude.'"

> The Court sees no reason why the expectation of privacy that comes from lawful possession and control and the attendant right to exclude would differ depending on whether the car in question is rented or privately owned by someone other than the person in current possession of it, much as it did not seem to matter whether the friend of the defendant in Jones owned or leased the apartment he permitted the defendant to use in his absence. Both would have the expectation of privacy that comes with the right to exclude. Indeed, the Government conceded at oral argument that an unauthorized driver in sole possession of a rental car would be permitted to exclude third parties from it, such as a carjacker. The central inquiry at this point turns on the concept of lawful possession, and this is where an important qualification of Byrd's proposed rule comes into play. *Rakas* makes clear that " 'wrongful' presence at the scene of a search would not enable a defendant to object to the legality of the search." "A burglar plying his trade in a summer cabin during the off season," for example, "may have a thoroughly justified subjective expectation of privacy, but it is not one which the law recognizes as 'legitimate.' "Likewise, "a person present in a stolen automobile at the time of the search may [not] object to the lawfulness of the search of the automobile." No matter the degree of possession and control, the car thief would not have a reasonable expectation of privacy in a stolen car.

> . . .

> The concept of standing in Fourth Amendment cases can be a useful shorthand for capturing the idea that a person must have a cognizable Fourth Amendment interest in the place searched before seeking relief for an unconstitutional search. . . .

> . . .

Fourth Amendment cases "require[d] of one who seeks to challenge the legality of a search as the basis for suppressing relevant evidence that he show that he himself was the victim of an invasion of privacy." "The Court subsequently departed from the concept of standing. Finding that "standing" served no useful analytical purpose, the Court has held that the issue of exclusion is to be determined solely upon a resolution of the substantive question whether the claimant's Fourth Amendment rights have been violated. *Rakas v. Illinois* (1978). The effect of the application of the Katz privacy rationale has been to narrow considerably the number of people who can complain of an unconstitutional search.

Though new, the fact pattern here continues a well-traveled path in this Court's Fourth Amendment jurisprudence. Those cases support the proposition, and the Court now holds, that the mere fact that a driver in lawful possession or control of a rental car is not listed on the rental agreement will not defeat his or her otherwise reasonable expectation of privacy."

Other Cases: Standing

Jones v. United States, 362 U.S. 257 (1960)

SUMMARY: Jones sought to exclude evidence resulting from a search of his friend's apartment that he had been given use of. He had clothing in the apartment, had slept there" 'maybe a night,'" and at the time was the sole occupant of the apartment. The Court established the rule that anyone legitimately on the premises could object to a search of the premises. Since Jones was on the premise with permission, he had his own key, his luggage was there, and had the right to exclude others, the Court found Jones had a legitimate expectation of privacy and, thus, standing. Note: the Court's *Jones* holding that anyone legitimately on the premises had standing to raise a Fourth Amendment claim was expressly overturned in *Rakas*. But, after *Byrd*, it may still have some "teeth."

United States v. Jeffers, 342 U.S. 48 (1951)

SUMMARY: Court found defendant had standing in a hotel room rented by defendant's aunts. He had a key and permission to store things

Mancusi v. DeForte, 392 U.S. 364 (1968)

SUMMARY: Defendant shared office with several others; though he had no reasonable expectation of absolute privacy, he could reasonably expect to be intruded on only by other occupants and not by police.

Rawlings v. Kentucky, 448 U.S. 98 (1980)

SUMMARY: Bowling Green police officers went to arrest Marquess with an arrest warrant for drug trafficking at Marquess' home. At the time, Marquess' housemate and four visitors were present, including Rawlings. Officers unsuccessfully searched the home for Marquess. In the course of the search, officers smelled marijuana smoke and saw marijuana seeds in plain sight. Two officers left to obtain a search warrant for the house, while the remaining officers detained the occupants.

(They were told they would be allowed to leave if they would consent to a body search, two did so and were allowed to leave.)

Officers returned with a search warrant for the entire house. An officer read the warrant to the remaining three occupants of the house, and also read them Miranda warnings. At that time, Rawlings was seated on the couch, next to one of the females, who was named Cox. Cox's purse was on the couch between them.

Officer Rainey instructed Rawlings to stand to be searched, and another officer instructed Cox to empty her purse onto the table. A large quantity of controlled substances, including LSD and methamphetamine, fell from the purse. Cox told Rawlings to "take what was his" and he claimed ownership of all of the drugs. Rawlings was also in possession of $4,500 in cash and a knife. He was arrested.

Rawlings stated at trial that he had asked Cox to "carry" the bag containing the drugs for him, and she had agreed. He claimed that the search of the purse invaded his privacy.

The Court found that Rawlings put the drugs in Cox's purse, having only known her a couple of days. He had no access to her purse prior to that time. He had no right to exclude others from her purse. Another individual had been in the purse earlier that same day, searching for a hairbrush. Rawlings admitted he did not expect privacy in the purse. For these reasons, the Court held that he did not have either a subjective or objective expectation of privacy in a purse belonging to another.

Minnesota v. Carter, 525 U.S. 83 (1998)

SUMMARY: A police informant saw some people, through the window of an apartment, bagging white powder. An officer then observed people for several minutes in a bagging operation through the apartment window. While officers were obtaining a warrant to enter the apartment, two men, later identified as Carter and Johns, left the building and got into a car. When the car was stopped, police found cocaine and cocaine paraphernalia.

A subsequent search of the apartment uncovered cocaine residue on the kitchen table. Thompson, the apartment lessee, said she had allowed Carter and Johns to use her apartment for their bagging operation for an amount of cocaine. Carter and Johns were in the apartment for about two and one-half hours and had never been to the apartment before. Carter and Johns moved to suppress all evidence, arguing that the officer's looking through the apartment window was an unreasonable search, thus violating their Fourth Amendment rights.

The Court held that Carter and Johns had no legitimate expectation of privacy in the apartment as they were only in the apartment one time, for a short time, and for were there for a commercial purpose only. Since they had no expectation of privacy, there is no need to determine whether the officer's looking through the window was a search.

The Fourth Amendment guarantees: "The right of the people to be secure in their persons, houses, papers, and effects, against unreasonable searches and seizures, shall not be violated, and no Warrants shall issue, but upon probable cause, supported by Oath or affirmation, and particularly describing the place to be searched, and the persons or things to be seized." The Amendment protects persons against unreasonable searches of "their persons [and] houses" and thus indicates that the Fourth Amendment is a personal right that must be invoked by an individual. See *Katz v. United States*, 389 U. S. 347, 351 (1967) ("[T]he Fourth Amendment protects people, not places"). But the extent to which the Fourth Amendment protects people may depend upon where those people are. We have held that "capacity to claim the protection of the Fourth Amendment depends ... upon whether the person who claims the protection of the Amendment has a legitimate expectation of privacy in the invaded place." *Rakas*, supra, at 143. See also *Rawlings v. Kentucky*, 448 U. S. 98, 106 (1980).

The text of the Amendment suggests that its protections extend only to people in "their" houses. But we have held that in some circumstances a person may have a legitimate expectation of privacy in the house of someone else. In *Minnesota v. Olson*, 495 U. S. 91 (1990), for example, we decided that an overnight guest in a house had the sort of expectation of privacy that the Fourth Amendment protects. We said:

> "To hold that an overnight guest has a legitimate expectation of privacy in his host's home merely recognizes the every day expectations of privacy that we all share. Staying overnight in another's home is a longstanding social custom that serves functions recognized as valuable by society. We stay in others' homes when we travel to a strange city for business or pleasure, when we visit our parents, children, or more distant relatives out of town, when we are in between jobs or homes, or when we house-sit for a friend ....

"From the overnight guest's perspective, he seeks shelter in another's home precisely because it provides him with privacy, a place where he and his possessions will not be disturbed by anyone but his host and those his host allows inside. We are at our most vulnerable when we are asleep because we cannot monitor our own safety or the security of our belongings. It is for this reason that, although we may spend all day in public places, when we cannot sleep in our own home we seek out another private place to sleep, whether it be a hotel room, or the home of a friend."

Cases Creating and Expanding the Exclusionary Rule

WEEKS v. UNITED STATES
232 U.S. 383 (1914)

JUSTICE DAY delivered the opinion of the Court:

The defendant was arrested by a police officer . . .without warrant, at the Union Station in Kansas City, Missouri, where he was employed by an express company. Other police officers had gone to the house of the defendant, and being told by a neighbor where the key was kept, found it and entered the house. They searched the defendant's room and took possession of various papers and articles found there, which were afterwards turned over to the United States marshal. Later in the same day police officers returned with the marshal, who thought he might find additional evidence, and, being admitted by someone in the house, probably a boarder, in response to a rap, the marshal searched the defendant's room and carried away certain letters and envelopes found in the drawer of a chiffonier. Neither the marshal nor the police officers had a search warrant.

After the jury had been sworn and before any evidence had been given, the defendant again urged his petition for the return of his property, which was denied by the court. Upon the introduction of such papers during the trial, the defendant objected on the ground that the papers had been obtained without a search warrant, and by breaking into his home, in violation of the 4th and 5th Amendments to the Constitution of the United States, which objection was overruled by the court.

…

The case in the aspect in which we are dealing with it involves the right of the court in a criminal prosecution to retain for the purposes of evidence the letters and correspondence of the accused, seized in his house in his absence and without his authority, by a United States marshal holding no warrant for his arrest and none for the search of his premises. If letters and private documents can thus be seized and held and used in evidence against a citizen accused of an offense, the protection of the 4th Amendment, declaring his right to be secure against such searches and seizures, is of no value, and, so far as those thus placed are concerned, might as well be stricken from the Constitution. The efforts of the courts and their officials to bring the guilty to punishment, praise-worthy as they are, are not to be aided by the sacrifice of those great principles established by years of endeavor and suffering which have resulted in their embodiment in the fundamental law of the land.

We therefore reach the conclusion that the letters in question were taken from the house of the accused by an official of the United States, acting under color of his office, in direct violation of the constitutional rights of the defendant; that having made a seasonable application for their return, which was heard and passed upon by the court, there was involved in the order refusing the application of denial of the constitutional rights of the accused, and that the court should have restored these letters to the accused. In holding them and permitting their use upon the trial, we think prejudicial error was committed.

MAPP v. OHIO
367 U.S. 643 (1961)

JUSTICE CLARK delivered the opinion of the Court.

On May 23, 1957, three Cleveland police officers arrived at appellant's residence in that city pursuant to information that "a person [was] hiding out in the home, who was wanted for questioning in connection with a recent bombing, and that there was a large amount of paraphernalia being hidden in the home." Miss Mapp and her daughter by a former marriage lived on the top floor of the two-family dwelling. Upon their arrival at that house, the officers knocked on the door and demanded entrance but appellant, after telephoning her attorney, refused to admit them without a search warrant. They advised their headquarters of the situation and undertook a surveillance of the house. The officers again sought entrance some three hours later when four or more additional officers arrived on the scene. When Miss Mapp did not come to the door immediately, at least one of the several doors to the house was forcibly opened and the policemen gained admittance. Meanwhile Miss Mapp's attorney arrived, but the officers, having secured their own entry, and continuing in their defiance of the law, would permit him neither to see Miss Mapp nor to enter the house. It appears that Miss Mapp was halfway down the stairs from the upper floor to the front door when the officers, in this highhanded manner, broke into the hall. She demanded to see the search warrant. A paper, claimed to be a warrant, was held up by one of the officers. She grabbed the "warrant" and placed it in her bosom. A struggle ensued in which the officers recovered the piece of paper and as a result of which they handcuffed appellant because she had been "belligerent" in resisting their official rescue of the "warrant" from her person. Running roughshod over appellant, a policeman "grabbed" her, "twisted [her] hand," and she "yelled [and] pleaded with him" because "it was hurting." Appellant, in handcuffs, was then forcibly taken upstairs to her bedroom where the officers searched a dresser, a chest of drawers, a closet and some suitcases. They also looked into a photo album and through personal papers belonging to the appellant. The search spread to the rest of the second floor including the child's bedroom, the living room, the kitchen and a dinette. The basement of the building and a trunk found therein were also searched. The obscene materials for possession of which she was ultimately convicted were discovered in the course of that widespread search.

At the trial no search warrant was produced by the prosecution, nor was the failure to produce one explained or accounted for. At best, "There is, in the record, considerable doubt as to whether there ever was any warrant for the search of defendant's home."

The State says that even if the search were made without authority, or otherwise unreasonably, it is not prevented from using the unconstitutionally seized evidence at trial, in which this Court did indeed hold "that in a prosecution in a State court for a State crime the Fourteenth Amendment does not forbid the admission of evidence obtained by an unreasonable search and seizure." On this appeal, of which we have noted probable jurisdiction, it is urged once again that we review that holding.

[I]n the year 1914, in the *Weeks* case, this Court "for the first time" held that "in a federal prosecution the Fourth Amendment barred the use of evidence secured through an illegal search and seizure." This Court has ever since required of federal law officers a strict adherence to that command which this Court has held to be a clear, specific, and constitutionally required - even if judicially implied - deterrent safeguard without insistence upon which the Fourth Amendment would have been reduced to "a form of words." It meant, quite simply, that "conviction by means of unlawful seizures and enforced confessions . . . should find no sanction in the judgments of the courts . . . ," and that such evidence "shall not be used at all."

There are in the cases of this Court some passing references to the *Weeks* rule as being one of evidence. But the plain and unequivocal language of *Weeks* - and its later paraphrase in *Wolf* - to the effect that the Weeks rule is of constitutional origin, remains entirely undisturbed.

In 1949, 35 years after *Weeks* was announced, this Court, in *Wolf v. Colorado*, supra, again for the first time, discussed the effect of the Fourth Amendment upon the States through the operation of the Due Process Clause of the Fourteenth Amendment. It said:

> "[W]e have no hesitation in saying that were a State affirmatively to sanction such police incursion into privacy it would run counter to the guaranty of the Fourteenth Amendment."

Nevertheless, after declaring that the "security of one's privacy against arbitrary intrusion by the police" is "implicit in the concept of ordered liberty' and as such enforceable against the States through the Due Process Clause," and announcing that it "stoutly adhere[d]" to the *Weeks* decision, the Court decided that the *Weeks* exclusionary rule would not then be imposed upon the States as "an essential ingredient of the right."

. . . .

Since the Fourth Amendment's right of privacy has been declared enforceable against the States through the Due Process Clause of the Fourteenth, it is enforceable against them by the same sanction of exclusion as is used against the Federal Government. Were it otherwise, then just as without the *Weeks* rule the assurance against unreasonable federal searches and seizures would be "a form of words," valueless and undeserving of mention in a perpetual charter of inestimable human liberties, so too, without that rule the freedom from state invasions of privacy would be so ephemeral and so neatly severed from its conceptual nexus with the freedom from all brutish means of coercing evidence as not to merit this Court's high regard as a freedom "implicit in the concept of ordered liberty." . . . Therefore, in extending the substantive protections of due process to all constitutionally unreasonable searches - state or federal - it was logically and constitutionally necessary that the exclusion doctrine - an essential part of the right to privacy - be also insisted upon as an essential ingredient of the right newly recognized by the *Wolf* case. In short, the admission of the new constitutional right by *Wolf* could not consistently tolerate denial of its most important constitutional privilege, namely, the exclusion of the evidence which an accused had been forced to give by reason of the unlawful seizure. To hold otherwise is to grant the right but in reality to withhold its privilege and enjoyment. Only last year the Court itself recognized that the purpose of the exclusionary rule "is to deter - to compel respect for the constitutional guaranty in the only effectively available way - by removing the incentive to disregard it."

Moreover, our holding that the exclusionary rule is an essential part of both the Fourth and Fourteenth Amendments is not only the logical dictate of prior cases, but it also makes very good sense. There is no war between the Constitution and common sense. Presently, a federal prosecutor may make no use of evidence illegally seized, but a State's attorney across the street may, although he supposedly

is operating under the enforceable prohibitions of the same Amendment. Thus the State, by admitting evidence unlawfully seized, serves to encourage disobedience to the Federal Constitution which it is bound to uphold.

There are those who say, as did Justice (then Judge) Cardozo, that under our constitutional exclusionary doctrine "[t]he criminal is to go free because the constable has blundered." In some cases this will undoubtedly be the result. But, as was said in *Elkins*, "there is another consideration - the imperative of judicial integrity." The criminal goes free, if he must, but it is the law that sets him free. Nothing can destroy a government more quickly than its failure to observe its own laws, or worse, its disregard of the charter of its own existence.

Having once recognized that the right to privacy embodied in the Fourth Amendment is enforceable against the States, and that the right to be secure against rude invasions of privacy by state officers is, therefore, constitutional in origin, we can no longer permit that right to remain an empty promise. Because it is enforceable in the same manner and to like effect as other basic rights secured by the Due Process Clause, we can no longer permit it to be revocable at the whim of any police officer who, in the name of law enforcement itself, chooses to suspend its enjoyment. Our decision, founded on reason and truth, gives to the individual no more than that which the Constitution guarantees him, to the police officer no less than that to which honest law enforcement is entitled, and, to the courts, that judicial integrity so necessary in the true administration of justice. . . .

JUSTICE HARLAN, whom JUSTICE FRANKFURTER and JUSTICE WHITTAKER join, dissenting.

I would not impose upon the States this federal exclusionary remedy. The reasons given by the majority for now suddenly turning its back on Wolf seem to me notably unconvincing.

Cases Limiting the Exclusionary Rule: The Exceptions

NIX v. WILLIAMS
467 U.S. 431 (1984)

CHIEF JUSTICE BURGER delivered the opinion of the Court.

[SUMMARY: Williams was arrested for the murder of 12-year-old Pamela Powers. He quickly called an attorney who told police not to question Williams as they transported him from Davenport, Iowa to Des Moines, Iowa. During the trip, police initiated a conversation that the Court (in Williams first trial) concluded was tantamount to questioning which violated his right to counsel. Police had played on defendant's sympathies and caused him to lead the officers to the girl's body which a large-scale search party (200 volunteers out looking for her) had yet to find. At the first trial the U.S. Supreme Court found that Williams right to counsel was violated and held the statements should have been excluded. At a motion to suppress prior to the second trial Williams claimed that the evidence of the body was fruit of the poisonous tree and should be excluded. The motion was denied. At the second trial, the statements were not entered, but the condition of the girl's body was.]

We granted certiorari …

…

Williams contends that evidence of the body's location and condition is "fruit of the poisonous tree," i.e., the "fruit" or product of Detective Leaming's plea to help the child's parents give her "a Christian burial," which this Court had already held equated to interrogation. He contends that admitting the challenged evidence violated the Sixth Amendment whether it would have been inevitably discovered or not. Williams also contends that, if the inevitable discovery doctrine is constitutionally permissible, it must

include a threshold showing of police good faith.

The doctrine requiring courts to suppress evidence as the tainted "fruit" of unlawful governmental conduct had its genesis in *Silverthorne Lumber Co. v. United States* (1920); there, the Court held that the exclusionary rule applies not only to the illegally obtained evidence itself, but also to other incriminating evidence derived from the primary evidence. The holding of Silverthorne was carefully limited, however, for the Court emphasized that such information does not automatically become "sacred and inaccessible." …

Wong Sun v. United States (1963), extended the exclusionary rule to evidence that was the indirect product or "fruit" of unlawful police conduct, but there again the Court emphasized that evidence that has been illegally obtained need not always be suppressed.

…

Although *Silverthorne* and *Wong Sun* involved violations of the Fourth Amendment, the "fruit of the poisonous tree" doctrine has not been limited to cases in which there has been a Fourth Amendment violation. The Court has applied the doctrine where the violations were of the Sixth Amendment... as well as of the Fifth Amendment.

The core rationale consistently advanced by this Court for extending the exclusionary rule to evidence that is the fruit of unlawful police conduct has been that this admittedly drastic and socially costly course is needed to deter police from violations of constitutional and statutory protections. This Court has accepted the argument that the way to ensure protection is to exclude evidence seized as a result of such violations notwithstanding the high social cost of letting persons obviously guilty go unpunished for their crimes. On this rationale, the prosecution is not to be put in a better position than it would have been in if no illegality had transpired.

By contrast, the derivative evidence analysis ensures that the prosecution is not put in a worse position simply because of some earlier police error or misconduct. The independent source doctrine allows admission of evidence that has been discovered by means wholly independent of any constitutional violation. That doctrine, although closely related to the inevitable discovery doctrine, does not apply here; Williams' statements to Leaming indeed led police to the child's body, but that is not the whole story. The independent source doctrine teaches us that the interest of society in deterring unlawful police conduct and the public interest in having juries receive all probative evidence of a crime are properly balanced by putting the police in the same, not a worse, position than they would have been in if no police error or misconduct had occurred. . . .When the challenged evidence has an independent source, exclusion of such evidence would put the police in a worse position than they would have been in absent any violation. There is a functional similarity between these two doctrines in that exclusion of evidence that would inevitably have been discovered would also put the government in a worse position, because the police would have obtained that evidence if no misconduct had taken place. Thus, while the independent source exception would not justify admission of evidence in this case, its rationale is wholly consistent with and justifies our adoption of the ultimate or inevitable discovery exception to the Exclusionary Rule.

It is clear that the cases implementing the exclusionary rule "began with the premise that the challenged evidence is in some sense the product of illegal governmental activity." . . .Of course, this does not end the inquiry. If the prosecution can establish by a preponderance of the evidence that the information ultimately or inevitably would have been discovered by lawful means — here

the volunteers' search — then the deterrence rationale has so little basis that the evidence should be received. Anything less would reject logic, experience, and common sense.

…

Exclusion of physical evidence that would inevitably have been discovered adds nothing to either the integrity or fairness of a criminal trial. The Sixth Amendment right to counsel protects against unfairness by preserving the adversary process in which the reliability of proffered evidence may be tested in cross-examination. … Here, however, Detective Leaming's conduct did nothing to impugn the reliability of the evidence in question — the body of the child and its condition as it was found, articles of clothing found on the body, and the autopsy. No one would seriously contend that the presence of counsel in the police car when Leaming appealed to Williams' decent human instincts would have had any bearing on the reliability of the body as evidence. Suppression, in these circumstances, would do nothing whatever to promote the integrity of the trial process, but would inflict a wholly unacceptable burden on the administration of criminal justice.

[I]f the government can prove that the evidence would have been obtained inevitably and, therefore, would have been admitted regardless of any overreaching by the police, there is no rational basis to keep that evidence from the jury in order to ensure the fairness of the trial proceedings. In that situation, the State has gained no advantage at trial and the defendant has suffered no prejudice. Indeed, suppression of that evidence would operate to undermine the adversary system by putting the State in a worse position than it would have occupied without any police misconduct. …

On [the] record it is clear that the search parties were approaching the actual location of the body, and we are satisfied, along with three courts earlier, that the volunteer search teams would have resumed the search had Williams not earlier led the police to the body and the body inevitably would have been found. …

JUSTICE BRENNAN, with whom JUSTICE MARSHALL joins, dissenting.

To the extent that today's decision adopts this "inevitable discovery" exception to the exclusionary rule, it simply acknowledges a doctrine that is akin to the "independent source" exception first recognized by the Court in *Silverthorne Lumber Co. v. United States*. … In particular, the Court concludes that unconstitutionally obtained evidence may be admitted at trial if it inevitably would have been discovered in the same condition by an independent line of investigation that was already being pursued when the constitutional violation occurred. As has every federal Court of Appeals previously addressing this issue, … I agree that in these circumstances the "inevitable discovery" exception to the exclusionary rule is consistent with the requirements of the Constitution.

In its zealous efforts to emasculate the exclusionary rule, however, the Court loses sight of the crucial difference between the "inevitable discovery" doctrine and the "independent source" exception from which it is derived. When properly applied, the "independent source" exception allows the prosecution to use evidence only if it was, in fact, obtained by fully lawful means. It therefore does no violence to the constitutional protections that the exclusionary rule is meant to enforce. The "inevitable discovery" exception is likewise compatible with the Constitution, though it differs in one key respect from its next of kin: specifically, the evidence sought to be introduced at trial has not actually been obtained from an independent source, but rather would have been discovered as a matter of course if independent investigations were allowed to proceed.

In my view, this distinction should require that the government satisfy a heightened burden of proof before it is allowed to use such evidence. The inevitable discovery exception necessarily implicates a hypothetical finding that differs in kind from the factual findings that precedes application of the independent source rule. To ensure that this hypothetical finding is narrowly confined to circumstances that are functionally equivalent to an independent source, and to protect fully the fundamental rights served by the exclusionary rule, I would require clear and convincing evidence before concluding that the government had met its burden of proof on this issue. . . .Increasing the burden of proof serves to impress the factfinder with the importance of the decision and thereby reduces the risk that illegally obtained evidence will be admitted. . . .Because the lower courts did not impose such a requirement, I would remand this case for application of this heightened burden of proof by the lower courts in the first instance. I am therefore unable to join either the Court's opinion or its judgment.

MURRAY v. UNITED STATES
487 U.S. 533 (1988)

JUSTICE SCALIA delivered the opinion of the Court.

In *Segura v. United States* (1984), we held that police officers' illegal entry upon private premises did not require suppression of evidence subsequently discovered at those premises when executing a search warrant obtained on the basis of information wholly unconnected with the initial entry. In these consolidated cases we are faced with the question whether, again assuming evidence obtained pursuant to an independently obtained search warrant, the portion of such evidence that had been observed in plain view at the time of a prior illegal entry must be suppressed.

Based on information received from informants, federal law enforcement agents had been surveilling petitioner Murray and several of his co-conspirators. At about 1:45

p.m. on April 6, 1983, they observed Murray drive a truck and Carter drive a green camper, into a warehouse in South Boston. When the petitioners drove the vehicles out about 20 minutes later, the surveilling agents saw within the warehouse two individuals and a tractor-trailer rig bearing a long, dark container. Murray and Carter later turned over the truck and camper to other drivers, who were in turn followed and ultimately arrested, and the vehicles lawfully seized. Both vehicles were found to contain marijuana.

After receiving this information, several of the agents converged on the South Boston warehouse and forced entry. They found the warehouse unoccupied, but observed in plain view numerous burlap-wrapped bales that were later found to contain marijuana. They left without disturbing the bales, kept the warehouse under surveillance, and did not reenter it until they had a search warrant. In applying for the warrant, the agents did not mention the prior entry, and did not rely on any observations made during that entry. When the warrant was issued - at 10:40 p.m., approximately eight hours after the initial entry - the agents immediately reentered the warehouse and seized 270 bales of marijuana and notebooks listing customers for whom the bales were destined.

…

The dispute here is over the scope of …[the independent discovery]… doctrine. Petitioners contend that it applies only to evidence obtained for the first time during an independent lawful search. The Government argues that it applies also to evidence initially discovered during, or as a consequence of, an unlawful search, but later obtained independently from activities untainted by the initial illegality. We think the Government's view has better support in both precedent and policy.

Our cases have used the concept of "independent source" in a more general and a more specific sense. The more general sense identifies all evidence acquired in a fashion untainted by the illegal evidence-gathering activity. Thus, where an unlawful entry has given investigators knowledge of facts x and y, but fact z has been learned by other means, fact z can be said to be admissible because derived from an "independent source." This is how we used the term in *Segura v. United States*. In that case, agents unlawfully entered the defendant's apartment and remained there until a search warrant was obtained. The admissibility of what they discovered while waiting in the apartment was not before us, but we held that the evidence found for the first time during the execution of the valid and untainted search warrant was admissible because it was discovered pursuant to an "independent source."

The original use of the term, however, and its more important use for purposes of these cases, was more specific. It was originally applied in the exclusionary rule context, by Justice Holmes, with reference to that particular category of evidence acquired by an untainted search which is identical to the evidence unlawfully acquired - that is, in the example just given, to knowledge of facts x and y derived from an independent source:

> "In the classic independent source situation, information which is received through an illegal source is considered to be cleanly obtained when it arrives through an independent source."

Petitioners' asserted policy basis for excluding evidence which is initially discovered during an illegal search, but is subsequently acquired through an independent and lawful source, is that a contrary rule will remove all deterrence to, and indeed positively encourage, unlawful police searches. As petitioners see the incentives, law enforcement officers will routinely enter without a warrant to make sure that what they expect to be on the premises is in fact there. If it is not, they will have spared themselves the time and trouble of getting a warrant; if it is, they can get the warrant and use the evidence despite the unlawful entry. We see the incentives differently. An officer with probable cause sufficient to obtain a search warrant would be foolish to enter the premises first in an unlawful manner. By doing so, he would risk suppression of all evidence on the premises, both seen and unseen, since his action would add to the normal burden of convincing a magistrate that there is probable cause the much more onerous burden of convincing a trial court that no information gained from the illegal entry affected either the law enforcement officers' decision to seek a warrant or the magistrate's decision to grant it.. Nor would the officer without sufficient probable cause to obtain a search warrant have any added incentive to conduct an unlawful entry, since whatever he finds cannot be used to establish probable cause before a magistrate.

So long as a later, lawful seizure is genuinely independent of an earlier, tainted one (which may well be difficult to establish where the seized goods are kept in the police's possession) there is no reason why the independent source doctrine should not apply.

The ultimate question, therefore, is whether the search pursuant to warrant was in fact a genuinely independent source of the information and tangible evidence at issue here. This would not have been the case if the agents' decision to seek the warrant was prompted by what they had seen during the initial entry, or if information obtained during that entry was presented to the Magistrate and affected his decision to issue the warrant.

. . . .

We . . . remand to the District Court for determination whether the warrant-authorized search of the warehouse was an independent source of the challenged evidence in the sense we have described.

JUSTICE MARSHALL, with whom JUSTICE STEVENS and JUSTICE O'CONNOR join, dissenting.

To ensure that the source of the evidence is genuinely independent, the basis for a finding that a search was untainted by a prior illegal search must focus, as with the inevitable discovery doctrine, on "demonstrated historical facts capable of ready verification or impeachment." In the instant cases, there are no "demonstrated historical facts" capable of supporting a finding that the subsequent warrant search was wholly unaffected by the prior illegal search. The same team of investigators was involved in both searches. The warrant was obtained immediately after the illegal search, and no effort was made to obtain a warrant prior to the discovery of the marijuana during the illegal search. The only evidence available that the warrant search was wholly independent is the testimony of the agents who conducted the illegal search. Under these circumstances, the threat that the subsequent search was tainted by the illegal search is too great to allow for the application of the independent source exception. The Court's contrary holding lends itself to easy abuse, and offers an incentive to bypass the constitutional requirement that probable cause be assessed by a neutral and detached magistrate before the police invade an individual's privacy.

When the very law enforcement officers who participate in an illegal search immediately thereafter obtain a warrant to search the same premises, I believe the evidence discovered during the initial illegal entry must be suppressed. Any other result emasculates the Warrant Clause and provides an intolerable incentive for warrantless searches. I respectfully dissent.

JUSTICE STEVENS, dissenting, omitted.

UTAH v. STRIEFF
579 U.S. ___ (2016)

JUSTICE THOMAS delivered the opinion of the Court.

To enforce the Fourth Amendment's prohibition against "unreasonable searches and seizures," this Court has at times required courts to exclude evidence obtained by unconstitutional police conduct. But the Court has also held that, even when there is a Fourth Amendment violation, this exclusionary rule does not apply when the costs of exclusion outweigh its deterrent benefits. In some cases, for example, the link between the unconstitutional conduct and the discovery of the evidence is too attenuated to justify suppression. The question in this case is whether this attenuation doctrine applies when an officer makes an unconstitutional investigatory stop; learns during that stop that the suspect is subject to a valid arrest warrant; and proceeds to arrest the suspect and seize incriminating evidence during a search incident to that arrest. We hold that the evidence the officer seized as part of the search incident to arrest is admissible because the officer's discovery of the arrest warrant attenuated the connection between the unlawful stop and the evidence seized incident to arrest.

Facts Summarized: An anonymous call led Narcotics detective Fackrell to investigate a tip about narcotics activity occurring at a residence. He went and surveilled, then decied to follow Strieff (a visitor to the residence) as he walked to a nearby convenience store. Fackrell detained Strieff, asked him what he was doing at the residence, requetsted identification, did a warrants check and found there was an outstanding warrant for Strieff's arrest. He was searched incident to that arrest and drugs were found. Strieff was charged and moved to suppress evidence claiming there it was derived from an unlawful investigatory stop. The prosecutors conceded that Fackrell lacked reasonable suspicion but claimed evidence should not be suppressed

because the existence of a valid arrest warrant attenuated the connection between the unlawful stop and the discovery of contraband.]

…

The trial court agreed with the State and admitted the evidence. The court found that the short time between the illegal stop and the search weighed in favor of suppressing the evidence, but that two countervailing considerations made it admissible. First, the court considered the presence of a valid arrest warrant to be an " 'extraordinary intervening circumstance.' " Second, the court stressed the absence of flagrant misconduct by Officer Fackrell, who was conducting a legitimate investigation of a suspected drug house.

Strieff conditionally pleaded guilty to reduced charges of attempted possession of a controlled substance and possession of drug paraphernalia, but reserved his right to appeal the trial court's denial of the suppression motion. …

[Procedural history omitted. The case wound up at the U.S. Supreme Court]

We granted certiorari to resolve disagreement about how the attenuation doctrine applies where an unconstitutional detention leads to the discovery of a valid arrest warrant.

II
A

[T]he exclusionary rule — the rule that often requires trial courts to exclude unlawfully seized evidence in a criminal trial — became the principal judicial remedy to deter Fourth Amendment violations.

Under the Court's precedents, the exclusionary rule encompasses both the "primary evidence obtained as a direct result of an illegal search or seizure" and, relevant here, "evidence later discovered and found to be derivative of an illegality," the so-called " 'fruit of the poisonous tree.' " But the significant costs of this rule have led us to deem it "applicable only . . . where its deterrence benefits outweigh its substantial social costs." "Suppression of evidence . . . has always been our last resort, not our first impulse."

We have accordingly recognized several exceptions to the rule. Three of these exceptions involve the causal relationship between the unconstitutional act and the discovery of evidence. First, the independent source doctrine allows trial courts to admit evidence obtained in an unlawful search if officers independently acquired it from a separate, independent source. Second, the inevitable discovery doctrine allows for the admission of evidence that would have been discovered even without the unconstitutional source. Third, and at issue here, is the attenuation doctrine: Evidence is admissible when the connection between unconstitutional police conduct and the evidence is remote or has been interrupted by some intervening circumstance, so that "the interest protected by the constitutional guarantee that has been violated would not be served by suppression of the evidence obtained."

B

Turning to the application of the attenuation doctrine to this case, we first address a threshold question: whether this doctrine applies at all to a case like this, where the intervening circumstance that the State relies on is the discovery of a valid, pre-existing, and untainted arrest warrant. ...[The Court concluded the doctrine *could* apply.]

It remains for us to address whether the discovery of a valid arrest warrant was a sufficient intervening event to break the causal chain between the unlawful stop and the discovery of drug-related evidence on Strieff's person. The three factors articulated in *Brown v. Illinois* . . . guide our analysis. First, we look to the "temporal proximity" between the unconstitutional conduct and the discovery of evidence to determine how

closely the discovery of evidence followed the unconstitutional search. Second, we consider "the presence of intervening circumstances." Third, and "particularly" significant, we examine "the purpose and flagrancy of the official misconduct." In evaluating these factors, we assume without deciding (because the State conceded the point) that Officer Fackrell lacked reasonable suspicion to initially stop Strieff. And, because we ultimately conclude that the warrant breaks the causal chain, we also have no need to decide whether the warrant's existence alone would make the initial stop constitutional even if Officer Fackrell was unaware of its existence.

1

The first factor, temporal proximity between the initially unlawful stop and the search, favors suppressing the evidence. Our precedents have declined to find that this factor favors attenuation unless "substantial time" elapses between an unlawful act and when the evidence is obtained. Here, however, Officer Fackrell discovered drug contraband on Strieff's person only minutes after the illegal stop. As the Court explained in *Brown*, such a short time interval counsels in favor of suppression; there, we found that the confession should be suppressed, relying in part on the "less than two hours" that separated the unconstitutional arrest and the confession.

In contrast, the second factor, the presence of intervening circumstances, strongly favors the State. In *Segura* the Court addressed similar facts to those here and found sufficient intervening circumstances to allow the admission of evidence. There, agents had probable cause to believe that apartment occupants were dealing cocaine. They sought a warrant. In the meantime, they entered the apartment, arrested an occupant, and discovered evidence of drug activity during a limited search for security reasons. The next evening, the Magistrate Judge issued the search warrant. This Court deemed the evidence admissible notwithstanding the illegal search because the information supporting the warrant was "wholly unconnected with the [arguably illegal] entry and was known to the agents well before the initial entry."

Segura, of course, applied the independent source doctrine because the unlawful entry "did not contribute in any way to discovery of the evidence seized under the warrant." But the *Segura* Court suggested that the existence of a valid warrant favors finding that the connection between unlawful conduct and the discovery of evidence is "sufficiently attenuated to dissipate the taint." That principle applies here.

In this case, the warrant was valid, it predated Officer Fackrell's investigation, and it was entirely unconnected with the stop. And once Officer Fackrell discovered the warrant, he had an obligation to arrest Strieff . . . Officer Fackrell's arrest of Strieff thus was a ministerial act that was independently compelled by the pre-existing warrant. And once Officer Fackrell was authorized to arrest Strieff, it was undisputedly lawful to search Strieff as an incident of his arrest to protect Officer Fackrell's safety.

Finally, the third factor, "the purpose and flagrancy of the official misconduct," . . . also strongly favors the State. The exclusionary rule exists to deter police misconduct. The third factor of the attenuation doctrine reflects that rationale by favoring exclusion only when the police misconduct is most in need of deterrence — that is, when it is purposeful or flagrant.

Officer Fackrell was at most negligent. In stopping Strieff, Officer Fackrell made two good-faith mistakes. First, he had not observed what time Strieff entered the suspected drug house, so he did not know how long Strieff had been there. . . . Second, . . . Officer Fackrell should have asked Strieff whether he would speak with him, instead of demanding that Strieff do so. Officer Fackrell's stated purpose was to "find out what was going on [in] the house." Nothing prevented him from approaching Strieff simply to ask. But these errors in judgment hardly rise to a purposeful

or flagrant violation of Strieff's Fourth Amendment rights.

While Officer Fackrell's decision to initiate the stop was mistaken, his conduct thereafter was lawful. The officer's decision to run the warrant check was a "negligibly burdensome precautio[n]" for officer safety. And Officer Fackrell's actual search of Strieff was a lawful search incident to arrest.

Moreover, there is no indication that this unlawful stop was part of any systemic or recurrent police misconduct. To the contrary, all the evidence suggests that the stop was an isolated instance of negligence that occurred in connection with a bona fide investigation of a suspected drug house. Officer Fackrell saw Strieff leave a suspected drug house. And his suspicion about the house was based on an anonymous tip and his personal observations.

Applying these factors, we hold that the evidence discovered on Strieff's person was admissible because the unlawful stop was sufficiently attenuated by the pre-existing arrest warrant. Although the illegal stop was close in time to Strieff's arrest, that consideration is outweighed by two factors supporting the State. The outstanding arrest warrant for Strieff's arrest is a critical intervening circumstance that is wholly independent of the illegal stop. The discovery of that warrant broke the causal chain between the unconstitutional stop and the discovery of evidence by compelling Officer Fackrell to arrest Strieff. And, it is especially significant that there is no evidence that Officer Fackrell's illegal stop reflected flagrantly unlawful police misconduct.

2

. . . .

We hold that the evidence Officer Fackrell seized as part of his search incident to arrest is admissible because his discovery of the arrest warrant attenuated the connection between the unlawful stop and the evidence seized from Strieff incident to arrest. ...

JUSTICE SOTOMAYOR, with whom JUSTICE GINSBURG joins as to Parts I, II, and III, dissenting.

The Court today holds that the discovery of a warrant for an unpaid parking ticket will forgive a police officer's violation of your Fourth Amendment rights. Do not be soothed by the opinion's technical language: This case allows the police to stop you on the street, demand your identification, and check it for outstanding traffic warrants — even if you are doing nothing wrong. If the officer discovers a warrant for a fine you forgot to pay, courts will now excuse his illegal stop and will admit into evidence anything he happens to find by searching you after arresting you on the warrant. Because the Fourth Amendment should prohibit, not permit, such misconduct, I dissent.

I

II

It is tempting in a case like this, where illegal conduct by an officer uncovers illegal conduct by a civilian, to forgive the officer. After all, his instincts, although unconstitutional, were correct. But a basic principle lies at the heart of the Fourth Amendment: Two wrongs don't make a right. When "lawless police conduct" uncovers evidence of lawless civilian conduct, this Court has long required later criminal trials to exclude the illegally obtained evidence. For example, if an officer breaks into a home and finds a forged check lying around, that check may not be used to prosecute the homeowner for bank fraud. We would describe the check as " 'fruit of the poisonous tree.' " Fruit that must be cast aside includes not only evidence directly found by an illegal search but also evidence "come at by exploitation of that illegality."

This "exclusionary rule" removes an incentive for officers to search us without proper justification. It also keeps courts from being "made party to lawless invasions of the constitutional rights of citizens by permitting unhindered governmental use of the fruits of such invasions." When courts admit only lawfully obtained evidence, they encourage "those who formulate law enforcement polices, and the officers who implement them, to incorporate Fourth Amendment ideals into their value system." But when courts admit illegally obtained evidence as well, they reward "manifest neglect if not an open defiance of the

…

The warrant check, . . . was not an "intervening circumstance" separating the stop from the search for drugs. It was part and parcel of the officer's illegal "expedition for evidence in the hope that something might turn up." Under our precedents, because the officer found Strieff's drugs by exploiting his own constitutional violation, the drugs should be excluded.

…

IV

This case involves a suspicionless stop, one in which the officer initiated this chain of events without justification. As the Justice Department notes, . . . many innocent people are subjected to the humiliations of these unconstitutional searches. The white defendant in this case shows that anyone's dignity can be violated in this manner. But it is no secret that people of color are disproportionate victims of this type of scrutiny. For generations, black and brown parents have given their children "the talk" — instructing them never to run down the street; always keep your hands where they can be seen; do not even think of talking back to a stranger — all out of fear of how an officer with a gun will react to them.

By legitimizing the conduct that produces this double consciousness, this case tells everyone, white and black, guilty and innocent, that an officer can verify your legal status at any time. It says that your body is subject to invasion while courts excuse the violation of your rights. It implies that you are not a citizen of a democracy but the subject of a carceral state, just waiting to be cataloged.

JUSTICE KAGAN, with whom JUSTICE GINSBURG joins, dissenting.

If a police officer stops a person on the street without reasonable suspicion, that seizure violates the Fourth Amendment. And if the officer pats down the unlawfully detained individual and finds drugs in his pocket, the State may not use the contraband as evidence in a criminal prosecution. That much is beyond dispute. The question here is whether the prohibition on admitting evidence dissolves if the officer discovers, after making the stop but before finding the drugs, that the person has an outstanding arrest warrant. Because that added wrinkle makes no difference under the Constitution, I respectfully dissent.

This Court has established a simple framework for determining whether to exclude evidence obtained through a Fourth Amendment violation: Suppression is necessary when, but only when, its societal benefits outweigh its costs. The exclusionary rule serves a crucial function — to deter unconstitutional police conduct. By barring the use of illegally obtained evidence, courts reduce the temptation for police officers to skirt the Fourth Amendment's requirements. But suppression of evidence also "exacts a heavy toll": Its consequence in many cases is to release a criminal without just punishment. Our decisions have thus endeavored to strike a sound balance between those two competing considerations — rejecting the "reflexive" impulse to exclude evidence every time an officer runs afoul of the Fourth Amendment, but insisting on suppression when it will lead to "appreciable deterrence" of police misconduct.

This case thus requires the Court to determine whether excluding the fruits of Officer Douglas Fackrell's unjustified stop of Edward Strieff would significantly deter police from committing similar constitutional violations in the future. And as the Court states, that inquiry turns on application of the "attenuation doctrine," — our effort to "mark the point" at which the discovery of evidence "become[s] so attenuated" from the police misconduct that the deterrent benefit of exclusion drops below its cost. Since *Brown v. Illinois* . . . three

factors have guided that analysis. . . . Here, as shown below, each of those considerations points toward suppression: Nothing in Fackrell's discovery of an outstanding warrant so attenuated the connection between his wrongful behavior and his detection of drugs as to diminish the exclusionary rule's deterrent benefits.

Start where the majority does: The temporal proximity factor, it forthrightly admits, "favors suppressing the evidence." After all, Fackrell's discovery of drugs came just minutes after the unconstitutional stop. And in prior decisions, this Court has made clear that only the lapse of "substantial time" between the two could favor admission. So the State, by all accounts, takes strike one.

Move on to the purposefulness of Fackrell's conduct, where the majority is less willing to see a problem for what it is. The majority chalks up Fackrell's Fourth Amendment violation to a couple of innocent "mistakes." But . . . Fackrell's seizure of Strieff was a calculated decision, taken with so little justification that the State has never tried to defend its legality . . . .

. . . .

Finally, consider whether any intervening circumstance "br[oke] the causal chain" between the stop and the evidence. The notion of such a disrupting event comes from the tort law doctrine of proximate causation. And as in the tort context, a circumstance counts as intervening only when it is unforeseeable — not when it can be seen coming from miles away. . . .

… Fackrell's discovery of an arrest warrant — the only event the majority thinks intervened — was an eminently foreseeable consequence of stopping Strieff. As Fackrell testified, checking for outstanding warrants during a stop is the "normal" practice of South Salt Lake City police. In other words, the department's standard detention procedures — stop, ask for identification, run a check — are partly designed to find outstanding warrants. And find them they will, given the staggering number of such warrants on the books. . . . In short, they are nothing like what intervening circumstances are supposed to be. Strike three.

The majority's misapplication of *Brown's* three-part inquiry creates unfortunate incentives for the police — indeed, practically invites them to do what Fackrell did here. Consider an officer who, like Fackrell, wishes to stop someone for investigative reasons, but does not have what a court would view as reasonable suspicion. If the officer believes that any evidence he discovers will be inadmissible, he is likely to think the unlawful stop not worth making — precisely the deterrence the exclusionary rule is meant to achieve. But when he is told of today's decision? Now the officer knows that the stop may well yield admissible evidence: So long as the target is one of the many millions of people in this country with an outstanding arrest warrant, anything the officer finds in a search is fair game for use in a criminal prosecution. The officer's incentive to violate the Constitution thus increases: From here on, he sees potential advantage in stopping individuals without reasonable suspicion — exactly the temptation the exclusionary rule is supposed to remove. Because the majority thus places Fourth Amendment protections at risk, I respectfully dissent.

Other Cases: Exclusionary Rule

Wong Sun v. United States 371 U.S. 471 (1963)

SUMMARY: Federal narcotics agents, acting on a tip, broke into Toy's apartment and handcuffed him. The entry was illegal because the police did not have probable cause. During the police entry, Toy made statements implicating Yee of selling narcotics. The police then went to Yee's, and Yee gave the police some heroin and stated he had been sold the drugs by Toy and Wong Sun. Wong Sun was then arrested (without probable cause). Wong Sun and Toy were arraigned on the drug charges and released on their own recognizance.

Several days later, Wong Sun voluntarily went back to the offices of the Bureau of Narcotics. He was warned of his right to remain silent and to have an attorney (this was actually before Miranda), and he nevertheless confessed.

The court held that Toy's statements were *derivative evidence* of the illegal home entry, and thus, the police could not introduce them — nor could police introduce evidence of the drugs seized from Yee since they were a direct result of Toy's statement.

The drugs, however, were admissible against Wong Sun, even though their seizure had been the direct product of the illegal entry into Toy's house because Wong Sun lacked standing to complain of that illegality.

The Court held that Wong Sun's own arrest was illegal, but found that his confession was admissible because he had been released for several days and the connection between the arrest and his statements several days later had "become so attenuated as to dissipate the taint."

Herring v. United States, 555 U.S. 1 (2009)

[Note the many "other cases" discussed in this case: *Evans, Leon, Sheppard, Krull, Mapp, Franks, Silverthorne*]

The Fourth Amendment forbids "unreasonable searches and seizures," and this usually requires the police to have probable cause or a warrant before making an arrest. What if an officer reasonably believes there is an outstanding arrest warrant, but that belief turns out to be wrong because of a negligent bookkeeping error by another police employee? The parties here agree that the ensuing arrest is still a violation of the Fourth Amendment, but dispute whether contraband found during a search incident to that arrest must be excluded in a later prosecution.

Our cases establish that such suppression is not an automatic consequence of a Fourth Amendment violation. Instead, the question turns on the culpability of the police and the potential of exclusion to deter wrongful police conduct. Here the error was the result of isolated negligence attenuated from the arrest. We hold that in these circumstances the jury should not be barred from considering all the evidence.

[Facts Summarized: Herring was arrested based on information that there was an outstanding warrant for his arrest. The warrant had actually been cleared but was still in the active warrant data base. Herring was searched incident to his arrest and drugs and a weapon were found. Herring was indicted and he filed a motion to suppress the drugs and weapon on the ground that his initial arrest had been illegal because the warrant had been rescinded. The Magistrate Judge recommended denied the motion because the arresting officers had acted in a good-faith belief that the warrant was still outstanding. Finding that there was "no reason to believe that application of the exclusionary rule here would deter the occurrence of any future mistakes." The Court accepted review to resolve a split in the lower courts on whether to exclude or not]

…

For the purpose of deciding this case, we accept the parties' assumption that there was a Fourth Amendment violation. This issue is whether the exclusionary rule should be applied.

…

The fact that a Fourth Amendment violation occurred — *i.e.*, that a search or arrest was unreasonable — does not necessarily mean that the exclusionary rule applies. Indeed, exclusion "has always been our last resort, not our first impulse," and our precedents establish important principles that constrain application of the exclusionary rule.

First, the exclusionary rule is not an individual right and applies only where it "'result[s] in appreciable deterrence.'" We have repeatedly rejected the argument that exclusion is a necessary consequence of a Fourth Amendment violation. Instead we have focused on the efficacy of the rule in deterring Fourth Amendment violations in the future.

In addition, the benefits of deterrence must outweigh the costs. "We have never suggested that the exclusionary rule must apply in every circumstance in which it might provide marginal deterrence." . . . "[T]o the extent that application of the exclusionary rule could provide some incremental deterrent, that possible benefit must be weighed against [its] substantial social costs." . . .

. . . .

In *Massachusetts* v. *Sheppard*, we held that the exclusionary rule did not apply when a warrant

was invalid because a judge forgot to make "clerical corrections" to it.

Shortly thereafter we extended these holdings to warrantless administrative searches performed in good-faith reliance on a statute later declared unconstitutional. *Krull, supra.* Finally, in *Evans*, we applied this good-faith rule to police who reasonably relied on mistaken information in a court's database that an arrest warrant was outstanding. We held that a mistake made by a judicial employee could not give rise to exclusion for three reasons: The exclusionary rule was crafted to curb police rather than judicial misconduct; court employees were unlikely to try to subvert the Fourth Amendment; and "most important, there [was] no basis for believing that application of the exclusionary rule in [those] circumstances" would have any significant effect in deterring the errors. *Evans* left unresolved "whether the evidence should be suppressed if police personnel were responsible for the error," an issue not argued by the State in that case, but one that we now confront.

The extent to which the exclusionary rule is justified by these deterrence principles varies with the culpability of the law enforcement conduct. As we said in *Leon*, "an assessment of the flagrancy of the police misconduct constitutes an important step in the calculus" of applying the exclusionary rule. Similarly, in *Krull* we elaborated that "evidence should be suppressed 'only if it can be said that the law enforcement officer had knowledge, or may properly be charged with knowledge, that the search was unconstitutional under the Fourth Amendment.'"

…

Indeed, the abuses that gave rise to the exclusionary rule featured intentional conduct that was patently unconstitutional. In *Weeks*, a foundational exclusionary rule case, the officers had broken into the defendant's home (using a key shown to them by a neighbor), confiscated incriminating papers, then returned again with a U. S. Marshal to confiscate even more. Not only did they have no search warrant, which the Court held was required, but they could not have gotten one had they tried. They were so lacking in sworn and particularized information that "not even an order of court would have justified such procedure." *Silverthorne Lumber Co.* v. *United States*, on which petitioner repeatedly relies, was similar; federal officials "without a shadow of authority" went to the defendants' office and "made a clean sweep" of every paper they could find. Even the Government seemed to acknowledge that the "seizure was an outrage."

Equally flagrant conduct was at issue in *Mapp* v. *Ohio*, which overruled *Wolf* v. *Colorado*, and extended the exclusionary rule to the States. Officers forced open a door to Ms. Mapp's house, kept her lawyer from entering, brandished what the court concluded was a false warrant, then forced her into handcuffs and canvassed the house for obscenity.

To trigger the exclusionary rule, police conduct must be sufficiently deliberate that exclusion can meaningfully deter it, and sufficiently culpable that such deterrence is worth the price paid by the justice system. As laid out in our cases, the exclusionary rule serves to deter deliberate, reckless, or grossly negligent conduct, or in some circumstances recurring or systemic negligence. The error in this case does not rise to that level.

Our decision in *Franks* v. *Delaware*, provides an analogy. In *Franks*, we held that police negligence in obtaining a warrant did not even rise to the level of a Fourth Amendment violation, let alone meet the more stringent test for triggering the exclusionary rule. We held that the Constitution allowed defendants, in some circumstances, "to challenge the truthfulness of factual statements made in an affidavit supporting the warrant," even after the warrant had issued. If those false statements were necessary to the Magistrate Judge's probable-cause determination, the warrant would be "voided.". But we did not find all false statements relevant: "There must be allegations of deliberate falsehood or of reckless disregard for the truth," and "[a]llegations of negligence or innocent mistake are insufficient."

Both this case and *Franks* concern false information provided by police. Under *Franks*, negligent police miscommunications in the course of acquiring a warrant do not provide a basis to rescind a warrant and render a search or arrest invalid. Here, the miscommunications occurred in a different context — after the warrant had been issued and recalled — but that fact should not require excluding the evidence obtained.

The pertinent analysis of deterrence and culpability is objective, not an "inquiry into the subjective awareness of arresting officers," We have already held that "our good-faith inquiry is confined to the objectively ascertainable question whether a reasonably well trained officer would have known that the search was illegal" in light of "all of the circumstances." These circumstances frequently include a particular officer's knowledge and experience, but that does not make the test any more subjective than the one for probable cause, which looks to an officer's knowledge and experience, but not his subjective intent.

We do not suggest that all recordkeeping errors by the police are immune from the exclusionary rule. In this case, however, the conduct at issue was not so objectively culpable as to require exclusion. . . .

If the police have been shown to be reckless in maintaining a warrant system, or to have knowingly made false entries to lay the groundwork for future false arrests, exclusion would certainly be justified under our cases should such misconduct cause a Fourth Amendment violation. . . .

. . . [W]e conclude that when police mistakes are the result of negligence such as that described here, rather than systemic error or reckless disregard of constitutional requirements, any marginal deterrence does not "pay its way." In such a case, the criminal should not "go free because the constable has blundered."

JUSTICE GINSBURG, with whom JUSTICE STEVENS, JUSTICE SOUTER, and JUSTICE BREYER join, dissenting.

. . .

Beyond doubt, a main objective of the rule "is to deter — to compel respect for the constitutional guaranty in the only effectively available way — by removing the incentive to disregard it." *Elkins* v. *United States*. But the rule also serves other important purposes: It "enabl[es] the judiciary to avoid the taint of partnership in official lawlessness," and it "assur[es] the people — all potential victims of unlawful government conduct — that the government would not profit from its lawless behavior, thus minimizing the risk of seriously undermining popular trust in government."

The exclusionary rule . . . is often the only remedy effective to redress a Fourth Amendment violation. Civil liability will not lie for "the vast majority of [F]ourth [A]mendment violations — the frequent infringements motivated by commendable zeal, not condemnable malice." Criminal prosecutions or administrative sanctions against the offending officers and injunctive relief against widespread violations are an even farther cry.

The Court maintains that Herring's case is one in which the exclusionary rule could have scant deterrent effect and therefore would not "pay its way." I disagree.

…

That the mistake here involved the failure to make a computer entry hardly means that application of the exclusionary rule would have minimal value. "Just as the risk of *respondeat superior* liability encourages employers to supervise . . . their employees' conduct [more carefully], so the risk of exclusion of evidence encourages policymakers and systems managers to monitor the performance of the systems they install and the personnel employed to operate those systems.

…

Is the potential deterrence here worth the costs it imposes? In light of the paramount importance of accurate recordkeeping in law enforcement, I would answer yes, and next explain why, as I see it, Herring's motion presents a particularly strong case for suppression. . . Law enforcement has an increasing supply of information within its easy electronic reach. The risk of error stemming from these databases is not slim. Herring's *amici* warn that law enforcement databases are insufficiently monitored and often out of date. Government reports describe, for example, flaws in NCIC Databases, terrorist watchlist databases and databases associated with the Federal Government's employment eligibility verification system.

Inaccuracies in expansive, interconnected collections of electronic information raise grave concerns for individual liberty. "The offense to the dignity of the citizen who is arrested, handcuffed, and searched on a public street simply because some bureaucrat has failed to maintain an accurate computer data base" is evocative of the use of general warrants that so outraged the authors of our Bill of Rights.

The Court assures that "exclusion would certainly be justified" if "the police have been shown to be reckless in maintaining a warrant system, or to have knowingly made false entries to lay the groundwork for future false arrests." This concession provides little comfort. First, by restricting suppression to bookkeeping errors that are deliberate or reckless, the majority leaves Herring, and others like him, with no remedy for violations of their constitutional rights. There can be no serious assertion that relief is available under 42 U. S. C. §1983. The arresting officer would be sheltered by qualified immunity, and the police department itself is not liable for the negligent acts of its employees. Moreover, identifying the department employee who committed the error may be impossible.

Second, I doubt that police forces already possess sufficient incentives to maintain up-to-date records. The Government argues that police have no desire to send officers out on arrests unnecessarily, because arrests consume resources and place officers in danger. The facts of this case do not fit that description of police motivation. Here the officer wanted to arrest Herring and consulted the Department's records to legitimate his predisposition.

Third, even when deliberate or reckless conduct is afoot, the Court's assurance will often be an empty promise: How is an impecunious defendant to make the required showing? If the answer is that a defendant is entitled to discovery (and if necessary, an audit of police databases) then the Court has imposed a considerable administrative burden on courts and law enforcement.

…

JUSTICE BREYER, with whom JUSTICE SOUTER joins, dissenting.

In *Arizona* v. *Evans*, 514 U. S. 1 (1995), we held that recordkeeping errors made by a court clerk do not trigger the exclusionary rule, so long as the police reasonably relied upon the court clerk's recordkeeping. The rationale for our decision was premised on a distinction between judicial errors and police errors. ….

Distinguishing between police recordkeeping errors and judicial ones not only is consistent with our precedent, but also is far easier for courts to administer than THE CHIEF JUSTICE's case-by-case, multifactored inquiry into the degree of police culpability. I therefore would apply the exclusionary rule when police personnel are responsible for a recordkeeping error that results in a Fourth Amendment violation. The need for a clear line, and the recognition of such a line in our precedent, are further reasons in support of the outcome … .

Silverthorne Lumber Co. v. United States, 251 U.S. 385 (1920)

SUMMARY: Defendants were indicted and arrested. While being detained, federal agents illegally entered their company business and made a clean sweep of all their books, papers, documents. They complained and a Court made the agents return what they had taken, but before they did, they made copies and photographs of what they had seized. The government attempted to use those copies against them. (Someone this case came about due to a contempt of a contempt of court by the Silverthornes who refused to give back to the government the originals that were taken and then returned, but that point of the case is obscure). This case became known as the "fruit of the poisonous tree" case (See Nardone v. United States, a 1939 case in which the Court first started referring to "fruit of the poisonous tree" evidence in Silverthorne).

The court stated,

"The proposition could not be presented more nakedly. It is that although of course its seizure was an outrage which the Government now regrets, it may study the papers before it returns them, copy them, and then may use the knowledge that it has gained to call upon the owners in a more regular form to produce them; that the protection of the Constitution covers the physical possession but not any advantages that the Government can gain over the object of its pursuit. Weeks v. United States . . . had established that laying the papers directly before the grand jury was unwarranted, but it is taken to mean only that two steps are required instead of one. In our opinion, such is not the law. It reduces the Fourth Amendment to a form of words. The essence of a provision forbidding the acquisitions of evidence in a certain way is that not merely the evidence so acquired shall not be used before the Court but that it should not be used at all."

The court went on to lay seeds for the independent discovery exception:

"Of course this does not mean that the facts thus obtained become sacred and inaccessible. If knowledge of them is gained from an independent source they may be proved like any others, but the knowledge gained by the Government's own wrong cannot be used by it in the way proposed."

.

Chapter Six: Confessions And Interrogations

Confessions and interrogations are governed by the Fourteenth, the Fifth, and the Sixth Amendments. In a series of cases, the Court has interpreted, but not necessarily consistently, how these Amendments limit the ability of police to get confessions from suspects.

The due process guarantees of the Fifth Amendment and Fourteenth Amendment speak to confessions that are coerced and involuntary. The Fourteenth Amendment states, The use of coerced confessions in federal prosecutions has been barred since 1897 (*Bram v. United Sates*), and since 1936 in state prosecutions (*Brown v. Mississippi)*. The Court reasoned that coerced or involuntary confessions violate fundamental fairness and admitting them in state court proceedings violates due process.

The "self-incrimination" protection of the Fifth Amendment guarantees that, "[n]o person shall be compelled in any criminal case to be a witness against himself." This Fifth Amendment federal guarantee was incorporated to the states (and made applicable to the states) because of the due process clause of the Fourteenth Amendment in *Malloy v. Hogan*, 378 U.S. 1 (1964).

The Sixth Amendment's right to counsel guarantee has been found to cover confession and interrogation scenarios. *Miranda v. Arizona,* 384 U.S. 436 (1966). It states, "In all criminal prosecutions, the accused shall . . . have the assistance of counsel for his defense."

Miranda is the key case in confession and interrogations jurisprudence and is one of the most significant cases in criminal procedure. Under *Miranda*, statements made by a defendant in response to custodial interrogation by a government official cannot be used to prove the defendant's guilt at trial unless the defendant was advised of the appropriate Fifth and Sixth Amendment rights. The *Miranda* case (which was really four joined cases) raises four key questions: Is the defendant in custody? Were the defendant's statements made in response to interrogation? Were the warnings given? Did the defendant validly waive the protections of the Fifth and Sixth Amendments after receiving the required warnings. Two follow up questions are: Is there any exceptions to the Miranda rule that would control in this case? What remedy is there for a constitutional violation which occur when police interrogate a suspect and obtain a confession?[68]

This chapter first examines the requirement that the defendant's confession be voluntary and explores the phenomenon of police-induced false confessions. It then explores the *Miranda* decision and what it meant by a "custodial interrogation," whether warnings were given, and how suspects invoke and waive their rights under *Miranda.* The chapter concludes by examining the Court's decisions revealing its willingness to recognize exceptions to *Miranda* as well as its later declaration

---

[68] The remedy for constitutional violations relating from confessions and interrogations is the excluding illegally obtained confessions from trial. The exclusionary rule, discussed in Chapter Five, is the same mechanism used to provide this remedy.

that Miranda espoused *constitutional rights* not just *prophylactic rights* (which meant that the holding could not be overturned by a mere act of Congress.)

THE FIFTH AND FOURTEENTH AMENDMENTS' DUE PROCESS AND VOLUNTARINESS REQUIREMENT

As just noted, the Court has overturned convictions involving involuntary and coerced confessions finding that they violate fundamental fairness that due process requires. Involuntarily-procured confessions not only violate the defendant's rights, but they lack reliability. And, because they are not reliable, involuntary confessions are not admissible against the defendant for any purpose — even impeachment.

Even when involuntary confessions have the indicia of reliability (meaning, they seem to be reliable), they will still be inadmissible because the police practices by which there were obtained violated fundamental decency. For example, in *Rogers v. Richmond*, 365 U.S. 534 (1961), the police obtained the defendant's confession by pretending to arrest his sick wife. The state court held that the confession was probably reliable and allowed it to be introduced at his trial as evidence of his guilt. The U.S. Supreme Court reversed, finding that the reliability of the confessions was not the only consideration. It said that confessions obtained by subterfuge and force must be disallowed "not because such confessions are unlikely to be true but because the methods used to extract them offend an underlying principle in the enforcement of our criminal law: that ours is an accusatorial and not an inquisitorial system." *Rodgers*, 365 U.S., at 540.

Some reliable and non-coerced confessions have been disallowed because they were not the product of the defendant's free choice, even when the police practices weren't necessarily objectionable. For example, in *Townsend v. Sain*, 372 U.S. 293 (1963) the defendant, who was sick, was given some medication which had the effect of a truth serum. The police were unaware of the drug's effects, and obtained a confession from the suspect after questioning him. Although reliable and not obtained through particularly coercive methods the Court held that "[a]ny questioning by police officers which *in fact* produces a confession which is not the product of free intellect renders that confession inadmissible."

State trial courts utilized the "voluntariness test" in analyzing whether a confession should be admitted from 1936 (*Brown*) until *(1964)* (*Malloy*). The voluntariness test has been criticized for not giving defendants enough protection because judges had tremendous discretion when employing the totality of the circumstance test in determining voluntariness. Federal trial courts also utilized the voluntariness test under the Fifth Amendment's due process clause).

The requirements set forth in *Miranda* supplemented, but did not replace, the requirement that confessions be voluntary. The *Mincey* Court specifically held that the due process voluntariness test remains in place after *Miranda*. "But *any* criminal trial use against a defendant of his *involuntary* statement is a denial of due process of law 'even though there is ample evidence aside from the confession to support the conviction.'" Even though police read a suspect the *Miranda* warnings, confessions taken by coercion that overbears a person's will are inadmissible. Accordingly, courts must still evaluate all the facts surrounding the taking of statements from a defendant and not just examine whether warnings were given and waived.

BROWN v. MISSISSIPPI
297 U.S. 278 (1936)

CHIEF JUSTICE HUGHES delivered the opinion of the Court.

The question in this case is whether convictions, which rest solely upon confessions shown to have been extorted by officers of the state by brutality and violence, are consistent with the due process of law required by the Fourteenth Amendment of the Constitution of the United States.

Petitioners were indicted for the murder of one Raymond Stewart, whose death occurred on March 30, 1934. They were indicted on April 4, 1934, and were then arraigned and pleaded not guilty. Counsel were appointed by the court to defend them. Trial was begun the next morning and was concluded on the following day, when they were found guilty and sentenced to death.

Aside from the confessions, there was no evidence sufficient to warrant the submission of the case to the jury. After a preliminary inquiry, testimony as to the confessions was received over the objection of defendants' counsel. Defendants then testified that the confessions were false and had been procured by physical torture. The case went to the jury with instructions, upon the request of defendants' counsel, that if the jury had reasonable doubt as to the confessions having resulted from coercion, they were not to be considered as evidence. …

There is no dispute as to the facts upon this point, and as they are clearly and adequately stated in the dissenting opinion. . . showing both the extreme brutality of the measures to extort the confessions and the participation of the state authorities. …

The crime with which these defendants, all ignorant negroes, are charged, was discovered about 1 o'clock p.m. on Friday, March 30, 1934. On that night one Dial, a deputy sheriff, accompanied by others, came to the home of Ellington, one of the defendants, and

requested him to accompany them to the house of the deceased, and there a number of white men were gathered, who began to accuse the defendant of the crime. Upon his denial they seized him, and with the participation of the deputy they hanged him by a rope to the limb of a tree, and, having let him down, they hung him again, and when he was let down the second time, and he still protested his innocence, he was tied to a tree and whipped, and, still declining to accede to the demands that he confess, he was finally released, and he returned with some difficulty to his home, suffering intense pain and agony. The record of the testimony shows that the signs of the rope on his neck were plainly visible during the so-called trial. A day or two thereafter the said deputy, accompanied by another, returned to the home of the said defendant and arrested him, and departed with the prisoner towards the jail in an adjoining county, but went by a route which led into the state of Alabama; and while on the way, in that state, the deputy stopped and again severely whipped the defendant, declaring that he would continue the whipping until he confessed, and the defendant then agreed to confess to such a statement as the deputy would dictate, and he did so, after which he was delivered to jail.

The other two defendants, Ed Brown and Henry Shields, were also arrested and taken to the same jail. On Sunday night, April 1, 1934, the same deputy, accompanied by a number of white men, one of whom was also an officer, and by the jailer, came to the jail, and the two last named defendants were made to strip and they were laid over chairs and their backs were cut to pieces with a leather strap with buckles on it, and they were likewise made by the said deputy definitely to understand that the whipping would be continued unless and until they confessed, and not only confessed, but confessed in every matter of detail as demanded by those present; and in this manner the defendants confessed he crime, and, as the whippings progressed and were repeated, they changed or adjusted their confession in all particulars of detail so as to conform to the demands of their torturers. When the confessions had been obtained in the exact form and contents as desired by the mob, they left with the parting admonition and warning that, if the defendants changed their story at any time in any respect from that last stated, the perpetrators of the outrage would administer the same or equally effective treatment.

Further details of the brutal treatment to which these helpless prisoners were subjected need not be pursued. It is sufficient to say that in pertinent respects the transcript reads more like pages torn from some medieval account than a record made within the confines of a modern civilization which aspires to an enlightened constitutional government.

All this having been accomplished, on the next day, that is, on Monday, April 2, when the defendants had been given time to recuperate somewhat from the tortures to which they had been subjected, the two sheriffs, one of the county where the crime was committed, and the other of the county of the jail in which the prisoners were confined, came to the jail, accompanied by eight other persons, some of them deputies, there to hear the free and voluntary confession of these miserable and abject defendants. The sheriff of the county of the crime admitted that he had heard of the whipping, but averred that he had no personal knowledge of it. He admitted that one of the defendants, when brought before him to confess, was limping and did not sit down, and that this particular defendant then and there stated that he had been strapped so severely that he could not sit down, and, as already stated, the signs of the rope on the neck of another of the defendants were plainly visible to all. Nevertheless the solemn farce of hearing the free and voluntary confessions was gone through with, and these two sheriffs and one other person then present were the three witnesses used in court to establish the so-called confessions, which were received by the court and admitted in evidence over the objections of the defendants duly entered of

record as each of the said three witnesses delivered their alleged testimony. There was thus enough before the court when these confessions were first offered to make known to the court that they were not, beyond all reasonable doubt, free and voluntary; and the failure of the court then to exclude the confessions is sufficient to reverse the judgment,....

The spurious confessions having been obtained-and the farce last mentioned having been gone through with on Monday, April 2d- the court, then in session, on the following day, Tuesday, April 3, 1934, ordered the grand jury to reassemble on the succeeding day, April 4, 1934, at 9 o'clock, and on the morning of the day last mentioned the grand jury returned an indictment against the defendants for murder. Late that afternoon the defendants were brought from the jail in the adjoining county and arraigned, when one or more of them offered to plead guilty, which the court declined to accept, and, upon inquiry whether they had or desired counsel, they stated that they had none, and did not suppose that counsel could be of any assistance to them. The court thereupon appointed counsel, and set the case for trial for the following morning at 9 o'clock, and the defendants were returned to the jail in the adjoining county about thirty miles away.

The defendants were brought to the courthouse of the county on the following morning, April 5th, and the so-called trial was opened, and was concluded on the next day, April 6, 1934, and resulted in a pretended conviction with death sentences. The evidence upon which the conviction was obtained was the so-called confessions. Without this evidence, a peremptory instruction to find for the defendants would have been inescapable. The defendants were put on the stand, and by their testimony the facts and the details thereof as to the manner by which the confessions were extorted from them were fully developed, and it is further disclosed by the record that the same deputy, Dial, under whose guiding hand and active participation the tortures to coerce the confessions were administered, was actively in the performance of the supposed duties of a court deputy in the courthouse and in the presence of the prisoners during what is denominated, in complimentary terms, the trial of these defendants. This deputy was put on the stand by the state in rebuttal, and admitted the whippings. It is interesting to note that in his testimony with reference to the whipping of the defendant Ellington, and in response to the inquiry as to how severely he was whipped, the deputy stated, 'Not too much for a negro; not as much as I would have done if it were left to me.' Two others who had participated in these whippings were introduced and admitted it-not a single witness was introduced who denied it. The facts are not only undisputed, they are admitted, and admitted to have been done by officers of the state, in conjunction with other participants, and all this was definitely well known to everybody connected with the trial, and during the trial, including the state's prosecuting attorney and the trial judge presiding.

The state stresses . . . that 'exemption from compulsory self-incrimination in the courts of the states is not secured by any part of the Federal Constitution,' and that 'the privilege against self-incrimination may be withdrawn and the accused put upon the stand as a witness for the state.' But the question of the right of the state to withdraw the privilege against self-incrimination is not here involved. The compulsion to which the quoted statements refer is that of the processes of justice by which the accused may be called as a witness and required to testify. Compulsion by torture to extort a confession is a different matter.

The state is free to regulate the procedure of its courts in accordance with its own conceptions of policy, unless in so doing it 'offends some principle of justice so rooted in the traditions and conscience of our people as to be ranked as fundamental.' The state may abolish trial by jury. It may dispense with indictment by a grand jury and substitute complaint or information. But the freedom of the state in establishing its policy is the freedom of constitutional government and is limited by the requirement of due process of law. Because a state may dispense with a jury trial, it does not follow that it may substitute trial by ordeal. The rack and torture chamber may not be substituted for the witness stand. The state may not permit an accused to be hurried to conviction under mob domination- where the whole proceeding is but a mask- without supplying corrective process. The state may not deny to the accused the aid of counsel. Nor may a state, through the action of its officers, contrive a conviction through the pretense of a trial which in truth is 'but used as a means of depriving a defendant of liberty through a deliberate deception of court and jury by the presentation of testimony known to be perjured.' And the trial equally is a mere pretense where the state authorities have contrived a conviction resting solely upon confessions obtained by violence. The due process clause requires 'that state action, whether through one agency or another, shall be consistent with the fundamental principles of liberty and justice which lie at the base of all our civil and political institutions.' It would be difficult to conceive of methods more revolting to the sense of justice than those taken to procure the confessions of these petitioners, and the use of the confessions thus obtained as the basis for conviction and sentence was a clear denial of due process.

[The state claims that defense counsel erred by not moving to exclude the confessions after it became known they were coerced and admitted (and defense counsel had objected to their admission.] … That complaint is not of the commission of mere error, but of a wrong so fundamental that it made the whole proceeding a mere pretense of a trial and rendered the conviction and sentence wholly void. We are not concerned with a mere question of state practice, or whether counsel assigned to petitioners were competent or mistakenly assumed that their first objections were sufficient. In an earlier case the Supreme Court of the State had recognized the duty of the court to supply corrective process where due process of law had been denied. … The duty of maintaining constitutional rights of a person on trial for his life rises above mere rules of procedure, and wherever the court is clearly satisfied that such violations exist, it will refuse to sanction such violations and will apply the corrective.

In the instant case, the trial court was fully advised by the undisputed evidence of the way in which the confessions had been procured. The trial court knew that there was no other evidence upon which conviction and sentence could be based. Yet it proceeded to permit conviction and to pronounce sentence. The conviction and sentence were void for want of the essential elements of due process, and the proceeding thus vitiated could be challenged in any appropriate manner.

Other Cases: Voluntariness of Confessions

Rochin v. California, 342 U.S. 165 (1952

SUMMARY: Police believed Rochin was selling drugs and went to his home, a two-story dwelling where Rochin lived with his his mother, wife, and other members of his family. Police entered through an open outside door, and then forced open the door to Rochin's room on the second floor. They found him sitting on the bed where his wife was lying.

"On a "night stand" beside the bed the deputies spied two capsules. When asked "Whose stuff is this?" Rochin seized the capsules and put them in his mouth. A struggle ensued, in the course of which the three officers "jumped upon him" and attempted to extract the capsules. The force they applied proved unavailing against Rochin's resistance. He was handcuffed and taken to a hospital. At the direction of one of the officers a doctor forced an emetic solution through a tube into Rochin's stomach against his will. This "stomach pumping" produced vomiting. In the vomited matter were found two capsules which proved to contain morphine."

"Rochin was brought to trial . . . and the . . . chief evidence against him was the two capsules. They were admitted over petitioner's objection, although the means of obtaining them was frankly set forth in the testimony by one of the deputies..."

The District Court of Appeal affirmed the conviction, despite the finding that the officers "were guilty of unlawfully breaking into and entering defendant's room and were guilty of unlawfully assaulting and battering defendant while in the room," and "were guilty of unlawfully assaulting, battering, torturing and falsely imprisoning the defendant at the alleged hospital." . . .

Before the Court was whether the government action violated the "limitations which the Due Process Clause of the Fourteenth Amendment imposes on the conduct of criminal proceedings by the States."

"Due process of law is a summarized constitutional guarantee of respect for those personal immunities which, as Mr. Justice Cardozo twice wrote for the Court, are "so rooted in the traditions and conscience of our people as to be ranked as fundamental," . . .or are "implicit in the concept of ordered liberty." . . .

The vague contours of the Due Process Clause do not leave judges at large. We may not draw on our merely personal and private notions and disregard the limits that bind judges in their judicial function. Even though the concept of due process of law is not final and fixed, these limits are derived from considerations that are fused in the whole nature of our judicial process. The Due Process Clause places upon this Court the duty of exercising a judgment, within the narrow confines of judicial power in reviewing State convictions, upon interests of society pushing in opposite directions.

Applying these general considerations to the circumstances of the present case, we are compelled to conclude that the proceedings by which this conviction was obtained do more than offend some fastidious squeamishness or private sentimentalism about combating crime too energetically. This is conduct that shocks the conscience. Illegally breaking into the privacy of the petitioner, the struggle to open his mouth and remove what was there, the forcible extraction of his stomach's contents — this course of proceeding by agents of government to obtain evidence is bound to offend even hardened sensibilities. They are methods too close to the rack and the screw to permit of constitutional differentiation.

It has long since ceased to be true that due process of law is heedless of the means by which otherwise relevant and credible evidence is obtained. This was not true even before the series of recent cases enforced the constitutional principle that the States may not base convictions upon confessions, however much verified, obtained by coercion. These decisions are not arbitrary exceptions to the comprehensive right of States to fashion their own rules of evidence for criminal trials. They are not sports in our constitutional law but applications of a general principle. They are only instances of the general requirement that States in their prosecutions respect certain decencies of civilized conduct. Due process of law, as a historic and generative principle, precludes defining, and thereby confining, these standards of conduct more precisely than to say that convictions cannot be brought about by methods that offend "a sense of justice." It would be a stultification of the responsibility which the course of constitutional history has cast upon this Court to hold that in order to convict a man the police cannot extract by force what is in his mind but can extract what is in his stomach.

To attempt in this case to distinguish what lawyers call "real evidence" from verbal evidence is to ignore the reasons for excluding coerced confessions. Use of involuntary verbal confessions in State criminal trials is constitutionally obnoxious not only because of their unreliability. They are inadmissible under the Due Process Clause even though statements contained in them may be independently established as true. Coerced confessions offend the community's sense of fair play and decency. So here, to sanction the brutal conduct which naturally enough was condemned by the court whose judgment is before us, would be to afford brutality the cloak of law. Nothing would be more calculated to discredit law and thereby to brutalize the temper of a society."

JUSTICE BLACK, concurring.

... I think a person is compelled to be a witness against himself not only when he is compelled to testify, but also when as here, incriminating evidence is forcibly taken from him by a contrivance of modern science. ...

JUSTICE DOUGLAS, concurring.

... The Framers made [the Fifth Amendment protection against self-incrimination] . . . a standard of due process for prosecutions by the Federal Government. If it is a requirement of due process for a trial in the federal courthouse, it is impossible for me to say it is not a requirement of due process for a trial in the state courthouse. The Court rejected the view that compelled testimony should be excluded and held in substance that the accused in a state trial can be forced to testify against himself. I disagree. Of course an accused can be compelled to be present at the trial, to stand, to sit, to turn this way or that, and to try on a cap or a coat. But I think that words taken from his lips, capsules taken from his stomach, blood taken from his veins are all inadmissible provided they are taken from him without his consent. They are inadmissible because of the command of the Fifth Amendment.

That is an unequivocal, definite and workable rule of evidence for state and federal courts. But we cannot in fairness free the state courts from that command and yet excoriate them for flouting the "decencies of civilized conduct" when they admit the evidence. That is to make the rule turn not on the Constitution but on the idiosyncrasies of the judges who sit here

Mincey v. Arizona, 437 U.S. 385 (1978)

SUMMARY: A drug-deal between undercover officers and Mincey went bad, and a shootout ensued. One officer was shot and later died and Mincey was shot and taken to the hospital and treated. While he was lying in the intensive care officers came to interrogate him.

"Mincey was unable to talk because of the tube in his mouth, and so he responded to Detective Hust's questions by writing answers on pieces of paper provided by the hospital. Hust told Mincey he was under arrest for the murder of a police officer, gave him the warnings required by *Miranda v. Arizona*, and began to ask questions about the events that had taken place in Mincey's apartment a few hours earlier. Although Mincey asked repeatedly that the interrogation stop until he could get a lawyer, Hust continued to question him until almost midnight.

. . . .

"Statements made by a defendant in circumstances violating the strictures of *Miranda v. Arizona*, supra, are admissible for impeachment if their "trustworthiness . . . satisfies legal standards." But any criminal trial use against a defendant of his involuntary statement is a denial of due process of law "even though there is ample evidence aside from the confession to support the conviction." If, therefore, Mincey's statements to Detective Hust were not "`the product of a rational intellect and a free will,'" his conviction cannot stand. . . . [T]his Court is under a duty to make an independent evaluation of the record.

It is hard to imagine a situation less conducive to the exercise of "a rational intellect and a free will" than Mincey's. He had been seriously wounded just a few hours earlier, and had arrived at the hospital "depressed almost to the point of coma," according to his attending physician. Although he had received some treatment, his condition at the time of Hust's interrogation was still sufficiently serious that he was in the intensive care unit. He complained to Hust that the pain in his leg was "unbearable." He was evidently confused and unable to think clearly about either the events of that afternoon or the circumstances of his interrogation, since some of his written answers were on their face not entirely coherent. Finally, while Mincey was being questioned he was lying on his back on a hospital bed, encumbered by tubes, needles, and breathing apparatus. He was, in short, "at the complete mercy" of Detective Hust, unable to escape or resist the thrust of Hust's interrogation.

In this debilitated and helpless condition, Mincey clearly expressed his wish not to be interrogated. As soon as Hust's questions turned to the details of the afternoon's events, Mincey wrote: "This is all I can say without a lawyer." Hust nonetheless continued to question him, and a nurse who was present suggested it would be best if Mincey answered. Mincey gave unresponsive or uninformative answers to several more questions, and then said again that he did not want to talk without a lawyer. Hust ignored that request and another made immediately thereafter.

It is apparent from the record in this case that Mincey's statements were not "the product of his free and rational choice." To the contrary, the undisputed evidence makes clear that Mincey wanted not to answer Detective Hust. But Mincey was weakened by pain and shock, isolated from family, friends, and legal counsel, and barely conscious, and his will was simply overborne. Due process of law requires that statements obtained as these were cannot be used in any way against a defendant at his trial."

JUSTICE REHNQUIST (concurring in part and dissenting in part) basically saw the facts a bit differently. He did not find that Mincey's statements were involuntary.

"The uncontradicted testimony of Detective Hust also reveals a questioning that was far from "relentless." While the interviews took place over a three-hour time span, the interviews were not "very long; probably not more than an hour total for everything." Hust would leave the room whenever Mincey received medical treatment "or if it looked like he was getting a little bit exhausted." According to Detective Hust, Mincey never "los[t] consciousness at any time."

. . . I believe that the trial court was entitled to conclude that, notwithstanding Mincey's medical condition, his statements in the intensive care unit were admissible. The fact that the same court might have been equally entitled to reach the opposite conclusion does not justify this Court's adopting the opposite conclusion.

Colorado v. Connelly, 479 U.S. 157 (1986)

SUMMRARY: Connelly suffered from chronic schizophrenia and in August 1983 he approached Denver Police Officer Anderson. Without any prompting, Connelly stated that he had murdered someone and wanted to talk about it. Immediately Anderson warned him of his rights under Miranda. Connelly stated he understood them but still wanted to talk; he stated he had not been drinking or taking drugs; he did state he had been a patient in several mental hospitals. Officer Anderson again warned Connelly that he was under no obligation to say anything, but Connelly replied that he wanted to talk to the Office because his conscience had been bothering him.

A homicide detective arrived shortly thereafer, and Connelly was again advised of his rights. The detective then asked "what he had on his mind." And Connelly he had come all the way from Boston to confess to murdering a young girl in November 1982. The officers confirmed that there was a body of an unidentified female who had been found in April 1983. Connelly discussed many of the details, and offered to take officers to the killing. They went to the crime location and Connelly pointed out the exact location of the murder. During this whole time, none of the officers got the sense that Connelly was suffering from any kind of mental illness.

Connelly was lodged in jail, and then was interviewed by the public defendner the next morning. He became confused and visibly disoriented and stated that the "voices" had told him to come to Denver. Ultimately, Connelly was sent to be evaluated for fitness to proceed (aid and assist in his own defense). At that time they concluded he wasn't. But, by March 1984, doctors concluded he was competent to proceed to trial.

There was a preliminary hearing in which Connelly moved to dismiss all of his statements. In essence his arguments for why those statements were not admissible is that they were the involuntary as command hallucinations which interfered with his ability to make free and rational choices and interfered with his cognitive abilities—thus, they were not voluntary.

The trial court suppressed the statements finding them not to be voluntary.

"The court ruled that a confession is admissible only if it is a product of the defendant's rational intellect and "free will." Although the court found that the police had done nothing wrong or coercive in securing respondent's confession, Connelly's illness destroyed his volition and compelled him to confess. The trial court also found that Connelly's mental state vitiated his attempted waiver of the right to counsel and the privilege against compulsory self-incrimination." . . .

The Court had to decide whether Connelly's statements were involuntary and needed to be suppressed. The Court stated,

"[C]ases considered by this Court over the 50 years since *Brown v. Mississippi* have focused upon the crucial element of police overreaching. While each confession case has turned on its own set of factors justifying the conclusion that

police conduct was oppressive, all have contained a substantial element of coercive police conduct. Absent police conduct causally related to the confession, there is simply no basis for concluding that any state actor has deprived a criminal defendant of due process of law.

. . . .

Our "involuntary confession" jurisprudence is entirely consistent with the settled law requiring some sort of "state action" to support a claim of violation of the Due Process Clause of the Fourteenth Amendment. . . .

. . . .

We hold that coercive police activity is a necessary predicate to the finding that a confession is not "voluntary" within the meaning of the Due Process Clause of the Fourteenth Amendment. We also conclude that the taking of respondent's statements, and their admission into evidence, constitute no violation of that Clause.

… The sole concern of the Fifth Amendment, on which Miranda was based, is governmental coercion. Indeed, the Fifth Amendment privilege is not concerned "with moral and psychological pressures to confess emanating from sources other than official coercion." The voluntariness of a waiver of this privilege has always depended on the absence of police overreaching, not on "free choice" in any broader sense of the word. "[T]he relinquishment of the right must have been voluntary in the sense that it was the product of a free and deliberate choice rather than intimidation, coercion or deception. . . . [T]he record is devoid of any suggestion that police resorted to physical or psychological pressure to elicit the statements."

JUSTICE STEVENS, dissenting opinion, omitted.

JUSTICE BRENNAN, with whom JUSTICE MARSHALL joins, dissenting.

The absence of police wrongdoing should not, by itself, determine the voluntariness of a confession by a mentally ill person. The requirement that a confession be voluntary reflects a recognition of the importance of free will and of reliability in determining the admissibility of a confession, and thus demands an inquiry into the totality of the circumstances surrounding the confession.

Today's decision restricts the application of the term "involuntary" to those confessions obtained by police coercion. Confessions by mentally ill individuals or by persons coerced by parties other than police officers are now considered "voluntary." The Court's failure to recognize all forms of involuntariness or coercion as antithetical to due process reflects a refusal to acknowledge free will as a value of constitutional consequence. But due process derives much of its meaning from a conception of fundamental fairness that emphasizes the right to make vital choices voluntarily: "The Fourteenth Amendment secures against state invasion . . . the right of a person to remain silent unless he chooses to speak in the unfettered exercise of his own will . . . ."

THE FIFTH AMENDMENT'S SELF-INCRIMINATION PROHIBITION

The crux of the Fifth Amendment's self-incrimination clause is that a person cannot be forced to be an instrument in his or her own prosecution. This protection applies only to natural persons (meaning humans); it cannot be claimed by a corporation or by its officers. *United States v. Doe,* 465 U.S. 605 (1984). This protection has also been used in civil cases whenever the witnesses' statement could subsequently be used against them in a criminal case. For example, On January 31, 2023 a video was released of the August 2022 deposition of former President Trump in a civil case proceeding against him in New York In it, he repeatedly invokes the Fifth Amendment saying he would be a fool not to.

Claiming The Fifth Amendment

A person who makes an incriminatory statement cannot take back the statement once it has been made. Thus, claiming the privilege is done by remaining silent. Once the statement is made, it can be used. At trial, the privilege against self-incrimination is invoked in different ways based on who is claiming the privilege. The criminal defendant asserts the privilege by refusing to be called to testify. A non-defendant witness, however, must take the stand and claim the protection from the witness stand. For example, in the O.J. Simpson case in which he was on trial for murder, Mark Furman, a state's witness repeatedly invoked the Fifth Amendment claiming something to the effect of: "I refuse to answer under the grounds that my answer might incriminate me.

Types Of Hearings In Which The Fifth Amendment Applies

The protection applies in civil cases if the statements could by used later in a criminal action against the witness. Additionally, the Court has held that a juvenile can claim the right to silence when facing a delinquency adjudication. Likewise, when a defendant speaks with a state psychiatrist in a pretrial competency hearing no incriminating statements can be introduced into the defendant's sentencing hearing unless the defendant waives his or her rights (*Estelle v. Smith*, 451 U.S. 454 (1981). The Court has not extended protection against self-incrimination to civil commitments. For example, in *Allen v. Illinois,* 478 U.S. 364 (1986), the Court held Allen's statements to a psychiatrist were admissible in a subsequent bench trial in which he was declared a sexually dangerous person and committed to a maximum-security institution. The Court reasoned that the label "civil commitment" controlled and the Fifth Amendment's protections did not apply. Inmates who answer potentially incriminating questions as a requirement to get into a treatment program are not protected by the privilege. Although inmates have Fifth Amendment rights, the program did not *compel* prisoners to testify because lost privileges and transfer to a maximum-security unit "are not [consequences] that compel a prisoner to speak about his past crimes despite a desire to remain silent." *McKune v. Lile,* 536 U.S. 24 (2002).

Types Of Evidence Covered By The Fifth Amendment

The Fifth Amendment protects testimonial evidence not physical evidence. In *Holt v. United States*, 218 U.S. 245 (1910), the Court held that the Fifth Amendment's protections do not provide the defendant the right to prevent the court, jury or witnesses from viewing the suspect's face. The government can compel a person to reenact a crime; shave his beard or mustache; try on clothing; dye his or her hair; demonstrate speech or other physical characteristics; furnish handwriting samples, hair samples, or fingerprints; have his or her gums examined; or submit to a blood alcohol, breathalyzer, or urine test. A suspect can be photographed and measured, have tattoos and scars examined, and be required to stand in a lineup. Police can require a person to provide blood samples taken by medical personnel where blood alcohol levels are relevant evidence. *Schmerber v. California* (below). A defendant can also be compelled to provide writing samples (*Gilbert v. California*, 388 U.S. 263 (1967)) and voice exemplars (*United States v. Wade,* 388 U.S. 218 (1967)) since these are not "testimony."

SCHMERBER v. CALIFORNIA
384 U.S. 757 (1966)

JUSTICE BRENNAN delivered the opinion of the Court.

SUMMARY: Defendant was being treated in a hospital after he was involved in a car crash. He refused to give a blood sample, but officers directed the hospital staff to do a blood draw and a chemical test of his blood for intoxicants. The analysis showed he was intoxicated, and at trial for driving under the influence of intoxicants, he objected to the use of the evidence. He was convicted and appealed the use of evidence at his trial claiming it violated his Fifth Amendment and Fourteenth Amendment due process rights, his Fifth Amendment privilege against self-incrimination as incorporated to the states through the Fourteenth Amendment, his Fourth Amendment right not to be subjected to unreasonable searches and seizures, and his Sixth Amendment right to the assistance of counsel. The Appellate Department of the California Superior Court rejected these contentions and affirmed the conviction.]

We affirm. . . .

[In] . . . *Malloy v. Hogan* . . . [we held] that "[t]he Fourteenth Amendment secures against state invasion the same privilege that the Fifth Amendment guarantees against federal infringement - the right of a person to remain silent unless he chooses to speak in the unfettered exercise of his own will, and to suffer no penalty . . . for such silence." We therefore must now decide whether the withdrawal of the blood and admission in evidence of the analysis involved in this case violated petitioner's privilege. We hold that the privilege protects an accused only from being compelled to testify against himself, or otherwise provide the State with evidence of a testimonial or communicative nature, and that the withdrawal of blood and use of the analysis in question in this case did not involve compulsion to these ends.

It is clear that the protection of the privilege reaches an accused's communications, whatever form they might take, and the compulsion of responses which are also communications, for example, compliance with a subpoena to produce one's papers. On the other hand, both federal and state courts have usually held that it offers no protection against compulsion to submit to fingerprinting, photographing, or measurements, to write or speak for identification, to appear in court, to stand, to assume a stance, to walk, or to make a particular gesture. The distinction which has emerged, often expressed in different ways, is that the privilege is a bar against compelling "communications" or "testimony," but that compulsion which makes a suspect or accused the source of "real or physical evidence" does not violate it.

...

In the present case, . . . [there is] . . . [n}ot even a shadow of testimonial compulsion upon or enforced communication by the accused was involved either in the extraction or in the chemical analysis. Petitioner's testimonial capacities were in no way implicated; indeed, his participation, except as a donor, was irrelevant to the results of the test, which depend on chemical analysis and on that alone. Since the blood test evidence, although an incriminating product of compulsion, was neither petitioner's testimony nor evidence relating to some communicative act or writing by the petitioner, it was not inadmissible on privilege grounds.

JUSTICE BLACK with whom JUSTICE DOUGLAS joins, dissenting.

[The] compulsory extraction of petitioner's blood for analysis so that the person who analyzed it could give evidence to convict him had both a "testimonial" and a "communicative nature." The sole purpose of this project which proved to be successful was to obtain "testimony" from some person to prove that petitioner had alcohol in his blood at the time he was arrested. And the purpose of the project was certainly "communicative" in that the analysis of the blood was to supply

information to enable a witness to communicate to the court and jury that petitioner was more or less drunk.

I think it unfortunate that the Court rests so heavily for its very restrictive reading of the Fifth Amendment's privilege against self-incrimination on the words "testimonial" and "communicative." These words are not models of clarity and precision as the Court's rather labored explication shows. ...

JUSTICE DOUGLAS, dissenting.

The Fifth Amendment marks "a zone of privacy" which the Government may not force a person to surrender. Likewise the Fourth Amendment recognizes that right when it guarantees the right of the people to be secure "in their persons." No clearer invasion of this right of privacy can be imagined than forcible bloodletting of the kind involved here.

JUSTICE FORTAS, dissenting.

I would reverse. In my view, petitioner's privilege against self-incrimination applies. I would add that, under the Due Process Clause, the State, in its role as prosecutor, has no right to extract blood from an accused or anyone else, over his protest. As prosecutor, the State has no right to commit any kind of violence upon the person, or to utilize the results of such a tort, and the extraction of blood, over protest, is an act of violence.

MIRANDA AND ITS PROGENY

Four cases led up to the Miranda v. Arizona decision: Crooker v. California, 357 U.S. 433 (1958), Spano v. New York, 360 U.S. 315 (1959), Massiah v. United States, 377 U.S. 201 (1964), and Escobedo v. Illinois, 378 U.S. 478 (1964). In Crooker a confession was held to have been voluntary and therefore admissible, despite the fact that the accused had unsuccessfully requested the right to call his lawyer. Four members of the Court dissented, stating "the accused who wants counsel should have one at any time after the moment of arrest." In Spano the Court held that a confession obtained after an overnight, eight-hour questioning session was involuntary—four justices joined in a concurring opinion indicating they felt that Spano's confession should have been excluded on right to counsel grounds. In Massiah, the defendant had been indicted, and while out on bail and riding in his co-defendant's car, he made incriminating statements that were overheard by the police via a concealed radio transmitter planted with the co-defendant's cooperation. The incriminating statements were held inadmissible. The 6-3 majority held that the overheard conversation was in effect a surreptitious investigation; the opinion noted that the right-to-counsel rationale in the Spano concurrence applied as forcefully to an undercover use of police tactics as it did to a jailhouse interrogation. Finally, in Escobedo, defendant's statements were obtained after he had made repeated requests to see his lawyer (and after the lawyer had actually come to the police station and been turned away). The Court stated,

> "We hold . . . that where, as here, the investigation is no longer a general inquiry into an unsolved crime but has begun to focus on a particular suspect, the suspect has been taken into police custody, the police carry out a process of interrogations that lends itself to eliciting incriminating statements, the suspect has requested and been denied an opportunity to consult with his lawyer, and the police have not effectively warned him of his absolute constitutional right to remain silent, the accused has been denied the 'Assistance of Counsel' in violation of the Sixth Amendment to the Constitution as made obligatory upon the states by the Fourteenth Amendment. . . and that no statement elicited by the police during the investigation may be used against him at trial."

Escobedo's short-lived "focal suspect" approach was a pivotal point in the move to abandon/supplement the voluntariness test with a cleaner, per se rule. The Miranda Court, unlike Escobedo, was not narrowly confined to particular facts. Instead, the Court considered four set of facts presented in four companion cases. In it, the Court found that police custodial interrogations are inherently compelling and pointed to the history of the "third degree" and the use of high-pressure psychological techniques to obtain confessions from arrested suspects. The Court, did not, however, rule that such techniques were a *per se* violation of the privilege against self-incrimination but found that such confessions would be inadmissible only if the police failed to warn suspects of their right to be free from self-incrimination.

MIRANDA v. ARIZONA
384 U.S. 436 (1966)

CHIEF JUSTICE WARREN delivered the opinion of the Court.

The cases before us raise questions which go to the roots of our concepts of American criminal jurisprudence: the restraints society must observe consistent with the Federal Constitution in prosecuting individuals for crime. More specifically, we deal with the admissibility of statements obtained from an individual who is subjected to custodial police interrogation and the necessity for procedures which assure that the individual is accorded his privilege under the Fifth Amendment to the Constitution not to be compelled to incriminate himself.

… We have undertaken a thorough re-examination of the Escobedo decision and the principles it announced, and we reaffirm it. That case was but an explication of basic rights that are enshrined in our Constitution — that "No person . . .shall be compelled in any

criminal case to be a witness against himself," and that "the accused shall . . .have the Assistance of Counsel" — rights which were put in jeopardy in that case through official overbearing. These precious rights were fixed in our Constitution only after centuries of persecution and struggle. And in the words of Chief Justice Marshall, they were secured "for ages to come, and . . .designed to approach immortality as nearly as human institutions can approach it." . . .

Our holding will be spelled out with some specificity in the pages which follow but briefly stated it is this: the prosecution may not use statements, whether exculpatory or inculpatory, stemming from custodial interrogation of the defendant unless it demonstrates the use of procedural safeguards effective to secure the privilege against self-incrimination. By custodial interrogation, we mean questioning initiated by law enforcement officers after a person has been taken into custody or otherwise deprived of his freedom of action in any significant way. As for the procedural safeguards to be employed, unless other fully effective means are devised to inform accused persons of their right of silence and to assure a continuous opportunity to exercise it, the following measures are required. Prior to any questioning, the person must be warned that he has a right to remain silent, that any statement he does make may be used as evidence against him, and that he has a right to the presence of an attorney, either retained or appointed. The defendant may waive effectuation of these rights, provided the waiver is made voluntarily, knowingly and intelligently. If, however, he indicates in any manner and at any stage of the process that he wishes to consult with an attorney before speaking there can be no questioning. Likewise, if the individual is alone and indicates in any manner that he does not wish to be interrogated, the police may not question him. The mere fact that he may have answered some questions or volunteered some statements on his own does not deprive him of the right to refrain from answering any further inquiries until he has consulted with an attorney and thereafter consents to be questioned.

The constitutional issue we decide . . .is the admissibility of statements obtained from a defendant questioned while in custody or otherwise deprived of his freedom of action in any significant way. In each, the defendant was questioned by police officers, detectives, or a prosecuting attorney in a room in which he was cut off from the outside world. In none of these cases was the defendant given a full and effective warning of his rights at the outset of the interrogation process. In all the cases, the questioning elicited oral admissions, and in three of them, signed statements as well which were admitted at their trials. They all thus share salient features — *incommunicado* interrogation of individuals in a police-dominated atmosphere, resulting in self-incriminating statements without full warnings of constitutional rights.

An understanding of the nature and setting of this in-custody interrogation is essential to our decisions today. The difficulty in depicting what transpires at such interrogations stems from the fact that in this country they have largely taken place *incommunicado*. From extensive factual studies undertaken in the early 1930's, including the famous Wickersham Report to Congress by a Presidential Commission, it is clear that police violence and the "third degree" flourished at that time. In a series of cases decided by this Court long after these studies, the police resorted to physical brutality — beating, hanging, whipping — and to sustained and protracted questioning *incommunicado* in order to extort confessions. The Commission on Civil Rights in 1961 found much evidence to indicate that "some policemen still resort to physical force to obtain confessions." The use of physical brutality and violence is not, unfortunately, relegated to the past or to any part of the country. Only recently in Kings County, New York, the police brutally beat, kicked and placed lighted cigarette butts on the back of a potential witness under interrogation for the purpose of securing a statement incriminating a third party. . . .

The examples given above are undoubtedly the exception now, but they are sufficiently widespread to be the object of concern. Unless a proper limitation upon custodial interrogation is achieved — such as these decisions will advance — there can be no assurance that practices of this nature will be eradicated in the foreseeable future.

Again we stress that the modern practice of in-custody interrogation is psychologically rather than physically oriented. Interrogation still takes place in privacy. Privacy results in secrecy and this in turn results in a gap in our knowledge as to what in fact goes on in the interrogation rooms. . . .

Even without employing brutality, the "third degree" or the specific stratagems described above, the very fact of custodial interrogation exacts a heavy toll on individual liberty and trades on the weakness of individuals.

In the cases before us today, given this background, we concern ourselves primarily with this interrogation atmosphere and the evils it can bring. In these cases, we might not find the defendants' statements to have been involuntary in traditional terms. Our concern for adequate safeguards to protect precious Fifth Amendment rights is, of course, not lessened in the slightest. In each of the cases, the defendant was thrust into an unfamiliar atmosphere and run through menacing police interrogation procedures. The potentiality for compulsion is forcefully apparent, for example, in *Miranda,* where the indigent Mexican defendant was a seriously disturbed individual with pronounced sexual fantasies. . . .

It is obvious that such an interrogation environment is created for no purpose other than to subjugate the individual to the will of his examiner. This atmosphere carries its own badge of intimidation. . . .The current practice of *incommunicado* interrogation is at odds with one of our Nation's most cherished principles — that the individual may not be compelled to incriminate himself. Unless adequate protective devices are employed to dispel the compulsion inherent in custodial surroundings, no statement obtained from the defendant can truly be the product of his free choice.

We are satisfied that all the principles embodied in the privilege apply to informal compulsion exerted by law-enforcement officers during in-custody questioning. An individual swept from familiar surroundings into police custody, surrounded by antagonistic forces, and subjected to the techniques of persuasion described above cannot be otherwise than under compulsion to speak. As a practical matter, the compulsion to speak in the isolated setting of the police station may well be greater than in courts or other official investigations, where there are often impartial observers to guard against intimidation or trickery.

The presence of counsel, in all the cases before us today, would be the adequate protective device necessary to make the process of police interrogation conform to the dictates of the privilege. His presence would insure that statements made in the government-established atmosphere are not the product of compulsion.

It is impossible for us to foresee the potential alternatives for protecting the privilege which might be devised by Congress or the States in the exercise of their creative rulemaking capacities. Therefore we cannot say that the Constitution necessarily requires adherence to any particular solution for the inherent compulsions of the interrogation process as it is presently conducted. Our decision in no way creates a constitutional straitjacket which will handicap sound efforts at reform, nor is it intended to have this effect. We encourage Congress and the States to continue their laudable search for increasingly effective ways of protecting the rights of the individual while promoting efficient enforcement of our criminal laws.

A recurrent argument made in these cases is that society's need for interrogation outweighs the privilege. This argument is not unfamiliar to this Court. . . .

In announcing these principles, we are not unmindful of the burdens which law enforcement officials must bear, often under trying circumstances. We also fully recognize the obligation of all citizens to aid in enforcing the criminal laws. This Court, while protecting individual rights, has always given ample latitude to law enforcement agencies in the legitimate exercise of their duties. The limit we have placed on the interrogation process should not constitute an undue interference with a proper system of law enforcement. As we have noted, our decision does not in any way preclude police from carrying out their traditional investigatory functions. Although confessions may play an important role in some convictions, the cases before us present graphic examples of the overstatement of the "need" for confessions.

Therefore, in accordance with the foregoing, the judgment of the Supreme Court of Arizona . . . [is] reversed. . . .

JUSTICE WHITE, with whom JUSTICE HARLAN and JUSTICE STEWART join, dissenting.

The obvious underpinning of the Court's decision is a deep-seated distrust of all confessions. As the Court declares that the accused may not be interrogated without counsel present, absent a waiver of the right to counsel, and as the Court all but admonishes the lawyer to advise the accused to remain silent, the result adds up to a judicial judgment that evidence from the accused should not be used against him in any way, whether compelled or not. This is the not so subtle overtone of the opinion — that it is inherently wrong for the police to gather evidence from the accused himself. And this is precisely the nub of this dissent. I see nothing wrong or immoral, and certainly nothing unconstitutional, in the police's asking a suspect whom they have reasonable cause to arrest whether or not he killed his wife or in confronting him with the evidence on which the arrest was based, at least where he has been plainly advised that he may remain completely silent. . . .

The rule announced today will measurably weaken the ability of the criminal law to perform these tasks. It is a deliberate calculus to prevent interrogations, to reduce the incidence of confessions and pleas of guilty and to increase the number of trials. . . .

In some unknown number of cases the Court's rule will return a killer, a rapist or other criminal to the streets and to the environment which produced him, to repeat his crime whenever it pleases him. As a consequence, there will not be a gain, but a loss, in human dignity. The real concern is not the unfortunate consequences of this new decision on the criminal law as an abstract, disembodied series of authoritative proscriptions, but the impact on those who rely on the public authority for protection and who without it can only engage in violent self-help with guns, knives and the help of their neighbors similarly inclined. There is, of course, a saving factor: the next victims are uncertain, unnamed and unrepresented in this case.

Nor can this decision do other than have a corrosive effect on the criminal law as an effective device to prevent crime. A major component in its effectiveness in this regard is its swift and sure enforcement. The easier it is to get away with rape and murder, the less the deterrent effect on those who are inclined to attempt it. This is still good common sense. If it were not, we should posthaste liquidate the whole law enforcement establishment as a useless, misguided effort to control human conduct.

And what about the accused who has confessed or would confess in response to simple, non-coercive questioning and whose guilt could not otherwise be proved? Is it so clear that release is the best thing for him in every case? Has it so unquestionably been resolved that in each and every case it would be better for him not to confess and to return to his environment with no attempt whatsoever to help him? I think not. It may well be that in many cases it will be no less than a callous disregard for his own welfare as well as for the interests of his next victim.

Much of the trouble with the Court's new rule is that it will operate indiscriminately in all criminal cases, regardless of the severity of the crime or the circumstances involved. It applies to every defendant, whether the professional criminal or one committing a crime of momentary passion who is not part and parcel of organized crime. It will slow down the investigation and the apprehension of confederates in those cases where time is of the essence, such as kidnapping, those involving the national security, and some of those involving organized crime. . . .

At the same time, the Court's *per se* approach may not be justified on the ground that it provides a "bright line" permitting the authorities to judge in advance whether interrogation may safely be pursued without jeopardizing the admissibility of any information obtained as a consequence. Nor can it be claimed that judicial time and effort, assuming that is a relevant consideration, will be conserved because of the ease of application of the new rule.

Today's decision leaves open such questions as whether the accused was in custody, whether his statements were spontaneous or the product of interrogation, whether the accused has effectively waived his rights, and whether nontestimonial evidence introduced at trial is the fruit of statements made during a prohibited interrogation, all of which are certain to prove productive of uncertainty during investigation and litigation during prosecution. For all these reasons, if further restrictions on police interrogation are desirable at this time, a more flexible approach makes much more sense than the Court's constitutional straitjacket which forecloses more discriminating treatment by legislative or rule-making pronouncements. ...

Custody

Miranda is limited to "custodial" interrogations. Below are key cases in which the court has elaborated on what it means to be a "custodial" interrogation, or when a person is "in custody for *Miranda* purposes."

OROZCO v. TEXAS
394 U.S. 324 (1969)

JUSTICE BLACK delivered the opinion of the Court.

The evidence introduced at trial showed that petitioner and the deceased had quarreled outside the El Farleto Cafe in Dallas shortly before midnight on the date of the shooting. The deceased had apparently spoken to petitioner's female companion inside the restaurant. In the heat of the quarrel outside, the deceased is said to have beaten petitioner about the face and called him "Mexican Grease." A shot was fired killing the deceased. Petitioner left the scene and returned to his boardinghouse to sleep. At about 4 a. m. four police officers arrived at petitioner's boardinghouse, were admitted by an unidentified woman, and were told that petitioner was asleep in the bedroom. All four officers entered the bedroom and began to question petitioner. From the moment he gave his name, according to the testimony of one of the officers, petitioner was not free to go where he pleased but was "under arrest." The officers asked him if he had been to the El Farleto restaurant that night and when he answered "yes" he was asked if he owned a pistol. Petitioner admitted owning one. After being asked a second time where the pistol was located, he admitted that it was in the washing machine in a backroom of the boardinghouse. Ballistics tests indicated that the gun found in the washing machine was the gun that fired the fatal shot. At petitioner's trial, the court allowed one of the officers, over the objection of petitioner's lawyer, to relate the statements made by petitioner concerning the gun and petitioner's presence at the scene of the shooting. The trial testimony clearly shows that the officers questioned petitioner about incriminating facts without first informing him of his right to remain silent, his right to have the advice of a lawyer before making any statement, and his right to have a lawyer appointed to assist him if he could not afford to hire one.

The State has argued here that since petitioner was interrogated on his own bed, in familiar surroundings, our *Miranda* holding should not apply. It is true that the Court did say in *Miranda* that "compulsion to speak in the isolated setting of the police station may well be greater than in courts or other official investigations, where there are often impartial observers to guard against intimidation or trickery." But the opinion iterated and reiterated the absolute necessity for officers interrogating people "in custody" to give the described warnings. According to the officer's testimony, petitioner was under arrest and not free to leave when he was questioned in his bedroom in the early hours of the morning. The *Miranda* opinion declared that the warnings were required when the person being interrogated was "in custody at the station or otherwise deprived of his freedom of action in any significant way." The decision of this Court in *Miranda* was reached after careful consideration and lengthy opinions were announced by both the majority and dissenting Justices. Reversed.

JUSTICE HARLAN, concurring.

Purely out of respect for *stare decisis*, I reluctantly feel compelled to acquiesce in today's decision of the Court, at the same time observing that the constitutional condemnation of this perfectly understandable, sensible, proper, and indeed commendable piece of police work highlights the unsoundness of *Miranda*.

JUSTICE WHITE, with whom JUSTICE STEWART joins, dissenting.

The Court now extends the same rules to all instances of in-custody questioning outside the station house. Once arrest occurs, the application of Miranda is automatic. The rule is simple but it ignores the purpose of Miranda to guard against what was thought to be the corrosive influence of practices which station house interrogation makes feasible.

Here, there was no prolonged interrogation, no unfamiliar surroundings, no opportunity for the police to invoke those procedures which moved the majority in *Miranda*. In fact, the conversation was by all accounts a very brief one. According to uncontradicted testimony, petitioner was awake when the officers entered his room, and they asked him four questions: his name, whether he had been at the El Farleto, whether he owned a pistol, and where it was. He gave his name, said he had been at the El Farleto, and admitted he owned a pistol without hesitation. He was slow in telling where the pistol was, and the question was repeated. He then took the police to the nearby washing machine where the gun was hidden. . . .

Memorandum of JUSTICE STEWART.

Although there is much to be said for MR. JUSTICE HARLAN'S position, I join my Brother WHITE in dissent. It seems to me that those of us who dissented in *Miranda v. Arizona*, remain free not only to express our continuing disagreement with that decision, but also to oppose any broadening of its impact.

OREGON v. MATHIASON
429 U.S. 492 (1977)

Per Curium

The Supreme Court of Oregon described the factual situation surrounding the confession as follows:

"An officer of the State Police investigated a theft at a residence near Pendleton. He asked the lady of the house which had been burglarized if she suspected anyone. She replied that the defendant was the only one she could think of. The defendant was a parolee and a `close associate' of her son. The officer tried to contact defendant on three or four occasions with no success. Finally, about 25 days after the burglary, the officer left his card at defendant's apartment with a note asking him to call because `I'd like to discuss something with you.' The next afternoon the defendant did call. The officer asked where it would be convenient to meet. The defendant had no preference; so the officer asked if the defendant could meet him at the state patrol office in about an hour and a half, about 5:00 p. m. The patrol office was about two blocks from defendant's apartment. The building housed several state agencies. "The officer met defendant in the hallway, shook hands and took him into an office. The defendant was told he was not under arrest. The door was closed. The two sat across a desk. The police radio in another room could be heard. The officer told defendant he wanted to talk to him about a burglary and that his truthfulness would possibly be considered by the district attorney or judge. The officer further advised that the police believed defendant was involved in the burglary and [falsely stated that] defendant's fingerprints were found at the scene. The defendant sat for a few minutes and then said he had taken the property. This occurred within five minutes after defendant had come to the office. The officer then advised defendant of his *Miranda* rights and took a taped confession.

"At the end of the taped conversation the officer told defendant he was not arresting him at this time; he was released to go about his job and return to his family. The officer said he was referring the case to the district attorney for him to determine whether criminal charges would be brought. It was 5:30 p. m. when the defendant left the office.

The Supreme Court of Oregon reasoned from these facts that:

"We hold the interrogation took place in a 'coercive environment.' The parties were in the offices of the State Police; they were alone behind closed doors; the officer informed the defendant he was a suspect in a theft and the authorities had evidence incriminating him in the crime; and the defendant was a parolee under supervision. We are of the opinion that this evidence is not overcome by the evidence that the defendant came to the office in response to a request and was told he was not under arrest."

Our decision in *Miranda* set forth rules of police procedure applicable to "custodial interrogation." "By custodial interrogation, we mean questioning initiated by law enforcement officers after a person has been taken into custody or otherwise deprived of his freedom of action in any significant way." Subsequently we have found the *Miranda* principle applicable to questioning which

takes place in a prison setting during a suspect's term of imprisonment on a separate offense, and to questioning taking place in a suspect's home, after he has been arrested and is no longer free to go where he pleases.

In the present case, however, there is no indication that the questioning took place in a context where respondent's freedom to depart was restricted in any way. He came voluntarily to the police station, where he was immediately informed that he was not under arrest. At the close of a 1/2-hour interview respondent did in fact leave the police station without hindrance. It is clear from these facts that Mathiason was not in custody "or otherwise deprived of his freedom of action in any significant way."

[P]olice officers are not required to administer *Miranda* warnings to everyone whom they question. Nor is the requirement of warnings to be imposed simply because the questioning takes place in the station house, or because the questioned person is one whom the police suspect. *Miranda* warnings are required only where there has been such a restriction on a person's freedom as to render him "in custody." It was that sort of coercive environment to which *Miranda* by its terms was made applicable, and to which it is limited.

The officer's false statement about having discovered Mathiason's fingerprints at the scene was found by the Supreme Court of Oregon to be another circumstance contributing to the coercive environment which makes the *Miranda* rationale applicable. Whatever relevance this fact may have to other issues in the case, it has nothing to do with whether respondent was in custody for purposes of the *Miranda* rule.

JUSTICE MARSHALL, dissenting.

The respondent in this case was interrogated behind closed doors at police headquarters in connection with a burglary investigation. He had been named by the victim of the burglary as a suspect, and was told by the police that they believed he was involved. He was falsely informed that his fingerprints had been found at the scene, and in effect was advised that by cooperating with the police he could help himself. Not until after he had confessed was he given the warnings set forth in *Miranda v. Arizona*.

The Court today holds that for constitutional purposes all this is irrelevant because respondent had not "'been taken into custody or otherwise deprived of his freedom of action in any significant way.'" I do not believe that such a determination is possible on the record before us. It is true that respondent was not formally placed under arrest, but surely formalities alone cannot control. At the very least, if respondent entertained an objectively reasonable belief that he was not free to leave during the questioning, then he was "deprived of his freedom of action in a significant way." Plainly the respondent could have so believed, after being told by the police that they thought he was involved in a burglary and that his fingerprints had been found at the scene.

More fundamentally, however, I cannot agree with the Court's conclusion that if respondent were not in custody no warnings were required.

In my view, even if respondent were not in custody, the coercive elements in the instant case were so pervasive as to require *Miranda*-type warnings. Respondent was interrogated in "privacy" and in "unfamiliar surroundings," factors on which *Miranda* places great stress.

The investigation had focused on respondent. And respondent was subjected to some of the "deceptive stratagems," I therefore agree with the Oregon Supreme Court that to excuse the absence of warnings given these facts is "contrary to the rationale expressed in *Miranda*."

I respectfully dissent.

JUSTICE STEVENS, dissenting.

In my opinion the issues presented by this case are too important to be decided summarily. Of particular importance is the fact that the respondent was on parole at the time of his interrogation in the police station.

The State surely has greater power to question a parolee about his activities than to question someone else. Moreover, as a practical matter, it seems unlikely that a *Miranda* warning would have much effect on a parolee's choice between silence and responding to police interrogation. Therefore, *Miranda* warnings are entirely inappropriate in the parole context.

On the other hand, a parolee is technically in legal custody continuously until his sentence has been served. Therefore, if a formalistic analysis of the custody question is to determine when the *Miranda* warning is necessary, a parolee should always be warned. Moreover, *Miranda* teaches that even if a suspect is not in custody, warnings are necessary if he is "otherwise deprived of his freedom of action in any significant way."

ILLINOIS v. PERKINS
496 U.S. 292 (1990)

JUSTICE KENNEDY delivered the opinion of the Court.

In November 1984, Richard Stephenson was murdered in a suburb of East St. Louis, Illinois. The murder remained unsolved until March 1986, when one Donald Charlton told police that he had learned about a homicide from a fellow inmate at the Graham Correctional Facility, where Charlton had

been serving a sentence for burglary. The fellow inmate was Lloyd Perkins, who is the respondent here. Charlton told police that, while at Graham, he had befriended respondent, who told him in detail about a murder that respondent had committed in East St. Louis. On hearing Charlton's account, the police recognized details of the Stephenson murder that were not well known, and so they treated Charlton's story as a credible one.

By the time the police heard Charlton's account, respondent had been released from Graham, but police traced him to a jail in Montgomery County, Illinois, where he was being held pending trial on a charge of aggravated battery, unrelated to the Stephenson murder. The police wanted to investigate further respondent's connection to the Stephenson murder, but feared that the use of an eavesdropping device would prove impracticable and unsafe. They decided instead to place an undercover agent in the cellblock with respondent and Charlton. The plan was for Charlton and undercover agent John Parisi to pose as escapees from a work release program who had been arrested in the course of a burglary. Parisi and Charlton were instructed to engage respondent in casual conversation and report anything he said about the Stephenson murder.

Parisi, using the alias "Vito Bianco," and Charlton, both clothed in jail garb, were placed in the cellblock with respondent at the Montgomery County jail. The cellblock consisted of 12 separate cells that opened onto a common room. Respondent greeted Charlton who, after a brief conversation with respondent, introduced Parisi by his alias. Parisi told respondent that he "wasn't going to do any more time" and suggested that the three of them escape. Respondent replied that the Montgomery County jail was "rinky-dink" and that they could "break out." The trio met in respondent's cell later that evening, after the other inmates were asleep, to refine their plan. Respondent said that his girlfriend could smuggle in a pistol. Charlton said: "Hey, I'm not a murderer, I'm a burglar. That's your guys' profession." After telling Charlton that he would be responsible for any murder that occurred, Parisi asked respondent if he had ever "done" anybody. Respondent said that he had and proceeded to describe at length the events of the Stephenson murder. Parisi and respondent then engaged in some casual conversation before respondent went to sleep. Parisi did not give respondent *Miranda* warnings before the conversations.

Respondent was charged with the Stephenson murder. Before trial, he moved to suppress the statements made to Parisi in the jail. The trial court granted the motion to suppress, and the State appealed. The Appellate Court of Illinois affirmed, holding that *Miranda v. Arizona* prohibits all undercover contacts with incarcerated suspects that are reasonably likely to elicit an incriminating response.

. . . .

Conversations between suspects and undercover agents do not implicate the concerns underlying *Miranda*. The essential ingredients of a "police-dominated atmosphere" and compulsion are not present when an incarcerated person speaks freely to someone whom he believes to be a fellow inmate. Coercion is determined from the perspective of the suspect. When a suspect considers himself in the company of cellmates and not officers, the coercive atmosphere is lacking. There is no empirical basis for the assumption that a suspect speaking to those whom he assumes are not officers will feel compelled to speak by the fear of reprisal for remaining silent or in the hope of more lenient treatment should he confess.

It is the premise of *Miranda* that the danger of coercion results from the interaction of custody and official interrogation. We reject the argument that *Miranda* warnings are required whenever a suspect is in custody in a technical sense and converses with someone who happens to be a government agent. . . . [W]here a suspect does not know that he is conversing with a government agent, these pressures do not exist. . . .

Miranda forbids coercion, not mere strategic deception by taking advantage of a suspect's misplaced trust in one he supposes to be a fellow prisoner. As we recognized in Miranda: "Confessions remain a proper element in law enforcement. Any statement given freely and voluntarily without any compelling influences is, of course, admissible in evidence." Ploys to mislead a suspect or lull him into a false sense of security that do not rise to the level of compulsion or coercion to speak are not within Miranda's concerns.

. . . .

JUSTICE BRENNAN, concurring in the judgment. (Omitted)

JUSTICE MARSHALL, dissenting.

. . .This exception is inconsistent with the rationale supporting Miranda and allows police officers intentionally to take advantage of suspects unaware of their constitutional rights. I therefore dissent.

Miranda was not . . . concerned solely with police coercion. It dealt with any police tactics that may operate to compel a suspect in custody to make incriminating statements without full awareness of his constitutional rights.

Custody works to the State's advantage in obtaining incriminating information. The psychological pressures inherent in

confinement increase the suspect's anxiety, making him likely to seek relief by talking with others. The inmate is thus more susceptible to efforts by undercover agents to elicit information from him. Similarly, where the suspect is incarcerated, the constant threat of physical danger peculiar to the prison environment may make him demonstrate his toughness to other inmates by recounting or inventing past violent acts. "Because the suspect's ability to select people with whom he can confide is completely within their control, the police have a unique opportunity to exploit the suspect's vulnerability. In short, the police can insure that if the pressures of confinement lead the suspect to confide in anyone, it will be a police agent."

The Court's adoption of the "undercover agent" exception to the *Miranda* rule thus is necessarily also the adoption of a substantial loophole in our jurisprudence protecting suspects' Fifth Amendment rights.

HOWES v. FIELDS
565 U.S. 499 (2012)

JUSTICE ALITO delivered the opinion of the Court.

. . . .

I

While serving a sentence in a Michigan jail, Randall Fields was escorted by a corrections officer to a conference room where two sheriff's deputies questioned him about allegations that, before he came to prison, he had engaged in sexual conduct with a 12-year-old boy. In order to get to the conference room, Fields had to go down one floor and pass through a locked door that separated two sections of the facility. Fields arrived at the conference room between 7 p.m. and 9 p.m. and was questioned for between five and seven hours.

At the beginning of the interview, Fields was told that he was free to leave and return to his cell. Later, he was again told that he could

leave whenever he wanted. The two interviewing deputies were armed during the interview, but Fields remained free of handcuffs and other restraints. The door to the conference room was sometimes open and sometimes shut.

About halfway through the interview, after Fields had been confronted with the allegations of abuse, he became agitated and began to yell. Fields testified that one of the deputies, using an expletive, told him to sit down and said that "if [he] didn't want to cooperate, [he] could leave." Fields eventually confessed to engaging in sex acts with the boy. According to Fields' testimony at a suppression hearing, he said several times during the interview that he no longer wanted to talk to the deputies, but he did not ask to go back to his cell prior to the end of the interview.

When he was eventually ready to leave, he had to wait an additional 20 minutes or so because a corrections officer had to be summoned to escort him back to his cell, and he did not return to his cell until well after the hour when he generally retired. At no time was Fields given *Miranda* warnings or advised that he did not have to speak with the deputies.

. . . .

In this case, it is abundantly clear that our precedents do not clearly establish the categorical rule on which the Court of Appeals relied, i.e., that the questioning of a prisoner is always custodial when the prisoner is removed from the general prison population and questioned about events that occurred outside the prison. On the contrary, we have repeatedly declined to adopt any categorical rule with respect to whether the questioning of a prison inmate is custodial.

In *Illinois v. Perkins*, where we upheld the admission of un-Mirandized statements elicited from an inmate by an undercover officer masquerading as another inmate, we noted that "[t]he bare fact of custody may not in every instance require a warning *even when the suspect is aware that he is speaking to an official, but we do not have occasion to explore that issue here.*" Instead, we simply "reject[ed] the argument that *Miranda* warnings are required whenever a suspect is in custody in a technical sense and converses with someone who happens to be a government agent."

Most recently, in *Maryland v. Shatzer*, we expressly declined to adopt a bright-line rule for determining the applicability of *Miranda* in prisons. Shatzer considered whether a break in custody ends the presumption of involuntariness established in *Edwards v. Arizona*, and, if so, whether a prisoner's return to the general prison population after a custodial interrogation constitutes a break in *Miranda* custody. In considering the latter question, we noted first that "[w]e have never decided whether incarceration constitutes custody for *Miranda* purposes, and have indeed explicitly declined to address the issue." The answer to this question, we noted, would "depen[d] upon whether [incarceration] exerts the coercive pressure that *Miranda* was designed to guard against — the 'danger of coercion [that] results from the interaction of custody and official interrogation.' "

. . . .

Miranda adopted a "set of prophylactic measures" designed to ward off the " 'inherently compelling pressures' of custodial interrogation," but *Miranda* did not hold that such pressures are always present when a prisoner is taken aside and questioned about events outside the prison walls. Indeed, *Miranda* did not even establish that police questioning of a suspect at the station house is always custodial. . . . (Citations omitted.)

In sum, our decisions do not clearly establish that a prisoner is always in custody for purposes of *Miranda* whenever a prisoner is isolated from the general prison population and questioned about conduct outside the prison. (Footnote omitted.)

. . . .

As used in our *Miranda* case law, "custody" is a term of art that specifies circumstances that are thought generally to present a serious danger of coercion. In determining whether a person is in custody in this sense, the initial step is to ascertain whether, in light of "the objective circumstances of the interrogation," . . . a "reasonable person [would] have felt he or she was not at liberty to terminate the interrogation and leave." . . . And in order to determine how a suspect would have "gauge[d]" his "freedom of movement," courts must examine "all of the circumstances surrounding the interrogation." . . . Relevant factors include the location of the questioning, its duration, statements made during the interview, the presence or absence of physical restraints during the questioning, and the release of the interviewee at the end of the questioning.

Determining whether an individual's freedom of movement was curtailed, however, is simply the first step in the analysis, not the last. Not all restraints on freedom of movement amount to custody for purposes of *Miranda*. We have "decline[d] to accord talismanic power" to the freedom-of-movement inquiry, and have instead asked the additional question whether the relevant environment presents the same inherently coercive pressures as the type of station house questioning at issue in *Miranda*. "Our cases make clear . . . that the freedom-of-movement test identifies only a necessary and not a sufficient condition for *Miranda* custody."

[I]n *Berkemer v. McCarty* . . . we held that the roadside questioning of a motorist who was pulled over in a routine traffic stop did not constitute custodial interrogation. We acknowledged that "a traffic stop significantly curtails the 'freedom of action' of the driver and the passengers," and that it is generally "a crime either to ignore a policeman's signal to stop one's car or, once having stopped, to drive away without permission." "[F]ew motorists," we noted, "would feel free either to disobey a directive to pull over or to leave the scene of a traffic stop without being told they might do so." Nevertheless, we held that a person detained as a result of a traffic stop is not in *Miranda* custody because such detention does not "sufficiently impair [the detained person's] free exercise of his privilege against self-incrimination to require that he be warned of his constitutional rights." As we later put it, the "temporary and relatively nonthreatening detention involved in a traffic stop or *Terry* stop does not constitute *Miranda* custody."

[In] *Shatzer* . . . we again distinguished between restraints on freedom of movement and *Miranda* custody. *Shatzer* . . . concerned the *Edwards* prophylactic rule, which limits the ability of the police to initiate further questioning of a suspect in *Miranda* custody once the suspect invokes the right to counsel. We held in *Shatzer* that this rule does not apply when there is a sufficient break in custody between the suspect's invocation of the right to counsel and the initiation of subsequent questioning. And, what is significant for present purposes, we further

held that a break in custody may occur while a suspect is serving a term in prison. If a break in custody can occur while a prisoner is serving an uninterrupted term of imprisonment, it must follow that imprisonment alone is not enough to create a custodial situation within the meaning of *Miranda*.

There are at least three strong grounds for this conclusion. First, questioning a person who is already serving a prison term does not generally involve the shock that very often accompanies arrest. . . . A person who is "cut off from his normal life and companions," and abruptly transported from the street into a "police-dominated atmosphere," may feel coerced into answering questions.

By contrast, when a person who is already serving a term of imprisonment is questioned, there is usually no such change. "Interrogated suspects who have previously been convicted of crime live in prison." For a person serving a term of incarceration, we reasoned in *Shatzer*, the ordinary restrictions of prison life, while no doubt unpleasant, are expected and familiar and thus do not involve the same "inherently compelling pressures" that are often present when a suspect is yanked from familiar surroundings in the outside world and subjected to interrogation in a police station.

Second, a prisoner, unlike a person who has not been sentenced to a term of incarceration, is unlikely to be lured into speaking by a longing for prompt release. When a person is arrested and taken to a station house for interrogation, the person who is questioned may be pressured to speak by the hope that, after doing so, he will be allowed to leave and go home. On the other hand, when a prisoner is questioned, he knows that when the questioning ceases, he will remain under confinement.

Third, a prisoner, unlike a person who has not been convicted and sentenced, knows that the law enforcement officers who question him probably lack the authority to affect the duration of his sentence. And "where the possibility of parole exists," the interrogating officers probably also lack the power to bring about an early release. "When the suspect has no reason to think that the listeners have official power over him, it should not be assumed that his words are motivated by the reaction he expects from his listeners." Under such circumstances, there is little "basis for the assumption that a suspect . . . will feel compelled to speak by the fear of reprisal for remaining silent or in the hope of [a] more lenient treatment should he confess."

. . . .

The two other elements included in the Court of Appeals' rule — questioning in private and questioning about events that took place outside the prison — are likewise insufficient.

Taking a prisoner aside for questioning — as opposed to questioning the prisoner in the presence of fellow inmates — does not necessarily convert a "noncustodial situation . . . to one in which *Miranda* applies." When a person who is not serving a prison term is questioned, isolation may contribute to a coercive atmosphere by preventing family members, friends, and others who may be sympathetic from providing either advice or emotional support. And without any such assistance, the person who is questioned may feel overwhelming pressure to speak and to refrain from asking that the interview be terminated.

By contrast, questioning a prisoner in private does not generally remove the prisoner from a supportive atmosphere. Fellow inmates are by no means necessarily friends. On the contrary, they may be hostile and, for a variety of reasons, may react negatively to what the questioning reveals. In the present case, for example, would respondent have felt more at ease if he had been questioned in the presence of other inmates about the sexual abuse of an adolescent boy? Isolation from the general prison population is often in the best interest of the interviewee and, in any event, does not suggest on its own the atmosphere of coercion that concerned the Court in *Miranda*.

It is true that taking a prisoner aside for questioning may necessitate some additional limitations on his freedom of movement. A prisoner may, for example, be removed from an exercise yard and taken, under close guard, to the room where the interview is to be held. But such procedures are an ordinary and familiar attribute of life behind bars. Escorts and special security precautions may be standard procedures regardless of the purpose for which an inmate is removed from his regular routine and taken to a special location. For example, ordinary prison procedure may require such measures when a prisoner is led to a meeting with an attorney.

. . . .

When a prisoner is questioned, the determination of custody should focus on all of the features of the interrogation. These include the language that is used in summoning the prisoner to the interview and the manner in which the interrogation is conducted. . . .

Confessions voluntarily made by prisoners in other situations should not be suppressed. "Voluntary confessions are not merely a proper element in law enforcement, they are an unmitigated good, essential to society's compelling interest in finding, convicting, and punishing those who violate the law." . . .

The record in this case reveals that respondent was not taken into custody for purposes of *Miranda*. To be sure, respondent did not invite the interview or consent to it in advance, and he was not advised that he was free to decline to speak with the deputies. The following facts also lend some support to respondent's argument that *Miranda's* custody requirement was met: The interview lasted for between five and seven hours in the evening and continued well past the hour when respondent generally went to bed; the deputies who questioned respondent were armed; and one of the deputies, according to respondent, "[u]sed a very sharp tone," and on one occasion, profanity.

These circumstances, however, were offset by others. Most important, respondent was told at the outset of the interrogation, and was reminded again thereafter, that he could leave and go back to his cell whenever he wanted. . . . Moreover, respondent was not physically restrained or threatened and was interviewed in a well-lit, average-sized conference room, where he was "not uncomfortable." He was offered food and water, and the door to the conference room was sometimes left open. "All of these objective facts are consistent with an interrogation environment in which a reasonable person would have felt free to terminate the interview and leave."

Because he was in prison, respondent was not free to leave the conference room by himself and to make his own way through the facility to his cell. Instead, he was escorted to the conference room and, when he ultimately decided to end the interview, he had to wait about 20 minutes for a corrections officer to arrive and escort him to his cell. But he would have been subject to this same restraint even if he had been taken to the conference room for some reason other than police questioning; under no circumstances could he have reasonably expected to be able to roam free. . . .

Taking into account all of the circumstances of the questioning — including especially the undisputed fact that respondent was told that he was free to end the questioning and to return to his cell — we hold that respondent was not in custody within the meaning of *Miranda*.

JUSTICE GINSBURG, with whom JUSTICE BREYER and JUSTICE SOTOMAYOR join, concurring in part and dissenting in part.

. . . .

Today, for people already in prison, the Court finds it adequate for the police to say: "You are free to terminate this interrogation and return to your cell." Such a statement is no substitute for one ensuring that an individual is aware of his rights.

For the reasons stated, I would hold that the "incommunicado interrogation [of Fields] in a police-dominated atmosphere," without informing him of his rights, dishonored the Fifth Amendment privilege *Miranda* was designed to safeguard.

Other Cases: Custody

Berkemer V. McCarty, 468 U.S. 420 (1984)

SUMMARY: Ohio State Trooper Williams stopped McCarty for weaving in and out of a lane of traffic on a state highway. During the stop, Williams asked McCarty some questions without first advising him of the Miranda warnings, and McCarty gave some incriminating responses. McCarty later moved to exclude the statements he had made to Williams.

The question before the court was "whether the roadside questioning of a motorist detained pursuant to a routine traffic stop should be considered "custodial interrogation."

See Court's holding quoted in *Howes v. Fields,* above.

OPINION

… Fidelity to the doctrine announced in *Miranda* requires that it be enforced strictly, but only in those types of situations in which the concerns that powered the decision are implicated. Thus, we must decide whether a traffic stop exerts upon a detained person pressures that sufficiently impair his free exercise of his privilege against self-incrimination to require that he be warned of his constitutional rights.

Two features of an ordinary traffic stop mitigate the danger that a person questioned will be induced "to speak where he would not otherwise do so freely," First, detention of a motorist pursuant to a traffic stop is presumptively temporary and brief. . . .In this respect, questioning incident to an ordinary traffic stop is quite different from stationhouse interrogation, which frequently is prolonged, and in which the detainee often is aware that questioning will continue until he provides his interrogators the answers they seek.

Second, circumstances associated with the typical traffic stop are not such that the motorist feels completely at the mercy of the police. To be sure, the aura of authority surrounding an armed, uniformed officer and the knowledge that the officer has some discretion in deciding whether to issue a citation, in combination, exert some pressure on the detainee to respond to questions. But other aspects of the situation substantially offset these forces. Perhaps most importantly, the typical traffic stop is public, at least to some degree. Passersby, on foot or in other cars, witness the interaction of officer and motorist. This exposure to public view both reduces the ability of an unscrupulous policeman to use illegitimate means to elicit self-incriminating statements and diminishes the motorist's fear that, if he does not cooperate, he will be subjected to abuse. The fact that the detained motorist typically is confronted by only one or at most two policemen further mutes his sense of vulnerability. In short, the atmosphere surrounding an ordinary traffic stop is substantially less "police dominated" than that surrounding the kinds of interrogation at issue in *Miranda* itself, and in the subsequent cases in which we have applied *Miranda*.

. . . .

Turning to the case before us, we find nothing in the record that indicates that respondent should have been given *Miranda* warnings at any point prior to the time Trooper Williams placed him under arrest. ...Although Trooper Williams apparently decided as soon as respondent stepped out of his car that respondent would be taken into custody and charged with a traffic offense, Williams never communicated his intention to respondent. A policeman's unarticulated plan has no bearing on the question whether a suspect was "in custody" at a particular time; the only relevant inquiry is how a reasonable man in the suspect's position would have understood his situation. ... [A] single police officer asked respondent a modest number of questions and requested him to perform a simple balancing test at a location visible to passing motorists. Treatment of this sort cannot fairly be characterized as the functional equivalent of formal arrest.

Beckwith v. United States, 425 U.S. 341 (1975),

SUMMARY: The Court held that a person interviewed by IRS agents at her home is not in custody when the agents had requested the interview and made it clear that Beckwith could terminate the interview at any time.

Minnesota v. Murphy, 465 U.S. 420 (1984)

SUMMARY: The Court held that a probationer required to attend a probation interview is not in custody for purposes of Miranda because the person is not under arrest

J.D.B. v. North Carolina, 564 U.S. 261 (2011)

SUMMARY: J.D.B was a 13-year-old seventh-grader questioned by the police after he was removed from his classroom by a uniformed officer and escorted to a closed door conference room. The questioning lasted at least half an hour and two officers and two administrators were present. J.D.B. grandparent (his care provider) was not. He was not given Miranda warnings nor the opportunity to speak with his grandmother. Nor was he told that he was free to leave the room.

OPINION:

"This case presents the question whether the age of a child subjected to police questioning is relevant to the custody analysis of *Miranda v. Arizona*. It is beyond dispute that children will often feel bound to submit to police questioning when an adult in the same circumstances would feel free to leave. Seeing no reason for police officers or courts to blind themselves to that commonsense reality, we hold that a child's age properly informs the *Miranda* custody analysis.

...

"Any police interview of an individual suspected of a crime has "coercive aspects to it." Only those interrogations that occur while a suspect is in police custody, however, "heighte[n] the risk" that statements obtained are not the product of the suspect's free choice.

. . . .

"Two discrete inquiries are essential to the determination: first, what were the circumstances surrounding the interrogation; and second, given those circumstances, would a reasonable person have felt he or she was at liberty to terminate the interrogation and leave. . . . [T]he court must apply an objective test to resolve the ultimate inquiry: was there a formal arrest or restraint on freedom of movement of the degree associated with formal arrest."

Rather than demarcate a limited set of relevant circumstances, we have required police officers and courts to "examine all of the circumstances surrounding the interrogation," including any circumstance that "would have affected how a reasonable person" in the suspect's position "would perceive his or her freedom to leave. . ."

B

. . . .

We have observed that children "generally are less mature and responsible than adults,". . . ; that they "often lack the experience, perspective, and judgment to recognize and avoid choices that could be detrimental to them,". . . ; that they "are more vulnerable or susceptible to . . .outside pressures" than adults . . . Addressing the specific context of police interrogation, we have observed that events that "would leave a man cold and unimpressed can overawe and overwhelm a lad in his early teens." . . . Describing no one child in particular, these observations restate what "any parent knows" — indeed, what any person knows — about children generally.

. . . .

Indeed, even where a "reasonable person" standard otherwise applies, the common law has reflected the reality that children are not adults. . . .

[O]ur history is replete with laws and judicial recognition" that children cannot be viewed simply as miniature adults. We see no justification for taking a different course here. So long as the child's age was known to the officer at the time of the interview, or would have been objectively apparent to any reasonable officer, including age as part of the custody analysis requires officers neither to consider circumstances "unknowable" to them, nor to

"anticipat[e] the frailties or idiosyncrasies" of the particular suspect whom they question. . . .

. . . .

[Including the child's age] . . . in the custody analysis is consistent with the objective nature of that test. This is not to say that a child's age will be a determinative, or even a significant, factor in every case. . . It is, however, a reality that courts cannot simply ignore.

Yarborough v. Alvarado, 541 U.S. 652 (2004)

SUMMARY: A murder investigation led LA County Sheriff detective Cheryl Comstock to wish to speak to Alvarado. She left word with Alvarado's parents that she wanted to speak with him, and then the parents brought Alvarado (a 17-year-old) to speak to officers at the station. Parents waited in the lobby while Alvarado was interviewed. He alleges that his parents wanted to be present during the interview but were not allowed to do so. The interview lasted about two hours, and involved only the detective and Alvarado. He was not given Miranda warnings. He moved to suppress his statements before trial, and the trial court denied the motion stating that the interview was noncustodial.

During trial, on cross exam, Alvarado admitted that the interview "was a pretty friendly conversation," that there was "sort of a free flow between [Alvarado] and Detective Comstock," and that Alvarado did not "feel coerced or threatened in any way" during the interview. Alvarado was convicted and appealed.

OPINION: The Court of Appeals held that the state court erred in failing to account for Alvarado's youth and inexperience when evaluating whether a reasonable person in his position would have felt free to leave. It noted that this Court has considered a suspect's juvenile status when evaluating the voluntariness of confessions and the waiver of the privilege against self-incrimination. The Court of Appeals held that in light of these authorities, Alvarado's age and experience must be a factor in the *Miranda* custody inquiry. A minor with no criminal record would be more likely to feel coerced by police tactics and conclude he is under arrest than would an experienced adult, the Court of Appeals reasoned. This required extra "safeguards . . . commensurate with the age and circumstances of a juvenile defendant." According to the Court of Appeals, the effect of Alvarado's age and inexperience was so substantial that it turned the interview into a custodial interrogation.

In light of the clearly established law considering juvenile status, it was "simply unreasonable to conclude that a reasonable 17-year-old, with no prior history of arrest or police interviews, would have felt that he was at liberty to terminate the interrogation and leave."

. . . .

It can be said that fair-minded jurists could disagree over whether Alvarado was in custody. On one hand, certain facts weigh against a finding that Alvarado was in custody. The police did not transport Alvarado to the station or require him to appear at a particular time. They did not threaten him or suggest he would be placed under arrest. Alvarado's parents remained in the lobby during the interview, suggesting that the interview would be brief. In fact, according to trial counsel for Alvarado, he and his parents were told that the interview was " 'not going to be long.' " During the interview, Comstock focused on Soto's crimes rather than Alvarado's. Instead of pressuring Alvarado with the threat of arrest and prosecution, she appealed to his interest in telling the truth and being helpful to a police officer. In addition, Comstock twice asked Alvarado if he wanted to take a break. At the end of the interview, Alvarado went home. All of these objective facts are consistent with an interrogation environment in which a reasonable person would have felt free to terminate the interview and leave.

Other facts point in the opposite direction. Comstock interviewed Alvarado at the police station. The interview lasted two hours.

Comstock did not tell Alvarado that he was free to leave. Alvarado was brought to the police station by his legal guardians rather than arriving on his own accord, making the extent of his control over his presence unclear. Counsel for Alvarado alleges that Alvarado's parents asked to be present at the interview but were rebuffed, a fact that — if known to Alvarado — might reasonably have led someone in Alvarado's position to feel more restricted than otherwise. These facts weigh in favor of the view that Alvarado was in custody.

These differing indications lead us to hold that the state court's application of our custody standard was reasonable. The Court of Appeals was nowhere close to the mark when it concluded otherwise.

JUSTICE O'CONNOR, concurring.

…There may be cases in which a suspect's age will be relevant to the *Miranda* "custody" inquiry. In this case, however, Alvarado was almost 18 years old at the time of his interview. It is difficult to expect police to recognize that a suspect is a juvenile when he is so close to the age of majority. Even when police do know a suspect's age, it may be difficult for them to ascertain what bearing it has on the likelihood that the suspect would feel free to leave. . . . Given these difficulties, I agree that the state court's decision in this case cannot be called an unreasonable application of federal law simply because it failed explicitly to mention Alvarado's age.

JUSTICE BREYER, with whom JUSTICE STEVENS, JUSTICE SOUTER, and JUSTICE GINSBURG join, dissenting.

The dissent analyzed the same facts and the same legal standard and just decided they fell on the other side of the line.

Interrogation

Miranda is limited to custodial "interrogations." The *Innis* case below defines what the Court means by interrogation which triggers the Miranda warnings.

RHODE ISLAND v. INNIS
446 U.S. 291 (1980)

JUSTICE STEWART delivered the opinion of the Court.

On the night of January 12, 1975, John Mulvaney, a Providence, R. I., taxicab driver, disappeared after being dispatched to pick up a customer. His body was discovered four days later buried in a shallow grave in Coventry, R. I. He had died from a shotgun blast aimed at the back of his head.

On January 17, 1975, shortly after midnight, the Providence police received a telephone call from Gerald Aubin, also a taxicab driver, who reported that he had just been robbed by a man wielding a sawed-off shotgun. Aubin further reported that he had dropped off his assailant near Rhode Island College in a section of Providence known as Mount Pleasant. While at the Providence police station waiting to give a statement, Aubin noticed a picture of his assailant on a bulletin board. Aubin so informed one of the police officers present. The officer prepared a photo array, and again Aubin identified a picture of the same person. That person was the respondent. Shortly thereafter, the Providence police began a search of the Mount Pleasant area.

At approximately 4:30 a. m. on the same date, Patrolman Lovell, while cruising the streets of Mount Pleasant in a patrol car, spotted the respondent standing in the street facing him. When Patrolman Lovell stopped his car, the respondent walked towards it. Patrolman Lovell then arrested the respondent, who was unarmed, and advised him of his so-called *Miranda* rights. While the two men waited in the patrol car for other police officers to arrive, Patrolman Lovell did not converse with the respondent other than to respond to the latter's request for a cigarette.

Within minutes, Sergeant Sears arrived at the scene of the arrest, and he also gave the respondent the *Miranda* warnings. Immediately thereafter, Captain Leyden and other police officers arrived. Captain Leyden advised the respondent of his *Miranda* rights. The respondent stated that he understood those rights and wanted to speak with a lawyer. Captain Leyden then directed that the respondent be placed in a "caged wagon," a four-door police car with a wire screen mesh between the front and rear seats, and be driven to the central police station. Three officers, Patrolmen Gleckman, Williams, and McKenna, were assigned to accompany the respondent to the central station. They placed the respondent in the vehicle and shut the doors. Captain Leyden then instructed the officers not to question the respondent or intimidate or coerce him in any way. The three officers then entered the vehicle, and it departed.

While en route to the central station, Patrolman Gleckman initiated a conversation with Patrolman McKenna concerning the missing shotgun. As Patrolman Gleckman later testified:

> "A. At this point, I was talking back and forth with Patrolman McKenna stating that I frequent this area while on patrol and [that because a school for handicapped children is located nearby,] there's a lot of handicapped children running around in this area, and God forbid one of them might find a weapon with shells and they might hurt themselves."

Patrolman McKenna apparently shared his fellow officer's concern:

> "A. I more or less concurred with him that it was a safety factor and that we should, you know, continue to search for the weapon and try to find it."

While Patrolman Williams said nothing, he overheard the conversation between the two officers:

> "A. He [Gleckman] said it would be too bad if the little - I believe he said a girl - would pick up the gun, maybe kill herself."

The respondent then interrupted the conversation, stating that the officers should turn the car around so he could show them where the gun was located. At this point, Patrolman McKenna radioed back to Captain Leyden that they were returning to the scene of the arrest, and that the respondent would inform them of the location of the gun. At the time the respondent indicated that the officers should turn back, they had traveled no more than a mile, a trip encompassing only a few minutes.

The police vehicle then returned to the scene of the arrest where a search for the shotgun was in progress. There, Captain Leyden again advised the respondent of his *Miranda* rights. The respondent replied that he understood those rights but that he "wanted to get the gun out of the way because of the kids in the area in the school." The respondent then led the police to a nearby field, where he pointed out the shotgun under some rocks by the side of the road.

. . . .

In the present case, the parties are in agreement that the respondent was fully informed of his *Miranda* rights and that he invoked his *Miranda* right to counsel when he told Captain Leyden that he wished to consult with a lawyer. It is also uncontested that the respondent was "in custody" while being transported to the police station.

The issue, therefore, is whether the respondent was "interrogated" by the police officers in violation of the respondent's undisputed right under *Miranda* to remain silent until he had consulted with a lawyer. In resolving this issue, we first define the term "interrogation" under *Miranda* before turning to a consideration of the facts of this case.

The starting point for defining "interrogation" in this context is, of course, the Court's *Miranda* opinion. There the Court observed that "[b]y custodial interrogation, we mean questioning initiated by law enforcement officers after a person has been taken into custody or otherwise deprived of his freedom of action in any significant way." This passage and other references throughout the opinion to "questioning" might suggest that the *Miranda* rules were to apply only to those police interrogation practices that involve express questioning of a defendant while in custody.

We do not, however, construe the *Miranda* opinion so narrowly. The concern of the Court in *Miranda* was that the "interrogation environment" created by the interplay of interrogation and custody would "subjugate the individual to the will of his examiner" and thereby undermine the privilege against compulsory self-incrimination. The police practices that evoked this concern included several that did not involve express questioning. For example, one of the practices discussed in *Miranda* was the use of line-ups in which a coached witness would pick the defendant as the perpetrator. This was designed to establish that the defendant was in fact guilty as a predicate for further interrogation. A variation on this theme discussed in *Miranda* was the so-called "reverse line-up" in which a defendant would be identified by coached witnesses as the perpetrator of a fictitious crime, with the object of inducing him to confess to the actual crime of which he was suspected in order to escape the false prosecution. The Court in Miranda also included in its survey of interrogation practices the use of psychological ploys, such as to "posi[t]" "the guilt of the subject," to "minimize the moral seriousness of the offense," and "to cast blame on the victim or on the society." It is clear that these techniques of persuasion, no less than express questioning, were thought, in a custodial setting, to amount to interrogation.

This is not to say, however, that all statements obtained by the police after a person has been taken into custody are to be considered the product of interrogation. As the Court in Miranda noted:

> "Confessions remain a proper element in law enforcement. Any statement given freely and voluntarily without any compelling influences is, of course, admissible in evidence. The fundamental

import of the privilege while an individual is in custody is not whether he is allowed to talk to the police without the benefit of warnings and counsel, but whether he can be interrogated. . . . Volunteered statements of any kind are not barred by the Fifth Amendment and their admissibility is not affected by our holding today."

It is clear therefore that the special procedural safeguards outlined in Miranda are required not where a suspect is simply taken into custody, but rather where a suspect in custody is subjected to interrogation. "Interrogation," as conceptualized in the Miranda opinion, must reflect a measure of compulsion above and beyond that inherent in custody itself.

We conclude that the Miranda safeguards come into play whenever a person in custody is subjected to either express questioning or its functional equivalent. That is to say, the term "interrogation" under Miranda refers not only to express questioning, but also to any words or actions on the part of the police (other than those normally attendant to arrest and custody) that the police should know are reasonably likely to elicit an incriminating response from the suspect. The latter portion of this definition focuses primarily upon the perceptions of the suspect, rather than the intent of the police. This focus reflects the fact that the *Miranda* safeguards were designed to vest a suspect in custody with an added measure of protection against coercive police practices, without regard to objective proof of the underlying intent of the police. A practice that the police should know is reasonably likely to evoke an incriminating response from a suspect thus amounts to interrogation. But, since the police surely cannot be held accountable for the unforeseeable results of their words or actions, the definition of interrogation can extend only to words or actions on the part of police officers that they should have known were reasonably likely to elicit an incriminating response.

Turning to the facts of the present case, we conclude that the respondent was not "interrogated" within the meaning of *Miranda*.

It is undisputed that the first prong of the definition of "interrogation" was not satisfied, for the conversation between Patrolmen Gleckman and McKenna included no express questioning of the respondent. Moreover, it cannot be fairly concluded that the respondent was subjected to the "functional equivalent" of questioning.

The case thus boils down to whether, in the context of a brief conversation, the officers should have known that the respondent would suddenly be moved to make a self-incriminating response. Given the fact that the entire conversation appears to have consisted of no more than a few offhand remarks, we cannot say that the officers should have known that it was reasonably likely that Innis would so respond. This is not a case where the police carried on a lengthy harangue in the presence of the suspect. Nor does the record support the respondent's contention that, under the circumstances, the officers' comments were particularly "evocative." It is our view, therefore, that the respondent was not subjected by the police to words or actions that the police should have known were reasonably likely to elicit an incriminating response from him.

CHIEF JUSTICE BURGER, concurring.

Since the result is not inconsistent with *Miranda v. Arizona,* I concur in the judgment. The meaning of *Miranda* has become reasonably clear and law enforcement practices have adjusted to its strictures; I would neither overrule *Miranda*, disparage it, nor extend it at this late date.

Trial judges have enough difficulty discerning the boundaries and nuances flowing from post-*Miranda* opinions, and we do not clarify that situation today.

JUSTICE MARSHALL, with whom JUSTICE BRENNAN joins, dissenting.

I am substantially in agreement with the Court's definition of "interrogation" within the meaning of *Miranda v. Arizona.* The Court requires an objective inquiry into the likely effect of police conduct on a typical individual, taking into account any special susceptibility of the suspect to certain kinds of pressure of which the police know or have reason to know.

I am utterly at a loss, however, to understand how this objective standard as applied to the facts before us can rationally lead to the conclusion that there was no interrogation. Innis was arrested at 4:30 a. m., handcuffed, searched, advised of his rights, and placed in the back seat of a patrol car. Within a short time he had been twice more advised of his rights and driven away in a four-door sedan with three police officers. Since the car traveled no more than a mile before Innis agreed to point out the location of the murder weapon, Officer Gleckman must have begun almost immediately to talk about the search for the shotgun.

One can scarcely imagine a stronger appeal to the conscience of a suspect than the assertion that if the weapon is not found an innocent person will be hurt or killed. And not just any innocent person, but an innocent child - a little girl - a helpless, handicapped little girl on her way to school. The notion that such an appeal could not be expected to have any effect unless the suspect were known to have some special interest in handicapped children verges on the ludicrous. As a matter of fact, the appeal to a suspect to confess for the sake of others, to "display some evidence of decency and honor," is a classic interrogation technique.

Gleckman's remarks would obviously have constituted interrogation if they had been explicitly directed to respondent, and the result should not be different because they were nominally addressed to McKenna. This is not a case where police officers speaking among themselves are accidentally overheard by a suspect. These officers were "talking back and forth" in close quarters with the handcuffed suspect, traveling past the very place where they believed the weapon was located. They knew respondent would hear and attend to their conversation, and they are chargeable with knowledge of and responsibility for the pressures to speak which they created.

JUSTICE STEVENS, dissenting.

. . . .

Under my view of the correct standard, the judgment of the Rhode Island Supreme Court should be affirmed because the statements made within Innis' hearing were as likely to elicit a response as a direct question.

Other Case – Interrogation

| **Arizona v. Mauro , 481 U.S. 520 (1987)**

SUMMARY: The Court held that it is not interrogation for police to permit the defendant who had requested counsel to speak with his wife in front of the police;

Illinois v. Perkins
(see above)
Dealt with interrogation as well as custody; | **Estelle v. Smith, 451 U.S. 454 (1981)**

SUMMARY: The Court held that defendant's statements to a psychiatrist to determine whether he was fit to stand trial should not have been admitted (considered for sentencing purposes) because the defendant had not been told of his right to remain silent. |

Warnings

Miranda warnings must be given in a clear and unambiguous manner so that the individual understands his rights and feels free to exercise them. The police do not have to quote the exact words of the *Miranda* decision, but the warning must make clear that the person has the right to have an attorney present during the questioning, that the defendant has the right to remain silent and that if he does choose to speak anything he says can be used against him. (See, *Commonwealth v. Singleton*, 266 A.2d 753 (Pa 1970) where the police told the defendant that anything he said could be used for or against him. . .the court found that an inadequate warning.) The Court has not required police to tell the defendant that their silence will not be used against him.

In *Duckworth v. Eagan* 492 U.S. 195 (1989) the police warned the defendant, "You have a right to talk to a lawyer for advice before we ask you any questions, and to have him with you during the questioning. You have the right to the advice and presence of a lawyer even if you cannot afford to hire one. We have no way of giving you a lawyer, but one will be appointed for you, if you wish, if and when you go to court." The defendant had argued that the statement was ambiguous whether he was entitled to a court-appointed lawyer before interrogation. Five members of the Court found this warning to be adequate albeit somewhat ambiguous. Four justices found that the warnings were clearly inadequate under *Miranda*. They believed that the "if and when you go to court" language led defendant to believe that he wouldn't be provided a lawyer until in the future after questioning.

The warnings must be given even if police believe that the suspect is already aware of his right to remain silent and to have a lawyer. However, if the suspect's lawyer is present during the interrogation, then the *Miranda* warnings do not have to be given. The Court in *Miranda* stated, "the presence of counsel . . . would be adequate protective device necessary to make the process of police interrogation conform to the dictates of the privilege. His presence would ensure that statements made in the government-established atmosphere are not the product of compulsion."

Miranda does not require that the police tell the suspect what he is charged with nor the seriousness of the crime. In *Colorado v. Spring*, 479 U.S. 564 (1987), for example, federal agents interrogated Spring about firearms violations knowing that he was suspected of a murder. They asked him if he had ever shot anyone, and Spring made an incriminating statement which was later used in the state murder prosecution. The Court held that the statements were admissible and the failure of the police to inform the suspect on a minor offense that he would be questioned on much more serious murder charges did not nullify his decision to waive his *Miranda* rights. Emanuel suggests that the police may not intentionally trick the suspect into thinking his crime is less serious than it is in order to induce him to confess. *Miranda* states, "any evidence that the accused was threatened, tricked, or cajoled into a waiver [of his right to silence or to a lawyer] will, of course, show that the defendant did not voluntarily waive his privilege."

Invoking And Waiving Miranda

The Court has consistently held that the defendant must himself express some desire to invoke *Miranda* (see, *Moran v. Burbine* (below) and *Montejo v. Louisiana*, 556 U.S. 778 (2009)). This next section explores how a suspect invokes the right to remain silent or the right to counsel, and examines cases in which the invocation was not "scrupulously honored" by the police.

MORAN v. BURBINE
475 U.S. 412 (1986)

JUSTICE O'CONNOR delivered the opinion of the Court.

On the morning of March 3, 1977, Mary Jo Hickey was found unconscious in a factory parking lot in Providence, Rhode Island. Suffering from injuries to her skull apparently inflicted by a metal pipe found at the scene,

she was rushed to a nearby hospital. Three weeks later she died from her wounds.

Several months after her death, the Cranston, Rhode Island, police arrested respondent and two others in connection with a local burglary. Shortly before the arrest, Detective Ferranti of the Cranston police force had learned from a confidential informant that the man responsible for Ms. Hickey's death lived at a certain address and went by the name of "Butch." Upon discovering that respondent lived at that address and was known by that name, Detective Ferranti informed respondent of his *Miranda* rights. When respondent refused to execute a written waiver, Detective Ferranti spoke separately with the two other suspects arrested on the breaking and entering charge and obtained statements further implicating respondent in Ms. Hickey's murder. At approximately 6 p.m., Detective Ferranti telephoned the police in Providence to convey the information he had uncovered. An hour later, three officers from that department arrived at the Cranston headquarters for the purpose of questioning respondent about the murder.

That same evening, at about 7:45 p.m., respondent's sister telephoned the Public Defender's Office to obtain legal assistance for her brother. Her sole concern was the breaking and entering charge, as she was unaware that respondent was then under suspicion for murder. She asked for Richard Casparian who had been scheduled to meet with respondent earlier that afternoon to discuss another charge unrelated to either the break-in or the murder. As soon as the conversation ended, the attorney who took the call attempted to reach Mr. Casparian. When those efforts were unsuccessful, she telephoned Allegra Munson, another Assistant Public Defender, and told her about respondent's arrest and his sister's subsequent request that the office represent him.

At 8:15 p.m., Ms. Munson telephoned the Cranston police station and asked that her call be transferred to the detective division. In the words of the Supreme Court of Rhode Island, whose factual findings we treat as presumptively correct, 28 U.S.C. 2254(d), the conversation proceeded as follows:

"A male voice responded with the word `Detectives.' Ms. Munson identified herself and asked if Brian Burbine was being held; the person responded affirmatively. Ms. Munson explained to the person that Burbine was represented by attorney Casparian who was not available; she further stated that she would act as Burbine's legal counsel in the event that the police intended to place him in a lineup or question him. The unidentified person told Ms. Munson that the police would not be questioning Burbine or putting him in a lineup and that they were through with him for the night. Ms. Munson was not informed that the Providence Police were at the Cranston police station or that Burbine was a suspect in Mary's murder."

At all relevant times, respondent was unaware of his sister's efforts to retain counsel and of the fact and contents of Ms. Munson's telephone conversation.

Less than an hour later, the police brought respondent to an interrogation room and conducted the first of a series of interviews concerning the murder. Prior to each session, respondent was informed of his *Miranda* rights, and on three separate occasions he signed a written form acknowledging that he understood his right to the presence of an attorney and explicitly indicating that he "[did] not want an attorney called or appointed for [him]" before he gave a statement.

Uncontradicted evidence at the suppression hearing indicated that at least twice during the course of the evening, respondent was left in a room where he had access to a telephone, which he apparently declined to use. Eventually, respondent signed three written statements fully admitting to the murder.

Prior to trial, respondent moved to suppress the statements. The court denied the motion, finding that respondent had received the *Miranda* warnings and had "knowingly, intelligently, and voluntarily waived his privilege against self-incrimination [and] his right to counsel."

The jury found respondent guilty of murder in the first degree, and he appealed to the Supreme Court of Rhode Island. A divided court rejected his contention that the Fifth and Fourteenth Amendments to the Constitution required the suppression of the inculpatory statements and affirmed the conviction. Failure to inform respondent of Ms. Munson's efforts to represent him, the court held, did not undermine the validity of the waivers. "It hardly seems conceivable that the additional information that an attorney whom he did not know had called the police station would have added significantly to the quantum of information necessary for the accused to make an informed decision as to waiver."

[Defendant] contends that the confessions must be suppressed because the police's failure to inform him of the attorney's telephone call deprived him of information essential to his ability to knowingly waive his Fifth Amendment rights. In the alternative, he suggests that to fully protect the Fifth Amendment values served by Miranda, we should extend that decision to condemn the conduct of the Providence police. We address each contention in turn.

Miranda holds that "[t]he defendant may waive effectuation" of the rights conveyed in the warnings "provided the waiver is made voluntarily, knowingly and intelligently." The inquiry has two distinct dimensions. First, the relinquishment of the right must have been voluntary in the sense that it was the product of a free and deliberate choice rather than intimidation, coercion, or deception. Second, the waiver must have been made with a full awareness of both the nature of the right being abandoned and the consequences of the decision to abandon it. Only if the "totality of the circumstances surrounding the interrogation" reveals both an uncoerced choice and the requisite level of comprehension may a court properly conclude that the *Miranda* rights have been waived.

Events occurring outside of the presence of the suspect and entirely unknown to him surely can have no bearing on the capacity to comprehend and knowingly relinquish a constitutional right. . . . Once it is determined that a suspect's decision not to rely on his rights was uncoerced, that he at all times knew he could stand mute and request a lawyer, and that he was aware of the State's intention to use his statements to secure a conviction, the analysis is complete and the waiver is valid as a matter of law. The Court of Appeals' conclusion to the contrary was in error.

Nor do we believe that the level of the police's culpability in failing to inform respondent of the telephone call has any bearing on the validity of the waivers.

Nor was the failure to inform respondent of the telephone call the kind of "trick[ery]" that can vitiate the validity of a waiver. Granting that the "deliberate or reckless" withholding of information is objectionable as a matter of ethics, such conduct is only relevant to the constitutional validity of a waiver if it deprives a defendant of knowledge essential to his ability to understand the nature of his rights and the consequences of abandoning them. Because respondent's voluntary decision to speak was made with full awareness and comprehension of all the information *Miranda* requires the police to convey, the waivers were valid.

…The purpose of the *Miranda* warnings … is to dissipate the compulsion inherent in custodial interrogation and, in so doing, guard against abridgment of the suspect's Fifth Amendment rights. Clearly, a rule that focuses on how the police treat an attorney — conduct that has no relevance at all to the degree of compulsion experienced by the defendant during interrogation — would ignore both *Miranda's* mission and its only source of legitimacy.

[R]eading *Miranda* to require the police in each instance to inform a suspect of an attorney's efforts to reach him would work a substantial and, we think, inappropriate shift in the subtle balance struck in that decision. Custodial interrogations implicate two competing concerns. On the one hand, "the need for police questioning as a tool for effective enforcement of criminal laws" cannot be doubted. Admissions of guilt are more than merely "desirable," they are essential to society's compelling interest in finding, convicting, and punishing those who violate the law. On the other hand, the Court has recognized that the interrogation process is "inherently coercive" and that, as a consequence, there exists a substantial risk that the police will inadvertently traverse the fine line between legitimate efforts to elicit admissions and constitutionally impermissible compulsion. *Miranda* attempted to reconcile these opposing concerns by giving the defendant the power to exert some control over the course of the interrogation. Police questioning, often an essential part of the investigatory process, could continue in its traditional form, the Court held, but only if the suspect clearly understood that, at any time, he could bring the proceeding to a halt or, short of that, call in an attorney to give advice and monitor the conduct of his interrogators.

JUSTICE STEVENS, with whom JUSTICE BRENNAN and JUSTICE MARSHALL join, dissenting.

Police interference with communications between an attorney and his client is a recurrent problem. The factual variations in the many state-court opinions condemning this interference as a violation of the Federal Constitution suggest the variety of contexts in which the problem emerges. In Oklahoma, police led a lawyer to several different locations while they interrogated the suspect; in Oregon, police moved a suspect to a new location when they learned that his lawyer was on his way; in Illinois, authorities failed to tell a suspect that his lawyer had arrived at the jail and asked to see him; in Massachusetts, police did not tell suspects that their lawyers were at or near the police station. In all these cases, the police not only failed to inform the suspect, but also misled the attorneys. The scenarios vary, but the core problem of police interference remains. "Its recurrence suggests that it has roots in some condition fundamental and general to our criminal system."

The near-consensus of state courts and the legal profession's Standards about this recurrent problem lends powerful support to the conclusion that police may not interfere with communications between an attorney and the client whom they are questioning.

Well-settled principles of law lead inexorably to the conclusion that the failure to inform Burbine of the call from his attorney makes the subsequent waiver of his constitutional rights invalid. Analysis should begin with an acknowledgment that the burden of proving the validity of a waiver of constitutional rights is always on the government. When such a waiver occurs in a custodial setting, that burden is an especially heavy one because custodial interrogation is inherently coercive, because disinterested witnesses are seldom available to describe what actually happened, and because history has taught us that the danger of overreaching during incommunicado interrogation is so real.

Like the failure to give warnings and like police initiation of interrogation after a request for counsel, police deception of a suspect through omission of information regarding attorney communications greatly exacerbates the inherent problems of incommunicado interrogation and requires a clear principle to safeguard the presumption against the waiver of constitutional rights. As in those situations, the police deception should render a subsequent waiver invalid.

In my view, as a matter of law, the police deception of Munson was tantamount to deception of Burbine himself. It constituted a violation of Burbine's right to have an attorney present during the questioning that began shortly thereafter.

. . .

I firmly believe that the right to counsel at custodial interrogation is infringed by police treatment of an attorney that prevents or impedes the attorney's representation of the suspect at that interrogation.

In my judgment, police interference in the attorney-client relationship is the type of governmental misconduct on a matter of central importance to the administration of justice that the Due Process Clause prohibits. Just as the police cannot impliedly promise a suspect that his silence will not be used against him and then proceed to break that promise, so too police cannot tell a suspect's attorney that they will not question the suspect and then proceed to question him. Just as the government cannot conceal from a suspect material and exculpatory evidence, so too the government cannot conceal from a suspect the material fact of his attorney's communication. …

Invoking Silence

In *Michigan v. Mosley*, 423 U.S. 96 (1975), Mosley was interrogated about two robberies after receiving his *Miranda* warnings, and he declined to answer. The police immediately ceased questioning Mosley. Several hours later, however, Mosley was taken to a different floor of a building where he was being held, and after again being given his *Miranda* warnings, was questioned by a different police officer about a fatal shooting which had occurred in a third robbery. Mosley implicated himself. He moved at trial to strike his statements on the ground that they were obtained in violation of his right not to be questioned after he invoked *Miranda*.

In a 7-2 decision, the Court held that Mosley's right not to be questioned had not been violated by the resumption of questioning. The Court emphasized that the second questioning was about a different crime, significant time had passed between the two interrogations, the interrogations took place in different locations, and the defendant was given his *Miranda* warnings before each of the sessions. (Keep in mind that *Mosley* involved only the defendant's invocation of his right to remain silent. Mosley did not assert during this time that he wanted counsel.)

The Supreme Court identified five *Mosley* factors that allow the use of an incriminating statement made in a second interrogation after a suspect has invoked the right of silence in a previous interrogation:

➤ whether initial *Miranda* warnings were given

➤ whether police immediately ceased interrogating when the suspect invoked silence,

➤ whether a significant time period had elapsed between the two interrogations,

➤ whether a fresh *Miranda* warning was given before the second interrogation.

➤ whether the second interrogation was for a different crime than that investigated in the first interrogation or was triggered by new circumstances (for example, the confession of a confederate).

Invoking Counsel

The Court treats a defendant's invocation of his right to counsel differently than his invocation of his right to remain silent. *Edwards v. Arizona*, (below) is the key case. It created a bright line rule: once a defendant invokes his right to an attorney, the police may not reapproach — regardless of how much time has passed. (As you read this, be aware that the court has modified the holding somewhat by creating the "break in custody" rule announced in Maryland v. Shatzer, below.)

EDWARDS v. ARIZONA
451 U.S. 477 (1981)

JUSTICE WHITE delivered the opinion of the Court.

[Facts Summarized:

Edwards was arrested from his home on a warrant. At the station he was read his rights. He said he understood them and was willing to submit to questioning. During the interrogation, police made known that another had implicated him in the crime, Edwards said he wanted to "make a deal." Interrogating officer said he didn't have the authority to negotiated, and ultimately gave Edwards the number of a county attorney. Edwards called that number, spoke briefly and then stated, "I want an attorney before making a deal." Police ceased questioning, and transported Edwards to the county jail. The next morning, officers went to the jail and asked to speak to Edwards. Edwards indicated he did not want to talk to anyone. Jail guards told him he "had to" talk and took him to meet the officers. Officers Mirandized Edwards, and Edwards indicated he was willing to talk but wanted to listen to the tape of the suspect who had implicated him. He listened, then agreed to make an unrecorded statement. Edwards ultimately made statements implicating himself the crime. Those statements were used at trial. Edwards was convicted and he appealed. He argued that he had invoked both rights on January 19th (the day he was arrested) and had not waived those rights on January 20th. Arizona appellate courts disagreed and found there was no violation of his constitutional rights. The U.S. Supreme Court, agreed with Edwards for two reasons.]

OPINION:

First, the Arizona Supreme Court applied an erroneous standard for determining waiver where the accused has specifically invoked his right to counsel. It is reasonably clear under our cases that waivers of counsel must not only be voluntary, but must also constitute a knowing and intelligent relinquishment or abandonment of a known right or privilege, a matter which depends in each case "upon the particular facts and circumstances surrounding that case, including the background, experience, and conduct of the accused."

Neither the trial court nor the Arizona Supreme Court undertook to focus on whether Edwards understood his right to counsel and intelligently and knowingly relinquished it. . . .

Second, although we have held that after initially being advised of his *Miranda* rights, the accused may himself validly waive his rights and respond to interrogation, the Court has strongly indicated that additional safeguards are necessary when the accused asks for counsel; and we now hold that when an accused has invoked his right to have counsel present during custodial interrogation, a valid waiver of that right cannot be established by showing only that he responded to further police-initiated custodial interrogation even if he has been advised of his rights. We further hold that an accused, such as Edwards, having expressed his desire to deal with the police only through counsel, is not subject to further interrogation by the authorities until counsel has been made available to him, unless the accused himself initiates further communication, exchanges, or conversations with the police.

...

In concluding that the fruits of the interrogation initiated by the police on January 20 could not be used against Edwards, we do not hold or imply that Edwards was powerless to countermand his election or that the authorities could in no event use any incriminating statements made by Edwards prior to his having access to counsel. Had Edwards initiated the meeting on January 20, nothing in the Fifth and Fourteenth Amendments would prohibit the police from merely listening to his voluntary, volunteered statements and using them against him at the trial. ...

...We think it is clear that Edwards was subjected to custodial interrogation on January 20 within the meaning of *Rhode Island v. Innis*, supra, and that this occurred at the instance of the authorities. His statement, made without having had access to counsel, did not amount to a valid waiver and hence was inadmissible.

Michigan v. Jackson, 475 U.S. 625 (1986)

SUMMARY: The Case involved companion cases of Rudy Bladel and Robert Jackson. Both Bladel and Jackson had spoken to police before their arraignments. Both affirmatively requested counsel at their arraignments (a court process in front of the judge in which the defendant is apprised of what charges have been filed). The court ruled that a suspect invoked the right to counsel for interrogation purposes when he requested a lawyer at a formal arraignment. Police officers were present at arraignment and observed defendants request the appointment of counsel.

The Court differentiated *Edwards* where defendant's request for counsel had been made during the interrogation and these cases where request for counsel was made in court, and opined that these two defendants should have at least as much protection under the Sixth Amendment's right to counsel during a post-arraignment interrogation as they do under the Fifth Amendment's right to counsel during a custodial interrogations. The Court held that any desire on defendant's part to speak after invoking counsel must be initiated by the defendant.

Arizona v. Roberson, 486 U.S. 675 (1988),

SUMMARY: The Court held that if a suspect asked to see a lawyer before speaking, all officers, not just the officer who first Mirandized the suspect, are deemed to be aware of the invocation and must heed it. If it were otherwise, officers could easily sidestep the Edwards rule by claiming ignorance of an initial invocation of the right to see an attorney. Roberson showed that the bright line rule of Edwards applied even though the police wanted to question the suspect about a different crime than the one they were questioning him about when he first requested the lawyer.

Minnick v. Mississippi, 498 U.S. 146 (1990)

SUMMARY: Minnick invoked the right to see counsel during an interrogation and was allowed to consult with a lawyer. He was thereafter interrogated without his counsel present. The Court found that this violated Minnick's rights

and that the right to counsel meant the right to have counsel present during the subsequent questioning.

Montejo v. Louisiana, 556 U.S. 778 (2009):

SUMMARY: Pursuant to state policy, Louisiana courts automatically appointed counsel to represent all indigent defendants. During the mandatory preliminary hearing, the indigent Montejo stood appeared before the judge but said nothing and did not request an attorney. But, as they did in all cases like this, the court appointed counsel on his behalf. Later that day — but before the defendant had yet met with his court appointed attorney — two detectives visited Montejo in prison. They requested that he go with them to locate the murder weapon (which Montejo had said he had thrown into a lake). Montejo was again read his Miranda rights and agreed to go with the detectives. During this trip, Montejo wrote a letter of apology to the victim's widow. Detectives took defendant back to the prison and Montejo finally met with his court-appointed attorney (who was "quite upset that detectives had interrogated his client in his absence.").

OPINION: The court held that the only purpose of *Edwards* was to protect the defendant from repeated badgering by police, and because that scenario was not present here, there was no requirement that police refrain from contacting the defendant. Had Montejo affirmatively requested an attorney, then Jackson would have applied. The court stated,

> "The question in *Jackson,* however, was not whether respondents were entitled to counsel (they unquestionably were), but "whether respondents validly waived their right to counsel," and even if it is reasonable to presume from a defendant's request for counsel that any subsequent waiver of the right was coerced, no such presumption can seriously be entertained when a lawyer was merely "secured" on the defendant's behalf, by the State itself, as a matter of course. . . .
>
> When a court appoints counsel for an indigent defendant in the absence of any request on his part, there is no basis for a

presumption that any subsequent waiver of the right to counsel will be involuntary. There is no "initial election" to exercise the right that must be preserved through a prophylactic rule against later waivers. No reason exists to assume that a defendant like Montejo, who has done nothing at all to express his intentions with respect to his Sixth Amendment rights, would not be perfectly amenable to speaking with the police without having counsel present. And no reason exists to prohibit the police from inquiring. *Edwards* and *Jackson* are meant to prevent police from badgering defendants into changing their minds about their rights, but a defendant who never asked for counsel has not yet made up his mind in the first instance.

Under *Miranda's* prophylactic protection of the right against compelled self-incrimination, any suspect subject to custodial interrogation has the right to have a lawyer present if he so requests, and to be advised of that right. Under *Edwards'* prophylactic protection of the *Miranda* right, once such a defendant "has invoked his right to have counsel present," interrogation must stop. And under *Minnick's* prophylactic protection of the *Edwards* right, no subsequent interrogation may take place until counsel is present, "whether or not the accused has consulted with his attorney."

These three layers of prophylaxis are sufficient. Under the *Miranda-Edwards-Minnick* line of cases (which is not in doubt), a defendant who does not want to speak to the police without counsel present need only say as much when he is first approached and given the *Miranda* warnings. At that point, not only must the immediate contact end, but "badgering" by later requests is prohibited. If that regime suffices to protect the integrity of "a suspect's voluntary choice not to speak outside his lawyer's presence" before his arraignment, it is hard to see why it would not also suffice to protect that same choice after arraignment, when Sixth Amendment rights have attached. And if so, then *Jackson* is simply superfluous."

Just because a defendant has been indicted, doesn't mean that police stop investigating a case. And they can continue to question the defendant about the crime for which he or she was indicted. They can question the defendant about other crimes as well. They may not, however, obtain evidence surreptitiously from an indicted defendant in a way that cuts the defendant off from the defense lawyer. So, for example, if police are investigating a suspect for burglary, and the suspect already has been indicted for distributing cocaine, an undercover agent may investigate the suspect for burglary (for which the suspect has not been charged.) That said, any evidence related to the cocaine charge for which defendant had already been incdicted and had counsel would not be admissible.

In *Maryland v. Shatzer*, the U.S. Supreme Court created a "break in custody" exception to the *Edwards* rule (once a defendant requests counsel, police may not reapproach unless defendant initiates contact). The *Shatzer* Court held that *Edwards* rule was not a constitutional mandate, but rather a "judicially prescribed prophylaxis," and that the judicial rule must be applied only when its benefits outweigh its costs.

MARYLAND V. SHATZER
559 U.S. 98 (2010)

JUSTICE SCALIA delivered the opinion of the court.

...[In balancing the benefits of the Edwards rule] . . . [w]e begin with the benefits. *Edwards'* presumption of involuntariness has the incidental effect of "conserv[ing] judicial resources which would otherwise be expended in making difficult determinations of voluntariness." . . . Its fundamental purpose, however, is to "[p]reserv[e] the integrity of an accused's choice to communicate with police only through counsel," by "prevent[ing] police from badgering a defendant into waiving his previously asserted *Miranda* rights," . . . Thus, the benefits of the rule are measured by the number of coerced confessions it suppresses that otherwise would have been admitted. . . .

It is easy to believe that a suspect may be coerced or badgered into abandoning his earlier refusal to be questioned without counsel in the paradigm *Edwards* case. That is a case in which the suspect has been arrested for a particular crime and is held in uninterrupted pretrial custody while that crime is being actively investigated. After the initial interrogation, and up to and including the second one, he remains cut off from his normal life and companions, "thrust into" and isolated in an "unfamiliar," "police-dominated atmosphere," where his captors "appear to control [his] fate," That was the situation confronted by the suspects in *Edwards*, *Roberson*, and *Minnick*, the three cases in which we have held the *Edwards* rule applicable. Edwards was arrested pursuant to a warrant and taken to a police station, where he was interrogated until he requested counsel. The officer ended the interrogation and took him to the county jail, but at 9:15 the next morning, two of the officer's colleagues reinterrogated Edwards at the jail. Roberson was arrested "at the scene of a just-completed burglary" and interrogated there until he requested a lawyer. A different officer interrogated him three days later while he "was still in custody pursuant to the arrest." Minnick was arrested by local police and taken to the San Diego jail, where two FBI agents interrogated him the next morning until he requested counsel. Two days later a Mississippi Deputy Sheriff reinterrogated him at the jail. None of these suspects regained a sense of control or normalcy after they were initially taken into custody for the crime under investigation.

When, unlike what happened in these three cases, a suspect has been released from his pretrial custody and has returned to his normal life for some time before the later attempted interrogation, there is little reason to think that his change of heart regarding interrogation without counsel has been coerced. He has no longer been isolated. He has likely been able to seek advice from an attorney, family members, and friends. And he knows from his earlier experience that he need only demand counsel to bring the interrogation to a halt; and that investigative custody does not last indefinitely. In these circumstances, it is far fetched to think that a police officer's asking the suspect whether he would like to waive his *Miranda* rights will any more "wear down the accused," . . . than did the first such request at the original attempted interrogation — which is of course not deemed coercive. His change of heart is less likely attributable to "badgering" than it is to the fact that further deliberation in familiar surroundings has caused him to believe (rightly or wrongly) that cooperating with the investigation is in his interest. Uncritical extension of Edwards to this situation would not significantly increase the number of genuinely coerced confessions excluded. …

At the same time that extending the *Edwards* rule yields diminished benefits, extending the rule also increases its costs: the in-fact voluntary confessions it excludes from trial, and the voluntary confessions it deters law enforcement officers from even trying to obtain. Voluntary confessions are not merely "a proper element in law enforcement," they are an "unmitigated good," . . . " 'essential to society's compelling interest in finding, convicting, and punishing those who violate the law,' ". . .

The protections offered by *Miranda*, … [which are] … sufficient to ensure that the police respect the suspect's desire to have an attorney present the first time police interrogate him, [also] adequately ensure that result when a suspect who initially requested counsel is reinterrogated after a break in custody that is of sufficient duration to dissipate its coercive effects.

If Shatzer's return to the general prison population qualified as a break in custody there is no doubt that it lasted long enough (2 years) to meet that durational requirement. . . . [W]hile it is certainly unusual for this Court to set forth precise time limits governing police action, it is not unheard-of.

[T]his is a case in which the requisite police action (. . . abstention from further interrogation) has not been prescribed by statute but has been established by opinion of this Court. We think it appropriate to specify a period of time to avoid the consequence that continuation of the Edwards presumption "will not reach the correct result most of the time." It seems to us that period is 14 days. That provides plenty of time for the suspect to get reacclimated to his normal life, to consult with friends and counsel, and to shake off any residual coercive effects of his prior custody."

One complicating factor in deciding whether defendant has invoked counsel revolves around whether defendant's statements are about a crime for which he or she already has a Sixth Amendment right to counsel[69] or concern a separate crime for which the defendant does not yet have a Sixth Amendment right to counsel.[70] The interplay between the Fifth Amendment's "right to counsel" implied by *Miranda* and the Sixth Amendment's right to counsel is tricky. It is possible that a statement made to an officer is admissible under the Fifth Amendment right against self-incrimination, but nevertheless inadmissible as a violation of the Sixth Amendment right to counsel. Consider, for example, this scenario. Bob is arrested; state files charges against Bob; Bob appears before the court with an attorney he hired while sitting in jail after he was arrested. Bob and his attorney show up for the arraignment and he is arraigned (told the charges that are pending). Judge decides to release Bob pending trial rather than keep Bob in custody. Bob is released. Three days later, police run into Bob on the street and ask, "Hey Bob, we know you committed that horrible crime, why? And, tell us, if you would be so kind, where you stowed the evidence." Bob admits the crime and takes the police to the stash of evidence. Bob, because he was not in custody (see the custody cases above), was not entitled to have been warned of his Miranda rights to silence/attorney under the Fifth Amendment. But Bob was entitled to have his attorney present under the Sixth Amendment because the state has initiated criminal proceedings against him. This situation is similar to the case of *Messiah v. United States* (decided before *Miranda*, but still good law). *Messiah* was indicted and requested and was represented by an attorney. The government put a listening device on his car and got statements from him. Since he was not in custody, there was no custodial interrogation, so his Fifth Amendment right was not violated. Nevertheless, his Sixth Amendment right to counsel was violated. The right is violated if, after adversary judicial proceedings have begun (for example, after indictment), the police question the defendant outside the presence of counsel or without a valid waiver of the right to counsel

This chapter tries to show that *Miranda* is about a suspect's Fifth Amendment right to be free from self-incrimination. The part of the *Miranda* warnings stating "you have the right to an attorney," is meant to warn the defendant to protect him or her against compulsory self-incrimination. (That is, if you know you have the right to talk to an attorney before you decide to talk to the police, maybe you will consult with an attorney to see if it is a good idea to continue to talk to the police). This is different than having an attorney to help you navigate the criminal justice process when and if you are charged with a crime—a Sixth Amendment right.

To make matters even a bit trickier, the Court notes that the Sixth Amendment right to counsel is specific to critical stages in a process (i.e., for example, the initiation of formal charges filed in court) and is offense/case specific. This means, that if the state is prosecuting a defendant for a burglary that occurred on New Year's Day, the defendant has a right to counsel to represent him on

---

[69] The Sixth Amendment's right to counsel is discussed more fully in Chapter XXX. That right "attaches" (becomes effective) as soon as the state initiates formal criminal proceedings (files charges against the defendant).

[70] Meaning, the state has not yet filed formal charges against the defendant.

that burglary. If defendant had also committed a battery against his wife two weeks later, that is a separate offense/case. Defendant would have the right to counsel to represent him for the battery if and when he is prosecuted for it. The test for determining whether there are two different offenses under the Sixth Amendment is the *Blockburger* Test. Under that test, two crimes are considered different offenses when each requires proof of an additional element that the other crime does not require. (If the crimes happened at two distinct times, as in the example above, this is also a good indicator.)

According to *Fellers v. United States* (2004), the proper standard to use when determining whether statements made by a defendant after an indictment (one of those critical stages in a process) are admissible is the Sixth Amendment right to counsel, not the Fifth Amendment right against self-incrimination. In *Fellers* police went to Feller's home, got him to talk, and had not given him his *Miranda* warnings. They took Fellers to jail, *Mirandized* him, and then he made some additional statements. Fellers had already been indicted by the grand jury. Under the Fifth Amendment Feller's statements at the jail would have been admissible because police gave the Miranda warnings. But, the Court instead found Feller's Sixth Amendment rights had been violated because they were fruit of an unlawful interrogation (at his home) "deliberately elicited" after he had been indicted and had an attorney.

The differences between Fifth and Sixth Amendment *Miranda*/Counsel.[71]

Miranda Warnings	Right to Counsel
Comes under the Fifth Amendment right against self-incrimination	Comes under the Sixth Amendment
Applies only during custodial interrogation	Applies in any proceedings-before trial, during trial, and during an appeal
Given by the police	Lawyer is either retained by the suspect or assigned by the judge because of indigency.
Given in the absence of a lawyer	Once defendant has a lawyer, defendant cannot be questioned in the absence of a lawyer unless the right to counsel has been waived
Must be given every time there is a custodial interrogation about any offense except routine traffic stops. (decide whether suspect was in custody; decide whether suspect was interrogated).	Once given, is violated only if the interrogation deals with the same offense for which the defendant is represented by an attorney, but not about other offenses, even if it is closely related.

As you can see from Fellers, even if a statement is admissible under the voluntariness test and under *Miranda*, it may still be excluded from trial if the taking of the statement violated the defendant's Sixth Amendment right to counsel. Note that the Sixth Amendment right to counsel can be violated even if the defendant was not explicitly questioned, as long as incriminating information was actually secured (deliberately elicited) from the defendant without the presence of counsel. The test is whether the government obtained incriminating statements by knowingly circumventing the accused's right to have counsel present in a confrontation between the accused and a government agent (for example, as in *Messiah*, where the police surreptitiously attached a listening device to a car)

---

[71]See, Del Carmen, R., Criminal Procedure: Law and Practice, Thomson Wadsworth, 7th Ed. (2007)

Brewer v. Williams, 430 U.S. 387 (1977), shows that courts will look carefully at confessions obtained from defendants who are represented by lawyers when those lawyers are not present. Completely passive listening (such as putting an informer in a cell to overhear comments of a cellmate) is probably not a violation of the Sixth Amendment. But, if the informer initiates a conversation designed to elicit incriminating remarks, it is.

Waiver Of Miranda

Miranda recognizes that defendants may expressly waive their *Miranda* rights. ("An express statement that the individual is willing to make a statement and does not want an attorney followed closely by a statement could constitute a waiver.") Express waivers are generally accepted by the courts. Implied waivers, however, are generally scrutinized carefully by the courts and evaluated strictly and on a case-by-case basis (no per se rules). Moreover, the prosecution has a "heavy burden" to demonstrate that any waiver was intelligent (the suspect knows what he is giving up) and voluntary (there is no coercion). Also, for a waiver to exist, prosecution must show that defendant understood his *Miranda* rights and intended to relinquish them.

The Court has made clear that silence does not constitute a waiver of *Miranda.* In *North Carolina v. Butler*, 441 U.S. 369 (1979) the court found that a suspect's refusal to sign a written waiver form did not automatically negate his waiver. In that case the suspect stated, "I will talk to you, but I am not signing the form." He did not say anything at all when advised of his right to a lawyer's assistance. The Supreme Court held that "an express waiver of *Miranda* rights is not necessary," and that in some circumstances can be "inferred from the actions and words of the person interrogated." The case was remanded back to the state to determine whether a waiver could be inferred. The dissenters argued that *Miranda* should be interpreted to require an express waiver otherwise ambiguous situations (like those in *Butler*) could arise in which it was not clear whether the suspect knowingly waived *Miranda.*

In *Connecticut v. Barrett,* 479 U.S. 523 (1987), a suspect expressed willingness to talk to police without a lawyer, but wanted to consult with a lawyer as to whether he should make a written statement. The Supreme Court held that this was only a partial waiver of rights. It did not serve as an invocation of his right to attorney for all purposes. The court upheld the introduction of incriminating statements because Barrett's statement of his willingness to answer oral questions without a lawyer was unambiguous.

In *Berghuis v. Thompkins,* 560 U.S. 370 (2010), the Court examined whether police may interrogate a suspect in custody when the suspect neither explicitly waived, nor explicitly invoked, his right to remain silent after receiving the *Miranda* warnings. In its opinion, the Court disparaged, "ambiguous, equivocal acts or omissions" as invocations of Miranda rights. The Court stated that even absent invocation, however, statements are only admissible if the prosecutor establishes that the rights were knowingly and voluntarily waived—"voluntarily in the sense that it was the product of a free and deliberate choice rather than intimidation, coercion or deception" and "made with the full awareness of both the nature of the right being abandoned and the consequences of the decision to abandon it." The court then analyzed the facts presented in this case.

> The record in this case shows that Thompkins waived his right to remain silent. There is no basis in this case to conclude that he did not understand his rights; and on these facts it follows that he chose not to invoke or rely on those rights when he did speak. First, there is no contention that Thompkins did not understand his rights; and from this it follows that he knew what he gave up when he spoke. . . . There was more than enough evidence in the record to conclude that Thompkins understood his Miranda rights. Thompkins received a written copy of the Miranda warnings; Detective Helgert determined that Thompkins could read and understand English; and Thompkins was given time to read the warnings. Thompkins, furthermore, read aloud the fifth warning, which stated that "you have the right

to decide at any time before or during questioning to use your right to remain silent and your right to talk with a lawyer while you are being questioned." . . . He was thus aware that his right to remain silent would not dissipate after a certain amount of time and that police would have to honor his right to be silent and his right to counsel during the whole course of interrogation. Those rights, the warning made clear, could be asserted at any time. Helgert, moreover, read the warnings aloud.

Second, Thompkins's answer to Detective Helgert's question about whether Thompkins prayed to God for forgiveness for shooting the victim is a "course of conduct indicating waiver" of the right to remain silent. . . . If Thompkins wanted to remain silent, he could have said nothing in response to Helgert's questions, or he could have unambiguously invoked his Miranda rights and ended the interrogation. The fact that Thompkins made a statement about three hours after receiving a Miranda warning does not overcome the fact that he engaged in a course of conduct indicating waiver. Police are not required to rewarn suspects from time to time. Thompkins's answer to Helgert's question about praying to God for forgiveness for shooting the victim was sufficient to show a course of conduct indicating waiver. This is confirmed by the fact that before then Thompkins had given sporadic answers to questions throughout the interrogation.

Third, there is no evidence that Thompkins's statement was coerced. . . . Thompkins does not claim that police threatened or injured him during the interrogation or that he was in any way fearful. The interrogation was conducted in a standard-sized room in the middle of the afternoon. It is true that apparently he was in a straight-backed chair for three hours, but there is no authority for the proposition that an interrogation of this length is inherently coercive. Indeed, even where interrogations of greater duration were held to be improper, they were accompanied, as this one was not, by other facts indicating coercion, such as an incapacitated and sedated suspect, sleep and food deprivation, and threats. . . . The fact that Helgert's question referred to Thompkins's religious beliefs also did not render Thompkins's statement involuntary. . . . In these circumstances, Thompkins knowingly and voluntarily made a statement to police, so he waived his right to remain silent.

In sum, a suspect who has received and understood the Miranda warnings, and has not invoked his Miranda rights, waives the right to remain silent by making an uncoerced statement to the police. Thompkins did not invoke his right to remain silent and stop the questioning. Understanding his rights in full, he waived his right to remain silent by making a voluntary statement to the police. The police, moreover, were not required to obtain a waiver of Thompkins's right to remain silent before interrogating him

LIMITATIONS (EXCEPTIONS) TO MIRANDA

Many conservative justices were against the holding in *Miranda,* but did not have sufficient votes to overrule the ruling outright. But, starting with *Michigan v. Tucker*, 417 U.S. 433 (1974), the Court was able to weaken its requirements by identifying exceptions to the rule. *Michigan v. Tucker*, 417 U.S. 433 (1974), held that *Miranda* did not have constitutional dimensions and that it was merely a prophylactic rule (a rule intended to prevent harm). The effect of this holding was that a failure to adhere to *Miranda's* requirements may not necessarily be a violation of the Constitution. The following cases highlight the exceptions to the *Miranda* rule, and one can see the chipping away of *Miranda's* protections over the years. In *Dickerson v. U.S.*, 530 U.S. 428 (2000) the Court faced squarely the question of whether *Miranda* should be overturned. In *Dickerson*, the Court breathed new life into *Miranda* and disavowed Justice Rehnquist's interpretation of *Miranda* as merely a prophylactic rule. *Miranda*, the Court noted, had taken on constitutional dimensions.

Public Safety Exception

NEW YORK v. QUARLES
467 US 649 (1984)

JUSTICE REHNQUIST delivered the opinion of the Court.

On September 11, 1980, at approximately 12:30 a. m., Officer Frank Kraft and Officer Sal Scarring were on road patrol in Queens, N. Y., when a young woman approached their car. She told them that she had just been raped by a black male, approximately six feet tall, who was wearing a black jacket with the name "Big Ben" printed in yellow letters on the back. She told the officers that the man had just entered an A&P supermarket located nearby and that the man was carrying a gun.

The officers drove the woman to the supermarket, and Officer Kraft entered the store while Officer Scarring radioed for assistance. Officer Kraft quickly spotted respondent, who matched the description given by the woman, approaching a checkout counter. Apparently upon seeing the officer, respondent turned and ran toward the rear of the store, and Officer Kraft pursued him with a drawn gun. When respondent turned the corner at the end of an aisle, Officer Kraft lost sight of him for several seconds, and upon regaining sight of respondent, ordered him to stop and put his hands over his head.

Although more than three other officers had arrived on the scene by that time, Officer Kraft was the first to reach respondent. He frisked him and discovered that he was wearing a shoulder holster which was then empty. After handcuffing him, Officer Kraft asked him where the gun was. Respondent nodded in the direction of some empty cartons and responded, "the gun is over there." Officer Kraft thereafter retrieved a loaded .38-caliber revolver from one of the cartons, formally placed respondent under arrest, and read him his *Miranda* rights from a printed card. Respondent indicated that he would be willing to answer questions without an attorney present. Officer Kraft then asked respondent if he owned the gun and where he had purchased it. Respondent answered that he did own it and that he had purchased it in Miami, Fla.

In the subsequent prosecution of respondent for criminal possession of a weapon, the judge excluded the statement, "the gun is over there," and the gun because the officer had not given respondent the warnings required by our decision in *Miranda v. Arizona*, before asking him where the gun was located. The judge excluded the other statements about respondent's ownership of the gun and the place of purchase, as evidence tainted by the prior *Miranda* violation.

The Court of Appeals . . . concluded that respondent was in "custody" within the meaning of *Miranda* during all questioning and rejected the State's argument that the exigencies of the situation justified Officer Kraft's failure to read respondent his *Miranda* rights until after he had located the gun.

Thus the only issue before us is whether Officer Kraft was justified in failing to make available to respondent the procedural safeguards associated with the privilege against compulsory self-incrimination since *Miranda.*

[R]espondent was in police custody. . . . [W]e have noted that "the ultimate inquiry is simply whether there is a `formal arrest or restraint on freedom of movement' of the degree associated with a formal arrest." Here Quarles was surrounded by at least four police officers and was handcuffed when the questioning at issue took place.

We hold that on these facts there is a "public safety" exception to the requirement that *Miranda* warnings be given before a suspect's answers may be admitted into evidence, and that the availability of that exception does not depend upon the motivation of the individual officers involved. In a kaleidoscopic situation such as the one confronting these officers, where spontaneity rather than adherence to a police manual is necessarily the order of the day, the application of the exception which we recognize today should not be made to depend on post hoc findings at a suppression hearing concerning the subjective motivation of the arresting officer. Undoubtedly most police officers, if placed in Officer Kraft's position, would act out of a host of different, instinctive, and largely unverifiable motives - their own safety, the safety of others, and perhaps as well the desire to obtain incriminating evidence from the suspect.

Whatever the motivation of individual officers in such a situation, we do not believe that the doctrinal underpinnings of *Miranda* require that it be applied in all its rigor to a situation in which police officers ask questions reasonably prompted by a concern for the public safety. The *Miranda* decision was based in large part on this Court's view that the warnings which it required police to give to suspects in custody would reduce the likelihood that the suspects would fall victim to constitutionally impermissible practices of police interrogation in the presumptively coercive environment of the station house.

The police in this case, in the very act of apprehending a suspect, were confronted with the immediate necessity of ascertaining the whereabouts of a gun which they had every reason to believe the suspect had just removed from his empty holster and discarded in the supermarket. So long as the gun was concealed somewhere in the supermarket, with its actual whereabouts unknown, it obviously posed more than one danger to the public safety: an accomplice might make use of it, a customer or employee might later come upon it.

.

We conclude that the need for answers to questions in a situation posing a threat to the public safety outweighs the need for the prophylactic rule protecting the Fifth Amendment's privilege against self-incrimination. We decline to place officers such as Officer Kraft in the untenable position of having to consider, often in a matter of seconds, whether it best serves society for them to ask the necessary questions without the *Miranda* warnings and render whatever probative evidence they uncover inadmissible, or for them to give the warnings in order to preserve the admissibility of evidence they might uncover but possibly damage or destroy their ability to obtain that evidence and neutralize the volatile situation confronting them.

JUSTICE O'CONNOR, concurring in the judgment in part and dissenting in part.

I would require suppression of the initial statement taken from respondent in this case. On the other hand, nothing in *Miranda* or the privilege itself requires exclusion of nontestimonial evidence derived from informal custodial interrogation, and I therefore agree with the Court that admission of the gun in evidence is proper.

...

JUSTICE MARSHALL, with whom JUSTICE BRENNAN and JUSTICE STEVENS join, dissenting.

[Summarized: In this dissent, the justices point to the findings of the state court that there was overwhelming evidence to support the conclusion that Quarles' hidden weapon did not pose a risk either to the arresting officers or to the public, and questions the majority for ignoring those factual findings. Then it discusses why the majority wrongly decides the case.]

The Collateral Uses of Un-Mirandized Statements

HARRIS v. NEW YORK
401 U.S. 222 (1971)

CHIEF JUSTICE BURGER delivered the opinion of the Court.

The State of New York charged petitioner in a two-count indictment with twice selling heroin to an undercover police officer. At a subsequent jury trial the officer was the State's chief witness, and he testified as to details of the two sales. A second officer verified collateral details of the sales, and a third offered testimony about the chemical analysis of the heroin.

Petitioner took the stand in his own defense. He admitted knowing the undercover police officer but denied a sale on January 4, 1966. He admitted making a sale of contents of a glassine bag to the officer on January 6 but claimed it was baking powder and part of a scheme to defraud the purchaser.

On cross-examination petitioner was asked … whether he had made specified statements to the police immediately following his arrest on January 7 - statements that partially contradicted petitioner's direct testimony at trial. In response to the cross-examination, petitioner testified that he could not remember virtually any of the questions or answers recited by the prosecutor. At the request of petitioner's counsel the written statement from which the prosecutor had read questions and answers in his impeaching process was placed in the record for possible use on appeal; the statement was not shown to the jury.

The trial judge instructed the jury that the statements attributed to petitioner by the prosecution could be considered only in passing on petitioner's credibility and not as evidence of guilt. In closing summations both counsel argued the substance of the impeaching statements. The jury then found petitioner guilty on the second count of the indictment.

…

Every criminal defendant is privileged to testify in his own defense, or to refuse to do so. But that privilege cannot be construed to include the right to commit perjury. Having voluntarily taken the stand, petitioner was under an obligation to speak truthfully and accurately, and the prosecution here did no more than utilize the traditional truth-testing devices of the adversary process. Had inconsistent statements been made by the accused to some third person, it could hardly be contended that the conflict could not be laid before the jury by way of cross-examination and impeachment.

The shield provided by *Miranda* cannot be perverted into a license to use perjury by way of a defense, free from the risk of confrontation with prior inconsistent utterances. We hold, therefore, that petitioner's credibility was appropriately impeached by use of his earlier conflicting statements.

The Grand Jury Statements Exception

In *United States v. Dionisio*, 410 U.S. 1 (1973) the court held that a suspect has the right to be free from self-incrimination in a grand jury proceeding, but the grand jury witness does not have to be warned of his right to remain silent or to have an attorney present. Additionally, the unmirandized statements by a suspect are admissible during a grand jury hearing.

The Routine Booking Questions Exception

In *Pennsylvania v. Munoz*, 496 U.S. 582 (1990) the Court held that routine questions asked by jail staff during the booking of a suspect do not require *Miranda* warnings, and that questions regarding defendant's name, address, height, weight, etc. did not require *Miranda* even though a video tape of the questions and defendant's answers was introduced at trial to show that defendant was drunk.

The Cured Statements Exception

In *Oregon v. Elstad*, *Fellers v. United States*, 540 U.S. 519 (2004) (above) and *Missouri v. Siebert* (below), the court dealt with the scenario where the defendant initially voluntarily made un-*Mirandized* statements, was later properly Mirandized, and then subsequently repeated essentially the initial statements. The Court in each case found the initial statements to be inadmissible, but the real question was whether the proper reading of *Miranda* "cured" the problem and/or removed the taint from the subsequent statements. (As you read *Elstad*, consider whether the Court's opinion suggests that Miranda is really just about voluntariness (by which, they seem to mean, lack of coercion) and that the Court really need only confine their inquiry as to whether coercion existed not to the effectiveness of warnings.

OREGON v. ELSTAD
470 U.S. 298 (1985)

JUSTICE O'CONNOR delivered the opinion of the Court.

This case requires us to decide whether an initial failure of law enforcement officers to administer the warnings required by *Miranda v. Arizona*, without more, "taints" subsequent admissions made after a suspect has been fully advised of and has waived his *Miranda* rights. Respondent, Michael James Elstad, was convicted of burglary by an Oregon trial court. The Oregon Court of Appeals reversed, holding that respondent's signed confession, although voluntary, was rendered inadmissible by a prior remark made in response to questioning without benefit of *Miranda* warnings. We granted certiorari, and we now reverse.

In December 1981, the home of Mr. and Mrs. Gilbert Gross, in the town of Salem, Polk Country, Ore., was burglarized. Missing were art objects and furnishings valued at $150,000. A witness to the burglary contacted the Polk County Sheriff's Office, implicating respondent Michael Elstad, an 18-year-old neighbor and friend of the Grosses' teenage son. Thereupon, Officers Burke and

McAllister went to the home of respondent Elstad, with a warrant for his arrest. Elstad's mother answered the door. She led the officers to her son's room where he lay on his bed, clad in shorts and listening to his stereo. The officers asked him to get dressed and to accompany them into the living room. Officer McAllister asked respondent's mother to step into the kitchen, where he explained that they had a warrant for her son's arrest for the burglary of a neighbor's residence. Officer Burke remained with Elstad in the living room. He later testified:

> "I sat down with Mr. Elstad and I asked him if he was aware of why Detective McAllister and myself were there to talk with him. He stated no, he had no idea why we were there. I then asked him if he knew a person by the name of Gross, and he said yes, he did, and also added that he heard that there was a robbery at the Gross house. And at that point I told Mr. Elstad that I felt he was involved in that, and he looked at me and stated, `Yes, I was there.'"

. . .

Elstad was transported to the Sheriff's headquarters and approximately one hour later, Officers Burke and McAllister joined him in McAllister's office. McAllister then advised respondent for the first time of his *Miranda* rights, reading from a standard card. Respondent indicated he understood his rights, and, having these rights in mind, wished to speak with the officers. Elstad gave a full statement, explaining that he had known that the Gross family was out of town and had been paid to lead several acquaintances to the Gross residence and show them how to gain entry through a defective sliding glass door. The statement was typed, reviewed by respondent, read back to him for correction, initialed and signed by Elstad and both officers. As an afterthought, Elstad added and initialed the sentence, "After leaving the house Robby & I went back to [the] van & Robby handed me a small bag of grass." Respondent concedes that the officers made no threats or promises either at his residence or at the Sheriff's office.

Respondent moved at once to suppress his oral statement and signed confession. He contended that the statement he made in response to questioning at his house "let the cat out of the bag," and tainted the subsequent confession as "fruit of the poisonous tree." The judge ruled that the statement, "I was there," had to be excluded because the defendant had not been advised of his *Miranda* rights. The written confession taken after Elstad's arrival at the Sheriff's office, however, was admitted in evidence. waiver was evidenced by the card which the defendant had signed. [It] was not tainted in any way by the previous brief statement between the defendant and the Sheriff's Deputies that had arrested him." . . .

Following his conviction, respondent appealed to the Oregon Court of Appeals, relying on *Wong Sun* and *Bayer*. The State conceded that Elstad had been in custody when he made his statement, "I was there," and accordingly agreed that this statement was inadmissible as having been given without the prescribed *Miranda* warnings. But the State maintained

that any conceivable "taint" had been dissipated prior to the respondent's written confession by McAllister's careful administration of the requisite warnings. The Court of Appeals reversed respondent's conviction, identifying the crucial constitutional inquiry as "whether there was a sufficient break in the stream of events between [the] inadmissible statement and the written confession to insulate the latter statement from the effect of what went before." The Oregon court concluded:

> "Regardless of the absence of actual compulsion, the coercive impact of the unconstitutionally obtained statement remains, because in a defendant's mind it has sealed his fate. It is this impact that must be dissipated in order to make a subsequent confession admissible. In determining whether it has been dissipated, lapse of time, and change of place from the original surroundings are the most important considerations."

Because of the brief period separating the two incidents, the "cat was sufficiently out of the bag to exert a coercive impact on [respondent's] later admissions."

. . . .

Prior to *Miranda*, the admissibility of an accused's in custody statements was judged solely by whether they were "voluntary" within the meaning of the Due Process Clause. If a suspect's statements had been obtained by "techniques and methods offensive to due process," or under circumstances in which the suspect clearly had no opportunity to exercise "a free and unconstrained will," the statements would not be admitted. The Court in *Miranda* required suppression of many statements that would have been admissible under traditional due process analysis by presuming that statements made while in custody and without adequate warnings were protected by the Fifth Amendment. The Fifth Amendment, of course, is not concerned with nontestimonial evidence. Nor is it concerned with moral and psychological pressures to confess emanating from sources other than official coercion. Voluntary statements "remain a proper element in law enforcement." "Indeed, far from being prohibited by the Constitution, admissions of guilt by wrongdoers, if not coerced, are inherently desirable. . . . Absent some officially coerced self-accusation, the Fifth Amendment privilege is not violated by even the most damning admissions." . . .

Respondent's contention that his confession was tainted by the earlier failure of the police to provide *Miranda* warnings and must be excluded as "fruit of the poisonous tree" assumes the existence of a constitutional violation. . . .

But as we explained in *Quarles* and *Tucker*, a procedural *Miranda* violation differs in significant respects from violations of the Fourth Amendment, which have traditionally mandated a broad application of the "fruits" doctrine.

The *Miranda* exclusionary rule, however, serves the Fifth Amendment and sweeps more broadly than the Fifth Amendment itself. It may be triggered even in the absence of a Fifth Amendment violation. The Fifth Amendment prohibits use by the prosecution in its case in chief only of compelled testimony. Failure to administer *Miranda* warnings creates a presumption of compulsion. Consequently, unwarned statements that are otherwise voluntary within the meaning of the Fifth Amendment must nevertheless be excluded from evidence under *Miranda*. Thus, in the individual case, *Miranda's* preventive medicine provides a remedy even to the defendant who has suffered no identifiable constitutional harm.

. . . .

Because *Miranda* warnings may inhibit persons from giving information, this Court has determined that they need be administered only after the person is taken into "custody" or his freedom has otherwise been significantly restrained. Unfortunately, the task of defining "custody" is a slippery one, and "policemen investigating serious crimes [cannot

realistically be expected to] make no errors whatsoever." If errors are made by law enforcement officers in administering the prophylactic *Miranda* procedures, they should not breed the same irremediable consequences as police infringement of the Fifth Amendment itself. It is an unwarranted extension of *Miranda* to hold that a simple failure to administer the warnings, unaccompanied by any actual coercion or other circumstances calculated to undermine the suspect's ability to exercise his free will, so taints the investigatory process that a subsequent voluntary and informed waiver is ineffective for some indeterminate period. Though *Miranda* requires that the unwarned admission must be suppressed, the admissibility of any subsequent statement should turn in these circumstances solely on whether it is knowingly and voluntarily made.

When a prior statement is actually coerced, the time that passes between confessions, the change in place of interrogations, and the change in identity of the interrogators all bear on whether that coercion has carried over into the second confession. The failure of police to administer *Miranda* warnings does not mean that the statements received have actually been coerced, but only that courts will presume the privilege against compulsory self-incrimination has not been intelligently exercised. Of the courts that have considered whether a properly warned confession must be suppressed because it was preceded by an unwarned but clearly voluntary admission, the majority have explicitly or implicitly recognized that Westover's requirement of a break in the stream of events is inapposite. In these circumstances, a careful and thorough administration of *Miranda* warnings serves to cure the condition that rendered the unwarned statement inadmissible. The warning conveys the relevant information and thereafter the suspect's choice whether to exercise his privilege to remain silent should ordinarily be viewed as an "act of free will." *Wong Sun v. United States*.

The Oregon court nevertheless identified a subtle form of lingering compulsion, the psychological impact of the suspect's conviction that he has let the cat out of the bag and, in so doing, has sealed his own fate. But endowing the psychological effects of voluntary unwarned admissions with constitutional implications would, practically speaking, disable the police from obtaining the suspect's informed cooperation even when the official coercion proscribed by the Fifth Amendment played no part in either his warned or unwarned confessions.

. . . .

This Court has never held that the psychological impact of voluntary disclosure of a guilty secret qualifies as state compulsion or compromises the voluntariness of a subsequent informed waiver. . . . When neither the initial nor the subsequent admission is coerced, little justification exists for permitting the highly probative evidence of a voluntary confession to be irretrievably lost to the factfinder.

There is a vast difference between the direct consequences flowing from coercion of a confession by physical violence or other deliberate means calculated to break the suspect's will and the uncertain consequences of disclosure of a "guilty secret" freely given in response to an unwarned but noncoercive question, as in this case.

Though belated, the reading of respondent's rights was undeniably complete. McAllister testified that he read the *Miranda* warnings aloud from a printed card and recorded Elstad's responses. There is no question that respondent knowingly and voluntarily waived his right to remain silent before he described his participation in the burglary. It is also beyond dispute that respondent's earlier remark was voluntary, within the meaning of the Fifth Amendment. Neither the environment nor the manner of either "interrogation" was coercive. The initial conversation took place at midday, in the living room area of respondent's own home, with his mother in the kitchen area, a few steps away. Although in retrospect the officers testified that respondent was then in custody,

at the time he made his statement he had not been informed that he was under arrest. The arresting officers' testimony indicates that the brief stop in the living room before proceeding to the station house was not to interrogate the suspect but to notify his mother of the reason for his arrest.

The State has conceded the issue of custody and thus we must assume that Burke breached *Miranda* procedures in failing to administer *Miranda* warnings before initiating the discussion in the living room. This breach may have been the result of confusion as to whether the brief exchange qualified as "custodial interrogation" or it may simply have reflected Burke's reluctance to initiate an alarming police procedure before McAllister had spoken with respondent's mother. Whatever the reason for Burke's oversight, the incident had none of the earmarks of coercion. Nor did the officers exploit the unwarned admission to pressure respondent into waiving his right to remain silent.

. . . .

This Court has never embraced the theory that a defendant's ignorance of the full consequences of his decisions vitiates their voluntariness. If the prosecution has actually violated the defendant's Fifth Amendment rights by introducing an inadmissible confession at trial, compelling the defendant to testify in rebuttal, the rule announced in *Harrison v. United States*, precludes use of that testimony on retrial. "Having `released the spring' by using the petitioner's unlawfully obtained confessions against him, the Government must show that its illegal action did not induce his testimony." But the Court has refused to find that a defendant who confesses, after being falsely told that his codefendant has turned State's evidence, does so involuntarily. The Court has also rejected the argument that a defendant's ignorance that a prior coerced confession could not be admitted in evidence compromised the voluntariness of his guilty plea. Likewise, in *California v. Beheler*, supra, the Court declined to accept defendant's contention that, because he was unaware of the potential adverse consequences of statements he made to the police, his participation in the interview was involuntary. Thus we have not held that the sine qua non for a knowing and voluntary waiver of the right to remain silent is a full and complete appreciation of all of the consequences flowing from the nature and the quality of the evidence in the case.

When police ask questions of a suspect in custody without administering the required warnings, *Miranda* dictates that the answers received be presumed compelled and that they be excluded from evidence at trial in the State's case in chief. The Court has carefully adhered to this principle, permitting a narrow exception only where pressing public safety concerns demanded. The Court today in no way retreats from the bright-line rule of *Miranda*. We do not imply that good faith excuses a failure to administer *Miranda* warnings; nor do we condone inherently coercive police tactics or methods offensive to due process that render the initial admission involuntary and undermine the suspect's will to invoke his rights once they are read to him. A handful of courts have, however, applied our precedents relating to confessions obtained under coercive circumstances to situations involving wholly voluntary admissions, requiring a passage of time or break in events

before a second, fully warned statement can be deemed voluntary. Far from establishing a rigid rule, we direct courts to avoid one; there is no warrant for presuming coercive effect where the suspect's initial inculpatory statement, though technically in violation of *Miranda*, was voluntary. The relevant inquiry is whether, in fact, the second statement was also voluntarily made. As in any such inquiry, the finder of fact must examine the surrounding circumstances and the entire course of police conduct with respect to the suspect in evaluating the voluntariness of his statements. The fact that a suspect chooses to speak after being informed of his rights is, of course, highly probative. We find that the dictates of *Miranda* and the goals of the Fifth Amendment proscription against use of compelled testimony are fully satisfied in the circumstances of this case by barring use of the unwarned statement in the case in chief. No further purpose is served by imputing "taint" to subsequent statements obtained pursuant to a voluntary and knowing waiver. We hold today that a suspect who has once responded to unwarned yet uncoercive questioning is not thereby disabled from waiving his rights and confessing after he has been given the requisite *Miranda* warnings. . . .

DICKERSON: MIRANDA IS "CONSTITUTIONAL"

In response to the *Miranda* holding, Congress immediately enacted legislation intended to overrule the Court's holding. The Act, 18 U.S.C., §3501, in essence reverted back to the Due Process/voluntariness analysis in determining whether the defendant's confessions in federal cases were to be admitted — without regard to whether *Miranda* warnings were given. Although passed in 1968, criminal justice practitioners did not rely on 18 U.S.C. §3501, suspecting the Act would not pass Court scrutiny in light of *Miranda* and the provision could possibly be found to violate the constitutional. Indeed, neither side argued on behalf of the constitutionality of the Act when the *Dickerson* case reached the U.S. Supreme Court, and the Court had to assign an attorney to "brief that argument" (prepare statements as to why the Act was constitutional). After *Dickerson*, many of the Court's crafted exceptions/limitations to the *Miranda* could be suspect (i.e., in jeopardy of being declared unconstitutional). *Missouri v. Siebert* shows how the Court has dealt with the cured statements exception after Dickerson.

DICKERSON v. UNITED STATES
530 U.S. 428 (2000)

CHIEF JUSTICE REHNQUIST delivered the opinion of the Court.

Petitioner Dickerson was indicted for bank robbery, conspiracy to commit bank robbery, and using a firearm in the course of committing a crime of violence, all in violation of the applicable provisions of Title 18 of the United States Code. Before trial, Dickerson moved to suppress a statement he had made at a Federal Bureau of Investigation field office, on the grounds that he had not received "*Miranda* warnings" before being interrogated. The District Court granted his motion to suppress, and the Government took an interlocutory appeal to the United States Court of Appeals for the Fourth Circuit. That court, by a divided vote, reversed the District Court's suppression order. It agreed with the District Court's conclusion that petitioner had not received *Miranda* warnings before making his statement. But it went on to hold that §3501, which in effect makes the admissibility of statements such as Dickerson's turn solely on whether they were made voluntarily, was satisfied in this case. It then concluded that our decision in *Miranda* was not a constitutional holding, and that therefore Congress could by statute have the final say on the question of admissibility.

Because of the importance of the questions raised by the Court of Appeals' decision, we granted certiorari, and now reverse.

We begin with a brief historical account of the law governing the admission of confessions. Prior to *Miranda*, we evaluated the admissibility of a suspect's confession under a voluntariness test. Over time, our cases recognized two constitutional bases for the requirement that a confession be voluntary to be admitted into evidence: the Fifth Amendment right against self-incrimination and the Due Process Clause of the Fourteenth Amendment.

We have never abandoned this due process jurisprudence, and thus continue to exclude confessions that were obtained involuntarily. But our decisions in *Malloy v. Hogan*, and *Miranda* changed the focus of much of the inquiry in determining the admissibility of suspects' incriminating statements. In *Malloy*, we held that the Fifth Amendment's Self-Incrimination Clause is incorporated in the Due Process Clause of the Fourteenth Amendment and thus applies to the States. We decided *Miranda* on the heels of *Malloy*.

Two years after *Miranda* was decided, Congress enacted §3501. That section provides, in relevant part:

> "(a) In any criminal prosecution brought by the United States or by the District of Columbia, a confession . . .shall be admissible in evidence if it is voluntarily given. Before such confession is received in evidence, the trial judge shall, out of the presence of the jury, determine any issue as to voluntariness. If the trial judge determines that the confession was voluntarily made it shall be admitted in evidence and the trial judge shall permit the jury to hear relevant evidence on the issue of voluntariness and shall instruct the jury to give such weight to the confession as the jury feels it deserves under all the circumstances.

> "(b) The trial judge in determining the issue of voluntariness shall take into consideration all the circumstances surrounding the giving of the confession, including (1) the time elapsing between arrest and arraignment of the defendant making the confession, if it was made after arrest and before arraignment, (2) whether such defendant knew the nature of the offense with which he was charged or of which he was suspected at the time of making the confession, (3) whether or not such defendant was advised or knew that he was not required to make any statement and that any such statement could be used against him, (4) whether or not such defendant had been advised

prior to questioning of his right to the assistance of counsel; and (5) whether or not such defendant was without the assistance of counsel when questioned and when giving such confession.

"The presence or absence of any of the above-mentioned factors to be taken into consideration by the judge need not be conclusive on the issue of voluntariness of the confession."

Given §3501's express designation of voluntariness as the touchstone of admissibility, its omission of any warning requirement, and the instruction for trial courts to consider a nonexclusive list of factors relevant to the circumstances of a confession, we agree with the Court of Appeals that Congress intended by its enactment to overrule *Miranda*. Because of the obvious conflict between our decision in *Miranda* and §3501, we must address whether Congress has constitutional authority to thus supersede Miranda. If Congress has such authority, §3501's totality-of-the-circumstances approach must prevail over *Miranda's* requirement of warnings; if not, that section must yield to *Miranda's* more specific requirements.

The law in this area is clear. This Court has supervisory authority over the federal courts, and we may use that authority to prescribe rules of evidence and procedure that are binding in those tribunals. However, the power to judicially create and enforce nonconstitutional "rules of procedure and evidence for the federal courts exists only in the absence of a relevant Act of Congress." Congress retains the ultimate authority to modify or set aside any judicially created rules of evidence and procedure that are not required by the Constitution.

But Congress may not legislatively supersede our decisions interpreting and applying the Constitution. This case therefore turns on whether the Miranda Court announced a constitutional rule or merely exercised its supervisory authority to regulate evidence in the absence of congressional direction. Recognizing this point, the Court of Appeals

surveyed Miranda and its progeny to determine the constitutional status of the Miranda decision. Relying on the fact that we have created several exceptions to Miranda's warnings requirement and that we have repeatedly referred to the Miranda warnings as "prophylactic," and "not themselves rights protected by the Constitution," the Court of Appeals concluded that the protections announced in Miranda are not constitutionally required.

We disagree with the Court of Appeals' conclusion, although we concede that there is language in some of our opinions that supports the view taken by that court. But first and foremost of the factors on the other side — that Miranda is a constitutional decision — is that both Miranda and two of its companion cases applied the rule to proceedings in state courts — to wit, Arizona, California, and New York. Since that time, we have consistently applied Miranda's rule to prosecutions arising in state courts. It is beyond dispute that we do not hold a supervisory power over the courts of the several States. With respect to proceedings in state courts, our "authority is limited to enforcing the commands of the United States Constitution."

The *Miranda* opinion itself begins by stating that the Court granted certiorari "to explore some facets of the problems . . .of applying the privilege against self-incrimination to in-custody interrogation, and to give concrete constitutional guidelines for law enforcement agencies and courts to follow." In fact, the majority opinion is replete with statements indicating that the majority thought it was announcing a constitutional rule. Indeed, the Court's ultimate conclusion was that the unwarned confessions obtained in the four cases before the Court in *Miranda* "were obtained from the defendant under circumstances that did not meet constitutional standards for protection of the privilege."

Additional support for our conclusion that *Miranda* is constitutionally based is found in the *Miranda* Court's invitation for legislative action to protect the constitutional right against coerced self-incrimination. After discussing the "compelling pressures" inherent in custodial police interrogation, the *Miranda* Court concluded that, "[i]n order to combat these pressures and to permit a full opportunity to exercise the privilege against self-incrimination, the accused must be adequately and effectively appraised of his rights and the exercise of those rights must be fully honored." However, the Court emphasized that it could not foresee "the potential alternatives for protecting the privilege which might be devised by Congress or the States," and it accordingly opined that the Constitution would not preclude legislative solutions that differed from the prescribed *Miranda* warnings but which were "at least as effective in apprising accused persons of their right of silence and in assuring a continuous opportunity to exercise it."

The Court of Appeals also relied on the fact that we have, after our *Miranda* decision, made exceptions from its rule in cases such as *New York v. Quarles*, and *Harris v. New York*. But we have also broadened the application of the *Miranda* doctrine in cases such as *Doyle v. Ohio*, and *Arizona v. Roberson*. These decisions illustrate the principle — not that *Miranda* is not a constitutional rule — but that no constitutional rule is immutable. No court laying down a general rule can possibly foresee the various circumstances in which counsel will seek to apply it, and the sort of modifications represented by these cases are as much a normal part of constitutional law as the original decision.

The Court of Appeals also noted that in *Oregon v. Elstad*, we stated that "'[t]he *Miranda* exclusionary rule . . .serves the Fifth Amendment and sweeps more broadly than the Fifth Amendment itself.'" Our decision in that case — refusing to apply the traditional "fruits" doctrine developed in Fourth Amendment cases — does not prove that *Miranda* is a nonconstitutional decision, but simply recognizes the fact that unreasonable searches under the Fourth Amendment are different from unwarned interrogation under the Fifth Amendment.

The dissent argues that it is judicial overreaching for this Court to hold §3501 unconstitutional unless we hold that the *Miranda* warnings are required by the Constitution, in the sense that nothing else will suffice to satisfy constitutional requirements. But we need not go farther than *Miranda* to decide this case. In *Miranda,* the Court noted that reliance on the traditional totality-of-the-circumstances test raised a risk of overlooking an involuntary custodial confession, a risk that the Court found unacceptably great when the confession is offered in the case in chief to prove guilt. The Court therefore concluded that something more than the totality test was necessary. As discussed above, §3501 reinstates the totality test as sufficient. Section 3501 therefore cannot be sustained if *Miranda* is to remain the law.

Whether or not we would agree with *Miranda's* reasoning and its resulting rule, were we addressing the issue in the first instance, the principles of stare decisis weigh heavily against overruling it now. While " `stare decisis is not an inexorable command,' " particularly when we are interpreting the Constitution, "even in constitutional cases, the doctrine carries such persuasive force that we have always required a departure from precedent to be supported by some `special justification."

We do not think there is such justification for overruling *Miranda. Miranda* has become embedded in routine police practice to the point where the warnings have become part of our national culture. While we have overruled our precedents when subsequent cases have undermined their doctrinal underpinnings, we do not believe that this has happened to the *Miranda* decision. If anything, our subsequent cases have reduced the impact of the *Miranda* rule on legitimate law enforcement while reaffirming the decision's core ruling that unwarned statements may not be used as evidence in the prosecution's case in chief.

The disadvantage of the *Miranda* rule is that statements which may be by no means involuntary, made by a defendant who is aware of his "rights," may nonetheless be excluded and a guilty defendant go free as a result. But experience suggests that the totality-of-the-circumstances test which §3501 seeks to revive is more difficult than *Miranda* for law enforcement officers to conform to, and for courts to apply in a consistent manner. The requirement that *Miranda* warnings be given does not, of course, dispense with the voluntariness inquiry. But as we said in *Berkemer v. McCarty,* "[c]ases in which a defendant can make a colorable argument that a self-incriminating statement was `compelled' despite the fact that the law enforcement authorities adhered to the dictates of *Miranda* are rare.

In sum, we conclude that *Miranda* announced a constitutional rule that Congress may not supersede legislatively. Following the rule of stare decisis, we decline to overrule *Miranda* ourselves. The judgment of the Court of Appeals is therefore reversed.

JUSTICE SCALIA, with whom JUSTICE THOMAS joins, dissenting.

(The dissent starts with sentiment that the decision was judicial over-reach) . . . The Court need only go beyond its carefully couched iterations that "*Miranda* is a constitutional decision," that "*Miranda* is constitutionally based," that *Miranda* has "constitutional underpinnings," and come out and say quite clearly: "We reaffirm today that custodial interrogation that is not preceded by *Miranda* warnings or their equivalent violates the Constitution of the United States." It

cannot say that, because a majority of the Court does not believe it. The Court therefore acts in plain violation of the Constitution when it denies effect to this Act of Congress.

. . .

Any conclusion that a violation of the *Miranda* rules necessarily amounts to a violation of the privilege against compelled self-incrimination can claim no support in history, precedent, or common sense, and as a result would at least presumptively be worth reconsidering even at this late date. But that is unnecessary, since the Court has (thankfully) long since abandoned the notion that failure to comply with *Miranda's* rules is itself a violation of the Constitution.

The Court asserts that *Miranda* must be a "constitutional decision" announcing a "constitutional rule," and thus immune to congressional modification, because we have since its inception applied it to the States. If this argument is meant as an invocation of stare decisis, it fails because, though it is true that our cases applying *Miranda* against the States must be reconsidered if *Miranda* is not required by the Constitution, it is likewise true that our cases (discussed above) based on the principle that *Miranda* is not required by the Constitution will have to be reconsidered if it is.

...

MISSOURI v. SIEBERT
542 U.S. 600 (2004)

JUSTICE SOUTER announced the judgment of the Court and delivered an opinion, in which JUSTICE STEVENS, JUSTICE GINSBURG, and JUSTICE BREYER join.

This case tests a police protocol for custodial interrogation that calls for giving no warnings of the rights to silence and counsel until interrogation has produced a confession. Although such a statement is generally

inadmissible, since taken in violation of *Miranda v. Arizona* , the interrogating officer follows it with *Miranda* warnings and then leads the suspect to cover the same ground a second time. The question here is the admissibility of the repeated statement. Because this midstream recitation of warnings after interrogation and unwarned confession could not effectively comply with *Miranda* 's constitutional requirement, we hold that a statement repeated after a warning in such circumstances is inadmissible.

I

Respondent Patrice Seibert's 12-year-old son Jonathan had cerebral palsy, and when he died in his sleep she feared charges of neglect because of bedsores on his body. In her presence, two of her teenage sons and two of their friends devised a plan to conceal the facts surrounding Jonathan's death by incinerating his body in the course of burning the family's mobile home, in which they planned to leave Donald Rector, a mentally ill teenager living with the family, to avoid any appearance that Jonathan had been unattended. Seibert's son Darian and a friend set the fire, and Donald died.

Five days later, the police awakened Seibert at 3 a.m. at a hospital where Darian was being treated for burns. In arresting her, Officer Kevin Clinton followed instructions from Rolla, Missouri, officer Richard Hanrahan that he refrain from giving *Miranda* warnings. After Seibert had been taken to the police station and left alone in an interview room for 15 to 20 minutes, Hanrahan questioned her without *Miranda* warnings for 30 to 40 minutes, squeezing her arm and repeating "Donald was also to die in his sleep." After Seibert finally admitted she knew Donald was meant to die in the fire, she was given a 20-minute coffee and cigarette break. Officer Hanrahan then turned on a tape recorder, gave Seibert the *Miranda* warnings, and obtained a signed waiver of rights from her. He resumed the questioning with "Ok, 'trice, we've been talking for a little while about what happened on Wednesday the twelfth, haven't we?," and confronted her with her prewarning statements:

. . . .

After being charged with first-degree murder for her role in Donald's death, Seibert sought to exclude both her prewarning and postwarning statements. At the suppression hearing, Officer Hanrahan testified that he made a "conscious decision" to withhold *Miranda* warnings, thus resorting to an interrogation technique he had been taught: question first, then give the warnings, and then repeat the question "until I get the answer that she's already provided once." He acknowledged that Seibert's ultimate statement was "largely a repeat of information . . . obtained" prior to the warning.

. . . .

We granted certiorari, 538 U. S. 1031 (2003), to resolve a split in the Courts of Appeals.

. . . .

II

In unifying the Fifth and Fourteenth Amendment voluntariness tests, *Malloy* "made clear what had already become apparent — that the substantive and procedural safeguards surrounding admissibility of confessions in state cases had become exceedingly exacting, reflecting all the policies embedded in the privilege" against self-incrimination.

In *Miranda* , we explained that the "voluntariness doctrine in the state cases . . . encompasses all interrogation practices which are likely to exert such pressure upon an individual as to disable him from making a free and rational choice," . . . We appreciated the difficulty of judicial enquiry post hoc into the circumstances of a police interrogation, *Dickerson v. United States* , 530 U. S. 428, 444 (2000), and recognized that "the coercion inherent in custodial interrogation blurs the line between voluntary and involuntary statements, and thus heightens the risk" that the privilege against self-incrimination will not be observed. Hence our concern that the "traditional totality-of-the-circumstances" test posed an "unacceptably great" risk that involuntary custodial confessions would escape detection.

Accordingly, "to reduce the risk of a coerced confession and to implement the Self-Incrimination Clause," this Court in *Miranda* concluded that "the accused must be adequately and effectively apprised of his rights and the exercise of those rights must be fully honored," 384 U. S., at 467. *Miranda* conditioned the admissibility at trial of any custodial confession on warning a suspect of his rights: failure to give the prescribed warnings and obtain a waiver of rights before custodial questioning generally requires exclusion of any statements obtained. Conversely, giving the warnings and getting a waiver has generally produced a virtual ticket of admissibility; maintaining that a statement is involuntary even though given after warnings and voluntary waiver of rights requires unusual stamina, and litigation over voluntariness tends to end with the finding of a valid waiver. …To point out the obvious, this common consequence would not be common at all were it not that *Miranda* warnings are customarily given under circumstances allowing for a real choice between talking and remaining silent.

III

There are those, of course, who preferred the old way of doing things, giving no warnings and litigating the voluntariness of any statement in nearly every instance. In the aftermath of *Miranda*, Congress even passed a statute seeking to restore that old regime, 18 U. S. C. §3501, although the Act lay dormant for years until finally invoked and challenged in *Dickerson v. United States. Dickerson* reaffirmed *Miranda* and held that its constitutional character prevailed against the statute.

The technique of interrogating in successive, unwarned and warned phases raises a new challenge to *Miranda*. Although we have no statistics on the frequency of this practice, it is not confined to Rolla, Missouri. …The upshot of all this advice is a question-first practice of some popularity, as one can see from the reported cases describing its use, sometimes in obedience to departmental policy.

IV

The object of question-first is to render *Miranda* warnings ineffective by waiting for a particularly opportune time to give them, after the suspect has already confessed.

Just as "no talismanic incantation [is] required to satisfy [*Miranda* 's] strictures," … it would be absurd to think that mere recitation of the litany suffices to satisfy *Miranda* in every conceivable circumstance. "The inquiry is simply whether the warnings reasonably 'conve[y] to [a suspect] his rights as required by *Miranda* .' " The threshold issue when interrogators question first and warn later is thus whether it would be reasonable to find that in these circumstances the warnings could function "effectively" as *Miranda* requires. Could the warnings effectively advise the suspect that he had a real choice about giving an admissible statement at that juncture? Could they reasonably convey that he could choose to stop talking even if he had talked earlier? For unless the warnings could place a suspect who has just been interrogated in a position to make such an informed choice, there is no practical justification for accepting the formal warnings as compliance with *Miranda*, or for treating the second stage of interrogation as distinct from the first, unwarned and inadmissible segment.

There is no doubt about the answer that proponents of question-first give to this question about the effectiveness of warnings given only after successful interrogation, and we think their answer is correct. By any objective measure, applied to circumstances exemplified here, it is likely that if the interrogators employ the technique of withholding warnings until after interrogation succeeds in eliciting a confession, the warnings will be ineffective in preparing the suspect for successive interrogation, close in time and similar in content. After all, the reason that question-first is catching on is as obvious as its manifest purpose, which is to get a confession the suspect would not make if he understood his rights at the outset; the sensible underlying assumption is that with one confession in hand before the warnings, the interrogator can count on getting its duplicate, with trifling additional trouble. Upon hearing warnings only in the aftermath of interrogation and just after making a confession, a suspect would hardly think he had a genuine right to remain silent, let alone persist in so believing once the police began to lead him over the same ground again. . . .

V

Missouri argues that a confession repeated at the end of an interrogation sequence envisioned in a question-first strategy is admissible on the authority of *Oregon v. Elstad* , 470 U. S. 298 (1985), but the argument disfigures that case. ...

The contrast between *Elstad* and this case reveals a series of relevant facts that bear on whether *Miranda* warnings delivered midstream could be effective enough to accomplish their object: the completeness and detail of the questions and answers in the first round of interrogation, the overlapping content of the two statements, the timing and setting of the first and the second, the continuity of police personnel, and the degree to which the interrogator's questions treated the second round as continuous with the first. In *Elstad*, it was not unreasonable to see the occasion for questioning at the station house as presenting a markedly different experience from the short conversation at home; since a reasonable person in the suspect's shoes could have seen the station house questioning as a new and distinct experience, the *Miranda* warnings could have made sense as presenting a genuine choice whether to follow up on the earlier admission.

At the opposite extreme are the facts here, which by any objective measure reveal a police strategy adapted to undermine the *Miranda* warnings. The unwarned interrogation was conducted in the station house, and the questioning was systematic, exhaustive, and managed with psychological skill. When the police were finished there was little, if anything, of incriminating potential left unsaid. The warned phase of questioning proceeded after a pause of only 15 to 20 minutes, in the same place as the unwarned

segment. When the same officer who had conducted the first phase recited the *Miranda* warnings, he said nothing to counter the probable misimpression that the advice that anything Seibert said could be used against her also applied to the details of the inculpatory statement previously elicited. In particular, the police did not advise that her prior statement could not be used. Nothing was said or done to dispel the oddity of warning about legal rights to silence and counsel right after the police had led her through a systematic interrogation, and any uncertainty on her part about a right to stop talking about matters previously discussed would only have been aggravated by the way Officer Hanrahan set the scene by saying "we've been talking for a little while about what happened on Wednesday the twelfth, haven't we?" The impression that the further questioning was a mere continuation of the earlier questions and responses was fostered by references back to the confession already given. It would have been reasonable to regard the two sessions as parts of a continuum, in which it would have been unnatural to refuse to repeat at the second stage what had been said before. These circumstances must be seen as challenging the comprehensibility and efficacy of the *Miranda* warnings to the point that a reasonable person in the suspect's shoes would not have understood them to convey a message that she retained a choice about continuing to talk.

Strategists dedicated to draining the substance out of *Miranda* cannot accomplish by training instructions what *Dickerson* held Congress could not do by statute. Because the question-first tactic effectively threatens to thwart *Miranda*'s purpose of reducing the risk that a coerced confession would be admitted, and because the facts here do not reasonably support a conclusion that the warnings given could have served their purpose, Seibert's postwarning statements are inadmissible.

Chapter Seven: Identification Procedures

Significant research from respected researchers over several years unequivocally demonstrate that many wrongful convictions in the United States are connected to faulty eyewitness identifications. Eyewitness identification is a powerful tool that police use in investigating crimes committed by strangers. Unfortunately, eyewitness identifications are plagued with one underlying problem. Eyewitnesses are humans. Eyewitness identification relies on human memory, which researchers have shown is less than reliable.[72]

LEGAL CHALLENGES TO IDENTIFICATION PROCEDURES

Police obtain physical identifications of suspects through a variety of methods: lineups, fingerprints, blood samples, voiceprints, the use of photographs, etc. Defendants identified through these methods have frequently raised constitutional objections to them stating 1) the identification procedure violates their privilege against self-incrimination (Fifth Amendment); 2) the identification procedure constitutes an unreasonable search and seizure (Fourth Amendment; 3) the identification procedure without the presence of their lawyer violates their right to counsel (Sixth Amendment); and 4) that these procedures violate the general due process protections found in the Fifth and Fourteenth Amendments.

Fifth Amendment Self-Incrimination Argument

The Court has held that physical identification procedures (for example, giving a voice sample or fingerprints) do not trigger the Fifth Amendment's privilege against self-incrimination. *Schmerber v. California,* 384 U.S. 757 (1966). The Court has extended *Schmerber* to include fingerprints, photography, measurements, physical movements, handwriting analysis, and examination by ultraviolet light. Suspect do not have a right to refuse to participate in an identification procedure since they are not within the privilege of self-incrimination, and if they do refuse, the court may hold them in contempt of court and jail them indefinitely. Moreover, prosecutors are not prohibited from commenting on this refusal during defendant's trial.

Fourth Amendment Unlawful Search And Seizure Argument

Defendants have been largely unsuccessful in asserting that identification procedures violate their Fourth Amendment right to be free from unreasonable searches and seizure (see, earlier chapters on search and seizure). Although decisions like *Rochin* (see above) have held that government goes too far when it seizes physical evidence from the body of a suspect, the Court has routinely approved the use of fingerprints, voice samples, and pictures evidence, without any concern that this evidence was the product of an unreasonable search or seizure. In *Maryland v. King*, 569 U.S.435 (2013) the Court reviewed the legality of the Maryland DNA Collection Act. The Act allowed for state and local law enforcement to collect DNA samples for individuals arrested for crimes of violence, attempted crimes of violence, burglary, or attempted burglary. The defendant had been arrested for first- and second-degree assault, and after his arrest (prior to trial/conviction) his DNA was collected through a cheek swab. It was logged into a database which matched his DNA to a DNA sample from an unsolved rape case. When prosecuted for the first-degree rape, King moved to suppress the DNA evidence -- the only evidence connecting him to the rape. His motion was denied, he was convicted and sentenced to life imprisonment. He claimed the test violated his rights under the Fourth Amendment. The Maryland Court of Appeals agreed and reversed his conviction stating that his

---

[72] Gary Wells, Elizabeth Loftus, and Steven Penrod, are cognative psychologists who have. with colleagues, conducted significant research in the field of mistaken eyewitness identification and have contributed numerous articles and books concerning faulty memory and identification.

expectation of privacy was greater than the State's interest in using his DNA for identification purposes. Justice Kennedy's 5-4 majority opinion from the U.S. Supreme Court held that, although Maryland's program of taking cheek swabs and testing DNA for individuals arrested for serious crimes (but not yet convicted) was a search, but it was permissible under the Fourth Amendment. The Court likened the taking and testing of DNA to other identification techniques such as fingerprinting and photographing the suspect. The majority justified the warrantless search and seizure using rationale supporting searches incident to lawful arrest and routine booking procedures already used by law enforcement.[73]

Sixth Amendment Right To Counsel Argument

The defendant may successfully argue that the identification procedure violates his Sixth Amendment right to counsel depending on at what stage of the process the identification procedure occurs. In two co-cases of *United States v. Wade*, 388 U.S. 218 (1967) and *Gilbert v. California*, 388 U.S. 263 (1967), the Court announced a rule that suspect who has already been indicted has the absolute right to have counsel present at any pretrial confrontation procedure (including lineups, one-person show ups). The *Wade-Gilbert* rule is a *per se* rule that any identification that occurs after the defendant has been indicted and without the presence of counsel must be excluded as evidence at trial. If the lineup is improper, not only may the prosecution not introduce into trial the fact that the defendant was picked out of a lineup, but the prosecution will even have to make a special showing before the witness who made the lineup identification will be allowed to testify in court that the person sitting in the desk is the person observed by the witness at the scene of the crime (make an in-court identification). In order to make this independent, in-court identification, the states will have to show by clear and convincing evidence that the in-court identification is not the fruit of the poisonous tree.

---

[73] Justice Scalia wrote a scathing dissent. He likened the DNA search as a general warrant proscribed by the Fourth Amendment. He noted that the procedures used under the Act, when followed, make it a particularly ineffective identification tool.

…

> The issue before us is not whether DNA can some day be used for identification; nor even whether it can today be used for identification; but whether it was used for identification here. Today, it can fairly be said that fingerprints really are used to identify people — so well, in fact, that there would be no need for the expense of a separate, wholly redundant DNA confirmation of the same information. What DNA adds — what makes it a valuable weapon in the law-enforcement arsenal — is the ability to solve unsolved crimes, by matching old crime-scene evidence against the profiles of people whose identities are already known. That is what was going on when King's DNA was taken, and we should not disguise the fact. Solving unsolved crimes is a noble objective, but it occupies a lower place in the American pantheon of noble objectives than the protection of our people from suspicionless law-enforcement searches. The Fourth Amendment must prevail.

> … Make no mistake about it: As an entirely predictable consequence of today's decision, your DNA can be taken and entered into a national DNA database if you are ever arrested, rightly or wrongly, and for whatever reason.

> Today's judgment will, to be sure, have the beneficial effect of solving more crimes; then again, so would the taking of DNA samples from anyone who flies on an airplane (surely the Transportation Security Administration needs to know the "identity" of the flying public), applies for a driver's license, or attends a public school. Perhaps the construction of such a genetic panopticon is wise. But I doubt that the proud men who wrote the charter of our liberties would have been so eager to open their mouths for royal inspection.

> I therefore dissent, and hope that today's incursion upon the Fourth Amendment, like an earlier one will some day be repudiated."

GILBERT v. CALIFORNIA
388 U.S. 263 (1967)

MR. JUSTICE BRENNAN delivered the opinion of the Court.

This case was argued with *United States v. Wade* and presents the same alleged constitutional error in the admission in evidence of in-court identifications there considered. In addition, petitioner alleges constitutional errors in the admission in evidence of testimony of some of the witnesses that they also identified him at the lineup, in the admission of handwriting exemplars taken from him after his arrest.... .

Petitioner was convicted in the Superior Court of California of the armed robbery of the Mutual Savings and Loan Association of Alhambra and the murder of a police officer who entered during the course of the robbery. There were separate guilt and penalty stages of the trial before the same jury, which rendered a guilty verdict and imposed the death penalty. The California Supreme Court affirmed. We granted certiorari, and set the case for argument with *Wade* and with *Stovall v. Denno*. If our holding today in *Wade* is applied to this case, the issue whether admission of the in-court and lineup identifications is constitutional error which requires a new trial could be resolved on this record only after further proceedings in the California courts. We must therefore first determine whether petitioner's other contentions warrant any greater relief.

I

THE HANDWRITING EXEMPLARS

Petitioner was arrested in Philadelphia by an FBI agent, and refused to answer questions about the Alhambra robbery without the advice of counsel. He later did answer questions of another agent about some Philadelphia robberies in which the robber used a handwritten note demanding that money be handed over to him, and, during that interrogation, gave the agent the handwriting

exemplars. They were admitted in evidence at trial over objection that they were obtained in violation of petitioner's Fifth and Sixth Amendment rights. ...

... [W]e conclude that the taking of the exemplars violated none of petitioner's constitutional rights.

First. The taking of the exemplars did not violate petitioner's Fifth Amendment privilege against self-incrimination. The privilege reaches only compulsion of "an accused's communications, whatever form they might take, and the compulsion of responses which are also communications, for example, compliance with a subpoena to produce one's papers," and not "compulsion which makes a suspect or accused the source of real or physical evidence'. ... *Schmerber v. California.* One's voice and handwriting are, of course, means of communication. It by no means follows, however, that every compulsion of an accused to use his voice or write compels a communication within the cover of the privilege. A mere handwriting exemplar, in contrast to the content of what is written, like the voice or body itself, is an identifying physical characteristic outside its protection. United States v. Wade. No claim is made that the content of the exemplars was testimonial or communicative matter.

Second. The taking of the exemplars was not a "critical" stage of the criminal proceedings entitling petitioner to the assistance of counsel. Putting aside the fact that the exemplars were taken before the indictment and appointment of counsel, there is minimal risk that the absence of counsel might derogate from his right to a fair trial. If, for some reason, an unrepresentative exemplar is taken, this can be brought out and corrected through the adversary process at trial, since the accused can make an unlimited number of additional exemplars for analysis and comparison by government and defense handwriting experts. Thus, "the accused has the opportunity for a meaningful confrontation of the [State's] case at trial through the ordinary processes of cross-examination of the [State's] expert [handwriting] witnesses and the presentation of the evidence of his own [handwriting] experts."

United States v. Wade, at 388 U. S. 227-228.

...

IV

THE IN-COURT AND LINEUP IDENTIFICATIONS

Since none of the petitioner's other contentions warrants relief, the issue becomes what relief is required by application to this case of the principles today announced in *United States v. Wade.*

Three eyewitnesses to the Alhambra crimes who identified Gilbert at the guilt stage of the trial had observed him at a lineup conducted without notice to his counsel in a Los Angeles auditorium 16 days after his indictment and after appointment of counsel. The manager of the apartment house in which incriminating evidence was found, and in which Gilbert allegedly resided, identified Gilbert in the courtroom and also testified, in substance, to her prior lineup identification on examination by the State. Eight witnesses who identified him in the courtroom at the penalty stage were not eyewitnesses to the Alhambra crimes, but to other robberies allegedly committed by him. In addition to their in-court identifications, these witnesses also testified that they identified Gilbert at the same lineup.

The lineup was on a stage behind bright lights which prevented those in the line from seeing the audience. Upwards of 100 persons were in the audience, each an eyewitness to one of the several robberies charged to Gilbert. The record is otherwise virtually silent as to what occurred at the lineup.

At the guilt stage, after the first witness, a cashier of the savings and loan association,

identified Gilbert in the courtroom, defense counsel moved, out of the presence of the jury, to strike her testimony on the ground that she identified Gilbert at the pretrial lineup conducted in the absence of counsel in violation of the Sixth Amendment made applicable to the States by the Fourteenth Amendment. He requested a hearing outside the presence of the jury to present evidence supporting his claim that her in-court identification was, and others to be elicited by the State from other eyewitnesses would be, "predicated at least in large part upon their identification or purported identification of Mr. Gilbert at the showup. . . ." The trial judge denied the motion as premature. Defense counsel then elicited the fact of the cashier's lineup identification on cross-examination and again moved to strike her identification testimony. Without passing on the merits of the Sixth Amendment claim, the trial judge denied the motion on the ground that, assuming a violation, it would not, in any event, entitle Gilbert to suppression of the in-court identification. Defense counsel thereafter elicited the fact of lineup identifications from two other eyewitnesses who on direct examination identified Gilbert in the courtroom. Defense counsel unsuccessfully objected at the penalty stage, to the testimony of the eight witnesses to the other robberies that they identified Gilbert at the lineup.

The admission of the in-court identifications without first determining that they were not tainted by the illegal lineup but were of independent origin was constitutional error. *United States v. Wade, supra.* We there held that a post-indictment pretrial lineup at which the accused is exhibited to identifying witnesses is a critical stage of the criminal prosecution; that police conduct of such a lineup without notice to, and in the absence of his counsel, denies the accused his Sixth Amendment right to counsel and calls in question the admissibility at trial of the in-court identifications of the accused by witnesses who attended the lineup. However, as in *Wade,* the record does not permit an informed judgment whether the in-court identifications at the two stages of the trial had an independent source. Gilbert is therefore entitled only to a vacation of his conviction pending the holding of such proceedings as the California Supreme Court may deem appropriate to afford the State the opportunity to establish that the in-court identifications had an independent source, or that their introduction in evidence was, in any event, harmless error.

Quite different considerations are involved as to the admission of the testimony of the manager of the apartment house at the guilt phase and of the eight witnesses at the penalty stage that they identified Gilbert at the lineup. That testimony is the direct result of the illegal lineup "come at by exploitation of [the primary] illegality." *Wong Sun v. United States*. The State is therefore not entitled to an opportunity to show that that testimony had an independent source. Only a *per se* exclusionary rule as to such testimony can be an effective sanction to assure that law enforcement authorities will respect the accused's constitutional right to the presence of his counsel at the critical lineup. In the absence of legislative regulations adequate to avoid the hazards to a fair trial which inhere in lineups as presently conducted, the desirability of deterring the constitutionally objectionable practice must prevail over the undesirability of excluding relevant evidence. That conclusion is buttressed by the consideration that the witness' testimony of his lineup identification will enhance the impact of his in-court identification on the jury and seriously aggravate whatever derogation exists of the accused's right to a fair trial. Therefore, unless the California Supreme Court is "able to declare a belief that it was harmless beyond a reasonable doubt," *Chapman v. California* Gilbert will be entitled on remand to a new trial or, if no prejudicial error is found on the guilt stage but only in the penalty stage, to whatever relief California law affords where the penalty stage must be set aside.

Limitations Of Wade-Gilbert

In *Kirby v. Illinois*, 406 U.S. 682 (1972) the Court declined to extend (did not extend) the *Wade-Gilbert* to pre-indictment lineup situations and noted that the right to counsel in lineups and showings only occurs "a time at or after the initiation of adversary judicial criminal proceedings — whether by way of a formal charge, preliminary hearing, indictment, information or arraignment." Although they are not exactly certain when "initiation of a judicial criminal proceeding" begins, most lower courts have held that the issuance of an arrest warrant triggers *Wade-Gilbert*. Where the only police action against the subject has been a warrantless arrest, however, most courts have held the *Wade-Gilbert* right to counsel at lineup rule was not triggered.

In *U.S. v. Ash*, 413 U.S. 300 (1973) the Supreme Court ruled that the right to counsel does not apply where witnesses view still or moving pictures of the suspect for identification purposes. The Court reasoned that, unlike a line-up or show-up situation, the suspect is not present when the witness views the photographs. The major purpose of the right-to-counsel in the Wade lineup situation is to prevent the suspect from being penalized for his ignorance and inability to ascertain and object to prejudicial conditions.

Due Process Argument

In *Stovall v. Denno*, 388 U.S. 293 (1967) the Court recognized a constitutional due process protection as a means to challenge an identification procedure --independent of any right to counsel claim. The question is "whether the confrontation was so unnecessarily suggestive and conducive to irreparable mistaken identification" as to deny a suspect due process of law. The Court found that unnecessarily suggestive lineups were fundamentally unfair. Because due process is a general standard rather than a clear-cut rule, determining due process violations, the Court looks at the totality of the circumstances presented in each case. *Perry v. New Hampshire*, examined whether due process concerns limit the admissibility of suggestive eyewitness identifications which were not staged nor set up by the police. This case provides a nice summary of all the identification procedures cases.

PERRY v. NEW HAMPSHIRE
565 U.S. 228 (2012)

JUSTICE GINSBURG delivered the opinion of the Court.

In our system of justice, fair trial for persons charged with criminal offenses is secured by the Sixth Amendment, which guarantees to defendants the right to counsel, compulsory process to obtain defense witnesses, and the opportunity to cross-examine witnesses for the prosecution. Those safeguards apart, admission of evidence in state trials is ordinarily governed by state law, and the reliability of relevant testimony typically falls within the province of the jury to determine. This Court has recognized, in addition, a due process check on the admission of eyewitness identification, applicable when the police have arranged suggestive circumstances leading the witness to identify a particular person as the perpetrator of a crime.

An identification infected by improper police influence, our case law holds, is not automatically excluded. Instead, the trial judge must screen the evidence for reliability pretrial. If there is "a very substantial likelihood of irreparable misidentification. . . " the judge must disallow presentation of the evidence at trial. But if the indicia of reliability are strong enough to outweigh the corrupting effect of the police-arranged suggestive circumstances, the identification evidence ordinarily will be admitted, and the jury will ultimately determine its worth.

We have not extended pretrial screening for reliability to cases in which the suggestive circumstances were not arranged by law enforcement officers. Petitioner requests that we do so because of the grave risk that mistaken identification will yield a miscarriage of justice. Our decisions, however, turn on the presence of state action and aim to deter police from rigging identification procedures, for example, at a lineup, showup, or photograph array. When no improper law enforcement activity is involved, we hold, it suffices to test reliability through the rights and opportunities generally designed for that purpose, notably, the presence of counsel at postindictment lineups, vigorous cross-examination, protective rules of evidence, and jury instructions on both the fallibility of eyewitness identification and the requirement that guilt be proved beyond a reasonable doubt. . . .

Around 3 a.m. on August 15, 2008, Joffre Ullon called the Nashua, New Hampshire, Police Department and reported that an African-American male was trying to break into cars parked in the lot of Ullon's apartment building. Officer Nicole Clay responded to the call. Upon arriving at the parking lot, Clay heard what "sounded like a metal bat hitting the ground." She then saw petitioner Barion Perry standing between two cars. Perry walked toward Clay, holding two car-stereo amplifiers in his hands. A metal bat lay on the ground behind him. Clay asked Perry where the amplifiers came from. "[I] found them on the ground," Perry responded.

Meanwhile, Ullon's wife, Nubia Blandon, woke her neighbor, Alex Clavijo, and told him she had just seen someone break into his car. Clavijo immediately went downstairs to the parking lot to inspect the car. He first observed that one of the rear windows had been shattered. On further inspection, he discovered that the speakers and amplifiers from his car stereo were missing, as were his bat and wrench. Clavijo then approached Clay and told her about Blandon's alert and his own subsequent observations.

By this time, another officer had arrived at the scene. Clay asked Perry to stay in the parking lot with that officer, while she and Clavijo went to talk to Blandon. Clay and Clavijo then entered the apartment building[SEP] and took the stairs to the fourth floor, where Blandon's and Clavijo's apartments were located. They met Blandon in the hallway just outside the open door to her apartment.

Asked to describe what she had seen, Blandon stated that, around 2:30 a.m., she saw from her kitchen window a tall, African-American man roaming the parking lot and looking into cars. Eventually, the man circled Clavijo's car, opened the trunk, and removed a large box.

Clay asked Blandon for a more specific description of the man. Blandon pointed to her kitchen window and said the person she saw breaking into Clavijo's car was standing in the parking lot, next to the police officer. Perry's arrest followed this identification.

About a month later, the police showed Blandon a photographic array that included a picture of Perry and asked her to point out the man who had broken into Clavijo's car. Blandon was unable to identify Perry.

B

Perry . . . moved to suppress Blandon's identification on the ground that admitting it at trial would violate due process. Blandon witnessed what amounted to a one-person showup in the parking lot, Perry asserted, which all but guaranteed that she would identify him as the culprit.

. . . .

We granted certiorari to resolve a division of opinion on[SEP] the question whether the Due Process Clause requires a trial judge to conduct a preliminary assessment of the reliability of an eyewitness identification made under suggestive circumstances not arranged by the police.

…

The Constitution … protects a defendant against a conviction based on evidence of questionable reliability, not by prohibiting introduction of the evidence, but by affording the defendant means to persuade the jury that the evidence should be discounted[SEP] as unworthy of credit. Constitutional safeguards available to defendants to counter the State's evidence include[SEP] the Sixth Amendment rights to counsel, compulsory process, and confrontation plus cross-examination of witnesses. … Only when evidence "is so extremely unfair that its admission violates fundamental conceptions of justice …" have we imposed a constraint tied to the Due Process Clause. …

Contending that the Due Process Clause is implicated here, Perry relies on a series of decisions involving police-arranged identification procedures. In *Stovall v. Denno* …a witness identified the defendant as her assailant after police officers brought the defendant to the witness' hospital room. At the time the witness made the identification, the defendant — the only African-American in the room — was handcuffed and surrounded by police officers. Although the police-arranged showup was undeniably suggestive, the Court held that no due process violation occurred. Crucial to the Court's decision was the procedure's necessity: The witness was the only person who could identify or exonerate the defendant; the witness could not leave her hospital room; and it was uncertain whether she would live to identify the defendant in more neutral circumstances.

A year later, in *Simmons v. United States*, the Court addressed a due process challenge to police use of a photographic array. When a witness identifies the defendant in a police-organized photo lineup, the Court ruled, the identification should be suppressed only where "the photographic identification procedure was so [unnecessarily] suggestive as to give rise to a very substantial likelihood of irreparable misidentification." Satisfied that the photo array used by Federal Bureau of Investigation agents in Simmons was both necessary and unlikely to have led to a mistaken identification, the Court rejected the defendant's due process challenge to admission of the identification. In contrast, the Court held in *Foster v. California*, that due process required the exclusion of an eyewitness identification obtained through police-arranged procedures that "made it all but inevitable that [the witness] would identify [the defendant]."

Synthesizing previous decisions, we set forth in *Neil v. Biggers*, and reiterated in *Manson v. Brathwaite*, the approach appropriately used to determine whether the Due Process Clause requires suppression of an eyewitness identification tainted by police arrangement. …[D]ue process concerns arise only when law enforcement officers use an identification procedure that is both suggestive and unnecessary. Even when the police use such a procedure, …suppression of the resulting identification is not the inevitable consequence.

A rule requiring automatic exclusion …would "g[o] too far," for it would "kee[p] evidence from the jury that is reliable and relevant," and "may result, on occasion, in the guilty going free." …

Instead of mandating a per se exclusionary rule, the Court held that the Due Process Clause requires courts to assess, on a case-by-case basis, whether improper police conduct created a "substantial likelihood of misidentification." "[R]eliability [of the eyewitness identification] is the linchpin" of that evaluation, the Court stated in Brathwaite. Where the "indicators of [a witness'] ability to make an accurate identification" are "outweighed by the corrupting effect" of law enforcement suggestion, the identification should be suppressed. Otherwise, the evidence (if admissible in all other respects) should be submitted to the jury.

Applying this "totality of the circumstances" approach, the Court held in *Biggers* that law enforcement's use of an unnecessarily suggestive showup did not require suppression of the victim's identification of her assailant. Notwithstanding the improper procedure, the victim's identification was reliable: She saw her assailant for a considerable period of time under adequate light, provided police with a detailed description of her attacker long before the showup, and had "no doubt" that the

defendant was the person she had seen. Similarly, the Court concluded in *Brathwaite* that police use of an unnecessarily suggestive photo array did not require exclusion of the resulting identification. The witness, an undercover police officer, viewed the defendant in good light for several minutes, provided a thorough description of the suspect, and was certain of his identification. Hence, the "indicators of [the witness'] ability to make an accurate identification [were] hardly outweighed by the corrupting effect of the challenged identification." …

Perry concedes that . . . law enforcement officials did not arrange the suggestive circumstances surrounding Blandon's identification. … He contends, however, that it was mere happenstance that each of the *Stovall* cases involved improper police action. The rationale underlying our decisions, Perry asserts, supports a rule requiring trial judges to prescreen eyewitness evidence for reliability any time an identification is made under suggestive circumstances. We disagree.

If reliability is the linchpin of admissibility under the Due Process Clause, Perry maintains, it should make no difference whether law enforcement was responsible for creating the suggestive circumstances that marred the identification.

Perry has removed our statement in *Brathwaite* from its mooring, and thereby attributes to the statement a meaning a fair reading of our opinion does not bear. … The due process check for reliability, Brathwaite made plain, comes into play only after the defendant establishes improper police conduct. The very purpose of the check. . . was to avoid depriving the jury of identification evidence that is reliable, notwithstanding improper police conduct.

Perry's contention that improper police action was not essential to the reliability check Brathwaite required is echoed by the dissent. Both ignore a key premise of the Brathwaite decision: A primary aim of excluding identification evidence obtained under unnecessarily suggestive circumstances … is to deter law enforcement use of improper lineups, showups, and photo arrays in the first place. Alerted to the prospect that identification evidence improperly obtained may be excluded, the Court reasoned, police officers will "guard against unnecessarily suggestive procedures." This deterrence rationale is inapposite in cases, like Perry's, in which the police engaged in no improper conduct.

...

Perry and the dissent place significant weight on *United States v. Wade*, describing it as a decision not anchored to improper police conduct. In fact, the risk of police rigging was the very danger to which the Court responded in *Wade* when it recognized a defendant's right to counsel at postindictment, police-organized identification procedures. "[T]he confrontation compelled by the State between the accused and the victim or witnesses," the Court began, "is peculiarly riddled with innumerable dangers and variable factors which might seriously, even crucially, derogate from a fair trial." "A major factor contributing to the high incidence of miscarriage of justice from mistaken identification," the Court continued, "has been the degree of suggestion inherent in the manner in which the prosecution presents the suspect to witnesses for pretrial identification."... Beyond genuine debate, then, prevention of unfair police practices prompted the Court to extend a defendant's right to counsel to cover postindictment lineups and showups.

...

C

In urging a broadly applicable due process check on eyewitness identifications, Perry maintains that eyewitness identifications are a uniquely unreliable form of evidence. . . . We do not doubt either the importance or the fallibility of eyewitness identifications. Indeed, in recognizing that defendants have a constitutional right to counsel at postindictment police lineups, we observed

that "the annals of criminal law are rife with instances of mistaken identification."

We have concluded in other contexts, however, that the potential unreliability of a type of evidence does not alone render its introduction at the defendant's trial fundamentally unfair. ... We reach a similar conclusion here: The fallibility of eyewitness evidence does not, without the taint of improper state conduct, warrant a due process rule requiring a trial court to screen such evidence for reliability before allowing the jury to assess its creditworthiness.

Our unwillingness to enlarge the domain of due process as Perry and the dissent urge rests, in large part, on our recognition that the jury, not the judge, traditionally determines the reliability of evidence. We also take account of other safeguards built into our adversary system that caution juries against placing undue weight on eyewitness testimony of questionable reliability. These protections include the defendant's Sixth Amendment right to confront the eyewitness. ... Another is the defendant's right to the effective assistance of an attorney, who can expose the flaws in the eyewitness' testimony during cross-examination and focus the jury's attention on the fallibility of such testimony during opening and closing arguments. Eyewitness-specific jury instructions, which many federal and state courts have adopted likewise warn the jury to take care in appraising identification evidence. . . . The constitutional requirement that the government prove the defendant's guilt beyond a reasonable doubt also impedes convictions based on dubious identification evidence.

State and federal rules of evidence, moreover, permit trial judges to exclude relevant evidence if its probative value is substantially outweighed by its prejudicial impact or potential for misleading the jury. In appropriate cases, some States also permit defendants to present expert testimony on the hazards of eyewitness identification evidence. . . .

Many of the safeguards just noted were at work at Perry's trial. During her opening statement, Perry's court-appointed attorney cautioned the jury about the vulnerability of Blandon's identification. ...While cross-examining Blandon and Officer Clay, Perry's attorney constantly brought up the weaknesses of Blandon's identification. She highlighted: (1) the significant distance between Blandon's window and the parking lot, (2) the lateness of the hour, (3) the van that partly obstructed Blandon's view, (4) Blandon's concession that she was "so scared [she] really didn't pay attention" to what Perry was wearing, (5) Blandon's inability to describe Perry's facial features or other identifying marks, (6) Blandon's failure to pick Perry out of a photo array, . . . and (7) Perry's position next to a uniformed, gun-bearing police officer at the moment Blandon made her identification. . . . Perry's counsel reminded the jury of these frailties during her summation.

After closing arguments, the trial court read the jury a lengthy instruction on identification testimony and the factors the jury should consider when evaluating it. The court also instructed the jury that the defendant's guilt must be proved beyond a reasonable doubt ... and specifically cautioned that "one of the things the State must prove [beyond a reasonable doubt] is the identification of the defendant as the person who committed the offense ... ."

Given the safeguards generally applicable in criminal trials, protections availed of by the defense in Perry's case, we hold that the introduction of Blandon's eyewitness testimony, without a preliminary judicial assessment of its reliability, did not render Perry's trial fundamentally unfair.

Finding no convincing reason to alter our precedent, we hold that the Due Process Clause does not require a preliminary judicial inquiry into the reliability of an eyewitness identification when the identification was not procured under unnecessarily suggestive circumstances arranged by law enforcement.

JUSTICE THOMAS, concurring, omitted.

JUSTICE SOTOMAYOR, dissenting.

This Court has long recognized that eyewitness identifications' unique confluence of features — their unreliability, susceptibility to suggestion, powerful impact on the jury, and resistance to the ordinary tests of the adversarial process — can undermine the fairness of a trial. Our cases thus establish a clear rule: The admission at trial of out-of-court eyewitness identifications derived from impermissibly suggestive circumstances that pose a very substantial likelihood of misidentification violates due process. The Court today announces that that rule does not even "com[e] into play" unless the suggestive circumstances are improperly "police-arranged."

Our due process concern, however, arises not from the act of suggestion, but rather from the corrosive effects of suggestion on the reliability of the resulting identification. By rendering protection contingent on improper police arrangement of the suggestive circumstances, the Court effectively grafts a mens rea inquiry onto our rule. The Court's holding enshrines a murky distinction — between suggestive confrontations intentionally orchestrated by the police and, as here, those inadvertently caused by police actions — that will sow confusion. It ignores our precedents' acute sensitivity to the hazards of intentional and unintentional suggestion alike and unmoors our rule from the very interest it protects, inviting arbitrary results. And it recasts the driving force of our decisions as an interest in police deterrence, rather than reliability. Because I see no warrant for declining to assess the circumstances of this case under our ordinary approach, I respectfully dissent.

I

The "driving force" behind *United States v. Wade*, *Gilbert v. California*, and *Stovall v. Denno*, was "the Court's concern with the problems of eyewitness identification" — specifically, "the concern that the jury not hear eyewitness testimony unless that evidence has aspects of reliability." We have pointed to the

" 'formidable' " number of "miscarriage[s] of justice from mistaken identification" in the annals of criminal law. We have warned of the "vagaries" and " 'proverbially untrustworthy' " nature of eyewitness identifications. And we have singled out a "major factor contributing" to that proverbial unreliability: "the suggestibility inherent in the context of the pretrial identification."

Our precedents make no distinction between intentional and unintentional suggestion. To the contrary, they explicitly state that "[s]uggestion can be created intentionally or unintentionally in many subtle ways." Rather than equate suggestive conduct with misconduct, we specifically have disavowed the assumption that suggestive influences may only be "the result of police procedures intentionally designed to prejudice an accused." ... "Persons who conduct the identification procedure may suggest, intentionally or unintentionally, that they expect the witness to identify the accused." The implication is that even police acting with the best of intentions can inadvertently signal "'that's the man.'"

...

More generally, our precedents focus not on the act of suggestion, but on suggestion's "corrupting effect" on reliability. Eyewitness evidence derived from suggestive circumstances, we have explained, is uniquely resistant to the ordinary tests of the adversary process. An eyewitness who has made an identification often becomes convinced of its accuracy. "Regardless of how the initial misidentification comes about, the witness thereafter is apt to retain in his memory the image of the photograph rather than of the person actually seen, reducing the trustworthiness of subsequent ... courtroom identification." Suggestion bolsters that confidence.

At trial, an eyewitness' artificially inflated confidence in an identification's accuracy complicates the jury's task of assessing witness credibility and reliability. It also impairs the defendant's ability to attack the eyewitness' credibility. That in turn jeopardizes the defendant's basic right to subject his accuser to meaningful cross-examination. ... The end result of suggestion, whether intentional or unintentional, is to fortify testimony bearing directly on guilt that juries find extremely convincing and are hesitant to discredit. ...

Consistent with our focus on reliability, we have declined to adopt a per se rule excluding all suggestive identifications. Instead, "reliability is the linchpin" in deciding admissibility. We have explained that a suggestive identification procedure "does not in itself intrude upon a constitutionally protected interest." ..."Suggestive confrontations are disapproved because they increase the likelihood of misidentification" — and "[i]t is the likelihood of misidentification which violates a defendant's right to due process." ... In short, "'what the Stovall due process right protects is an evidentiary interest.'"

To protect that evidentiary interest, we have applied a two-step inquiry: First, the defendant has the burden of showing that the eyewitness identification was derived through "impermissibly suggestive" means. Second, if the defendant meets that burden, courts consider whether the identification was reliable under the totality of the circumstances. That step entails considering the witness' opportunity to view the perpetrator, degree of attention, accuracy of description, level of certainty, and the time between the crime and pretrial confrontation, then weighing such factors against the "corrupting effect of the suggestive identification." Most identifications will be admissible. The standard of "fairness as required by the Due Process Clause," however, demands that a subset of the most unreliable identifications — those carrying a "'very substantial likelihood of ... misidentification'" — will be excluded.

II

...

B

[I]t is the likelihood of misidentification which violates a defendant's right to due process," and we are concerned with suggestion insofar as it has "corrupting effect[s]" on the identification's reliability. Accordingly, whether the police have created the suggestive circumstances intentionally or inadvertently, the resulting identification raises the same due process concerns. It is no more or less likely to misidentify the perpetrator. It is no more or less powerful to the jury. And the defendant is no more or less equipped to challenge the identification through cross-examination or prejudiced at trial. The arrangement-focused inquiry thus untethers our doctrine from the very " 'evidentiary interest' " it was designed to protect, inviting arbitrary results.

…

C

…

It would be one thing if the passage of time had cast doubt on the empirical premises of our precedents. But just the opposite has happened. A vast body of scientific literature has reinforced every concern our precedents articulated nearly a half-century ago, though it merits barely a parenthetical mention in the majority opinion. Over the past three decades, more than two thousand studies related to eyewitness identification have been published. One state supreme court recently appointed a special master to conduct an exhaustive survey of the current state of the scientific evidence and concluded that "[t]he research … is not only extensive," but "it represents the 'gold standard in terms of the applicability of social science research to law.' " "Experimental methods and findings have been tested and retested, subjected to scientific scrutiny through peer-reviewed journals, evaluated through the lens of meta-analyses, and replicated at times in real-world settings."…

The empirical evidence demonstrates that eyewitness misidentification is " 'the single greatest cause of wrongful convictions in this country.' " Researchers have found that a staggering 76% of the first 250 convictions overturned due to DNA evidence since 1989 involved eyewitness misidentification. Study after study demonstrates that eyewitness recollections are highly susceptible to distortion by postevent information or social cues; that jurors routinely overestimate the accuracy of eyewitness identifications; that jurors place the greatest weight on eyewitness confidence in assessing identifications even though confidence is a poor gauge of accuracy; and that suggestiveness can stem from sources beyond police-orchestrated procedures. The majority today nevertheless adopts an artificially narrow conception of the dangers of suggestive identifications at a time when our concerns should have deepened.

III

There are many reasons why Perry's particular situation might not violate due process. The trial court found that the circumstances surrounding Blandon's identification did not rise to an impermissibly suggestive level. It is not at all clear, moreover, that there was a very substantial likelihood of misidentification, given Blandon's lack of equivocation on the scene, the short time between crime and confrontation, and the "fairly well lit" parking lot. The New Hampshire Supreme Court, however, never made findings on either point and, under the majority's decision today, never will.

The Court's opinion today renders the defendant's due process protection contingent on whether the suggestive circumstances giving rise to the eyewitness identification stem from improper police arrangement. That view lies in tension with our precedents' more holistic conception of the dangers of suggestion and is untethered from the evidentiary interest the due process right protects. In my view, the ordinary two-step inquiry should apply, whether the police created the suggestive circumstances intentionally or inadvertently. Because the New Hampshire Supreme Court truncated its inquiry at the threshold, I would remand…. .

Foster v. California, 394 U.S. 440 (1969)

SUMMARY: Foster was charged by information [the title of a type of charging document] with the armed robbery of a Western Union. The day after the robbery one of the robbers, Clay, surrendered to the police and implicated Foster and Grice. Allegedly, Foster and Clay had entered the office while Grice waited in a car. Foster and Grice were tried together. Grice was acquitted. Foster was convicted. The California District Court of Appeal affirmed the conviction; the State Supreme Court denied review. We granted certiorari, limited to the question whether the conduct of the police lineup resulted in a violation of petitioner's constitutional rights.

The only witness to the crime was Joseph David, the late-night manager of the Western Union office. After Foster had been arrested, David was called to the police station to view a lineup. There were three men in the lineup. One was petitioner. He is a tall man — close to six feet in height. The other two men were short - five feet, five or six inches. Petitioner wore a leather jacket which David said was similar to the one he had seen underneath the coveralls worn by the robber. After seeing this lineup, David could not positively identify petitioner as the robber. He "thought" he was the man, but he was not sure. David then asked to speak to petitioner, and petitioner was brought into an office and sat across from David at a table. Except for prosecuting officials there was no one else in the room. Even after this one-to-one confrontation David still was uncertain whether petitioner was one of the robbers: "truthfully - I was not sure," he testified at trial. A week or 10 days later, the police arranged for David to view a second lineup. There were five men in that lineup. Petitioner was the only person in the second lineup who had appeared in the first lineup. This time David was "convinced" petitioner was the man.

At trial, David testified to his identification of petitioner in the lineups, as summarized above. He also repeated his identification of petitioner in the courtroom. The only other evidence against petitioner which concerned the particular robbery with which he was charged was the testimony of the alleged accomplice Clay.

[The Court discussed why the holdings in Wade and Gilbert weren't yet applicable to this case (it was decided on the same day as they were) and stated,] . . . we recognized that, judged by the "totality of the circumstances," the conduct of identification procedures may be "so unnecessarily suggestive and conducive to irreparable mistaken identification" as to be a denial of due process of law.

The suggestive elements in this identification procedure made it all but inevitable that David would identify petitioner whether or not he was in fact "the man." In effect, the police repeatedly said to the witness, "This is the man." This procedure so undermined the reliability of the eyewitness identification as to violate due process.

Neil v. Biggers, 409 U.S 188 (1972)

OPINION: In 1965, after a jury trial in a Tennessee court, respondent was convicted of rape and was sentenced to 20 years' imprisonment. The State's evidence consisted in part of testimony concerning a station-house identification of respondent by the victim.

The District Court held . . . that the station-house identification procedure was so suggestive as to violate due process. The Court of Appeals affirmed. We granted certiorari . . . [to decide] whether the identification procedure violated due process.

We proceed, then, to consider respondent's due process claim. As the claim turns upon the facts, we must first review the relevant testimony at the jury trial and at the habeas corpus hearing regarding the rape and the identification. The victim testified at trial that on the evening of January 22, 1965, a youth with a butcher knife grabbed her in the doorway to her kitchen:

"A. [H]e grabbed me from behind, and grappled - twisted me on the floor. Threw me down on the floor.

"Q. And there was no light in that kitchen?

"A. Not in the kitchen.

"Q. So you couldn't have seen him then?

"A. Yes, I could see him, when I looked up in his face.

"Q. In the dark?

"A. He was right in the doorway - it was enough light from the bedroom shining through. Yes, I could see who he was.

"Q. You could see? No light? And you could see him and know him then?

"A. Yes."

When the victim screamed, her 12-year-old daughter came out of her bedroom and also began to scream. The assailant directed the victim to "tell her [the daughter] to shut up, or I'll kill you both." She did so, and was then walked at knifepoint about two blocks along a railroad track, taken into the woods, and raped there. She testified that "the moon was shining brightly, full moon." After the rape, the assailant ran off, and she returned home, the whole incident having taken between 15 minutes and half an hour.

She then gave the police . . . a very general description," describing him as "being fat and flabby with smooth skin, bushy hair and a youthful voice." Additionally . . . she testified at the habeas corpus hearing that she had described her assailant as being between 16 and 18 years old and between five feet ten inches and six feet tall, as weighing between 180 and 200 pounds, and as having a dark brown complexion. This testimony was substantially corroborated by that of a police officer who was testifying from his notes.

On several occasions over the course of the next seven months, she viewed suspects in her home or at the police station, some in lineups and others in showups, and was shown between 30 and 40 photographs. She told the police that a man pictured in one of the photographs had features similar to those of her assailant, but identified none of the suspects. On August 17, the police called her to the station to view respondent, who was being detained on another charge. In an effort to construct a suitable lineup, the police checked the city jail and the city juvenile home. Finding no one at either place fitting respondent's unusual physical description, they conducted a showup instead.

The showup itself consisted of two detectives walking respondent past the victim. At the victim's request, the police directed respondent to say "shut up or I'll kill you." The testimony at trial was not altogether clear as to whether the victim first identified him and then asked that he repeat the words or made her identification after he had spoken. In any event, the victim testified that she had "no doubt" about her identification. At the habeas corpus hearing, she elaborated in response to questioning.

"A. That I have no doubt, I mean that I am sure that when I - see, when I first laid eyes on him, I knew that it was the individual, because his face - well, there was just something that I don't think I could ever forget. I believe _____

"Q. You say when you first laid eyes on him, which time are you referring to?

"A. When I identified him - when I seen him in the courthouse when I was took up to view the suspect."

We must decide whether, as the courts below held, this identification and the circumstances surrounding it failed to comport with due process requirements.

We have considered on four occasions the scope of due process protection against the admission of evidence deriving from suggestive identification procedures. In *Stovall*, the Court held that the defendant could claim that "the confrontation conducted . . . was so unnecessarily suggestive and conducive to irreparable mistaken identification that he was denied due process of law." This, we held, must be determined "on the totality of the circumstances." We went on to find that on the facts of the case then before us, due process was not violated, emphasizing that the critical condition of the injured witness justified a showup in her hospital room. At trial, the witness, whose view of the suspect at the time of the crime was brief, testified to the out-of-court identification, as did several police officers present in her hospital room, and also made an in-court identification.

Subsequently, in a case where the witnesses made in-court identifications arguably stemming from previous exposure to a suggestive photographic array, the Court restated the governing test:

"[W]e hold that each case must be considered on its own facts, and that convictions based on eyewitness identification at trial following a pretrial identification by photograph will be set aside on that ground only if the photographic identification procedure was so impermissibly suggestive as to give rise to a very substantial likelihood of irreparable misidentification."

Again we found the identification procedure to be supportable, relying both on the need for prompt utilization of other investigative leads and on the likelihood that the photographic identifications were reliable, the witnesses having viewed the bank robbers for periods of up to five minutes under good lighting conditions at the time of the robbery.

The only case to date in which this Court has found identification procedures to be violative of due process is *Foster*. There, the witness failed to identify *Foster* the first time he confronted him, despite a suggestive lineup. The police then arranged a showup, at which the witness could make only a tentative identification. Ultimately, at yet another confrontation, this time a lineup, the witness was able to muster a definite identification. We held all of the identifications inadmissible, observing that the identifications were "all but inevitable" under the circumstances.

In the most recent case of *Coleman*, we held admissible an in-court identification by a witness who had a fleeting but "real good look" at his assailant in the headlights of a passing car. The witness testified at a pretrial suppression hearing that he identified one of the petitioners among the participants in the lineup before the police placed the participants in a formal line. MR. JUSTICE BRENNAN for four members of the Court stated that this evidence could support a finding that the in-court identification was "entirely based upon observations at the time of the assault and not at all induced by the conduct of the lineup."

Some general guidelines emerge from these cases as to the relationship between suggestiveness and misidentification. It is, first of all, apparent that the primary evil to be avoided is "a very substantial likelihood of irreparable misidentification." While the phrase was coined as a standard for determining whether an in-court identification would be admissible in the wake of a suggestive out-of-court identification, with the deletion of "irreparable" it serves equally well as a standard for the admissibility of testimony concerning the

out-of-court identification itself. It is the likelihood of misidentification which violates a defendant's right to due process, and it is this which was the basis of the exclusion of evidence in Foster.

Suggestive confrontations are disapproved because they increase the likelihood of misidentification, and unnecessarily suggestive ones are condemned for the further reason that the increased chance of misidentification is gratuitous. But as *Stovall* makes clear, the admission of evidence of a showup without more does not violate due process.

What is less clear from our cases is whether unnecessary suggestiveness alone requires the exclusion of evidence. While we are inclined to agree with the courts below that the police did not exhaust all possibilities in seeking persons physically comparable to respondent, we do not think that the evidence must therefore be excluded. The purpose of a strict rule barring evidence of unnecessarily suggestive confrontations would be to deter the police from using a less reliable procedure where a more reliable one may be available, and would not be based on the assumption that in every instance the admission of evidence of such a confrontation offends due process.). …

We turn, then, to the central question, whether under the "totality of the circumstances" the identification was reliable even though the confrontation procedure was suggestive. As indicated by our cases, the factors to be considered in evaluating the likelihood of misidentification include the opportunity of the witness to view the criminal at the time of the crime, the witness' degree of attention, the accuracy of the witness' prior description of the criminal, the level of certainty demonstrated by the witness at the confrontation, and the length of time between the crime and the confrontation. Applying these factors, we disagree with the District Court's conclusion.

. . . .

[The court applied each of those criteria to the litany of facts surrounding the identification here and concluded,] . . . weighing all the factors, we find no substantial likelihood of misidentification. The evidence was properly allowed to go to the jury.

Manson v. Brathwaite, 432 U.S. 98 (1977),

SUMMARY: This case involved an identification based upon viewing of a single photograph by police officer, Glover, the eyewitness. The state supreme court found that "no substantial injustice" resulted from the identification, but a federal court excluded the photograph saying that examining a single photograph was unnecessary, suggestive, and possibly unreliable, even though it might have been reliable under the circumstances. The U.S. Supreme Court reversed and said a photographic array was preferable, but under *Biggers* even inherently suggestive show-ups do not require the per se exclusion of such identifications.

The Court applied the five-factor analysis from *Biggers* and concluded that the eyewitness (an undercover police narcotics officer) had the ability to make an accurate identification:

The opportunity to view. ("The facts indicated that Glover had natural lighting and two to three minutes to observe Brathwaite from two feet away.')

The degree of attention ("Glover was a trained on duty police officer specializing in narcotics enforcement, was an African American, and could be expected to pay scrupulous attention to detail, for he knew that subsequently he would have to find and arrest his vendor" and testify about this in court.")

The accuracy of the description (Glover's description was given to D'Onofrio (the officer who provided the photograph to Glover based on Glover's description) within minutes after the transaction and included the vendor's race, height, build, the color and style of his hair, and the high cheekbone facial feature. It also included clothing the vendor wore. D'Onofrio reacted positively, and two days later, when Glover was alone, he viewed the photograph and identified its subject as the narcotics seller).

The witness's level of certainty (Glover, in response to a question as to whether the photograph was that of the seller, testified: "There is no question whatsoever.")

The time between the crime and the confrontation identification. (The Court concluded that "we cannot say that under all the circumstances of this case there is a 'very substantial likelihood of irreparable misidentification.'")

SECTION FIVE: CONSTITUTIONAL RIGHTS IN THE ACCUSATORIAL PHASE

Chapter Eight: Pretrial

This chapter reviews the Court's rulings concerning pre-trial procedures. Generally, pretrial guarantees are found in the Fifth Amendment to the U.S. Constitution, but pretrial procedures are also governed by state statutes, local court rules, and federal congressional acts.

PROBABLE CAUSE-TO-DETAIN DETERMINATIONS

Probable cause-to-detain determinations are required only when suspects are arrested without a warrant. Where an arrest warrant has been issued, a magistrate has already determined that probable cause exists to arrest and detain the suspect.[74] Generally these determinations are made by a judicial officer (judge or magistrate) who review an affidavit/statement by the arresting officer which articulate the reasons why there was probable cause to arrest the detainee. The arresting officer's statement should set out the specific facts that demonstrate probable cause rather than make generalized conclusory statements.

COUNTY OF RIVERSIDE v. McLAUGHLIN
500 U.S. 44 (1991)

JUSTICE O'CONNOR delivered the opinion of the Court.

In *Gerstein v. Pugh*, this Court held that the Fourth Amendment requires a prompt judicial determination of probable cause as a prerequisite to an extended pretrial detention following a warrantless arrest. This case requires us to define what is "prompt" under *Gerstein*.

This is a class action brought under 42 U.S.C. 1983 challenging the manner in which the

County of Riverside, California (County) provides probable cause determinations to persons arrested without a warrant. At issue is the County's policy of combining probable cause determinations with its arraignment procedures. Under County policy . . . arraignments must be conducted without unnecessary delay and, in any event, within two days of arrest. This two-day requirement excludes from computation weekends and holidays. Thus, an individual arrested without a warrant late in the week may, in some cases,

---

[74] Confusingly, these determinations are sometimes inaccurately called preliminary hearings or first appearances. A probable cause-to-detain hearing (pc hearing) is generally neither. The arrested individual has no right to appear before the judge (this is a first appearance), nor is there any type of hearing in which the sufficiency of the evidence to go forward into felony court is tested (this is a preliminary hearing). The judge need only review a statement of probable cause written by the police officer showing why the suspect was arrested and is now being detained. In some cases, *Rothergery v. Gillespie County* for instance (see below), you may see that a court has a practice of making probable cause to detain determinations at a first appearance. But, due to the timing discussed in County of Riverside v. McLaughlin case below, shows that there are limitations on this practice.

be held for as long as five days before receiving a probable cause determination. Over the Thanksgiving holiday, a 7-day delay is possible.

We granted certiorari to resolve this conflict among the Circuits as to what constitutes a "prompt" probable cause determination under Gerstein.

. . . .

In *Gerstein*, this Court held unconstitutional Florida procedures under which persons arrested without a warrant could remain in police custody for 30 days or more without a judicial determination of probable cause. In reaching this conclusion, we attempted to reconcile important competing interests. On the one hand, States have a strong interest in protecting public safety by taking into custody those persons who are reasonably suspected of having engaged in criminal activity, even where there has been no opportunity for a prior judicial determination of probable cause. On the other hand, prolonged detention based on incorrect or unfounded suspicion may unjustly "imperil [a] suspect's job, interrupt his source of income, and impair his family relationships." We sought to balance these competing concerns by holding that States "must provide a fair and reliable determination of probable cause as a condition for any significant pretrial restraint of liberty and this determination must be made by a judicial officer either before or promptly after arrest."

The Court thus established a "practical compromise" between the rights of individuals and the realities of law enforcement. Under *Gerstein*, warrantless arrests are permitted, but persons arrested without a warrant must promptly be brought before a neutral magistrate for a judicial determination of probable cause. Significantly, the Court stopped short of holding that jurisdictions were constitutionally compelled to provide a probable cause hearing immediately upon taking a suspect into custody and completing booking procedures. We acknowledged the burden that proliferation of pretrial proceedings places on the criminal justice system, and recognized that the interests of everyone involved, including those persons who are arrested, might be disserved by introducing further procedural complexity into an already intricate system. Accordingly, we left it to the individual States to integrate prompt probable cause determinations into their differing systems of pretrial procedures.

Our purpose in *Gerstein* was to make clear that the Fourth Amendment requires every State to provide prompt determinations of probable cause, but that the Constitution does not impose on the States a rigid procedural framework. Rather, individual States may choose to comply in different ways.

Inherent in *Gerstein's* invitation to the States to experiment and adapt was the recognition that the Fourth Amendment does not compel an immediate determination of probable cause upon completing the administrative steps incident to arrest. Plainly, if a probable cause hearing is constitutionally compelled the moment a suspect is finished being "booked," there is no room whatsoever for "flexibility and experimentation by the States." Incorporating probable cause determinations "into the procedure for setting bail or fixing other conditions of pretrial release" - which *Gerstein* explicitly contemplated, - would be impossible. Waiting even a few hours so that a bail hearing or arraignment could take place at the same time as the probable cause determination would amount to a constitutional violation. Clearly, *Gerstein* is not that inflexible.

[T]he Ninth Circuit Court of Appeals ... construed *Gerstein* as "requir[ing] a probable cause determination to be made as soon as the administrative steps incident to arrest were completed, and that such steps should require only a brief period." This same reading is advanced by the dissent. The foregoing discussion readily demonstrates the error of this approach ... *Gerstein* struck a balance between competing interests; a proper understanding of the decision is possible only if one takes into account both sides of the equation.

As mentioned at the outset, the question before us today is what is "prompt" under *Gerstein*. We answer that question by recognizing that *Gerstein* struck a balance between competing interests.

Given that *Gerstein* permits jurisdictions to incorporate probable cause determinations into other pretrial procedures, some delays are inevitable. For example, where, as in Riverside County, the probable cause determination is combined with arraignment, there will be delays caused by paperwork and logistical problems. Records will have to be reviewed, charging documents drafted, appearance of counsel arranged, and appropriate bail determined. On weekends, when the number of arrests is often higher and available resources tend to be limited, arraignments may get pushed back even further. In our view, the Fourth Amendment permits a reasonable postponement of a probable cause determination while the police cope with the everyday problems of processing suspects through an overly burdened criminal justice system.

But flexibility has its limits; *Gerstein* is not a blank check. A State has no legitimate interest in detaining for extended periods individuals who have been arrested without probable cause. The Court recognized in *Gerstein* that a person arrested without a warrant is entitled to a fair and reliable determination of probable cause, and that this determination must be made promptly.

[I]t is not enough to say that probable cause determinations must be "prompt." This vague standard simply has not provided sufficient guidance. Instead, it has led to a flurry of systemic challenges to city and county practices, putting federal judges in the role of making legislative judgments and overseeing local jailhouse operations.

Our task in this case is to articulate more clearly the boundaries of what is permissible under the Fourth Amendment. Although we hesitate to announce that the Constitution compels a specific time limit, it is important to provide some degree of certainty so that States

and counties may establish procedures with confidence that they fall within constitutional bounds. Taking into account the competing interests articulated in *Gerstein*, we believe that a jurisdiction that provides judicial determinations of probable cause within 48 hours of arrest will, as a general matter, comply with the promptness requirement of *Gerstein*. ...

This is not to say that the probable cause determination in a particular case passes constitutional muster simply because it is provided within 48 hours. Such a hearing may nonetheless violate *Gerstein* if the arrested individual can prove that his or her probable cause determination was delayed unreasonably. Examples of unreasonable delay are delays for the purpose of gathering additional evidence to justify the arrest, a delay motivated by ill-will against the arrested individual, or delay for delay's sake. In evaluating whether the delay in a particular case is unreasonable, however, courts must allow a substantial degree of flexibility. Courts cannot ignore the often unavoidable delays in transporting arrested persons from one facility to another, handling late-night bookings where no magistrate is readily available, obtaining the presence of an arresting officer who may be busy processing other suspects or securing the premises of an arrest, and other practical realities.

Where an arrested individual does not receive a probable cause determination within 48 hours, the calculus changes. In such a case, the arrested individual does not bear the burden of proving an unreasonable delay. Rather, the burden shifts to the government to demonstrate the existence of a bona fide emergency or other extraordinary circumstance. The fact that, in a particular case, it may take longer than 48 hours to consolidate pretrial proceedings does not qualify as an extraordinary circumstance. Nor, for that matter, do intervening weekends. A jurisdiction that chooses to offer combined proceedings must do so as soon as is reasonably feasible, but in no event later than 48 hours after arrest.

Everyone agrees that the police should make every attempt to minimize the time a presumptively innocent individual spends in jail. One way to do so is to provide a judicial determination of probable cause immediately upon completing the administrative steps incident to arrest - i.e., as soon as the suspect has been booked, photographed, and fingerprinted. ...[S]everal states, laudably, have adopted this approach. The Constitution does not compel so rigid a schedule, however. Under *Gerstein*, jurisdictions may choose to combine probable cause determinations with other pretrial proceedings, so long as they do so promptly. This necessarily means that only certain proceedings are candidates for combination. Only those proceedings that arise very early in the pretrial process - such as bail hearings and arraignments - may be chosen. Even then, every effort must be made to expedite the combined proceedings.

[T]he County's current policy and practice do not comport fully with the principles we have outlined. The County's current policy is to offer combined proceedings within two days, exclusive of Saturdays, Sundays, or holidays.

As a result, persons arrested on Thursdays may have to wait until the following Monday before they receive a probable cause determination. The delay is even longer if there is an intervening holiday. Thus, the County's regular practice exceeds the 48-hour period we deem constitutionally permissible, meaning that the County is not immune from systemic challenges, such as this class action.

JUSTICE SCALIA, dissenting.

…

In my view, absent extraordinary circumstances, it is an "unreasonable seizure" within the meaning of the Fourth Amendment for the police, having arrested a suspect without a warrant, to delay a determination of probable cause for the arrest either (1) for reasons unrelated to arrangement of the probable cause determination or completion of the steps incident to arrest, or (2) beyond 24 hours after the arrest. Like the Court, I would treat the time limit as a presumption; when the 24 hours are exceeded, the burden shifts to the police to adduce unforeseeable circumstances justifying the additional delay.

ARRAIGNMENTS

Arraignments are open court proceedings at which the court notifies the defendant what formal charges were filed by the state. Generally, the accused is required to be present at arraignments, but in minor cases defense counsel may send in a 'notice of appearance' and make alternate arrangements. As seen in *Rothgery v. Gillespie County* (below), the defendant is entitled to have counsel represent him or her during this proceeding. Often, arraignments are referred to as "first appearance" or "initial appearance." But, if defendant shows up at court the first time (a first appearance) without a defense attorney, the court cannot proceed with the arraignment until an attorney is present or the defendant waives an attorney. Because this is inefficient, courts have started using "stand by" attorneys during these first appearances so that the defendant may be arraigned. The defendant will then be appointed an attorney (not necessarily the stand-by attorney) if indigent, or will be able to hire an attorney if not indigent. If the defendant tells the court at first appearance that he or she wants to hire an attorney (or already has), the court will delay the arraignment process until that attorney can be present.

At arraignments the defendant is told what charges have been filed and she will be given a copy the charges. The judge will inquire if the defendant is correctly named on the charging document; the judge will also determine whether the defendant should be in custody or not and if not, whether there should be bail or conditions to the release. Finally, the defendant may be asked to enter a not guilty plea and request a trial—this triggers the start of the official proceedings against her.

BAIL AND PREVENTIVE DETENTION

The Eighth Amendment limits the government (the courts) from setting excessive bail (defined by *Stack v. Boyle* 342 U.S. 1 (1951) as a sum greater than necessary to assure defendant's reappearance at further court proceedings), but does not require that bail be set. Indeed, courts routinely deny bail when the defendant is accused of murder. Historically, it was recognized that the right of bail was qualified and the federal government and states had considerable latitude in how they structured their bail systems (for example, outsourcing to private commercial bail bondsmen). There had been some abuses of this system over time and by 1966 the federal government responded by enacting the Federal Bail Reform Act of 1966. The gist of that legislation was that everyone should be released pending trial ("OR'd") unless such release would not secure their reappearance. The Act did not mention that judges could consider the dangerousness of the offender, but in fact, judges were doing so. The 1984 Federal Bail Act was one part of a comprehensive Crime Control Act from that year, and it specified that there was a presumption of release, but judges could detain defendants who presented no flight risks but were determined, after an adversarial hearing, to pose a risk of danger to the community.

Gernstein (2013) argues that the setting of bail should be considered a critical stage of the criminal justice process (thus carrying with it the right to the assistance of counsel. See, Chapter Nine). He observes,

> "Among other adverse consequences, a bad outcome at a bail hearing can force an indigent defendant to plead guilty. Many indigent defendants cannot post even minimum bail. Defendants who are required to post bail that they cannot afford may end up pleading guilty to avoid waiting in jail. If the sentence offered by the prosecutor in a plea deal is shorter than the expected wait for trial or bail review, all but the most stubborn of defendants would plead guilty. For a defendant charged with a relatively minor offense, the bail hearing can be the main event; a bad outcome can seal his fate. Because the bail determination is likely unrelated to the defendant's culpability, its effect on his plea decision is prejudicial. It does not cause him to plead guilty because he is guilty; it causes him to plead guilty because he has been held on bail.

> Surprisingly, there is no federal right to appointed counsel for indigent defendants at bail hearings, and most states do not appoint counsel at all in such hearings. So most indigent (who represent the overwhelming majority of criminal defendants in this country) face bail hearings without counsel. But, according to a study in Baltimore, defendants with counsel are more than twice as likely to be released on their own recognizance. And, when represented defendants are granted bail, it is on average around six hundred dollars less than what is set for unrepresented defendants. Appointing counsel at bail hearings, then, will substantially reduce the amount of time a substantial number of indigent defendants spend in jail awaiting their trials. And that will cut down on the number of plea deals those defendants have to take just to get out of deal — regardless of their guilty or innocence."[75]

United States v. Salerno, 481 U.S. 739 (1987), dealt with the constitutionality of preventive detention — the denial of bail based upon defendant's dangerousness as opposed to his likelihood of reappearance. *United States v. Salerno* stemmed from the prosecution of two organized crime figures under the federal Racketeer Influenced and Corrupt Organizations (RICO) Act. The backstory of "Fat Tony Salerno" and "Fish Cafaro's" prosecution led by U.S. Attorney for the Southern District of New York, Rudy Giuliani, is touched upon in the facts section in the case, but it is more scintillating than

---

[75] Gernstein, C. Plea Bargaining and the Right to Counsel at Bail Hearings, Michigan Law Review, Vol. 111, June 2013 (p. 1515-1516).

described. Fat Tony was one of the 50 biggest Mafia bosses at the time, and he had been out on release (on $2 million dollars bail) on tax charges which had two times resulted in mistrials. During his release, these RICO charges -- involving using control over the concrete workers unions to control concrete jobs in New York City, were filed. At the release hearing on those RICO charges, "Jimmy the Weasel" Frattioni's" turncoat testimony linked Fat Tony to some murderous activities that had occurred during his release on the tax cases. As to the adversarial detention hearing itself, although he two dozen witnesses testified that he was not dangerous, District Court Judge Walker concluded the government had met its burden for preventive detention and locked up Fat Tony and Fish Cafaro. The trial judge, Mary Johnson refused to reconsider Judge Walker's refusal to release order, this was appealed, and a 3- judge Court of Appeals opinion upheld his detention but said the Act violated the Constitution. As a "rest of the story" report: Cafaro had agreed to work for the government, but then he wouldn't, but then, he did. Salerno was ultimately convicted of the RICO charges but not the murder charges. He was given a 70-year prison sentence to run consecutive to a 100-year sentence on other charges. He died in 1992 at 80 years of age and in federal custody.[76]

UNITED STATES v. SALERNO
481 U.S. 739 (1987)

CHIEF JUSTICE REHNQUIST delivered the opinion of the Court.

The Bail Reform Act of 1984 allows a federal court to detain an arrestee pending trial if the government demonstrates by clear and convincing evidence after an adversary hearing that no release conditions "will reasonably assure the safety of any other person and the community." . . . We hold that, as against the facial attack mounted by these respondents, the Act fully comports with constitutional requirements. We therefore reverse.

Responding to "the alarming problem of crimes committed by persons on release," Congress formulated the Bail Reform Act of 1984 as the solution to a bail crisis in the federal courts. . . . Congress hoped to "give the courts adequate authority to make release decisions that give appropriate recognition to the danger a person may pose to others if released."

To this end, Sec. 314(a) of the Act requires a judicial officer to determine whether an arrestee shall be detained. Section 3142(e) provides that "[i]f, after a hearing pursuant to the provisions of subsection (f), the judicial officer finds that no condition or combination of conditions will reasonably assure the appearance of the person as required and the safety of any other person and the community, he shall order the detention of the person prior to trial." Section 3142(f) provides the arrestee with a number of procedural safeguards. He may request the presence of counsel at the detention hearing, he may testify and present witnesses in his behalf, as well as proffer evidence, and he may cross-examine other witnesses appearing at the hearing. If the judicial officer finds that no conditions of pretrial release can reasonably assure the safety of other persons and the community, he must state his findings of fact in writing, § 3142(i), and support his conclusion with "clear and convincing evidence." § 3142(f).

The judicial officer is not given unbridled discretion in making the detention determination. Congress has specified the considerations relevant to that decision. These factors include the nature and seriousness of the charges, the substantiality of the government's evidence against the arrestee, the arrestee's background and characteristics, and the nature and seriousness of the danger posed by the suspect's release. Should a judicial officer order detention, the detainee is

---

[76] See, Criminal Justice Stories in Criminal Procedure.

entitled to expedited appellate review of the detention order.

Respondents Anthony Salerno and Vincent Cafaro were arrested on March 21, 1986, after being charged in a 29-count indictment alleging various Racketeer Influenced and Corrupt Organizations Act (RICO) violations, mail and wire fraud offenses, extortion, and various criminal gambling violations. The RICO counts alleged 35 acts of racketeering activity, including fraud, extortion, gambling, and conspiracy to commit murder. At respondents' arraignment, the Government moved to have Salerno and Cafaro detained pursuant to § 3142(e), on the ground that no condition of release would assure the safety of the community or any person. The District Court held a hearing at which the Government made a detailed proffer of evidence. The Government's case showed that Salerno was the "boss" of the Genovese Crime Family of La Cosa Nostra and that Cafaro was a "captain" in the Genovese Family. Accordingly, to the Government's proffer, based in large part on conversations intercepted by a court-ordered wiretap, the two respondents had participated in wide-ranging conspiracies to aid their illegitimate enterprises through violent means. The Government also offered the testimony of two of its trial witnesses, who would assert that Salerno personally participated in two murder conspiracies. Salerno opposed the motion for detention, challenging the credibility of the Government's witnesses. He offered the testimony of several character witnesses as well as a letter from his doctor stating that he was suffering from a serious medical condition. Cafaro presented no evidence at the hearing, but instead characterized the wiretap conversations as merely "tough talk."

The District Court granted the Government's detention motion, concluding that the Government had established by clear and convincing evidence that no condition or combination of conditions of release would ensure the safety of the community or any person. Respondents appealed, contending that to the extent that the Bail Reform Act permits pretrial detention on the ground that the arrestee is likely to commit future crimes, it is unconstitutional on its face. . . .

Respondents contend that the Bail Reform Act violates the Excessive Bail Clause of the Eighth Amendment. . . . We think that the Act survives a challenge founded upon the Eighth Amendment. The Eighth Amendment addresses pretrial release by providing merely that "Excessive bail shall not be required." The Clause, of course, says nothing about whether bail shall be available at all. Respondents nevertheless contend that this Clause grants them a right to bail calculated solely upon considerations of flight. They rely on *Stack v. Boyle* (1951), in which the Court stated that "bail set at a figure higher than an amount reasonably calculated [to ensure the defendant's presence at trial] is 'excessive' under the Eighth Amendment." . . .

While we agree that a primary function of bail is to safeguard the courts' role in adjudicating the guilt or innocence of defendants, we reject the proposition that the Eighth Amendment categorically prohibits the government from pursuing other admittedly compelling interests through regulation of pretrial release. The above-quoted dicta in *Stack v. Boyle* is far too slender a reed on which to rest this argument. The Court in *Stack* had no occasion to consider whether the Excessive Bail Clause requires courts to admit all defendants to bail. . . Thus, the Court had to determine only whether bail, admittedly available in that case, was excessive if set at a sum greater than that necessary to ensure the arrestees' presence at trial.

In our society liberty is the norm, and detention prior to trial or without trial is the carefully limited exception. We hold that the provisions for pretrial detention in the Bail Reform Act of 1984 fall within that carefully limited exception. The Act authorizes the detention prior to trial of arrestees charged with serious felonies who are found after an adversary hearing to pose a threat to the safety of individuals or to the community which no condition of release can dispel. The numerous procedural safeguards detailed above must attend this adversary hearing. . . .

JUSTICE MARSHALL, with whom JUSTICE BRENNAN joins, dissenting.

This case brings before the Court for the first time a statute in which Congress declares that a person innocent of any crime may be jailed indefinitely, pending the trial of allegations which are legally presumed to be untrue, if the Government shows to the satisfaction of a judge that the accused is likely to commit crimes, unrelated to the pending charges, at any time in the future. Such statutes, consistent with the usages of tyranny and the excesses of what bitter experience teaches us to call the police state, have long been thought incompatible with the fundamental human rights protected by our Constitution. Today a majority of this Court holds otherwise. Its decision disregards basic principles of justice established centuries ago and enshrined beyond the reach of governmental interference in the Bill of Rights.

Other Cases: Bail and Preventive Detention

Stack v. Boyle, 342 U.S. 1 (1951)

Petitioners moved to reduce bail on the ground that bail as fixed was excessive under the Eighth Amendment. In support of their motion, petitioners submitted statements as to their financial resources, family relationships, health, prior criminal records, and other information. The only evidence offered by the Government was a certified record showing that four persons previously convicted under the Smith Act in the Southern District of New York had forfeited bail. No evidence was produced relating those four persons to the petitioners in this case. ...

First. From the passage of the Judiciary Act of 1789 to the present Federal Rules of Criminal Procedure, Rule 46 (a) (1), federal law has unequivocally provided that a person arrested for a non-capital offense shall be admitted to bail. This traditional right to freedom before conviction permits the unhampered preparation of a defense, and serves to prevent the infliction of punishment prior to conviction. ... Unless this right to bail before trial is preserved, the presumption of innocence, secured only after centuries for struggle, would lose its meaning.

The right to release before trial is conditioned upon the accused's giving adequate assurance that he will stand trial and submit to sentence if found guilty. ... [T]he modern practice of requiring a bail bond or the deposit of a sum of money subject to forfeiture serves as additional assurance of the presence of an accused. Bail set at a figure higher than an amount reasonably calculated to fulfill this purpose is "excessive" under the Eighth Amendment. Since the function of bail is limited, the fixing of bail for any individual defendant must be based upon standards relevant to the purpose of assuring the presence of that defendant. ... Upon final judgment of conviction, petitioners face imprisonment of not more than five years and a fine of not more than $10,000. It is not denied that bail for each petitioner has been fixed in a sum much higher than that usually imposed for offenses with like penalties and yet there has been no factual showing to justify such action in this case. The Government asks the courts to depart from the norm by assuming, without the introduction of evidence, that each petitioner is a pawn in a conspiracy and will, in obedience to a superior, flee the jurisdiction. To infer from the fact of indictment alone a need for bail in an unusually high amount is an arbitrary act. Such conduct would inject into our own system of government the very principles of totalitarianism which Congress was seeking to guard against in passing the statute under which petitioners have been indicted.

If bail in an amount greater than that usually fixed for serious charges of crimes is required in the case of any of the petitioners, that is a matter to which evidence should be directed in a hearing so that the constitutional rights of each petitioner may be preserved. In the absence of such a showing, we are of the opinion that the fixing of bail before trial in these cases cannot be squared with the statutory and constitutional standards for admission to bail.

Jennings v. Rodriguez, 583 U.S. ___ (2018)

SUMMARY: After a 2004 conviction, Rodriguez, a Mexican citizen and a lawful U.S. permanent resident, was detained under 8 U.S.C. 1226 while the government sought his removal. In 2007, Rodriguez sought habeas relief, claiming that he was entitled to a bond hearing to determine whether his continued detention was justified, alleging that [specific sections of federal laws] do not authorize "prolonged" detention without an individualized bond hearing at which the government proves by clear and convincing evidence that detention remains justified.

The Court held that non-citizens who were subject to mandatory pretrial detention under the Immigration Act were not entitled to a bond hearing if they are detained for longer than 6 months.

GRAND JURY

The Fifth Amendment grand jury provides defendants the right to have their case reviewed by a grand jury before continuing to a full-blown criminal trial in federal prosecutions. In *Hurtado v. California*, 110 U.S. 516 (1884), the Court considered whether the Fifth Amendment's grand jury requirement applied to state criminal prosecutions through the Fourteenth Amendment. (Hurtado was charged in California on an information (the name of the charging document) for killing Jose Antonio Stuardo. He contended that California's constitution requiring that cases be charged on an information rather than a grand jury indictment violated the U.S. Constitution.) The Court stated,

> "The proposition of law we are asked to affirm is, that an indictment or presentment by a grand jury … is essential to that "due process of law," when applied to prosecutions for felonies, which is secured and guarantied (sic) by this provision of the Constitution of the United States, and which accordingly it is forbidden to the States respectively to dispense with in the administration of criminal law.

> . . .["D]ue process of law" was not meant or intended to include the institution and procedure of a grand jury in any case. . . [I]f in the adoption of [the Fourteenth] Amendment it had been part of its purpose to perpetuate the institution of the grand jury in all the States, it would have embodied, as did the 5th Amendment, express declarations to that effect. … The 14th Amendment, by parity of reason, it refers to that law of the land in each State, which derives its authority from the inherent and reserved powers of the State, exerted within the limits of those fundamental principles of liberty and justice which lie at the base of all our civil and political institutions, and the greatest security for which resides in the right of the people to make their own laws, and alter them at their pleasure.

States use either grand jury, preliminary hearings, or both. Both procedures are designed to test the sufficiency of the state's evidence to go forward in felony court. The grand jury differs from preliminary hearing in the following ways:

➢ grand jurors rather than a judge determine whether the state has sufficient evidence,

➢ the charging document filed is called an "indictment" rather than an "information,"

➢ the defendant has no right to appear or present evidence before the grand jury but has the right to appear (but not present evidence) at the preliminary hearing,

➢ The defense is not present at the grand jury and cannot challenge the evidence presented by the state, but the defendant may cross-examine witnesses at the preliminary hearing,

➤ the grand jury proceeding is a closed proceeding (not open to the public) but the preliminary hearing is an open proceeding and usually recorded. Some grand jury proceedings are recorded, but others are not.

	Grand Jury	Preliminary Hearing
Who decides sufficiency of evidence	Grand Jurors (as few as 7, as many as 23)	Judge
Present at hearing	State, witnesses (one at a time), no defendant	Judge, Defendant/Counsel, Prosecutor, Witnesses
Cross examination of witnesses	No	Yes
Decision (terms of art)	"Return a True Bill," "Return a Not True Bill"	"Bind the Defendant Over"
Title of charging document	Indictment	Information

In *United States v. Calandra*, 414 U.S. 338 (1974), the Supreme Court considered whether a grand jury witness may refuse to answer questions about evidence obtained from an unlawful search and seizure. In his opinion for the Court, Justice Powell discusses the role and function of the grand jury.

UNITED STATES v. CALANDRA
414 U.S. 338 (1974)

JUSTICE POWELL delivered the opinion of the court.

The institution of the grand jury is deeply rooted in Anglo-American history. In England, the grand jury served for centuries both as a body of accusers sworn to discover and present for trial persons suspected of criminal wrongdoing and as a protector of citizens against arbitrary and oppressive governmental action. In this country the Founders thought the grand jury so essential to basic liberties that they provided in the Fifth Amendment that federal prosecution for serious crimes can only be instituted by "a presentment or indictment of a Grand Jury." The grand jury's historic functions survive to this day. Its responsibilities continue to include both the determination whether there is probable cause to believe a crime has been committed and the protection of citizens against unfounded criminal prosecutions.

Traditionally the grand jury has been accorded wide latitude to inquire into violations of criminal law. No judge presides to monitor its proceedings. It deliberates in secret and may determine alone the course of its inquiry. The grand jury may compel the production of evidence or the testimony of witnesses as it considers appropriate, and its operation generally is unrestrained by the technical procedural and evidentiary rules governing the conduct of criminal trials. "It is a grand inquest, a body with powers of investigation and inquisition, the scope of whose inquiries is not to be limited narrowly by questions of propriety or forecasts of the probable result of the investigation, or by doubts whether any particular individual will be found properly subject to an accusation of crime."

The scope of the grand jury's powers reflects its special role in insuring fair and effective law enforcement. A grand jury proceeding is not an adversary hearing in which the guilt or innocence of the accused is adjudicated. Rather, it is an *ex parte* investigation to determine whether a crime has been committed and whether criminal proceedings should be instituted against any person. The grand jury's investigative power must be broad if its public responsibility is adequately to be discharged.

The grand jury's sources of information are widely drawn, and the validity of an indictment is not affected by the character of the evidence considered. Thus, an indictment valid on its face is not subject to challenge on the ground that the grand jury acted on the basis of inadequate or incompetent evidence, or even on the basis of information obtained in violation of a defendant's Fifth Amendment privilege against self-incrimination.

The power of a federal court to compel persons to appear and testify before a grand jury is also firmly established. The duty to testify has long been recognized as a basic obligation that every citizen owes his Government. The duty to testify may on occasion be burdensome and even embarrassing. It may cause injury to a witness' social and economic status. Yet the duty to testify has been regarded as "so necessary to the administration of justice" that the witness' personal interest in privacy must yield to the public's overriding interest in full disclosure. Furthermore, a witness may not interfere with the course of the grand jury's inquiry. He "is not entitled to urge objections of incompetency or irrelevancy, such as a party might raise, for this is no concern of his." Nor is he entitled "to challenge the authority of the court or of the grand jury" or "to set limits to the investigation that the grand jury may conduct."

Of course, the grand jury's subpoena power is not unlimited. It may consider incompetent evidence, but it may not itself violate a valid privilege, whether established by the Constitution, statutes, or the common law. Although, for example, an indictment based on evidence obtained in violation of a defendant's Fifth Amendment privilege is nevertheless valid, the grand jury may not force a witness to answer questions in violation of that constitutional guarantee. Rather, the grand jury may override a Fifth Amendment claim only if the witness is

granted immunity co-extensive with the privilege against self-incrimination. Similarly, a grand jury may not compel a person to produce books and papers that would incriminate him. The grand jury is also without power to invade a legitimate privacy interest protected by the Fourth Amendment. A grand jury's subpoena *duces tecum* will be disallowed if it is "far too sweeping in its terms to be regarded as reasonable" under the Fourth Amendment. Judicial supervision is properly exercised in such cases to prevent the wrong before it occurs.

In the instant case, the Court of Appeals held that the exclusionary rule of the Fourth Amendment limits the grand jury's power to compel a witness to answer questions based on evidence obtained from a prior unlawful search and seizure. The exclusionary rule was adopted to effectuate the Fourth Amendment right of all citizens "to be secure in their persons, houses, papers, and effects, against unreasonable searches and seizures." Under this rule, evidence obtained in violation of the Fourth Amendment cannot be used in a criminal proceeding against the victim of the illegal search and seizure. This prohibition applies as well to the fruits of the illegally seized evidence.

The purpose of the exclusionary rule is not to redress the injury to the privacy of the search victim. Instead, the rule's prime purpose is to deter future unlawful police conduct and thereby effectuate the guarantee of the Fourth Amendment against unreasonable search and seizures. In sum, the rule is a judicially created remedy designed to safeguard Fourth Amendment rights generally through its deterrent effect, rather than a personal constitutional right of the party aggrieved.

Despite its broad deterrent purpose, the exclusionary rule has never been interpreted to proscribe the use of illegally seized evidence in all proceedings or against all persons. As with any remedial device, the application of the rule has been restricted to those areas where its remedial objectives are thought most efficaciously served.

In deciding whether to extend the exclusionary rule to grand jury proceedings, we must weigh the potential injury to the historic role and functions of the grand jury against the potential benefits of the rule as applied in this context. It is evident that this extension of the exclusionary rule would seriously impede the grand jury. Because the grand jury does not finally adjudicate guilt or innocence, it has traditionally been allowed to pursue its investigative and accusatorial functions unimpeded by the evidentiary and procedural restrictions applicable to a criminal trial. Permitting witnesses to invoke the exclusionary rule before a grand jury would precipitate adjudication of issues hitherto reserved for the trial on the merits and would delay and disrupt grand jury proceedings. Suppression hearings would halt the orderly progress of an investigation and might necessitate extended litigation of issues only tangentially related to the grand jury's primary objective. The probable result would be "protracted interruption of grand jury proceedings," effectively transforming them into preliminary trials on the merits. In some cases the delay might be fatal to the enforcement of the criminal law.

[W]e believe that allowing a grand jury witness to invoke the exclusionary rule would unduly interfere with the effective and expeditious discharge of the grand jury's duties. Against this potential damage to the role and functions of the grand jury, we must weigh the benefits to be derived from this proposed extension of the exclusionary rule. Suppression of the use of illegally seized evidence against the search victim in a criminal trial is thought to be an important method of effectuating the Fourth Amendment. But it does not follow that the Fourth Amendment requires adoption of every proposal that might deter police misconduct.

Any incremental deterrent effect which might be achieved by extending the rule to grand jury proceedings is uncertain at best. Whatever deterrence of police misconduct may result from the exclusion of illegally seized evidence from criminal trials, it is unrealistic to assume that application of the rule to grand jury proceedings would significantly further that goal. Such an extension would deter only police investigation consciously directed toward the discovery of evidence solely for use in a grand jury investigation. The incentive to disregard the requirement of the Fourth Amendment solely to obtain an indictment from a grand jury is substantially negated by the inadmissibility of the illegally seized evidence in a subsequent criminal prosecution of the search victim. For the most part, a prosecutor would be unlikely to request an indictment where a conviction could not be obtained. We therefore decline to embrace a view that would achieve a speculative and undoubtedly minimal advance in the deterrence of police misconduct at the expense of substantially impeding the role of the grand jury.

Other Cases: Grand Jury

Branzburg v. Hayes, 408 U.S. 655 (1972).

SUMMARY: The government had subpoena'd Branzburg, a newspaper reporter, to testify at grand jury believing he could identify certain persons he had seen using and selling illicit drugs, during an undercover investigation of the local drug scene. Branzburg, argued he had a newspaper source privilege under the First Amendment and refused to disclose his confidential sources to the grand jury. The Court stated,

> "Grand juries address themselves to the issues of whether crimes have been committed and who committed them. ... [T]he Constitution does not, as it never has, exempt the newsman from performing the citizen's normal duty of appearing and furnishing information relevant to the grand jury's task."

PRELIMINARY HEARINGS

As you have just learned from *Hurtado*, some states, use a preliminary hearing instead of a grand jury. In those cases, the defendant is entitled to a preliminary hearing before a magistrate within a reasonably short time after arrest. These preliminary hearings resemble trials, but their purpose is for a judge to decide whether there is enough evidence to allow the felony case to go forward. If so, the judge will "bind the defendant over for trial." The defendant, through counsel, is entitled to be present at the preliminary hearing and to cross examine the state's witnesses who give testimony at the preliminary hearing. In *Petersen v. California*, 604 F.3d 1166 (9th Cir, May 17, 2010) the court held that the defendant's Sixth Amendment right to confrontation is not violated when the state presents hearsay evidence which the defendant cannot challenge through cross examination during the preliminary hearing. Similarly, *California v. Green, 399 U.S. 149 (1970)* noted that "the inability to cross-examine the witness at the time he made his prior statement …[at preliminary hearing] … cannot easily be shown to be of crucial significance as long as the defendant is assured of full and effective cross-examination at the time of trial."

During a preliminary hearing, the defendant is not entitled to present any evidence. Additionally, the state does not have to present all the evidence it has, but rather needs to show only a *prima facie* (on its face) case that sufficient evidence exists to go forward. The defendant is entitled to have counsel represent him during a preliminary hearing. *Coleman v. Alabama,* 399 U.S. 1 (1970).

PLEA BARGAINING

In the 1970s plea bargaining was controversial. Across the nation prosecutors were making deals with defendants, but the courts had not yet determined whether plea bargaining was constitutionally permissible. Strong sentiments about plea bargaining existed, and as late as the 1980s, attempts to abolish plea bargaining garnered support. Indeed, in 1984-1985 Alaska instituted a ban on plea bargaining. The courts resolved the constitutionality of plea bargaining in cases set out below, and interests in plea bargaining as a field for social science research waned. That said, at the November 2012 American Criminological Society Conference in Chicago, some researchers called for a renewed examination in plea bargaining. They noted the number of cases resolved by plea bargaining (perhaps as high as 95%), the advent of mandatory minimum sentencing schemes that push discretion to the prosecutors, and the advent of specialized courts all warranted a renewed interest in plea bargaining as a research topic.

The following cases examine aspects of plea bargaining and the entry of a guilty plea (either "negotiated pleas," or "straight up pleas"). To accept a guilty plea (negotiated or otherwise), the judge must be satisfied that the defendant is competent to enter the plea and that the plea is voluntary. The judge must determine that the defendant understands the charges and the consequences of entering the plea (generally this means the judge will explain the maximum possible sentence that might be imposed, the minimum sentence that might be imposed, etc). In many states and the federal system, the court must find that there is a factual basis for the plea. The defendant must say something to the effect of "I did the acts I am charged with committing." If the defendant continues to maintain innocence while attempting to enter a guilty plea, the court will not accept the guilty plea. The one exception to this is called an "*Alford* plea."

BORDENKIRCHER v. HAYES
434 U.S. 357 (1978)

Justice Stewart Delivered the opinion of the Court.

The respondent, Paul Lewis Hayes, was indicted by a Fayette County, Ky., grand jury on a charge of uttering a forged instrument in the amount of $88.30, an offense then punishable by a term of two to 10 years in prison ... After arraignment, Hayes, his retained counsel, and the Commonwealth's attorney met in the presence of the clerk of the court to discuss a possible plea agreement. During these conferences the prosecutor offered to recommend a sentence of five years in prison if Hayes would plead guilty to the indictment. He also said that if Hayes did not plead guilty and "save the court the inconvenience of a trial," he would return to the grand jury to seek an indictment under the Kentucky Habitual Criminal Act, which would subject Hayes to a mandatory sentence of life imprisonment by reason of his two prior felony convictions. Hayes chose not to plead guilty, and the prosecutor did obtain an indictment charging him under the Habitual Criminal Act. ...

A jury found Hayes guilty ... and ... [a]s required by the habitual offender statute; he was sentenced to a life term in the penitentiary. ...

...

To punish a person because he has done what the law plainly allows him to do is a due process violation of the most basic sort, and for an agent of the State to pursue a course of action whose objective is to penalize a person's reliance on his legal rights is "patently unconstitutional." But in the "give-and-take" of plea bargaining, there is no such element of punishment or retaliation so long as the accused is free to accept or reject the prosecution's offer.

Plea bargaining flows from "the mutuality of advantage" to defendants and prosecutors, each with his own reasons for wanting to avoid trial. Defendants advised by competent counsel and protected by other procedural safeguards are presumptively capable of intelligent choice in response to prosecutorial persuasion, and unlikely to be driven to false self-condemnation. Indeed, acceptance of the basic legitimacy of plea bargaining necessarily implies rejection of any notion that a guilty plea is involuntary in a constitutional sense simply because it is the end result of the bargaining process. By hypothesis, the plea may have been induced by promises of a recommendation of a lenient sentence or a reduction of charges, and thus by fear of the possibility of a greater penalty upon conviction after a trial.

While confronting a defendant with the risk of more severe punishment clearly may have a "discouraging effect on the defendant's assertion of his trial rights, the imposition of these difficult choices [is] an inevitable — and permissible —attribute of any legitimate system which tolerates and encourages the negotiation of pleas." It follows that, by tolerating and encouraging the negotiation of pleas, this Court has necessarily accepted as constitutionally legitimate the simple reality that the prosecutor's interest at the bargaining table is to persuade the defendant to forego his right to plead not guilty.

In our system, so long as the prosecutor has probable cause to believe that the accused committed an offense defined by statute, the decision whether or not to prosecute, and what charge to file or bring before a grand jury, generally rests entirely in his discretion. Within the limits set by the legislature's constitutionally valid definition of chargeable offenses, "the conscious exercise of some selectivity in enforcement is not in itself a federal constitutional violation" so long as "the selection was [not] deliberately based upon an unjustifiable standard such as race, religion, or other arbitrary classification."

[A] rigid constitutional rule that would prohibit a prosecutor from acting forthrightly in his dealings with the defense could only invite unhealthy subterfuge that would drive the practice of plea bargaining back into the shadows from which it has so recently emerged.

There is no doubt that the breadth of discretion that our country's legal system vests in prosecuting attorneys carries with it the potential for both individual and institutional abuse. And broad though that discretion may be there are undoubtedly constitutional limits upon its exercise. We hold only that the course of conduct engaged in by the prosecutor in this case, which no more than openly presented the defendant with the unpleasant alternatives of foregoing trial or facing charges on which he was plainly subject to prosecution, did not violate the Due Process Clause of the Fourteenth Amendment. Accordingly, the judgment of the Court of Appeals is reversed.

JUSTICE BLACKMUN, with whom JUSTICE BRENNAN and JUSTICE MARSHALL join, dissenting.

Prosecutorial vindictiveness. . . is the fact against which the Due Process Clause ought to protect. I perceive little difference between vindictiveness after what the Court describes as the exercise of a "legal right to attack his original conviction," and vindictiveness in the " 'give-and-take

negotiation common in plea bargaining.' "Prosecutorial vindictiveness in any context is still prosecutorial vindictiveness. The Due Process Clause should protect an accused against it, however it asserts itself.

JUSTICE POWELL, dissenting.

There may be situations in which a prosecutor would be fully justified in seeking a fresh indictment for a more serious offense. The most plausible justification might be that it would have been reasonable and in the public interest initially to have charged the defendant with the greater offense. ...

But this is not such a case. Here, any inquiry into the prosecutor's purpose is made unnecessary by his candid acknowledgment that he threatened to procure and in fact procured the habitual criminal indictment because of respondent's insistence on exercising his constitutional rights.

...

Only in the most exceptional case should a court conclude that the scales of the bargaining are so unevenly balanced as to arouse suspicion. In this case, the prosecutor's actions denied respondent due process because their admitted purpose was to discourage and then to penalize with unique severity his exercise of constitutional rights. Implementation of a strategy calculated solely to deter the exercise of constitutional rights is not a constitutionally permissible exercise of discretion.

BOYKIN v. ALABAMA
395 U.S. 238 (1969)

JUSTICE DOUGLAS delivered the opinion of the Court.

In the spring of 1966, within the period of a fortnight, a series of armed robberies occurred in Mobile, Alabama. The victims, in each case, were local shopkeepers open at night who were forced by a gunman to hand over money. While robbing one grocery store, the assailant fired his gun once, sending a bullet

through a door into the ceiling. A few days earlier in a drugstore, the robber had allowed his gun to discharge in such a way that the bullet, on ricochet from the floor, struck a customer in the leg. Shortly thereafter a local grand jury returned five indictments against petitioner, a 27-year-old Negro, for common-law robbery — an offense punishable in Alabama by death.

Before the matter came to trial, the court determined that petitioner was indigent and appointed counsel to represent him. Three days later, at his arraignment, petitioner pleaded guilty to all five indictments. So far as the record shows, the judge asked no questions of petitioner concerning his plea, and petitioner did not address the court.

A plea of guilty is more than a confession which admits that the accused did various acts; it is itself a conviction; nothing remains but to give judgment and determine punishment. Admissibility of a confession must be based on a "reliable determination on the voluntariness issue which satisfies the constitutional rights of the defendant." The requirement that the prosecution spread on the record the prerequisites of a valid waiver is no constitutional innovation. "The record must show, or there must be an allegation and evidence which show, that an accused was offered counsel but intelligently and understandingly rejected the offer. Anything less is not waiver."

We think that the same standard must be applied to determining whether a guilty plea is voluntarily made. For, as we have said, a plea of guilty is more than an admission of conduct; it is a conviction. Ignorance, incomprehension, coercion, terror, inducements, subtle or blatant threats might be a perfect cover-up of unconstitutionality. The question of an effective waiver of a federal constitutional right in a proceeding is of course governed by federal standards.

Several federal constitutional rights are involved in a waiver that takes place when a plea of guilty is entered in a state criminal trial. First, is the privilege against compulsory self-incrimination guaranteed by the Fifth Amendment and applicable to the States by reason of the Fourteenth. Second, is the right to trial by jury. Third, is the right to confront one's accusers. We cannot presume a waiver of these three important federal rights from a silent record. What is at stake for an accused facing death or imprisonment demands the utmost solicitude of which courts are capable in canvassing the matter with the accused to make sure he has a full understanding of what the plea connotes and of its consequence. When the judge discharges that function, he leaves a record adequate for any review that may be later sought and forestalls the spin-off of collateral proceedings that seek to probe murky memories.

JUSTICE HARLAN, whom JUSTICE BLACK joins, dissenting, omitted.

Other Cases: Plea Bargaining

Missouri v. Frye, 566 U.S. ___ (2012)

SUMMARY: The Court found ineffective assistance of counsel when defendant failed to accept a favorable plea bargain because his attorney failed to communicate the offer to him.

Rothgery v. Gillespie County, 554 U.S. 191, 217 (2008)

JUSTICE ALITO CONCURRING OPINION: [W]e have recognized that certain pretrial events may so prejudice the outcome of the defendant's prosecution, that as a practical matter, the defendant must be represented at those events in order to enjoy genuinely effective assistance at trial." Defendants need the assistance of counsel during plea negotiations.

North Carolina v. Alford, 400 U.S. 25 (1970),

SUMMARY: The defendant was charged with murder and claimed that he did not commit the crime, but he nevertheless wanted to accept the prosecution's offer to allow him to plead guilty in exchange for a life sentence (rather than seeking the death penalty).

The court ruled that Alford's plea (entering a guilty plea while maintaining innocence) was valid because a valid guilty plea requires only a knowing waiver of rights, not an admission of guilt. In those jurisdictions requiring a factual basis be established, the court, in accepting an *Alford* plea, will ask the prosecutor to recite the facts rather than requiring the defendant to "cave" and admit guilt. The court also noted that a "criminal defendant does not have the absolute right under the Constitution to have his guilty plea accepted by the court."

Santobello v New York, 404 U.S. 257 (1971)

SUMMARY: In June 1969 Santobello entered a plea to lesser included charges based on negotiations with the Assistant District Attorney after being indicted in New York. The prosecutor agreed to make not sentence recommendations. During entry of his plea, Santobello represented that his plea was voluntary and that there was a factual basis for them. The judge took the plea and set the matter over for sentencing.

There was then a series of delays, and in September 1969 Santobello had a new attorney, and Santobello moved to withdraw his guilty plea which was denied by the court.

In June 1970 the case was set for sentencing in front of a different judge. Santobello again moved to have his plea withdrawn. This was again denied by the new judge, who then moved on to consider sentencing. The original prosecutor was not present and the new prosecutor—instead of making no recommendation—recommended the maximum one-year sentence and cited several reasons why this new judge should follow that recommendation. Defense counsel objected stating that the State had promised the petitioner as part of the negotiated plea that there would be no recommendation. Defense attorney moved to adjourn so that he could provide the court proof of the first prosecutor's promise. The second prosecutor argued there was nothing in the record to support petitioner's claim of a promise (but in later proceedings the State did not contest that a promise was made.)

"The sentencing judge ended discussion, with the following statement, quoting extensively from the presentence report:

"Mr. Aronstein [Defense Counsel], I am not at all influenced by what the District Attorney says, so that there is no need to adjourn the sentence, and there is no need to have any testimony. It doesn't make a particle of difference what the District Attorney says he will do, or what he doesn't do."

After reviewing on the record the pre-sentence report, the judge imposed the maximum sentence of one year.

OPINION:

Disposition of charges after plea discussions is not only an essential part of the process but a highly desirable part for many reasons. It leads to prompt and largely final disposition of most criminal cases; it avoids much of the corrosive impact of enforced idleness during pretrial confinement for those who are denied release pending trial; it protects the public from those accused persons who are prone to continue criminal conduct even while on pretrial release; and, by shortening the time between charge and disposition, it enhances whatever may be the rehabilitative prospects of the guilty when they are ultimately imprisoned.

However, all of these considerations presuppose fairness in securing agreement between an accused and a prosecutor. It is now clear, for example, that the accused pleading guilty must be counseled, absent a waiver. The sentencing judge must develop, on the record, the factual basis for the plea, as, for example, by having the accused describe the conduct that gave rise to the charge. The plea must, of course, be voluntary and knowing and if it was induced by promises, the essence of those promises must in some way be made known. There is, of course, no absolute right to have a guilty plea accepted. A court may reject a plea in exercise of sound judicial discretion.

This phase of the process of criminal justice, and the adjudicative element inherent in accepting a plea of guilty, must be attended by safeguards to insure the defendant what is reasonably due in the circumstances. Those circumstances will vary, but a constant factor is that when a plea rests in any significant degree on a promise or agreement of the prosecutor, so that it can be said to be part of the inducement or consideration, such promise must be fulfilled.

On this record, petitioner "bargained" and negotiated for a particular plea in order to secure dismissal of more serious charges, but also on Condition that no sentence recommendation would be made by the prosecutor. It is now conceded that the promise to abstain from a recommendation was made, and at this stage the prosecution is not in a good position to argue that its inadvertent breach of agreement is immaterial. The staff lawyers in a prosecutor's office have the burden of "letting the left hand know what the right hand is doing" or has done. That the breach of agreement was inadvertent does not lessen its impact.

We need not reach the question whether the sentencing judge would or would not have been influenced had he known all the details of the negotiations for the plea. He stated that the prosecutor's recommendation did not influence him and we have no reason to doubt that. Nevertheless, we conclude that the interests of justice and appropriate recognition of the duties of the prosecution in relation to promises made in the negotiation of pleas of guilty will be best served by remanding the case to the state courts for further consideration. The ultimate relief to which petitioner is entitled we leave to the discretion of the state court, which is in a better position to decide whether the circumstances of this case require only that there be specific performance of the agreement on the plea, in which case petitioner should be resentenced by a different judge, or whether, in the view of the state court, the circumstances require granting the relief sought by petitioner, i. e., the opportunity to withdraw his plea of guilty. We emphasize that this is in no sense to question the fairness of the sentencing judge; the fault here rests on the prosecutor, not on the sentencing judge.

JUSTICE DOUGLAS, concurring.

I join the opinion of the Court and add only a word. I agree that New York did not keep its "plea bargain" with petitioner and that it is no excuse for the default merely because a member of the prosecutor's staff who was not a party to the "plea bargain" was in charge of the case when it came before the New York court. The staff of the prosecution is a unit and each member must be presumed to know the commitments made by any other member.

This Court has recognized that "unfairly obtained" guilty pleas in the federal courts ought to be vacated. In the course of holding that withdrawn guilty pleas were not admissible in subsequent federal prosecutions, the Court opined:

"[O]n timely application, the court will vacate a plea of guilty shown to have been unfairly obtained or given through ignorance, fear or inadvertence. Such an application does not involve any question of guilt or innocence."

([W]e have) clearly held that a federal prisoner who had pleaded guilty despite his ignorance of and his being uninformed of his right to a lawyer was deprived of that Sixth Amendment right, or if he had been tricked by the prosecutor through misrepresentations into pleading guilty then his due process rights were offended …

JUSTICE MARSHALL, with whom JUSTICE BRENNAN and JUSTICE STEWART join, concurring in part and dissenting in part.

…Petitioner must be permitted to withdraw his guilty plea. This is the relief petitioner requested, and, on the facts set out by the majority, it is a form of relief to which he is entitled.

…

Class v. United States, 583 U.S. ___ (2018)

SUMMARY: Class was indicted for possessing firearms which were locked in his jeep which was parked on U.S. Capitol grounds. He doesn't dispute that he possessed the guns, but alleges the statute for which he was charged violated the Second Amendment and Due Process Clause. He nevertheless, plead guilty. In his plea he indicated his understanding of all the rights he gave up by entering a plea and not going to trial. His plea agreement was silent on the right to challenge on direct appeal the constitutionality of the statute under which he was charged.

Class entered his plea, the judge sentenced him, and then he filed a direct appeal asserting the unconstitutionality of the statute. The Court of Appeals held that Class could not appeal because by pleading guilty, he had waived his constitutional claims. The U.S. Supreme Court accepted review.

OPINION: A guilty plea, by itself, does not bar a federal criminal defendant from challenging the constitutionality of his statute of conviction on direct appeal.

In *Blackledge* v. *Perry*, 417 U. S. 21, the Court recognized that a guilty plea bars some " 'antecedent constitutional violations,' " related to events that " 'occu[r] prior to the entry of the guilty plea.' " However, where the claim implicates "the very power of the State" to prosecute the defendant, a guilty plea cannot by itself bar it. Likewise, in *Menna* v. *New York*, … the Court held that because the defendant's claim was that "the State may not convict [him] no matter how validly his factual guilt is established," his "guilty plea, therefore, [did] not bar the claim." In more recent years, the Court has reaffirmed the *Menna-Blackledge* doctrine's basic teaching that " 'a plea of guilty to a charge does not waive a claim that—judged on its face—the charge is one which the State may not constitutionally prosecute.' " *United States* v. *Broce*.

In this case, Class neither expressly nor implicitly waived his constitutional claims by pleading guilty. As this Court understands them, the claims at issue here do not contradict the terms of the indictment or the written plea agreement and they can be resolved "on the basis of the existing record." Class challenges the Government's power to criminalize his (admitted) conduct and thereby calls into question the Government's power to " 'constitutionally prosecute' " him. A guilty plea does not bar a direct appeal in these circumstances.

Kernan v. Cuero,, 583 U.S. ___ -(2017)

SUMMARY: (This California case involved federal habeas review of a state sentence.) Although the state had agreed to a sentence of just over 14 years, it belatedly discovered that prosecutors miscalculated the defendant's prior criminal history (the defendant had a prior "strike" conviction which elevated the mandatory minimum sentence to 25 year). State then amended the criminal complaint after defendant had already entered a guilty plea. Defendant argued that he was entitled to specific performance (to force the state to follow the deal). The Ninth Circuit Court of Appeals agreed, but the U.S. Supreme Court held that defendant was not entitled to specific performance. Instead, the Court was satisfied that the remedy, allowing the defendant to withdraw his plea, was appropriate, and that specific performance was not required by "clearly established federal law"

PRETRIAL MOTIONS

Discussed below are the several potential pretrial motions the defendant can raise. If the defendant claims of constitutional violations, they must be raised prior to trial or they are deemed waived.

Motions To Suppress Or Exclude Evidence

Illegal search and seizure claims, for example are raised in a motion to suppress. The defendant alleges that the state violated the Fourth Amendment and moves the court to suppress, or exclude, the evidence citing the judicially-created exclusionary rule (discussed in Chapter Five). Defendants also move to exclude pre-trial confessions (discussed in Chapter Six) and pre-trial identification procedures (discussed in Chapter Seven).

Motion For Change Of Venue

Venue is the location of the trial which is generally held where the crime occurred. The defendant can request that the trial be held, and jurors drawn from, another venue. Only a few states allow the prosecution to move for a change of venue, but all states and the federal government allow the defendant to move for a venue change. A defendant waives the right to proper venue by an express statement consenting to be tried in a different judicial district even though the crime has no connections to that district. The right to be tried in a particular venue, is not considered a fundamental right, and the federal government and the states have statutes authorizing a trial court to move the trial from the original district to another district. In determining whether to change venue, the courts consider the feasibility of a fair trial in the place where the crime was committed as well as the desire for a convenient forum. *Skilling v. United States,* 561 U.S. 358 (2010), (discussed more in Chapter Ten) examined the trial court's refusal to allow Enron CEO Jeffy Skilling's change of venue motion and whether the venue resulted in an unfair trial. In *Skilling* the Court refused to find that the pretrial publicity and community prejudice prevented Skilling from receiving a fair trial after the trial court denied Skilling's motion for a change of venue.

Motion For Joinder Or Severance

Motions for joinder or severance of the offenses are frequently filed when there are multiple defendants, or the defendant has several offenses that arise out of the same conduct. Joinder and severance motions are fairly technical and beyond the scope this text (unless they raise due process concerns), but you should be aware of their existence and functions. The prosecution, in seeking the indictment or information has a great deal of latitude in joining cases, defendants, and charges, so motions to join or sever are filed by defendants and not prosecutors. Defendants frequently file motions for joinder or severance when there are multiple defendants or charges as it is generally assumed that defendants are disadvantaged when they face multiple charges or are tried with other defendants. One reason that a court might grant a motion to sever is if it believes the state intends to use one co-defendant's statements against another. See, e.g., *Bruton v. United States*, 391 U.S. 123 (1968) (below), and *Courier v. Virginia*, (below).

Motion For A Speedy Trial

A speedy trial motion is a pretrial motion, but it is discussed in Chapter Ten since it relates to defendant's ability to have a fair trial.

Motion For Discovery

One difference in the practice of civil law and the practice of criminal law is how information is shared or "discovered" by opposing sides. In civil practice, it is common for an attorney to "depose" the other side's witnesses before trial. The opportunity to "take a deposition" (get a preview of what an opposing witness will say) is not available to the criminal defense attorney or prosecutor.[77] Instead, there are rules of discovery, generally set forth by statute or court rules that dictate the sharing of information. There is no general constitutional obligation of the prosecutor to disclose material evidence to the defense, and federal law and states' laws vary tremendously as to what the defense and prosecution must disclose to each other, but it is a two-way street.

The state generally must provide more in discovery to the defendant than the defendant must provide to the state, but it is a common fallacy that the state must turn over everything it has to the defendant. The types of pre-trial disclosure covered by a defendant's motion for discovery include:

➢ Defendant's statements. Nearly all states and the federal government require the prosecution upon request to give the defense copies of prior recorded statements by the defendant.

➢ Scientific reports. The federal government and most states require the prosecution to turn over reports of medical and physical examinations and scientific tests done on behalf of the the prosecution.

➢ Documents and tangible evidence. Generally, the defendant will have at least the right to inspect these, and where feasible, obtain copies.

➢ Witness lists. Many jurisdictions require the prosecution give the defense a list of witnesses (names, dates of birth, addresses) whom the prosecution intends to call at trial; some states require the disclosure of prior written and recorded statements of these witnesses;

---

[77] The preliminary hearing, since it involves sworn statements by state witnesses, may give defense some idea of the evidence the state intends to use at trial, but it is certainly not complete. Nor is the questioning directed by the defense (although there can be cross-examination of those witnesses the prosecutor has questioned).

➢ Police reports. Most jurisdictions do not require the prosecution to turn over police reports — viewing these as work product, however, most prosecutors disclose official police reports but not police officer's notes).

Although the state has no constitutional right to information held by the defense, statutes and court rules give the prosecution some right to discovery. The scope of discovery defendants must provide to the state is generally less broad than what the state must provide to the defendant. The defense may be required to disclose to the prosecution the names and addresses of witnesses it plans to call during the trial, witness statements (some states), and notices of any affirmative defense the defendant plans to call.

Failure to give discovery as required by law or the order of the court in response to a motion to compel discovery can result in dismissals (very rare) or continuances (more frequent) or simply a short postponement of the proceeding to allow the side to review the discovery given (very frequent). Violations of discovery rules can also result in a Brady motion and grounds for collateral attack on the conviction if the violation is discovered after the trial. *Brady v. Maryland*, 373 U.S. 83 (1963).

In *Brady*, defendant admitted participating in the crime but claimed that his companion did the actual killing. Prior to the trial, Brady's lawyer requested that the prosecutor allow him to examine the companion's extrajudicial statements. The prosecutor showed these to Brady's lawyer but withheld the statement in which the companion admitted doing the actual killing. Brady did not find out about the statement until he had been tried and sentenced. On appeal, the Court reversed his conviction saying, "the suppression by the prosecution of evidence favorable to the accused upon request violates due process where the evidence is material either to guilt or to punishment, irrespective of good faith or bad faith of the prosecution."

The *Brady* rule is not without limits. If the prosecution fails to turn over Brady material and the violation is not determined until after trial, the defendant will get a new trial — but only if the non-disclosure is found to have been "material." In 2017 in *Turner et al. v. United States*, 582 U.S. _____ (2017) the Court addressed the *Brady* rule's requirement that the undisclosed evidence be material. It stated,

> "Petitioners and the Government, however, do contest the materiality of the undisclosed Brady information. "[E]vidence is 'material' within the meaning of Brady when there is a reasonable probability that, had the evidence been disclosed, the result of the proceeding would have been different." *Cone v. Bell*, (2009). "A 'reasonable probability' of a different result" is one in which the suppressed evidence "'undermines confidence in the outcome of the trial.'" *Kyles*. In other words, petitioners here are entitled to a new trial only if they "establis[h] the prejudice necessary to satisfy the 'materiality' inquiry." Strickler. Consequently, the issue before us here is legally simple but factually complex. We must examine the trial record, "evaluat[e]" the withheld evidence "in the context of the entire record," *Agurs*, and determine in light of that examination whether "there is a reasonable probability that, had the evidence been disclosed, the result of the proceeding would have been different." *Cone*. Although the *Brady* case itself arose on direct appeal, frequently the defendant does not discover the failure of the state to disclose until after the time period for filing an appeal has lapsed and must raise discovery issues as a collateral attack."

CONNICK v. THOMPSON
563 U.S. 51 (2011)

Justice Thomas delivered the opinion of the Court

[Facts Summarized: Thompson was charged with murder. Witnesses erroneously identified Thompson (due to murder publicity?) for a robbery charge. He was tried for the robbery based on forensic evidence. Prosecutors were aware that blood testing that could show that Thompson was not the robber, but it never turned that evidence over to the defense team, and Thompson was convicted of the robbery. Due to his prior felony conviction, Thompson elected not to testify in his murder trial. He was convicted and sentenced to die. Investigation to support his stay of execution revealed the undisclosed crime lab report in the armed robbery investigation. The blood evidence that proved it was not Thompson lead to a stay of execution, and the court to vacate the robbery conviction.

The Louisiana Court of Appeals reversed his murder conviction concluding that the armed robbery conviction unconstitutionally deprived Thompson of his right to testify in his own defense at the murder trial. Thompson was retried, and acquitted of the murder.]

OPINION:

After his release from prison, Thompson sued petitioner Harry Connick, in his official capacity as the Orleans Parish District Attorney, for damages. Thompson alleged that Connick had failed to train his prosecutors adequately about their duty to produce exculpatory evidence and that the lack of training had caused the nondisclosure in Thompson's robbery case. The jury awarded Thompson $14 million, and the Court of Appeals for the Fifth Circuit affirmed by an evenly divided en banc court. We granted certiorari to decide whether a district attorney's office may be held liable under §1983 for failure to train based on a single Brady violation. We hold that it cannot.

. . .

Thompson's . . . only claim that proceeded to trial was Thompson's claim under §1983 that the district attorney's office had violated Brady by failing to disclose the crime lab report in his armed robbery trial. Thompson alleged liability under two theories: (1) the Brady violation was caused by an unconstitutional policy of the district attorney's office; and (2) the violation was caused by Connick's deliberate indifference to an obvious need to train the prosecutors in his office in order to avoid such constitutional violations.

Before trial, Connick conceded that the failure to produce the crime lab report constituted a Brady violation. Accordingly, the District Court instructed the jury that the "only issue" was whether the nondisclosure was caused by either a policy, practice, or custom of the district attorney's office or a deliberately indifferent failure to train the office's prosecutors.

Although no prosecutor remembered any specific training session regarding Brady prior to 1985, it was undisputed at trial that the prosecutors were familiar with the general Brady requirement that the State disclose to the defense evidence in its possession that is favorable to the accused. Prosecutors testified that office policy was to turn crime lab reports and other scientific evidence over to the defense. They also testified that, after the discovery of the undisclosed crime lab report in 1999, prosecutors disagreed about whether it had to be disclosed under Brady absent knowledge of Thompson's blood type.

…

The Brady violation conceded in this case occurred when one or more of the four prosecutors involved with Thompson's armed robbery prosecution failed to disclose the crime lab report to Thompson's counsel.

…

The role of a prosecutor is to see that justice is done. "It is as much [a prosecutor's] duty to refrain from improper methods calculated to produce a wrongful conviction as it is to use every legitimate means to bring about a just one." By their own admission, the prosecutors who tried Thompson's armed robbery case failed to carry out that responsibility. But the only issue before us is whether Connick, as the policymaker for the district attorney's office, was deliberately indifferent to the need to train the attorneys under his authority.

We conclude that this case does not fall within the narrow range of "single-incident" liability … as a possible exception to the pattern of violations necessary to prove deliberate indifference in §1983 actions alleging failure to train. The District Court should have granted Connick judgment as a matter of law on the failure-to-train claim because Thompson did not prove a pattern of similar violations that would "establish that the 'policy of inaction' [was] the functional equivalent of a decision by the city itself to violate the Constitution."

JUSTICE SCALIA, with whom JUSTICE ALITO joins, concurring.

The withholding of evidence in his case was almost certainly caused not by a failure to give prosecutors specific training, but by miscreant prosecutor Gerry Deegan's willful suppression of evidence he believed to be exculpatory, in an effort to railroad Thompson.

…

JUSTICE GINSBURG, with whom JUSTICE BREYER, JUSTICE SOTOMAYOR, and JUSTICE KAGAN join, dissenting.

In *Brady v. Maryland*, this Court held that due process requires the prosecution to turn over evidence favorable to the accused and material to his guilt or punishment. That obligation, the parties have stipulated, was dishonored in this case; consequently, John Thompson spent 18 years in prison, 14 of them isolated on death row, before the truth came to light: He was innocent of the charge of attempted armed robbery, and his subsequent trial on a murder charge, by prosecutorial design, was fundamentally unfair.

The Court holds that the Orleans Parish District Attorney's Office (District Attorney's Office or Office) cannot be held liable, in a civil rights action under 42 U. S. C. §1983, for the grave injustice Thompson suffered. That is so, the Court tells us, because Thompson has shown only an aberrant Brady violation, not a routine practice of giving short shrift to Brady's requirements. The evidence presented to the jury that awarded compensation to Thompson, however, points distinctly away from the Court's assessment. As the trial record in the §1983 action reveals, the conceded, long-concealed prosecutorial transgressions were neither isolated nor atypical.

From the top down, the evidence showed, members of the District Attorney's Office, including the District Attorney himself, misperceived Brady's compass and therefore inadequately attended to their disclosure obligations. Throughout the pretrial and trial proceedings against Thompson, the team of four engaged in prosecuting him for armed robbery and murder hid from the defense and the court exculpatory information Thompson requested and had a constitutional right to receive. The prosecutors did so despite multiple opportunities, spanning nearly two decades, to set the record straight. Based on the prosecutors' conduct relating to Thompson's trials, a fact trier could reasonably conclude that inattention to Brady was standard operating procedure at the District Attorney's Office.

What happened here, the Court's opinion obscures, was no momentary oversight, no single incident of a lone officer's misconduct. Instead, the evidence demonstrated that misperception and disregard of Brady's disclosure requirements were pervasive in Orleans Parish. That evidence, I would hold, established persistent, deliberately indifferent conduct for which the District Attorney's Office bears responsibility under §1983.

. . . .

Over 20 years ago, we observed that a municipality's failure to provide training may be so egregious that, even without notice of prior constitutional violations, the failure "could properly be characterized as 'deliberate indifference' to constitutional rights . . . .

. . .

...[T]he evidence permitted the jury to reach the following conclusions. First, Connick did not ensure that prosecutors in his Office knew their *Brady* obligations; he neither confirmed their familiarity with *Brady* when he hired them, nor saw to it that training took place on his watch. Second, the need for *Brady* training and monitoring was obvious to Connick. Indeed he so testified. Third, Connick's cavalier approach to his staff's knowledge and observation of *Brady* requirements contributed to a culture of inattention to *Brady* in Orleans Parish.

Connick resisted an effort to hold prosecutors accountable for *Brady* compliance because he felt the effort would "make [his] job more difficult." He never disciplined or fired a single prosecutor for violating *Brady*. The jury was told of this Court's decision in *Kyles* v. *Whitley*, a capital case prosecuted by Connick's Office that garnered attention because it featured "so many instances of the state's failure to disclose exculpatory evidence." When questioned about *Kyles*, Connick told the jury he was satisfied with his Office's practices and saw no need, occasioned by *Kyles*, to make any changes. In both quantity and quality, then, the evidence canvassed here was more than sufficient to warrant a jury determination that Connick and the prosecutors who served under him were not merely negligent regarding *Brady*. Rather, they were deliberately indifferent to what the law requires.

. . .

Brady, this Court has long recognized, is among the most basic safeguards brigading a criminal defendant's fair trial right. Vigilance in superintending prosecutors' attention to *Brady*'s requirement is all the more important for this reason: A *Brady* violation, by its nature, causes suppression of evidence beyond the defendant's capacity to ferret out. Because the absence of the withheld evidence may result in the conviction of an innocent defendant, it is unconscionable not to impose reasonable controls impelling prosecutors to bring the information to light.

…

A District Attorney aware of his office's high turnover rate, who recruits prosecutors fresh out of law school and promotes them rapidly through the ranks, bears responsibility for ensuring that on-the-job training takes place. In short, the buck stops with him. As the Court recognizes, "the duty to produce Brady evidence to the defense" is "[a]mong prosecutors' unique ethical obligations." The evidence in this case presents overwhelming support for the conclusion that the Orleans Parish Office slighted its responsibility to the profession and to the State's system of justice by providing no on-the-job Brady training. Connick was not "entitled to rely on prosecutors' professional training," for Connick himself should have been the principal insurer of that training

Other Cases: Discovery and Brady v. Maryland

Smith v. Cain, 565 U.S. 73 (2012)

SUMMARY: Smith was charged and convicted of killing five people during an armed robbery due to the testimony of only one witness who linked him to the crime. The witness, Boatner, testified at trial that he was socializing at a friend's house when Smith and two other gunmen entered the home, demanded money and drugs, and shortly thereafter began shooting, resulting in the death of five of Boatner's friends. In court Boatner identified Smith as the first gunman to come through the door. He claimed that he had been face to face with Smith during the initial moments of the robbery. No other witnesses and no physical evidence implicated Smith in the crime.

After being convicted, Smith sought postconviction relief in the state courts and obtained files from the police investigation of his case, including those of the lead investigator, Detective Ronquillo.

OPINION: Detective Ronquillo's notes contain statements by Boatner that conflict with his testimony identifying Smith as a perpetrator. The notes from the night of the murder state that Boatner "could not . . . supply a description of the perpetrators other then [sic] they were black males." Ronquillo also made a handwritten account of a conversation he had with Boatner five days after the crime, in which Boatner said he "could not ID anyone because [he] couldn't see faces" and "would not know them if [he] saw them." And Ronquillo's typewritten report of that conversation states that Boatner told Ronquillo he "could not identify any of the perpetrators of the murder."

Smith requested that his conviction be vacated, arguing ... that the prosecution's failure to disclose Ronquillo's notes violated this Court's decision in *Brady v. Maryland*. . . .

Under *Brady*, the State violates a defendant's right to due process if it withholds evidence that is favorable to the defense and material to the defendant's guilt or punishment. The State does not dispute that Boatner's statements in

Ronquillo's notes were favorable to Smith and that those statements were not disclosed to him. The sole question before us is thus whether Boatner's statements were material to the determination of Smith's guilt. We have explained that "evidence is 'material' within the meaning of Brady when there is a reasonable probability that, had the evidence been disclosed, the result of the proceeding would have been different." A reasonable probability does not mean that the defendant "would more likely than not have received a different verdict with the evidence," only that the likelihood of a different result is great enough to "undermine[] confidence in the outcome of the trial."

We have observed that evidence impeaching an eyewitness may not be material if the State's other evidence is strong enough to sustain confidence in the verdict. That is not the case here. Boatner's testimony was the only evidence linking Smith to the crime. And Boatner's undisclosed statements directly contradict his testimony: Boatner told the jury that he had "[n]o doubt" that Smith was the gunman he stood "face to face" with on the night of the crime, but Ronquillo's notes show Boatner saying that he "could not ID anyone because [he] couldn't see faces" and "would not know them if [he] saw them." Boatner's undisclosed statements were plainly material ...

.

FILING A DEMURRER

Defendants may also attack the charging document (either an information or an indictment) by filing a demurrer. Demurrers challenge the constitutionality of the statute the defendant is charged with violating. These challenges include void for vagueness, void for overbreadth, and freedom of speech (discussed in Chapter Two).

CLAIMING IMMUNITY

The defendant may raise issues of immunity at pre-trial. Issues of immunity often surround a witness's grand jury testimony, or whether they will be called at trial.

"There are many situations in which the government grants immunity to a witness or a codefendant in return for his or her testimony. Immunity in criminal cases means that the person granted immunity will not be prosecuted in a criminal case, either fully or partially — depending on what type of immunity is granted — for testimony given before a grand jury, in court, or in some other proceeding from which prosecution could otherwise have resulted. Immunity is usually given when the testimony of the witness is crucial to proving the government's case or when the government needs further information for investigative purposes, particularly in cases involving organized crime." Del Carmen, R., Criminal Procedure: Law and Practice (2007), 476.

The two types of immunity are transactional immunity (a broader grant of immunity protecting the witness from prosecution for any offense arising out of the act or transaction they testified about) or use immunity (a narrower form of immunity protecting the witness only from a prosecution wherein their testimony and evidence derived from it are used against them). *Kastigar v. United States*, 406 U.S. 441 (1972) held that prosecutors only have to grant use immunity to compel an unwilling witness to testify.

RAISING A CLAIM OF DOUBLE JEOPARDY

Under certain circumstances, the defendant may raise a claim of double jeopardy. Double jeopardy issues are generally raised in pre-trial motions to dismiss. The protection against double jeopardy is found in the Fifth Amendment and has been held to be applicable to the states. *Benton v. Maryland*, 395 U.S. 784 (1969). The protection against double jeopardy raises several questions including:

> ➢ what does "double jeopardy" mean and when does it apply

> ➢ when does it "attach" or start

> ➢ what is meant by "same offense" and does that include lesser included offenses, and

> ➢ when is it waived.

What Double Jeopardy Means

Double jeopardy is the successive (repeated) prosecution of a defendant for the same offense by the same jurisdiction. The Fifth Amendment and state double jeopardy provisions protect defendants against a second prosecution for the same offense after acquittal, and also protects defendants against multiple punishments for the same offense. See, *North Carolina v. Pearce*, 395 U.S. 711 (1969). The constitutional prohibition against double jeopardy has many limitations: the double jeopardy prohibition stops one jurisdiction from repeatedly trying an offender for the same crime, but it does not prevent a person from being sued for civil damages after being convicted or acquitted; the double jeopardy prohibition does not stop prosecution of cases that are not the "same offense" (if the elements of the crimes differ, there is no double jeopardy prohibition); and, conviction or acquittal by one jurisdiction does not bar a prosecution in another jurisdiction (the federal government can prosecute the defendant for the same offense the defendant was already convicted of in state court; one state can prosecute defendant after another state has already prosecuted, and under *United States v. Lara*, 541 U.S. 193 (2004) the federal government can prosecute a defendant who has been tried in a sovereign Indian court).

When Double Jeopardy "Attaches"

Double jeopardy "attaches" or starts when the jury is sworn in a jury trial, or when the first witness has given the testimonial oath (being sworn in) during a bench trial. In 2005 the Court held that double jeopardy prohibited the trial judge from reconsidering his earlier decision to acquit the defendant on one during the course of the trial after hearing further evidence on other charges because the double jeopardy protection had already attached. *Smith v. Massachusettes*, 543 U.S. 462 (2005).

The "Same Offense"

Double jeopardy only applies to prosecutions for the "same offense." The key case on what qualifies as "the same offense" is *Blockburger v. United States*, 284 U.S. 299 (1932). *Blockburger* indicates that double jeopardy bars two prosecutions for crimes which have identical statutory elements or when crime is a lesser included offense of the other. "Lesser included offense" is defined as an offense that is "composed of some, but not all, of the elements of the greater crime, and which does not have any element not included in the greater offense."

Brown v. Ohio, 432 U.S. 161 (1977) provides a good example of what the court means by same offense or lesser included offense. On November 29th Brown stole a car from the parking lot of one Ohio county, and he was arrested on December 8th for driving the car in another county. Brown was charged with having "joy ridden" on December 8th, and he plead guilty. Brown was then prosecuted for auto theft and joy riding for taking the car on the 29th of November. The Court held that the Double Jeopardy Clause prohibits Brown from being prosecuted for the auto theft and joy riding because auto theft consists of joy riding plus the intent to permanently deprive the owner of possession. Since the initial guilty plea to joy riding was an offense all of whose elements were contained within the later auto theft charge, the subsequent prosecution for auto theft was the "same offense" and thus barred.

Defendants have raised the issue of whether the Double Jeopardy Clause bars their prosecution under three strikes type of sentencing. (See, California's three strikes mandatory minimum sentencing scheme). They have argued that their sentence for their current crime is longer because of their past conviction — so, in effect, they are being punished a second time for the earlier crime. The Court does not agree, finding that persistent offender statutes do not violate Double Jeopardy. "An enhanced sentence imposed on a persistent offender … 'is not to be viewed as either a new jeopardy or additional penalty for the earlier crimes' but as a 'stiffened penalty for the latest crime which is considered to be an aggravated offense because a repetitive one.'" *Monge v. California*, 524 U.S. 721 (1998)

CURRIER v. VIRGINIA
585 U.S. ___ (2018)

JUSTICE GORSUCH delivered the opinion of the Court …

[Facts Summarized: Michael Courier and his friend stole a safe with money and guns from the friend's uncle. He was charged with burglary, grand larceny, and unlawful possession of a weapon by a convicted felon. Wanting to avoid possible prejudice the jury might have in hearing he had a previous felony conviction, Courier requested the trial on the burglary and larceny charges be separated from the trial on the weapons charge. The court agreed, and defendant was acquitted on the burglary and larceny charges. Courier then claimed the State was prohibited from trying him on the weapons charge as it would be a violation of the double jeopardy protections found in the Fifth Amendment. He claimed that prior Court precedent in *Ashe v. Swenson* (a case where the defendant was tried for each separate robbery victim in a separate trial) controlled. In Ashe, the Court

suggested that any relitigation of the issue whether the defendant participated as "one of the robbers" would be tantamount to the forbidden relitigation of the same offense resolved at the first trial. Court noted that *Ashe* forbids a second trial only if to secure a conviction the prosecution must prevail on an issue the jury necessarily resolved in the defendant's favor in the first trial.

The question before the court was whether a defendant who agrees to have the charges against him considered in two trials, can later successfully argue that the second trial offends the Fifth Amendment's Double Jeopardy Clause?]

Opinion:

The Double Jeopardy Clause, applied to the States through the Fourteenth Amendment, provides that no person may be tried more than once "for the same offence." This guarantee recognizes the vast power of the sovereign, the ordeal of a criminal trial, and the injustice our criminal justice system would invite if prosecutors could treat trials as dress rehearsals until they secure the convictions they seek. At the same time, this Court has said, the Clause was not written or originally understood to pose "an insuperable obstacle to the administration of justice" in cases where "there is no semblance of [these] type[s] of oppressive practices."

…

Bearing all that in mind, a critical difference immediately emerges between our case and *Ashe*. Even assuming without deciding that Mr. Currier's second trial qualified as the retrial of the same offense under *Ashe*, he consented to it. Nor does anyone doubt that trying all three charges in one trial would have prevented any possible *Ashe* complaint Mr. Currier might have had.

How do these features affect the double jeopardy calculus? A precedent points the way. In *Jeffers* v. *United States* . . . (1977), the defendant sought separate trials on each of the counts against him to reduce the possibility of prejudice. The court granted his request. After the jury convicted the defendant in the first trial of a lesser-included offense, he argued that the prosecution could not later try him for a greater offense. In any other circumstance the defendant likely would have had a good argument. Historically, courts have treated greater and lesser-included offenses as the same offense for double jeopardy purposes, so a conviction on one normally precludes a later trial on the other. But, *Jeffers* concluded, it's different when the defendant consents to two trials where one could have done. If a single trial on multiple charges would suffice to avoid a double jeopardy complaint, "there is no violation of the Double Jeopardy Clause when [the defendant] elects to have the . . . offenses tried separately and persuades the trial court to honor his election."

What was true in *Jeffers*, we hold, can be no less true here. If a defendant's consent to two trials can overcome concerns lying at the historic core of the Double Jeopardy Clause,

so too we think it must overcome a double jeopardy complaint under *Ashe*. Nor does anything in *Jeffers* suggest that the outcome should be different if the first trial yielded an acquittal rather than a conviction when a defendant consents to severance. While we acknowledge that *Ashe*'s protections apply only to trials following acquittals, as a general rule, the Double Jeopardy Clause " 'protects against a second prosecution for the same offense after conviction' " as well as " 'against a second prosecution for the same offense after acquittal.' " Because the Clause applies equally in both situations, consent to a second trial should in general have equal effect in both situations.

…

Mr. Currier replies that he had no real choice but to seek two trials. Without a second trial, he says, evidence of his prior convictions would have tainted the jury's consideration of the burglary and larceny charges… [But] this simply isn't a case where the defendant had to give up one constitutional right to secure another. Instead, Mr. Currier faced a lawful choice between two courses of action that each bore potential costs and rationally attractive benefits. It might have been a hard choice. But litigants every day face difficult decisions. …

III

… Mr. Currier's problems begin with the text of the Double Jeopardy Clause. …

…The Double Jeopardy Clause took its cue from English common law pleas that prevented courts from retrying a criminal defendant previously acquitted or convicted of the crime in question. … But those pleas barred only repeated "prosecution for the same identical act *and* crime," not the retrial of particular issues or evidence

…

This Court's contemporary double jeopardy cases confirm what the text and history suggest. Under *Blockburger* v. *United States*, 284 U. S. 299 (1932), the courts apply today much the same double jeopardy test they did at the founding. To prevent a second trial on a new charge, the defendant must show an identity of *statutory elements* between the two charges against him; it's not enough that "a substantial overlap [exists] in the *proof* offered to establish the crimes." Of course, *Ashe* later pressed *Blockburger*'s boundaries by suggesting that, in narrow circumstances, the retrial of an issue can be considered tantamount to the retrial of an offense. But, as we've seen, even there a court's ultimate focus remains on the practical identity of offenses, and the only available remedy is the traditional double jeopardy bar against the retrial of the same offense—not a bar against the relitigation of issues or evidence. Even at the outer reaches of our double jeopardy jurisprudence, then, this Court has never sought to regulate the retrial of issues or evidence in the name of the Double Jeopardy Clause.

Mistrials

Double jeopardy protections are waived under certain circumstances. First, the defendant waives double jeopardy protections if he or she moves for, or consents to, a mistrial during the initial trial—even if the motion for mistrial is based on prosecutorial misconduct. Additionally, when the defendant did not consent to a mistrial, courts have invoked the doctrine of manifest necessity holding that re-prosecution is not barred. Manifest necessity is a vague concept, but generally, the court will declare manifest necessity when a jury cannot reach a verdict (a hung jury) requiring the court to declare a mistrial.

In *Blueford v. Arkansas,* 566 U.S. 599 (2012), the Court considered the Double Jeopardy Clause in Arkansas an "acquittal first" jurisdiction -- one which dictates how the jury is to decide multiple lesser-included charges -- Justice Sotomayor wrote about manifest necessity in her dissent. She stated,

> [M]anifest necessity" is a high bar: "[T]he power ought to be used with the greatest caution, under urgent circumstances, and for very plain and obvious causes." . . . Before declaring a mistrial, therefore, a trial judge must weigh heavily a "defendant's valued right to have his trial completed by a particular tribunal." And in light of the historical abuses against which the Double Jeopardy Clause guards, a trial judge must tread with special care where a mistrial would "help the prosecution, at a trial in which its case is going badly, by affording it another, more favorable opportunity to convict the accused.

> A jury's genuine inability to reach a verdict constitutes manifest necessity. But in an acquittal-first jurisdiction, a jury that advances to the consideration of a lesser included offense has not demonstrated an inability to decide a defendant's guilt or innocence on a greater — it has acquitted on the greater. ...

> ...[T]he facts of this case confirm that there was no necessity, let alone manifest necessity, for a mistrial. There was no reason for the judge not to have asked the jury, prior to discharge, whether it remained "unanimous against" conviction on capital and first-degree murder. There would have been no intrusion on the jury's deliberative process. . . . Because the judge failed to take even this modest step — or indeed, to explore any alternatives to a mistrial, or even to make an on-the-record finding of manifest necessity — I conclude that there was an abuse of discretion.

Renico v. Lett, 559 U.S. 766 (2010)

SUMMARY: The Court held it was reasonable for the Michigan Supreme Court to determine that the trial judge had exercised sound discretion in declaring a mistrial. The case, a first-degree murder prosecution, took only 9 hours for the entire trial (from jury selection through jury instruction). After 4 hours of deliberation, the court received a note that questioned what would happen if the jurors could not agree. Based on that note, the judge declared a mistrial. The defendant argued that the judge had declared a mistrial without manifest necessity.

"Trial judges may declare a mistrial when "in their opinion, taking all the circumstances into consideration, there is a manifest necessity for doing so. ... i.e., a high degree of necessity. ... 'The decision to declare a mistrial is left to the sound discretion' of the judge, but 'the power ought to be used with the greatest caution, under urgent circumstances, and for plain and obvious cases.' ..."

The Court reiterated the importance of granting deference to the trial judge as long as discretion was sound. The Court noted that there "is not a rigid formula to determining when declaring a mistrial is appropriate. Nor must the judge make explicit findings concerning manifest necessity to do so.

Appealing Convictions

Courts will also find that double jeopardy is waived when defendants appeal their convictions or ask for the conviction to be set aside. By appealing or asking for review, the defendant implicitly waives his or her right to protection against double jeopardy. For example, in *Miranda*), Ernesto Miranda's conviction was reversed because the Court held that his confession was obtained in violation of the right against self-incrimination and right to consult with an attorney before being interrogated while he was in custody. Arizona tried him again (under an assumed name) and he was again convicted—this time on evidence that did not include his illegally obtained confession. There was no double jeopardy because, by appealing his conviction, he waived his right to be free from double jeopardy.

Writs Of Habeas Corpus

Defendants who file petitions for writs of habeas corpus (see, Chapter One) to challenge conditions of confinement can be retried if their habeas corpus petition is successful. The Court's holdings that a defendant may be re-prosecuted if the verdict is set aside on appeal or through a writ of habeas corpus has important exceptions. If the appellate court reverses the defendant's convictions finding the evidence at trial was insufficient to support a conviction, then re-prosecution is not allowed. Additionally, the Double Jeopardy Clause may limit the sentence that can be imposed after a retrial. For example, the Court held that the constitution requires the state award the defendant credit for the time served under the first charge before it was overturned. *North Carolina v. Pearce*, 395 U.S. 711 (1969). The judge hearing the second trial may, nevertheless, impose a longer sentence than was imposed upon the first conviction. "A corollary of the power to retry a defendant is the power, upon the defendant's reconviction, is to impose whatever sentence may be legally authorized, whether or not it is greater than the sentence imposed after the first conviction." *North Carolina v. Pearce*. If, however, the jury in the defendant's first trial voted against the death penalty, the Double Jeopardy Clause bars the court from sentencing the defendant to death upon conviction on retrial. *Bullington v. Missouri, 451 U.S. 430 (1981).*

Chapter Nine: The Right To Counsel

This chapter examines the development and expansion of the right to counsel. This chapter discusses the right to counsel that flows from the Sixth Amendment. The Sixth Amendment states, "In all criminal prosecutions, the accused shall enjoy. . . the right to have the Assistance of Counsel for his defense."

Originally, what the drafters of the Bill of Rights had in mind was that people tried in federal court who could (afford to) hire an attorney, could have the attorney's assistance during their trial. Since 1791, the right to counsel has been interpreted to mean much more than just the right to hire an attorney. As you read in *Wade* and *Gilbert* (above), the right to counsel attaches to all "critical stages" of the criminal justice process, thus it begins during the investigative phase, continues through accusatory/pre-trial and adjudicatory/trial phase, and continues in some post-adjudication hearings (some appeals, some collateral attacks, and parole and probation violation hearings).

THE RIGHT TO COUNSEL IN STATE PROSECUTIONS

In *Powell v. Alabama,* 287 U.S. 45 (1932), the Court examined whether defendants, charged with crimes for which the state sought the death penalty, were entitled to the assistance of counsel at trial because of fundamental fairness guarantees implicit in the Due Process Clause. In *Gideon v. Wainwright* 372 U.S. 33 (1963), the Court, overturning an earlier case (*Betts v. Bradey*, 316 U.S. 455 (1942), held that when the defendant is charged with a felony in state court, he was entitled to the assistance of counsel. In *Argersinger v. Hamlin,* 407 U.S. 23 (1972) and *Scott v. Illinois, 440 U.S. 367 (1979)* the Court examined the extent of defendant's right to assistance of counsel when charged with a misdemeanor crime.

POWELL v. ALABAMA
287 U.S. 45 (1932)

JUSTICE SUTHERLAND delivered the opinion of the Court.

The record shows that on the day when the offense is said to have been committed, these defendants, together with a number of other negroes, were upon a freight train on its way through Alabama. On the same train were seven white boys and two white girls. A fight took place between the negroes and the white boys, in the course of which the white boys, with the exception of one named Gilley, were thrown off the train. A message was sent ahead, reporting the fight and asking that every negro be gotten off the train. The participants in the fight, and the two girls, were in an open gondola car. The two girls testified that each of them was assaulted by six different negroes in turn, and they identified

the seven defendants as having been among the number. None of the white boys was called to testify, with the exception of Gilley, who was called in rebuttal.

Before the train reached Scottsboro, Alabama, a sheriff's posse seized the defendants and two other negroes. Both girls and the negroes then were taken to Scottsboro, the county seat. Word of their coming and of the alleged assault had preceded them, and they were met at Scottsboro by a large crowd. It does not sufficiently appear that the defendants were seriously threatened with, or that they were actually in danger of, mob violence; but it does appear that the attitude of the community was one of great hostility. The sheriff thought it necessary to call for the militia to assist in safeguarding the prisoners. Chief Justice

Anderson pointed out in his opinion that every step taken from the arrest and arraignment to the sentence was accompanied by the military. Soldiers took the defendants to Gadsden for safekeeping, brought them back to Scottsboro for arraignment, returned them to Gadsden for safekeeping while awaiting trial, escorted them to Scottsboro for trial a few days later, and guarded the courthouse and grounds at every stage of the proceedings. It is perfectly apparent that the proceedings, from beginning to end, took place in an atmosphere of tense, hostile and excited public sentiment. During the entire time, the defendants were closely confined or were under military guard. The record does not disclose their ages, except that one of them was nineteen; but the record clearly indicates that most, if not all, of them were youthful, and they are constantly referred to as "the boys." They were ignorant and illiterate. All of them were residents of other states, where alone members of their families or friends resided.

However guilty defendants, upon due inquiry might prove to have been, they were, until convicted, presumed to be innocent. It was the duty of the court having their cases in charge to see that they were denied no necessary incident of a fair trial. With any error of the state court involving alleged contravention of the state statutes or constitution we, of course, have nothing to do. The sole inquiry which we are permitted to make is whether the federal Constitution was contravened and as to that, we confine ourselves, as already suggested, to the inquiry whether the defendants were in substance denied the right to counsel, and if so, whether such denial infringes the Due Process Clause of the Fourteenth Amendment.

First. The record shows that immediately upon the return of the indictment defendants were arraigned and pleaded not guilty. Apparently they were not asked whether they had, or were able to employ, counsel, or wished to have counsel appointed; or whether they had friends or relatives who might assist in that regard if communicated with. It is hardly necessary to say that the right to counsel being conceded, a defendant should be afforded a fair

opportunity to secure counsel of his own choice. Not only was that not done here, but such designation of counsel as was attempted was either so indefinite or so close upon the trial as to amount to a denial of effective and substantial aid in that regard. This will be amply demonstrated by a brief review of the record.

On April 6, six days after indictment, the trial began. When the first case was called, the court inquired whether the parties were ready for trial. The state's attorney replied that he was ready to proceed. No one answered for the defendants or appeared to represent or defend them. Mr. Roddy, a Tennessee lawyer, not a member of the local bar, addressed the court, saying that he had not been employed, but that people who were interested had spoken to him about the case. He was asked by the court whether he intended to appear for the defendants, and answered that he would like to appear along with counsel that the court might appoint. The record then proceeds:

> The Court: If you appear for these defendants, then I will not appoint counsel: if local counsel are willing to appear and assist you under the circumstances all right, but I will not appoint them.
>
> Mr. Roddy: Your Honor has appointed counsel, is that correct?
>
> The Court: I appointed all the members of the bar for the purpose of arraigning the defendants and then of course I anticipated them to continue to help them if no counsel appears.
>
> Mr. Roddy: Then I don't appear then as counsel but I do want to stay in and not be ruled out in this case.
>
> The Court: Of course I would not do that —
>
> Mr. Roddy: I just appear here through the courtesy of Your Honor.
>
> The Court: Of course I give you that right;

[T]his action of the trial judge in respect of appointment of counsel was little more than an expansive gesture, imposing no substantial or definite obligation upon any one during perhaps the most critical period of the proceedings against these defendants, that is to say, from the time of their arraignment until the beginning of their trial, when consultation, thorough-going investigation and preparation were vitally important, the defendants did not have the aid of counsel in any real sense, although they were as much entitled to such aid during that period as at the trial itself.

Nor do we think the situation was helped by what occurred on the morning of the trial. At that time, as appears from the colloquy printed above, Mr. Roddy stated to the court that he did not appear as counsel, but that he would like to appear along with counsel that the court might appoint; that he had not been given an opportunity to prepare the case; that he was not familiar with the procedure in Alabama, but merely came down as a friend of the people who were interested; that he thought the boys would be better off if he should step entirely out of the case. Mr. Moody, a member of the local bar, expressed a willingness to help Mr. Roddy in anything he would do under the circumstances. To this the court responded, "All right, all the lawyers that will; of course I would not require a lawyer to appear if —." And Mr. Moody continued, "I am willing to do that for him as a member of the bar; I will go ahead and help do anything I can do." With this dubious understanding, the trials immediately proceeded. The defendants, young, ignorant, illiterate, surrounded by hostile sentiment, haled back and forth under guard of soldiers, charged with an atrocious crime regarded with especial horror in the community where they were to be tried, were thus put in peril of their lives within a few moments after counsel for the first time charged with any degree of responsibility began to represent them.

It is not enough to assume that counsel thus precipitated into the case thought there was no defense, and exercised their best judgment in proceeding to trial without preparation.

Neither they nor the court could say what a prompt and thorough-going investigation might disclose as to the facts. No attempt was made to investigate. No opportunity to do so was given. Defendants were immediately hurried to trial. Chief Justice Anderson, after disclaiming any intention to criticize harshly counsel who attempted to represent defendants at the trials, said: "The record indicates that the appearance was rather *pro forma* than zealous and active." Under the circumstances disclosed, we hold that defendants were not accorded the right of counsel in any substantial sense. To decide otherwise, would simply be to ignore actualities.

The prompt disposition of criminal cases is to be commended and encouraged. But in reaching that result a defendant, charged with a serious crime, must not be stripped of his right to have sufficient time to advise with counsel and prepare his defense. To do that is not to proceed promptly in the calm spirit of regulated justice but to go forward with the haste of the mob.

Second. The Constitution of Alabama provides that in all criminal prosecutions the accused shall enjoy the right to have the assistance of counsel; and a state statute requires the court in a capital case, where the defendant is unable to employ counsel, to appoint counsel for him. The state supreme court held that these provisions had not been infringed.

…

… But how can a judge, whose functions are purely judicial, effectively discharge the obligations of counsel for the accused? He can and should see to it that in the proceedings before the court the accused shall be dealt with justly and fairly. He cannot investigate the facts, advise and direct the defense, or participate in those necessary conferences between counsel and accused which sometimes partake of the inviolable character of the confessional.

In light of the facts outlined in the forepart of this opinion — the ignorance and illiteracy of the defendants, their youth, the circumstances of public hostility, the imprisonment and the close surveillance of the defendants by the military forces, the fact that their friends and families were all in other states and communication with them necessarily difficult, and above all that they stood in deadly peril of their lives — we think the failure of the trial court to give them reasonable time and opportunity to secure counsel was a clear denial of due process.

But passing that, and assuming their inability, even if opportunity had been given, to employ counsel, as the trial court evidently did assume, we are of opinion that, under the circumstances just stated, the necessity of counsel was so vital and imperative that the failure of the trial court to make an effective appointment of counsel was likewise a denial of due process within the meaning of the Fourteenth Amendment. Whether this would be so in other criminal prosecutions, or under other circumstances, we need not determine. All that it is necessary now to decide, as we do decide, is that in a capital case, where the defendant is unable to employ counsel, and is incapable adequately of making his own defense because of ignorance, feeble-mindedness, illiteracy, or the like, it is the duty of the court, whether requested or not, to assign counsel for him as a necessary requisite of due process of law; and that duty is not discharged by an assignment at such a time or under such circumstances as to preclude the giving of effective aid in the preparation and trial of the case. To hold otherwise would be to ignore the fundamental postulate, already adverted to, "that there are certain immutable principles of justice which inhere in the very idea of free government which no member of the Union may disregard." In a case such as this, whatever may be the rule in other cases, the right to have counsel appointed, when necessary, is a logical corollary from the constitutional right to be heard by counsel.

The judgments must be reversed and the causes remanded for further proceedings not inconsistent with this opinion.

JUSTICE BUTLER, dissenting, omitted

GIDEON v. WAINWRIGHT
372 U.S. 33 (1963)

JUSTICE BLACK delivered the opinion of the Court.

Petitioner was charged in a Florida state court with having broken and entered a poolroom with intent to commit a misdemeanor. This offense is a felony under Florida law. Appearing in court without funds and without a lawyer, petitioner asked the court to appoint counsel for him, whereupon the following colloquy took place:

The Court: Mr. Gideon, I am sorry, but I cannot appoint Counsel to represent you in this case. Under the laws of the State of Florida, the only time the Court can appoint Counsel to represent a Defendant is when that person is charged with a capital offense. I am sorry, but I will have to deny your request to appoint Counsel to defend you in this case.

The Defendant: The United States Supreme Court says I am entitled to be represented by Counsel.

Put to trial before a jury, *Gideon* conducted his defense about as well as could be expected from a layman. He made an opening statement to the jury, cross-examined the State's witnesses, presented witnesses in his own defense, declined to testify himself, and made a short argument "emphasizing his innocence to the charge contained in the Information filed in this case." The jury returned a verdict of guilty, the petitioner was sentenced to serve five years in the state prison. Later, petitioner filed in the Florida Supreme Court this habeas corpus petition attacking his conviction and sentence on the ground that the trial court's refusal to appoint counsel for him denied him rights "guaranteed by the Constitution and the Bill of Rights by the United States

Government." Treating the petition for habeas corpus as properly before it, the State Supreme Court, "upon consideration thereof" but without an opinion, denied all relief. Since 1942, when *Betts v. Brady,* was decided by a divided Court, the problem of a defendant's federal constitutional right to counsel in a state court has been a continuing source of controversy and litigation in both state and federal courts. To give this problem another review here, we granted certiorari. Since *Gideon* was proceeding *in forma pauperis,* we appointed counsel to represent him and requested both sides to discuss in their briefs and oral arguments the following: "Should this Court's holding in *Betts v. Brady* be reconsidered?"

Since the facts and circumstances of the two cases are so nearly indistinguishable, we think the *Betts v. Brady* holding if left standing would require us to reject Gideon's claim that the Constitution guarantees him the assistance of counsel. Upon full reconsideration we conclude that *Betts v. Brady* should be overruled. The facts upon which Betts claimed that he had been unconstitutionally denied the right to have counsel appointed to assist him are strikingly like the facts upon which *Gideon* here bases his federal constitutional claim.

. . . .

We think the Court in *Betts* had ample precedent for acknowledging that those guarantees of the Bill of Rights which are fundamental safeguards of liberty immune from federal abridgment are equally protected against state invasion by the Due Process Clause of the Fourteenth Amendment. This same principle was recognized, explained, and applied in *Powell v. Alabama,* a case upholding the right of counsel, where the Court held that … the Fourteenth Amendment "embraced" those " 'fundamental principles of liberty and justice which lie at the base of all our civil and political institutions,' " even though they had been "specifically dealt with in another part of the federal Constitution." …

… The fact is that in deciding as it did — that "appointment of counsel is not a fundamental right, essential to a fair trial" the Court in *Betts v. Brady* made an abrupt break with its own well-considered precedents. In returning to these old precedents, sounder we believe than the new, we but restore constitutional principles established to achieve a fair system of justice. Not only these precedents but also reason and reflection require us to recognize that in our adversary system of criminal justice, any person haled into court, who is too poor to hire a lawyer, cannot be assured a fair trial unless counsel is provided for him. This seems to us to be an obvious truth. Governments, both state and federal, quite properly spend vast sums of money to establish machinery to try defendants accused of crime. Lawyers to prosecute are everywhere deemed essential to protect the public's interest in an orderly society. Similarly, there are few defendants charged with crime, few indeed, who fail to hire the best lawyers they can get to prepare and present their defenses. That government hires lawyers to prosecute and defendants who have the money hire lawyers to defend are the strongest indications of the widespread belief that lawyers in criminal courts are necessities, not luxuries. The right of one charged with crime to counsel may not be deemed fundamental and essential to fair trials in some countries, but it is in ours. From the very beginning, our state and national constitutions and laws have laid great emphasis on procedural and substantive safeguards designed to assure fair trials before impartial tribunals in which every defendant stands equal before the law. This noble ideal cannot be realized if the poor man charged with crime has to face his accusers without a lawyer to assist him.

Twenty-two States, as friends of the Court, argue that *Betts* was "an anachronism when handed down" and that it should now be overruled. We agree.

State Misdemeanor Trials

In *Argersinger v. Hamlin*, 407 U.S. 23 (1972), the Court noted that the Sixth Amendment did not distinguish between felonies and misdemeanors, nor was there any historical precedent for doing so. It rejected the state's argument that the shorter penalties meant that counsel wasn't needed, finding that some misdemeanor trials "bristle with thorny constitutional questions." The Court recognized that difficult questions of legal tactics are also in play during misdemeanor cases. Argersinger had been sentenced to jail, and the Court held the state should have appointed counsel for him, so still unresolved was whether the right to the assistance of counsel applied in situations where the defendant was tried for a misdemeanor but would not receive or did not receive jail.

The Court decided this issue in *Scott v. Illinois*, 440 U.S. 367 (1979). Scott was convicted of theft after a bench trial and was sentenced to a $50.00 fine. The Illinois statute provided a maximum punishment of $500.00 and up to one year jail. Scott appealed his conviction, relying on the Court's statement in *Argersinger*. ("We hold therefore that absent a knowing or intelligent waiver, no person may be imprisoned unless he was represented by counsel.") The Supreme Court of Illinois indicated that it was not inclined to "extend *Argersinger* to a case where imprisonment was authorized but not imposed." The U.S. Supreme Court agreed holding that states need not appoint counsel in cases where the defendant is not actually sentenced to jail — even if the offense is one that is punishable by imprisonment.

Many states have rejected the *Scott v. Illinois* approach because it is difficult to implement (how would the state necessarily know whether the defendant should be sentenced to jail at the very outset of the case?) These states provide appointed counsel to all indigent defendants who have the possibility of receiving a sentence of incarceration.

THE RIGHT TO COUNSEL IN FEDERAL TRIALS

The Court in *Johnson v. Zerbst,* 304 U.S. 458 (1938) held that in all federal felony trials, a defendant must be represented by counsel unless the defendant waives that right. The Court further found that the absence of counsel without a waiver is a *jurisdictional error* and that, accordingly, Zerbst's convictions was void (because court's lack of authority to even hear the case and thus lack of authority to deprive an accused of life or liberty.)

Zerbst also established rules for a proper waiver of the Sixth Amendment right to counsel in federal cases. The Court defined waiver as an "intelligent relinquishment or abandonment of a known right or privilege." It established a presumption against waiver. In order to adequately and constitutionally waive the right to counsel, the defendant must 1) know he or she has a right to counsel and 2) voluntarily give it up knowing that he or she has the right to claim it. Therefore, if the defendant only silently goes along with the conduct of the trial without complaining about the lack of counsel, his or her silence does not amount to a waiver.

In 1945 Congress passed the Federal Rules of Criminal Procedure (FRCP). Rule 44 of the FRCP assures that defendants have access and representation of counsel, either retained or appointed, at every stage of the proceedings from the initial appearance through appeal. The lack of a federal defense bar for appointed cases made this rule difficult to implement, so in 1964 Congress passed the Criminal Justice Act of 1964 establishing a national system for providing counsel to indigent defendants in federal courts (i.e., a federal public defender system).

CRITICAL STAGES OF THE CRIMINAL JUSTICE PROCESS

In *Rothgery v. Gillespie County*, the Court considered at what stage in the criminal justice process the defendant is entitled to have the assistance of counsel.

ROTHGERY V. GILLESPIE COUNTY
554 U.S. 191 (2008)

Justice Souter delivered the opinion of the Court.

...

Although petitioner Walter Rothgery has never been convicted of a felony, a criminal background check disclosed an erroneous record that he had been, and on July 15, 2002, Texas police officers relied on this record to arrest him as a felon in possession of a firearm. The officers lacked a warrant, and so promptly brought Rothgery before a magistrate judge, as required by... [Texas law]. Texas law has no formal label for this initial appearance before a magistrate, ... which is sometimes called the "article 15.17 hearing," it combines the Fourth Amendment's required probable-cause determination with the setting of bail, and is the point at which the arrestee is formally apprised of the accusation against him.

Rothgery's article 15.17 hearing followed routine. The arresting officer submitted a sworn "Affidavit Of Probable Cause" .... After reviewing the affidavit, the magistrate judge "determined that probable cause existed for the arrest." The magistrate judge informed Rothgery of the accusation, set his bail at $5,000, and committed him to jail, from which he was released after posting a surety bond. ... The release was conditioned on the defendant's personal appearance in trial court "for any and all subsequent proceedings that may be had relative to the said charge in the course of the criminal action based on said charge." [So, Rothgery bailed out before he got an attorney.]

Rothgery had no money for a lawyer and made several oral and written requests for appointed counsel which went unheeded. The following January, he was indicted by a Texas grand jury for unlawful possession of a firearm by a felon, resulting in rearrest the next day, and an order increasing bail to $15,000. When he could not post it, he was put in jail and remained there for three weeks.

On January 23, 2003, six months after the article 15.17 hearing, Rothgery was finally assigned a lawyer, who promptly obtained a bail reduction (so Rothgery could get out of jail), and assembled the paperwork confirming that Rothgery had never been convicted of a felony. Counsel relayed this information to the district attorney, who in turn filed a motion to dismiss the indictment, which was granted.

B

Rothgery then brought this 42 U. S. C. §1983 action against respondent Gillespie County, claiming that if the County had provided a lawyer within a reasonable time after the article 15.17 hearing, he would not have been indicted, rearrested, or jailed for three weeks. The County's failure is said to be owing to its unwritten policy of denying appointed counsel to indigent defendants out on bond until at least the entry of an information or indictment. Rothgery sees this policy as violating his Sixth Amendment right to counsel.

The District Court granted summary judgment to the County, and the Court of Appeals affirmed. The Court of Appeals felt itself bound by Circuit precedent, ... to the effect that the Sixth Amendment right to counsel did not attach at the article 15.17 hearing, because "the relevant prosecutors were not aware of or involved in Rothgery's arrest or appearance before the magistrate on July 16, 2002," and "[t]here is also no indication that the officer who filed the probable cause affidavit at Rothgery's appearance had any power to commit the state to prosecute without the knowledge or involvement of a prosecutor," 491 F. 3d, at 297.

We granted certiorari, 552 U. S. ___ (2007), and now vacate and remand.

II

The Sixth Amendment right of the "accused" to assistance of counsel in "all criminal prosecutions" is limited by its terms: "it does not attach until a prosecution is commenced." *McNeil* v. *Wisconsin*, (1991); see also *Moran* v. *Burbine*, (1986). We have, for purposes of the right to counsel, pegged commencement to " 'the initiation of adversary judicial criminal proceedings— whether by way of formal charge, preliminary hearing, indictment, information, or arraignment,' " The rule is not "mere formalism," but a recognition of the point at which "the government has committed itself to prosecute," "the adverse positions of government and defendant have solidified," and the accused "finds himself faced with the prosecutorial forces of organized society, and immersed in the intricacies of substantive and procedural criminal law." The issue is whether Texas's article 15.17 hearing marks that point, with the consequent state obligation to appoint counsel within a reasonable time once a request for assistance is made.

A

... [W]e have twice held that the right to counsel attaches at the initial appearance before a judicial officer, see *Jackson*; *Brewer*. This first time before a court, also known as the " 'preliminary arraignment' " or " 'arraignment on the complaint,' " is generally the hearing at which "the magistrate informs the defendant of the charge in the complaint, and of various rights in further proceedings," and "determine[s] the conditions for pretrial release," Texas's article 15.17 hearing is an initial appearance: Rothgery was taken before a magistrate judge, informed of the formal accusation against him, and sent to jail until he posted bail.

...

We flatly rejected the distinction between initial arraignment and arraignment on the indictment, the State's argument being "untenable" in light of the "clear language in our decisions about the significance of arraignment." ... [B]y the time a defendant is brought before a judicial officer, is informed of a formally lodged accusation, and has restrictions imposed on his liberty in aid of the prosecution, the State's relationship with the defendant has become solidly adversarial. And

that is just as true when the proceeding comes before the indictment (in the case of the initial arraignment on a formal complaint) as when it comes after it (at an arraignment on an indictment. See *Coleman* v. *Alabama*, 399 U. S. 1, 8 (1970) (plurality opinion) (right to counsel applies at preindictment preliminary hearing at which the "sole purposes ... are to determine whether there is sufficient evidence against the accused to warrant presenting his case to the grand jury, and, if so, to fix bail if the offense is bailable"). ...

B

... In *McNeil* . . . [we reaffirmed] . . . that "[t]he Sixth Amendment right to counsel attaches at the first formal proceeding against an accused," and observed that "in most States, at least with respect to serious offenses, free counsel is made available at that time ... ."

That was 17 years ago, the same is true today, and the overwhelming consensus practice conforms to the rule that the first formal proceeding is the point of attachment. We are advised without contradiction that not only the Federal Government, including the District of Columbia, but 43 States take the first step toward appointing counsel "before, at, or just after initial appearance." ... And even in the remaining 7 States (Alabama, Colorado, Kansas, Oklahoma, South Carolina, Texas, and Virginia) the practice is not free of ambiguity. ... In any event, to the extent these States have been denying appointed counsel on the heels of the first appearance, they are a distinct minority.

C

The only question is whether there may be some arguable justification for the minority practice. Neither the Court of Appeals in its opinion, nor the County in its briefing to us, has offered an acceptable one.

. . . .

presence of appointed counsel during any "critical stage" of the postattachment proceedings; what makes a stage critical is what shows the need for counsel's presence. Thus, counsel must be appointed within a reasonable time after attachment to allow for adequate representation at any critical stage before trial, as well as at trial itself.

[The Court held that Texas article 15.17 hearing signals an "attachment" -- government's signal that it is committed to prosecute the individual and "counsel must be appointed within a reasonable time after that attachment to allow for adequate representation at any critical stage before trial, as well as at trial itself."]

Our holding is narrow. . . We merely reaffirm what we have held before and what an overwhelming majority of American jurisdictions understand in practice: a criminal defendant's initial appearance before a judicial officer, where he learns the charge against him and his liberty is subject to restriction, marks the start of adversary judicial proceedings that trigger attachment of the Sixth Amendment right to counsel.

Prior to *Rothgery*, the Court in *White v. Maryland*, 373 U.S, 59 (1963) found that the right to counsel should be required at every **critical stage** of the criminal justice process. A critical stage, according to the Court is one in which the defendant is compelled to make a decision which may later formally be used against him. The *White* Court found that the initial appearance during which the defendant enters a non-binding plea was a critical stage, so White should have had access to appointed counsel. (In White's case, his statements during his initial plea were used against him at his trial.) A preliminary hearing is a critical stage. *Coleman v. Alabama*, 399 U.S. 1 (1970). Recall, a post-indictment line up or show up is similarly a critical stage. *Wade v. United States* 388 U.S. 218 (1967) and *Gilbert v. California* 388 U.S. 263 (1967).

THE RIGHT TO COUNSEL IN NON-TRIAL PROCEEDINGS

Psychiatric Examinations

Estelle v. Smith, 451 U.S. 454 (1981) held that a defendant charged with a capital crime and ordered by the court to be examined by a psychiatrist (to see whether he a poses a danger in the future) was entitled to consult with counsel. It was prejudicial error to fail to appoint defense counsel to represent a defendant subjected to a psychiatric evaluation, and counsel must have knowledge of the projected examination before it occurs. *Satterwhite v. Texas*, 486 U.S. 249 (1988).
"*Ake v. Oklahoma* . . . clearly established that when an indigent "defendant demonstrates . . . that his sanity at the time of the offense is to be a significant fact at trial, the State must" provide the defendant with "access to a competent psychiatrist who will conduct an appropriate examination and assist in evaluation, preparation, and presentation of the defense." *McWilliams v. Dunn et al.* ,582 U.S. ___ (2017).

Juvenile Delinquency And Civil Commitment Proceedings

Juveniles subject to juvenile delinquency proceedings are entitled to the right to appointed counsel if institutional commitment is a possibility. The rationale of *In re Gault*, 387 U.S. 1 (1967), seems to be applicable to other proceedings which are "comparable in seriousness to a felony prosecution," and the right to counsel has been extended by several courts to civil commitment proceedings in which a significant deprivation of freedom is involved.

Probation And Parole Revocation Hearings

In *Mempa* v. *Rhay*, 389 U.S. 128 (1967), the court deferred imposition of sentence, and placed defendant, who had plead guilty to "joyriding," on two years of probation with the first 30 days to be spent in jail. About four months later, the prosecutor moved to have petitioner's probation revoked on the ground that he had been involved with a subsequent burglary. The 17-year-old Mempa was not represented by counsel at the hearing during which he confessed to being involved in the burglary. The Court held that Mempa should have had counsel to assist him in his sentencing hearing. It noted that there may be a case where an accused agreed to plead guilty although he had a valid defense because he was offered probation; absence of counsel at the imposition of sentence might well result in loss of the right to appeal.

In *Gagnon v. Scarpelli*, 411 U.S. 778 (1973) the state revoked defendant's probation. The Court found that the revocation of probation hearing did not meet the standards of due process. Because a probation revocation does involve a loss of liberty, due process must be accorded the probationer. Nevertheless, the court did not adopt the position that a probationer must always be appointed a counsel in the due process hearings (thus rejecting a *per se* rule). Instead the Court stated,

> "We find no justification for a new, inflexible constitutional rule with respect to the requirement of counsel. We think rather, that the decision as to the need for counsel must be made on a case-by-case basis in the exercise of sound discretion by the state authority charged with responsibility for administering the probation and parole system. ... Presumptively, it may be said that counsel should be provided in cases where, after being informed of his right to request counsel, the probationer or parolee makes such a request based on a timely and colorable claim. ... In passing on a request for the appointment of counsel, the responsible agency should also consider, especially in doubtful cases, whether probationer appears to be capable of speaking effectively for himself. In every case in which a request for counsel at a preliminary or final hearing is refused, the grounds for refusal shall be stated succinctly in the record."

Post-Trial Proceedings

After a trial in which the jury finds the defendant guilty, the court will frequently revoke any bail and remand the defendant into custody. A sentencing date is usually set sometime after the trial. The attorney representing the defendant has the legal obligation to make post-trial motions to preserve the defendant's rights. Counsel must assist the defendant between the time of the reading of the verdict through the sentencing hearing. As you may recall from Chapter One, sometimes motions for a new trial is filed, a motion for a judgment of acquittal notwithstanding the verdict, etc. At sentencing, the Sixth Amendment right to counsel still is at play, and generally the defendant's pre-trial and trial attorney continues with the representation. After sentencing, however, the defendant's attorney's job frequently ends upon counseling the newly "convicted" person of the rights to appeal.

The Court has distinguished between the defendant's right to the assistance of counsel on mandatory appeals ("appeals of right") and discretionary appeals. In *Douglas v. California*, 372 U.S. 353 (1963) the Court found that the government should appoint indigent counsel to individuals for their first appeal which they are entitled as a matter of right through statute or state laws. But, once the first appeal has been dismissed or resolved, the indigent defendant is on his own. *Ross v. Moffitt*, 417 U.S. 600 (1974) held that an indigent person does not have a right to appointed counsel on his application for discretionary review by the state supreme court or on his petition for *writ of certiorari* to the United States Supreme Court. This decision seems inconsistent with the holding in *Douglas*, but the *Ross v. Moffitt* majority reasoned that the defendant did not need an attorney to have "meaningful access" to higher appellate courts." Any legal issues that could be raised on appeal should have been developed and briefed by counsel in the pleadings on the appeal of right. Discretionary appeals are "accepted or rejected usually on the basis, not of the likelihood that the original determination of guilt was wrong, but of the importance of the legal issues involved, a question which can be evaluated from the record of the intermediate appellate court proceedings.

Additionally, the court noted that the concept of equal protection does not require absolute equality, so that "the fact that a particular service might be of benefit to an indigent does not mean that the service is constitutionally required."

Prisoners have a limited right to legal assistance for the purpose of filing writs of habeas corpus. In *Bounds v. Smith*, 430 U.S. 817 (1977) the Court held that "the fundamental constitutional right of access to the courts requires prison authorities to assist inmates in the preparation and filing of meaningful legal papers by providing prisoners with adequate law libraries or adequate assistance from persons trained in the law." The obligation, however, can be fulfilled by training prisoners to be paralegal assistants to work under lawyer's supervision, law students, paralegals, volunteer lawyers." The difference between the Court's willingness to require access to legally trained persons for habeas corpus petitions and not for discretionary reviews (*Ross v. Moffitt*) may be due to the nature of collateral attack where a claim is often being advanced for the first time and therefore the need for legal assistance may be greater.

THE RIGHT TO COUNSEL OF ONE'S CHOICE

Whether a defendant is entitled to a counsel of his or her choice probably depends on the facts of the case. In *Wheat v. United States*, 486 U.S. 153 (1988) one defendant wanted to be represented by the same attorney who was representing his accomplice/co-conspirator in a complex drug distribution conspiracy. One of the co-defendants, who was represented by that counsel, had already pled guilty to one count of the indictment. Wheat and his other co-defendants were willing to waive their rights to 'conflict-free' counsel (the rules of professional ethics say attorneys cannot represent clients who may have conflicts of interest). Nevertheless, the Supreme Court denied the application for the counsel indicating that irreconcilable and unwaivable conflicts of interest would be created by the likelihood that the Wheat would be called to testify in one of his co-defendants' trials and that his co-defendant would be testifying in Wheat's trial.

In *United States v. Gonzalez-Lopez,* 458 U.S. 140 (2008), defendant hired an attorney from a different state. That attorney and the trial judge had disagreements prompting the trial judge to prohibited the attorney from taking part in the defendant's trial. The state conceded it had erroneously deprived the defendant of his choice of counsel but argued that this was harmless error. The Court instead found the denial of the defendant's right to the counsel he chose to hire was a structural error, and thus not subject to a harmless error analysis. Consequently, the defendant did not have to show that the counsel that actually represented him was ineffective or that he was prejudiced by that counsel's performance. He should have been able to have the counsel he hired, and because he did not, his conviction was reversed — despite the fact that the attorney who did represent him did not do a bad job.

RIGHT TO REPRESENT ONESELF

Defendants who choose to represent themselves are referred to as *"pro se"* defendants. So long as they waive their rights intelligently and voluntarily, defendants can do so. *Faretta v. California*, 422 U.S. 806 (1975). *Pro se* defendants don't always do a bad job in representing themselves, but in this author's opinion, they generally do a bad job — and they cannot claim ineffective assistance of counsel on appeal or writ of habeas corpus. Thus, they have no one to cast blame upon (but themselves).

FARETTA v. CALIFORNIA
422 U.S. 806 (1975)

JUSTICE STEWART delivered the opinion of the Court.

Anthony Faretta was charged with grand theft. At the arraignment, the Superior Court Judge assigned to preside at the trial appointed the public defender to represent Faretta. Well before the date of trial, however, Faretta requested that he be permitted to represent himself. Questioning by the judge revealed that Faretta had once represented himself in a criminal prosecution, that he had a high school education, and that he did not want to be represented by the public defender because he believed that that office was "very loaded down with . . . a heavy case load." The judge responded that he believed Faretta was "making a mistake" and emphasized that in further proceedings Faretta would receive no special favors. Nevertheless, after establishing that Faretta wanted to represent himself and did not want a lawyer, the judge, in a "preliminary ruling," accepted Faretta's waiver of the assistance of counsel. The judge indicated, however, that he might reverse this ruling if it later appeared that Faretta was unable adequately to represent himself.

Several weeks thereafter, but still prior to trial, the judge sua sponte [on its own motion] held a hearing to inquire into Faretta's ability to conduct his own defense, and questioned him specifically about both the hearsay rule and the state law governing the challenge of potential jurors. After consideration of Faretta's answers, and observation of his demeanor, the judge ruled that Faretta had not made an intelligent and knowing waiver of his right to the assistance of counsel, and also ruled that Faretta had no constitutional right to conduct his own defense. The judge, accordingly, reversed his earlier ruling permitting self-representation and again appointed the public defender to represent Faretta. Faretta's subsequent request for leave to act as cocounsel was rejected, as were his efforts to make certain motions on his own behalf. Throughout the subsequent trial, the judge required that Faretta's defense be conducted only through the appointed lawyer from the public defender's office. At the conclusion of the trial, the jury found Faretta guilty as charged, and the judge sentenced him to prison.

In the federal courts, the right of self-representation has been protected by statute since the beginnings of our Nation. The Judiciary Act of 1789, enacted by the First Congress and signed by President Washington one day before the Sixth Amendment was proposed, provided that "in all the courts of the United States, the parties may plead and manage their own causes personally or by the assistance of . . . counsel . . . ."

With few exceptions, each of the several States also accords a defendant the right to represent himself in any criminal case. The Constitutions of 36 States explicitly confer that right. Moreover, many state courts have expressed the view that the right is also supported by the Constitution of the United States.

We confront here a nearly universal conviction, on the part of our people as well as our courts, that forcing a lawyer upon an unwilling defendant is contrary to his basic right to defend himself if he truly wants to do so.

The Sixth Amendment includes a compact statement of the rights necessary to a full defense: "In all criminal prosecutions, the accused shall enjoy the right . . . to be informed of the nature and cause of the accusation; to be confronted with the witnesses against him; to have compulsory process for obtaining witnesses in his favor, and to have the Assistance of Counsel for his defence."

Because these rights are basic to our adversary system of criminal justice, they are part of the "due process of law" that is guaranteed by the Fourteenth Amendment to defendants in the criminal courts of the States. The rights to notice, confrontation, and compulsory process, when taken together, guarantee that a criminal charge may be answered in a manner now considered fundamental to the fair administration of American justice — through the calling and interrogation of favorable witnesses, the cross-examination of adverse witnesses, and the orderly introduction of evidence. In short, the Amendment constitutionalizes the right in an adversary criminal trial to make a defense as we know it.

The Sixth Amendment does not provide merely that a defense shall be made for the accused; it grants to the accused personally the right to make his defense. It is the accused, not counsel, who must be "informed of the nature and cause of the accusation," who must be "confronted with the witnesses against him," and who must be accorded "compulsory process for obtaining witnesses in his favor." Although not stated in the Amendment in so many words, the right to self-representation - to make one's own defense personally - is thus necessarily implied by the structure of the Amendment. The right to defend is given directly to the accused; for it is he who suffers the consequences if the defense fails.

There can be no blinking the fact that the right of an accused to conduct his own defense seems to cut against the grain of this Court's decisions holding that the Constitution requires that no accused can be convicted and imprisoned unless he has been accorded the right to the assistance of counsel. For it is surely true that the basic thesis of those decisions is that the help of a lawyer is essential to assure the defendant a fair trial. And a strong argument can surely be made that the whole thrust of those decisions must inevitably lead to the conclusion that a State may constitutionally impose a lawyer upon even an unwilling defendant.

But it is one thing to hold that every defendant, rich or poor, has the right to the assistance of counsel, and quite another to say that a State may compel a defendant to accept a lawyer he does not want. The value of state-appointed counsel was not unappreciated by the Founders, yet the notion of compulsory counsel was utterly foreign to them. And whatever else may be said of those who wrote the Bill of Rights, surely there can be no doubt that they understood the inestimable worth of free choice.

It is undeniable that in most criminal prosecutions defendants could better defend with counsel's guidance than by their own unskilled efforts. But where the defendant will not voluntarily accept representation by counsel, the potential advantage of a lawyer's training and experience can be realized, if at all, only imperfectly. To force a lawyer on a defendant can only lead him to believe that the law contrives against him. Moreover, it is not inconceivable that in some rare instances, the defendant might in fact present his case more effectively by conducting his own defense. Personal liberties are not rooted in the law of averages. The right to defend is personal. The defendant, and not his lawyer or the State, will bear the personal consequences of a conviction. It is the defendant, therefore, who must be free personally to decide whether in his particular case counsel is to his advantage.

When an accused manages his own defense, he relinquishes, as a purely factual matter, many of the traditional benefits associated with the right to counsel. For this reason, in order to represent himself, the accused must "knowingly and intelligently" forgo those relinquished benefits. Although a defendant need not himself have the skill and experience of a lawyer in order competently and intelligently to choose self-representation, he should be made aware of the dangers and disadvantages of self-representation, so that the record will establish that "he knows what he is doing and his choice is made with eyes open."

Here, weeks before trial, Faretta clearly and unequivocally declared to the trial judge that he wanted to represent himself and did not want counsel. The record affirmatively shows that Faretta was literate, competent, and understanding, and that he was voluntarily exercising his informed free will. The trial judge had warned Faretta that he thought it was a mistake not to accept the assistance of counsel, and that Faretta would be required to follow all the "ground rules" of trial procedure. We need make no assessment of how well or poorly Faretta had mastered the intricacies of the hearsay rule and the California code provisions that govern challenges of potential jurors on voir dire. For his technical legal knowledge, as such, was not relevant to an assessment of his knowing exercise of the right to defend himself.

In forcing Faretta, under these circumstances, to accept against his will a state-appointed public defender, the California courts deprived him of his constitutional right to conduct his own defense. Accordingly, the judgment before us is vacated, and the case is remanded for further proceedings not inconsistent with this opinion.

CHIEF JUSTICE BURGER, with whom JUSTICE BLACKMUN and JUSTICE REHNQUIST join, dissenting, omitted.

In *McKaskle v. Wiggins*, 465 U.S. 168 (1984), the Court found that a trial judge may appoint a standby counsel to assist a *pro se* defendant — even over the defendant's objections. The appointment of standby counsel is warranted by several concerns. First, if a defendant who is representing himself suddenly decides to ask for a lawyer during a trial, there will be no delay in getting counsel. Second, a standby counsel can advise the *pro se* defendant more effectively exercise his right to self-representation. Third, standby counsel can assist a defendant whose mental or emotional "fortitude" may be questioned to make a meaningful defense. Finally, standby counsel eliminates the need for a judge to give the appearance of bias by advising the defendant during the trial.

THE RIGHT TO THE "EFFECTIVE ASSISTANCE" OF COUNSEL

Defendants frequently raise ineffective assistance of counsel claims in their petitions for a writ of habeas corpus. The Sixth Amendment right to counsel guarantee means that the defendant has the right to *effective* assistance of counsel. *McMann v. Richardson,* 397 U.S. 759 (1970). The Court established the standard for evaluating effective assistance in *Strickland v. Washington*, 466 U.S. 668 (1984) referred to in *Lee v. United States* (below).

LEE v. UNITED STATES
582 U.S. ___ (2017)

Chief Justice Roberts delivered the opinion of the Court.

Petitioner Jae Lee was indicted on one count of possessing ecstasy with intent to distribute. Although he has lived in this country for most of his life, Lee is not a United States citizen, and he feared that a criminal conviction might affect his status as a lawful permanent resident. His attorney assured him there was nothing to worry about—the Government would not deport him if he pleaded guilty. So Lee, who had no real defense to the charge, opted to accept a plea that carried a lesser prison sentence than he would have faced at trial.

Lee's attorney was wrong: The conviction meant that Lee was subject to mandatory deportation from this country. Lee seeks to vacate his conviction on the ground that, in accepting the plea, he received ineffective assistance of counsel in violation of the Sixth Amendment. Everyone agrees that Lee received objectively unreasonable representation. The question presented is whether he can show he was prejudiced as a result.

I

...

At an evidentiary hearing on Lee's motion, both Lee and his plea-stage counsel testified that "deportation was the determinative issue in Lee's decision whether to accept the plea." . . . In fact, Lee explained, his attorney became "pretty upset because every time something comes up I always ask about immigration status," and the lawyer "always said why [are you] worrying about something that you don't need to worry about." According to Lee, the lawyer assured him that if deportation was not in the plea agreement, "the government cannot deport you." Lee's attorney testified that he thought Lee's case was a "bad case to try" because Lee's defense to the charge was weak. The attorney nonetheless acknowledged that if he had known Lee would be deported upon pleading guilty, he would have advised him to go to trial. Based on the hearing testimony, a Magistrate Judge recommended that Lee's plea be set aside and his conviction vacated because he had received ineffective assistance of counsel.

The District Court . . . [applying] . . . our two-part test for ineffective assistance claims from *Strickland* v. *Washington*, . . . concluded that Lee's counsel had performed deficiently by giving improper advice about the deportation consequences of the plea. But, "[i]n light of the overwhelming evidence of Lee's guilt," Lee "would have almost certainly" been found guilty and received "a significantly longer prison sentence, and subsequent deportation," had he gone to trial. Lee therefore could not show he was prejudiced by his attorney's erroneous advice. . . .

The Court of Appeals for the Sixth Circuit . . . [relying] . . . on Circuit precedent holding that "no rational defendant charged with a deportable offense and facing overwhelming evidence of guilt would proceed to trial rather than take a plea deal with a shorter prison

sentence," . . . concluded that Lee could not show prejudice We granted certiorari. 580 U. S. ___ (2016).

II

The Sixth Amendment guarantees a defendant the effective assistance of counsel at "critical stages of a criminal proceeding," including when he enters a guilty plea. *Lafler* v. *Cooper* . . . ; *Hill.* To demonstrate that counsel was constitutionally ineffective, a defendant must show that counsel's representation "fell below an objective standard of reasonableness" and that he was prejudiced as a result. *Strickland.* The first requirement is not at issue in today's case: The Government concedes that Lee's plea-stage counsel provided inadequate representation when he assured Lee that he would not be deported if he pleaded guilty. The question is whether Lee can show he was prejudiced by that erroneous advice.

A

...

...[W]hen a defendant claims that his counsel's deficient performance deprived him of a trial by causing him to accept a plea, the defendant can show prejudice by demonstrating a "reasonable probability that, but for counsel's errors, he would not have pleaded guilty and would have insisted on going to trial."

The dissent contends that a defendant must also show that he would have been better off going to trial. That is true when the defendant's decision about going to trial turns on his prospects of success and those are affected by the attorney's error—for instance, where a defendant alleges that his lawyer should have but did not seek to suppress an improperly obtained confession.

Not all errors, however, are of that sort. Here Lee knew, correctly, that his prospects of acquittal at trial were grim, and his attorney's error had nothing to do with that. The error was instead one that affected Lee's understanding of the consequences of pleading guilty. The Court confronted precisely this kind of error in *Hill* ("the claimed error of counsel is erroneous advice as to eligibility for parole"). Rather than asking how a hypothetical trial would have played out absent the error, the Court considered whether there was an adequate showing that the defendant, properly advised, would have opted to go to trial. The Court rejected the defendant's claim because he had "alleged no special circumstances that might support the conclusion that he placed particular emphasis on his parole eligibility in deciding whether or not to plead guilty."

Lee, on the other hand, argues he can establish prejudice under *Hill* because he never would have accepted a guilty plea had he known that he would be deported as a result. Lee insists he would have gambled on trial, risking more jail time for whatever small chance there might be of an acquittal that would let him remain in the United States. The Government responds that, since Lee had no viable defense at trial, he would almost certainly have lost and found himself still subject to deportation, with a lengthier prison sentence to boot. Lee, the Government contends, cannot show prejudice from accepting a plea where his only hope at trial was that something unexpected and unpredictable might occur that would lead to an acquittal.

B

The Government asks that we, like the Court of Appeals below, adopt a *per se* rule that a defendant with no viable defense cannot show prejudice from the denial of his right to trial. As a general matter, it makes sense that a defendant who has no realistic defense to a charge supported by sufficient evidence will be unable to carry his burden of showing prejudice from accepting a guilty plea. But in elevating this general proposition to a *per se* rule, the Government makes two errors. First, it forgets that categorical rules are ill suited to an inquiry that we have emphasized demands a "case-by-case examination" of the "totality of the evidence." *Williams* v. *Taylor*, … (2000); *Strickland*, And, more fundamentally, the Government overlooks that the inquiry we prescribed

in *Hill v. Lockhart* focuses on a defendant's decisionmaking, which may not turn solely on the likelihood of conviction after trial.

A defendant without any viable defense will be highly likely to lose at trial. And a defendant facing such long odds will rarely be able to show prejudice from accepting a guilty plea that offers him a better resolution than would be likely after trial. But that is not because the prejudice inquiry in this context looks to the probability of a conviction for its own sake. It is instead because defendants obviously weigh their prospects at trial in deciding whether to accept a plea. Where a defendant has no plausible chance of an acquittal at trial, it is highly likely that he will accept a plea if the Government offers one.

But common sense (not to mention our precedent) recognizes that there is more to consider than simply the likelihood of success at trial. The decision whether to plead guilty also involves assessing the respective consequences of a conviction after trial and by plea. When those consequences are, from the defendant's perspective, similarly dire, even the smallest chance of success at trial may look attractive. For example, a defendant with no realistic defense to a charge carrying a 20-year sentence may nevertheless choose trial, if the prosecution's plea offer is 18 years. Here Lee alleges that avoiding deportation was *the* determinative factor for him; deportation after some time in prison was not meaningfully different from deportation after somewhat less time. He says he accordingly would have rejected any plea leading to deportation—even if it shaved off prison time—in favor of throwing a "Hail Mary" at trial.

…

C

"Surmounting *Strickland*'s high bar is never an easy task," … and the strong societal interest in finality has "special force with respect to convictions based on guilty pleas." …. Courts should not upset a plea solely because of *post hoc* assertions from a defendant about how he would have pleaded but for his attorney's deficiencies. Judges should instead look to contemporaneous evidence to substantiate a defendant's expressed preferences.

In the unusual circumstances of this case, we conclude that Lee has adequately demonstrated a reasonable probability that he would have rejected the plea had he known that it would lead to mandatory deportation. There is no question that "deportation was the determinative issue in Lee's decision whether to accept the plea deal." …

Lee demonstrated as much at his plea colloquy: When the judge warned him that a conviction "could result in your being deported," and asked "[d]oes that at all affect your decision about whether you want to plead guilty or not," Lee answered "Yes, Your Honor." When the judge inquired "[h]ow does it affect your decision," Lee responded "I don't understand," and turned to his attorney for advice. Only when Lee's counsel assured him that the judge's statement was a "standard warning" was Lee willing to proceed to plead guilty.

There is no reason to doubt the paramount importance Lee placed on avoiding deportation. Deportation is always "a particularly severe penalty," … and we have "recognized that 'preserving the client's right to remain in the United States may be more important to the client than any potential jail sentence,' " … At the time of his plea, Lee had lived in the United States for nearly three decades, had established two businesses in Tennessee, and was the only family member in the United States who could care for his elderly parents—both naturalized American citizens. In contrast to these strong connections to the United States, there is no indication that he had any ties to South Korea; he had never returned there since leaving as a child.

…

We cannot agree that it would be irrational for a defendant in Lee's position to reject the plea offer in favor of trial. But for his attorney's incompetence, Lee would have known that accepting the plea agreement would *certainly* lead to deportation. Going to trial? *Almost* certainly. If deportation were the "determinative issue" for an individual in plea discussions, as it was for Lee; if that individual had strong connections to this country and no other, as did Lee; and if the consequences of taking a chance at trial were not markedly harsher than pleading, as in this case, that "almost" could make all the difference. Balanced against holding on to some chance of avoiding deportation was a year or two more of prison time. Not everyone in Lee's position would make the choice to reject the plea. But we cannot say it would be irrational to do so.

The Court decides ineffective assistance of counsel cases each year — generally capital cases based on habeas corpus motions. (Because of the stakes, the court may be more inclined to review these cases.) Ineffective assistance cases are obviously limited to the facts of the particular case, but the court has not varied from the standards and analysis set forth in *Strickland.*

Other Cases: Effective Assistance of Counsel

Wiggens v. Smith, 539 U.S. 510 (2003)

SUMMARY: The Court found that Wiggen's defense attorneys provided ineffective assistance of counsel in the sentencing portion of his trial for the capital murder of a 77-year-old woman because they failed to investigate and present information they had showing that he had been subject to regular (daily?) sexual abuse as a child.

"In finding that Schlaich and Nethercott's investigation did not meet Strickland's performance standards, we emphasize that Strickland does not require counsel to investigate every conceivable line of mitigating evidence no matter how unlikely the effort would be to assist the defendant at sentencing. Nor does Strickland require defense counsel to present mitigating evidence at sentencing in every case. Both conclusions would interfere with the "constitutionally protected independence of counsel" at the heart of Strickland. We base our conclusion on the much more limited principle that "strategic choices made after less than complete investigation are reasonable" only to the extent that "reasonable professional judgments support the limitations on investigation." . . . A decision not to investigate thus "must be directly assessed for reasonableness in all the circumstances."

Counsel's investigation into Wiggins' background did not reflect reasonable professional judgment. Their decision to end their investigation when they did was neither consistent with the professional standards that prevailed in 1989, nor reasonable in light of the evidence counsel uncovered in the social services records — evidence that would have led a reasonably competent attorney to investigate further. Counsel's pursuit of bifurcation until the eve of sentencing and their partial presentation of a mitigation case suggest that their incomplete investigation was the result of inattention, not reasoned strategic judgment. In deferring to counsel's decision not to pursue a mitigation case despite their unreasonable investigation, the Maryland Court of Appeals unreasonably applied Strickland."

Buck v. Davis, 580 U.S. ____ (2017),

SUMMARY: The Court found that defense counsel was ineffective and the two prongs of Strickland were met when he called a psychologist to testify to future dangerousness in the penalty phase of a capital prosecution. The expert stated testified that, because defendant was black, he had an increased probability of future dangerousness and that race was a factor in predicting future dangerousness. The prosecutor cross-examined the psychologist based on his testimony and report and relied on his evidence. The jury received the reports and returned a sentence of death.

OPINION: To satisfy Strickland, a defendant must first show that counsel performed deficiently. Buck's trial counsel knew that Dr. Quijano's report reflected the view that Buck's race predisposed him to violent conduct and that the principal point of dispute during the penalty phase was Buck's future dangerousness. Counsel nevertheless called Dr. Quijano to the stand, specifically elicited testimony about the connection between race and violence, and put Dr. Quijano's report into evidence. No competent defense attorney would introduce evidence that his client is liable to be a future danger because of his race.

Strickland further requires a defendant to demonstrate prejudice — "a reasonable probability that, but for counsel's unprofessional errors, the result of the proceeding would have been different." It is reasonably probable that without Dr. Quijano's testimony on race and violence, at least one juror would have harbored a reasonable doubt on the question of Buck's future dangerousness. This issue required the jury to make a predictive judgment inevitably entailing a degree of speculation. But Buck's race was not subject to speculation, and according to Dr. Quijano, that immutable characteristic carried with it an increased probability of future violence. Dr. Quijano's testimony appealed to a powerful racial stereotype and might well have been valued by jurors as the opinion of a medical expert bearing the court's imprimatur. For these reasons, the District Court's conclusion that any mention of race during the penalty phase was de minimis is rejected. So is the State's argument that Buck was not prejudiced by Dr. Quijano's testimony because it was introduced by his own counsel, rather than the prosecution. Jurors understand that prosecutors seek convictions and may reasonably be expected to evaluate the government's evidence in light of its motivations. When damaging evidence is introduced by a defendant's own lawyer, it is in the nature of an admission against interest, more likely to be taken at face value.

Nix v. Whiteside, 475 U.S. 157 (1986)

SUMMARY: The Court held that defense counsel is not required to, and indeed cannot, acquiesce to the defendant's desire to put on perjured testimony. Whiteside wanted to lie about seeing something metallic in the victim's hand as a means of raising self-defense. The lawyer, who knew this to be false and contrary to the defendant's other stories, refused to allow the defendant to testify. (This is generally a decision made by the defendant). The defendant maintained that his lawyer's refusal to put on his testimony violated his right to counsel. The court held that the rules of professional ethics prohibited the lawyer from putting on defendant's testimony, and that it could not be a violation of the defendant's Sixth Amendment rights for his counsel to act in accordance with professional rules.

McCoy v. Louisiana, 584 U.S. ___ (2018)

SUMMARY: Defendant was charged with first degree murder for killing his estranged wife's mother, stepfather, and son. He consistently maintained his innocence throughout the entirety of the pre-trial phase which lasted a several years (there were delays due to extradition, aid and assist hearings, firing of first attorney, a public defender assigned to represent him). His parents hired an attorney, English, who after reviewing the evidence concluded that the evidence against McCoy was overwhelming, and that the only hope he had of being spared the death penalty was for McCoy to concede guilt at the guilt/innocence phase and plead for mercy at the sentencing phase. McCoy was adamantly opposed to this, and attempted to fire English. At a hearing, two days before trial, the judge denied the motion to terminate English and have another attorney represent him. At trial English conceded McCoy's guilt (still against McCoy's wishes). The jury ultimately returned three death verdicts.

...

The Sixth Amendment guarantees to each criminal defendant "the Assistance of Counsel for his defence." At common law, self-representation was the norm. As the laws of England and the American Colonies developed, providing for a right to counsel in criminal cases, self-representation remained common and the right to proceed without counsel was recognized. Faretta. ... [A]n accused may insist upon representing herself-however counterproductive that course may be. As this Court explained, "[t]he right to defend is personal," and a defendant's choice in exercising that right "must be honored out of 'that respect for the individual which is the lifeblood of the law.'"

The choice is not all or nothing: To gain assistance, a defendant need not surrender control entirely to counsel. For the Sixth Amendment, in "grant[ing] to the accused personally the right to make his defense," "speaks of the 'assistance' of counsel, and an assistant, however expert, is still an assistant." Trial management is the lawyer's province: Counsel provides his or her assistance by making decisions such as "what arguments to pursue, what evidentiary objections to raise, and what agreements to conclude regarding the admission of evidence." Some decisions, however, are reserved for the client—notably, whether to plead guilty, waive the right to a jury trial, testify in one's own behalf, and forgo an appeal.

Autonomy to decide that the objective of the defense is to assert innocence belongs in this latter category. Just as a defendant may steadfastly refuse to plead guilty in the face of overwhelming evidence against her, or reject the assistance of legal counsel despite the defendant's own inexperience and lack of professional qualifications, so may she insist on maintaining her innocence at the guilt phase of a capital trial. These are not strategic choices about how best to achieve a client's objectives; they are choices about what the client's objectives in fact are. See Weaver v. Massachusetts, (2017) (self-representation will often increase the likelihood of an unfavorable outcome but "is based on the fundamental legal principle that a defendant must be allowed to make his own choices about the proper way to protect his own liberty"). ...

Counsel may reasonably assess a concession of guilt as best suited to avoiding the death penalty, as English did in this case. But the client may not share that objective. He may wish to avoid, above all else, the opprobrium that comes with admitting he killed family members. Or he may hold life in prison not worth living and prefer to risk death for any hope, however small, of exoneration. ...

Preserving for the defendant the ability to decide whether to maintain his innocence should not displace counsel's, or the court's, respective trial management roles. ... Counsel, in any case, must still develop a trial strategy and discuss it with her client, ... explaining why, in her view, conceding guilt would be the best option. In this case, the court had determined that McCoy was competent to stand trial, i.e., that McCoy had "sufficient present ability to consult with his lawyer with a reason- able degree of rational understanding." If, after consultations with English concerning the management of the defense, McCoy disagreed with English's proposal to concede McCoy committed three murders, it was not open to English to override McCoy's objection. English could not interfere with McCoy's telling the jury "I was not the murderer," although counsel could, if consistent with providing effective assistance, focus his own collaboration on urging that McCoy's mental state weighed against conviction. ...

...[T]hree other State Supreme Courts that have addressed this conflict in the past twenty years. ... In each of the three cases, as here, the defendant repeatedly and adamantly insisted on maintaining his factual innocence despite counsel's preferred course: concession of the defendant's commission of criminal acts and pursuit of diminished capacity, mental illness, or lack of premeditation defenses. These were not strategic disputes about whether to concede an element of a charged offense, they were intractable disagreements about the fundamental objective of the defendant's representation. For McCoy, that objective was to maintain "I did not kill the members of my family." In this stark scenario, we agree with the majority of state courts of last resort that counsel may not admit her client's guilt of a charged crime over the client's intransigent objection to that admission.

III

Because a client's autonomy, not counsel's competence, is in issue, we do not apply our ineffective-assistance-of-counsel jurisprudence to McCoy's claim. To gain redress for attorney error, a defendant ordinarily must show prejudice. Here, however, the violation of McCoy's protected autonomy right was complete when the court allowed counsel to usurp control of an issue within McCoy's sole prerogative.

Violation of a defendant's Sixth Amendment-secured autonomy ranks as error of the kind our decisions have called "structural"; when present,

such an error is not subject to harmless-error review. ... Structural error "affect[s] the framework within which the trial proceeds," as distinguished from a lapse or flaw that is "simply an error in the trial process itself." Arizona v. Fulminante, (1991). An error may be ranked structural, we have explained, "if the right at issue is not designed to protect the defendant from erroneous conviction but instead protects some other interest," such as "the fundamental legal principle that a defendant must be allowed to make his own choices about the proper way to protect his own liberty." Weaver. ... An error might also count as structural when its effects are too hard to measure, as is true of the right to counsel of choice, or where the error will inevitably signal fundamental unfairness, as we have said of a judge's failure to tell the jury that it may not convict unless it finds the defendant's guilt beyond a reasonable doubt. ...

Under at least the first two rationales, counsel's admission of a client's guilt over the client's express objection is error structural in kind. Such an admission blocks the defendant's right to make the fundamental choices about his own defense. And the effects of the admission would be immeasurable, because a jury would almost certainly be swayed by a lawyer's concession of his client's guilt. McCoy must therefore be accorded a new trial without any need first to show prejudice.

...

Larry English was placed in a difficult position; he had an unruly client and faced a strong government case. He reasonably thought the objective of his representation should be avoidance of the death penalty. But McCoy insistently maintained: "I did not murder my family." Once he communicated that to court and counsel, strenuously objecting to English's proposed strategy, a concession of guilt should have been off the table. The trial court's allowance of English's admission of McCoy's guilt despite McCoy's insistent objections was incompatible with the Sixth Amendment. Because the error was structural, a new trial is the required corrective.

Chapter Ten: Trial Procedures

CONSTITUTIONAL RIGHT TO JURY TRIAL

The Sixth Amendment to the U.S. Constitution guarantees the accused in a criminal trial the right to an impartial jury. The Court held that this right also applied in state prosecutions because of the Due Process Clause of the Fourteenth Amendment. *Duncan v. Louisiana*, 391 U.S. 145 (1968). In *Duncan v. Louisiana* the Court examined whether a trial by jury is fundamental to the American scheme of justice — the standard the Court used for incorporation at the time.

DUNCAN v. LOUISIANA
391 U.S. 145 (1968)

JUSTICE WHITE delivered the opinion of the Court.

[SUMMARY: Duncan, a 19-year-old black male was driving on a Louisiana highway when he saw his two younger cousins engaged in a conversation with four white boys along the side of the road. Duncan knew that his cousins had just recently transferred to a formerly all-white high school and knew of racial incidents at the school. Duncan got out of his car, approached the group. There were varying accounts of what exactly happened, but Duncan encouraged his cousins to break off the encounter and as he was getting back into his car he either touched (Duncan and his witness's testimony) or slapped (the white witness's testimony) Herman Landry (one of the whites) on the elbow.

Duncan was charged with simple battery, a misdemeanor punishable by up to two years imprisonment and a $300.00 fine. He requested a jury trial, but the judge denied a jury stating that Louisiana law only provided for a jury trial for death penalty cases and cases resulting in imprisonment in hard labor. Duncan was convicted and sentenced to 60 days imprisonment and a $150.00 fine. He appealed in state courts claiming that the denial of a jury deprived him of his Sixth Amendment rights under the U.S. Constitution. The Court had to decide whether the Fourteenth Amendment Dupe Process Clause guarantees a jury trial in state prosecutions.]

OPINION:

The Fourteenth Amendment denies the States the power to "deprive any person of life, liberty, or property, without due process of law." In resolving conflicting claims concerning the meaning of this spacious language, the Court has looked increasingly to the Bill of Rights for guidance; many of the rights guaranteed by the first eight Amendments to the Constitution have been held to be protected against state action by the Due Process Clause of the Fourteenth Amendment. ...

...The claim before us is that the right to trial by jury guaranteed by the Sixth Amendment meets these tests. The position of Louisiana, on the other hand, is that the Constitution imposes upon the States no duty to give a jury trial in any criminal case, regardless of the seriousness of the crime or the size of the punishment which may be imposed. Because we believe that trial by jury in criminal cases is fundamental to the American scheme of justice, we hold that the Fourteenth Amendment guarantees a right of jury trial in all criminal cases which were they to be tried in a federal court would come within the Sixth Amendment's guarantee. Since we consider the appeal before us to be such a case, we hold that the Constitution was violated when appellant's demand for jury trial was refused.

Jury trial continues to receive strong support. The laws of every State guarantee a right to jury trial in serious criminal cases; no State has dispensed with it; nor are there significant movements underway to do so. ...

...The guarantees of jury trial in the Federal and State Constitutions reflect a profound judgment about the way in which law should be enforced and justice administered. A right to jury trial is granted to criminal defendants in order to prevent oppression by the Government.

[I]n the American States, as in the federal judicial system, a general grant of jury trial for serious offenses is a fundamental right, essential for preventing miscarriages of justice and for assuring that fair trials are provided for all defendants. We would not assert, however, that every criminal trial or any particular trial held before a judge alone is unfair or that a defendant may never be as fairly treated by a judge as he would be by a jury. Thus we hold no constitutional doubts about the practices, common in both federal and state courts, of accepting waivers of jury trial and prosecuting petty crimes without extending a right to jury trial. However, the fact is that in most places more trials for serious crimes are to juries than to a court alone; a great many defendants prefer the judgment of a jury to that of a court. Even where defendants are satisfied with bench trials, the right to a jury trial very likely serves its intended purpose of making judicial or prosecutorial unfairness less likely.

[Louisiana contends that Duncan's conviction is valid] . . . and constitutional because here the petitioner was tried for simple battery and was sentenced to only 60 days in the parish prison. We are not persuaded. It is doubtless true that there is a category of petty crimes or offenses which is not subject to the Sixth Amendment jury trial provision and should not be subject to the Fourteenth Amendment jury trial requirement here applied to the States. Crimes carrying possible penalties up to six months do not require a jury trial if they otherwise qualify as petty offenses. The question, then, is whether a crime carrying such a penalty is an offense which Louisiana may insist on trying without a jury.

We think not.

We need not, however, settle in this case the exact location of the line between petty offenses and serious crimes. It is sufficient for our purposes to hold that a crime punishable by two years in prison is, based on past and contemporary standards in this country, a serious crime and not a petty offense. Consequently appellant was entitled to a jury trial and it was error to deny it.

JUSTICE FORTAS, concurring

I would make these points clear today. Neither logic nor history nor the intent of the draftsmen of the Fourteenth Amendment can possibly be said to require that the Sixth Amendment or its jury trial provision be applied to the States together with the total gloss that this Court's decisions have supplied. The draftsmen of the Fourteenth Amendment intended what they said, not more or less: that no State shall deprive any person of life, liberty, or property without due process of law. It is ultimately the duty of this Court to interpret, to ascribe specific meaning to this phrase. There is no reason whatever for us to conclude that, in so doing, we are bound slavishly to follow not only the Sixth Amendment but all of its bag and baggage, however securely or insecurely affixed they may be by law and precedent to federal proceedings. To take this course, in my judgment, would be not only unnecessary but mischievous because it would inflict a serious blow upon the principle of federalism.

The Due Process Clause commands us to apply its great standard to state court proceedings to assure basic fairness. It does not command us rigidly and arbitrarily to impose the exact pattern of federal proceedings upon the 50 States. On the contrary, the Constitution's command, in my view, is that in our insistence upon state observance of due process, we should, so far as possible, allow the greatest latitude for state differences. ...

JUSTICE BLACK, with whom JUSTICE DOUGLAS joins, concurring.

...

I believe as strongly as ever that the Fourteenth Amendment was intended to make the Bill of Rights applicable to the States. I have been willing to support the selective incorporation doctrine, however, as an alternative, although perhaps less historically supportable than complete incorporation. The selective incorporation process, if used properly, does limit the Supreme Court in the Fourteenth Amendment field to specific Bill of Rights' protections only and keeps judges from roaming at will in their own notions of what policies outside the Bill of Rights are desirable and what are not. And, most importantly for me, the selective incorporation process has the virtue of having already worked to make most of the Bill of Rights' protections applicable to the States.

JUSTICE HARLAN, whom JUSTICE STEWART joins, dissenting, omitted.

Other Cases: Right to a Jury Trial

Baldwin v. New York, 399 U.S. 117 (1970),	***Blanton v. City of North Las Vegas, 489 U.S. 538 (1989),***
HOLDING: The Court held that a jury trial is not required for trials of petty crimes and trials for crimes with penalties of imprisonment of six months or less did not require a jury.	HOLDING: The Court held that a crime punishable by up to six months in jail was a "petty crime" even though it carried additional penalty such as a minimum jail stay or community service.

Right To A Unanimous Jury (Ramos v. Louisiana)

Fifty years ago, the Court allowed for a non-unanimous, 10-2 jury verdict in *Apodaca v. Oregon,* 406 U.S. 404 (1972) and a 9-3 verdict in *Johnson v. Louisiana*, 406 U.S. 356 (1972). Decided the same day, these cases both involved non-death penalty charges, and the holdings were the result of a plurality, and very split opinion. Over the decades no state had embraced the Court's invitation to allow non-unanimous juries but for Oregon and Louisiana (where the cases had arisen). In 2019, Oregon alone did not require a unanimous verdict (In 2018 Louisiana voters approved bipartisan legislation requiring jury unanimity in all felony cases. This law took effect in January 2019.) In Oregon, the criminal defense bar had long lobbied for a constitutional amendment requiring jury unanimity and the Oregon District Attorney's Association had indicated its willingness to submit the amendment to the voters. In the meantime, the case of *Ramos v. Louisiana*, 590 U.S. ___ (2020) reached the Court. At issue was whether the requirement of unanimity demanded by the federal courts as part of the Sixth Amendment was also a requirement for state courts. The briefing filed in the case is fascinating and the oral arguments are worth listening to (on Oyez). What is clear from the reading of the cases and the briefs does is not necessarily reflected in the holding per se. These cases were The Court had been signaling its impression that there was no "light of day" between the federal Bill of Rights and the state's obligations under the due process clause. In *Timbs v. Indiana*, ___ U.S. ___ (2019) the Court noted,

The sole exception (to the holding that the Bill of Rights are enforced against the state under the same standard as in the federal government) is our holding that the Sixth Amendment requires jury unanimity in federal, but not state, criminal proceedings. *Apodaca v. Oregon,* 406 U.S. 404 (1972). As we have explained, that "exception to the general rule . . . was the result of an unusual division among the Justices.

Ramos was decided in April 2020. Ramos had been charged with second-degree murder and requested a jury trial. Ten of the jurors voted to convict, but two jurors voted to acquit. Under

Louisiana law, only ten jurors were needed to convict (enter a guilty verdict). Ramos was sentenced to life in prison without the possibility of parole. He appealed, claiming his rights to a jury trial under the Sixth Amendment, as incorporated against the states, requires that a jury find a criminal defendant guilty by a unanimous verdict. The Court agreed, and in a 6-3 complex decision,[78]the Court held that

<hr/>

[78] Justice Neil Gorsuch authored the primary opinion.

In Part I, Justice Neil Gorsuch (writing for a majority: himself and Justices Ruth Bader Ginsburg, Stephen Breyer, Sonia Sotomayor, and Brett Kavanaugh) noted that the original public meaning of the Sixth Amendment's right to trial by jury, as well as its history, support an interpretation that it requires guilt be determined by a unanimous jury. Because this right is "fundamental to the American scheme of justice," it is incorporated against the states (that is, it applies to state governments as well) by the Due Process Clause of the Fourteenth Amendment. Thus, the Sixth Amendment requires a unanimous verdict to support a conviction in state court.

In Part II-A, Justice Gorsuch, writing for the same majority, explained how the Court's jurisprudence came to allow Oregon and Louisiana to permit non-unanimous jury verdicts, describing the fractured plurality opinions in those cases (*Apodaca v. Oregon* and *Johnson v. Louisiana*) with a fifth vote from Justice Lewis Powell that was "neither here nor there" but effectively permitted those states to proceed with non-unanimous jury verdicts.

In Part II-B, Justice Gorsuch wrote for a plurality of the Court (himself, and Justices Ginsburg, Breyer, Sotomayor), describing the confusion surrounding the *Apodaca* decision and the apparent conflict in the Court's precedent as to whether the Sixth Amendment requires unanimous jury verdicts.

In Part III, Justice Gorsuch, again writing for the majority, rejected Louisana's arguments for non-unanimous jury verdicts, finding that the drafting history of the Sixth Amendment is ambiguous at best, the *Apodaca* plurality's reasoning was "skimpy," and most importantly, that the *Apodaca* plurality "subjected the ancient guarantee of a unanimous jury verdict to its own functionalist assessment."

In Part IV-A, Justice Gorsuch, writing for a plurality (himself and Justices Ginsburg and Breyer), addressed the dissent's argument that the principle of stare decisis required the Court to stand by its decision in *Apodaca* and uphold Louisiana's non-unanimous jury law. Justice Gorsuch argued that under no view can the plurality opinion in *Apodaca* be controlling on today's Court.

Writing again for a majority in Part IV-B-1, Justice Gorsuch noted that even if the Court accepted the premise that *Apodaca* established a precedent, no one on the Court today would say it was rightly decided, and "stare decisis isn't supposed to be the art of methodically ignoring what everyone knows to be true."

For the four-justice plurality (Justice Kavanaugh did not join this part), Justice Gorsuch in Part IV-B-2 addressed the reliance interest Louisiana and Oregon have in the security of their final criminal judgments. Justice Gorsuch minimized the significance of the state's reliance interests and pointed instead to the reliance interests of the American people in having a just criminal jury that uniformly requires a unanimous verdict for a finding of guilt.

Justice Sotomayor filed an opinion concurring as to all but Part IV-A, writing separately to raise three points: "First, overruling precedent here is not only warranted, but compelled. Second, the interests at stake point far more clearly to that outcome than those in other recent cases. And finally, the racially biased origins of the Louisiana and Oregon laws uniquely matter here."

Justice Brett Kavanaugh wrote an opinion concurring in part to explain his view of how stare decisis applies in this case, laying out seven factors, which he argued, support overruling *Apodaca* in this case.

Justice Clarence Thomas filed an opinion concurring in the judgment. Justice Thomas noted from the outset that the Sixth Amendment right to trial by jury includes protection against non-unanimous jury verdicts and would thus resolve the question there. He would further find that the Sixth Amendment's right to a jury trial requires a unanimous verdict to support a conviction in federal court, but would find that the Privileges or Immunities Clause incorporates it against the states.

Justice Samuel Alito filed a dissenting opinion, in which Chief Justice John Roberts joined, and which Justice Elena Kagan joined as to all but Part III-D. Justice Alito argued that stare decisis requires following *Apodaca* and that in overruling that case, the majority "cast[] aside an important and long-established decision with little regard for the enormous reliance the decision has engendered." In the part of the dissent that Justice Kagan did not join, Justice Alito argued that the reliance in this case "far outstrips" the reliance interests in other recent cases where the dissenters in those cases claimed reliance interests." See, *Ramos v. Louisiana*." Oyez, www.oyez.org/cases/2019/18-5924. Accessed 6 Feb. 2023.

a jury verdict of guilty must be a unanimous verdict. Interestingly, in Oregon the Constitution still has a provision for a 10-2 verdict, and although that has been struck down by Ramos under principle of constitutional supremacy, the possibility of a non-guilty nonunanimous verdict remains. (Meaning, it takes all twelve jurors to convict (agree that defendant is guilty), but it only takes 10 jurors to acquit (agree that defendant is not guilty).

One issue raised by the advocates arguing before the Supreme Court in oral argument in Ramos was whether it would be retroactive to all individuals who had been convicted by a less than unanimous verdict—would the courts even know? That issue was resolved in *Edwards v. Vannoy*, 593 U.S. ___ (2021). Thedrick Edwards was convicted and sentenced to life in prison on a 11-1 verdict in Louisiana in 2007. (The one black juror in the case voted to acquit). Justice Kavanaugh's majority opinion pointed to Ramos being a new rule which historically were not applied retroactively.

Other Cases: Size and Unanimity of Jury

Williams v. Florida, 399 U.S. 78 (1970)

(As summarized in Burch v. Louisiana) (below) "The Court held that this constitutional guarantee of trial by jury did not require a State to provide an accused with a jury of 12 members and that Florida did not violate the jury trial rights of criminal defendants charged with nonpetty offenses by affording them jury panels comprised of only 6 persons. After canvassing the common-law development of the jury and the constitutional history of the jury trial right, the Court concluded that the 12-person requirement was "a historical accident" and that there was no indication that the Framers intended to preserve in the Constitution the features of the jury system as it existed at common law. Thus freed from strictly historical considerations, the Court turned to examine the function that this particular feature performs and its relation to the purposes of jury trial. The purpose of trial by jury, as noted in Duncan, is to prevent government oppression by providing a "safeguard against the corrupt or overzealous prosecutor and against the compliant, biased, or eccentric judge." Given this purpose, the Williams Court observed that the jury's essential feature lies in the "interposition between the accused and his accuser of the commonsense judgment of a group of laymen, and in the community participation and shared responsibility that results from that group's determination of guilt or innocence." These purposes could be fulfilled, the Court believed, so long as the jury was of a sufficient size to promote group deliberation, free from outside intimidation, and to provide a fair possibility that a cross section of the community would be represented on it. The Court concluded, however, that there is "little reason to think that these goals are in any meaningful sense less likely to be achieved when the jury numbers six, than when it numbers 12 — particularly if the requirement of unanimity is retained."

Ballew v. Georgia, 425 U.S. 223 (1978),

(As summarized in Burch v. Louisiana):

We considered whether a jury of less than six members passes constitutional scrutiny. The Court, in separate opinions, held that conviction by a unanimous five-person jury in a trial for a nonpetty offense deprives an accused of his right to trial by jury. While readily admitting that the line between six members and five was not altogether easy to justify, at least five Members of the Court believed that reducing a jury to five persons in nonpetty cases raised sufficiently substantial doubts as to the fairness of the proceeding and proper functioning of the jury to warrant drawing the line at six.

Burch v. Louisiana, 441 U.S. 130 (1979)

SUMMARY: Burch, an individual, and a Louisiana corporation (Wrestle) were jointly charged for showing two obscene motion pictures. Pursuant to Louisiana law, they were tried before a six-person jury, which found both guilty. A poll of the jury after verdict indicated that the jury had voted unanimously to convict petitioner Wrestle, Inc., and had voted 5-1 to convict petitioner Burch. Burch was sentenced to two consecutive 7-month prison terms, which were suspended, and fined $1,000; Wrestle, Inc., was fined $600 on each count.

Burch argued that permitting conviction by a nonunanimous six-member jury violated the rights of persons accused of nonpetty criminal offenses to trial by jury guaranteed by the Sixth and Fourteenth Amendments. The Louisiana Supreme Court, although finding that the question presented was a close one, allowed the conviction to stand.

OPINION: We agree with the Louisiana Supreme Court that the question presented is a "close" one. Nonetheless, we believe that conviction by a nonunanimous six-member jury in a state criminal trial for a nonpetty offense deprives an accused of his constitutional right to trial by jury.

Only in relatively recent years has this Court had to consider the practices of the several States relating to jury size and unanimity. The Court in Duncan held that because trial by jury in "serious" criminal cases is "fundamental to the American scheme of justice" and essential to due process of law, the Fourteenth Amendment guarantees a state criminal defendant the right to a jury trial in any case which, if tried in a federal court, would require a jury under the Sixth Amendment.

…[T]his case lies at the intersection of our decisions concerning jury size and unanimity. …[W]e do not pretend the ability to discern a priori a bright line below which the number of jurors participating in the trial or in the verdict would not permit the jury to function in the manner required by our prior cases. But having already departed from the strictly historical requirements of jury trial, it is inevitable that lines must be drawn somewhere if the substance of the jury trial right is to be preserved

This line-drawing process, "although essential, cannot be wholly satisfactory, for it requires attaching different consequences to events which, when they lie near the line, actually differ very little." However, much the same reasons that led us in *Ballew* to decide that use of a five-member jury threatened the fairness of the proceeding and the proper role of the jury, lead us to conclude now that conviction for a nonpetty offense by only five members of a six-person jury presents a similar threat to preservation of the substance of the jury trial guarantee and justifies our requiring verdicts rendered by six-person juries to be unanimous. We are buttressed in this view by the current jury practices of the several States. It appears that of those States that utilize six-member juries in trials of nonpetty offenses, only two, including Louisiana, also allow nonunanimous verdicts. We think that this near-uniform judgment of the Nation provides a useful guide in delimiting the line between those jury practices that are constitutionally permissible and those that are not.

[The State's interest in reducing time and expense of the administration of justice] … cannot prevail here. First, any benefits that might accrue by allowing five members of a six-person jury to render a verdict, as compared with requiring unanimity of a six-member jury, are speculative. More importantly, we think that when a State has reduced the size of its juries to the minimum number of jurors permitted by the Constitution, the additional authorization of nonunanimous verdicts by such juries sufficiently threatens the constitutional principles that led to the establishment of the size threshold that any countervailing interest of the State should yield.

JURY SELECTION

Some attorneys feel that a case is won or lost by what happens during voir dire (questioning of the petit jury (the trial jury)). Some judges allow attorneys wide latitude in questioning the jury, and so they use voir dire to educate the jury on their theory of the case or the difficult issues which may arise — under the guise of exploring a juror's possible bias and ability to follow the law. Other judges severely limit the types of questioning that can be done. Attorneys may be able to push onto the judge the difficult task of approaching highly sensitive questions claiming that if jurors are to be offended better to have them mad at the judge rather than one side or the other. Jury selection practices vary widely among jurisdictions, as do the qualifications required of jurors and the source of the *venire* (large jury panel). (Note that the grand jurors who indicted the defendant will never be the trial jurors.)

Each side can challenge a potential juror either by exercising a "challenge for cause" or a "peremptory challenge" A challenge for cause involves the party striking off a juror from the petit jury because of either express bias or implied bias. Because bias affects the outcome of a case and the possibility of a fair trial, challenges for cause are unlimited. Each party may challenge off of the jury as many people as it can show demonstrate either *express bias* (prejudice against one side or person) or *implied bias* (based upon the relationship of the juror to one of the parties or participants in the trial). Challenges for cause are generally exercised by the judge at the request of one of the parties.

The second type of challenge is a peremptory challenge. Peremptory challenges are discretionary, and the party need not demonstrate that the juror it wishes to challenge has either express or implied bias. Because peremptory challenges can be used without regard to any particular quality of a juror, they have been used as a tool to exclude certain segments of the citizenry from serving as jurors. Early cases have invalidated the use of peremptory challenges: *Strauder v. West Virginia,* 100 U.S. 303 (1880) (a state statute that explicitly excluded African Americans from jury service violated the Equal Protection Clause); *Norris v. Alabama* 294 U.S. 587 (1935) (a virtual exclusion of African Americans from grand juries violated the Equal Protections Clause); *Swain v. Alabama,* 380 U.S. 202(1965) (the exclusion of a prospective juror because of race violates the defendant's equal protection rights, but violations must be proven by a pattern of exclusions over a number of cases).

On January 1, 2022 a rule passed by the Arizona Supreme Court eliminated the peremptory challenge in all jury trials in Arizona (including criminal, civil, and eviction cases).[79] The rule was in response to a statewide task force that evaluated whether Arizona juries were fair representations of their communities. Attorneys are still able to exercise challenges for cause, but they have to bear the burden by preponderance of the evidence to show a juror could not render a fair and impartial verdict. See, Ariz. R. Civ. P. 47(d)(3). In light of these rule changes, a more robust voir dire is critical to better ascertain possible conflicts and biases among potential jurors. In recognition of this need, the Arizona Supreme Court considered the results of the study conducted by the state task force. The task force made three specific findings:

➤ Research indicates that prospective jurors are more willing to provide candid information in a written response format (versus open questioning in front of the panel).

➤ Research also suggests that jurors are more willing to provide candid and useful information when asked open-ended questions about their personal opinions and life experiences rather than questions about undefined terms such as "bias" "prejudice" and whether they will follow the law. (Most people believe they are fair and impartial and are unsuccessful at identifying when they have bias or prejudice.)

➤ Research suggests that jurors are willing to provide a basis for disqualification, but they must be asked the right questions.

In response to this rule, House Bill 2413 was proposed to reinstate peremptory challenges in criminal cases. It advanced to the House Judicial Committee with a 6-4 vote, but apparently failed or was deleted in June of 2022. So, it seems as February 2023, at least one state is trying to reform their jury selection process.

---

[79]). https://www.righilaw.com/news-events/2022/february/arizona-eliminates-peremptory-challenges-in-all-/

In the key case of *Batson v. Kentucky,* 476 U.S. 79 (1986), the Court held that peremptory challenges may not be used to exclude a potential juror based solely on race. Batson overturned *Swain* by allowing proof of discrimination in a single case (rather than several cases showing a pattern of exclusions).

BATSON v. KENTUCKY
476 U.S. 79 (1986)

JUSTICE POWELL delivered the opinion of the Court.

This case requires us to reexamine that portion of *Swain v. Alabama* concerning the evidentiary burden placed on a criminal defendant who claims that he has been denied equal protection through the State's use of peremptory challenges to exclude members of his race from the petit jury.

Petitioner, a black man, was indicted in Kentucky on charges of second-degree burglary and receipt of stolen goods. On the first day of trial in Jefferson Circuit Court, the judge conducted *voir dire* examination of the venire, excused certain jurors for cause, and permitted the parties to exercise peremptory challenges. The prosecutor used his peremptory challenges to strike all four black persons on the venire, and a jury composed only of white persons was selected. Defense counsel moved to discharge the jury before it was sworn on the ground that the prosecutor's removal of the black veniremen violated petitioner's rights under the Sixth and Fourteenth Amendments to a jury drawn from a cross-section of the community, and under the Fourteenth Amendment to equal protection of the laws. Counsel requested a hearing on his motion. Without expressly ruling on the request for a hearing, the trial judge observed that the parties were entitled to use their peremptory challenges to "strike anybody they want to." The judge then denied petitioner's motion, reasoning that the cross-section requirement applies only to selection of the venire and not to selection of the petit jury itself. The jury convicted petitioner on both counts. The Supreme Court of Kentucky affirmed. We granted certiorari and now reverse.

In *Swain v. Alabama,* this Court recognized that a "State's purposeful or deliberate denial to Negroes on account of race of participation as jurors in the administration of justice violates the Equal Protection Clause." This principle has been "consistently and repeatedly" reaffirmed, in numerous decisions of this Court both preceding and following *Swain.* We reaffirm the principle today.

More than a century ago, the Court decided that the State denies a black defendant equal protection of the laws when it puts him on trial before a jury from which members of his race have been purposefully excluded. *Strauder v. West Virginia* (1880). That decision laid the foundation for the Court's unceasing efforts to eradicate racial discrimination in the procedures used to select the venire from which individual jurors are drawn. In *Strauder,* the Court explained that the central concern of the recently ratified Fourteenth Amendment was to put an end to governmental discrimination on account of race. Exclusion of black citizens from service as jurors constitutes a primary example of the evil the Fourteenth Amendment was designed to cure.

In holding that racial discrimination in jury selection offends the Equal Protection Clause, the Court in *Strauder* recognized, however, that a defendant has no right to a "petit jury composed in whole or in part of persons of his own race." "The number of our races and nationalities stands in the way of evolution of such a conception" of the demand of equal protection. But the defendant does have the right to be tried by a jury whose members are selected pursuant to nondiscriminatory criteria. The Equal Protection Clause guarantees the defendant that the State will not exclude members of his race from the jury venire on account of race, or on the false assumption that members of his race as a group are not qualified to serve as jurors.

Purposeful racial discrimination in selection of the venire violates a defendant's right to equal protection because it denies him the protection that a trial by jury is intended to secure. "The very idea of a jury is a body composed of the peers or equals of the person whose rights it is selected or summoned to determine; that is, of his neighbors, fellows, associates, persons having the same legal status in society as that which he holds." The petit jury has occupied a central position in our system of justice by safeguarding a person accused of crime against the arbitrary exercise of power by prosecutor or judge. Those on the venire must be "indifferently chosen" to secure the defendant's right under the Fourteenth Amendment to "protection of life and liberty against race or color prejudice."

Racial discrimination in selection of jurors harms not only the accused whose life or liberty they are summoned to try. Competence to serve as a juror ultimately depends on an assessment of individual qualifications and ability impartially to consider evidence presented at a trial. A person's race simply "is unrelated to his fitness as a juror." As long ago as *Strauder,* therefore, the Court recognized that by denying a person participation in jury service on account of his race, the State unconstitutionally discriminated against the excluded juror.

The harm from discriminatory jury selection extends beyond that inflicted on the defendant and the excluded juror to touch the entire community. Selection procedures that purposefully exclude black persons from juries undermine public confidence in the fairness of our system of justice. Discrimination within the judicial system is most pernicious because it is "a stimulant to that race prejudice which is an impediment to securing to [black citizens] that equal justice which the law aims to secure to all others."

As in any equal protection case, the "burden is, of course," on the defendant who alleges

discriminatory selection of the venire "to prove the existence of purposeful discrimination." In deciding if the defendant has carried his burden of persuasion, a court must undertake "a sensitive inquiry into such circumstantial and direct evidence of intent as may be available." Circumstantial evidence of invidious intent may include proof of disproportionate impact. We have observed that under some circumstances proof of discriminatory impact "may for all practical purposes demonstrate unconstitutionality because in various circumstances the discrimination is very difficult to explain on nonracial grounds." For example, "total or seriously disproportionate exclusion of Negroes from jury venires is itself such an 'unequal application of the law as to show intentional discrimination.'"

Moreover, since *Swain,* we have recognized that a black defendant alleging that members of his race have been impermissibly excluded from the venire may make out a *prima facie* case of purposeful discrimination by showing that the totality of the relevant facts gives rise to an inference of discriminatory purpose. Once the defendant makes the requisite showing, the burden shifts to the State to explain adequately the racial exclusion. The State cannot meet this burden on mere general assertions that its officials did not discriminate or that they properly performed their official duties. Rather, the State must demonstrate that "permissible racially neutral selection criteria and procedures have produced the monochromatic result." The standards for assessing a *prima facie* case in the context of discriminatory selection of the venire have been fully articulated since *Swain.* These principles support our conclusion that a defendant may establish a *prima facie* case of purposeful discrimination in selection of the petit jury solely on evidence concerning the prosecutor's exercise of peremptory challenges at the defendant's trial. To establish such a case, the defendant first must show that he is a member of a cognizable racial group, and that the prosecutor has exercised peremptory challenges to remove from the venire members of the defendant's race.

Second, the defendant is entitled to rely on the fact, as to which there can be no dispute, that peremptory challenges constitute a jury selection practice that permits "those to discriminate who are of a mind to discriminate." Finally, the defendant must show that these facts and any other relevant circumstances raise an inference that the prosecutor used that practice to exclude the veniremen from the petit jury on account of their race. This combination of factors in the empanelling of the petit jury, as in the selection of the venire, raises the necessary inference of purposeful discrimination.

In deciding whether the defendant has made the requisite showing, the trial court should consider all relevant circumstances. For example, a "pattern" of strikes against black jurors included in the particular venire might give rise to an inference of discrimination. Similarly, the prosecutor's questions and statements during *voir dire* examination and in exercising his challenges may support or refute an inference of discriminatory purpose. These examples are merely illustrative. We have confidence that trial judges, experienced in supervising *voir dire,* will be able to decide if the circumstances concerning the prosecutor's use of peremptory challenges creates a *prima facie* case of discrimination against black jurors.

Once the defendant makes a *prima facie* showing, the burden shifts to the State to come forward with a neutral explanation for challenging black jurors. ...[T]he prosecutor may not rebut the defendant's *prima facie* case of discrimination by stating merely that he challenged jurors of the defendant's race on the assumption — or his intuitive judgment — that they would be partial to the defendant because of their shared race. ... The core guarantee of equal protection, ensuring citizens that their State will not discriminate on account of race, would be meaningless were we to approve the exclusion of jurors on the basis of such assumptions, which arise solely from the jurors' race. Nor may the prosecutor rebut the defendant's case merely by denying that he had a discriminatory

motive or "affirming his good faith in individual selections." If these general assertions were accepted as rebutting a defendant's *prima facie* case, the Equal Protection Clause "would be but a vain and illusory requirement." The prosecutor therefore must articulate a neutral explanation related to the particular case to be tried. The trial court then will have the duty to determine if the defendant has established purposeful discrimination.

. . . .

In this case, petitioner made a timely objection to the prosecutor's removal of all black persons on the venire. Because the trial court flatly rejected the objection without requiring the prosecutor to give an explanation for his action, we remand this case for further proceedings. If the trial court decides that the facts establish, *prima facie,* purposeful discrimination and the prosecutor does not come forward with a neutral explanation for his action, our precedents require that petitioner's conviction be reversed.

JUSTICE REHNQUIST, with whom THE CHIEF JUSTICE joins, dissenting.

I cannot subscribe to the Court's unprecedented use of the Equal Protection Clause to restrict the historic scope of the peremptory challenge, which has been described as "a necessary part of trial by jury." In my view, there is simply nothing "unequal" about the State using its peremptory challenges to strike blacks from the jury in cases involving black defendants, so long as such challenges are also used to exclude whites in cases involving white defendants, Hispanics in cases involving Hispanic defendants, Asians in cases involving Asian defendants, and so on. This case-specific use of peremptory challenges by the State does not single out blacks, or members of any other race for that matter, for discriminatory treatment. Such use of preemptories is at best based upon seat-of-the-pants instincts, which are undoubtedly crudely stereotypical and may in many cases be hopelessly mistaken. But as long as they are applied across the board to jurors of all races and nationalities, I do not see — and the Court most certainly has not explained — how their use violates the Equal Protection.

Nor does such use of peremptory challenges by the State infringe upon any other constitutional interests. . . . [B]ecause the case-specific use of peremptory challenges by the State does not deny blacks the right to serve as jurors in cases involving non-black defendants, it harms neither the excluded jurors nor the remainder of the community.

. . . .

The Court has extended the rationale in *Batson* to ethnicity (*Hernandez v. New York*, 500 U.S. 352 (1991)) and gender (*J.E.B v. Alabama ex rel. T.B.*, 511 U.S. 127 (1994)). The Court's rationale pointed to a a party's right to have a certain mix of jurors and also to the Equal Protection Clause's ensuring a person's ability to sit on a jury without regard for race or gender. In Hernandez the Court expanded Batson to include peremptory challenges of Hispanic jurors since this ethnic category was akin to a cognizable racial group for purposes of exclusion from jury service during voir dire. J.E.B. involved a paternity suit by the state on behalf of T.B., the mother of a minor child. After challenges for cause, only ten of thirty-three jurors were male; the "State then used 9 of its 10 peremptory strikes to remove male jurors; petitioner used all but one of his strikes to remove female jurors. As a result, all the selected jurors were female." The Supreme Court upheld J.E.B.'s contention that the pattern of striking male jurors by the state, solely on the basis of gender, constituted the kind of purposeful discrimination that violated the Equal Protection Clause. To excuse male or female jurors by the use of peremptory challenges solely on the basis of their gender assumes men and women "hold particular views simply because of their gender." This stereotype reflects and reinforces patterns of historical discrimination that are contrary to the equal protection of laws.

The Court has applied *Batson* to a variety of situations. For example, in *Powers v. Ohio*, 499 U.S. 400 (1991) the Court held that a defendant has standing to challenge a prosecutor's peremptory challenges to remove a juror from the jury on account of race, notwithstanding the fact that the juror is not of the same race as the defendant. In *Powers,* the defendant was white, but the removed juror was African American. The Court stated, "A prosecutor's discriminatory use of peremptory challenges harms the excluded jurors and the community at large."

In *Edmonson v. Leesville Concrete Company,* 500 U.S. 614 (1991) the Court applied *Batson* to all parties in a civil lawsuit and also held that because it (the Supreme Court) was a federal court, it could only apply a constitutional provision to a state lawsuit if there was a state action. Prosecutors are state actors, but civil litigants are not. Nevertheless, the Court found that the judge's action in dismissing the challenged juror at the party's request was held to be a state action since the judge was a state actor.

In 1992 *Georgia v. McCollum,* 505 U.S. 42 (1992), applied the ruling of *Batson* to the defendant's exercise of a peremptory challenge by holding that the defense attorney who exercised a peremptory challenge was engaged in a state action. The Court reiterated that protection of the defendant was only one goal of Batson — the harm to the excluded juror and the community's confidence in a fair and impartial jury was at least as important.

The first step in the process of a Batson challenge is for the challenging party to make a showing of *prima facia* discrimination — that is, discrimination on its face. Since *Batson*, the Court has found *prima facia* discrimination in several cases. For example, in *Miller-El v. Cockrell*, 537 U.S. 322 (2003), the Court found that the prosecutor violated *Batson* when he struck 91% of the eligible black jurors with peremptory strikes compared with just 13% of eligible nonblack prospective jurors.

The second step in the process of a *Batson* challenge is for the opposing party to offer a race-neutral reason why the juror was struck. In *Purkett v. Elem,* 514 U.S. 765 (1995), a prosecutor eliminated two African American jurors, and when challenged under Batson, said the potential jurors were excluded, not because of their race, but because of long unkempt hair, their mustaches and goatee beards. The U.S. Court of Appeals said that these were not legitimate race-neutral explanations, but the Supreme Court reversed. It noted that the proffer of a race-neutral explanation for supporting a peremptory challenge is the second step after the opponent of a peremptory challenge made out a prima facie cause of racial discrimination. At this step, any race-neutral explanation for striking a juror must at first be accepted by a trial judge.

The third step involves the court evaluating whether the opponent of the strike has proved purposeful racial discrimination and whether the proffered explanation is a pretext or cover for purposeful discrimination. In a 2006 Ninth Circuit case, *Yee v. Duncan,* 441 F.3d 851(9th Cir. 2006), the court found that

> "When a criminal defendant has established a *prima facie* case of gender discrimination in the prosecutor's use of a peremptory challenge during jury selection, and the prosecutor is unable to recall the basis for her challenge, a trial court may not substitute findings of the prosecutor's sincerity, together with circumstantial evidence indicating a lack of gender-based motive, for the prosecutor's failure to offer a gender-neutral explanation for the challenge."

In 2005, the Court decided *Miller-El v. Dretke* 545 U.S. 231 (2005) which examined the peremptory challenges based on race. *Miller-El* involved the Dallas County (Texas) prosecutor's use of peremptory strikes against 10 of the 11 qualified black venire members during jury selection for Miller-El's capital murder trial. He objected, claiming that the strikes were based on race and could not be presumed legitimate since the District Attorney's Office had a history of excluding blacks from criminal juries. The Court noted,

> "More powerful than the bare statistics are side-by-side comparisons of some black venire panelists who were struck and white ones who were not. If a prosecutor's proffered reason for striking a black panelist applies just as well to a white panelist allowed to serve, that is evidence tending to prove purposeful discrimination." . . . "The details of two panel member comparisons bear out this Court's observation that the prosecution's reason for exercising peremptory strikes against some black panel members appeared to apply equally to some white jurors." . . . "As for law, the *Batson* rule provides the prosecutor an opportunity to give the reason for striking a juror and requires the judge to assess the reason's plausibility in light of all of the evidence, but it does not does not call for a mere exercise in thinking up any rational basis."

The Court also reviewed the prosecutor's use of the Texas law allowing either side to "shuffle the cards" with jury panel member's names and concluded,

> "The prosecution's broader patterns of practice during jury selection also support the case for discrimination. . . . No racially neutral reason for the shuffling has ever been offered, and nothing stops the suspicion of discriminatory intent from rising to an inference."

Additionally, the court looked at the type of questions and statements the prosecutor made to the potential jurors and found,

> "The contrasting voir dire questions posed respectively to black and nonblack panel members also indicate that the State was trying to avoid black jurors.". . . "The final body of evidence confirming the conclusion here is that the Dallas County District Attorney's Office had, for decades, followed a specific policy of systematically excluding blacks from juries. The

Miller-El prosecutors' notes of the race of each panel member show that they took direction from a jury selection manual that included racial stereotypes."

The court concluded,

"The prosecutors' chosen race-neutral reasons for the strikes do not hold up and are so far at odds with the evidence that pretext is the fair conclusion. The selection process was replete with evidence that prosecutors were selecting and rejecting potential jurors because of race. And the prosecutors took their cues from a manual on jury selection with an emphasis on race. It blinks reality to deny that the State struck Fields and Warren because they were black. The facts correlate to nothing as well as to race."

In the past few years, the Court has routinely accepted review and issued opinions in cases involving *Batson* challenges. These cases are fact-specific, and the Court continues to follow the analysis in *Batson* and *Miller-El* in its decisions. One recent case, involving the repeated prosecution of Curtis Flowers. Since the Court's ruling in the case: Mr. Flowers has sued the district attorney, Doug Evans;[80] District attorney Evans ran for a county court judgeship and was beat in a landslide[81]; Mr. Flowers' case was dismissed *with prejudice*—meaning that the state cannot retry him for the seventh time;[82] Mr. Flower's has settled with the state for $500.000 for the 23 years he spent incarcerated,[83] and there was a two-season podcast, *In the Dark*, about his case.[84]

FLOWERS V. MISSISSIPPI,
588 U.S. ___ (2019)

Kavanaugh, J., delivered the opinion of the Court, in which Roberts, C. J., and Ginsburg, Breyer, Alito, Sotomayor, and Kagan, JJ., joined.

Official Summary:

Petitioner Curtis Flowers has been tried six separate times for the murder of four employees of a Mississippi furniture store. Flowers is black; three of the four victims were white. At the first two trials, the State used its peremptory strikes on all of the qualified black prospective jurors. In each case, the jury convicted Flowers and sentenced him to death, but the convictions were later reversed by the Mississippi Supreme Court based on prosecutorial misconduct. At the third trial, the State used all of its 15 peremptory strikes against black prospective

jurors, and the jury convicted Flowers and sentenced him to death. The Mississippi Supreme Court reversed again, this time concluding that the State exercised its peremptory strikes on the basis of race in violation of Batson v. Kentucky, 476 U.S. 79. Flowers' fourth and fifth trials ended in mistrials. At the fourth, the State exercised 11 peremptory strikes—all against black prospective jurors. No available racial information exists about the prospective jurors in the fifth trial. At the sixth trial, the State exercised six peremptory strikes—five against black prospective jurors, allowing one black juror to be seated. Flowers again raised a Batson claim, but the trial court concluded that the State had offered race-neutral reasons for each of the five peremptory strikes. The

---

[80] In June,2022 an appeal was taken from the U.S. District Court which had dismissed Flower's suit against Doug Evans (chrome-extension://efaidnbmnnnibpcajpcglclefindmkaj/https://www.ca5.uscourts.gov/opinions/pub/20/20-60913-CV0.pdf) to the Fifth Circuit Court of Appeals. In September 2022, the Fifth Circuit affirmed the District Court's dismissal.

[81] See, https://deathpenaltyinfo.org/news/curtis-flowers-prosecutor-defeated-in-bid-to-become-county-judge

[82] See, https://www.americanbar.org/groups/committees/death_penalty_representation/project_press/2020/fall-2020/curtis-flowers-all-charges-dropped/

[83] https://www.usatoday.com/story/news/nation/2021/03/03/curtis-flowers-wrongfully-imprisoned-compensation-mississippi-death-row/6908892002/

[84] https://features.apmreports.org/in-the-dark/

jury convicted Flowers and sentenced him to death. ...

Held: All of the relevant facts and circumstances taken together establish that the trial court at Flowers' sixth trial committed clear error in concluding that the State's peremptory strike of black prospective juror Carolyn Wright was not motivated in substantial part by discriminatory intent.

(a) Under Batson, once a prima facie case of discrimination has been shown by a defendant, the State must provide race-neutral reasons for its peremptory strikes. The trial judge then must determine whether the prosecutor's stated reasons were the actual reasons or instead were a pretext for discrimination. The Batson Court rejected four arguments. First, the Batson Court rejected the idea that a defendant must demonstrate a history of racially discriminatory strikes in order to make out a claim of race discrimination. Second, the Batson Court rejected the argument that a prosecutor could strike a black juror based on an assumption or belief that the black juror would favor a black defendant. Third, the Batson Court rejected the argument that race-based peremptories should be permissible because black, white, Asian, and Hispanic defendants and jurors were all "equally" subject to race-based discrimination. Fourth, the Batson Court rejected the argument that race-based peremptories are permissible because both the prosecution and defense could employ them in any individual case and in essence balance things out.

(b) Four categories of evidence loom large in assessing the Batson issue here, where the State had a persistent pattern of striking black prospective jurors from Flowers' first through his sixth trial.

(1) A review of the history of the State's peremptory strikes in Flowers' first four trials strongly supports the conclusion that the State's use of peremptory strikes in Flowers' sixth trial was motivated in substantial part by discriminatory intent. The State tried to strike all 36 black prospective jurors over the course of the first four trials. And the state courts

themselves concluded that the State had violated Batson on two separate occasions. The State's relentless, determined effort to rid the jury of black individuals strongly suggests that the State wanted to try Flowers before a jury with as few black jurors as possible, and ideally before an all-white jury.

(2) The State's use of peremptory strikes in Flowers' sixth trial followed the same pattern as the first four trials.

(3) Disparate questioning can be probative of discriminatory intent. Miller-El v. Cockrell .... Here, the State spent far more time questioning the black prospective jurors than the accepted white jurors—145 questions asked of 5 black prospective jurors and 12 questions asked of 11 white seated jurors. The record refutes the State's explanation that it questioned black and white prospective jurors differently only because of differences in the jurors' characteristics. Along with the historical evidence from the earlier trials, as well as the State's striking of five of six black prospective jurors at the sixth trial, the dramatically disparate questioning and investigation of black prospective jurors and white prospective jurors at the sixth trial strongly suggest that the State was motivated in substantial part by a discriminatory intent.

(4) Comparing prospective jurors who were struck and not struck can be an important step in determining whether a Batson violation occurred. See Snyder v. Louisiana. ... Here, Carolyn Wright, a black prospective juror, was struck, the State says, in part because she knew several defense witnesses and had worked at Wal-Mart where Flowers' father also worked. But three white prospective jurors also knew many individuals involved in the case, and the State asked them no individual questions about their connections to witnesses. White prospective jurors also had relationships with members of Flowers' family, but the State did not ask them follow-up questions in order to explore the depth of those relationships. The State also incorrectly explained that it exercised a peremptory strike against Wright because she had worked with

one of Flowers' sisters and made apparently incorrect statements to justify the strikes of other black prospective jurors. When considered with other evidence, a series of factually inaccurate explanations for striking black prospective jurors can be another clue showing discriminatory intent. The overall context here requires skepticism of the State's strike of Carolyn Wright. The trial court at Flowers' sixth trial committed clear error in concluding that the State's peremptory strike of black prospective juror Carolyn Wright was not motivated in substantial part by discriminatory intent.

Alito, J., filed a concurring opinion.

As the Court takes pains to note, this is a highly unusual case. Indeed, it is likely one of a kind. In 1996, four defenseless victims, three white and one black, were slaughtered in a furniture store in a small town in Montgomery County, Mississippi, a jurisdiction with fewer than 11,000 inhabitants. One of the victims was the owner of the store, which was widely frequented by residents of the community. The person prosecuted for this crime, petitioner Curtis Flowers, an African-American, comes from a local family whose members make up a gospel group and have many community ties.

By the time jury selection began in the case now before us, petitioner had already been tried five times for committing that heinous and inflammatory crime. Three times, petitioner was convicted and sentenced to death, but all three convictions were reversed by the State Supreme Court. Twice, the jurors could not reach a unanimous verdict. In all of the five prior trials, the State was represented by the same prosecutor, and as the Court recounts, many of those trials were marred by racial discrimination in the selection of jurors and prosecutorial misconduct. Nevertheless, the prosecution at the sixth trial was led by the same prosecutor, and the case was tried in Montgomery County where, it appears, a high

percentage of the potential jurors have significant connections to either petitioner, one or more of the victims, or both.

These connections and the community's familiarity with the case were bound to complicate a trial judge's task in trying to determine whether the prosecutor's asserted reason for striking a potential juror was a pretext for racial discrimination, and that is just what occurred. Petitioner argues that the prosecution improperly struck five black jurors, but for each of the five, the prosecutor gave one or more reasons that were not only facially legitimate but were of a nature that would be of concern to a great many attorneys. If another prosecutor in another case in a larger jurisdiction gave any of these reasons for exercising a peremptory challenge and the trial judge credited that explanation, an appellate court would probably have little difficulty affirming that finding. And that result, in all likelihood, would not change based on factors that are exceedingly difficult to assess, such as the number of voir dire questions the prosecutor asked different members of the venire.

But this is not an ordinary case, and the jury selection process cannot be analyzed as if it were. In light of all that had gone before, it was risky for the case to be tried once again by the same prosecutor in Montgomery County. Were it not for the unique combinations of circumstances present here, I would have no trouble affirming the decision of the Supreme Court of Mississippi, which conscientiously applied the legal standards applicable in less unusual cases. But viewing the totality of the circumstances present here, I agree with the Court that petitioner's capital conviction cannot stand.

Thomas, J., filed a dissenting opinion, in which Gorsuch, J., joined as to Parts I, II, and III., omitted

FAIR CROSS SECTION JURY COMPOSITION

In 2010, the National Center for State Courts published "Jury Manager's Toolbox, a Primer on Fair Cross Section Jurisprudence." It provides an excellent discussion of the Court's case holdings on the requirement of a fair cross section as implicated by the right to a fair trial provided in the Sixth Amendment. One of the primary tasks of a state court system is making sure potential jurors are summoned to sit on "jury duty." There is a great deal of variation among the states concerning who is eligible, how the courts get the list of individuals, how jurors are summoned, how long their term of service is.

"The phrase "a jury of one's peers" brings to mind an image of a jury that perfectly mirrors its community in terms of demographic and attitudinal characteristics. In an ideal world, a perfectly representative jury would be best able to fulfill its role as the conscience of the community in judicial decision-making. As a practical matter, however, the legal requirements governing the composition of the jury do not mandate perfect representation of the jury pool. Rather, they set the minimum standards that state and federal courts must achieve to guarantee the Sixth Amendment and Equal Protection rights of criminal defendants to a jury drawn from a fair cross section of the community. Originally, the Sixth Amendment right to "a speedy and public trial, by an impartial jury of the State and district wherein the crime shall have been committed" focused on the ability of individual jurors to judge the cases before them fairly and impartially. Over time, however, courts came to recognize the reality that jurors have preexisting life experiences, attitudes and opinions that affect the way they perceive and interpret information. Courts abandoned their insistence on unrealistically stringent criteria for the impartiality of individual jurors (e.g., no relevant life experience, attitude or opinions related to the case). Instead, the theory supporting jury diversity is that biases held by individual jurors will be balanced or canceled out by competing biases held by other jurors. Gradually, they adopted the idea that the best way to ensure a fair and impartial jury is to ensure a diverse jury pool from which to select juries. An important caveat concerning the fair cross section requirement is that it only applies to the pool from which juries are selected, not to composition of the jury itself."

The contemporary test to determine whether a violation of the fair cross section has occurred is the *Duren* test, named for *Duren v. Missouri*, a 1979 case decided by the U.S. Supreme Court. In *Duren*, the Court addressed the question of whether an automatic exemption from jury service offered to women was unconstitutional given that it reduced the percentage of women from 46% of the community to 15% of the pool from which the defendant's jury was selected. The Court described three criteria that a defendant must show to establish a prima facie violation of the fair cross section requirement: (1) the group alleged to be excluded is a "distinctive" group in the community; (2) the group's representation in the jury pool is not fair and reasonable in relation to the number of such persons in the population; and (3) the under-representation of the group results from systematic exclusion of the group in the jury selection process. Once the defendant has established a prima facie violation of the fair cross section requirement, the burden shifts to the State to provide a compelling justification for the systematic exclusion of the distinctive group. Duren made it clear, however, that the States retained broad discretion to define eligibility qualifications and exemption criteria for jury service.

A "distinctive" group for fair cross section purposes generally refers to groups that see themselves as distinct from other groups, that are seen by others as a distinct group, and that hold values not necessarily held by other groups. Many court opinions also refer to these groups using Equal Protection terminology of "cognizable" groups. In most instances, these groups are defined by immutable characteristics, especially gender, race, and ethnicity

(Hispanic/Latino) and are recognized as valid groups under both Sixth Amendment and Equal Protection Clause criteria. In addition to gender, race, and ethnicity, some courts have found groups characterized by religious affiliation or national origin to be distinctive groups under the Sixth Amendment. In most instances, however, distinctive groups characterized by religious affiliation have such a strongly cohesive community that the religious affiliation is similar to ethnicity in terms of its cultural significance (e.g., Jews in New York City and Amish persons in Ohio)." (Jury Manager's Toolbox, a Primer on Fair Cross Section Jurisprudence, National Center for State Courts, 2010)[85].

Other Cases: Fair Cross Section

Berghuis v. Smith, 559 U.S. 314 (2010)

SUMMARY: Diapolis Smith, was a black man who was charged with murder for shooting and killing Christopher Rumbly in a bar brawl in Grand Rapids Michigan. The bar was crowded, with 200-300 people on the premise at the time -- all of whom were black. The state charged Smith with murder in Kent County Circuit Court.

The voir dire for Smith's trial took place in September 1993. The venire panel included between 60 and 100 individuals. At most, three venire members were African-American. Smith unsuccessfully objected to the composition of the venire panel.

At the time of Smith's trial, African-Americans constituted 7.28% of Kent County's jury-eligible population, and 6% of the pool from which potential jurors were drawn.

 Smith's case proceeded to trial before an all-white jury. The case for the prosecution turned on the identity of the man who shot Rumbley. Thirty-seven witnesses from the bar, including Smith, testified at the trial. Of those, two testified that Smith fired the gun. Five testified that the shooter was not Smith, and the remainder made no identifications of the shooter. The jury convicted Smith of second-degree murder and possession of a firearm during a felony, and the court sentenced him to life imprisonment with the possibility of parole.

The defendant appealed his conviction. On his first appeal, the Michigan Court of Appeals ordered the trial court to conduct an evidentiary hearing on Smith's fair-cross-section claim. At the hearing Smith introduced the testimony of an expert in demographics and economics, who tied the underrepresentation to social and economic factors. In Kent County, the expert explained, these forces made African-Americans less likely than whites to receive or return juror-eligibility questionnaires, and more likely to assert a hardship excuse.

The hearing convinced the trial court that African-Americans were underrepresented in Circuit Court venires. But Smith's evidence was insufficient, that court held, to prove that the juror-assignment order, or any other part of the jury-selection process, had systematically excluded African-Americans. The court therefore rejected Smith's fair-cross-section claim.

The Michigan Court of Appeals concluded that the juror-allocation system in place at the relevant time did result in the underrepresentation of African-Americans. . . .

The Michigan Supreme Court, in turn, reversed the Court of Appeals' judgment, concluding that Smith "ha[d] not established a prima facie violation of the Sixth Amendment fair-cross-section requirement."

The Court noted the Sixth Amendment secures to criminal defendants the right to be tried by an impartial jury drawn from sources reflecting a fair cross section of the community. The question presented in this case is whether that right was accorded to respondent Diapolis Smith.

The Court followed the *Duren* test of evaluating challenges to fair-cross-section requirement. It disagreed with Smith's argument that to "establish systematic exclusion the defendant must show only that the underrepresentation is persistent and "produced by the method or

---

[85] /https://www.ncsc-jurystudies.org/__data/assets/pdf_file/0026/7478/a-primer-on-fair-cross-section.pdf

'system' used to select [jurors]," rather than by chance."

No "clearly established" precedent of this Court supports Smith's claim that he can make out a prima facie case merely by pointing to a host of factors that, individually or in combination, might contribute to a group's underrepresentation. . . .

ROLE OF JURIES IN SENTENCING: DEATH QUALIFIED JURIES

The Court has decided several cases concerning the role of juries in capital (death penalty) cases. Defendants are entitled to be tried by a jury of their peers, but the Court has never held this to mean that the actual composition of the trial jury in any given case must be specifically representative of the demographics of the community from which it is chosen. For example, if a community is comprised of 53% women and 47% men, 80% Caucasian, 10% African American and 10% Hispanic, 30% Protestant, 30% Catholic, 15% Atheist, 5% Muslim, 5% Jews, 5% Hindus, and 5% other religions, the defendant, as you have just seen in *Berghuis v. Smith,* cannot insist a jury demographic match this. Similarly, the defendant isn't entitled to a jury that is representative of the public opinion polls regarding capital punishment. Approximately two-thirds of the states have the death penalty, and approximately forty percent of all those polled nationwide are against the death penalty.[86] In those states having the death penalty, the defendant cannot insist that at least four of twelve jurors (one-third) are against the death penalty. Why? Because death sentences must be from unanimous verdicts. Just one person who cannot or would not impose the death penalty prevents a jury from ever imposing the death penalty.

In death penalty cases the same jurors who decided the defendant was guilty decide the sentence. Thus, if potential-juror Abe Jones states from the beginning that he could be impartial in deciding whether the defendant committed the crime but couldn't ever, under any circumstance, impose the death penalty, it would be a colossal waste of time and energy to put on the sentencing hearing. One could predict the outcome from the beginning. Abe Jones would not vote for death, the jury would not be unanimous, and the jury would "hang" as to the sentence. Because of this, the Court has allowed "death qualified juries." A death qualified jury is one which is comprised only of jurors who indicate that they can follow the law the judge instructs, and where warranted could impose the death penalty.

In *Witherspoon v. Illinois*, 391 US 510 (1968) the Court overturned Witherspoon's death sentence and declared unconstitutional a state statute that allowed dismissal of any juror with conscientious scruples against the death penalty. During Witherspoon's trial, the prosecutor, using this statute, had excused half of the jurors that had mentioned having qualms about the death penalty (he did not inquire whether they could actually impose a death sentence). Witherspoon was convicted and appealed his death sentence saying the statute violated his Sixth Amendment right to an impartial jury and the Fourteenth Amendment's right to to due process. The Court agreed, finding that while jurors who say they will not impose a death sentence may appropriately be dismissed (now known as "Witherspoon excludables"), those jurors who simply oppose the death penalty as a personal belief may not.

In *Lockhart v. McCree*, 476 U.S. 162 (1986), Lockhart was on trial for capital murder, and the judge excused for cause all prospective jurors who stated that they could not vote for the imposition of the death penalty under any circumstances. The jury convicted Lockhart, but it did not impose the death penalty as the state had requested. The Court, held that a death qualified jury did not violate the "fair cross section" requirement of the Sixth Amendment so long as the jury reflected the composition of the community at large. Justice Rehnquist argued that the state has a legitimate

---

[86] https://deathpenaltyinfo.org/news/2021-gallup-poll-public-support-for-capital-punishment-remains-at-half-century-low

interest to impanel jurors who "can properly and impartially apply the law to the facts of the case at both the guilt and sentencing phases of a capital trial." Thus, as long as a jury is selected from a fair cross-section of the community, is impartial, and can properly apply the law to a case's circumstances, then a defendant's constitutional right to a fair trial is protected.

One concern that arises from *Witherspoon* and *Lockhart* is whether a death qualified jury is more "prosecution prone." Are folks who say they can impose the death penalty more likely from the outset to be pro-state or pro-prosecution? If so, then they may not be impartial nor well-suited to determine guilt or innocence of the particular defendant. (Some research indicates this may be the case.)

In *Arizona v. Ring*, 536 U.S. 584 (2002), the Court struck down an Arizona death penalty scheme under which the judge, not the jury, decided whether to impose the death penalty. *Ring* followed a series of cases starting with *Apprendi v. New Jersey*, 530 U.S. 466 (1998), which gave jurors a greater role in sentencing. Prior to *Apprendi*, jurors only decided sentences in capital cases, but after *Apprendi* jurors must decide whether aggravating factors exist (and must indicate that they were convinced beyond a reasonable doubt) that allow the judge to give sentences longer than normal sentences. *Apprendi* had several important consequences, one of which is to expand the role of the jury beyond that of guilt or non-guilt determination.

WAIVING A JURY

States vary as to whether the defendant can insist on having a "bench trial" (one where the judge sits as the jury). In some states, the prosecution has the right to demand a jury trial even if the defendant waives it. The Court has determined that there is no federal constitutional right for the criminal defendant to be tried by a judge alone. *Singer v. United States*, 380 U.S. 24 (1965). When defendants do get to waive the jury, their waiver must be express and intelligent.

IMPEACHING A JURY'S VERDICT

Most states and the federal government follow the Federal Rules of Evidence's "no impeachment" rules. Under this rule, the court is not to set aside a verdict based upon some irregularity in how the jury reached its verdict and what may have happened or been said during deliberations. The exception is when there has been some external influence (for example, a bribe) on the jury. In 2017 this virtually hard and fast rule was at issue in *Pena-Rodriguez v. Colorado* (below).

PENA-RODRIGUEZ V. COLORADO
583 U.S. ____ (2017)

[Official syllabus]

A Colorado jury convicted petitioner Peña-Rodriguez of harassment and unlawful sexual contact. Following the discharge of the jury, two jurors told defense counsel that, during deliberations, Juror H. C. had expressed anti-Hispanic bias toward petitioner and petitioner's alibi witness. Counsel, with the trial court's supervision, obtained affidavits from the two jurors describing a number of biased statements by H. C. The court acknowledged H. C.'s apparent bias but denied petitioner's motion for a new trial on the ground that Colorado Rule of Evidence 606(b) generally prohibits a juror from testifying as to statements made during deliberations in a proceeding inquiring into the validity of the verdict. The Colorado Court of Appeals affirmed, agreeing that H. C.'s alleged statements did not fall within an exception to Rule 606(b). The Colorado Supreme Court also affirmed, relying on *Tanner* v. *United States* and *Warger* v. *Shauers*, both of which rejected constitutional challenges to the federal no-impeachment rule as applied to evidence of juror misconduct or bias.

Held: Where a juror makes a clear statement indicating that he or she relied on racial stereotypes or animus to convict a criminal defendant, the Sixth Amendment requires that the no-impeachment rule give way in order to permit the trial court to consider the evidence of the juror's statement and any resulting denial of the jury trial guarantee.

(a) At common law jurors were forbidden to impeach their verdict, either by affidavit or live testimony. Some American jurisdictions adopted a more flexible version of the no-impeachment bar, known as the "Iowa rule," which prevented jurors from testifying only about their own subjective beliefs, thoughts, or motives during deliberations. An alternative approach, later referred to as the federal approach, permitted an exception only for events extraneous to the deliberative process. This Court's early decisions did not establish a clear preference for a particular version of the no-impeachment rule, appearing open to the Iowa rule in *United States v. Reid* and *Mattox v. United States*, but rejecting that approach in *McDonald v. Pless*.

The common-law development of the rule reached a milestone in 1975 when Congress adopted Federal Rule of Evidence 606(b), which sets out a broad no-impeachment rule, with only limited exceptions. This version of the no-impeachment rule has substantial merit, promoting full and vigorous discussion by jurors and providing considerable assurance that after being discharged they will not be summoned to recount their deliberations or otherwise harassed. The rule gives stability and finality to verdicts.

(b) Some version of the no-impeachment rule is followed in every State and the District of Columbia, most of which follow the Federal Rule. At least 16 jurisdictions have recognized an exception for juror testimony about racial bias in deliberations. Three Federal Courts of Appeals have also held or suggested there is a

constitutional exception for evidence of racial bias.

In addressing the common-law no-impeachment rule, this Court noted the possibility of an exception in the "gravest and most important cases." *United States v. Reid*; *McDonald v. Pless*. The Court has addressed the question whether the Constitution mandates an exception to Rule 606(b) just twice, rejecting an exception each time. In *Tanner*, where the evidence showed that some jurors were under the influence of drugs and alcohol during the trial, the Court identified "long-recognized and very substantial concerns" supporting the no-impeachment rule. The Court also outlined existing, significant safeguards for the defendant's right to an impartial and competent jury beyond post-trial juror testimony: members of the venire can be examined for impartiality during *voir dire*; juror misconduct may be observed the court, counsel, and court personnel during the trial; and jurors themselves can report misconduct to the court before a verdict is rendered. In *Warger*, a civil case where the evidence indicated that the jury forewoman failed to disclose a prodefendant bias during *voir dire*, the Court again put substantial reliance on existing safeguards for a fair trial. But the Court also warned, as in *Reid* and *McDonald*, that the no-impeachment rule may admit of exceptions for "juror bias so extreme that, almost by definition, the jury trial right has been abridged." *Reid*, *McDonald*, and *Warger* left open the question here: whether the Constitution requires an exception to the no-impeachment rule when a juror's statements indicate that racial animus was a significant motivating factor in his or her finding of guilt.

(c) The imperative to purge racial prejudice from the administration of justice was given new force and direction by the ratification of the Civil War Amendments. "[T]he central purpose of the Fourteenth Amendment was to eliminate racial discrimination emanating from official sources in the States." *McLaughlin* v. *Florida*. Time and again, this Court has enforced the Constitution's guarantee against state-sponsored racial discrimination in the jury system. The Court has interpreted the Fourteenth Amendment to prohibit the exclusion of jurors based on race, *Strauder* v. *West Virginia*; struck down laws and practices that systematically exclude racial minorities from juries, see, *e.g., Neal* v. *Delaware*; ruled that no litigant may exclude a prospective juror based on race, see, *e.g., Batson* v. *Kentucky*; and held that defendants may at times be entitled to ask about racial bias during *voir dire,* see, *e.g., Ham* v. *South Carolina*. The unmistakable principle of these precedents is that discrimination on the basis of race, "odious in all aspects, is especially pernicious in the administration of justice," *Rose* v. *Mitchell*, damaging "both the fact and the perception" of the jury's role as "a vital check against the wrongful exercise of power by the State," *Powers* v. *Ohio*.

(d) This case lies at the intersection of the Court's decisions endorsing the no-impeachment rule and those seeking to eliminate racial bias in the jury system. Those lines of precedent need not conflict. Racial bias, unlike the behavior in *McDonald*, *Tanner*, or *Warger,* implicates unique historical, constitutional, and institutional concerns and, if left unaddressed, would risk systemic injury to the administration of justice. It is also distinct in a pragmatic sense, for the *Tanner* safeguards may be less effective in rooting out racial bias. But while all forms of improper bias pose challenges to the trial process, there is a sound basis to treat racial bias with added precaution. A constitutional rule that racial bias in the justice system must be addressed—including, in some instances, after a verdict has been entered—is necessary to prevent a systemic loss of confidence in jury verdicts, a confidence that is a central premise of the Sixth Amendment trial right.

(e) Before the no-impeachment bar can be set aside to allow further judicial inquiry, there must be a threshold showing that one or more jurors made statements exhibiting overt racial bias that cast serious doubt on the fairness and impartiality of the jury's deliberations and resulting verdict. To qualify, the statement must tend to show that racial animus was a significant motivating factor in the juror's vote to convict. Whether the threshold showing has been satisfied is committed to the substantial discretion of the trial court in light of all the circumstances, including the content and timing of the alleged statements and the reliability of the proffered evidence.

The practical mechanics of acquiring and presenting such evidence will no doubt be shaped and guided by state rules of professional ethics and local court rules, both of which often limit counsel's post-trial contact with jurors. The experience of those jurisdictions that have already recognized a racial-bias exception to the no-impeachment rule, and the experience of courts going forward, will inform the proper exercise of trial judge discretion. The Court need not address what procedures a trial court must follow when confronted with a motion for a new trial based on juror testimony of racial bias or the appropriate standard for determining when such evidence is sufficient to require that the verdict be set aside and a new trial be granted. Standard and existing safeguards may also help prevent racial bias in jury deliberations, including careful *voir dire* and a trial court's instructions to jurors about their duty to review the evidence, deliberate together, and reach a verdict in a fair and impartial way, free from bias of any kind.

After *Pena-Rodriguez* the Court issued a per curium opinion in *Tharpe v. Sellers, 583 U.S. ___ (2018)*. Tharpe had been convicted in Georgia for the 1990 murder of his sister-in-law, Jacqueline Freeman. A jury sentenced him to death, and the Georgia Supreme Court affirmed his conviction and sentence. After his sentencing, it was revealed that a white juror from Tharpe's trial,

Barney Gattie, made several highly discriminatory statements regarding African Americans. Tharpe, who is black, petitioned for state habeas relief alleging that improper racial animus had influenced the jury's deliberations. The state courts denied his petition finding that he had procedurally defaulted on his claim by failing to raise the racial bias issue in earlier proceedings, and because he did not adequately support his claim that ineffective assistance of counsel was to blame for the omission. The habeas court also noted that juror testimony was inadmissible to prove Tharpe's racial animus claim.

Tharpe next petitioned the federal courts for a writ of habeas corpus alleging that racial bias among the jury had rendered his conviction and sentence unable to withstand constitutional scrutiny. Ultimately, the federal courts denied granting him habeas relief. The Court then decided *Pena-Rodriguez v. Colorado.* Thereafter Tharpe petitioned the district court reopen his case arguing that *Pena-Rodriguez* should apply retroactively, allowing him to present the juror testimony that had previously been deemed inadmissible.

Tharpe's case eventually ended up in the U.S. Supreme Court. It considered whether Tharpe's capital case should be reopened because the trial judge would now have sufficient evidence because of the juror's racially discriminatory statements would show that racial animus had influenced the jury's conviction and imposition of the death penalty. The Court issued a summary ruling granting the petition and remanding the case back to the state courts explaining that, while the state court's factual determinations were binding on federal courts in the absence of clear and convincing countervailing evidence, the sworn affidavit produced by Tharpe provided compelling evidence that racial bias had influenced his vote to impose the death sentence. The Supreme Court stated that "Gattie's remarkable affidavit—which he never retracted—presents a strong factual basis for the argument that Tharpe's race affected Gattie's vote for a death verdict. At the very least, jurists of reason could debate whether Tharpe has shown by clear and convincing evidence that the state court's factual determination was wrong."

A PUBLIC TRIAL

The Sixth Amendment provides that the accused shall enjoy the right to a public trial. Although federal and state rules of evidence allow judges to "sequester" witnesses (exclude individuals who will be called as witnesses from the courtroom until they have testified in order to prevent them from altering their testimony based on the testimony of other witnesses), trials and most courtroom proceedings are generally open to the public. See, e.g., FRE 615. Typically, there are few spectators watching trials. Trials in which there is a lot of publicity are the exception, and small courtrooms can be quickly filled. *Weaver v. Massachusetts* explores closure of the courtroom to accommodate potential jurors during jury selection.

WEAVER v. MASSACHUSETTS
582 U.S. ___ (2017)

When petitioner was tried in a Massachusetts trial court, the courtroom could not accommodate all the potential jurors. As a result, for two days of jury selection, an officer of the court excluded from the courtroom any member of the public who was not a potential juror, including petitioner's mother and her minister. Defense counsel neither objected to the closure at trial nor raised the issue on direct review. Petitioner was convicted of murder and a related charge. Five years later, he filed a motion for a new trial in state court, arguing . . . that his attorney had provided ineffective assistance by failing to object to the courtroom closure.

Not every public-trial violation will lead to a fundamentally unfair trial. And the failure to object to that violation does not always deprive the defendant of a reasonable probability of a different outcome. Thus, a defendant raising a public-trial violation via an ineffective assistance claim must show either a reasonable probability of a different outcome in his or her case or, as assumed here, that the particular violation was so serious as to render the trial fundamentally unfair.

When a defendant objects to a courtroom closure, the trial court can either order the courtroom opened or explain the reasons for keeping it closed, but when a defendant first raises the closure in an ineffective-assistance claim, the trial court has no chance to cure the violation. The costs and uncertainties of a new trial are also greater because more time will have elapsed in most cases.

Because petitioner has not shown a reasonable probability of a different outcome but for counsel's failure to object or that counsel's shortcomings led to a fundamentally unfair trial, he is not entitled to a new trial. Although potential jurors might have behaved differently had petitioner's family or the public been present, petitioner has offered no

evidence suggesting a reasonable probability of a different outcome but for counsel's failure to object. He has also failed to demonstrate fundamental unfairness. His mother and her minister were indeed excluded during jury selection.

But his trial was not conducted in secret or in a remote place; closure was limited to the jury voir dire; the courtroom remained open during the evidentiary phase of the trial; the closure decision apparently was made by court officers, not the judge; venire members who did not become jurors observed the proceedings; and the record of the proceedings indicates no basis for concern, other than the closure itself. There was no showing, furthermore, that the potential harms flowing from a courtroom closure came to pass in this case, e.g., misbehavior by the prosecutor, judge, or any other party. Thus, even though this case comes here on the assumption that the closure was a Sixth Amendment violation, the violation here did not pervade the whole trial or lead to basic unfairness

A SPEEDY TRIAL

The Sixth Amendment guarantees criminal defendants a speedy trial. The speedy trial time clock begins running once the defendant is formally charged with the crime. Delay, in and of itself, does not necessarily mean a constitutional violation. The Court is concerned with unnecessary and unwanted delay. *Barker v. Wingo* (below) enunciates the factors the court will consider in determining whether defendant was deprived of the right to a speedy trial.

BARKER v. WINGO
407 U.S. 514 (1972)

JUSTICE POWELL delivered the opinion of the Court.

On July 20, 1958, in Christian County, Kentucky, an elderly couple was beaten to death by intruders wielding an iron tire tool. Two suspects, Manning and Barker, the petitioner, were arrested shortly thereafter. The grand jury indicted them on September 15. Counsel was appointed on September 17, and Barker's trial was set for October 21. The Commonwealth had a stronger case against Manning, and it believed that Barker could not be convicted unless Manning testified against

him. Manning was naturally unwilling to incriminate himself. Accordingly, on October 23, the day Manning was brought to trial, the Commonwealth sought and obtained the first of what was to be a series of 16 continuances of Barker's trial. Barker made no objection. By first convicting Manning, the Commonwealth would remove possible problems of self-incrimination and would be able to assure his testimony against Barker.

The Commonwealth encountered more than a few difficulties in its prosecution of Manning. The first trial ended in a hung jury. A second trial resulted in a conviction, but the Kentucky Court of Appeals reversed because of the admission of evidence obtained by an illegal search. At his third trial, Manning was again convicted, and the Court of Appeals again reversed because the trial court had not granted a change of venue. A fourth trial resulted in a hung jury. Finally, after five trials, Manning was convicted, in March 1962, of murdering one victim, and after a sixth trial, in December 1962, he was convicted of murdering the other.

The Christian County Circuit Court holds three terms each year - in February, June, and September. Barker's initial trial was to take place in the September term of 1958. The first continuance postponed it until the February 1959 term. The second continuance was granted for one month only. Every term thereafter for as long as the Manning prosecutions were in process, the Commonwealth routinely moved to continue Barker's case to the next term. When the case was continued from the June 1959 term until the following September, Barker, having spent 10 months in jail, obtained his release by posting a $5,000 bond. He thereafter remained free in the community until his trial. Barker made no objection, through his counsel, to the first 11 continuances.

When on February 12, 1962, the Commonwealth moved for the twelfth time to continue the case until the following term, Barker's counsel filed a motion to dismiss the indictment. The motion to dismiss was denied two weeks later, and the Commonwealth's motion for a continuance was granted. The Commonwealth was granted further continuances in June 1962 and September 1962, to which Barker did not object.

In February 1963, the first term of court following Manning's final conviction, the Commonwealth moved to set Barker's trial for March 19. But on the day scheduled for trial, it again moved for a continuance until the June term. It gave as its reason the illness of the ex-sheriff who was the chief investigating officer in the case. To this continuance, Barker objected unsuccessfully.

The witness was still unable to testify in June, and the trial, which had been set for June 19, was continued again until the September term over Barker's objection. This time the court announced that the case would be dismissed for lack of prosecution if it were not tried during the next term. The final trial date was set for October 9, 1963. On that date, Barker again moved to dismiss the indictment, and this time specified that his right to a speedy trial had been violated. The motion was denied; the trial commenced with Manning as the chief prosecution witness; Barker was convicted and given a life sentence.

The right to a speedy trial is generically different from any of the other rights enshrined in the Constitution for the protection of the accused. In addition to the general concern that all accused persons be treated according to decent and fair procedures, there is a societal interest in providing a speedy trial which exists separate from, and at times in opposition to, the interests of the accused. The inability of courts to provide a prompt trial has contributed to a large backlog of cases in urban courts which, among other things, enables defendants to negotiate more effectively for pleas of guilty to lesser offenses and otherwise manipulate the system. In addition, persons released on bond for lengthy periods awaiting trial have an opportunity to commit other crimes. It must be of little comfort to the residents of Christian County, Kentucky, to know that Barker was at large on bail for over four years while accused of a vicious and brutal murder of which he was ultimately convicted. Moreover, the longer an accused is free awaiting trial, the more tempting becomes his opportunity to jump bail and escape.

If an accused cannot make bail, he is generally confined, as was Barker for 10 months, in a local jail. This contributes to the overcrowding and generally deplorable state of those institutions. Lengthy exposure to these conditions "has a destructive effect on human character and makes the rehabilitation of the individual offender much more difficult." At times the result may even be violent rioting.

Finally, lengthy pretrial detention is costly. The cost of maintaining a prisoner in jail varies from $3 to $9 per day, and this amounts to millions across the Nation. In addition, society loses wages which might have been earned, and it must often support families of incarcerated breadwinners.

A second difference between the right to speedy trial and the accused's other constitutional rights is that deprivation of the right may work to the accused's advantage. Delay is not an uncommon defense tactic. As the time between the commission of the crime and trial lengthens, witnesses may become unavailable or their memories may fade. If the witnesses support the prosecution, its case will be weakened, sometimes seriously so. And it is the prosecution which carries the burden of proof. Thus, unlike the right to counsel or the right to be free from compelled self-incrimination, deprivation of the right to speedy trial does not per se prejudice the accused's ability to defend himself.

Finally, and perhaps most importantly, the right to speedy trial is a more vague concept than other procedural rights. It is, for example, impossible to determine with precision when the right has been denied. We cannot definitely say how long is too long in a system where justice is supposed to be swift but deliberate. As a consequence, there is no fixed point in the criminal process when the State can put the defendant to the choice of either exercising or waiving the right to a speedy trial. If, for example, the State moves for a 60-day continuance, granting that continuance is not a violation of the right to speedy trial unless the circumstances of the case are such that further delay would endanger the values the right protects. It is impossible to do more than generalize about when those circumstances exist. There is nothing comparable to the point in the process when a defendant exercises or waives his right to counsel or his right to a jury trial. Any inquiry into a speedy trial claim necessitates a functional analysis of the right in the particular context of the case:

"The right of a speedy trial is necessarily relative. It is consistent with delays and depends upon circumstances. It secures rights to a defendant. It does not preclude the rights of public justice."

The amorphous quality of the right also leads to the unsatisfactorily severe remedy of dismissal of the indictment when the right has been deprived. This is indeed a serious consequence because it means that a defendant who may be guilty of a serious crime will go free, without having been tried. Such a remedy is more serious than an exclusionary rule or a reversal for a new trial, but it is the only possible remedy.

Perhaps because the speedy trial right is so slippery, two rigid approaches are urged upon us as ways of eliminating some of the uncertainty which courts experience in protecting the right. The first suggestion is that we hold that the Constitution requires a criminal defendant to be offered a trial within a specified time period. The result of such a ruling would have the virtue of clarifying when the right is infringed and of simplifying courts' application of it.

We find no constitutional basis for holding that the speedy trial right can be quantified into a specified number of days or months. The States, of course, are free to prescribe a reasonable period consistent with constitutional standards, but our approach must be less precise.

The second suggested alternative would restrict consideration of the right to those cases in which the accused has demanded a speedy trial. . . . We shall refer to the former approach as the demand-waiver doctrine. The demand-waiver doctrine provides that a defendant waives any consideration of his right to speedy trial for any period prior to which he has not demanded a trial. Under this rigid approach, a prior demand is a necessary condition to the consideration of the speedy trial right. This essentially was the approach the Sixth Circuit took below.

Such an approach, by presuming waiver of a fundamental right from inaction, is inconsistent with this Court's pronouncements on waiver of constitutional rights. The Court has defined waiver as "an intentional relinquishment or abandonment of a known right or privilege." The Court has ruled similarly with respect to waiver of other rights designed to protect the accused.

In excepting the right to speedy trial from the rule of waiver we have applied to other fundamental rights, courts that have applied the demand-waiver rule have relied on the assumption that delay usually works for the benefit of the accused and on the absence of any readily ascertainable time in the criminal process for a defendant to be given the choice of exercising or waiving his right. But it is not necessarily true that delay benefits the defendant. There are cases in which delay appreciably harms the defendant's ability to defend himself. Moreover, a defendant confined to jail prior to trial is obviously disadvantaged by delay as is a defendant released on bail but unable to lead a normal life because of community suspicion and his own anxiety.

We reject the rule that a defendant who fails to demand a speedy trial forever waives his right. This does not mean, however, that the defendant has no responsibility to assert his right. We think the better rule is that the defendant's assertion of or failure to assert his right to a speedy trial is one of the factors to be considered in an inquiry into the deprivation of the right. Such a formulation avoids the rigidities of the demand-waiver rule and the resulting possible unfairness in its application. It allows the trial court to exercise a judicial discretion based on the circumstances, including due consideration of any applicable formal procedural rule. It would permit, for example, a court to attach a different weight to a situation in which the defendant knowingly fails to object from a situation in which his attorney acquiesces in long delay without adequately informing his client, or from a situation in which no counsel is appointed. It would also allow a court to

weigh the frequency and force of the objections as opposed to attaching significant weight to a purely pro forma objection.

We, therefore, reject both of the inflexible approaches - the fixed-time period because it goes further than the Constitution requires; the demand-waiver rule because it is insensitive to a right which we have deemed fundamental. The approach we accept is a balancing test, in which the conduct of both the prosecution and the defendant are weighed.

A balancing test necessarily compels courts to approach speedy trial cases on an ad hoc basis. We can do little more than identify some of the factors which courts should assess in determining whether a particular defendant has been deprived of his right. Though some might express them in different ways, we identify four such factors: Length of delay, the reason for the delay, the defendant's assertion of his right, and prejudice to the defendant.

The length of the delay is to some extent a triggering mechanism. Until there is some delay which is presumptively prejudicial, there is no necessity for inquiry into the other factors that go into the balance. Nevertheless, because of the imprecision of the right to speedy trial, the length of delay that will provoke such an inquiry is necessarily dependent upon the peculiar circumstances of the case. To take but one example, the delay that can be tolerated for an ordinary street crime is considerably less than for a serious, complex conspiracy charge.

Closely related to length of delay is the reason the government assigns to justify the delay. Here, too, different weights should be assigned to different reasons. A deliberate attempt to delay the trial in order to hamper the defense should be weighted heavily against the government. A more neutral reason such as negligence or overcrowded courts should be weighted less heavily but nevertheless should be considered since the ultimate responsibility for such circumstances must rest with the government rather than with the defendant. Finally, a valid reason, such as a missing witness, should serve to justify appropriate delay.

We have already discussed the third factor, the defendant's responsibility to assert his right. Whether and how a defendant asserts his right is closely related to the other factors we have mentioned. The strength of his efforts will be affected by the length of the delay, to some extent by the reason for the delay, and most particularly by the personal prejudice, which is not always readily identifiable, that he experiences. The more serious the deprivation, the more likely a defendant is to complain. The defendant's assertion of his speedy trial right, then, is entitled to strong evidentiary weight in determining whether the defendant is being deprived of the right. We emphasize that failure to assert the right will make it difficult for a defendant to prove that he was denied a speedy trial.

A fourth factor is prejudice to the defendant. Prejudice, of course, should be assessed in the light of the interests of defendants which the speedy trial right was designed to protect. This Court has identified three such interests: (i) to prevent oppressive pretrial incarceration; (ii) to minimize anxiety and concern of the accused; and (iii) to limit the possibility that the defense will be impaired. Of these, the most serious is the last, because the inability of a defendant adequately to prepare his case skews the fairness of the entire system. If witnesses die or disappear during a delay, the prejudice is obvious. There is also prejudice if defense witnesses are unable to recall accurately events of the distant past. Loss of memory, however, is not always reflected in the record because what has been forgotten can rarely be shown.

We regard none of the four factors identified above as either a necessary or sufficient condition to the finding of a deprivation of the right of speedy trial. Rather, they are related factors and must be considered together with such other circumstances as may be relevant. In sum, these factors have no talismanic qualities; courts must still engage in a difficult and sensitive balancing process. But, because we are dealing with a fundamental right of the accused, this process must be carried out with full recognition that the accused's interest in a speedy trial is specifically affirmed in the Constitution.

We do not hold that there may never be a situation in which an indictment may be dismissed on speedy trial grounds where the defendant has failed to object to continuances. There may be a situation in which the defendant was represented by incompetent counsel, was severely prejudiced, or even cases in which the continuances were granted ex parte. But barring extraordinary circumstances, we would be reluctant indeed to rule that a defendant was denied this constitutional right on a record that strongly indicates, as does this one, that the defendant did not want a speedy trial. We hold, therefore, that Barker was not deprived of his due process right to a speedy trial.

Federal Speedy Trials

In federal prosecutions, the speedy trial provision of the Sixth Amendment has been essentially superseded by very elaborate legislation, the Speedy Trial Act. The Act sets out two separate time limits, one for the period from arrest to charge, and the other from the period from charge to trial. [Note that the period of time from the offense to the arrest is covered not by speedy trial provisions but rather by pertinent statutes of limitations.] Under the Speedy Trial Act, the time between arrest and indictment must be no more than 30 days. The time between indictment or information and the commencement of trial must normally be no more than 70 days. However, there are a series of periods of delay which do not count. Some of these are very elastic. For instance, delay due to the unavailability of essential witness does not count. Delay due to a continuance granted at the prosecution's request by the trial judge, if the judge puts findings on the record as to why the "ends of justice served by granting such a continuance outweigh the best interests of the public and the defendant in a speedy trial" does not count. See, Emanuel, S, *Emanuel Law Outlines: Criminal Procedure,* pp 362-363.

The remedy for a speedy trial violation is that the government must dismiss the charges. There is no requirement that the dismissal be "with prejudice" [dismissal with prejudice means the inability to refile charges). Thus, the prosecutor can obtain a new indictment, and in effect start the prosecution all over again (assuming no statute of limitation prevents this).

States generally have statutory laws or constitutional provisions setting forth their speedy trial provisions. If the state is not ready to proceed to trial within that framework then the remedy is to release the defendant from custody (generally on a conditional release) -- not that the case be dismissed. Out-of-custody speedy trial guidelines follow *Barker v. Wingo,* and the general rule is to get the case to trial "as soon as possible."

Vermont v. Brillon 556 U.S. __ (2009), held that, because a public defender represents his client and not the state, delay caused by the defense attorney needs to be attributed to the defendant. Michael Brillon was jailed for three years and went through six defense attorneys before his trial for assaulting his girlfriend. The Vermont Supreme Court had thrown out the conviction as a speedy trial violation, but the U.S. Supreme Court held that delay caused by a public defender in a criminal trial does not amount to a constitutional violation requiring dismissal of an indictment. The Court suggested that the Vermont court look at whether the breakdown in Vermont's public defender system played a role in Brillon's case and, if so, whether his rights were violated.

FAIR TRIAL

Comments On Defendant's Not Testifying

Even seemingly innocuous comments about the defendant not testifying at trial can incur the wrath of the judge – it is almost a sure-fire way for the court to at least consider declaring a mistrial.[87] Prosecutors learn this as somewhat as an absolute rule and generally take great care to avoid even hinting at it ("wouldn't you like to know this? Well, the only person who can tell us is the defendant."). A quick review of cases and legal articles discussing prosecutorial comments on defendants' refusal to testify reveal "not much action" in this area since the 1970s. This indicates that perhaps it is such a well-entrenched principle and such a clear-cut directive from the Court that defendants' rights to a fair trial are not routinely being violated by this governmental action. The Griffin case mentioned in the following *Chapman* decision is the seminal case on improper commenting.

CHAPMAN v. CALIFORNIA
386 U.S. 18 (1967)

JUSTICE BLACK delivered the opinion of the Court.

Petitioners, Ruth Elizabeth Chapman and Thomas LeRoy Teale, were convicted in a California state court upon a charge that they robbed, kidnapped, and murdered a bartender. She was sentenced to life imprisonment and he to death. At the time of the trial, the State's Constitution provided that "in any criminal case, whether the defendant testifies or not, his failure to explain or to deny by his testimony any evidence or facts in the case against him may be commented upon by the court and by counsel, and may be considered by the court or the jury." Both petitioners in this case chose not to testify at their trial, and the State's attorney prosecuting them took full advantage of his right under the State Constitution to

---

[87] https://www.ojp.gov/ncjrs/virtual-library/abstracts/prosecutors-comment-defendants-pretrial-silence-impeach-his

comment upon their failure to testify, filling his argument to the jury from beginning to end with numerous references to their silence and inferences of their guilt resulting therefrom. The trial court also charged the jury that it could draw adverse inferences from petitioners' failure to testify. Shortly after the trial, but before petitioners' cases had been considered on appeal by the California Supreme Court, this Court decided *Griffin v. California*, in which we held California's constitutional provision and practice invalid on the ground that they put a penalty on the exercise of a person's right not to be compelled to be a witness against himself, guaranteed by the Fifth Amendment to the United States Constitution and made applicable to California and the other States by the Fourteenth Amendment. On appeal, the State Supreme Court, admitting that petitioners had been denied a federal constitutional right by the comments on their silence, nevertheless affirmed, applying the State Constitution's harmless-error provision, which forbids reversal unless "the court shall be of the opinion that the error complained of has resulted in a miscarriage of justice."

We granted certiorari limited to these questions: "Where there is a violation of the rule of *Griffin v. California*, 380 U.S. 609, (1) can the error be held to be harmless, and (2) if so, was the error harmless in this case?"

We have no hesitation in saying that the right of these petitioners not to be punished for exercising their Fifth and Fourteenth Amendment right to be silent expressly created by the Federal Constitution itself is a federal right which, in the absence of appropriate congressional action, it is our responsibility to protect by fashioning the necessary rule.

We are urged by petitioners to hold that all federal constitutional errors, regardless of the facts and circumstances, must always be deemed harmful. Such a holding, as petitioners correctly point out, would require an automatic reversal of their convictions and make further discussion unnecessary. We decline to adopt any such rule. . .

… Certainly error, constitutional error, in illegally admitting highly prejudicial evidence or comments, casts on someone other than the person prejudiced by it a burden to show that it was harmless.

. . .We hold . . . that before a federal constitutional error can be held harmless, the court must be able to declare a belief that it was harmless beyond a reasonable doubt. While appellate courts do not ordinarily have the original task of applying such a test, it is a familiar standard to all courts, and we believe its adoption will provide a more workable standard …

Applying the foregoing standard, we have no doubt that the error in these cases was not harmless to petitioners.

The state prosecutor's argument and the trial judge's instruction to the jury continuously and repeatedly impressed the jury that from the failure of petitioners to testify, to all intents and purposes, the inferences from the facts in evidence had to be drawn in favor of the State in short, that by their silence petitioners had served as irrefutable witnesses against themselves. And though the case in which this occurred presented a reasonably strong "circumstantial web of evidence" against petitioners, it was also a case in which, absent the constitutionally forbidden comments, honest, fair-minded jurors might very well have brought in not-guilty verdicts. Under these circumstances, it is completely impossible for us to say that the State has demonstrated, beyond a reasonable doubt, that the prosecutor's comments and the trial judge's instruction did not contribute to petitioners' convictions. Such a machine-gun repetition of a denial of constitutional rights, designed and calculated to make petitioners' version of the evidence worthless, can no more be considered harmless than the introduction against a defendant of a coerced confession. Petitioners are entitled to a trial free from the pressure of unconstitutional inferences.

Courtroom Attire

Does what the defendant wears at trial impact whether he or she got a fair trial? Does the clothing worn influence the juror or prejudice them against the defendant? What if the defendant is shackled? What about the presence of law enforcement in the courtroom? What about the attire of courtroom spectators? The following cases explore these issues. (Note, pay attention to the *Estelle v. Williams* and the *Flynn* case cited in *Musladin*).[88]

CAREY v. MUSLADIN
549 U.S. 70 (2006)

JUSTICE THOMAS delivered the opinion of the Court.

This Court has recognized that certain courtroom practices are so inherently prejudicial that they deprive the defendant of a fair trial. . . . In this case, a state court held that buttons displaying the victim's image worn by the victim's family during respondent's trial did not deny respondent his right to a fair trial. We must decide whether that holding was contrary to or an unreasonable application of clearly established federal law, as determined by this Court. ... We hold that it was not.

On May 13, 1994, respondent Mathew Musladin shot and killed Tom Studer outside the home of Musladin's estranged wife, Pamela. At trial, Musladin admitted that he killed Studer but argued that he did so in self-defense. A California jury rejected Musladin's self-defense argument and convicted him of first-degree murder and three related offenses.

During Musladin's trial, several members of Studer's family sat in the front row of the spectators' gallery. On at least some of the trial's 14 days, some members of Studer's family wore buttons with a photo of Studer on them. (Footnote omitted). Prior to opening statements, Musladin's counsel moved the court to order the Studer family not to wear the buttons during the trial. The court denied the motion, stating that it saw "no possible prejudice to the defendant." . . .

Musladin appealed his conviction to the California Court of Appeal in 1997. He argued that the buttons deprived him of his Fourteenth Amendment and Sixth Amendment rights. At the outset of its analysis, the Court of Appeal stated that Musladin had to show actual or inherent prejudice to succeed on his claim. The Court of Appeal, made clear that it "consider[ed] the wearing of photographs of victims in a courtroom to be an 'impermissible factor coming into play,' the practice of which should be discouraged." . . . Nevertheless, the court concluded that the buttons had not "branded defendant 'with an unmistakable mark of guilt' in the eyes of the jurors" because "[t]he simple photograph of Tom Studer was unlikely to have been taken as a sign of anything other than the normal grief occasioned by the loss of [a] family member.". . .

Musladin argued that the buttons were inherently prejudicial and that . . . the Studers' wearing of the buttons deprived him of a fair trial.

. . . .

---

[88] In a 2018 case (*United States v. Sanchez-Gomez*) the Court ultimately dodged deciding whether full shackles in non-jury proceedings with U.S. Marshalls which had been used per policy of U.S. District Court for the Southern District of California violated the constitution. The defendants challenged the use of handcuffs connected to waist chains, but before the case could be heard, their criminal convictions ended. The case moved forward as a quasi class-action case and the Ninth Circuit Court of Appeals held the policy unconstitutional. The U.S. Supreme Court held that the case was moot. Chief Justice Roberts wrote for a unanimous court examining prior precedent in Gernstein v. Pugh, Federal Rules of Criminal Procedure, and indicated that the two individuals (Sanchez-Gomez and Patricio Guzman) were no longer in pretrial custody, so there was no longer a pending controversy. (The Court did NOT embrace the idea that this policy was capable of repetition yet evading review).

Both *Williams* and *Flynn* dealt with government-sponsored practices: In *Williams*, the State compelled the defendant to stand trial in prison clothes, and in *Flynn*, the State seated the troopers immediately behind the defendant. Moreover, in both cases, this Court noted that some practices are so inherently prejudicial that they must be justified by an "essential state" policy or interest. . . .

In contrast to state-sponsored courtroom practices, the effect on a defendant's fair-trial rights of the spectator conduct to which Musladin objects is an open question in our jurisprudence. This Court has never addressed a claim that such private-actor courtroom conduct was so inherently prejudicial that it deprived a defendant of a fair trial. And although the Court articulated the test for inherent prejudice that applies to state conduct in *Williams* and *Flynn*, we have never applied that test to spectators' conduct. Indeed, part of the legal test of *Williams* and *Flynn* — asking whether the practices furthered an essential state interest — suggests that those cases apply only to state-sponsored practices.

Reflecting the lack of guidance from this Court, lower courts have diverged widely in their treatment of defendants' spectator-conduct claims. . . .

Given the lack of holdings from this Court regarding the potentially prejudicial effect of spectators' courtroom conduct of the kind involved here, it cannot be said that the state court "unreasonabl[y] appli[ed] clearly established Federal law." . . .

JUSTICE KENNEDY, concurring in the judgment.

Trials must be free from a coercive or intimidating atmosphere. This fundamental principle of due process is well established. . . . The disruptive presence of the press required reversal in *Sheppard v. Maxwell* . . . where "newsmen took over practically the entire courtroom, hounding most of the participants in the trial," and *Estes v. Texas* . . . where the presence of cameras distracted jurors throughout the proceedings.

The rule against a coercive or intimidating atmosphere at trial exists because "we are committed to a government of laws and not of men," under which it is "of the utmost importance that the administration of justice be absolutely fair and orderly," and "the constitutional safeguards relating to the integrity of the criminal process attend every stage of a criminal proceeding . . .culminating with a trial 'in a courtroom presided over by a judge.' " *Cox v. Louisiana* . . . .

The rule settled by these cases requires a court, on either direct or collateral review, to order a new trial when a defendant shows his conviction has been obtained in a trial tainted by an atmosphere of coercion or intimidation similar to that documented in the foregoing cases. This would seem to be true whether the pressures were from partisans, or, as seems to have been the case in Sheppard, from persons reacting to the drama of the moment who created an environment so raucous that calm deliberation by the judge or jury was likely compromised in a serious way.

In the case before us there is no indication the atmosphere at respondent's trial was one of coercion or intimidation to the severe extent demonstrated in the cases just discussed. The instant case does present the issue whether as a preventative measure, or as a general rule to preserve the calm and dignity of a court, buttons proclaiming a message relevant to the case ought to be prohibited as a matter of course.

JUSTICE SOUTER, concurring in the judgment.

[T]he question is whether the practice or condition presents " 'an unacceptable risk . . .of impermissible factors coming into play' " in the jury's consideration of the case. . . . The Court's intent to adopt a standard at this general and comprehensive level could not be much clearer.

As for the applicability of this standard, there is no serious question that it reaches the behavior of spectators. The focus of the later cases is on appearances within the courtroom open to the jurors' observation. There is no suggestion in the opinions, and no reason to think now, that it should matter whether the State or an individual may be to blame for some objectionable sight; either way, the trial judge has an affirmative obligation to control the courtroom and keep it free of improper influence. . . .And since the *Williams-Flynn* standard is a guide for trial judges, not for laypersons without schooling in threats to the fairness of trials, its general formulation is enough to tell trial judges that it applies to the behavior of courtroom visitors.

[O]ne could not seriously deny that allowing spectators at a criminal trial to wear visible buttons with the victim's photo can raise a risk of improper considerations. The display is no part of the evidence going to guilt or innocence, and the buttons are at once an appeal for sympathy for the victim (and perhaps for those who wear the buttons) and a call for some response from those who see them. On the jurors' part, that expected response could well seem to be a verdict of guilty, and a sympathetic urge to assuage the grief or rage of survivors with a conviction would be the paradigm of improper consideration.

The only debatable question is whether the risk in a given case reaches the "unacceptable" level. While there is a fair argument that any level of risk from wearing buttons in a courtroom is unacceptable, two considerations keep me from concluding that the state court acted unreasonably in failing to see the issue this way and reverse the conviction. First, of the several courts that have considered the influence of spectators' buttons, the majority have left convictions standing. . . . Second, an interest in protected expression on the part of the spectators wearing mourners' buttons has been raised, but not given focus or careful attention in this or any other case that has come to our notice. Although I do not find such a First Amendment interest intuitively strong here, in the absence of developed argument it would be preferable not to decide whether protection of speech could require acceptance of some risk raised by spectators' buttons.

For these reasons, I think Musladin has not shown the state judge's application of our law to be unreasonable, and on that ground concur in the Court's judgment.

DECK V. MISSOURI
544 U. S. 622 (2005)

JUSTICE BREYER delivered the opinion of the court.

We here consider whether shackling a convicted offender during the penalty phase of a capital case violates the Federal Constitution. We hold that the Constitution forbids the use of visible shackles during the penalty phase, as it forbids their use during the guilt phase, *unless* that use is "justified by an essential state interest"—such as the interest in courtroom security—specific to the defendant on trial.

I

In July 1996, petitioner Carman Deck robbed, shot, and killed an elderly couple. In 1998, the

State of Missouri tried Deck for the murders and the robbery. At trial, state authorities required Deck to wear leg braces that apparently were not visible to the jury. Deck was convicted and sentenced to death. The State Supreme Court upheld Deck's conviction but set aside the sentence. The State then held a new sentencing proceeding.

From the first day of the new proceeding, Deck was shackled with leg irons, handcuffs, and a belly chain. Before the jury voir dire began, Deck's counsel objected to the shackles. The objection was overruled. During the voir dire, Deck's counsel renewed the objection. The objection was again overruled, the court stating that Deck "has been convicted and will remain in legirons and a belly chain." After the voir dire, Deck's counsel once again objected, moving to strike the jury panel "because of the fact that Mr. Deck is shackled in front of the jury and makes them think that he is … violent today." The objection was again overruled, the court stating that his "being shackled takes any fear out of their minds." The penalty phase then proceeded with Deck in shackles. Deck was again sentenced to death.

On appeal, Deck claimed that his shackling violated both Missouri law and the Federal Constitution. The Missouri Supreme Court rejected these claims, writing that there was "no record of the extent of the jury's awareness of the restraints"; there was no "claim that the restraints impeded" Deck "from participating in the proceedings"; and there was "evidence" of "a risk" that Deck "might flee in that he was a repeat offender" who may have "killed his two victims to avoid being returned to custody." Thus, there was "sufficient evidence in the record to support the trial court's exercise of its discretion" to require shackles, and in any event Deck "has not demonstrated that the outcome of his trial was prejudiced… . Neither being viewed in shackles by the venire panel prior to trial, nor being viewed while restrained throughout the entire trial, alone, is proof of prejudice." The court rejected Deck's other claims of error and affirmed the sentence.

We granted certiorari to review Deck's claim that his shackling violated the Federal Constitution.

II

We first consider whether, as a general matter, the Constitution permits a State to use visible shackles routinely in the guilt phase of a criminal trial. The answer is clear: The law has long forbidden routine use of visible shackles during the guilt phase; it permits a State to shackle a criminal defendant only in the presence of a special need.

. . . . While these earlier courts disagreed about the degree of discretion to be afforded

trial judges, they settled virtually without exception on a basic rule embodying notions of fundamental fairness: trial courts may not shackle defendants routinely, but only if there is a particular reason to do so.

More recently, this Court has suggested that a version of this rule forms part of the Fifth and Fourteenth Amendments' due process guarantee. Thirty-five years ago, when considering the trial of an unusually obstreperous criminal defendant, the Court held that the Constitution sometimes permitted special measures, including physical restraints. *Allen*. The Court wrote that "binding and gagging might possibly be the fairest and most reasonable way to handle" such a defendant. But the Court immediately added that "even to contemplate such a technique … arouses a feeling that no person should be tried while shackled and gagged except as a last resort."

Sixteen years later, the Court considered a special courtroom security arrangement that involved having uniformed security personnel sit in the first row of the courtroom's spectator section. The Court held that the Constitution allowed the arrangement, stating that the deployment of security personnel during trial is not "the sort of inherently prejudicial practice that, like shackling, should be permitted only where justified by an essential state interest specific to each trial." *Holbrook*. See also *Estelle v. Williams* (making a defendant appear in prison garb poses such a threat to the "fairness of the factfinding process" that it must be justified by an "essential state policy").

…Courts and commentators share close to a consensus that, during the guilt phase of a trial, a criminal defendant has a right to remain free of physical restraints that are visible to the jury; that the right has a constitutional dimension; but that the right may be overcome in a particular instance by essential state interests such as physical security, escape prevention, or courtroom decorum.

Lower courts have disagreed about the specific procedural steps a trial court must take prior to shackling, about the amount and type of evidence needed to justify restraints, and about what forms of prejudice might warrant a new trial, but they have not questioned the basic principle. They have emphasized the importance of preserving trial court discretion…, but they have applied the limits on that discretion…. In light of this precedent, and of a lower court consensus disapproving routine shackling…, it is clear that this Court's prior statements gave voice to a principle deeply embedded in the law. We now conclude that those statements identify a basic element of the "due process of law" protected by the Federal Constitution. Thus, the Fifth and Fourteenth Amendments prohibit the use of physical restraints visible to the jury absent a trial court determination, in the exercise of its discretion, that they are justified by a state interest specific to a particular trial. Such a determination may of course take into account the factors that courts have traditionally relied on in gauging potential security problems and the risk of escape at trial.

III

We here consider shackling not during the guilt phase of an ordinary criminal trial, but during the punishment phase of a capital case. And we must decide whether that change of circumstance makes a constitutional difference. To do so, we examine the reasons that motivate the guilt-phase constitutional rule and determine whether they apply with similar force in this context.

A

. . . .

First, the criminal process presumes that the defendant is innocent until proved guilty. . . . Visible shackling undermines the presumption of innocence and the related fairness of the factfinding process. It suggests to the jury that the justice system itself sees a "need to separate a defendant from the community at large."

Second, the Constitution, in order to help the accused secure a meaningful defense, provides him with a right to counsel. The use of physical restraints diminishes that right. Shackles can interfere with the accused's "ability to communicate" with his lawyer. Indeed, they can interfere with a defendant's ability to participate in his own defense, say by freely choosing whether to take the witness stand on his own behalf.

Third, judges must seek to maintain a judicial process that is a dignified process. The courtroom's formal dignity, which includes the respectful treatment of defendants, reflects the importance of the matter at issue, guilt or innocence, and the gravity with which Americans consider any deprivation of an individual's liberty through criminal punishment. And it reflects a seriousness of purpose that helps to explain the judicial system's power to inspire the confidence and to affect the behavior of a general public whose demands for justice our courts seek to serve. The routine use of shackles in the presence of juries would undermine these symbolic yet concrete objectives. As this Court has said, the use of shackles at trial "affront[s]" the "dignity and decorum of judicial proceedings that the judge is seeking to uphold."

There will be cases, of course, where these perils of shackling are unavoidable. We do not underestimate the need to restrain dangerous defendants to prevent courtroom attacks, or the need to give trial courts latitude in making individualized security determinations. We are mindful of the tragedy that can result if judges are not able to protect themselves and their courtrooms. But given their prejudicial effect, due process does not permit the use of visible restraints if the trial court has not taken account of the circumstances of the particular case.

B

The considerations that militate against the routine use of visible shackles during the guilt phase of a criminal trial apply with like force to penalty proceedings in capital cases. This is obviously so in respect to the latter two considerations mentioned, securing a meaningful defense and maintaining dignified proceedings. It is less obviously so in respect to the first consideration mentioned, for the defendant's conviction means that the presumption of innocence no longer applies. Hence shackles do not undermine the jury's effort to apply that presumption.

Nonetheless, shackles at the penalty phase threaten related concerns. Although the jury is no longer deciding between guilt and innocence, it is deciding between life and death.

Neither is accuracy in making that decision any less critical. The Court has stressed the "acute need" for reliable decisionmaking when the death penalty is at issue The appearance of the offender during the penalty phase in shackles, however, almost inevitably implies to a jury, as a matter of common sense, that court authorities consider the offender a danger to the community—often a statutory aggravator and nearly always a relevant factor in jury decisionmaking, even where the State does not specifically argue the point. It also almost inevitably affects adversely the jury's perception of the character of the defendant. And it thereby inevitably undermines the jury's ability to weigh accurately all relevant considerations—considerations that are often unquantifiable and elusive—when it determines whether a defendant deserves death. In these ways, the use of shackles can be a "thumb [on] death's side of the scale."

Given the presence of similarly weighty considerations, we must conclude that courts cannot routinely place defendants in shackles or other physical restraints visible to the jury during the penalty phase of a capital proceeding. The constitutional requirement, however, is not absolute. It permits a judge, in the exercise of his or her discretion, to take account of special circumstances, including security concerns, that may call for shackling. In so doing, it accommodates the important need to protect the courtroom and its occupants. But any such determination must be case specific; that is to say, it should reflect particular concerns, say special security needs or escape risks, related to the defendant on trial..

Judge Or Jury Misconduct

Wellons v. Hall, 558 U.S. ___ (2010) presents a disturbing fact pattern upon which the defense attorney attempted to raise fair trial and discovery issues through a writ of habeas corpus. The defense attorney, after the culmination of the trial and after his client was sentenced to death, discovered there had been improper *ex parte* contact between the judge and jury. The jury and bailiff, he determined, had planned a reunion either during or after the penalty phase of the trial. He also discovered that jury members had given the judge a penis-shaped chocolate and the bailiff a breast-shaped chocolate. The judge had not, during the course of the trial or penalty phase mentioned these improprieties. The District Court held that "the gifts given were inappropriate and represented an unusual display of poor taste in the context of a proceeding so grave as a capital trial;" nevertheless, that court denied the discovery request. The U.S. Supreme Court's discussion, however, centered on the proper procedural mechanism to raise the claim and did not weigh in on whether the defendant's fair trial rights were violated by the misconduct.

In the next cases, the Court examines judges' failure to recuse themselves. This issue has become a political lightening rod, and since Spring 2022 there has been a lot of heat on Justice Thomas for his failure to recuse himself on cases connected to his wife's political consulting activities (which predate and include the events of January 6th attack on the Capitol). Note that Justice Thomas' dissent on the Williams case—he did not find defendant's rights violated when the Pennsylvania Supreme Court Justice did not recuse himself.[89]

WILLIAMS v. PENNSYLVANIA
579 U.S. ___ (2016)

JUSTICE KENNEDY delivered the opinion of the Court.

I

[Facts Summarized: In 1984 Defendant was charged with murder, and the deputy district attorney assigned to prosecute the case requested and obtained permission to seek the death penalty from her boss, District Attorney Ronald Castille. Williams was convicted and the death penalty was imposed. It was later determined when Williams filed a petition for post-conviction relief that the government improperly used co-defendant's false testimony against Williams in gaining the conviction. At a post-conviction hearing, the court ordered the district attorney's files be released. They were, and it became clear that the trial prosecutor had suppressed material and exculpatory material in violation of *Brady v. Maryland* and had engaged in "prosecutorial gamesmanship." The PCR court issued a stay of Williams execution and ordered a new sentencing hearing.]

…

Seeking to vacate the stay of execution, the Commonwealth submitted an emergency application to the Pennsylvania Supreme Court. By this time, almost three decades had passed since Williams's prosecution. Castille had been elected to a seat on the State Supreme Court and was serving as its chief justice. Williams filed a response to the Commonwealth's application. The disclosure of the trial prosecutor's sentencing memorandum in the PCRA proceedings had alerted Williams to Chief Justice Castille's involvement in the decision to seek a death sentence in his case. For this reason, Williams also filed a motion asking Chief Justice Castille to recuse himself or, if he declined to do so, to refer the recusal motion to the full court for decision. The Commonwealth opposed Williams's recusal motion. Without explanation, Chief Justice Castille denied the motion for recusal and the request for its referral. Two days later, the Pennsylvania Supreme Court denied the application to vacate the stay and ordered full briefing on the issues raised in the appeal. The State Supreme Court then vacated the PCRA court's order granting penalty-phase relief and reinstated Williams's death sentence. Chief Justice Castille and Justices Baer and Stevens joined the majority opinion written by Justice Eakin.

…

Chief Justice Castille authored a concurrence. He lamented that the PCRA court had "lost sight of its role as a neutral judicial officer" and had stayed Williams's execution "for no valid reason." "[B]efore condemning officers of the court," the chief justice stated, "the tribunal should be aware of the substantive status of Brady law," which he believed the PCRA court had misapplied. In addition, Chief Justice Castille denounced what he perceived as the "obstructionist anti-death penalty agenda" of Williams's attorneys from the Federal Community Defender Office. PCRA courts "throughout Pennsylvania need to be vigilant and circumspect when it comes to the activities of this particular advocacy group," he wrote, lest Defender Office lawyers turn postconviction proceedings "into a circus where [they] are the

---

[89] See, Paul Blumenthal's article in the Huffington Post on March 29, 2022 in which he discusses the many times Justice Clarence has recused himself (surrounding his son's activities) but not his wife's activities at https://www.huffpost.com/entry/clarence-thomas-recuse-jan-6_n_6243372ee4b03516d4288d1

ringmasters, with their parrots and puppets as a sideshow."

Two weeks after the Pennsylvania Supreme Court decided Williams's case, Chief Justice Castille retired from the bench. This Court granted Williams's petition for certiorari.

II
A

Williams contends that Chief Justice Castille's decision as district attorney to seek a death sentence against him barred the chief justice from later adjudicating Williams's petition to overturn that sentence. Chief Justice Castille, Williams argues, violated the Due Process Clause of the Fourteenth Amendment by acting as both accuser and judge in his case.

The Court's due process precedents do not set forth a specific test governing recusal when, as here, a judge had prior involvement in a case as a prosecutor. For the reasons explained below, however, the principles on which these precedents rest dictate the rule that must control in the circumstances here. The Court now holds that under the Due Process Clause there is an impermissible risk of actual bias when a judge earlier had significant, personal involvement as a prosecutor in a critical decision regarding the defendant's case.

Due process guarantees "an absence of actual bias" on the part of a judge. Bias is easy to attribute to others and difficult to discern in oneself. To establish an enforceable and workable framework, the Court's precedents apply an objective standard that, in the usual case, avoids having to determine whether actual bias is present. The Court asks not whether a judge harbors an actual, subjective bias, but instead whether, as an objective matter, "the average judge in his position is 'likely' to be neutral, or whether there is an unconstitutional 'potential for bias.' " Of particular relevance to the instant case, the Court has determined that an unconstitutional potential for bias exists when the same person serves as both accuser and adjudicator in a case. This objective risk of bias is reflected in the due process maxim that "no man can be a

judge in his own case and no man is permitted to try cases where he has an interest in the outcome."

The due process guarantee that "no man can be a judge in his own case" would have little substance if it did not disqualify a former prosecutor from sitting in judgment of a prosecution in which he or she had made a critical decision. . . .

No attorney is more integral to the accusatory process than a prosecutor who participates in a major adversary decision. When a judge has served as an advocate for the State in the very case the court is now asked to adjudicate, a serious question arises as to whether the judge, even with the most diligent effort, could set aside any personal interest in the outcome. There is, furthermore, a risk that the judge "would be so psychologically wedded" to his or her previous position as a prosecutor that the judge "would consciously or unconsciously avoid the appearance of having erred or changed position." In addition, the judge's "own personal knowledge and impression" of the case, acquired through his or her role in the prosecution, may carry far more weight with the judge than the parties' arguments to the court.

. . . .

. . .The involvement of multiple actors and the passage of time do not relieve the former prosecutor of the duty to withdraw in order to ensure the neutrality of the judicial process in determining the consequences that his or her own earlier, critical decision may have set in motion.

B

This leads to the question whether Chief Justice Castille's authorization to seek the death penalty against Williams amounts to significant, personal involvement in a critical trial decision. The Court now concludes that it was a significant, personal involvement; and, as a result, Chief Justice Castille's failure to recuse from Williams's case presented an unconstitutional risk of bias.

As an initial matter, there can be no doubt that the decision to pursue the death penalty is a critical choice in the adversary process. Indeed, after a defendant is charged with a death-eligible crime, whether to ask a jury to end the defendant's life is one of the most serious discretionary decisions a prosecutor can be called upon to make.

Nor is there any doubt that Chief Justice Castille had a significant role in this decision. Without his express authorization, the Commonwealth would not have been able to pursue a death sentence against Williams. The importance of this decision and the profound consequences it carries make it evident that a responsible prosecutor would deem it to be a most significant exercise of his or her official discretion and professional judgment.

. . . .

Chief Justice Castille's own comments while running for judicial office refute the Commonwealth's claim that he played a mere ministerial role in capital sentencing decisions. During the chief justice's election campaign, multiple news outlets reported his statement that he "sent 45 people to death rows" as district attorney. Chief Justice Castille's willingness to take personal responsibility for the death sentences obtained during his tenure as district attorney indicate that, in his own view, he played a meaningful role in those sentencing decisions and considered his involvement to be an important duty of his office.

Although not necessary to the disposition of this case, the PCRA court's ruling underscores the risk of permitting a former prosecutor to be a judge in what had been his or her own case. The PCRA court determined that the trial prosecutor — Chief Justice Castille's former subordinate in the district attorney's office — had engaged in multiple, intentional Brady violations during Williams's prosecution. While there is no indication that Chief Justice Castille was aware of the alleged prosecutorial misconduct, it would be difficult for a judge in his position not to view the PCRA court's findings as a criticism of his former office and, to some extent, of his own leadership and supervision as district attorney.

The potential conflict of interest posed by the PCRA court's findings illustrates the utility of statutes and professional codes of conduct that "provide more protection than due process requires." It is important to note that due process "demarks only the outer boundaries of judicial disqualifications." Most questions of recusal are addressed by more stringent and detailed ethical rules, which in many jurisdictions already require disqualification under the circumstances of this case. At the time Williams filed his recusal motion with the Pennsylvania Supreme Court, for example, Pennsylvania's Code of Judicial Conduct disqualified judges from any proceeding in which "they served as a lawyer in the matter in controversy, or a lawyer with whom they previously practiced law served during such association as a lawyer concerning the matter. . . ." The fact that most jurisdictions have these rules in place suggests that today's decision will not occasion a significant change in recusal practice.

Chief Justice Castille's significant, personal involvement in a critical decision in Williams's case gave rise to an unacceptable risk of actual bias. This risk so endangered the appearance of neutrality that his participation in the case "must be forbidden if the guarantee of due process is to be adequately implemented."

III

Having determined that Chief Justice Castille's participation violated due process, the Court must resolve whether Williams is entitled to relief. In past cases, the Court has not had to decide the question whether a due process violation arising from a jurist's failure to recuse amounts to harmless error if the jurist is on a multimember court and the jurist's vote was not decisive. For the reasons discussed below, the Court holds that an unconstitutional failure to recuse constitutes structural error even if the judge in question did not cast a deciding vote.

The Court has little trouble concluding that a due process violation arising from the participation of an interested judge is a defect "not amenable" to harmless-error review, regardless of whether the judge's vote was dispositive. The deliberations of an appellate panel, as a general rule, are confidential. As a result, it is neither possible nor productive to inquire whether the jurist in question might have influenced the views of his or her colleagues during the decisionmaking process. Indeed, one purpose of judicial confidentiality is to assure jurists that they can reexamine old ideas and suggest new ones, while both seeking to persuade and being open to persuasion by their colleagues. As Justice Brennan wrote in his Lavoie concurrence,

> "The description of an opinion as being 'for the court' connotes more than merely that the opinion has been joined by a majority of the participating judges. It reflects the fact that these judges have exchanged ideas and arguments in deciding the case. It reflects the collective process of deliberation which shapes the court's perceptions of which issues must be addressed and, more importantly, how they must be addressed. And, while the influence of any single participant in this process can never be measured with precision, experience teaches us that each member's involvement plays a part in shaping the court's ultimate disposition."

. . . The fact that the interested judge's vote was not dispositive may mean only that the judge was successful in persuading most members of the court to accept his or her position. That outcome does not lessen the unfairness to the affected party.

A multimember court must not have its guarantee of neutrality undermined, for the appearance of bias demeans the reputation and integrity not just of one jurist, but of the larger institution of which he or she is a part. An insistence on the appearance of neutrality is not some artificial attempt to mask imperfection in the judicial process, but rather an essential means of ensuring the reality of a fair adjudication. Both the appearance and reality of impartial justice are necessary to the public legitimacy of judicial pronouncements and thus to the rule of law itself. When the objective risk of actual bias on the part of a judge rises to an unconstitutional level, the failure to recuse cannot be deemed harmless.

. . . .

Chief Justice Castille's participation in Williams's case was an error that affected the State Supreme Court's whole adjudicatory framework below. Williams must be granted an opportunity to present his claims to a court unburdened by any "possible temptation . . . not to hold the balance nice, clear and true between the State and the accused."

CHIEF JUSTICE ROBERTS, with whom JUSTICE ALITO joins, dissenting, omitted.

JUSTICE THOMAS, dissenting.

The Court concludes that it violates the Due Process Clause for the chief justice of the Supreme Court of Pennsylvania, a former district attorney who was not the trial prosecutor in petitioner Terrance Williams' case, to review Williams' fourth petition for state postconviction review. That conclusion is flawed. The specter of bias alone in a judicial proceeding is not a deprivation of due process. Rather than constitutionalize every judicial disqualification rule, the Court has left such rules to legislatures, bar associations, and the judgment of individual adjudicators. Williams, moreover, is not a criminal defendant. His complaint is instead that the due process protections in his state postconviction proceedings — an altogether new civil matter, not a continuation of his criminal trial — were lacking. Ruling in Williams' favor, the Court ignores this posture and our precedents commanding less of state postconviction proceedings than of criminal prosecutions involving defendants whose convictions are not yet final. I respectfully dissent.

. . . .

III

Even if I were to assume that an error occurred in Williams' state postconviction proceedings, the question remains whether there is anything left for the Pennsylvania courts to remedy. There is not.

The majority remands the case to "[a]llo[w] an appellate panel to reconsider a case without the participation of the interested member," which it declares "will permit judges to probe lines of analysis or engage in discussions they may have felt constrained to avoid in their first deliberations." The majority neglects to mention that the Supreme Court of Pennsylvania might have done just that. It entertained Williams' motion for reargument without Castille, who had retired months before the court denied the motion. The Supreme Court of Pennsylvania is free to decide on remand that it cured any alleged deprivation of due process in Williams' postconviction proceeding by considering his motion for reargument without Castille's participation.

This is not a case about the " 'accused.' " It is a case about the due process rights of the already convicted. Whatever those rights might be, they do not include policing alleged violations of state codes of judicial ethics in postconviction proceedings. The Due Process Clause does not require any and all conceivable procedural protections that Members of this Court think "Western liberal democratic government ought to guarantee to its citizens." I respectfully dissent.

RIPPO v. BAKER
582 U.S. ___ (2017)

Per Curiam.

Facts Summarized: Rippo was prosecuted by the Clark County District Attorney in Nevada. The judge who presided over his case was under investigation in a federal bribery probe, and the district attorney prosecuting Rippo was playing a role in that investigation. Rippo sought to disqualify the judge asserting that a judge could not be fair in a case where one of the parties was investigating him. That motion was denied.

A new judge was assigned to the case after the initial judge was indicted, and he denied Rippo's motion for a new trial. After conviction, Rippo appealed. The Nevada Supreme Court affirmed conviction on direct appeal noting that Rippo hadn't shown that the district attorney was involved in the investigation. Rippo later sought state postconviction relief and advanced his bias claim once more -- pointing to documents from the judge's criminal trial indicating that the district attorney's office had participated in The investigation of the trial judge . . . Nevertheless, the Nevada Supreme Court held that although Rippo had raised claims, he hadn't shown any evidence of actual bias.

OPINION: We vacate the Nevada Supreme Court's judgment because it applied the wrong legal standard. Under our precedents, the Due Process Clause may sometimes demand recusal even when a judge " 'ha[s] no actual bias.' " Recusal is required when, objectively speaking, "the probability of actual bias on the part of the judge or decisionmaker is too high to be constitutionally tolerable." ... see *Williams* v. *Pennsylvania*, ("The Court asks not whether a judge harbors an actual, subjective bias, but instead whether, as an objective matter, the average judge in his position is likely to be neutral, or whether there is an unconstitutional potential for bias" . . . Although ...[in *Bracy*] we explained that the petitioner there *had* pointed to facts suggesting actual, subjective bias, we did not hold that a litigant *must* show as a matter of course that a judge was "actually biased in [the litigant's] case," ... [The proper question is] ...whether, considering all the circumstances alleged, the risk of bias was too high to be constitutionally tolerable.

Prosecutorial Misconduct

In *Berger v. United States* (below), the Court examines the prosecutor's trial behavior and its effect on the defendant's right to a fair trial. In *Banks v. Dretke,* a case in which the defendant received the death penalty, the court examines whether a prosecutor's violated defendant's right to a fair trial by failing to set the record straight when a prosecution witness gave inaccurate testimony.

BERGER v. UNITED STATES
295 U.S. 78 (1935)

JUSTICE SUTHERLAND delivered the opinion of the Court.

That the United States prosecuting attorney overstepped the bounds of that propriety and fairness which should characterize the conduct of such an officer in the prosecution of a criminal offense is clearly shown by the record. He was guilty of misstating the facts in his cross- examination of witnesses; of putting into the mouths of such witnesses things which they had not said; of suggesting by his questions that statements had been made to him personally out of court, in respect of which no proof was offered; of pretending to understand that a witness had said something which he had not said and persistently cross-examining the witness upon that basis; of assuming prejudicial facts not in evidence; of bullying and arguing with witnesses; and, in general, of conducting himself in a thoroughly indecorous and improper manner. . . . It is impossible, however, without reading the testimony at some length, and thereby obtaining a knowledge of the setting in which the objectionable matter occurred, to appreciate fully the extent of the misconduct. The trial judge, it is true, sustained objections to some of the questions, insinuations and misstatements, and instructed the jury to disregard them. But the situation was one which called for stern rebuke and repressive measures and, perhaps, if these were not successful, for the granting of a mistrial. It is impossible to say that the evil influence upon the jury of these acts of misconduct was removed by such mild judicial action as was taken.

The prosecuting attorney's argument to the jury was undignified and intemperate, containing improper insinuations and assertions calculated to mislead the jury. . . .

The United States Attorney is the representative not of an ordinary party to a controversy, but of a sovereignty whose obligation to govern impartially is as compelling as its obligation to govern at all; And whose interest, therefore, in a criminal prosecution is not that it shall win a case, but that justice shall be done. As such, he is in a peculiar and very definite sense the servant of the law, the twofold aim of which is that guilt shall not escape or innocence suffer. He may prosecute with earnestness and vigor-indeed, he should do so. But, while he may strike hard blows, he is not at liberty to strike foul ones. It is as much his duty to refrain from improper methods calculated to produce a wrongful conviction as it is to use every legitimate means to bring about a just one.

It is fair to say that the average jury, in a greater or less degree, has confidence that these obligations, which so plainly rest upon the prosecuting attorney, will be faithfully observed. Consequently, improper suggestions, insinuations, and, especially, assertions of personal knowledge are apt to carry much weight against the accused when they should properly carry none. . . .

In these circumstances prejudice to the cause of the accused is so highly probable that we are not justified in assuming its nonexistence. If the case against Berger had been strong, or, as some courts have said, the evidence of his guilt 'overwhelming,' a different conclusion might be reached. Moreover, we have not here a case where the misconduct of the prosecuting attorney was slight or confined to a single instance, but one where such misconduct was pronounced and persistent, with a probable cumulative effect upon the jury which cannot be disregarded as inconsequential. A new trial must be awarded.

BANKS v. DRETKE
540 U.S. 668 (2004)

JUSTICE GINSBURG delivered the opinion of the court.

After police found a gun-shot corpse near Texarkana, Texas, Deputy Sheriff Willie Huff learned that the decedent had been seen with petitioner Banks three days earlier. When a paid informant told Deputy Huff that Banks was driving to Dallas to fetch a weapon, Deputy Huff followed Banks to a residence there. On the return trip, police stopped Banks's vehicle, found a handgun, and arrested the car's occupants. Returning to the Dallas residence, Deputy Huff encountered Charles Cook and recovered a second gun, which Cook said Banks had left at the residence several days earlier. On testing, the second gun proved to be the murder weapon.

Prior to Banks's trial, the State advised defense counsel that, without necessity of motions, the State would provide Banks with all discovery to which he was entitled. Nevertheless, the State withheld evidence that would have allowed Banks to discredit two essential prosecution witnesses. At the trial's guilt phase, Cook testified, *inter alia,* that Banks admitted "kill[ing a] white boy." On cross-examination, Cook thrice denied talking to anyone about his testimony.

In fact, Deputy Huff and prosecutors intensively coached Cook about his testimony during at least one pretrial session. The prosecution allowed Cook's misstatements to stand uncorrected. After Banks's capital murder conviction, the penalty-phase jury found that Banks would probably commit criminal acts of violence that would constitute a continuing threat to society. One of the State's two penalty-phase witnesses, Robert Farr, testified that Banks had retrieved a gun from Dallas in order to commit robberies. According to Farr, Banks had said he would "take care of it" if trouble arose during those crimes. Two defense witnesses impeached Farr, but were, in turn, impeached.

Banks testified, among other things, that, although he had traveled to Dallas to obtain a gun, he had no intent to participate in the robberies, which Farr alone planned to commit.

In summation, the prosecution suggested that Banks had not traveled to Dallas only to supply Farr with a weapon. Stressing Farr's testimony that Banks said he would "take care" of trouble arising during the robberies, the prosecution urged the jury to find Farr credible. Farr's admission that he used narcotics, the prosecution suggested, indicated that he had been open and honest in every way. The State did not disclose that Farr was the paid informant who told Deputy Huff about the Dallas trip. The judge sentenced Banks to death.

Through Banks's direct appeal, the State continued to hold secret Farr's and Cook's links to the police. In a 1992 state-court postconviction motion, Banks alleged for the first time that the prosecution knowingly failed to turn over exculpatory evidence that would have revealed Farr as a police informant and Banks's arrest as a "set-up." Banks also alleged that during the trial's guilt phase, the State deliberately withheld information of a deal prosecutors made with Cook, which would have been critical to the jury's assessment of Cook's credibility. Banks asserted that the State's actions violated *Brady v. Maryland*, which held that the prosecution's suppression of evidence requested by and favorable to an accused violates due process where the evidence is material to either guilt or punishment, irrespective of the prosecution's good or bad faith. The State denied Banks's allegations, and the state post-conviction court rejected his claims.

In 1996, Banks filed the instant federal habeas petition, alleging, as relevant, that the State had withheld material exculpatory evidence revealing Farr to be a police informant and Banks' arrest as a "set-up." Banks further alleged that the State had concealed Cook's incentive to testify in a manner favorable to the prosecution

. . . .

When police or prosecutors conceal significant exculpatory or impeaching material in the State's possession, it is ordinarily incumbent on the State to set the record straight.

A *Brady* prosecutorial misconduct claim has three essential elements. Beyond debate, the first such element — that the evidence at issue be favorable to the accused as exculpatory or impeaching — is satisfied here. Farr's paid informant status plainly qualifies as evidence advantageous to Banks. Cause and prejudice in this case parallel the second and third of the three *Brady* components. Corresponding to the second *Brady* element — that the State suppressed the evidence at issue — a petitioner shows cause when the reason for the failure to develop facts in state-court proceedings was the State's suppression of the relevant evidence. Coincident with the third *Brady* component — that prejudice ensued — prejudice within the compass of the "cause and prejudice" requirement exists when suppressed evidence is "material" for *Brady* purposes. Thus, if Banks succeeds in demonstrating cause and prejudice, he will also succeed in establishing the essential elements of his Farr *Brady* claim.

First, the State knew of, but kept back, Farr's arrangement with Deputy Huff. Second, the State asserted, on the eve of trial, that it would disclose all *Brady* material. Banks cannot be faulted for relying on that representation.

Third, in its answer to Banks's, the State denied Banks's assertions that Farr was a police informant and Banks's arrest a "set-up." The State thereby confirmed Banks's reliance on the prosecution's representation that it had disclosed all *Brady* material. Each time Farr misrepresented his dealings with police, the prosecution allowed that testimony to stand uncorrected. Banks appropriately assumed police would not engage in improper litigation conduct to obtain a conviction.

The State's suppression of Farr's informant status is "material" for *Brady* purposes. The materiality standard for *Brady* claims is met when "the favorable evidence could reasonably be taken to put the whole case in such a different light as to undermine confidence in the verdict." Farr was paid for a critical role in the scenario that led to Banks's indictment. . . . Farr's trial testimony was the centerpiece of the Banks prosecution's penalty-phase case. That testimony was cast in large doubt by the declaration Banks ultimately obtained from Farr and introduced in the federal habeas proceeding. Had jurors known of Farr's continuing interest in obtaining Deputy Huff's favor and his receipt of funds to set Banks up, they might well have distrusted Farr's testimony, and, insofar as it was uncorroborated, disregarded it.

The jury, moreover, did not benefit from customary, truth-promoting precautions that generally accompany informant testimony. Such testimony poses serious credibility questions. This Court, therefore, has long allowed defendants broad latitude to cross-examine informants and has counseled the use of careful instructions on submission of the credibility issue to the jury. The State's argument that Farr's informant status was rendered cumulative by his impeachment at trial is contradicted by the record. Neither witness called to impeach Farr gave evidence directly relevant to Farr's part in Banks's prosecution. The impeaching witnesses, moreover, were themselves impeached, as the prosecution stressed on summation. Further, the prosecution turned to its advantage remaining impeachment evidence by suggesting that Farr's admission of drug use demonstrated his openness and honesty.

[The district court granted habeas relief with respect to Banks' death sentence based on the state's failure to disclose Farr's informant status. but refused to reverse the guilt verdict, rejecting Banks' Brady claim relating to Cook's testimony.

The Fifth Circuit Court of Appeals reversed the district court's decision to grant Banks relief as to his death sentence based on his Brady claim relating to Farr's testimony. The Court held that Banks first had to press his claims in state court.

The Supreme Court held 7-2 that the Fifth Circuit was wrong to dismiss Banks' claim under *Brady* relating to Farr's testimony and 9–0 that the Fifth Circuit was wrong to deny Banks' appeal based on Cook's testimony.]

Pretrial Publicity

One of the fundamental principles of the United States criminal justice system is the principle of orality. This principle holds that defendants may only be convicted on the basis of evidence developed and admitted at trial. Although principle of orality is generally considered in terms of the way evidence is developed during the trial, it also includes the notion that jurors should not decide guilt or innocence based on publicity given to the case prior to, or during, the trial. *Sheppard v. Maxwell*, 384 U.S. 333 (1966), involved the trial of Sam Sheppard — the story upon which the movie "The Fugitive" was based. This decision chronicled the intense pre-trial and trial publicity surrounding the case and found that the intense publicity prevented the defendant from getting a fair trial.

SHEPPARD v. MAXWELL
384 U.S. 333 (1966)

JUSTICE CLARK, delivered the opinion of the court

"The question . . . [before the Court is] . . . whether Sheppard was deprived of a fair trial in his state conviction for the second-degree murder of his wife because of the trial judge's failure to protect Sheppard sufficiently from the massive, pervasive and prejudicial publicity that attended his prosecution. . . . Sheppard did not receive a fair trial consistent with the Due Process Clause of the Fourteenth Amendment. . . .

"[L]egal trials are not like elections, to be won through the use of the meeting-hall, the radio, and the newspaper." And the Court has insisted that no one be punished for a crime without "a charge fairly made and fairly tried in a public tribunal free of prejudice, passion, excitement, and tyrannical power." "Freedom of discussion should be given the widest range compatible with the essential requirement of the fair and orderly administration of justice." But it must not be allowed to divert the trial from the "very purpose of a court system to adjudicate controversies, both criminal and civil, in the calmness and solemnity of the courtroom according to legal procedures." Among these "legal procedures" is the requirement that the jury's verdict be based on evidence received in open court, not from outside sources.

The undeviating rule of this Court was expressed by Mr. Justice Holmes over half a century ago in *Patterson v. Colorado,* 205 U.S. 454, 462 (1907): "The theory of our system is that the conclusions to be reached in a case will be induced only by evidence and argument in open court, and not by any outside influence, whether of private talk or public print." Moreover, "the burden of showing essential unfairness as a demonstrable reality," need not be undertaken when television has exposed the community "repeatedly and in depth to the spectacle of [the accused] personally confessing in detail to the crimes with which he was later to be charged."

In *Turner v. Louisiana,* 379 U.S. 466 (1965), two key witnesses were deputy sheriffs who doubled as jury shepherds during the trial. The deputies swore that they had not talked to the jurors about the case, but the Court nonetheless held that, "even if it could be assumed that the deputies never did discuss the case directly with any members of the jury, it would be blinking reality not to recognize the extreme prejudice inherent in this continual association."

Only last Term in *Estes v. Texas,* 381 U.S. 532 (1965), we set aside a conviction despite the absence of any showing of prejudice. We said there: "It is true that in most cases involving claims of due process deprivations we require a showing of identifiable prejudice to the accused. Nevertheless, at times a procedure employed by the State involves such a probability that prejudice will result that it is deemed inherently lacking in due process."

It is clear that the totality of circumstances in this case also warrants such an approach. Unlike *Estes,* Sheppard was not granted a change of venue to a locale away from where the publicity originated; nor was his jury sequestered. The *Estes* jury saw none of the television broadcasts from the courtroom. On the contrary, the Sheppard jurors were subjected to newspaper, radio and television coverage of the trial while not taking part in the proceedings. They were allowed to go their separate ways outside of the courtroom, without adequate directions not to read or listen to anything concerning the case. The judge's "admonitions" at the beginning of the trial are representative: "I would suggest to you and caution you that you do not read any newspapers during the progress of this trial, that you do not listen to radio comments nor watch or listen to television comments, insofar as this case is concerned. You will feel very much better as the trial proceeds. I am sure that we shall all feel very much better if we do not indulge in any newspaper reading or

listening to any comments whatever about the matter while the case is in progress. After it is all over, you can read it all to your heart's content."

At intervals during the trial, the judge simply repeated his "suggestions" and "requests" that the jurors not expose themselves to comment upon the case. Moreover, the jurors were thrust into the role of celebrities by the judge's failure to insulate them from reporters and photographers. The numerous pictures of the jurors, with their addresses, which appeared in the newspapers before and during the trial itself exposed them to expressions of opinion from both cranks and friends. The fact that anonymous letters had been received by prospective jurors should have made the judge aware that this publicity seriously threatened the jurors' privacy.

The press coverage of the *Estes* trial was not nearly as massive and pervasive as the attention given by the Cleveland newspapers and broadcasting stations to Sheppard's prosecution. Sheppard stood indicted for the murder of his wife; the State was demanding the death penalty. For months the virulent publicity about Sheppard and the murder had made the case notorious. Charges and countercharges were aired in the news media besides those for which Sheppard was called to trial. In addition, only three months before trial, Sheppard was examined for more than five hours without counsel during a three-day inquest which ended in a public brawl. The inquest was televised live from a high school gymnasium seating hundreds of people. Furthermore, the trial began two weeks before a hotly contested election at which both Chief Prosecutor Mahon and Judge Blythin were candidates for judgeships.

While we cannot say that Sheppard was denied due process by the judge's refusal to take precautions against the influence of pretrial publicity alone, the court's later rulings must be considered against the setting in which the trial was held. In light of this background, we believe that the arrangements made by the judge with the news media caused Sheppard to be deprived of that "judicial serenity and calm to which [he] was entitled." . . . The fact is that bedlam reigned at the courthouse during the trial and newsmen took over practically the entire courtroom, hounding most of the participants in the trial, especially Sheppard. At a temporary table within a few feet of the jury box and counsel table sat some 20 reporters staring at Sheppard and taking notes. The erection of a press table for reporters inside the bar is unprecedented. The bar of the court is reserved for counsel, providing them a safe place in which to keep papers and exhibits, and to confer privately with client and co-counsel. It is designed to protect the witness and the jury from any distractions, intrusions or influences, and to permit bench discussions of the judge's rulings away from the hearing of the public and the jury. Having assigned almost all of the available seats in the courtroom to the news media the judge lost his ability to supervise that environment. The movement of the reporters in and out of the courtroom caused frequent confusion and disruption of the trial. And the record reveals constant commotion within the bar. Moreover, the judge gave the throng of newsmen gathered in the corridors of the courthouse absolute free rein. Participants in the trial, including the jury, were forced to run a gantlet of reporters and photographers each time they entered or left the courtroom. The total lack of consideration for the privacy of the jury was demonstrated by the assignment to a broadcasting station of space next to the jury room on the floor above the courtroom, as well as the fact that jurors were allowed to make telephone calls during their five-day deliberation.

Indeed, every court that has considered this case, save the court that tried it, has deplored the manner in which the news media inflamed and prejudiced the public.

Nor is there doubt that this deluge of publicity reached at least some of the jury. On the only occasion that the jury was queried, two jurors admitted in open court to hearing the highly inflammatory charge that a prison inmate claimed Sheppard as the father of her illegitimate child. Despite the extent and nature of the publicity to which the jury was exposed during trial, the judge refused defense counsel's other requests that the jurors be asked whether they had read or heard specific prejudicial comment about the case, including the incidents we have previously summarized. In these circumstances, we can assume that some of this material reached members of the jury.

The court's fundamental error is compounded by the holding that it lacked power to control the publicity about the trial. From the very inception of the proceedings the judge announced that neither he nor anyone else could restrict prejudicial news accounts. And he reiterated this view on numerous occasions. Since he viewed the news media as his target, the judge never considered other means that are often utilized to reduce the appearance of prejudicial material and to protect the jury from outside influence. We conclude that these procedures would have been sufficient to guarantee Sheppard a fair trial and so do not consider what sanctions might be available against a recalcitrant press nor the charges of bias now made against the state trial judge.

The carnival atmosphere at trial could easily have been avoided since the courtroom and courthouse premises are subject to the control of the court. . . . As we stressed in *Estes,* the presence of the press at judicial proceedings must be limited when it is apparent that the accused might otherwise be prejudiced or disadvantaged. Bearing in mind the massive pretrial publicity, the judge should have adopted stricter rules governing the use of the courtroom by newsmen, as Sheppard's counsel requested. The number of reporters in the courtroom itself could have been limited at the first sign that their presence would disrupt the trial. They certainly should not have been placed inside the bar. Furthermore, the judge should have more closely regulated the conduct of newsmen in the courtroom. For instance, the judge belatedly asked them not to handle and photograph trial exhibits lying on the counsel table during recesses.

Secondly, the court should have insulated the witnesses. All of the newspapers and radio stations apparently interviewed prospective witnesses at will, and in many instances disclosed their testimony. . . . Although the witnesses were barred from the courtroom during the trial the full verbatim testimony was available to them in the press. This completely nullified the judge's imposition of the rule.

Thirdly, the court should have made some effort to control the release of leads, information, and gossip to the press by police officers, witnesses, and the counsel for both sides. Much of the information thus disclosed was inaccurate, leading to groundless rumors and confusion. . . .

Defense counsel immediately brought to the court's attention the tremendous amount of publicity in the Cleveland press that "misrepresented entirely the testimony" in the case. Under such circumstances, the judge should have at least warned the newspapers to check the accuracy of their accounts. And it is obvious that the judge should have further sought to alleviate this problem by imposing control over the statements made to the news media by counsel, witnesses, and especially the Coroner and police officers. The prosecution repeatedly made evidence available to the news media which was never offered in the trial. Much of the "evidence" disseminated in this fashion was clearly inadmissible. The exclusion of such evidence in court is rendered meaningless when news media make it available to the public. . . .

The fact that many of the prejudicial news items can be traced to the prosecution, as well as the defense, aggravates the judge's failure to take any action. Effective control of these sources — concededly within the court's power — might well have prevented the divulgence of inaccurate information, rumors, and accusations that made up much of the inflammatory publicity, at least after Sheppard's indictment.

More specifically, the trial court might well have proscribed extrajudicial statements by any lawyer, party, witness, or court official which divulged prejudicial matters . . . Had the judge, the other officers of the court, and the police placed the interest of justice first, the news media would have soon learned to be content with the task of reporting the case as it unfolded in the courtroom — not pieced together from extrajudicial statements.

From the cases coming here we note that unfair and prejudicial news comment on pending trials has become increasingly prevalent. Due process requires that the accused receive a trial by an impartial jury free from outside influences. Given the pervasiveness of modern communications and the difficulty of effacing prejudicial publicity from the minds of the jurors, the trial courts must take strong measures to ensure that the balance is never weighed against the accused. And appellate tribunals have the duty to make an independent evaluation of the circumstances. Of course, there is nothing that proscribes the press from reporting events that transpire in the courtroom. But where there is a reasonable likelihood that prejudicial news prior to trial will prevent a fair trial, the judge should continue the case until the threat abates, or transfer it to another county not so permeated with publicity. In addition, sequestration of the jury was something the judge should have raised sua sponte with counsel. If publicity during the proceedings threatens the fairness of the trial, a new trial should be ordered. But we must remember that reversals are but palliatives; the cure lies in those remedial measures that will prevent the prejudice at its inception. The courts must take such steps by rule and regulation that will protect their processes from prejudicial outside interferences. Neither prosecutors, counsel for defense, the accused, witnesses, court staff, nor enforcement officers coming under the jurisdiction of the court should be permitted to frustrate its function. Collaboration between counsel and the press as to information affecting the fairness of a criminal trial is not only subject to regulation, but is highly censurable and worthy of disciplinary measures.

Since the state trial judge did not fulfill his duty to protect Sheppard from the inherently prejudicial publicity which saturated the community and to control disruptive influences in the courtroom, we must reverse . . ."

As discussed in *Sheppard* a court can control publicity so as to ensure a fair trial in several ways including change of venue, sequestration of the jury, a gag order prohibiting parties in the trial from releasing information to the press or saying anything in public about the trial, and finally, excluding the media from the trial. Although the press has a right to attend a criminal trial, the media may be excluded if the court specifically finds that closure is necessary for a fair trial.

The Court in *Skilling v. United States,* 561 U.S. ____ (2010), refused to find that trial publicity and community prejudice prevented Enron CEO, Jeffrey Skilling, from receiving a fair trial. Skilling had moved to change venue from Houston, claiming that adverse pre-trial publicity had poisoned potential jurors. The Court distinguished *Sheppard v. Maxwell, Estes v. Texas*, and *Rideau v. Louisiana*, cases in which convictions were obtained in trial atmospheres utterly corrupted by press coverage. Pretrial publicity — even persuasive, adverse publicity does not inevitably lead to an unfair trial. *Nebraska Press Assn. v. Stuart,* 427 U.S. 539 (1979). The Court found that Skilling had not established that a presumption of juror prejudice arose nor that actual bias infected the jury that had tried him. The trial court, it noted, had stressed impartiality at voir dire and had imposed adequate safeguards. The Court pointed to factors to be considered in determining whether there was a presumption of prejudice which is warranted in only the extreme case.

> ➤ The size and character of the community in which the crime occurred. Houston was the 4th most populus city in the United States at the time of the trial, and 4.5 million people qualified for jury duty.

> ➤ Whether news story contained a confession by the defendant or blatantly prejudicial information of the type readers or viewers could not reasonably be expected to shut from sight.

> ➤ The time between the crime and the trial. The Court noted that the level of media attention in Skilling's case diminished over time.

> ➤ Evidence from the verdict which would undermine a finding of bias. In this case, the jury acquitted Skilling of nine counts of insider-trading.

In sum, the Court deferred to the trial court's ability to assess through voir dire whether actual prejudice infected the jury. The court stated, "In this case ... news stories about Enron did not present the kind of vivid, unforgettable information we have recognized as particularly likely to produce prejudice, and Houston's size and diversity diluted the media impact."

In January 2019, Roger Stone, political advisor and commentator, was indicted for obstruction of justice, witness tampering, and other offenses as part of a seven-count indictment. The judge conditionally released Mr. Stone, but imposed a gag order on the attorneys in the case. Shortly thereafter, Mr. Stone posted on his Instagram account a picture of the judge, D.C. District Court Judge Amy Berman Jackson with crosshairs in the corner of the picture. Judge Berman Jackson ordered Mr. Stone back to court to discuss his continued release under the Bail Reform Act, 18 U.S. Code Section 3142. After the hearing, the judge ruled from the bench, and discussed the purposes of conditional release under the act, the restrictions a judge can place on a person released (pre-trial) so as to ensure the right to a free trial. She stated,

. . .

For all these reasons, then, I find, pursuant to 18 U.S. Code Section 3142 (c)(1), based on this record and the Instagram post that will be entered under seal as part of the record, that released under the current set of conditions without modification does pose a danger to the safety of other persons associated with this case or the community. In addition as case law set forth in the February 15 media communications order, at docket 36, explains, I have a number of duties and responsibilities. I have the duty -- notwithstanding any steps that defendant takes to frustrate this goal – to preserve his right to a fair trial by an impartial jury.

The publicity generated by the defendant's own actions had precisely the effect I warned him about. The attempt to stoke up his followers also stoked up those who disagree with his views. And by continuing to ensure that he would be the subject of a story, he provoked a series of unflattering posts and comments in response to those stories. When the defense asks me not to impose any restrictions on the defendant, it assured me, on page 7 of its submission, that, quote, the first wave of publicity, close quote, considering the indictment and the execution of the search warrant, quote, will subside, close quote. And that the court's ability to seat a fair jury will not be compromised by the press or by Mr. Stone.

That turned out quickly to be a highly inaccurate prediction. The publicity cannot possibly subside if it's the defendant out there fanning the flames. The Supreme Court case law cited in my order also makes it clear that the responsibility lies with me in the first instance to craft appropriate rules to ensure that the trial does not devolve into a circus. The *Gentile* case and cases cited by the Office of Special Counsel in its submission support the Court's ability to impose restrictions on all participants, not just attorneys. And the Supreme Court and the D.C. Circuit have also emphasized the Court's responsibility. It notes that order and decorum and dignity are not just old-fashioned pleasantries, they're fundamental to the fair administration of justice, which enures to the benefit of everyone, including the defendant. And it's my responsibility to uphold that order. And it includes making sure that the people who work in this building, the people who need to access the building for their own cases, and prosecutors, jurors, witnesses, parties — and, yes, judges —can come and go from this building safely.

So, no, Mr. Stone, I am not giving you another chance. I have serious doubts about whether you've learned any lesson at all.

Therefore, the conditions of the defendant's pretrial release are hereby modified to include the condition that, and the February 15th, 2019 media communications order is hereby modified to provide that, from this moment on, the defendant may not speak publicly about the investigation or the case or any of the participants in the investigation or the case. Period. The prohibition includes, but is not limited to, no statements about the case during radio broadcasts of his own. No statements about the case during interviews on TV, and on the radio, with print reporters or on internet-based media. No press releases or press conferences. No blogs or letters to the editor. No posts on Facebook, Twitter, Instagram, Snapchat or any other form of social media. And the defendant may not comment publicly about the case indirectly, by having statements made on his behalf by surrogates, family members, spokespersons, representatives, or his, quote, many volunteers, close quote.

You may send out as many emails, Tweets, post as you choose that say, Please donate to the Roger Stone defense fund to help me defend myself against these charges. And you may add that you deny or are innocent of the charges, but that's the extent of it. You apparently need clear boundaries, so there they are.

Please note that I am not prohibiting you from being part of the public discourse or from earning a living. You told me yourself that you will not lose a cent of income if I bar you from speaking about this case. You may continue to publish, to write, and to speak, and to be, as your lawyer put it, a voice about any other matter of public interest; not this case, not the people in it. Not while you are under my supervision.

Under U.S. Code Section 1342(c)(1) and (3), I find that this additional condition is necessary and that it is the least restrictive means possible to reasonably assure the safety of persons associated with this case and the community. I also find that the order is supported by all the reasons and authority set out in my original media communications order. Under Local Rule 57.7(c), I find that extrajudicial statements by the defendant are likely to interfere with his right to have a fair trial by an impartial jury. And I further find, based on this record, that additional public comments about this case by this defendant pose a substantial risk of material prejudice to the case and the due administration of justice.

I agree with the special counsel that the effect and very likely the intent of the post was to denigrate this process and taint the jury pool. What this all means, Mr. Stone, is that any violation of this order will be a basis for revoking your bond and detaining you pending trial. So, I want to be clear, today I gave you a second chance. But this is not baseball. There will not be a third chance. If you cannot or will not or do no comply with today's orders, I will find it necessary to adjust your environment so that you don't have access to the temptations posed by cameras, phones, computers and microphones.

I fully recognize that you have, as you've emphasized, the right to defend yourself. But the charges are not pending out there; they're pending in here." (Transcript of Show Cause Hearing in Criminal Action Number 19-CR-018, before the Honorable Judge Amy Berman Jackson; U.S. District Court for the District of Columbia, February 21st, 2019.) [90]

RIGHT TO CONFRONTATION

The Sixth Amendment provides: In all criminal prosecutions the accused shall enjoy the . . . right to be confronted with the witnesses against him." One of the most important cases in recent history is *Crawford v. Washington*, 541 U.S. 36 (2004). The case examines the interplay between evidentiary rules (hearsay and privilege) and the Sixth Amendment's guarantee of the right to confrontation in criminal trials. The facts are essentially this: Michael Crawford was convicted for stabbing Kenneth Lee a man who had tried to rape Sylvia Crawford, Michael's wife. At Michael's trial, Sylvia invoked the spousal testimony privilege and refused to be called to testify. In lieu of Sylvia's testimony concerning the stabbing, the State played for the jury her tape-recorded statement to the police describing the stabbing. Michael Crawford's objected claiming this violated his right to confrontation. Although agreeing that the statements were hearsay, the trial judge allowed the statements to come in as they met the requirements of a "well-established exception to the hearsay rule having indicia of reliability" (the standard of admissibility types of hearsay at that time). The question presented to the Court was whether Crawford's Sixth Amendment rights to confrontation were violated by the admission of the taped statements over his objections.

The Court found that Crawford's Sixth Amendment right to confrontation had indeed been violated. It held, "where testimonial statements are at issue, the only indicium of reliability sufficient to satisfy constitutional demands is confrontation." Although the *Crawford* decision itself is not excerpted here, the following cases discuss its import and "unpack" its holding.

---

[90] Follow up on this case: Roger Stone was convicted at trial, sentenced, then pardoned by former President Trump.

DAVIS V. WASHINGTON
547 U. S. 813 (2006)

Justice Scalia delivered the opinion of the Court.

These cases require us to determine when statements made to law enforcement personnel during a 911 call or at a crime scene are "testimonial" and thus subject to the requirements of the Sixth Amendment's Confrontation Clause.

I

A

The relevant statements in *Davis* v. *Washington*, No. 05–5224, were made to a 911 emergency operator on February 1, 2001. When the operator answered the initial call, the connection terminated before anyone spoke. She reversed the call, and Michelle McCottry answered. In the ensuing conversation, the operator ascertained that McCottry was involved in a domestic disturbance with her former boyfriend Adrian Davis, the petitioner in this case:

As the conversation continued, the operator learned that Davis had "just r[un] out the door" after hitting McCottry, and that he was leaving in a car with someone else. McCottry started talking, but the operator cut her off, saying, "Stop talking and answer my questions." She then gathered more information about Davis (including his birthday), and learned that Davis had told McCottry that his purpose in coming to the house was "to get his stuff," since McCottry was moving. McCottry described the context of the assault, after which the operator told her that the police were on their way. "They're gonna check the area for him first," the operator said, "and then they're gonna come talk to you."

The police arrived within four minutes of the 911 call and observed McCottry's shaken state, the "fresh injuries on her forearm and her face," and her "frantic efforts to gather her belongings and her children so that they could leave the residence."

The State charged Davis with felony violation of a domestic no-contact order. "The State's only witnesses were the two police officers who responded to the 911 call. Both officers testified that McCottry exhibited injuries that appeared to be recent, but neither officer could testify as to the cause of the injuries." McCottry presumably could have testified as to whether Davis was her assailant, but she did not appear. Over Davis's objection, based on the Confrontation Clause of the Sixth Amendment, the trial court admitted the recording of her exchange with the 911 operator, and the jury convicted him. The Supreme Court of Washington, ... [concluded] that the portion of the 911 conversation in which McCottry identified Davis was not testimonial, and that if other portions of the conversation were testimonial, admitting them was harmless beyond a reasonable doubt.

B

In *Hammon* v. *Indiana*, police responded late on the night of February 26, 2003, to a "reported domestic disturbance" at the home of Hershel and Amy Hammon. They found Amy alone on the front porch, appearing " 'somewhat frightened,' " but she told them that " 'nothing was the matter,' " ... . She gave them permission to enter the house, where an officer saw "a gas heating unit in the corner of the living room" that had "flames coming out of the ... partial glass front. There were pieces of glass on the ground in front of it and there was flame emitting from the front of the heating unit."

Hershel, meanwhile, was in the kitchen. He told the police "that he and his wife had 'been in an argument' but 'everything was fine now' and the argument 'never became physical.' " By this point Amy had come back inside. One of the officers remained with Hershel; the other went to the living room to talk with

Amy, and "again asked [her] what had occurred." Hershel made several attempts to participate in Amy's conversation with the police, but was rebuffed. The officer later testified that Hershel "became angry when I insisted that [he] stay separated from Mrs. Hammon so that we can investigate what had happened." After hearing Amy's account, the officer "had her fill out and sign a battery affidavit." Amy handwrote the following: "Broke our Furnace & shoved me down on the floor into the broken glass. Hit me in the chest and threw me down. Broke our lamps & phone. Tore up my van where I couldn't leave the house. Attacked my daughter."

The State charged Hershel with domestic battery and with violating his probation. Amy was subpoenaed, but she did not appear at his subsequent bench trial. The State called the officer who had questioned Amy, and asked him to recount what Amy told him and to authenticate the affidavit. Hershel's counsel repeatedly objected to the admission of this evidence. At one point, after hearing the prosecutor defend the affidavit because it was made "under oath," defense counsel said, "That doesn't give us the opportunity to cross examine [the] person who allegedly drafted it. Makes me mad." Nonetheless, the trial court admitted the affidavit as a "present sense impression," and Amy's statements as "excited utterances" that "are expressly permitted in these kinds of cases even if the declarant is not available to testify." The officer thus testified that Amy "informed me that she and Hershel had been in an argument. That he became irrate [sic] over the fact of their daughter going to a boyfriend's house. The argument became ... physical after being verbal and she informed me that Mr. Hammon, during the verbal part of the argument was breaking things in the living room and I believe she stated he broke the phone, broke the lamp, broke the front of the heater. When it became physical he threw her down into the glass of the heater.

"She informed me Mr. Hammon had pushed her onto the ground, had shoved her head into the broken glass of the heater and that he had punched her in the chest twice I believe."

The trial judge found Hershel guilty on both charges. ... The Indiana Supreme Court also affirmed, concluding that Amy's statement was admissible for state-law purposes as an excited utterance, that "a 'testimonial' statement is one given or taken in significant part for purposes of preserving it for potential future use in legal proceedings," where "the motivations of the questioner and declarant are the central concerns," and that Amy's oral statement was not "testimonial" under these standards. It also concluded that, although the affidavit was testimonial and thus wrongly admitted, it was harmless beyond a reasonable doubt, largely because the trial was to the bench. We granted certiorari.

II

The Confrontation Clause of the Sixth Amendment provides: "In all criminal prosecutions, the accused shall enjoy the right … to be confronted with the witnesses against him." In *Crawford* v. *Washington* we held that this provision bars "admission of testimonial statements of a witness who did not appear at trial unless he was unavailable to testify, and the defendant had had a prior opportunity for cross-examination." A critical portion of this holding, and the portion central to resolution of the two cases now before us, is the phrase "testimonial statements." Only statements of this sort cause the declarant to be a "witness" within the meaning of the Confrontation Clause. It is the testimonial character of the statement that separates it from other hearsay that, while subject to traditional limitations upon hearsay evidence, is not subject to the Confrontation Clause.

Our opinion in *Crawford* set forth "[v]arious formulations" of the core class of " 'testimonial' " statements, but found it unnecessary to endorse any of them, because "some statements qualify under any definition," Among those, we said, were "[s]tatements taken by police officers in the course of interrogations," The questioning that generated the deponent's statement in *Crawford*—which was made and recorded while she was in police custody, after having been given *Miranda* warnings as a possible suspect herself—"qualifies under any conceivable definition" of an " 'interrogation,' " We therefore did not define that term, except to say that "[w]e use [it] . . . in its colloquial, rather than any technical legal, sense," and that "one can imagine various definitions . . . , and we need not select among them in this case." The character of the statements in the present cases is not as clear, and these cases require us to determine more precisely which police interrogations produce testimony.

Without attempting to produce an exhaustive classification of all conceivable statements— or even all conceivable statements in response to police interrogation—as either testimonial or nontestimonial, it suffices to decide the present cases to hold as follows: Statements are nontestimonial when made in the course of police interrogation under circumstances objectively indicating that the primary purpose of the interrogation is to enable police assistance to meet an ongoing emergency. They are testimonial when the circumstances objectively indicate that there is no such ongoing emergency, and that the primary purpose of the interrogation is to establish or prove past events potentially relevant to later criminal prosecution.

III

A

… We must decide, therefore, whether the Confrontation Clause applies only to testimonial hearsay; and, if so, whether the recording of a 911 call qualifies.

The answer to the first question was suggested in Crawford, even if not explicitly held:

"The text of the Confrontation Clause reflects this focus [on testimonial hearsay]. It applies to 'witnesses' against the accused—in other words, those who 'bear testimony.' … 'Testimony,' in turn, is typically 'a solemn declaration or affirmation made for the purpose of establishing or proving some fact.'

An accuser who makes a formal statement to government officers bears testimony in a sense that a person who makes a casual remark to an acquaintance does not."

A limitation so clearly reflected in the text of the constitutional provision must fairly be said to mark out not merely its "core," but its perimeter.

We are not aware of any early American case invoking the Confrontation Clause or the common-law right to confrontation that did not clearly involve testimony as thus defined. Well into the 20th century, our own Confrontation Clause jurisprudence was carefully applied only in the testimonial context.…

Even our later cases, conforming to the reasoning of *Ohio* v. *Roberts* never in practice dispensed with the Confrontation Clause requirements of unavailability and prior cross-examination in cases that involved testimonial hearsay. …

…

The question before us in *Davis*, then, is whether, objectively considered, the interrogation that took place in the course of the 911 call produced testimonial statements. When we said in *Crawford*, that "interrogations by law enforcement officers fall squarely within [the] class" of testimonial hearsay, we had immediately in mind (for that was the case before us) interrogations solely directed at establishing the facts of a past crime, in order to identify (or provide evidence to convict) the perpetrator. The product of such interrogation, whether reduced to a writing signed by the declarant or embedded in the memory (and perhaps notes) of the interrogating officer, is testimonial. It is, … " '[a] solemn declaration or affirmation made for the purpose of establishing or proving some fact.' " … A 911 call, on the other hand, and at least the initial interrogation conducted in connection with a 911 call, is ordinarily not designed primarily to "establis[h] or prov[e]" some past fact, but to describe current circumstances requiring police assistance.

The difference between the interrogation in *Davis* and the one in *Crawford* is apparent on the face of things. In *Davis,* McCottry was speaking about events *as they were actually happening*, rather than "describ[ing] past events," Sylvia Crawford's interrogation, on the other hand, took place hours after the events she described had occurred. Moreover, any reasonable listener would recognize that McCottry (unlike Sylvia Crawford) was facing an ongoing emergency. Although one *might* call 911 to provide a narrative report of a crime absent any imminent danger, McCottry's call was plainly a call for help against bona fide physical threat. Third, the nature of what was asked and answered in *Davis*, again viewed objectively, was such that the elicited statements were necessary to be able to *resolve* the present emergency, rather than simply to learn (as in *Crawford*) what had happened in the past. That is true even of the operator's effort to establish the identity of the assailant, so that the dispatched officers might know whether they would be encountering a violent felon. And finally, the difference in the level of formality between the two interviews is striking. Crawford was responding calmly, at the station house, to a series of questions, with the officer-interrogator taping and making notes of her answers; McCottry's frantic answers were provided over the phone, in an environment that was not tranquil, or even (as far as any reasonable 911 operator could make out) safe.

We conclude from all this that the circumstances of McCottry's interrogation objectively indicate its primary purpose was to enable police assistance to meet an ongoing emergency. She simply was not acting as a *witness;* she was not *testifying.*

...

This is not to say that a conversation which begins as an interrogation to determine the need for emergency assistance cannot, as the Indiana Supreme Court put it, "evolve into testimonial statements," once that purpose has been achieved. In this case, for example, after the operator gained the information needed to address the exigency of the moment, the emergency appears to have ended (when Davis drove away from the premises). The operator then told McCottry to be quiet, and proceeded to pose a battery of questions. It could readily be maintained that, from that point on, McCottry's statements were testimonial, not unlike the "structured police questioning" that occurred in *Crawford.* ... [T]rial courts will recognize the point at which, for Sixth Amendment purposes, statements in response to interrogations become testimonial. Through *in limine* procedure, they should redact or exclude the portions of any statement that have become testimonial, as they do, for example, with unduly prejudicial portions of otherwise admissible evidence. Davis's jury did not hear the *complete* 911 call, although it may well have heard some testimonial portions. We were asked to classify only McCottry's early statements identifying Davis as her assailant, and we agree with the Washington Supreme Court that they were not testimonial. That court also concluded that, even if later parts of the call were testimonial, their admission was harmless beyond a reasonable doubt. Davis does not challenge that holding, and we therefore assume it to be correct.

B

Determining the testimonial or nontestimonial character of the statements that were the product of the interrogation in *Hammon* is a much easier task, since they were not much different from the statements we found to be testimonial in *Crawford.* It is entirely clear from the circumstances that the interrogation was part of an investigation into possibly criminal past conduct — as, indeed, the testifying officer expressly acknowledged. ... There was no emergency in progress; the interrogating officer testified that he had heard no arguments or crashing and saw no one throw or break anything. When the officers first arrived, Amy told them that things were fine, and there was no immediate threat to her person. When the officer questioned Amy for the second time, and elicited the challenged statements, he was not seeking to determine (as in *Davis*) "what is happening," but rather "what happened." Objectively viewed, the primary, if not indeed the sole, purpose of the interrogation was to investigate a possible crime—which is, of course, precisely what the officer *should* have done.

It is true that the *Crawford* interrogation was more formal. It followed a *Miranda* warning, was tape-recorded, and took place at the station house While these features certainly strengthened the statements' testimonial aspect—made it more objectively apparent, that is, that the purpose of the exercise was to nail down the truth about past criminal events—none was essential to the point. It was formal enough that Amy's interrogation was conducted in a separate room, away from her husband (who tried to intervene), with the officer receiving her replies for use in his "investigat[ion]." What we called the "striking resemblance" of the *Crawford* statement is shared by Amy's statement here. Both declarants were actively separated from the defendant — officers forcibly prevented Hershel from participating in the interrogation. Both statements deliberately recounted, in response to police questioning, how

potentially criminal past events began and progressed. And both took place sometime after the events described were over. Such statements under official interrogation are an obvious substitute for live testimony, because they do precisely *what a witness does* on direct examination; they are inherently testimonial.

…

Although we necessarily reject the Indiana Supreme Court's implication that virtually any "initial inquiries" at the crime scene will not be testimonial, we do not hold the opposite—that *no* questions at the scene will yield nontestimonial answers. We have already observed of domestic disputes that "[o]fficers called to investigate … need to know whom they are dealing with in order to assess the situation, the threat to their own safety, and possible danger to the potential victim." Such exigencies may *often* mean that "initial inquiries" produce nontestimonial statements. But in cases like this one, where Amy's statements were neither a cry for help nor the provision of information enabling officers immediately to end a threatening situation, the fact that they were given at an alleged crime scene and were "initial inquiries" is immaterial.

In *Michigan v. Bryant*, 562 US 344 (2011) the Court further articulated the meaning of "testimonial" versus "non-testimonial" when faced with a potential "on-going emergency" in a non-domestic scenario. Police responded to a scene where they found a gunshot victim, Anthony Covington, who was in great pain and spoke with difficulty. The police questioned what had happened to him, who had shot him, and where the shooting occurred. Covington stated that "Rick" shot him. Covington also stated he had had a conversation with Bryant who he recognized by his voice, through the back of Bryant's home, and when he turned to leave he was shot through the door. Covington drove to the gas station where police found him. His conversation with the police ended within 10 minutes when emergency medical services arrived. He was transported to the hospital where he died a few hours later. After leaving the gas station, police went to Bryant's house where they did not find Bryant but did find blood and a bullet on the back porch, a bullet hole in the back door, and Covington's wallet and identification outside the house. At Bryant's trial (which was prior to the Court's decision in Crawford), the police testified what Covington had told them at the gas station.

Justice Sotomayor's majority decision focused on whether the primary purpose of the police interrogation was to allow police to meet with an ongoing emergency. The Court concluded the viewpoint was from both the declarant (Covington) and the police officer's perspective. The majority ultimately held that Covington's statements were not testimonial and their admission at Bryant's trial did not violate the Confrontation Clause.

Justice Scalia (the author of *Crawford*) dissented.

"Today's tale — a story of five officers conducting successive examinations of a dying man with the primary purpose, not of obtaining and preserving his testimony regarding his killer, but of protecting him, them, and others from a murderer somewhere on the loose — is so transparently false that professing to believe it demeans this institution. But reaching a patently incorrect conclusion on the facts is a relatively benign judicial mischief; it affects, after all, only the case at hand. In its vain attempt to make the incredible plausible, however — or perhaps as an intended second goal — today's opinion distorts our Confrontation Clause jurisprudence and leaves it in a shambles. Instead of clarifying the law, the Court makes itself the obfuscator of last resort. Because I continue to adhere to the Confrontation Clause that the People adopted . . . . I dissent.

In *Davis*, we explained how to identify testimonial hearsay prompted by police questioning in the field. A statement is testimonial "when the circumstances objectively indicate . . .that the primary purpose of the interrogation is to establish or prove past events potentially relevant to later criminal prosecution." When, however, the circumstances objectively indicate that the declarant's statements were "a cry for help [o]r the provision of information enabling officers immediately to end a threatening situation," they bear little resemblance to in-court testimony. "No 'witness' goes into court to proclaim an emergency and seek help."

Crawford and *Davis* did not address whose perspective matters — the declarant's, the interrogator's, or both — when assessing "the primary purpose of [an] interrogation." In those cases the statements were testimonial from any perspective. I think the same is true here, but because the Court picks a perspective so will I: The declarant's intent is what counts. In-court testimony is more than a narrative of past events; it is a solemn declaration made in the course of a criminal trial. For an out-of-court statement to qualify as testimonial, the declarant must intend the statement to be a solemn declaration rather than an unconsidered or offhand remark; and he must make the statement with the understanding that it may be used to invoke the coercive machinery of the State against the accused.

A declarant-focused inquiry is also the only inquiry that would work in every fact pattern implicating the Confrontation Clause. The Clause applies to volunteered testimony as well as statements solicited through police interrogation.

Looking to the declarant's purpose (as we should), this is an absurdly easy case. Roughly 25 minutes after Anthony Covington had been shot, Detroit police responded to a 911 call reporting that a gunshot victim had appeared at a neighborhood gas station. They quickly arrived at the scene, and in less than 10 minutes five different Detroit police officers questioned Covington about the shooting. Each asked him a similar battery of questions: . . . The battery relented when the paramedics arrived and began tending to Covington's wounds.

From Covington's perspective, his statements had little value except to ensure the arrest and eventual prosecution of Richard Bryant. He knew the "threatening situation," had ended six blocks away and 25 minutes earlier when he fled from Bryant's back porch. . . . [I]t was entirely beyond imagination that Bryant would again open fire while Covington was surrounded by five armed police officers. And Covington knew the shooting was the work of a drug dealer, not a spree killer who might randomly threaten others.

. . .

[T]oday's decision is not only a gross distortion of the facts. It is a gross distortion of the law — a revisionist narrative in which reliability continues to guide our Confrontation Clause jurisprudence, at least where emergencies and faux emergencies are concerned.

Justice Ginsburg also dissented, agreeing with Justice Scalia that Covington's statements were testimonial and it is the declarant's intent that matters. "Today's decision, *Justice Scalia* rightly notes, 'creates an expansive exception to the Confrontation Clause for violent crimes . . . In so doing, the decision confounds our recent Confrontation Clause jurisprudence, which made it plain that '[r]eliability tells us nothing about whether a statement is testimonial'."

Cicchini (2011) analyzed the Courts holdings in *Crawford, Davis,* and *Bryant.*[91] He wrote,

"The Sixth Amendment's Confrontation Clause guarantees, quite simply and clearly, that "[i]n all criminal prosecutions, the accused shall enjoy the right . . . to be confronted with the witnesses against him." This right to cross-examine one's accuser is so basic to our fundamental sense of fairness that the U.S. Supreme Court has called it a "bedrock procedural guarantee." But despite its simplicity and clarity, the Confrontation Clause has been the subject of thousands of articles and court opinions, each debating or deciding its proper reach and scope in every imaginable circumstance. Furthermore, its importance is easily understood. Few among us would have confidence in the typical criminal conviction unless, at a bare minimum, the accuser appeared at trial, took an oath (or made an affirmation) to tell the truth, and was cross-examined about his biases, motives, and ability to accurately recall the events about which he testified. And although law reviews and courts continue to publish these articles and opinions, the Confrontation Clause, for all practical purposes, died in 1980 with the Court's decision in *Ohio v. Roberts*.

In *Roberts*, the Court held that a prosecutor could use hearsay evidence at trial to convict a defendant if a judge, using a multi-factor balancing test, first found the hearsay to be reliable. For reasons explained later in this Essay, this highly subjective, fact-intensive, malleable standard "fail[ed] to provide meaningful protection from even core confrontation violations." Prosecutors, with the blessing of trial judges, routinely ran roughshod over defendants' rights and often won convictions based primarily, if not entirely, on untested hearsay allegations. The Confrontation Clause was dead.

In 2004, however, the Court decided *Crawford v. Washington* and (temporarily) breathed new life into the Confrontation Clause. In *Crawford*, the Court conceded that it had been misinterpreting the Constitution for the past twenty-five years, in part because it had allowed trial judges to use multi-factor balancing tests and their own judgments about reliability to replace actual cross-examination at trial. While the Court's admission was of little consolation to the many thousands of individuals who had been convicted and imprisoned (or worse) based on hearsay they could not cross-examine, it was a welcome concession nonetheless. In fact, many hailed *Crawford* as a great "sea change" in Confrontation Clause jurisprudence.

But the more things changed, the more they stayed the same. Despite the Court's mea culpa, *Crawford* failed to cure the numerous ills of *Roberts*, and instead created a new standard that classified hearsay as either testimonial or nontestimonial. A new day, it seemed, was dawning. If, and only if, the hearsay was testimonial, the Confrontation Clause banned its use at trial; otherwise, a prosecutor could use the nontestimonial hearsay as he wished. But what exactly is this newly created concept—testimonial hearsay—on which the

---

[91] Michael D. Cicchini, Dead Again: The Latest Demise of the Confrontation Clause, 80 Fordham L. Rev. 1301 (2011). Available at: http://ir.lawnet.fordham.edu/flr/vol80/iss3/12

Constitution's "bedrock procedural guarantee" now turns? The Court's answer: "We leave for another day any effort to spell out a comprehensive definition of 'testimonial.'"

After *Crawford*, over the course of seven years and two cases—first *Davis v. Washington* in 2006 and then *Michigan v. Bryant* in 2011—the Court attempted to put some meat on the bones of its revamped Confrontation Clause. But instead of resuscitating it as many had hoped, the Court slowly and painfully developed yet another highly subjective, fact-intensive, malleable standard—the very thing it condemned in *Crawford*. This, unfortunately, is the current state of Confrontation Clause jurisprudence under *Crawford-Davis-Bryant*. The Confrontation Clause is dead again.

The purpose of this Essay is not to make sense of a defendant's confrontation rights in this *Crawford-Davis-Bryant* world; that is not possible. Law professor Daniel Blinka accurately describes the Court's most recent case, *Bryant*, as "a train wreck," and sympathizes that "[f]or the defense lawyers and prosecutors who must eat this mush . . . every day, you have my best wishes and these words of solace." Similarly, law professor Richard Friedman describes *Bryant* as "remarkably mushy, unjustified by any sound reasoning and virtually incoherent." Likewise, Justice Scalia acknowledges in his *Bryant* dissent that the Court "distorts our Confrontation Clause jurisprudence and leaves it in a shambles."

After *Crawford* the Court decided *Melendez-Diaz v. Massachusetts* (2009) which examined whether the right to confrontation was violated by the introduction of lab report affidavits rather than the testimony of a lab analyst. In *Melendez-Diaz*, the Court stated,

> "There is little doubt that the documents at issue in this case fall within the "core class of testimonial statements" thus described. . . . The documents at issue here, while denominated by Massachusetts law as "certificates," are quite plainly affidavits . . . They are incontrovertibly a " 'solemn declaration or affirmation made for the purpose of establishing or proving some fact.' " . . . . The fact in question is that the substance found in the possession of Melendez-Diaz and his codefendants was, as the prosecution claimed, cocaine — the precise testimony the analysts would be expected to provide if called at trial. The "certificates" are functionally identical to live, in-court testimony, doing "precisely what a witness does on direct examination." . . . Here, moreover, not only were the affidavits "made under circumstances which would lead an objective witness reasonably to believe that the statement would be available for use at a later trial," but under Massachusetts law the sole purpose of the affidavits was to provide "prima facie evidence of the composition, quality, and the net weight" of the analyzed substance. We can safely assume that the analysts were aware of the affidavits' evidentiary purpose, since that purpose — as stated in the relevant state-law provision — was reprinted on the affidavits themselves."

The Court found a violation of the defendant's Sixth Amendment right to confrontation by allowing the report without the analyst being subject to cross examination. Years before *Melendez-Diaz* was decided, however, Donald Bullcoming had been arrested and tried for driving while intoxicated. His appeal reached the Court shortly after the Court issued its opinion in *Melendez-Diaz*, and the Court reaffirmed its holding in that case.

BULLCOMING v. NEW MEXICO
564 U.S. 647 (2011)

***Justice Ginsburg delivered the opinion of the Court, except as to Part IV and footnote 6.* * ***

[Facts Summarized: Bullcoming drove a car into the back of a pickup in August 2005, and he was arrested at the scene for driving a vehicle while "under the influence of intoxicating liquor" (DWI).

Because Bullcoming refused to take a breath test, the police obtained a warrant authorizing a blood-alcohol analysis. Pursuant to the warrant, a sample of Bullcoming's blood was drawn at a local hospital. To determine Bullcoming's blood-alcohol concentration (BAC), the police sent the sample to the New Mexico Department of Health, Scientific Laboratory Division (SLD). The lab report revealed that Bullcoming's blood alcohol concentration was well above the limit for aggravated DWI.

The case was tried to a jury in November 2005, (after *Crawford v. Washington* but before Melendez-Diaz). On the day of trial the State announced that it would not be calling the analyst (Caylor) who tested the Bullcoming's blood sample and signed the lab certificate ("because he was on unpaid leave for a reason not revealed") but instead would be calling another analyst who worked at the lab and was familiar with their testing procedures (but did not participate in the testing). Defense counsel objected and complained that the prosecution had ..."

> never disclosed, until trial commenced, that the witness "out there . . . [was] not the analyst [of Bullcoming's sample]." Counsel stated that, "had [she] known that the analyst [who tested Bullcoming's blood] was not available," her opening, indeed, her entire defense "may very well have been dramatically different."

The State, however, proposed to introduce Caylor's finding as a "business record" during the testimony of Gerasimos Razatos, an SLD

scientist who had neither observed nor reviewed Caylor's analysis.

Bullcoming's counsel opposed the State's proposal. Without Caylor's testimony, defense counsel maintained, introduction of the analyst's finding would violate Bullcoming's Sixth Amendment right "to be confronted with the witnesses against him." The trial court overruled the objection and admitted the SLD report as a business record. The jury convicted Bullcoming of aggravated DWI, and the New Mexico Court of Appeals upheld the conviction, concluding that "the blood alcohol report in the present case was non-testimonial and prepared routinely with guarantees of trustworthiness."]

OPINION: In *Melendez-Diaz v. Massachusetts*, this Court held that a forensic laboratory report stating that a suspect substance was cocaine ranked as testimonial for purposes of the Sixth Amendment's Confrontation Clause. The report had been created specifically to serve as evidence in a criminal proceeding. Absent stipulation, the Court ruled, the prosecution may not introduce such a report without offering a live witness competent to testify to the truth of the statements made in the report.

...

We granted certiorari to address this question: Does the Confrontation Clause permit the prosecution to introduce a forensic laboratory report containing a testimonial certification, made in order to prove a fact at a criminal trial, through the in-court testimony of an analyst who did not sign the certification or personally perform or observe the performance of the test reported in the certification. Our answer is in line with controlling precedent: As a rule, if an out-of-court statement is testimonial in nature, it may not be introduced against the accused at trial unless the witness who made the statement is unavailable and the accused has had a prior opportunity to confront that witness. Because the New Mexico Supreme Court permitted the testimonial statement of one witness, i.e. , Caylor, to enter into evidence through the in-court testimony of a second person, i.e. , Razatos, we reverse that court's judgment.

II

The Sixth Amendment 's Confrontation Clause confers upon the accused "[i]n all criminal prosecutions, . . . the right . . . to be confronted with the witnesses against him." In a pathmarking 2004 decision, *Crawford v. Washington* , we overruled Ohio v. Roberts, which had interpreted the Confrontation Clause to allow admission of absent witnesses' testimonial statements based on a judicial determination of reliability. Rejecting *Roberts* ' "amorphous notions of 'reliability,' " Crawford held that fidelity to the Confrontation Clause permitted admission of "[t]estimonial statements of witnesses absent from trial . . . only where the declarant is unavailable, and only where the defendant has had a prior opportunity to cross-examine," . . . *Melendez-Diaz* , relying on *Crawford* 's rationale, refused to create a "forensic evidence" exception to this rule. An analyst's certification prepared in connection with a criminal investigation or prosecution, the Court held, is "testimonial," and therefore within the compass of the Confrontation Clause.

The State in the instant case never asserted that the analyst who signed the certification, Curtis Caylor, was unavailable. The record showed only that Caylor was placed on unpaid leave for an undisclosed reason. Nor did Bullcoming have an opportunity to cross-examine Caylor. Crawford and Melendez-Diaz , therefore, weigh heavily in Bullcoming's favor. The New Mexico Supreme Court, however, although recognizing that the SLD report was testimonial for purposes of the Confrontation Clause, considered SLD analyst Razatos an adequate substitute for Caylor.

. . . .

B

Recognizing that admission of the blood-alcohol analysis depended on "live, in-court testimony [by] a qualified analyst," the New Mexico Supreme Court believed that Razatos could substitute for Caylor because Razatos "qualified as an expert witness with respect to the gas chromatograph machine and the SLD's laboratory procedures." But surrogate testimony of the kind Razatos was equipped to give could not convey what Caylor knew or observed about the events his certification concerned, i.e. , the particular test and testing process he employed. Nor could such surrogate testimony expose any lapses or lies on the certifying analyst's part. Significant here, Razatos had no knowledge of the reason why Caylor had been placed on unpaid leave. With Caylor on the stand, Bullcoming's counsel could have asked questions designed to reveal whether incompetence, evasiveness, or dishonesty accounted for Caylor's removal from his work station. Notable in this regard, the State never asserted that Caylor was "unavailable"; the prosecution conveyed only that Caylor was on uncompensated leave. Nor did the State assert that Razatos had any "independent opinion" concerning Bullcoming's BAC. …

More fundamentally, as this Court stressed in Crawford, "[t]he text of the Sixth Amendment does not suggest any open-ended exceptions from the confrontation requirement to be developed by the courts." Nor is it "the role of courts to extrapolate from the words of the [Confrontation Clause] to the values behind it, and then to enforce its guarantees only to the extent they serve (in the courts' views) those underlying values." Accordingly, the Clause does not tolerate dispensing with confrontation simply because the court believes that questioning one witness about another's testimonial statements provides a fair enough opportunity for cross-examination.

. . . .

In short, when the State elected to introduce Caylor's certification, Caylor became a witness Bullcoming had the right to confront.

Our precedent cannot sensibly be read any other way. . . .

III

We turn, finally, to the State's contention that the SLD's blood-alcohol analysis reports are nontestimonial in character, therefore no Confrontation Clause question even arises in this case. ...

...

In all material respects, the laboratory report in this case resembles those in *Melendez-Diaz*. Here, as in *Melendez-Diaz*, a law-enforcement officer provided seized evidence to a state laboratory required by law to assist in police investigations. Like the analysts in *Melendez-Diaz*, analyst Caylor tested the evidence and prepared a certificate concerning the result of his analysis. Like the *Melendez-Diaz* certificates, Caylor's certificate is "formalized" in a signed document, *Davis*, headed a "report," . . . . Noteworthy as well, the SLD report form contains a legend referring to municipal and magistrate courts' rules that provide for the admission of certified blood-alcohol analyses.

In sum, the formalities attending the "report of blood alcohol analysis" are more than adequate to qualify Caylor's assertions as testimonial. . . .

IV

The State and its amici urge that unbending application of the Confrontation Clause to forensic evidence would impose an undue burden on the prosecution. . . .The constitutional requirement, we reiterate, "may not [be] disregard[ed] . . . at our convenience," and the predictions of dire consequences, we again observe, are dubious. . . .

New Mexico law, it bears emphasis, requires the laboratory to preserve samples, which can be retested by other analysts, and neither party questions SLD's compliance with that requirement. Retesting "is almost always an option . . . in [DWI] cases," and the State had that option here: New Mexico could have

avoided any Confrontation Clause problem by asking Razatos to retest the sample, and then testify to the results of his retest rather than to the results of a test he did not conduct or observe.

Furthermore, notice-and-demand procedures, long in effect in many jurisdictions, can reduce burdens on forensic laboratories. Statutes governing these procedures typically "render . . . otherwise hearsay forensic reports admissible[,] while specifically preserving a defendant's right to demand that the prosecution call the author/ analyst of [the] report.". . .

Even before this Court's decision in *Crawford*, moreover, it was common prosecutorial practice to call the forensic analyst to testify. Prosecutors did so "to bolster the persuasive power of [the State's] case[,] . . . [even] when the defense would have preferred that the analyst did not testify."

We note also the "small fraction of . . . cases" that "actually proceed to trial." . . . And, "when cases in which forensic analysis has been conducted [do] go to trial," defendants "regularly . . . [stipulate] to the admission of [the] analysis." "[A]s a result, analysts testify in only a very small percentage of cases," for "[i]t is unlikely that defense counsel will insist on live testimony whose effect will be merely to highlight rather than cast doubt upon the forensic analysis.

Tellingly, in jurisdictions in which "it is the [acknowledged] job of . . . analysts to testify in court . . . about their test results," the sky has not fallen. State and municipal laboratories "make operational and staffing decisions" to facilitate analysts' appearance at trial. Prosecutors schedule trial dates to accommodate analysts' availability, and trial courts liberally grant continuances when unexpected conflicts arise. In rare cases in which the analyst is no longer employed by the laboratory at the time of trial, "the prosecution makes the effort to bring that analyst . . . to court." And, as is the practice in New Mexico, laboratories ordinarily retain additional samples, enabling them to run tests again when necessary.

Defendant's Right To Be Present At Trial

The right to confrontation includes the opportunity of the defendant to be physically present in the courtroom at the time any testimony is given against him. However, this right may be waived under certain circumstances such as the defendant's deliberate absence or disruptive behavior in the courtroom. The Court in *Taylor v. United States*, 414 U.S. 17 (1973), held that Taylor, a defendant who appeared for trial but then voluntarily absented himself once the trial began, could be tried *in absentia* (without being present). It is unclear whether the Court would find the right to confrontation was met when a defendant was not present at any point of the trial. *Illinois v. Allen* (below) examined the right of a disruptive defendant to stay in the courtroom.

ILLINOIS v. ALLEN
397 U.S. 337 (1970)

JUSTICE BLACK delivered the opinion of the Court.

The Confrontation Clause of the Sixth Amendment to the United States Constitution provides that: 'In all criminal prosecutions, the accused shall enjoy the right . . .to be confronted with the witnesses against him ....' We have held that the Fourteenth Amendment makes the guarantees of this clause obligatory upon the States. One of the most basic of the rights guaranteed by the Confrontation Clause is the accused's right to be present in the courtroom at every stage of his trial. The question presented in this case is whether an accused can claim the benefit of this constitutional right to remain in the courtroom while at the same time he engages in speech and conduct which is so noisy, disorderly, and disruptive that it is exceedingly difficult or wholly impossible to carry on the trial.

The issue arose in the following way. The respondent, Allen, was convicted by an Illinois jury of armed robbery and was sentenced to serve 10 to 30 years in the Illinois State Penitentiary. The evidence against him showed that on August 12, 1956, he entered a tavern in Illinois and took $200 from the bartender at gunpoint. . . . Allen . . . alleg[ed] that he had been wrongfully deprived . . . of his constitutional right to remain present throughout his trial.

The facts surrounding Allen's expulsion from the courtroom are set out in the Court of Appeals' opinion sustaining Allen's contention:

'After his indictment and during the pretrial stage, the petitioner refused court-appointed counsel and indicated to the trial court on several occasions that he wished to conduct his own defense. After considerable argument by the petitioner, the trial judge told him, 'I'll let you be your own lawyer, but I'll ask Mr. Kelly (court- appointed counsel) (to) sit in and protect the record for you, insofar as possible.'

'The trial began on September 9, 1957. After the State's Attorney had accepted the first four jurors following their voir dire examination, the petitioner began examining the first juror and continued at great length. Finally, the trial judge interrupted the petitioner, requesting him to confine his questions solely to matters relating to the prospective juror's qualifications. At that point, the petitioner started to argue with the judge in a most abusive and disrespectful manner. At last, and seemingly in desperation, the judge asked appointed counsel to proceed with the examination of the jurors. The petitioner continued to talk, proclaiming that the appointed attorney was not going to act as his lawyer. He terminated his remarks by saying, 'When I go out for lunchtime, you're (the judge) going to be a corpse here.' At that point he tore the file which his attorney had and threw the papers on the floor. The trial judge thereupon stated to the petitioner, 'One more outbreak of that sort and I'll remove you from the courtroom.' This warning had no effect on the petitioner. He continued to talk back to the judge, saying, 'There's not going to be no trial, either. I'm going to sit here and you're going to talk and you can bring your shackles out and straight jacket and put them on me and tape my mouth, but it will do no good because there's not going to be no trial.' After more abusive remarks by the petitioner, the trial judge ordered the trial to proceed in the petitioner's absence. The petitioner was removed from the courtroom. The voir dire examination then continued and the jury was selected in the absence of the petitioner.

'After a noon recess and before the jury was brought into the courtroom, the petitioner, appearing before the judge, complained about the fairness of the trial and his appointed attorney. He also said he wanted to be present in the court during his trial. In reply, the judge said that the petitioner would be permitted to remain in the courtroom if he 'behaved (himself) and (did) not interfere with the introduction of the case.' The jury was brought in and seated. Counsel for the petitioner then moved to exclude the witnesses from the courtroom. The (petitioner) protested this effort on the part of his attorney, saying: 'There is going to be no proceeding. I'm going to start talking and I'm going to keep on talking all through the trial. There's not going to be no trial like this. I want my sister and my friends here in court to testify for me.' The trial judge thereupon ordered the petitioner removed from the courtroom.'

After this second removal, Allen remained out of the courtroom during the presentation of the State's case-in-chief, except that he was brought in on several occasions for purposes of identification. During one of these latter appearances, Allen responded to one of the judge's questions with vile and abusive language. After the prosecution's case had been presented, the trial judge reiterated his promise to Allen that he could return to the courtroom whenever he agreed to conduct himself properly. Allen gave some assurances of proper conduct and was permitted to be present through the remainder of the trial, principally his defense, which was conducted by his appointed counsel.

The Court of Appeals went on to hold that the Supreme Court of Illinois was wrong in ruling that Allen had by his conduct relinquished his constitutional right to be present, declaring that:

'No conditions may be imposed on the absolute right of a criminal defendant to be present at all stages of the proceeding. The insistence of a defendant that he exercise this right under unreasonable conditions does not amount to a waiver. Such conditions, if insisted upon, should and must be dealt with in a manner that does not compel the relinquishment of his right.

'We are of the view that the defendant should not have been excluded from the courtroom during his trial despite his disruptive and disrespectful conduct. The proper course for the trial judge was to have restrained the defendant by whatever means necessary, even if those means included his being shackled and gagged.'

The Court of Appeals felt that the defendant's Sixth Amendment right to be present at his own trial was so 'absolute' that, he could never be held to have lost that right so long as he continued to insist upon it, as Allen clearly did. Therefore the Court of Appeals concluded that a trial judge could never expel a defendant from his own trial and that the judge's ultimate remedy when faced with an obstreperous defendant like Allen who determines to make his trial impossible is to bind and gag him. We cannot agree that the Sixth Amendment, the cases upon which the Court of Appeals relied, or any other cases of this Court so handicap a trial judge in conducting a criminal trial. We accept instead the statement of Mr. Justice Cardozo who, speaking for the Court in *Snyder* said: 'No doubt the privilege (of personally confronting witnesses) may be lost by consent or at times even by misconduct.' Although mindful that courts must indulge every reasonable presumption against the loss of constitutional rights, we explicitly hold today that a defendant can lose his right to be present at trial if, after he has been warned by the judge that he will be removed if he continues his disruptive behavior, he nevertheless insists on conducting himself in a manner so disorderly, disruptive, and disrespectful of the court that his trial cannot be carried on with him in the courtroom. Once lost, the right to be present can, of course, be reclaimed as soon as the defendant is willing to conduct himself consistently with the decorum and respect inherent in the concept of courts and judicial proceedings.

It is essential to the proper administration of criminal justice that dignity, order, and decorum be the hallmarks of all court proceedings in our country. The flagrant disregard in the courtroom of elementary standards of proper conduct should not and cannot be tolerated. We believe trial judges confronted with disruptive, contumacious, stubbornly defiant defendants must be given sufficient discretion to meet the circumstances of each case. No one formula for maintaining the appropriate courtroom atmosphere will be best in all situations. We think there are at least three constitutionally permissible ways for a trial judge to handle an obstreperous defendant like Allen: (1) bind and gag him, thereby keeping him present; (2) cite him for contempt; (3) take him out of the courtroom until he promises to conduct himself properly.

Trying a defendant for a crime while he sits bound and gagged before the judge and jury would to an extent comply with that part of the Sixth Amendment's purposes that accords the defendant an opportunity to confront the witnesses at the trial. But even to contemplate such a technique, much less see it, arouses a feeling that no person should be tried while shackled and gagged except as a last resort. Not only is it possible that the sight of shackles and gags might have a significant effect on the jury's feelings about the defendant, but the use of this technique is itself something of an affront to the very dignity and decorum of judicial proceedings that the judge is seeking to uphold. Moreover, one of the defendant's primary advantages of being present at the trial, his ability to communicate with his counsel, is greatly reduced when the defendant is in a condition of total physical restraint. It is in part because of these inherent disadvantages and limitations in this method of dealing with disorderly defendants that we decline to hold with the Court of Appeals that a defendant cannot under any possible circumstances be deprived of his right to be present at trial. However, in some situations which we need not attempt to foresee, binding and gagging might possibly be the fairest and most reasonable way to handle a defendant who acts as Allen did here.

The trial court in this case decided under the circumstances to remove the defendant from the courtroom and to continue his trial in his absence until and unless he promised to conduct himself in a manner befitting an American courtroom. As we said earlier, we find nothing unconstitutional about this procedure. Allen's behavior was clearly of such an extreme and aggravated nature as to justify either his removal from the courtroom or his total physical restraint. Prior to his removal he was repeatedly warned by the trial judge that he would be removed from the courtroom if he persisted in his unruly conduct, and the record demonstrates that Allen would not have been at all dissuaded by the trial judge's use of his criminal contempt powers. Allen was constantly informed that he could return to the trial when he would agree to conduct himself in an orderly manner. Under these circumstances we hold that Allen lost his right guaranteed by the Sixth and

Fourteenth Amendments to be present throughout his trial.

We do not hold that removing this defendant from his own trial was the only way the Illinois judge could have constitutionally solved the problem he had. We do hold, however, that there is nothing whatever in this record to show that the judge did not act completely within his discretion. Deplorable as it is to remove a man from his own trial, even for a short time, we hold that the judge did not commit legal error in doing what he did.

The judgment of the Court of Appeals is reversed.

JUSTICE BRENNAN, concurring.

To allow the disruptive activities of a defendant like respondent to prevent his trial is to allow him to profit from his own wrong. The Constitution would protect none of us if it prevented the courts from acting to preserve the very processes that the Constitution itself prescribes.

Of course, no action against an unruly defendant is permissible except after he has been fully and fairly informed that his conduct is wrong and intolerable, and warned of the possible consequences of continued misbehavior. The record makes clear that respondent was so informed and warned in this case. Thus there can be no doubt that respondent, by persisting in his reprehensible conduct, surrendered his right to be present at the trial.

I join the Court's opinion. The constitutional right to be present can be surrendered if it is abused for the purpose of frustrating the trial. Due process does not require the presence of the defendant if his presence means that there will be no orderly process at all.

I would add only that when a defendant is excluded from his trial, the court should make reasonable efforts to enable him to communicate with his attorney and, if possible, to keep apprised of the progress of his trial. Once the court has removed the contumacious defendant, it is not weakness to mitigate the disadvantages of his expulsion as far as technologically possible in the circumstances.

The Right To Face Witnesses

The right to confrontation also includes the right to face witnesses at trial. State law that allowed testimony during trial via a closed-circuit television or behind a screen has been held to violate the defendant's Sixth Amendment rights. *Coy v. Iowa*, 487 U.S. 1012 (1988). In *Coy* the Court found that the use of a semi-transparent screen placed between the defendant and two youthful victims in a child sex abuse trial violated Coy's rights. However, two years later in *Maryland v. Craig*, 497 U.S. 836 (1990) the court carved out an exception to this rule, holding that face-to-face confrontation may be dispensed with "when preventing such confrontation is necessary to further important public policy and the reliability of the testimony is otherwise assured." *Craig* was a child sex abuse case in which the six-year-old victim was allowed to testify in a different room because courtroom testimony would result in the child's suffering such serious emotional distress that she could not reasonably communicate. The testimony was seen and heard via one-way, closed-circuit television. The Court stated that although face-to-face confrontation forms the "core" of this constitutional right, it is not an indispensible element."

The Right To Cross Examine Co-Defendant's Statements

The right to confrontation has, at its core, the right to cross examine statements of witnesses. In prosecuting co-defendants, the state loses the ability to call to the stand any co-defendants due to the Fifth Amendment protection against self-incrimination. However, co-defendants frequently make very incriminating statements against their partners in crime, and the state needs to be able to use those statements in its prosecution. The following case of *Bruton v. United States* deals with whether the state can permissibly use statements of one defendant against the others when both are prosecuted in one trial.

BRUTON v. UNITED STATES
391 U.S. 123 (1968)

JUSTICE BRENNAN delivered the opinion of the Court.

This case presents the question, last considered in *Delli Paoli v. United States*, 352 U.S. 232 [1957], whether the conviction of a defendant at a joint trial should be set aside although the jury was instructed that a codefendant's confession inculpating the defendant had to be disregarded in determining his guilt or innocence.

A joint trial of petitioner and one Evans in the District Court for the Eastern District of Missouri resulted in the conviction of both by a jury on a federal charge of armed postal robbery. A postal inspector testified that Evans orally confessed to him that Evans and petitioner committed the armed robbery. The postal inspector obtained the oral confession, and another in which Evans admitted he had an accomplice whom he would not name, in the course of two interrogations of Evans at the city jail in St. Louis, Missouri, where Evans was held in custody on state criminal charges. Both petitioner and Evans appealed their convictions to the Court of Appeals for the Eighth Circuit. That court set aside Evans' conviction on the ground that his oral confessions to the postal inspector should not have been received in evidence against him. However, the court, relying upon *Delli Paoli*, affirmed petitioner's conviction because the trial judge instructed the jury that although Evans' confession was competent evidence against Evans it was inadmissible hearsay against petitioner and therefore had to be disregarded in determining petitioner's guilt or innocence.

We granted certiorari to reconsider *Delli Paoli*. . . . We hold that, because of the substantial risk that the jury, despite instructions to the contrary, looked to the incriminating extrajudicial statements in determining petitioner's guilt, admission of Evans' confession in this joint trial violated petitioner's right of cross-examination secured by the Confrontation Clause of the Sixth Amendment. We therefore overrule *Delli Paoli* and reverse.

The basic premise of *Delli Paoli* was that it is "reasonably possible for the jury to follow" sufficiently clear instructions to disregard the confessor's extrajudicial statement that his codefendant participated with him in committing the crime. If it were true that the jury disregarded the reference to the codefendant, no question would arise under the Confrontation Clause, because by hypothesis the case is treated as if the confessor made no statement inculpating the nonconfessor. But since *Delli Paoli* was decided this Court has effectively repudiated its basic premise. . . .

. . . .

"The fact of the matter is that too often such admonition against misuse is intrinsically ineffective in that the effect of such a nonadmissible declaration cannot be wiped from the brains of the jurors. The admonition therefore becomes a futile collocation of words and fails of its purpose as a legal protection to defendants against whom such a declaration should not tell." . . . "The government should not have the windfall of having the jury be influenced by evidence against a defendant which, as a matter of law, they should not consider but which they cannot put out of their minds."

[Federal Rule of Criminal Procedure] Rule 14 authorizes a severance where it appears that a defendant might be prejudiced by a joint trial. The Rule was amended in 1966 to provide expressly that "[i]n ruling on a motion by a defendant for severance the court may order the attorney for the government to deliver to the court for inspection in camera any statements or confessions made by the defendants which the government intends to introduce in evidence at the trial."

The Advisory Committee on Rules said in explanation of the amendment: "A defendant may be prejudiced by the admission in evidence against a co-defendant of a statement or confession made by that co-defendant. This prejudice cannot be dispelled by cross-examination if the co-defendant does not take the stand. Limiting instructions to the jury may not in fact erase the prejudice. "The purpose of the amendment is to provide a procedure whereby the issue of possible prejudice can be resolved on the motion for severance."

[I]n *Jackson v. Denno,* there are some contexts in which the risk that the jury will not, or cannot, follow instructions is so great, and the consequences of failure so vital to the defendant, that the practical and human limitations of the jury system cannot be ignored. Such a context is presented here, where the powerfully incriminating extrajudicial statements of a codefendant, who stands accused side-by-side with the defendant, are deliberately spread before the jury in a joint trial. Not only are the incriminations devastating to the defendant but their credibility is inevitably suspect, a fact recognized when accomplices do take the stand and the jury is instructed to weigh their testimony carefully given the recognized motivation to shift blame onto others. The unreliability of such evidence is intolerably compounded when the alleged accomplice, as here, does not testify and cannot be tested by cross-examination. It was against such threats to a fair trial that the Confrontation Clause was directed.

Here the introduction of Evans' confession posed a substantial threat to petitioner's right to confront the witnesses against him, and this is a hazard we cannot ignore. . . .

RIGHT TO COMPULSORY PROCESS

The Sixth Amendment provides that the accused in a criminal prosecution shall have the right to compulsory process for obtaining witnesses in his or her favor. The right to obtain witnesses includes the power to require the appearance of witnesses and the right to present a defense. Excluding substantially trustworthy evidence crucial to the defense violates the right to present a defense. *Chambers v. Mississippi*, 410 US 284 (1973). In *Washington v. Texas*, 388 U.S. 14 (1967), Washington was convicted of murder and sentenced to 50 years in prison. He claimed that Charles Fuller, who had already been convicted of the same murder, had actually been the shooter and that Washington had attempted to stop the shooting. Washington claimed that Fuller would testify to these facts, but, based on a state statute preventing from persons charged in the same crime from testifying on behalf of one another, the prosecution objected. The trial court refused to allow Fuller to testify, and Washington claimed his Sixth Amendment right to compulsory process was violated. The Court agreed. The majority found that the Sixth Amendment right to compulsory process was so fundamental that it is incorporated to the states through the Due Process Clause of the Fourteenth Amendment. In *Holmes v. South Carolina*, 347 U.S. 319 (2006), Bobby Holmes was not allowed to present third party evidence (evidence suggesting another person had committed the crime (of murder) for which he was charged) due to a state statute. In a unanimous decision, the Court reversed the conviction. Justice Alito's majority opinion found that evidence of third-party guilt brought by the defendant could not be excluded only on the basis of the strength of the prosecutions case because it denied him the meaningful opportunity to present a complete defense.

SECTION SEVEN: CONSTITUTIONAL LIMITS ON PUNISHMENTS

Chapter Eleven: Punishment

CRUEL AND UNUSUAL PUNISHMENT

The Eighth Amendment tells the government that it cannot make punishment cruel or unusual. The terms "cruel and unusual," according to the Court, may change over time. In *Trop v. Dulles,* 356 U.S. 86 (1958), Chief Justice Warren wrote that the Cruel and Unusual Punishments Clause "must draw its meaning from the evolving standards of decency that mark the progress of a maturing society." *Trop* involved removing a soldier's citizenship after he had been found guilty of desertion. The Court found the penalty too extreme. The Court has cited extensively to *Trop* in cases in which it interprets what the words "cruel and unusual" mean. Professor LaFave lists three approaches the Court has used in interpreting the clause:

> ➤ limiting the methods employed to inflict punishment,

> ➤ restricting the "amount of punishment" that may be imposed, and

> ➤ prohibiting the criminal punishment of certain acts. LaFave, at 187.

BARBARIC PUNISHMENT

Punishment that is "barbaric" (meaning it involves needless pain) is cruel and unusual punishment. Barbaric punishment describes the form of punishment. "The Eighth Amendment was designed to prohibit certain forms of punishment, such as torture, that had been practiced in England and were widely viewed as reprehensible." Kerper, *supra* at 334. When the Eighth Amendment passed, barbaric punishment included: burning at the stake, crucifixion, breaking on the wheel, drawing and quartering, the rack and the thumbscrew. Now most courts are willing to consider that some punishments that were not included in that original list may, nevertheless, be cruel and unusual. The passage of time may alter whether a type of punishment is considered cruel and unusual. For example, corporal punishment was acceptable when the Eighth Amendment was passed in 1791, but was abolished in 1972 when Delaware, the last state to allow corporal punishment, repealed its statute allowing whipping.

Capital punishment has been challenged as inherently barbaric, but the death penalty has historically been viewed as a constitutionally acceptable form of punishment. The Court has noted that punishments are "cruel when they involve torture or lingering death; but the punishment of death is not cruel within the meaning of that word or as used in the constitution. Cruelty implies there is something inhuman or barbarous—something more than the mere extinguishment of life." *In re Kemmler*, 136 U.S. 436, at 436 (1897) (electrocution was unusual, but not cruel.) Even the *Furman v. Georgia*, the case which temporarily invalidated all death sentences, did not find that capital punishment was inherently unconstitutional. The five methods of execution used in the United States (hanging, firing squad, electrocution, the gas chamber, and lethal injection) have all been found by the Court to not be inherently cruel and unusual. In *Coker v. Georgia*, 433 U.S. 584 (1977), the Court held that a punishment is unconstitutional if it (1) makes no measurable contribution to acceptable goals of punishment and hence is nothing more than the purposeless and needless imposition of pain and suffering."

IRICK v. TENNESSEE,
585 U.S. ____ (2018)

JUSTICE SOTOMAYOR, dissenting from the denial of the application for stay.

Tonight the State of Tennessee intends to execute Billy Ray Irick using a procedure that he contends will amount to excruciating torture. During a recent 10-day trial in the state court, medical experts explained in painstaking detail how the three-drug cocktail Tennessee plans to inject into Irick's veins will cause him to experience sensations of drowning, suffocating, and being burned alive from the inside out. . . . The entire process will last at least 10 minutes, and perhaps as many as 18, before the third drug (potassium chloride) finally induces fatal cardiac arrest. Meanwhile, as a result of the second drug (vecuronium bromide), Irick will be "entirely paralyzed, unable to move or scream."

But Irick may well be aware of what is happening to him. In theory, the first drug in the three-drug protocol, midazolam, is supposed to render a person unable to feel pain during an execution. But the medical experts who testified here explained that midazolam would not work, and the trial court credited that testimony. If the drug indeed fails, the consequences for Irick will be extreme: Although the midazolam may temporarily render Irick unconscious, the onset of pain and suffocation will rouse him. And it may do so just as the paralysis sets in, too late for him to alert bystanders that his execution has gone horribly (if predictably) wrong.

...[T]he trial court credited the evidence put on by Irick and his co-plaintiffs, finding that they "established that midazolam does not elicit strong analgesic [i.e., pain-inhibiting] effects," and that therefore Irick "may be able to feel pain from the administration of the second and third drugs." Id., at 21. Those are the drugs that will paralyze him and create

sensations of suffocation and of burning that "'may well be the chemical equivalent of being burned at the stake'" before eventually stopping his heart. Accounts from other executions carried out using midazolam lend troubling credence to the trial court's finding. See No. 18–183–II(III), at 28 (noting testimony describing inmates' "grimaces, clenched fists, furrowed brows, and moans" during lethal injection executions, including by use of midazolam); Glossip, 576 U. S., at ___ (SOTOMAYOR, J., dissenting) (slip op., at 19– 20).

Given the Eighth Amendment's prohibition on "cruel and unusual punishments," one might think that such a finding would resolve this case in Irick's favor. And to stay or delay Irick's execution, the Tennessee Supreme Court needed only to conclude that it is likely (not certain) that Irick can persuade an appellate court that his claim has merit.

But the Tennessee Supreme Court did not find any such likelihood and declined to postpone Irick's execution to allow appellate review of his claims. Id., at 3–5. The court instead effectively let stand the trial court's order, which held that Irick's extensive and persuasive evidence describing the ordeal that awaits him raised no constitutional concerns. The trial court offered two independent reasons for its holding: first, that Irick had not proven that another, less painful method of killing him was available to the State; and second, even assuming Irick had proven a readily available alternative, that this Court would not consider the painful ordeal that Irick faces sufficiently torturous to violate the Eighth Amendment. Thereafter, the Tennessee Supreme Court refused to postpone Irick's execution on the ground that he was unlikely to succeed in disturbing the trial court's no-available-alternative holding on appeal. The court did not directly address the trial court's second rationale, but implied that it agreed. See id., at 5.

. . .

As to the prediction that this Court would deem up to 18 minutes of needless torture anything less than cruel, unusual, and unconstitutional, I fervently hope the state courts were mistaken. At a minimum, their conclusion that the Constitution tolerates what the State plans to do to Irick is not compelled by Glossip, which did not categorically determine whether a lethal injection protocol using midazolam is a constitutional method of execution. Glossip's majority concluded only that, based on the evidence presented in that case, there was no clear error in the District Court's factual finding that midazolam was highly likely to prevent a person from feeling pain. As noted, the trial court here came to a different factual conclusion based on a different factual record, as have others. …

If it turns out upon more sober appellate review that this case presents the question, I would grant certiorari to decide the important question whether the Constitution truly tolerates executions carried out by such quite possibly torturous means.

In refusing to grant Irick a stay, the Court today turns a blind eye to a proven likelihood that the State of Tennessee is on the verge of inflicting several minutes of torturous pain on an inmate in its custody, while shrouding his suffering behind a veneer of paralysis. I cannot in good conscience join in this "rush to execute" without first seeking every assurance that our precedent permits such a result. If the law permits this execution to go forward in spite of the horrific final minutes that Irick may well experience, then we have stopped being a civilized nation and accepted barbarism. I dissent.

Other Cases: Barbaric Punishment

Hope v. Pelzer, 536 U.S. 730 (2002).

Hope's, a prisoner in Alabama, was handcuffed to a hitching post for seven-hours in the hot sun; he was painfully handcuffed at shoulder level to a horizontal bar without a shirt, taunted, and provided with water only once or twice and denied bathroom breaks. There was no effort to monitor his condition despite the risks of dehydration and sun damage. The Court held that Alabama's use of the "hitching post" to discipline inmates constituted "wanton and unnecessary pain." The Court held that the use of the hitching post was painful and punitive retribution which served no legitimate and necessary penal purpose

Brown v. Plata, 593 U.S. 493 (2011)

FACTS (Official Summary)

Marciano Plata and other prisoners filed a class action suit against California prison alleging that due to serious and continued overcrowding, lack of proper health care, serious mental health care in California prisons was deteriorating. They argued that these conditions amounted to cruel and unusual punishment and that California was violating their constitutional rights under the Eighth Amendment to the U.S. Constitution.

OPINION

If a prison deprives prisoners of basic sustenance, including adequate medical care, the courts have a responsibility to remedy the resulting Eighth Amendment Violation. "The trial record documents the severe impact of burgeoning demand on the provision of care. The evidence showed that there were high vacancy rates for medical and mental health staff and that the numbers understated the severity of the crisis because the State has not budgeted sufficient staff to meet demand. … Such a shortfall contributes to significant delays in treating mentally ill prisoners, who are housed in administrative segregation for extended periods while awaiting transfer to scarce mental health treatment beds. There are also backlogs of up to 700 prisoners waiting to see a doctor for physical care. Crowding creates unsafe and unsanitary conditions that hamper effective delivery of medical and mental health care. It also promotes unrest and violence and can cause prisoners with latent mental illnesses to worsen and develop overt symptoms. Increased violence required increased reliance on lockdowns to keep order, and lockdowns further impede the effective delivery of care. Overcrowding's effects are particularly acute in prison reception centers, which process 140,000 new or returning prisoners annually, and which house some prisoners for their entire incarceration. Numerous experts testified that crowding is the primary cause of the constitutional violations.

The Prison Litigation Reform Act (PLRA) requires courts to set a population limit at the lightest level consistent with an efficacious remedy and order the population reduction to be achieved in the shortest time reasonably consistent with public safety. The Court upheld the three-judge court's order releasing enough prisoners to bring the inmate population to 137.5% of the prison's total design capacity and establishing a 2-year deadline for relief.

DISPROPORTIONATE PUNISHMENT

Disproportionate punishment also violates the Cruel and Unusual Punishment Clause of the Eighth Amendment to the U.S. Constitution. In *Coker*, the Court looked at whether the death penalty was grossly out of proportion to the severity of the crime when the defendant had raped an adult woman. The Court found that it was. In striking down the death penalty, Justice White wrote, "The death penalty, which is unique in its severity and its irrevocability, is an excessive penalty for a rapist who does not take a human life." 433 U.S. at 598 (1977). *Coker* left open the question of whether death was an appropriate sentence for rape of a child victim. *Kennedy v. Louisiana*, 554 U.S. 407 (2008), involving a horrific rape of a twelve-year-old girl by her step-father, answered that question. The Court decided that Kennedy's death sentence also was disproportionate since the crime did not result in the death of the victim. So, what we know from those cases is that the Court will likely find that a sentence of death for a crime that does not result in the victim's death is cruel and unusual because it is grossly disproportionate and therefore violates the Eighth Amendment.

Punishment may also be disproportionate if it is imposed in an uneven manner. The 1970s' death penalty cases before the Court highlight this. In *Furman v. Georgia,* 408 U.S. 238 (1972), the Court ultimately struck down capital punishment laws across the nation, finding they were applied in an uneven, arbitrary and capricious manner. The states immediately reacted by enacting mandatory death penalty laws that required capital punishment for all defendants convicted of intentional homicide. The Court held that these mandatory laws were similarly unconstitutional--mandatory death for all homicides may not be arbitrary punishment, but these statutes may result in death being inflicted on undeserving defendants. Instead, the Court held, the jury must fit the punishment to the circumstances of the particular offense and the character and record of the individual offender. *Woodson v. North Carolina*, 438 U.S.280 (1976).

The Court has also grappled with the question of whether a lengthy sentence (not a death sentence) of incarceration could be considered cruel and unusual punishment under the disproportionality test. Some federal appellate judges believe that it is perfectly acceptable for federal courts to evaluate states' non-death penalty statutes to determine if they impose disproportionate punishment. Other disagree, believing that the length of a criminal sentence is the province of the elected state legislators and that judicial intervention should be extremely rare.

HUMPHREY v. WILSON,
228 Ga. 520 (Ga.Sup.Ct., 2007)

Facts Summarized: Wilson, a 17-year-old was convicted of aggravated child molestation for having consensual oral sex with a willing 15-year-old girl. Georgia law at that time authorized a maximum of 30 years of incarceration, and Wilson was sentenced to the statutory minimum sentence of ten years with one year probation. The crime for which he was convicted also required him to register as a sex offender. The court opinion noted the consequences of that requirement:

[U]nder OCGA §42-1-12, Wilson would be required, before his release from prison, to provide prison officials with, among other things, his new address, his fingerprints, his social security number, his date of birth, and his photograph. Prison officials would have to forward this information to the sheriff of Wilson's intended county of residence, and Wilson, within seventy-two hours of his release, would have to register with that sheriff, and he would be required to update the information each year for the rest of his life. Moreover, upon Wilson's release from prison, information regarding Wilson's residence, his photograph, and his offense would be posted in numerous public places in the county in which he lives and on the internet. Significantly, Wilson could not live or work within 1,000 feet of any child care facility, church, or area where minors congregate.

Motions were filed, appeals were made (the official facts of the case present a very complex procedural history), and ultimately this case came before the Georgia Supreme Court after Humphrey, the warden where Wilson was housed, appealed a verdict favorable to Wilson from a court that had heard the petition for writ of habeas corpus filed by Wilson. That habeas court had considered that while up on appeal, the Georgia governor had signed into law a House Bill that had made the conduct Wilson was convicted of a misdemeanor and also considered an Amendment to the reporting law that granting teenagers convicted of that new law relief from having to register as a sex offender.

"In this regard, the 2006 Amendment to OCGA §16-6-4 provides that, if a person engages in sodomy with a victim who "is at least 13 but less than 16 years of age" and, if the person who engages in the conduct is "18 years of age or younger

and is no more than four years older than the victim," the person is guilty of the new crime of misdemeanor aggravated child molestation. Moreover, the 2006 Amendment to OCGA § 42-1-12 provided that teenagers whose conduct is a misdemeanor under the 2006 Amendment to OCGA § 16-6-4 do not have to register as sex offenders."

Opinion:

…

The warden . . . contends that the habeas court erred in ruling that Wilson's sentence constituted cruel and unusual punishment. We disagree.

(a) Under the Eighth Amendment to the United States Constitution and under Art. I, Sec. I, Par. XVII of the Georgia Constitution, a sentence is cruel and unusual if it " ' "is grossly out of proportion to the severity of the crime." ' " Moreover, whether "a particular punishment is cruel and unusual is not a static concept, but instead changes in recognition of the ' "evolving standards of decency that mark the progress of a maturing society." ' " Legislative enactments are the clearest and best evidence of a society's evolving standard of decency and of how contemporary society views a particular punishment.

In determining whether a sentence set by the legislature is cruel and unusual, this Court has cited with approval Justice Kennedy's concurrence in *Harmelin v. Michigan*. Under Justice Kennedy's concurrence in *Harmelin*, as further developed in *Ewing v. California*, in order to determine if a sentence is grossly disproportionate, a court must first examine the "gravity of the offense compared to the harshness of the penalty" and determine whether a threshold inference of gross disproportionality is raised. In making this determination, courts must bear in mind the primacy of the legislature in setting punishment and seek to determine whether the sentence furthers a "legitimate penological goal" considering the offense and the offender in question. If a sentence does not further a legitimate penological goal, it does not "reflect [ ] a rational legislative judgment, entitled to deference," and a threshold showing of disproportionality has been made. If this threshold analysis reveals an inference of gross disproportionality, a court must proceed to the second step and determine whether the initial judgment of disproportionality is confirmed by a comparison of the defendant's sentence to sentences imposed for other crimes within the jurisdiction and for the same crime in other jurisdictions.

(b)

. . .

(c) We turn now to the threshold inquiry of disproportionality as developed in *Harmelin* and *Ewing*. [W]e conclude that . . . considering the nature of Wilson's offense, his ten-year sentence does not further a legitimate penological goal and thus the threshold inquiry of gross disproportionality falls in Wilson's favor.

[The court then cites two controlling Georgia cases where the court had before it the question of cruel and unusual punishment demonstrated by a change in law. First, a case (Fleming) involving death penalty for mentally ill offender. Second a case (Dawson) examining lethal injection as a method of execution replacing electrocution.] . . .

Here, the legislature has recently amended OCGA § 16-6-4 to substitute misdemeanor punishment for Wilson's conduct in place of the felony punishment of a minimum of ten years in prison (with the maximum being 30 years in prison) with no possibility of probation or parole. Moreover, the legislature has relieved such teenage offenders from registering as a sex offender. It is beyond dispute that these changes represent a seismic shift in the legislature's view of the gravity of oral sex between two willing teenage participants. Acknowledging, as we must under Fleming, that no one has a better sense of the evolving standards of decency in this State than our elected representatives, we conclude that the amendments to OCGA §§

16-6-4 and 42-1-12 reflect a decision by the people of this State that the severe felony punishment and sex offender registration imposed on Wilson make no measurable contribution to acceptable goals of punishment.

Stated in the language of *Ewing* and *Harmelin*, our legislature compared the gravity of the offense of teenagers who engage in oral sex but are within four years of age of each other and determined that a minimum ten-year sentence is grossly disproportionate for that crime. This conclusion appears to be a recognition by our General Assembly that teenagers are engaging in oral sex in large numbers; that teenagers should not be classified among the worst offenders because they do not have the maturity to appreciate the consequences of irresponsible sexual conduct and are readily subject to peer pressure; and that teenage sexual conduct does not usually involve violence and represents a significantly more benign situation than that of adults preying on children for sex. Similarly, the Model Penal Code adopted a provision de-criminalizing oral or vaginal sex with a person under sixteen years old where that person willingly engaged in the acts with another person who is not more than four years older. The commentary to the Model Penal Code explains that the criminal law should not target "[s]exual experimentation among social contemporaries"; that "[i]t will be rare that the comparably aged actor who obtains the consent of an underage person to sexual conduct . will be an experienced exploiter of immaturity"; and that the "more likely case is that both parties will be willing participants and that the assignment of culpability only to one will be perceived as unfair."

In addition to the extraordinary reduction in punishment for teenage oral sex reflected in the 2006 Amendment to OCGA § 16-6-4, the 2006 Amendment to that statute also provided for a large increase in the punishment for adults who engage in child molestation and aggravated child molestation. The new punishment for adults who engage in child molestation is ten years to life in prison, whereas the punishment under the prior law was imprisonment "for not less than five nor more than 20 years." For aggravated child molestation, the punishment for adults is now twenty-five years to life, followed by life on probation, with no possibility of probation or parole for the minimum prison time of twenty-five years. The significant increase in punishment for adult offenders highlights the legislature's view that a teenager engaging in oral sex with a willing teenage partner is far from the worst offender and is, in fact, not deserving of similar punishment to an adult offender.

Although society has a significant interest in protecting children from premature sexual activity, we must acknowledge that Wilson's crime does not rise to the level of culpability of adults who prey on children and that, for the law to punish Wilson as it would an adult, with the extraordinarily harsh punishment of ten years in prison without the possibility of probation or parole, appears to be grossly disproportionate to his crime.

Based on the foregoing factors and, in particular, based on the significance of the sea change in the General Assembly's view of the appropriate punishment for teenage oral sex, we could comfortably conclude that Wilson's punishment, as a matter of law, is grossly disproportionate to his crime without undertaking the further comparisons outlined in *Harmelin* and *Ewing*. However, we nevertheless will undertake those comparisons to complete our analysis.

(d) A comparison of Wilson's sentence with sentences for other crimes in this State buttresses the threshold inference of gross disproportionality. For example, a defendant who gets in a heated argument and shoving match with someone, walks away to retrieve a weapon, returns minutes later with a gun, and intentionally shoots and kills the person may be convicted of voluntary manslaughter and sentenced to as little as one year in prison. A person who plays Russian Roulette with a loaded handgun and causes the death of another person by shooting him or her with the loaded weapon may be convicted of

involuntary manslaughter and receive a sentence of as little as one year in prison and no more than ten years. A person who intentionally shoots someone with the intent to kill, but fails in his aim such that the victim survives, may be convicted of aggravated assault and receive as little as one year in prison. A person who maliciously burns a neighbor's child in hot water, causing the child to lose use of a member of his or her body, may be convicted of aggravated battery and receive a sentence of as little as one year in prison. Finally, at the time Wilson committed his offense, a fifty-year-old man who fondled a five-year-old girl for his sexual gratification could receive as little as five years in prison, and a person who beat, choked, and forcibly raped a woman against her will could be sentenced to ten years in prison. There can be no legitimate dispute that the foregoing crimes are far more serious and disruptive of the social order than a teenager receiving oral sex from another willing teenager. The fact that these more culpable offenders may receive a significantly smaller or similar sentence buttresses our initial judgment that Wilson's sentence is grossly disproportionate to his crime.

(e) Finally, we compare Wilson's sentence to sentences imposed in other states for the same conduct. A review of other jurisdictions reveals that most states either would not punish Wilson's conduct at all or would, like Georgia now, punish it as a misdemeanor. Although some states retain a felony designation for Wilson's conduct, we have found no state that imposes a minimum punishment of ten years in prison with no possibility of probation or parole, such as that provided for by former OCGA § 16-6-4. This review thus also reinforces our initial judgment of gross disproportionality between Wilson's crime and his sentence.

(f) At this point, the Supreme Court's decision in *Weems v. United States*, merits discussion. In that case, Weems forged signatures on several public documents. The Supreme Court found that a minimum sentence of twelve years in chains at hard labor for falsifying public documents, combined with lifetime surveillance by appropriate authorities after Weems's release from prison, constituted cruel and unusual punishment. The Court stated that, because the minimum punishment imposed on Weems was more severe than or similar to punishments for some "degrees of homicide" and other more serious crimes, Weems's punishment was cruel and unusual. According to the Court,

> [t]his contrast shows more than different exercises of legislative judgment. It is greater than that. It condemns the sentence in this case as cruel and unusual. It exhibits a difference between unrestrained power and that which is

exercised under the spirit of constitutional limitations formed to establish justice.

(g) All of the foregoing considerations compel the conclusion that Wilson's sentence is grossly disproportionate to his crime and constitutes cruel and unusual punishment under both the Georgia and United States Constitutions. We emphasize that it is the "rare case [ ]" in which the threshold inference of gross disproportionality will be met and a rarer case still in which that threshold inference stands after further scrutiny. The present case, however, is one of those rare cases. ...

MILLER v. ALABAMA, 567 U.S. 460 (2012)

FACTS (Official Summary)

In each of these cases, a 14-year-old was convicted of murder and sentenced to a mandatory term of life imprisonment without the possibility of parole. In No. 10–9647, petitioner Jackson accompanied two other boys to a video store to commit a robbery; on the way to the store, he learned that one of the boys was carrying a shotgun. Jackson stayed outside the store for most of the robbery, but after he entered, one of his co-conspirators shot and killed the store clerk. Arkansas charged Jackson as an adult with capital felony murder and aggravated robbery, and a jury convicted him of both crimes. The trial court imposed a statutorily mandated sentence of life imprisonment without the possibility of parole. Jackson filed a state habeas petition, arguing that a mandatory life-without-parole term for a 14-year-old violates the Eighth Amendment. Disagreeing, the court granted the State's motion to dismiss. The Arkansas Supreme Court affirmed.

In No. 10–9646, petitioner Miller, along with a friend, beat Miller's neighbor and set fire to his trailer after an evening of drinking and drug use. The neighbor died. Miller was initially charged as a juvenile, but his case was removed to adult court, where he was charged with murder in the course of arson. A jury found Miller guilty, and the trial court imposed a statutorily mandated punishment of life without parole. The Alabama Court of Criminal Appeals affirmed, holding that Miller's sentence was not overly harsh when compared to his crime, and that its mandatory nature was permissible under the Eighth Amendment.

KAGAN, J., delivered the opinion of the Court, in which KENNEDY, GINSBURG, BREYER, and SOTOMAYOR, JJ., joined.

HELD: The Eighth Amendment forbids a sentencing scheme that mandates life in prison without possibility of parole for juvenile homicide offenders.

(a) The Eighth Amendment's prohibition of cruel and unusual punishment "guarantees individuals the right not to be subjected to excessive sanctions." *Roper v. Simmons*, 543 U. S. 551, 560. That right "flows from the basic 'precept of justice that punishment for crime should be graduated and proportioned' " to both the offender and the offense.

Two strands of precedent reflecting the concern with proportionate punishment come together here. The first has adopted categorical bans on sentencing practices based on mismatches between the culpability of a class of offenders and the severity of a penalty. ... Several cases in this group have specially focused on juvenile offenders, because of their lesser culpability. Thus, *Roper v. Simmons* held that the Eighth Amendment bars capital punishment for children, and *Graham v. Florida*, 560 U. S. ___, concluded that the Amendment prohibits a sentence of life without the possibility of parole for a juvenile convicted of a nonhomicide offense. *Graham* further likened life without parole for juveniles to the death penalty, thereby evoking a second line of cases. In those decisions, this Court has required sentencing authorities to consider the characteristics of a defendant and the details of his offense before sentencing him to death. Here, the confluence of these two lines of precedent leads to the conclusion that mandatory life without parole for juveniles violates the Eighth Amendment.

As to the first set of cases: *Roper* and *Graham* establish that children are constitutionally different from adults for sentencing purposes. Their " 'lack of maturity' " and " 'underdeveloped sense of responsibility' " lead to recklessness, impulsivity, and heedless risk-taking. *Roper.* They "are more vulnerable . . . to negative influences and outside pressures," including from their family and peers; they have limited "contro[l] over their own environment" and lack the ability to extricate themselves from horrific, crime-producing settings. And because a child's character is not as "well formed" as an adult's, his traits are "less fixed" and his actions are less likely to be "evidence of irretrievabl[e] deprav[ity]." *Roper* and *Graham* emphasized that the distinctive attributes of youth diminish the penological justifications for imposing the harshest sentences on juvenile offenders, even when they commit terrible crimes.

While *Graham*'s flat ban on life without parole was for nonhomicide crimes, nothing that *Graham* said about children is crime-specific. Thus, *[Graham's]* reasoning

implicates any life-without-parole sentence for a juvenile, even as its categorical bar relates only to nonhomicide offenses. Most fundamentally, *Graham* insists that youth matters in determining the appropriateness of a lifetime of incarceration without the possibility of parole. The mandatory penalty schemes at issue here, however, prevent the sentencer from considering youth and from assessing whether the law's harshest term of imprisonment proportionately punishes a juvenile offender. This contravenes *Graham*'s (and also *Roper*'s) foundational principle: that imposition of a State's most severe penalties on juvenile offenders cannot proceed as though they were not children.

Graham also likened life-without-parole sentences for juveniles to the death penalty. That decision recognized that life-without-parole sentences "share some characteristics with death sentences that are shared by no other sentences." 560 U. S., at ___. And it treated life without parole for juveniles like this Court's cases treat the death penalty, imposing a categorical bar on its imposition for nonhomicide offenses. By likening life-without-parole sentences for juveniles to the death penalty, *Graham* makes relevant this Court's cases demanding individualized sentencing in capital cases. In particular, those cases have emphasized that sentencers must be able to consider the mitigating qualities of youth. In light of *Graham*'s reasoning, these decisions also show the flaws of imposing mandatory life-without-parole sentences on juvenile homicide offenders.

(1) The State first contend that *Harmelin* v. *Michigan* forecloses a holding that mandatory life-without-parole sentences for juveniles violate the Eighth Amendment. *Harmelin* declined to extend the individualized sentencing requirement to noncapital cases "because of the qualitative difference between death and all other penalties." But *Harmelin* had nothing to do with children, and did not purport to apply to juvenile offenders. Indeed, since *Harmelin*, this Court has held on multiple occasions that sentencing

practices that are permissible for adults may not be so for children.

The States next contend that mandatory life-without-parole terms for juveniles cannot be unconstitutional because 29 jurisdictions impose them on at least some children convicted of murder. In considering categorical bars to the death penalty and life without parole, this Court asks as part of the analysis whether legislative enactments and actual sentencing practices show a national consensus against a sentence for a particular class of offenders. But where, as here, this Court does not categorically bar a penalty, but instead requires only that a sentencer follow a certain process, this Court has not scrutinized or relied on legislative enactments in the same way.

In any event, the "objective indicia of society's standards," that the States offer do not distinguish these cases from others holding that a sentencing practice violates the Eighth Amendment. Fewer States impose mandatory life-without-parole sentences on juvenile homicide offenders than authorized the penalty (life-without-parole for nonhomicide offenders) that this Court invalidated in *Graham*. And as *Graham* and *Thompson* v. *Oklahoma* explain, simply counting legislative enactments can present a distorted view. In those cases, as here, the relevant penalty applied to juveniles based on two separate provisions: One allowed the transfer of certain juvenile offenders to adult court, while another set out penalties for any and all individuals tried there. In those circumstances, this Court

reasoned, it was impossible to say whether a legislature had endorsed a given penalty for children (or would do so if presented with the choice). The same is true here.

(2) The States next argue that courts and prosecutors sufficiently consider a juvenile defendant's age, as well as his background and the circumstances of his crime, when deciding whether to try him as an adult. But this argument ignores that many States use mandatory transfer systems. In addition, some lodge the decision in the hands of the prosecutors, rather than courts. And even where judges have transfer-stage discretion, it has limited utility, because the decisionmaker typically will have only partial information about the child or the circumstances of his offense. Finally, because of the limited sentencing options in some juvenile courts, the transfer decision may present a choice between a light sentence as a juvenile and standard sentencing as an adult. It cannot substitute for discretion at post-trial sentencing.

BREYER, J., **concurring** opinion in which SOTOMAYOR, J., joined, omitted.

ROBERTS, C. J., **dissenting** opinion, in which SCALIA, THOMAS, and ALITO, JJ., joined, omitted.

THOMAS, J., **dissenting** opinion, in which SCALIA, J., joined., omitted.

ALITO, J., **dissenting** opinion, in which SCALIA, J., joined, omitted.

EWING v. CALIFORNIA, 538 U.S. 11 (2003)

FACTS (Official Summary)

Under California's three strikes law, a defendant who is convicted of a felony and has previously been convicted of two or more serious or violent felonies must receive an indeterminate life imprisonment term. Such a defendant becomes eligible for parole on a date calculated by reference to a minimum term, which, in this case, is 25 years. While on parole, petitioner

Ewing was convicted of felony grand theft for stealing three golf clubs, worth $399 apiece. As required by the three strikes law, the prosecutor formally alleged, and the trial court found, that Ewing had been convicted previously of four serious or violent felonies. In sentencing him to 25 years to life, the court refused to exercise its discretion to reduce the conviction to a misdemeanor--under a state law that permits certain offenses, known as "wobblers," to be classified as either misdemeanors or felonies--or to dismiss the allegations of some or all of his prior relevant convictions. The State Court of Appeal . . . rejected Ewing's claim that his sentence was grossly disproportionate under the Eighth Amendment and reasoned that enhanced sentences under the three strikes law served the State's legitimate goal of deterring and incapacitating repeat offenders. The State Supreme Court denied review.

OPINION (Official Summary)

Justice O'Connor, joined by The Chief Justice and Justice Kennedy, concluded that Ewing's sentence is not grossly disproportionate and therefore does not violate the Eighth Amendment's prohibition on cruel and unusual punishments.

(a) The Eighth Amendment has a "narrow proportionality principle" that "applies to noncapital sentences." The Amendment's application in this context is guided by the principles distilled in Justice Kennedy's concurrence in *Harmelin:* "[T]he primacy of the legislature, the variety of legitimate penological schemes, the nature of our federal system, and the requirement that proportionality review be guided by objective factors" inform the final principle that the "Eighth Amendment does not require strict proportionality between crime and sentence [but] forbids only extreme sentences that are 'grossly disproportionate' to the crime."

(b) State legislatures enacting three strikes laws made a deliberate policy choice that individuals who have repeatedly engaged in serious or violent criminal behavior, and whose conduct has not been deterred by more conventional punishment approaches, must be isolated from society to protect the public safety. Though these laws are relatively new, this Court has a longstanding tradition of deferring to state legislatures in making and implementing such important policy decisions. The Constitution "does not mandate adoption of any one penological theory," and nothing in the Eighth Amendment prohibits California from choosing to incapacitate criminals who have already been convicted of at least one serious or violent crime. Recidivism has long been recognized as a legitimate basis for increased punishment and is a serious public safety concern in California and the Nation. Any criticism of the law is appropriately directed at the legislature, which is primarily responsible for making the policy choices underlying any criminal sentencing scheme.

(c) In examining Ewing's claim that his sentence is grossly disproportionate, the gravity of the offense must be compared to the harshness of the penalty. Even standing alone, his grand theft should not be taken lightly. The California Supreme Court has noted that crime's seriousness in the context of proportionality review; that it is a "wobbler" is of no moment, for it remains a felony unless the trial court imposes a misdemeanor sentence. The trial judge justifiably exercised her discretion not to extend lenient treatment given Ewing's long criminal history. In weighing the offense's gravity, both his current felony and his long history of felony recidivism must be placed on the scales. Any other approach would not accord proper deference to the policy judgments that find expression in the legislature's choice of sanctions. Ewing's sentence is justified by the State's public-safety interest in incapacitating and deterring recidivist felons, and amply supported by his own long, serious criminal record. He has been convicted of numerous offenses, served nine separate prison terms, and committed most of his crimes while on probation or parole. His prior strikes were serious felonies including robbery and residential burglary. Though long, his current sentence reflects a rational legislative judgment that is entitled to deference.

Justice Scalia agreed that petitioner's sentence does not violate the Eighth Amendment's prohibition against cruel and unusual punishments, but on the ground that that prohibition was aimed at excluding only certain modes of punishment.

Justice Thomas concludes the Eighth Amendment contains no proportionality principle.

Weems v. United States, 217 U.S. 349 (1910).

Court held that a 12-year-sentence of hard labor for the crime of passing a forged check was cruel and unusual punishment.

Madison v. Alabama, 586 U.S. ___ (2019)

Vernon Madison had been on death row for over 30 years for killing a police officer. While on death row, he suffered a series of strokes, was diagnosed with vascular dementia, and could not remember killing the police officer. The Court held that the Eighth Amendment does not prohibit a state from executing a prisoner who, due to mental disability, cannot remember committing the crime. The Court also had to decide whether it was cruel and unusual punishment to execute a prisoner who cannot rationally understand the reasons for his execution whether that inability is due to psychosis or dementia. The Court found that it was. Justice Kagan's opinion stated,

> First, a person lacking in memory of his crime may yet rationally understand why the State seeks to execute him; if so, the Eighth Amendment poses no bar to his execution. Second a person suffering from dementia may be unable to rationally understand the reasons for his sentence; if so, the Eighth Amendment does not allow his

execution. What matters is whether a person has a rational understanding. . .not whether he has any particular memory or any particular mental illness.

Bucklew v. Precythe, 587 U.S. ___ (2019)

Bucklew was convicted by a state court jury and sentenced to death. He was scheduled to be executed in 2014. In federal court he claimed that Missouri's lethal injection protocol would constitute cruel and unusual punishment as applied to him because of his unique congenital medical condition. He claimed that the injection would likely cause him to hemorrhage during the execution causing him to choke on his own blood. He proposed nitrogen hypoxia as an alternative method for his execution. A state court prisoner can successfully request an alternative method (or claim that the state's method constitutes a violation of the Eighth Amendment) if he can show that there is a feasible and readily implemented alternative that would significantly reduce a substantial risk of pain, and that the state had refused to adopt it without any legitimate penological reason. The Court held 5-4 that Bucklew had failed to meet his burden in proving that nitrogen hypoxia was a viable, readily implemented alternative…And, even if he had, he had failed to show that it would significantly reduce a substantial risk of severe pain.

RELIEF FROM CRUEL AND UNUSUAL PUNISHMENT

Courts aren't the only entity able to provide relief for violations of constitutional protections. Non-judicial relief may sometimes be found in the executive branch through the use of federal and state pardons, commutations, moratoriums. Such was the case involving an inexperienced truck driver who, when twenty-three-years old, lost control of his semi coming down a pass on Interstate 70 in Colorado causing a horrific crash resulting in four deaths and several additional injuries. Unable to stop his rig, he careened into several cars and other semi-trucks in what was, undisputedly, an unintentional, but careless, act. Under Colorado law, the judge imposed the minimum sentence of 110 years. Shortly thereafter, Colorado governor Jared Polis granted clemency to Rogel Aguilera-Mederos, reducing his sentence to 10 years.[92]

---

[92] See, https://www.denver7.com/news/local-news/gov-polis-reduces-truckers-sentence-to-10-years#:~:text=Polis%20granted%20clemency%20to%20Rogel,state's%20mandatory%20minimum%20sentencing%20rules.

INDEX

Made in the USA
Columbia, SC
11 March 2024